HARPER TORCHBOOKS / The University Library

John R. Alden	THE AMERICAN REVOLUTION: 1775-1783. Illus. TB/3011
Ray A. Billington	THE FAR WESTERN FRONTIER: 1830-1860. Illus. TB/3012
J. Bronowski & Bruce Mazlish	THE WESTERN INTELLECTUAL TRADITION: *From Leonardo to Hegel* TB/3001
Edward P. Cheyney	THE DAWN OF A NEW ERA: 1250-1453. Illus. TB/3002
Carl J. Friedrich	THE AGE OF THE BAROQUE: 1610-1660. Illus. TB/3004
Myron P. Gilmore	THE WORLD OF HUMANISM: 1453-1517. Illus. TB/3003
Lawrence Henry Gipson	THE COMING OF THE [AMERICAN] REVOLUTION: 1763-1775. Illus. TB/3007
Wallace Notestein	THE ENGLISH PEOPLE ON THE EVE OF COLONIZATION: 1603-1630. Illus. TB/3006
Joseph A. Schumpeter	CAPITALISM, SOCIALISM AND DEMOCRACY. Third edition. TB/3008
Frederick L. Nussbaum	THE TRIUMPH OF SCIENCE AND REASON: 1660-1685. Illus. TB/3009
Louis B. Wright	THE CULTURAL LIFE OF THE AMERICAN COLONIES: 1607-1763. Illus. TB/3005
M. D. Zabel, *Ed.*	LITERARY OPINION IN AMERICA. 3rd Edition. *Vol. I*, TB/3013; *Vol. II*, TB/3014

HARPER TORCHBOOKS / The Academy Library

[Selected Titles]

Jacques Barzun	THE HOUSE OF INTELLECT TB/1051
Jeremy Bentham	THE HANDBOOK OF POLITICAL FALLACIES. Intro. by Crane Brinton TB/1069
Henri Bergson	TIME AND FREE WILL: *The Immediate Data of Consciousness* TB/1021
H. J. Blackham	SIX EXISTENTIALIST THINKERS TB/1002
Crane Brinton	ENGLISH POLITICAL THOUGHT IN THE NINETEENTH CENTURY TB/1071
Joseph Charles	THE ORIGINS OF THE AMERICAN PARTY SYSTEM TB/1049
Thomas C. Cochran	THE AMERICAN BUSINESS SYSTEM: *A Historical Perspective* TB/1080
Cochran & Miller	THE AGE OF ENTERPRISE: *A Social History of Industrial America* TB/1054
G. G. Coulton	MEDIEVAL VILLAGE, MANOR, AND MONASTERY TB/1022
Wilhelm Dilthey	PATTERN AND MEANING IN HISTORY TB/1075
St. Clair Drake & Horace Cayton	BLACK METROPOLIS: *A Study of Negro Life in a Northern City.* Introductions by Richard Wright and Everett C. Hughes. Revised edition. *Vol. I*, TB/1086; *Vol. II*, TB/1087
Peter F. Drucker	THE NEW SOCIETY: *The Anatomy of Industrial Order* TB/1082
W. Ferguson, et al.	THE RENAISSANCE: *Six Essays* TB/1084
F. L. Ganshof	FEUDALISM TB/1058
W. K. C. Guthrie	THE GREEK PHILOSOPHERS: *From Thales to Aristotle* TB/1008
John Higham, *Ed.*	THE RECONSTRUCTION OF AMERICAN HISTORY TB/1068
Dan N. Jacobs, *Ed.*	THE NEW COMMUNIST MANIFESTO *and related documents* TB/1078
Henry James	THE PRINCESS CASAMASSIMA. A novel. Intro. by Clinton Oliver TB/1005
Hans Kohn, *Ed.*	THE MIND OF MODERN RUSSIA TB/1065
Samuel Noah Kramer	SUMERIAN MYTHOLOGY. Illustrated TB/1055
Oskar Kristeller	RENAISSANCE THOUGHT: *Classic, Scholastic, Humanist Strains* TB/1048
Arthur O. Lovejoy	THE GREAT CHAIN OF BEING: *A Study of the History of an Idea* TB/1009
Paul Mantoux	THE INDUSTRIAL REVOLUTION IN THE EIGHTEENTH CENTURY TB/1079
William Miller, *Ed.*	MEN IN BUSINESS: *The Historical Role of the Entrepreneur* TB/1081
J. E. Neale	THE AGE OF CATHERINE DE MEDICI TB/1085
Erwin Panofsky	STUDIES IN ICONOLOGY: *Humanistic Themes in Renaissance Art.* Illus. TB/1077
Parsons & Shils, *Eds.*	TOWARD A GENERAL THEORY OF ACTION TB/1083
Priscilla Robertson	REVOLUTIONS OF 1848: *A Social History* TB/1025
Ferdinand Schevill	THE MEDICI. Illustrated TB/1010
C. P. Snow	TIME OF HOPE. A novel. TB/1040
N. N. Sukhanov	THE RUSSIAN REVOLUTION, 1917: *Eyewitness Account Vol. I*, TB/1066; *Vol. II*, TB/1067
Dorothy Van Ghent	THE ENGLISH NOVEL: *Form and Function* TB/1050
W. Lloyd Warner	SOCIAL CLASS IN AMERICA: *The Evaluation of Status* TB/1013
Alfred N. Whitehead	PROCESS AND REALITY: *An Essay in Cosmology* TB/1033

HARPER TORCHBOOKS / The Bollingen Library

Rachel Bespaloff	ON THE ILIAD. *Introduction by Hermann Broch* TB/2006
Joseph Campbell, *Ed.*	PAGAN AND CHRISTIAN MYSTERIES: *Papers from Eranos Yearbooks.* Illus. TB/2013
Elliott Coleman, *Ed.*	LECTURES IN CRITICISM TB/2003

HARPER TORCHBOOKS / The Cloister Library

HARPER TORCHBOOKS / The Science Library

Religion in Primitive Culture

13 44

EDWARD BURNETT TYLOR

with an introduction by Paul Radin

HARPER TORCHBOOKS

HARPER & ROW, PUBLISHERS

New York, Evanston, and London

Advisory Editor in the Humanities and Social Sciences: Benjamin Nelson

CONTENTS

OF THE SECOND VOLUME

CHAPTER XI

ANIMISM

PAGE

CHAPTER XII

ANIMISM (*continued*)

CHAPTER XIII

ANIMISM (*continued*)

CHAPTER XIV

ANIMISM (*continued*)

CHAPTER XV

ANIMISM (*continued*)

CHAPTER XVI

ANIMISM (*continued*)

CHAPTER XVII

ANIMISM (*continued*)

CHAPTER XVIII

RITES AND CEREMONIES

CHAPTER XIX

CONCLUSION

INTRODUCTION
TO THE TORCHBOOK EDITION

————

Tylor's most signal contribution to anthropology lies, it is generally agreed, in his discussion of religion. Many people, anthropologists as well as laymen, seem to think that this aspect of thought begins and ends with his doctrine of animism. But that is hardly the case. Tylor's achievement is much greater than that. It may be said that he was the first to give us a well-thought-out history of religions from the beginnings up to the time of the great Egyptian and Sumerian-Babylonian civilizations. He was the first, moreover, to demonstrate in adequate fashion how many of the concepts, beliefs, and rites of what might possibly be called the paleolithic-neolithic phase of man's history are to be found not only in the Egyptian and Sumerian-Babylonian but in the Greek, Roman, and Christian religions as well.

Despite his stress on an essentially orderly and progressive evolution, Tylor knew where to begin. One might expect a mid-nineteenth century exponent of evolution to be tempted to begin his evolutionary sequence by postulating a period when no religion existed. In Tylor's day it was a widespread belief that many primitive peoples had been without religion. Tylor realized that logically and historically this might be a reasonable assumption. But as he wisely and acutely says, "Though the theoretical niche is ready and convenient, the actual statue to fill it is not forthcoming." He did not deny that the statue might some day be found.

The first and the most fundamental problem with which he was confronted was the very difficult one of finding a minimum definition for religion. It was not his Christian background so much as a careful examination of the facts at his disposal that led him to make the belief in spiritual beings this minimum definition. The term he applied to this belief in spiritual beings, *animism,* was not invented by Tylor. But, as usual, he gave it a new meaning and a new scope. For him animism was the groundwork of all philosophy from savages to civilized man.

Tylor regarded his theory of animism as falling into two parts, forming a consistent whole. The first part was concerned with the souls of individual creatures, "capable of continued existence after the death or destruction of the body"; the second was concerned with "other spirits, upward to the rank of powerful deities." Here we have then the predication of a universal belief in souls and immortality, and of souls to be distinguished from spiritual beings. The functions of spiritual beings he defines as follows:

> [They] are held to affect or control the events of the material world, and man's life here and hereafter; and it being considered that they hold intercourse with men, and receive pleasure or displeasure from human actions, the belief in their existence leads naturally, and it might almost be said inevitably, sooner or later to active reverence and propitiation.

He is defining here what he calls animism in its full development. It thus can be said that he postulates for animism a number of stages and finds tribes representing these various stages. I should say that the majority of students of comparative religion and many of those anthropologists—their number is very small, unfortunately—who occupy themselves with this subject would agree with him. In this respect Tylor, the students of comparative religion and the anthropologists are all straight-line and somewhat naïve evolutionists.

Tylor's doctrine of animism has often been criticized as representing a purely intellectualistic approach and there is some justice in this criticism. He himself seems to imply this when he states that he is treating the doctrines and practices of primitive peoples as belonging to "theological systems devised by human reason without supernatural aid or revelation," that is, on the assumption that they were developments of natural religion. But here he is simply protesting against those who could see religious evolution only in terms of the dogmas and implications of revealed religion.

His concept of human reason, as the perusal of *Primitive Culture* makes abundantly clear, included all forms of religious experience. To a person brought up in the Quaker tradition, reason and a mystical experience could be easily combined. His doctrine of animism need not imply a purely intellectualistic approach at all. In fact Tylor came to be criticized on this score only after the theory of pre-animism had been developed, that is, after the appearance of R. R. Marett's book on *The Threshold of Religion* (1909) and after the so-called early stages of religion were discussed obsessively in terms of the Melanesian *mana*, the Iroquoian *orenda*, the Central Algonquian *manito* and the Siouan *wakanda*. It was only after the publication of Lévy-Bruhl's famous book and the influence it had upon such distinguished students of religion and philosophy as Cassirer, van der Leeuw and Mircea Eliade, that it became something of a dogma to ascribe to Tylor a purely intellectualistic approach.

The doctrine of souls occupies a central position in the animistic theory. Where Tylor is describing it concretely, little exception need be taken to his statement. Unfortunately he sought, as a rationalist of his time might be expected to do, to delve into the ultimate origin of the conceptions of the soul. The temptation to do so has always been irresistible to anyone dealing with the history of religion and the temptation to attempt this in terms of the apparent meaning the word for soul possesses seems to be even more irresistible.

The dangers inherent in any such attempt are, of course, tremendous. But neither Tylor nor later theorists were frightened. All of these scholars have, in different degrees, felt it necessary to assume that no matter what the level of culture, thinking men—even nonthinkers—must have been impressed by a number of biological and psychological problems. What is the difference between a living body and a dead one; what is it that causes waking, sleep, trance, disease, death; and what are the human shapes which appear in dreams and visions? Having asked these questions, Tylor goes on to say, and it is best to quote him, that our primitive philosopher made

> the obvious inference that every man has two things belonging to him, namely a life and a phantom. These two are evidently in close connexion with the body, the life as enabling it to feel and think and act, the phantom as being its image or second self.

This, however, is only the first step in our primitive philosopher's reasoning. The second step would be to combine the life and the phantom. We have then arrived at the well-known conception of an apparitional soul and a ghost soul. In this definition of the personal soul or spirit we assuredly have the influence of Herbert Spencer.

There is no need to enter here into the details of Tylor's doctrine of soul. In his view, the doctrine answers to the plain evidence of man's senses. So well, indeed, does the notion of soul account for the facts of nature that it extends into the higher levels of civilization. Moreover although the notion has been modified greatly by Greco-Roman and medieval philosophy it always has retained traces of its original character. To Tylor, then, animism was not simply a religion but a basic philosophy whose history can be traced in man's development. He wrote:

> Out of the vast mass of evidence, collected among the most various and distant races of mankind, typical details may now be selected to display the earlier theory of the soul, the relation of the parts of this theory, and the manner in which these parts have been abandoned, modified, or kept up, along the course of culture.

Those of us currently engaged in the study of religion would not begin with an examination of the conceptions of the soul. We would incline to place such conceptions in the category of religious beliefs with quite a number of comparable beliefs and we would regard it as futile to attempt specifically to trace the antecedents of the belief in spiritual beings. Strangely enough this is not to be attributed to the influence of the theory of evolution but to Tylor's insistence that one belief flows naturally from another. Here we are again in the presence of Leibniz's doctrine that apparently so impressed Tylor; namely, that nothing ever happens without sufficient reason and that nature never acts by leaps. But perhaps more is involved here. Tylor seems to have believed that primitive peoples possessed the capacity for drawing the proper inferences from the concept of souls. He quotes Jacob Boehme whose ideas had so much influence on the Quakers to the effect that early man found everything easy. On this view, logical thinking belonged to a stage of innocence. Early man is assumed to have experienced great happiness in attempting to explain the causes of things.

How are we to understand Tylor's reasoning here? It is not a form of intellectualistic approach as so many later critics have believed. It flowed, on the contrary, directly from his own personality. Tylor was himself, at times, this simple, hypothetical ancient man. Moreover, the romantic period had not ended nor had Rousseau been forgotten. Fortunately the acceptance of the animistic doctrine does not depend upon the assumption that spiritual beings are an outgrowth of the belief in souls. Although Tylor is unfortunately always returning to this doubtful theory, his discussion of the innumerable phases through which the belief in spiritual beings passed on its way to become a faith in a Supreme Creator continues to merit attention.

At the end of his final chapter on animism Tylor gives a resumé that deserves special comment for it clearly shows two things: that his interest in aboriginal civilizations was entirely secondary, and that he was more concerned than is generally recognized with the philosophical aspects of religion. Animism for him was a philosophy with a definite value and, I suspect, one tinged with personal meaning. It always had had a value, Tylor was convinced. Only its scope and its stresses had changed. It began as a philosophy of the universe and ended as the principle of a moral institution. In Tylor's view, it is the emphasis on the ethical level of the great civilizations—presumably he is speaking here of the Judeo-Christian religions—that is a more fundamental mark of progress than the increase of natural scientific theory and mature theories of knowledge. It is because practically no aboriginal peoples ever developed a divine sanction of ethical laws, because there existed among them no theological enforcement of morality, no teaching of moral government of the universe, that they are inferior to modern civilized Western man among whom we find the law of righteousness and holiness the inspiration of duty and of love. Despite his simplicity and his Quaker upbringing, Tylor remained a mid-Victorian.

If it is ethical advancement, then, that matters, and if this advancement is to be interpreted in terms of the religions of the great civilizations, it is easy to understand how this would adversely affect Tylor's whole theory and his evaluations of primitive cultures. Yet even here he could have escaped some of the unfortunate consequences of his assumptions if he had not included in this higher ethical level the provision that there must be a divine sanction for ethical laws; if he had realized that such a higher level could be obtained by the group sanction as well. However, we need not criticize him too much for this. Andrew Lang and Father Wilhelm Schmidt and innumerable contemporary scholars agree with him in this respect. The result unfortunately has been the distortion of the whole ethnological record.

One cannot conclude a summary and evaluation of Tylor's work without some remarks about later developments in the approach toward aboriginal religions. The most important of such developments are concerned with the attempts to push back the history of religions one step further. Antecedent to the belief in spiritual beings, it was contended, there existed the concept of supernatural power, called *mana*. Codrington in his famous book on the Melanesians (1891) defined it as "a force altogether distinct from physical power which acts in all kinds of ways for good and evil and which it is of the greatest advantage to possess and control." Kindred conceptions were discovered all over the world. It was seized upon by students of comparative religion with uncritical avidity and regarded as demolishing for all time Tylor's theory that religion began with a belief in spiritual beings. Yet it is now beginning to be realized that this belief in *mana*, insofar as it can be defined in Codrington's terms, exists side by side with the belief in spiritual beings and may in fact postdate this belief. At best it belongs more to the development of magical rather than to that of religious beliefs. Whether magic preceded religion is an open question. That it did not develop into religion is reasonably certain.

Tylor is quite right then in insisting that one cannot

study religion in terms of what is not religion. Here he finds himself in what would assuredly have seemed to him very strange company; in that of the foremost promulgator of the theory, Father Wilhelm Schmidt, that from the very beginning man has believed in a Supreme Deity. Although actually this theory had first been clearly formulated by Andrew Lang, Father Schmidt freed it from the remnants of the degeneration theory which still persisted in Lang's presentation.

There seems to be little question but that such a belief exists among a large number of the simplest primitive peoples. The only question that must be resolved is whether we are here dealing with monotheism or monolatry and whether all individuals in a group share this belief or only a few. The answer seems to be quite clear; namely, that a belief in a Supreme Creator is confined to a small number of people in any given group and that even they will not be consistent monotheists. Under certain historical circumstances it may very well happen that the formulation of the few believers in a Supreme Deity becomes the belief of the whole tribe. But this is extremely rare and the monotheism then becomes highly diluted.

In the overwhelming number of cases animism in its various forms is the basic religion of primitive peoples. In that respect Tylor was quite right. Where he erred is that he did not sufficiently distinguish the essentially religious individual from the nonreligious one and that he did not fully realize that to such a religious individual religion would mean what it does to a deeply religious person among ourselves. Yet that he nevertheless had some understanding of this is proved by a passage in his last chapter on animism. There he expressly says:

> Even in the life of the rudish savage, religious belief is associated with intense emotion, with awful reverence, with agonizing terror, with rapt ecstasy when sense and thought utterly transcend the common level of daily life.

Here we have almost everything that Rudolf Otto stated in his famous book *The Idea of the Holy*. Indeed, in some respects his insight may indeed be regarded as superior to that of Otto. Why then did Tylor neglect this aspect of religion? He gives us the answer himself. It is "the intellectual rather than the emotional side of religion that has here [that is, in *Primitive Culture*] been kept in view." The rationalist and the Quaker had got in his way.

Yet Tylor's shortcomings in no way need diminish his achievement. As Marett has well said in his biography of Tylor, we are dealing here with a plain man, but with a man of genius, one who, "like Moses and Joshua in one, not only described the promised land but with sublime vision devised and actually tried out the means of conquest." It was due to him that British and American anthropology before the Durkheimian and psychoanalytical invasions remained loyal for so long a time to facts and common sense.

PAUL RADIN

Brandeis University
November, 1957

PREFACE TO THE SECOND EDITION

SINCE the publication of this work in 1871, translations have appeared in German and Russian. In the present edition the form of page has been slightly altered, for convenience of re-issue at once in England and America. The matter, however, remains substantially the same. A few passages have been amplified or altered for greater clearness, and on some points additional or improved evidence has been put in. Among the anthropologists whose published reviews or private communications have enabled me to correct or strengthen various points, I will only mention by name Professor Felix Liebrecht, of Liége, Mr. Clements R. Markham, Professor Calderwood, Mr. Ralston, and Mr. Sebastian Evans.

It may have struck some readers as an omission, that in a work on civilization insisting so strenuously on a theory of development or evolution, mention should scarcely have been made of Mr. Darwin and Mr. Herbert Spencer, whose influence on the whole course of modern thought on such subjects should not be left without formal recognition. This absence of particular reference is accounted for by the present work, arranged on its own lines, coming scarcely into contact of detail with the previous works of these eminent philosophers.

An objection made by several critics as to the accumulation of evidence in these volumes leads me to remark, with sincere gratification, that this objection has in fact been balanced by solid advantage. The plan of collecting wide and minute evidence, so that readers may have actually before them the means of judging the theory put forward, has been justified by the reception of the book, even in circles to whose views many of its arguments are strongly adverse, and that in matters of the first importance. Writers of most various philosophical and theological schools now admit that the ethnological facts are real, and vital, and have to be accounted for. It is not too much to say that a perceptible movement of public opinion has here justified the belief that the English mind, not readily swayed by rhetoric, moves freely under the pressure of facts.

E. B. T.

September, 1873.

CHAPTER XI

ANIMISM

Religious ideas generally appear among low races of Mankind—Negative statements on this subject frequently misleading and mistaken : many cases uncertain—Minimum definition of Religion—Doctrine of Spiritual Beings, here termed Animism—Animism treated as belonging to Natural Religion—Animism divided into two sections, the philosophy of Souls, and of other Spirits—Doctrine of Souls, its prevalence and definition among the lower races—Definition of Apparitional Soul or Ghost-Soul— It is a theoretical conception of primitive Philosophy, designed to account for phenomena now classed under Biology, especially Life and Death, Health and Disease, Sleep and Dreams, Trance and Visions— Relation of Soul in name and nature to Shadow, Blood, Breath— Division of Plurality of Souls—Soul cause of Life ; its restoration to body when supposed absent—Exit of Soul in Trances—Dreams and Visions : theory of exit of dreamer's or seer's own soul ; theory of visits received by them from other souls—Ghost-Soul seen in Apparitions—Wraiths and Doubles—Soul has form of body ; suffers mutilation with it—Voice of Ghost—Soul treated and defined as of Material Substance ; this appears to be the original doctrine—Transmission of Souls to service in future life by Funeral Sacrifice of wives, attendants, &c.—Souls of Animals—Their transmission by Funeral Sacrifice—Souls of Plants— Souls of Objects—Their transmission by Funeral Sacrifice—Relation of doctrine of Object-Souls to Epicurean theory of Ideas—Historical development of Doctrine of Souls, from the Ethereal Soul of primitive Biology to the Immaterial Soul of modern Theology.

ARE there, or have there been, tribes of men so low in culture as to have no religious conceptions whatever ? This is practically the question of the universality of religion, which for so many centuries has been affirmed and denied, with a confidence in striking contrast to the imperfect evidence on which both affirmation and denial have been based. Ethnographers, if looking to a theory of development to explain civilization, and regarding its successive

stages as arising one from another, would receive with
peculiar interest accounts of tribes devoid of all religion.
Here, they would naturally say, are men who have no religion because their forefathers had none, men who represent
a præ-religious condition of the human race, out of which
in the course of time religious conditions have arisen.   It
does not, however, seem advisable to start from this ground
in an investigation of religious development.   Though the
theoretical niche is ready and convenient, the actual statue
to fill it is not forthcoming.   The case is in some degree
similar to that of the tribes asserted to exist without language
or without the use of fire; nothing in the nature of things
seems to forbid the possibility of such existence, but as a
matter of fact the tribes are not found.   Thus the assertion
that rude non-religious tribes have been known in actual
existence, though in theory possible, and perhaps in fact
true, does not at present rest on that sufficient proof
which, for an exceptional state of things, we are entitled
to demand.

It is not unusual for the very writer who declares in
general terms the absence of religious phenomena among
some savage people, himself to give evidence that shows
his expressions to be misleading.   Thus Dr. Lang not only
declares that the aborigines of Australia have no idea of a
supreme divinity, creator, and judge, no object of worship,
no idol, temple, or sacrifice, but that ' in short, they have
nothing whatever of the character of religion, or of religious observance, to distinguish them from the beasts that
perish.'   More than one writer has since made use of this
telling statement, but without referring to certain details
which occur in the very same book.   From these it appears
that a disease like small-pox, which sometimes attacks the
natives, is ascribed by them ' to the influence of Budyah,
an evil spirit who delights in mischief ; ' that when the
natives rob a wild bees' hive, they generally leave a little of
the honey for Buddai ; that at certain biennial gatherings
fo the Queensland tribes, young girls are slain in sacrifice

to propitiate some evil divinity ; and that, lastly, according to the evidence of the Rev. W. Ridley, ' whenever he has conversed with the aborigines, he found them to have definite traditions concerning supernatural beings—Baiame, whose voice they hear in thunder, and who made all things, Turramullum the chief of demons, who is the author of disease, mischief, and wisdom, and appears in the form of a serpent at their great assemblies, &c.'[1] By the concurring testimony of a crowd of observers, it is known that the natives of Australia were at their discovery, and have since remained, a race with minds saturated with the most vivid belief in souls, demons, and deities. In Africa, Mr. Moffat's declaration as to the Bechuanas is scarcely less surprising —that ' man's immortality was never heard of among that people,' he having remarked in the sentence next before, that the word for the shades or manes of the dead is ' liriti.'[2] In South America, again, Don Felix de Azara comments on the positive falsity of the ecclesiastics' assertion that the native tribes have a religion. He simply declares that they have none ; nevertheless in the course of his work he mentions such facts as that the Payaguas bury arms and clothing with their dead and have some notions of a future life, and that the Guanas believe in a Being who rewards good and punishes evil. In fact, this author's reckless denial of religion and law to the lower races of this region justifies D'Orbigny's sharp criticism, that, ' this is indeed what he says of all the nations he describes, while actually proving the contrary of his thesis by the very facts he alleges in its support.'[3]

Such cases show how deceptive are judgments to which breadth and generality are given by the use of wide words in narrow senses. Lang, Moffat, and Azara are authors to whom ethnography owes much valuable knowledge of the tribes

[1] J. D. Lang, ' Queensland,' pp. 340, 374, 380, 388, 444 (Buddai appears, p. 379, as causing a deluge ; he is probably identical with Budyah).

[2] Moffat, ' South Africa,' p. 261.

[3] Azara, ' Voy. dans l'Amérique Méridionale,' vol. ii. pp. 3, 14, 25, 51, 60, 91, 119, &c. ; D'Orbigny, ' L'Homme Américain,' vol. ii. p. 318.

they visited, but they seem hardly to have recognized anything short of the organized and established theology of the
higher races as being religion at all. They attribute irreligion to tribes whose doctrines are unlike theirs, in much
the same manner as theologians have so often attributed
atheism to those whose deities differed from their own, from
the time when the ancient invading Aryans described the
aboriginal tribes of India as *adeva*, i.e. ' godless,' and
the Greeks fixed the corresponding term ἄθεοι on the early
Christians as unbelievers in the classic gods, to the comparatively modern ages when disbelievers in witchcraft and
apostolical succession were denounced as atheists; and down
to our own day, when controversialists are apt to infer, as in
past centuries, that naturalists who support a theory of
development of species therefore necessarily hold atheistic
opinions.[1] These are in fact but examples of a general
perversion of judgment in theological matters, among the
results of which is a popular misconception of the religions
of the lower races, simply amazing to students who have
reached a higher point of view. Some missionaries, no
doubt, thoroughly understand the minds of the savages
they have to deal with, and indeed it is from men like
Cranz, Dobrizhoffer, Charlevoix, Ellis, Hardy, Callaway,
J. L. Wilson, T. Williams, that we have obtained our best
knowledge of the lower phases of religious belief. But for
the most part the ' religious world ' is so occupied in
hating and despising the beliefs of the heathen whose vast
regions of the globe are painted black on the missionary
maps, that they have little time or capacity left to understand them. It cannot be so with those who fairly seek to
comprehend the nature and meaning of the lower phases of
religion. These, while fully alive to the absurdities believed and the horrors perpetrated in its name, will yet

---

[1] Muir, ' Sanskrit Texts,' part ii. p. 435; Euseb. ' Hist. Eccl.' iv. 15;
Bingham, book i. ch. ii.; Vanini, ' De Admirandis Naturae Arcanis,' dial. 37;
Lecky, ' Hist. of Rationalism,' vol. i. p. 126; Encyclop. Brit. (5th ed.) s.v.
' Superstition.'

regard with kindly interest all record of men's earnest seeking after truth with such light as they could find. Such students will look for meaning, however crude and childish, at the root of doctrines often most dark to the believers who accept them most zealously ; they will search for the reasonable thought which once gave life to observances now become in seeming or reality the most abject and super-stitious folly. The reward of these enquirers will be a more rational comprehension of the faiths in whose midst they dwell, for no more can he who understands but one religion understand even that religion, than the man who knows but one language can understand that language. No religion of mankind lies in utter isolation from the rest, and the thoughts and principles of modern Christianity are attached to intellectual clues which run back through far præ-Christian ages to the very origin of human civilization, perhaps even of human existence.

While observers who have had fair opportunities of studying the religion of savages have thus sometimes done scant justice to the facts before their eyes, the hasty denials of others who have judged without even facts can carry no great weight. A 16th-century traveller gave an account of the natives of Florida which is typical of such : ' Touching the religion of this people, which wee have found, for want of their language wee could not understand neither by signs nor gesture that they had any religion or lawe at all. . . . We suppose that they have no religion at all, and that they live at their own libertie.' [1] Better knowledge of these Floridans nevertheless showed that they had a religion, and better knowledge has reversed many another hasty assertion to the same effect ; as when writers used to declare that the natives of Madagascar had no idea of a future state, and no word for soul or spirit ; [2] or when Dampier enquired after the religion of the natives of Timor, and was told

[1] J. de Verrazano in Hakluyt, vol. iii. p. 300.
[2] See W. Ellis, ' Hist. of Madagascar,' vol. i. p. 429 ; Flacourt, ' Hist. de Madagascar,' p. 59.

that they had none ;[1] or when Sir Thomas Roe landed in Saldanha Bay on his way to the court of the Great Mogul, and remarked of the Hottentots that ' they have left off their custom of stealing, but know no God or religion.'[2] Among the numerous accounts collected by Lord Avebury as evidence bearing on the absence or low development of religion among low races,[3] some may be selected as lying open to criticism from this point of view. Thus the statement that the Samoan Islanders had no religion cannot stand, in face of the elaborate description by the Rev. G. Turner of the Samoan religion itself ; and the assertion that the Tupinambas of Brazil had no religion is one not to be received on merely negative evidence, for the religious doctrines and practices of the Tupi race have been recorded by Lery, De Laet, and other writers. Even with much time and care and knowledge of language, it is not always easy to elicit from savages the details of their theology. They try to hide from the prying and contemptuous foreigner their worship of gods who seem to shrink, like their worshippers, before the white man and his mightier Deity. Mr. Sproat's experience in Vancouver's Island is an apt example of this state of things. He says : ' I was two years among the Ahts, with my mind constantly directed towards the subject of their religious beliefs, before I could discover that they possessed any ideas as to an overruling power or a future state of existence. The traders on the coast, and other persons well acquainted with the people, told me that they had no such ideas, and this opinion was confirmed by conversation with many of the less intelligent savages ; but at last I succeeded in getting a satisfactory clue.'[4] It then appeared that the Ahts had all the time been hiding a whole characteristic system of religious doctrines as to souls and their migrations, the

---

[1] Dampier, ' Voyages,' vol. ii. part ii. p. 76.

[2] Roe in Pinkerton, vol. viii. p. 2.

[3] Lubbock, ' Prehistoric Times,' p. 564 : see also ' Origin of Civilization,' p. 138.

[4] Sproat, ' Scenes and Studies of Savage Life,' p. 205.

spirits who do good and ill to men, and the great gods above all. Thus, even where no positive proof of religious ideas among any particular tribe has reached us, we should distrust its denial by observers whose acquaintance with the tribe in question has not been intimate as well as kindly. It is said of the Andaman Islanders that they have not the rudest elements of a religious faith ; yet it appears that the natives did not even display to the foreigners the rude music which they actually possessed, so that they could scarcely have been expected to be communicative as to their theology, if they had any.[1] In our time the most striking negation of the religion of savage tribes is that published by Sir Samuel Baker, in a paper read in 1866 before the Ethnological Society of London, as follows : ' The most northern tribes of the White Nile are the Dinkas, Shillooks, Nuehr, Kytch, Bohr, Aliab, and Shir. A general description will suffice for the whole, excepting the Kytch. Without any exception, they are without a belief in a Supreme Being, neither have they any form of worship or idolatry ; nor is the darkness of their minds enlightened by even a ray of superstition.' Had this distinguished explorer spoken only of the Latukas, or of other tribes hardly known to ethnographers except through his own intercourse with them, his denial of any religious consciousness to them would have been at least entitled to stand as the best procurable account, until more intimate communication should prove or disprove it. But in speaking thus of comparatively well known tribes such as the Dinkas, Shilluks and Nuehr, Sir S. Baker ignores the existence of published evidence, such as describes the sacrifices of the Dinkas, their belief in good and evil spirits (adjok and djyok), their good deity and heaven-dwelling creator, Dendid, as likewise Néar the Deity of the Nuehr, and the Shilluk's creator, who is described as visiting, like other spirits, a sacred wood or tree. Kaufmann, Brun-

---

[1] Mouat, ' Andaman Islanders,' pp. 2, 279, 303. Since the above was written, the remarkable Andaman religion has been described by Mr. E. H. Man, in ' Journ. Anthrop. Inst.' vol. xii. (1883) p. 156. [Note to 3rd ed.]

Rollet, Lejean, and other observers, had thus placed on record details of the religion of these White Nile tribes, years before Sir S. Baker's rash denial that they had any religion at all.[1]

The first requisite in a systematic study of the religions of the lower races, is to lay down a rudimentary definition of religion. By requiring in this definition the belief in a supreme deity or of judgment after death, the adoration of idols or the practice of sacrifice, or other partially-diffused doctrines or rites, no doubt many tribes may be excluded from the category of religious. But such narrow definition has the fault of identifying religion rather with particular developments than with the deeper motive which underlies them. It seems best to fall back at once on this essential source, and simply to claim, as a minimum definition of Religion, the belief in Spiritual Beings. If this standard be applied to the descriptions of low races as to religion, the following results will appear. It cannot be positively asserted that every existing tribe recognizes the belief in spiritual beings, for the native condition of a considerable number is obscure in this respect, and from the rapid change or extinction they are undergoing, may ever remain so. It would be yet more unwarranted to set down every tribe mentioned in history, or known to us by the discovery of antiquarian relics, as necessarily having passed the defined minimum of religion. Greater still would be the unwisdom of declaring such a rudimentary belief natural or instinctive in all human tribes of all times ; for no evidence

---

[1] Baker, ' Races of the Nile Basin,' in Tr. Eth. Soc. vol. v. p. 231 ; ' The Albert Nyanza,' vol. i. p. 246. See Kaufmann, ' Schilderungen aus Central-afrika,' p. 123 ; Brun-Rollet, ' Le Nil Blanc et le Soudan,' pp. 100, 222, also pp. 164, 200, 234 ; G. Lejean in ' Rev. des Deux M.' April 1, 1862, p. 760 ; Waitz, ' Anthropologie,' vol. ii. pp. 72-5 ; Bastian, ' Mensch,' vol. iii. p. 208. Other recorded cases of denial of religion of savage tribes on narrow definition or inadequate evidence may be found in Meiners, ' Gesch. der Rel.' vol. i. pp. 11-15 (Australians and Californians); Waitz, ' Anthropologie,' vol. i. p. 323 (Aru Islanders, &c.) ; Farrar in ' Anthrop. Rev.' Aug. 1864, p. ccxvii. (Kafirs, &c.); Martius, ' Ethnog. Amer.' vol. i. p. 583 (Manaos); J. G. Palfrey, ' Hist. of New England,' vol. i. p. 46 (New England tribes).

justifies the opinion that man, known to be capable of so vast an intellectual development, cannot have emerged from a non-religious condition, previous to that religious condition in which he happens at present to come with sufficient clearness within our range of knowledge. It is desirable, however, to take our basis of enquiry in observation rather than from speculation. Here, so far as I can judge from the immense mass of accessible evidence, we have to admit that the belief in spiritual beings appears among all low races with whom we have attained to thoroughly intimate acquaintance; whereas the assertion of absence of such belief must apply either to ancient tribes, or to more or less imperfectly described modern ones. The exact bearing of this state of things on the problem of the origin of religion may be thus briefly stated. Were it distinctly proved that non-religious savages exist or have existed, these might be at least plausibly claimed as representatives of the condition of Man before he arrived at the religious state of culture. It is not desirable, however, that this argument should be put forward, for the asserted existence of the non-religious tribes in question rests, as we have seen, on evidence often mistaken and never conclusive. The argument for the natural evolution of religious ideas among mankind is not invalidated by the rejection of an ally too weak at present to give effectual help. Non-religious tribes may not exist in our day, but the fact bears no more decisively on the development of religion, than the impossibility of finding a modern English village without scissors or books or lucifer-matches bears on the fact that there was a time when no such things existed in the land.

I propose here, under the name of Animism, to investigate the deep-lying doctrine of Spiritual Beings, which embodies the very essence of Spiritualistic as opposed to Materialistic philosophy. Animism is not a new technical term, though now seldom used.[1] From its special relation to the doctrine

---

[1] The term has been especially used to denote the doctrine of Stahl, the promulgator also of the phlogiston-theory. The Animism of Stahl is a

of the soul, it will be seen to have a peculiar appropriateness to the view here taken of the mode in which theological ideas have been developed among mankind. The word Spiritualism, though it may be, and sometimes is, used in a general sense, has this obvious defect to us, that it has become the designation of a particular modern sect, who indeed hold extreme spiritualistic views, but cannot be taken as typical representatives of these views in the world at large. The sense of Spiritualism in its wider acceptation, the general belief in spiritual beings, is here given to Animism.

Animism characterizes tribes very low in the scale of humanity, and thence ascends, deeply modified in its transmission, but from first to last preserving an unbroken continuity, into the midst of high modern culture. Doctrines adverse to it, so largely held by individuals or schools, are usually due not to early lowness of civilization, but to later changes in the intellectual course, to divergence from, or rejection of, ancestral faiths ; and such newer developments do not affect the present enquiry as to the fundamental religious condition of mankind. Animism is, in fact, the groundwork of the Philosophy of Religion, from that of savages up to that of civilized men. And although it may at first sight seem to afford but a bare and meagre definition of a minimum of religion, it will be found practically sufficient; for where the root is, the branches will generally be produced. / It is habitually found that the theory of Animism divides into two great dogmas, forming parts of one consistent doctrine; first, concerning souls of individual creatures, capable of continued existence after the death or destruction of the body ; second, concerning other spirits, upward to the rank of powerful deities.) Spiritual beings are held to affect or control the events of the material world, and man's life here and hereafter; and it being considered

revival and development in modern scientific shape of the classic theory identifying vital principle and soul. See his ' Theoria Medica Vera,' Halle, 1737 ; and the critical dissertation on his views, Lemoine, ' Le Vitalisme et l'Animisme de Stahl,' Paris, 1864.

that they hold intercourse with men, and receive pleasure or displeasure from human actions, the belief in their existence leads naturally, and it might almost be said inevitably, sooner or later to active reverence and propitiation. Thus Animism in its full development, includes the belief in souls and in a future state, in controlling deities and subordinate spirits, these doctrines practically resulting in some kind of active worship. One great element of religion, that moral element which among the higher nations forms its most vital part, is indeed little represented in the religion of the lower races. It is not that these races have no moral sense or no moral standard, for both are strongly marked among them, if not in formal precept, at least in that traditional consensus of society which we call public opinion, according to which certain actions are held to be good or bad, right or wrong. It is that the conjunction of ethics and Animistic philosophy, so intimate and powerful in the higher culture, seems scarcely yet to have begun in the lower. I propose here hardly to touch upon the purely moral aspects of religion, but rather to study the animism of the world so far as it constitutes, as unquestionably it does constitute, an ancient and world-wide philosophy, of which belief is the theory and worship is the practice. Endeavouring to shape the materials for an enquiry hitherto strangely undervalued and neglected, it will now be my task to bring as clearly as may be into view the fundamental animism of the lower races, and in some slight and broken outline to trace its course into higher regions of civilization. Here let me state once for all two principal conditions under which the present research is carried on. First, as to the religious doctrines and practices examined, these are treated as belonging to theological systems devised by human reason, without supernatural aid or revelation ; in other words, as being developments of Natural Religion. Second, as to the connexion between similar ideas and rites in the religions of the savage and the civilized world. While dwelling at some length on doctrines and ceremonies of the lower races, and sometimes particularizing for special reasons the related doctrines and ceremonies of the higher nations, it has not seemed my proper task to work out in detail the problems thus suggested among the philosophies and creeds of Christendom. Such applications, extending farthest from the direct scope of a work on primitive culture, are briefly stated in general terms, or touched in slight allusion, or taken for granted without remark. Educated readers possess the information required to work out their general bearing on theology, while more technical discussion is left to philosophers and theologians specially occupied with such arguments.

The first branch of the subject to be considered is the doctrine of human and other Souls, an examination of which will occupy the rest of the present chapter. What the doctrine of the soul is among the lower races, may be explained in stating the animistic theory of its development. It seems as though thinking men, as yet at a low level of culture, were deeply impressed by two groups of biological problems. In the first place, what is it that makes the difference between a living body and a dead one ; what causes waking, sleep, trance, disease, death ? In the second place, what are those human shapes which appear in dreams and visions ? Looking at these two groups of phenomena, the ancient savage philosophers probably made their first step by the obvious inference that every man has two things belonging to him, namely, a life and a phantom. These two are evidently in close connexion with the body, the life as enabling it to feel and think and act, the phantom as being its image or second self ; both, also, are perceived to be things separable from the body, the life as able to go away and leave it insensible or dead, the phantom as appearing to people at a distance from it. The second step would seem also easy for savages to make, seeing how extremely difficult civilized men have found it to unmake. It is merely to combine the life and the phantom. As both belong to the body, why should they not also belong to one another, and be manifestations of one and the same soul ? Let them then be considered as united, and the result is that well-known conception which may be described as an apparitional-soul, a ghost-soul. This, at any rate, corresponds with the actual conception of the personal soul or spirit among the lower races, which may be defined as follows : It is a thin unsubstantial human image, in its nature a sort of vapour, film, or shadow ; the cause of life and thought in the individual it animates ; independently possessing the personal consciousness and volition of its corporeal owner, past or present ; capable of leaving the body far behind, to flash swiftly from place to place; mostly impalpable and invisible, yet also manifesting physical power, and especially appearing to men waking or asleep as a phantasm separate from the body of which it bears the likeness; continuing to exist and appear to men after the death of that body; able to enter into, possess, and act in the bodies of other men, of animals, and even of things. Though this definition is by no means of universal application, it has sufficient generality to be taken as a standard, modified by more or less divergence among any particular people. Far from these world-wide opinions being arbitrary or conventional products, it is seldom even justifiable to consider their uniformity among distant races as proving communication of any sort. They are doctrines answering in the most forcible way to the plain evidence of men's senses, as interpreted by a fairly consistent and rational primitive philosophy. So well, indeed, does primitive animism account for the facts of nature, that it has held its place into the higher levels of education. Though classic and mediæval philosophy modified it much, and modern philosophy has handled it yet more unsparingly, it has so far retained the traces of its original character, that heirlooms of primitive ages may be claimed in the existing psychology of the civilized world. Out of the vast mass of evidence, collected among the most various and distant races of mankind, typical details may now be selected to display the earlier theory of the soul, the relation of the parts of this theory, and the manner in which these parts have been abandoned, modified, or kept up, along the course of culture.

To understand the popular conceptions of the human soul or spirit, it is instructive to notice the words which have been found suitable to express it. The ghost or phantasm seen by the dreamer or the visionary is an unsubstantial form, like a shadow or reflexion, and thus the familiar term of the *shade* comes in to express the soul. Thus the Tasmanian word for the shadow is also that for the spirit;[1] the Algonquins describe a man's soul as *otahchuk*, ' his shadow;'[2] the Quiché language uses *natub* for ' shadow, soul;'[3] the Arawak *ueja* means ' shadow, soul, image;'[4] the Abipones made the one word *loákal* serve for ' shadow, soul, echo, image.'[5] The Zulus not only use the word *tunzi* for ' shadow, spirit, ghost,' but they consider that at death the shadow of a man will in some way depart from the corpse, to become an ancestral spirit.[6] The Basutos not only call the spirit remaining after death the *seriti* or ' shadow,' but they think that if a man walks on the river bank, a crocodile may seize his shadow in the water and draw him in;[7] while in Old Calabar there is found the same identification of the spirit with the *ukpon* or ' shadow,' for a man to lose which is fatal.[8] There are thus found among the lower races not only the types of those familiar classic terms, the *skia* and *umbra*, but also what seems the fundamental thought of the stories of shadowless men still current in the folklore of Europe, and familiar to modern readers in Chamisso's tale of Peter

[1] Bonwick, ' Tasmanians,' p. 182.
[2] Tanner's ' Narr.' p. 291, Cree atchâk = soul.
[3] Brasseur, ' Langue Quichée,' s.v.
[4] Martius, ' Ethnog. Amer.' vol. i. p. 705 ; vol. ii. p. 310.
[5] Dobrizhoffer, ' Abipones,' vol. ii. p. 194.
[6] Döhne, ' Zulu Dic.' s.v. ' tunzi ; ' Callaway, ' Rel. of Amazulu,' pp. 91, 126 ; ' Zulu Tales,' vol. i. p. 342.
[7] Casalis, ' Basutos,' p. 245 ; Arbousset and Daumas, ' Voyage,' p. 12.
[8] Goldie, ' Efik Dictionary,' s.v. ; see Kölle, ' Afr. Native Lit.' p. 324 (Kanuri). Also ' Journ. Ind. Archip.' vol. v. p. 713 (Australian).

Schlemihl. Thus the dead in Purgatory knew that Dante was alive when they saw that, unlike theirs, his figure cast a shadow on the ground.[1] Other attributes are taken into the notion of soul or spirit, with especial regard to its being the cause of life. Thus the Caribs, connecting the pulses with spiritual beings, and especially considering that in the heart dwells man's chief soul, destined to a future heavenly life, could reasonably use the one word *iouanni* for ' soul, life, heart.'[2] The Tongans supposed the soul to exist throughout the whole extension of the body, but particularly in the heart. On one occasion, the natives were declaring to a European that a man buried months ago was nevertheless still alive. ' And one, endeavouring to make me understand what he meant, took hold of my hand, and squeezing it, said, "This will die, but the life that is within you will never die ; " with his other hand pointing to my heart.'[3] So the Basutos say of a dead man that his heart is gone out, and of one recovering from sickness that his heart is coming back.[4] This corresponds to the familiar Old World view of the heart as the prime mover in life, thought, and passion. The connexion of soul and blood, familiar to the Karens and Papuas, appears prominently in Jewish and Arabic philosophy.[5] To educated moderns the idea of the Macusi Indians of Guiana may seem quaint, that although the body will decay, ' the man in our eyes ' will not die, but wander about.[6] Yet the association of personal animation with the pupil of the eye is familiar to European folklore, which not unreasonably discerned a sign of bewitchment or approaching death in the disappearance of the image, pupil, or baby, from the dim eyeballs of the sick man.[7]

---

[1] Dante, ' Div. Comm. Purgatorio,' canto iii. Compare Grohmann, ' Aberglauben aus Böhmen,' p. 221. See *ante*, p. 85.

[2] Rochefort, pp. 429, 516 ; J. G. Müller, p. 207.

[3] Mariner, ' Tonga Is.' vol. ii. p. 135 ; S. S. Farmer, ' Tonga,' &c. p. 131.

[4] Casalis, l.c. See also Mariner, ibid.

[5] Bastian, ' Psychologie,' pp. 15-23.

[6] J. H. Bernau, ' Brit. Guiana,' p. 134.

[7] Grimm, ' D. M.' pp. 1028, 1133. Anglo-Saxon *man-lica*.

The act of breathing, so characteristic of the higher
animals during life, and coinciding so closely with life in its
departure, has been repeatedly and naturally identified with
the life or soul itself. Laura Bridgman showed in her instructive way the analogy between the effects of restricted
sense and restricted civilization, when one day she made
the gesture of taking something away from her mouth : ' I
dreamed,' she explained in words, ' that God took away
my breath to heaven.'[1] It is thus that West Australians
used one word *waug* for ' breath, spirit, soul;'[2] that in the
Netela language of California, *piuts* means ' life, breath,
soul;'[3] that certain Greenlanders reckoned two souls to
man, namely his shadow and his breath ;[4] that the Malays
say the soul of the dying man escapes through his nostrils,
and in Java use the same word *ñawa* for ' breath, life,
soul.'[5] How the notions of life, heart, breath, and phantom
unite in the one conception of a soul or spirit, and at the
same time how loose and vague such ideas are among
barbaric races, is well brought into view in the answers to
a religious inquest held in 1528 among the natives of
Nicaragua. ' When they die, there comes out of their
mouth something that resembles a person, and is called
julio [Aztec *yuli*=to live]. This being goes to the place
where the man and woman are. It is like a person, but
does not die, and the body remains here.' *Question*. ' Do
those who go up on high keep the same body, the same
face, and the same limbs, as here below ? ' *Answer*. ' No ;
there is only the heart.' *Question*. ' But since they tear
out their hearts [i.e. when a captive was sacrificed], what
happens then ? ' *Answer*. ' It is not precisely the heart,
but that in them which makes them live, and that quits the
body when they die.' Or, as stated in another interro-

[1] Lieber, ' Laura Bridgman,' in Smithsonian Contrib. vol. ii. p. 8.
[2] G. F. Moore, ' Vocab. of W. Australia,' p. 103.
[3] Brinton, p. 50, see p. 235 ; Bastian, ' Psychologie,' p. 15.
[4] Cranz, ' Grönland,' p. 257.
[5] Crawfurd, ' Malay Gr. and Dic.' s.v. ; Marsden, ' Sumatra,' p. 386.

gatory, ' It is not their heart that goes up above, but what makes them live, that is to say, the breath that issues from their mouth and is called *julio*.'[1] The conception of the soul as breath may be followed up through Semitic and Aryan etymology, and thus into the main streams of the philosophy of the world. Hebrew shows *nephesh*, ' breath,' passing into all the meanings of ' life, soul, mind, animal,' while *ruach* and *neshamah* make the like transition from ' breath ' to ' spirit ' ; and to these the Arabic *nefs* and *ruh* correspond. The same is the history of Sanskrit *âtman* and *prâna*, of Greek *psychē* and *pneuma*, of Latin *animus*, *anima*, *spiritus*. So Slavonic *duch* has developed the meaning of ' breath ' into that of soul or spirit ; and the dialects of the Gypsies have this word *dūk* with the meanings of ' breath, spirit, ghost,' whether these pariahs brought the word from India as part of their inheritance of Aryan speech, or whether they adopted it in their migration across Slavonic lands.[2] German *geist* and English *ghost*, too, may possibly have the same original sense of breath. And if any should think such expressions due to mere metaphor, they may judge the strength of the implied connexion between breath and spirit by cases of most unequivocal significance. Among the Seminoles of Florida, when a woman died in childbirth, the infant was held over her face to receive her parting spirit, and thus acquire strength and knowledge for its future use. These Indians could have well understood why at the death-bed of an ancient Roman, the nearest kinsman leant over to inhale the last breath of the departing (et excipies hanc animam ore pio). Their state of mind is kept up to this day among Tyrolese peasants, who can still fancy a good man's soul to issue from his mouth at death like a little white cloud.[3]

---

[1] Oviedo, ' Hist. du Nicaragua,' pp. 21-51.

[2] Pott, ' Zigeuner,' vol. ii. p. 306 ; ' Indo-Germ. Wurzel-Wörterbuch, vol. i. p. 1073 ; Borrow, ' Lavengro,' vol. ii. ch. xxvi. ' write the lil of him whose *dook* gallops down that hill every night,' see vol. iii. ch. iv.

[3] Brinton, ' Myths of New World,' p. 253 ; Comm. in Virg. Æn. iv. 684 ;

It will be shown that men, in their composite and confused notions of the soul, have brought into connexion a
list of manifestations of life and thought even more multifarious than this. But also, seeking to avoid such perplexity of combination, they have sometimes endeavoured
to define and classify more closely, especially by the theory
that man has a combination of several kinds of spirit, soul,
or image, to which different functions belong. Already
in the barbaric world such classification has been invented
or adopted. Thus the Fijians distinguished between a man's
' dark spirit ' or shadow, which goes to Hades, and his
' light spirit ' or reflexion in water or a mirror, which stays
near where he dies.[1] The Malagasy say that the *saina* or
mind vanishes at death, the *aina* or life becomes mere air,
but the *matoatoa* or ghost hovers round the tomb.[2] In
North America, the duality of the soul is a strongly marked
Algonquin belief ; one soul goes out and sees dreams while
the other remains behind ; at death one of the two abides
with the body, and for this the survivors leave offerings of
food, while the other departs to the land of the dead. A
division into three souls is also known, and the Dakotas
say that man has four souls, one remaining with the corpse,
one staying in the village, one going in the air, and one to
the land of spirits.[3] The Karens distinguish between the ' là '
or ' kelah,' the personal life-phantom, and the ' thah,' the
responsible moral soul.[4] More or less under Hindu influence,
the Khonds have a fourfold division, as follows : the first soul
is that capable of beatification or restoration to Boora the
Good Deity; the second is attached to a Khond tribe on earth
and is re-born generation after generation, so that at the

Cic. Verr. v. 45 ; Wuttke, ' Volksaberglaube,' p. 210 ; Rochholz, ' Deutscher
Glaube,' &c. vol. i. p. 111.

[1] Williams, ' Fiji,' vol. i. p. 241.

[2] Ellis, ' Madagascar,' vol. i. p. 393.

[3] Charlevoix, ' Nouvelle France,' vol. vi. pp. 75-8 ; Schoolcraft, ' Indian
Tribes,' part i. pp. 33, 83, part iv. p. 70 ; Waitz, vol. iii. p. 194; J. G.
Müller, pp. 66, 207-8.

[4] Cross in ' Journ. Amer. Oriental Soc.' vol. iv. p. 310.

birth of each child the priest asks who has returned ; the third goes out to hold spiritual intercourse, leaving the body in a languid state, and it is this soul which can pass for a time into a tiger, and transmigrates for punishment after death ; the fourth dies on the dissolution of the body.[1] Such classifications resemble those of higher nations, as for instance the three-fold division of shade, manes, and spirit :

> ' Bis duo sunt homini, manes, caro, spiritus, umbra :
> Quatuor ista loci bis duo suscipiunt.
> Terra tegit carnem, tumulum circumvolat umbra,
> Orcus habet manes, spiritus astra petit.'

Not attempting to follow up the details of such psychical division into the elaborate systems of literary nations, I shall not discuss the distinction which the ancient Egyptians seem to have made in the Ritual of the Dead between the man's *ba*, *akh*, *ka*, *khaba*, translated by Dr. Birch as his ' soul,' ' mind,' ' image,' ' shade,' or the Rabbinical division into what may be roughly described as the bodily, spiritual, and celestial souls, or the distinction between the emanative and genetic souls in Hindu philosophy, or the distribution of life, apparition, ancestral spirit, among the three souls of the Chinese, or the demarcations of the *nous*, *psychē*, and *pneuma*, or of the *anima* and *animus*, or the famous classic and mediæval theories of the vegetal, sensitive, and rational souls. Suffice it to point out here that such specu- lation dates back to the barbaric condition of our race, in a state fairly comparing as to scientific value with much that has gained esteem within the precincts of higher culture. It would be a difficult task to treat such classification on a consistent logical basis. Terms corresponding with those of life, mind, soul, spirit, ghost, and so forth, are not thought of as describing really separate entities, so much as the several forms and functions of one individual being. Thus

---

[1] Macpherson, pp. 91-2. See also Klemm, ' C. G.' vol. iii. p. 71 (Lapp) ; St. John, ' Far East,' vol. i. p. 189 (Dayaks).

the confusion which here prevails in our own thought and language, in a manner typical of the thought and language of mankind in general, is in fact due not merely to vagueness of terms, but to an ancient theory of substantial unity which underlies them. Such ambiguity of language, however, will be found to interfere little with the present enquiry, for the details given of the nature and action of spirits, souls, phantoms, will themselves define the exact sense such words are to be taken in.

The early animistic theory of vitality, regarding the functions of life as caused by the soul, offers to the savage mind an explanation of several bodily and mental conditions, as being effects of a departure of the soul or some of its constituent spirits. This theory holds a wide and strong position in savage biology. The South Australians express it when they say of one insensible or unconscious, that he is ' wilyamarraba,' i.e., ' without soul.'[1] Among the Algonquin Indians of North America, we hear of sickness being accounted for by the patient's ' shadow ' being unsettled or detached from his body, and of the convalescent being reproached for exposing himself before his shadow was safely settled down in him ; where we should say that a man was ill and recovered, they would consider that he died, but came again. Another account from among the same race explains the condition of men lying in lethargy or trance ; their souls have travelled to the banks of the River of Death, but have been driven back and return to reanimate their bodies.[2] Among the Fijians, ' when any one faints or dies, their spirit, it is said, may sometimes be brought back by calling after it ; and occasionally the ludicrous scene is witnessed of a stout man lying at full length, and bawling out lustily for the return of his own soul.'[3] To the negroes of North Guinea, derange-

---

[1] Shürmann, ' Vocab. of Parnkalla Lang.' s.v.
[2] Tanner's ' Narr.' p. 291 ; Keating, ' Narr. of Long's Exp.' vol. ii. p. 154.
[3] Williams, ' Fiji,' vol. i. p. 242 ; see the converse process of catching away a man's soul, causing him to pine and die, p. 250.

ment or dotage is caused by the patient being prematurely
deserted by his soul, sleep being a more temporary with-
drawal.[1] Thus, in various countries, the bringing back of
lost souls becomes a regular part of the sorcerer's or priest's
profession. The Salish Indians of Oregon regard the spirit
as distinct from the vital principle, and capable of quitting
the body for a short time without the patient being conscious of its absence ; but to avoid fatal consequences it
must be restored as soon as possible, and accordingly the
medicine-man in solemn form replaces it down through the
patient's head.[2] The Turanian or Tatar races of Northern
Asia strongly hold the theory of the soul's departure in
disease, and among the Buddhist tribes the Lamas carry
out the ceremony of soul-restoration in most elaborate
form. When a man has been robbed by a demon of his
rational soul, and has only his animal soul left, his senses
and memory grow weak and he falls into a dismal state.
Then the Lama undertakes to cure him, and with quaint
rites exorcises the evil demon. But if this fails, then it is the
patient's soul itself that cannot or will not find its way back.
So the sick man is laid out in his best attire and surrounded
with his most attractive possessions, the friends and relatives go thrice round the dwelling, affectionately calling back
the soul by name, while as a further inducement the Lama
reads from his book descriptions of the pains of hell, and
the dangers incurred by a soul which wilfully abandons its
body, and then at last the whole assembly declare with one
voice that the wandering spirit has returned and the patient
will recover.[3] The Karens of Burma will run about pretending to catch a sick man's wandering soul, or as they
say with the Greeks and Slavs, his ' butterfly ' (leip-pya),
and at last drop it down upon his head. The Karen doctrine of the ' là ' is indeed a perfect and well-marked

[1] J. L. Wilson, ' W. Afr.' p. 220.
[2] Bastian, ' Mensch,' vol. ii. p. 319 ; also Sproat, p. 213 (Vancouver's I.).
[3] Bastian, ' Psychologie,' p. 34; Gmelin, ' Reisen durch Sibirien,' vol. ii.
p. 359 (Yakuts) ; Ravenstein, ' Amur,' p. 351 (Tunguz).

vitalistic system. This là, soul, ghost, or genius, may be separated from the body it belongs to, and it is a matter of the deepest interest to the Karen to keep his là with him, by calling it, making offerings of food to it, and so forth. It is especially when the body is asleep, that the soul goes out and wanders ; if it is detained beyond a certain time, disease ensues, and if permanently, then its owner dies. When the ' wee ' or spirit-doctor is employed to call back the departed shade or life of a Karen, if he cannot recover it from the region of the dead, he will sometimes take the shade of a living man and transfer it to the dead, while its proper owner, whose soul has ventured out in a dream, sickens and dies. Or when a Karen becomes sick, languid and pining from his là having left him, his friends will perform a ceremony with a garment of the invalid's and a fowl which is cooked and offered with rice, invoking the spirit with formal prayers to come back to the patient.[1] This ceremony is perhaps ethnologically connected, though it is not easy to say by what manner of diffusion or when, with a rite still practised in China. When a Chinese is at the point of death, and his soul is supposed to be already out of his body, a relative may be seen holding up the patient's coat on a long bamboo, to which a white cock is often fastened, while a Tauist priest by incantations brings the departed spirit into the coat, in order to put it back into the sick man. If the bamboo after a time turns round slowly in the holder's hands, this shows that the spirit is inside the garment.[2]

Such temporary exit of the soul has a world-wide application to the proceedings of the sorcerer, priest, or seer himself. He professes to send forth his spirit on distant

[1] Bastian, ' Oestl. Asien,' vol. i. p. 143 ; vol. ii. pp. 388, 418 ; vol. iii. p. 236. Mason, ' Karens,' l.c. p. 196, &c. ; Cross, ' Karens,' in ' Journ. Amer. Oriental Soc.' vol. iv. 1854, p. 307. See also St. John, ' Far East,' l.c. (Dayaks).

[2] Doolittle, ' Chinese,' vol. i. p. 150.

journeys, and probably often believes his soul released for a time from its bodily prison, as in the case of that remarkable dreamer and visionary Jerome Cardan, who describes himself as having the faculty of passing out of his senses as into ecstasy whenever he will, feeling when he goes into this state a sort of separation near the heart as if his soul were departing, this state beginning from his brain and passing down his spine, and he then feeling only that he is out of himself.[1] Thus the Australian native doctor is alleged to obtain his initiation by visiting the world of spirits in a trance of two or three days' duration;[2] the Khond priest authenticates his claim to office by remaining from one to fourteen days in a languid and dreamy state, caused by one of his souls being away in the divine presence;[3] the Greenland angekok's soul goes forth from his body to fetch his familiar demon;[4] the Turanian shaman lies in lethargy while his soul departs to bring hidden wisdom from the land of spirits.[5] The literature of more progressive races supplies similar accounts. A characteristic story from old Scandinavia is that of the Norse chief Ingimund, who shut up three Finns in a hut for three nights, that they might visit Iceland and inform him of the lie of the country where he was to settle ; their bodies became rigid, they sent their souls on the errand, and awakening after the three days they gave a description of the Vatnsdæl.[6] The typical classic case is the story of Hermotimos, whose prophetic soul went out from time to time to visit distant regions, till at last his wife burnt the lifeless body on the funeral pile, and when the poor soul came back, there was no longer a dwelling for it to animate.[7] A group of the legendary visits to the

---

[1] Cardan, ' De Varietate Rerum,' Basel, 1556, cap. xliii.

[2] Stanbridge, ' Abor. of Victoria,' in ' Tr. Eth. Soc.' vol. i. p. 300.

[3] Macpherson, ' India,' p. 103.

[4] Cranz, ' Grönland,' p. 269. See also Sproat, l.c.

[5] Rühs, ' Finland,' p. 303 ; Castrén, ' Finn. Myth.' p. 134 ; Bastian, Mensch,' vol. ii. p. 319.

[6] Vatnsdæla Saga ; Baring-Gould, ' Werewolves,' p. 29.

[7] Plin. vii. 53 ; Lucian. Hermotimus, Musc. Encom. 7.

spirit-world, which will be described in the next chapter, belong to this class. A typical spiritualistic instance may be quoted from Jung-Stilling, who says that examples have come to his knowledge of sick persons who, longing to see absent friends, have fallen into a swoon during which they have appeared to the distant objects of their affection.[1] As an illustration from our own folklore, the well-known superstition may serve, that fasting watchers on St. John's Eve may see the apparitions of those doomed to die during the year come with the clergyman to the church door and knock ; these apparitions are spirits who come forth from their bodies, for the minister has been noticed to be much troubled in his sleep while his phantom was thus engaged, and when one of a party of watchers fell into a sound sleep and could not be roused, the others saw his apparition knock at the church door.[2] Modern Europe has indeed kept closely enough to the lines of early philosophy, for such ideas to have little strangeness to our own time. Language preserves record of them in such expressions as ' out of oneself,' ' beside oneself,' ' in an ecstasy,' and he who says that his spirit goes forth to meet a friend, can still realize in the phrase a meaning deeper than metaphor.

This same doctrine forms one side of the theory of dreams prevalent among the lower races. Certain of the Greenlanders, Cranz remarks, consider that the soul quits the body in the night and goes out hunting, dancing, and visiting ; their dreams, which are frequent and lively, having brought them to this opinion.[3] Among the Indians of North America, we hear of the dreamer's soul leaving his body and wandering in quest of things attractive to it. These things the waking man must endeavour to obtain,

---

[1] R. D. Owen, ' Footfalls on the Boundary of another World,' p. 259. See A. R. Wallace, ' Scientific Aspect of the Supernatural,' p. 43.

[2] Brand, ' Pop. Ant.' vol. i. p. 331, vol. iii. p. 236. See Calmet, ' Diss. sur les Esprits ; ' Maury, ' Magie,' part ii. ch. iv.

[3] Cranz, ' Grönland,' p. 257.

lest his soul be troubled, and quit the body altogether.[1]
The New Zealanders considered the dreaming soul to leave
the body and return, even travelling to the region of the
dead to hold converse with its friends.[2] The Tagals of
Luzon object to waking a sleeper, on account of the absence
of his soul.[3] The Karens, whose theory of the wandering
soul has just been noticed, explain dreams to be what this
là sees and experiences in its journeys when it has left the
body asleep. They even account with much acuteness for
the fact that we are apt to dream of people and places
which we knew before ; the leip-pya, they say, can only
visit the regions where the body it belongs to has been
already.[4] Onward from the savage state, the idea of the
spirit's departure in sleep may be traced into the speculative philosophy of higher nations, as in the Vedanta
system, and the Kabbala.[5] St. Augustine tells one of the
double narratives which so well illustrate theories of this
kind. The man who tells Augustine the story relates that,
at home one night before going to sleep, he saw coming to
him a certain philosopher, most well known to him, who
then expounded to him certain Platonic passages, which
when asked previously he had refused to explain. And
when he (afterwards) enquired of this philosopher why he
did at his house what he had refused to do when asked at
his own : ' I did not do it,' said the philosopher, ' but I
dreamt I did.' And thus, says Augustine, that was ex-
hibited to one by phantastic image while waking, which the
other saw in a dream.[6] European folklore, too, has preserved
interesting details of this primitive dream-theory, such as

---

[1] Waitz, vol. iii. p. 195.

[2] Taylor, ' New Zealand,' pp. 104, 184, 333 ; Baker in ' Tr. Eth. Soc.' vol.
i. p. 57.

[3] Bastian, ' Mensch,' vol. ii. p. 319 ; Jagor in ' Journ. Eth. Soc.,' vol. ii.
p. 175.

[4] Mason, ' Karens,' l.c. p. 199 ; Cross, l.c. ; Bastian, ' Oestl. Asien,' vol. i.
p. 144, vol. ii. p. 389, vol. iii. p. 266.

[5] Bastian, ' Psychologie,' pp. 16-20 ; Eisenmenger, vol. i. p. 458, vol. ii.
pp. 13, 20, 453 ; Franck, ' Kabbale,' p. 235.

[6] Augustin. De Civ. Dei, xviii. 18.

the fear of turning a sleeper over lest the absent soul should miss the way back. King Gunthram's legend is one of a group interesting from the same point of view. The king lay in the wood asleep with his head in his faithful hench-man's lap ; the servant saw as it were a snake issue from his lord's mouth and run to the brook, but it could not pass, so the servant laid his sword across the water, and the creature ran along it and up into a mountain; after a while it came back and returned into the mouth of the sleeping king, who waking told him how he had dreamt that he went over an iron bridge into a mountain full of gold.[1] This is one of those instructive legends which preserve for us, as in a museum, relics of an early intellectual condition of our Aryan race, in thoughts which to our modern minds have fallen to the level of quaint fancy, but which still remain sound and reasonable philosophy to the savage. A Karen at this day would appreciate every point of the story ; the familiar notion of spirits not crossing water which he ex-emplifies in his Burmese forests by stretching threads across the brook for the ghosts to pass along ; the idea of the soul going forth embodied in an animal; and the theory of the dream being a real journey of the sleeper's soul. Finally, this old belief still finds, as such beliefs so often do, a refuge in modern poetry :

> 'Yon child is dreaming far away,
> And is not where he seems.'

This opinion, however, only constitutes one of several parts of the theory of dreams in savage psychology. An-other part has also a place here, the view that human souls come from without to visit the sleeper, who sees them as dreams. These two views are by no means incompatible. The North American Indians allowed themselves the alterna-tive of supposing a dream to be either a visit from the soul of the person or object dreamt of, or a sight seen by the rational soul, gone out for an excursion while the sensi-

[1] Grimm, 'D. M.' p. 1036.

tive soul remains in the body.[1] So the Zulu may be visited
in a dream by the shade of an ancestor, the itongo, who
comes to warn him of danger, or he may himself be taken
by the itongo in a dream to visit his distant people, and see
that they are in trouble; as for the man who is passing into
the morbid condition of the professional seer, phantoms are
continually coming to talk to him in his sleep, till he becomes,
as the expressive native phrase is, ' a house of dreams.'[2]
In the lower range of culture, it is perhaps most frequently
taken for granted that a man's apparition in a dream is a
visit from his disembodied spirit, which the dreamer, to use
an expressive Ojibwa idiom, ' sees when asleep.' Such a
thought comes out clearly in the Fijian opinion that a living
man's spirit may leave the body, to trouble other people in
their sleep;[3] or in a recent account of an old Indian woman
of British Columbia sending for the medicine-man to drive
away the dead people who came to her every night.[4] A
modern observer's description of the state of mind of the
negroes of West Africa in this respect is extremely characteristic and instructive. ' All their dreams are construed
into visits from the spirits of their deceased friends. The
cautions, hints, and warnings which come to them through
this source are received with the most serious and deferential
attention, and are always acted upon in their waking hours.
The habit of relating their dreams, which is universal,
greatly promotes the habit of dreaming itself, and hence
their sleeping hours are characterized by almost as much
intercourse with the dead as their waking are with the
living. This is, no doubt, one of the reasons of their exces-
sive superstitiousness. Their imaginations become so lively
that they can scarcely distinguish between their dreams and
their waking thoughts, between the real and the ideal, and

[1] Charlevoix, ' Nouvelle France,' vol. vi. p. 78 ; Lafitau, ' Mœurs des
Sauvages,' vol. i. p. 363.
[2] Callaway, ' Relig. of Amazulu,' pp. 228, 260, 316 ; ' Journ. Anthrop.
Inst.' vol. i. p. 170. See also St. John, ' Far East,' vol. i. p. 199 (Dayaks).
[3] Williams, ' Fiji,' vol. i. p. 242.
[4] Mayne, ' Brit. Columbia,' p. 261 ; see Sproat, l.c.

they consequently utter falsehood without intending, and profess to see things which never existed.'[1]

To the Greek of old, the dream-soul was what to the modern savage it still is. Sleep, loosing cares of mind, fell on Achilles as he lay by the sounding sea, and there stood over him the soul of Patroklos, like to him altogether in stature, and the beauteous eyes, and the voice, and the garments that wrapped his skin ; he spake, and Achilles stretched out to grasp him with loving hands, but caught him not, and like a smoke the soul sped twittering below the earth. Along the ages that separate us from Homeric times, the apparition in dreams of men living or dead has been a subject of philosophic speculation and of superstitious fear.[2] Both the phantom of the living and the ghost of the dead figure in Cicero's typical tale. Two Arcadians came to Megara together, one lodged at a friend's house, the other at an inn. In the night this latter appeared to his fellow-traveller, imploring his help, for the innkeeper was plotting his death ; the sleeper sprang up in alarm, but thinking the vision of no consequence went to sleep again. Then a second time his companion appeared to him, to entreat that though he had failed to help, he would at least avenge, for the innkeeper had killed him and hidden his body in a dung-cart, wherefore he charged his fellow-traveller to be early next morning at the city-gate before the cart passed out. Struck with this second dream, the traveller went as bidden, and there found the cart ; the body of the murdered man was in it, and the innkeeper was brought to justice. ' Quid hoc somnio dici potest divinius ! '[3] Augustine discusses with reference to the nature of the soul various dream-stories of his time, where the apparitions of men dead or living are seen in dreams.

[1] J. L. Wilson, ' W. Africa,' pp. 210, 395 ; M. H. Kingsley, ' W. African Studies,' p. 205. See also Ellis, ' Polyn. Res.' vol. i. p. 396 ; J. G. Müller, ' Amer. Urrel.' p. 287 ; Buchanan, ' Mysore,' in Pinkerton, vol. viii. p. 677 ; ' Early Hist. of Mankind,' p. 8.

[2] Homer. Il. xxiii. 59. See also Odyss. xi. 207, 222 ; Porphyr. De Antro Nympharum ; Virgil. Æn. ii. 794 ; Ovid. Fast. v. 475.

[3] Cicero De Divinatione, i. 27.

In one of the latter he himself figured, for when a disciple of his, Eulogius the rhetor of Carthage, once could not get to sleep for thinking of an obscure passage in Cicero's Rhetoric, that night Augustine came to him in a dream and explained it. But Augustine's tendency was toward the modern theory of dreams, and in this case he says it was certainly his image that appeared, not himself, who was far across the sea, neither knowing nor caring about the matter.[1] As we survey the immense series of dream-stories of similar types in patristic, mediæval, and modern literature, we may find it difficult enough to decide which are truth and which are fiction. But along the course of these myriad narratives of human phantoms appearing in dreams to cheer or torment, to warn or inform, or to demand fulfilment of their own desires, the problem of dream-apparitions may be traced in progress of gradual determination, from the earlier conviction that a disembodied soul really comes into the presence of the sleeper, toward the later opinion that such a phantasm is produced in the dreamer's mind without the perception of any external objective figure.

The evidence of visions corresponds with the evidence of dreams in their bearing on primitive theories of the soul,[2] and the two classes of phenomena substantiate and supplement one another. Even in healthy waking life, the savage or barbarian has never learnt to make that rigid distinction between subjective and objective, between imagination and reality, to enforce which is one of the main results of scientific education. Still less, when disordered in body and mind he sees around him phantom human forms, can he distrust the evidence of his very senses. Thus it comes to pass that throughout the lower civilization men believe, with the most vivid and intense belief, in the objective reality of the human spectres which they see in sickness, exhaustion, or excitement. As will be hereafter noticed, one main reason of the practices of fasting, penance, narcotising by drugs, and

[1] Augustin. De Curâ pro Mortuis, x.-xii. Epist. clviii.
[2] Compare Voltaire's remarks, ' Dict. Phil.' art. ' ame,' &c.

other means of bringing on morbid exaltation, is that the patients may obtain the sight of spectral beings, from whom they look to gain spiritual knowledge and even worldly power. Human ghosts are among the principal of these phantasmal figures. There is no doubt that honest visionaries describe ghosts as they really appear to their perception, while even the impostors who pretend to see them conform to the descriptions thus established ; thus, in West Africa, a man's *kla* or soul, becoming at his death a *sisa* or ghost, can remain in the house with the corpse, but is only visible to the wong-man, the spirit-doctor.[1] Sometimes the phantom has the characteristic quality of not being visible to all of an assembled company. Thus the natives of the Antilles believed that the dead appeared on the roads when one went alone, but not when many went together;[2] thus among the Finns the ghosts of the dead were to be seen by the shamans, but not by men generally unless in dreams.[3] Such is perhaps the meaning of the description of Samuel's ghost, visible to the witch of Endor, but not to Saul, for he has to ask her what it is she sees.[4] Yet this test of the nature of an apparition is one which easily breaks down. We know well how in civilized countries a current rumour of some one having seen a phantom is enough to bring a sight of it to others whose minds are in a properly receptive state. The condition of the modern ghost-seer, whose imagination passes on such slight excitement into positive hallucination is rather the rule than the exception among uncultured and intensely imaginative tribes, whose minds may be thrown off their balance by a touch, a word, a gesture, an unaccustomed noise. Among savage tribes, however, as among civilized races who have inherited remains of early philosophy formed under similar conditions, the doctrine of visibility or

[1] Steinhauser, ' Religion des Negers,' in ' Magazin der Evang. Missionen, Basel, 1856, No. 2, p. 135.

[2] ' Historie del S. D. Fernando Colombo,' tr. Alfonso Ulloa, Venice, 1571, p. 127, Eng. Tr. in Pinkerton, vol. xii. p. 80.

[3] Castrén, ' Finn. Myth.' p. 120.

[4] 1 Sam. xxviii. 12.

invisibility of phantoms has been obviously shaped with reference to actual experience. To declare that souls or ghosts are necessarily either visible or invisible, would directly contradict the evidence of men's senses. But to assert or imply, as the lower races do, that they are visible sometimes and to some persons, but not always or to every one, is to lay down an explanation of facts which is not indeed our usual modern explanation, but which is a perfectly rational and intelligible product of early science.

Without discussing on their merits the accounts of what is called ' second sight,' it may be pointed out that they are related among savage tribes, as wi_en Captain Jonathan Carver obtained from a Cree medicine-man a true prophecy of the arrival of a canoe with news next day at noon ; or when Mr. J. Mason Brown, travelling with two voyageurs on the Coppermine River, was met by Indians of the very band he was seeking, these having been sent by their medicine-man, who, on enquiry, stated that ' He saw them coming, and heard them talk on their journey.' [1] These are analogous to accounts of the Highland second-sight, as when Pennant heard of a gentleman of the Hebrides, said to have the convenient gift of foreseeing visitors in time to get ready for them, or when Dr. Johnson was told by another laird 'that a labouring man of his had predicted his return to the island, and described the peculiar livery his servant had been newly dressed in.[2]

As a general rule, people are apt to consider it impossible for a man to be in two places at once, and indeed a saying to that effect has become a popular saw. But the rule is so far from being universally accepted, that the word ' bilocation ' has been invented to express the miraculous faculty possessed by certain Saints of the Roman Church, of being in two places at once ; like St. Alfonso di Liguori, who had the useful power of preaching his sermon in church while

[1] Brinton, ' Myths of New World,' p. 269.
[2] Pennant, ' 2nd Tour in Scotland,' in Pinkerton, vol. iii. p. 315 ; Johnson, ' Journey to the Hebrides.'

he was confessing penitents at home.[1] The reception and explanation of these various classes of stories fit perfectly with the primitive animistic theory of apparitions, and the same is true of the following most numerous class of the second-sight narratives.

Death is the event which, in all stages of culture, brings thought to bear most intensely, though not always most healthily, on the problems of psychology. The apparition of the disembodied soul has in all ages been thought to bear especial relation to its departure from its body at death. This is well shown by the reception not only of a theory of ghosts, but of a special doctrine of ' wraiths ' or ' fetches.' Thus the Karens say that a man's spirit, appearing after death, may thus announce it.[2] In New Zealand it is ominous to see the figure of an absent person, for if it be shadowy and the face not visible, his death may ere long be expected, but if the face be seen he is dead already. A party of Maoris (one of whom told the story) were seated round a fire in the open air, when there appeared, seen only by two of them, the figure of a relative left ill at home ; they ex-claimed, the figure vanished, and on the return of the party it appeared that the sick man had died about the time of the vision.[3] Examining the position of the doctrine of wraiths among the higher races, we find it especially prominent in three intellectual districts, Christian hagiology, popular folk-lore, and modern spiritualism. St. Anthony saw the soul of St. Ammonius carried to heaven in the midst of choirs of angels, the same day that the holy hermit died five days' journey off in the desert of Nitria ; when St. Ambrose died on Easter Eve, several newly-baptized children saw the holy bishop, and pointed him out to their parents, but these with their less pure eyes could not behold him ; and so forth.[4]

[1] J. Gardner, ' Faiths of the World,' s.v. ' bilocation.'

[2] Mason, ' Karens,' l.c. p. 198.

[3] Shortland, ' Trads. of New Zealand,' p. 140 ; Polack, ' M. and C. of New Zealanders,' vol. i. p. 268. See also Ellis, ' Madagascar,' vol. i. p. 393 ; J. G. Müller, p. 261.

[4] Calmet, ' Diss. sur les Esprits,' vol. i. ch. xl.

Folklore examples abound in Silesia and the Tyrol, where the gift of wraith-seeing still flourishes, with the customary details of funerals, churches, four-cross-roads, and headless phantoms, and an especial association with New Year's Eve. The accounts of ' second-sight ' from North Britain mostly belong to a somewhat older date. Thus the St. Kilda people used to be haunted by their own spectral doubles, forerunners of impending death, and in 1799 a traveller writes of the peasants of Kirkcudbrightshire, ' It is common among them to fancy that they see the wraiths of persons dying, which will be visible to one and not to others present with him. Within these last twenty years, it was hardly possible to meet with any person who had not seen many wraiths and ghosts in the course of his experience.' Those who discuss the authenticity of the second-sight stories as actual evidence, must bear in mind that they prove a little too much ; they vouch not only for human apparitions, but for such phantoms as demon-dogs, and for still more fanciful symbolic omens. Thus a phantom shroud seen in spiritual vision on a living man predicts his death, immediate if it is up to his head, less nearly approaching if it is only up to his waist ; and to see in spiritual vision a spark of fire fall upon a person's arm or breast, is a forerunner of a dead child to be seen in his arms.[1] As visionaries often see phantoms of living persons without any remarkable event coinciding with their hallucinations, it is naturally admitted that a man's phantom or ' double ' may be seen without portending anything in particular. The spiritualistic theory specially insists on cases of apparition where the person's death corresponds more or less nearly with the time when some friend perceives his phantom.[2] Narratives of this class, which I can here only specify without arguing on them, are

[1] Wuttke, ' Volksaberglaube,' pp. 44, 56, 208 ; Brand, ' Popular Antiquities,' vol. iii. pp. 155, 235 ; Johnson, ' Journey to the Hebrides ; ' Martin, ' Western Islands of Scotland,' in Pinkerton, vol. iii. p. 670.

[2] See R. D. Owen, ' Footfalls on the Boundary of another World ; ' Mrs. Crowe, ' Night-Side of Nature ; ' Howitt's Tr. of Ennemoser's ' Magic,' &c.

abundantly in circulation. Thus, I have an account by a lady, who ' saw, as it were, the form of some one laid out,' near the time when a brother died at Melbourne, and who mentions another lady known to her, who thought she saw her own father look in at the church window at the moment he was dying in his own house. Another account is sent me by a Shetland lady, who relates that about twenty years ago she and a girl leading her pony recognized the familiar figure of one Peter Sutherland, whom they knew to be at the time in ill-health in Edinburgh; he turned a corner and they saw no more of him, but next week came the news of his sudden death.

That the apparitional human soul bears the likeness of its fleshly body, is the principle implicitly accepted by all who believe it really and objectively present in dreams and visions. My own view is that nothing but dreams and visions could have ever put into men's minds such an idea as that of souls being ethereal images of bodies. It is thus habitually taken for granted in animistic philosophy, savage or civilized, that souls set free from the earthly body are recognized by a likeness to it which they still retain, whether as ghostly wanderers on earth or inhabitants of the world beyond the grave. Man's spirit, says Swedenborg, is his mind, which lives after death in complete human form, and this is the poet's dictum in ' In Memoriam : '

> ' Eternal form shall still divide
> The eternal soul from all beside ;
> And I shall know him when we meet.'

This world-wide thought, coming into view here in a multitude of cases from all grades of culture, needs no collection of ordinary instances to illustrate it.[1] But a quaint and special group of beliefs will serve to display the thorough-

---

[1] The conception of the soul as a small human image is found in various districts ; see Eyre, ' Australia,' vol. ii. p. 356 ; St. John, ' Far East,' vol. i. p. 189 (Dayaks) ; Waitz, vol. iii. p. 194 (N. A. Ind.). The idea of a soul as a sort of ' thumbling ' is familiar to the Hindus and to German folklore ; compare the representations of tiny souls in mediæval pictures.

ness with which the soul is thus conceived as an image of the body. As a consistent corollary to such an opinion, it is argued that the mutilation of the body will have a corresponding effect upon the soul, and very low savage races have philosophy enough to work out this idea. Thus it was recorded of the Indians of Brazil by one of the early European visitors, that they ' believe that the dead arrive in the other world wounded or hacked to pieces, in fact just as they left this.'[1] Thus, too, the Australian who has slain his enemy will cut off the right thumb of the corpse, so that although the spirit will become a hostile ghost, it cannot throw with its mutilated hand the shadowy spear, and may be safely left to wander, malignant but harmless.[2] The negro fears long sickness before death, such as will send him lean and feeble into the next world. His theory of the mutilation of soul with body could not be brought more vividly into view than in that ugly story of the West Indian planter, whose slaves began to seek in suicide at once relief from present misery and restoration to their native land ; but the white man was too cunning for them, he cut off the heads and hands of the corpses, and the survivors saw that not even death could save them from a master who could maim their very souls in the next world.[3] The same rude and primitive belief continues among nations risen far higher in intellectual rank. The Chinese hold in especial horror the punishment of decapitation, considering that he who quits this world lacking a member will so arrive in the next, and a case is recorded lately of a criminal at Amoy who for this reason begged to die instead by the cruel death of crucifixion, and was crucified accordingly.[4] The series ends as usual in the folklore of the civilized world. The phantom skeleton in chains that haunted the house at

[1] Magalhanes de Gandavo, p. 110 ; Maffei, ' Indie Orientali,' p. 107.

[2] Oldfield in ' Tr. Eth. Soc.' vol. iii. p. 287.

[3] Waitz, vol. ii. p. 194 ; Römer, ' Guinea,' p. 42.

[4] Meiners, vol. ii. pp. 756, 763 ; Purchas, vol. iii. p. 495 ; J. Jones in ' Tr. Eth. Soc.' vol. iii. p. 138.

Bologna, showed the way to the garden where was buried the real chained fleshless skeleton it belonged to, and came no more when the remains had been duly buried. When the Earl of Cornwall met the fetch of his friend William Rufus carried black and naked on a black goat across the Bodmin moors, he saw that it was wounded through the midst of the breast ; and afterwards he heard that at that very hour the king had been slain in the New Forest by the arrow of Walter Tirell.[1]

In studying the nature of the soul as conceived among the lower races, and in tracing such conceptions onward among the higher, circumstantial details are available. It is as widely recognized among mankind that souls or ghosts have voices, as that they have visible forms, and indeed the evidence for both is of the same nature. Men who perceive evidently that souls do talk when they present themselves in dream or vision, naturally take for granted at once the objective reality of the ghostly voice, and of the ghostly form from which it proceeds. This is involved in the series of narratives of spiritual communications with living men, from savagery onward to civilization, while the more modern doctrine of the subjectivity of such phenomena recognizes the phenomena themselves, but offers a different explanation of them. One special conception, however, requires particular notice. This defines the spirit-voice as being a low murmur, chirp, or whistle, as it were the ghost of a voice. The Algonquin Indians of North America could hear the shadow-souls of the dead chirp like crickets.[2] The divine spirits of the New Zealand dead, coming to converse with the living, utter their words in whistling tones, and such utterances by a squeaking noise are mentioned elsewhere in Polynesia.[3] The Zulu diviner's familiar

[1] Calmet, vol. i. ch. xxxvi. ; Plin. Ep. vii. 27 ; Hunt, ' Pop. Romances,' vol. ii. p. 156.
[2] Le Jeune in ' Rel. des Jésuites,' 1639, p. 43 ; see 1634, p. 13.
[3] Shortland, ' Trads. of N. Z.' p. 92 ; Yate, p. 140 ; R. Taylor, pp. 104, 153 ; Ellis, ' Polyn. Res.' vol. i. p. 406.

spirits are ancestral manes, who talk in a low whistling
tone short of a full whistle, whence they have their name
of ' imilozi ' or whistlers.[1] These ideas correspond with
classic descriptions of the ghostly voice, as a ' twitter '
or ' thin murmur : '

$$\Psi υχὴ \ δὲ \ κατὰ \ χθονὸς \ ἠῦτε \ καπνὸς,$$
ᾤχετο τετριγυῖα.' [2]

' Umbra cruenta Remi visa est assistere lecto,
   Atque haec exiguo murmure verba loqui.' [3]

As the attributes of the soul or ghost extend to other
spiritual beings, and the utterances of such are to a great
extent given by the voice of mediums, we connect these
accounts with the notion that the language of demons is
also a low whistle or mutter, whence the well-known practice
of whispering or murmuring charms, the ' susurrus necro-
manticus ' of sorcerers, to whom the already cited description of ' wizards that peep (i.e. chirp) and mutter ' is
widely applicable.[4]

The conception of dreams and visions as caused by
present objective figures, and the identification of such
phantom souls with the shadow and the breath, has led
to the treatment of souls as substantial material beings.
Thus it is a usual proceeding to make openings through
solid materials to allow souls to pass. The Iroquois in
old times used to leave an opening in the grave for the
lingering soul to visit its body, and some of them still

---

[1] Callaway, ' Rel. of Amazulu,' pp. 265, 348, 370.
[2] Homer, Il. xxiii. 100.
[3] Ovid, Fast. v. 457.
[4] Isaiah viii. 19 ; xxix. 4. The Arabs hate whistling (el sifr), it is talking
to devils (Burton, ' First Footsteps in East Africa,' p. 142). ' Nicolaus Remi-
gius, whose " Daemonolatreia " is one of the ghastliest volumes in the ghastly
literature of witchcraft, cites Hermolaus Barbarus as having heard the voice
sub-sibilantis daemonis, and, after giving other instances, adduces the authority of Psellus to prove that the devils generally speak very low and con-
fusedly in order not to be caught fibbing,' Dr Sebastian Evans in ' Nature,'
June 22, 1871, p. 140. (Nicolai Remigii Daemonolatreia, Col. Agripp. 1596,
lib. i. c. 8, ' pleraeque aliae vocem illis esse aiunt qualem emittunt qui os
in dolium aut restam rimosam insertum habent '—' ut Daemones e pelvi
stridulâ voce ac tenui sibilo verba ederent ').

bore holes in the coffin for the same purpose.[1] The Malagasy sorcerer, for the cure of a sick man who had lost his
soul, would make a hole in a burial-house to let out a
spirit, which he would catch in his cap and so convey to
the patient's head.[2] The Chinese make a hole in the roof
to let out the soul at death.[3] And lastly, the custom
of opening a window or door for the departing soul when
it quits the body is to this day a very familiar superstition
in France, Germany, and England.[4] Again, the souls of
the dead are thought susceptible of being beaten, hurt
and driven like any other living creatures. Thus the
Queensland aborigines would beat the air in an annual
mock fight, held to scare away the souls that death had
let loose among the living since last year.[5] Thus North
American Indians, when they had tortured an enemy to
death, ran about crying and beating with sticks to scare
the ghost away ; they have been known to set nets round
their cabins to catch and keep out neighbours' departed
souls ; fancying the soul of a dying man to go out at the
wigwam roof, they would habitually beat the sides with
sticks to drive it forth ; we even hear of the widow going
off from her husband's funeral followed by a person flourishing a handful of twigs about her head like a flyflapper, to
drive off her husband's ghost and leave her free to marry
again.[6] With a kindlier feeling, the Congo negroes abstained for a whole year after a death from sweeping the
house, lest the dust should injure the delicate substance of
the ghost;[7] the Tonquinese avoided house-cleaning during
the festival when the souls of the dead came back to their

---

[1] Morgan, ' Iroquois,' p. 176.

[2] Flacourt, ' Madagascar,' p. 101.

[3] N. B. Dennys, ' Folk-Lore of China,' p. 22.

[4] Monnier, ' Traditions Populaires,' p. 142 ; Wuttke, ' Volksaberglaube,'
p. 209 ; Grimm, ' D. M.' p. 801 ; Meiners, vol. ii. p. 761.

[5] Lang, ' Queensland,' p. 441 ; Bonwick ,' Tasmanians,' p. 187.

[6] Charlevoix, ' Nouvelle France,' vol. vi. pp. 76, 122 ; Le Jeune in ' Rel.
des Jésuites,' 1634, p. 23 ; 1639, p. 44 ; Tanner's ' Narr.' p. 292 ; Peter Jones,
' Hist. of Ojebway Indians,' p. 99.

[7] Bastian, ' Mensch,' vol. ii. p. 323.

houses for the New Year's visit;[1] and it seems likely that the special profession of the Roman ' everriatores ' who swept the houses out after a funeral, was connected with a similar idea.[2] To this day, it remains a German peasants' saying that it is wrong to slam a door, lest one should pinch a soul in it.[3] The not uncommon practice of strewing ashes to show the footprints of ghosts or demons takes for granted that they are substantial bodies. In the literature of animism, extreme tests of the weight of ghosts are now and then forthcoming. They range from the declaration of a Basuto diviner that the late queen had been bestriding his shoulders, and he never felt such a weight in his life, to Glanvil's story of David Hunter the neatherd, who lifted up the old woman's ghost, and she felt just like a bag of feathers in his arms, or the pathetic German superstition that the dead mother's coming back in the night to suckle the baby she has left on earth, may be known by the hollow pressed down in the bed where she lay, and at last down to the alleged modern spiritualistic reckoning of the weight of a human soul at from 3 to 4 ounces.[4]

Explicit statements as to the substance of soul are to be found both among low and high races, in an instructive series of definitions. The Tongans imagined the human soul to be the finer or more aeriform part of the body, which leaves it suddenly at the moment of death ; something comparable to the perfume and essence of a flower as related to the more solid vegetable fibre.[5] The Greenland seers described the soul as they habitually perceived it in their visions ; it is pale and soft, they said, and he who tries to seize it feels nothing, for it has no flesh nor bone

[1] Meiners, vol. i. p. 318.
[2] Festus, s.v. ' everriatores ; ' see Bastian, l.c., and compare Hartknoch, cited below, vol. ii. p. 40.
[3] Wuttke, ' Volksaberglaube,' pp. 132, 216.
[4] Casalis, ' Basutos,' p. 285 ; Glanvil, ' Saducismus Triumphatus,' part ii. p. 161 ; Wuttke, p. 216; Bastian ' Psychologie ' p. 192.
[5] Mariner, ' Tonga Is.' vol. ii. p. 135.

nor sinew.[1] The Caribs did not think the soul so immaterial as to be invisible, but said it was subtle and thin like
a purified body.[2] Turning to higher races, we may take
the Siamese as an example of a people who conceive of
souls as consisting of subtle matter escaping sight and
touch, or as united to a swiftly moving aerial body.[3] In
the classic world, it is recorded as an opinion of Epicurus
that 'they who say the soul is incorporeal talk folly, for it
could neither do nor suffer anything were it such.'[4] Among
the Fathers, Irenæus describes souls as incorporeal in comparison with mortal bodies,[5] and Tertullian relates a vision
or revelation of a certain Montanist prophetess, of the soul
seen by her corporeally, thin and lucid, aerial in colour and
human in form.[6] For an example of mediæval doctrine,
may be cited a 14th-century English poem, the 'Ayenbite
of Inwyt' (i.e. 'Remorse of Conscience') which points
out how the soul, by reason of the thinness of its substance,
suffers all the more in purgatory :

> 'The soul is more tendre and nesche
> Than the bodi that hath bones and fleysche ;
> Thanne the soul that is so tendere of kinde,
> Mote nedis hure penaunce hardere y-finde,
> Than eni bodi that evere on live was.'[7]

The doctrine of the ethereal soul passed on into more
modern philosophy, and the European peasant holds fast to
it still ; as Wuttke says, the ghosts of the dead have to him
a misty and evanescent materiality, for they have bodies as
we have, though of other kind: they can eat and drink,
they can be wounded and killed.[8] Nor was the ancient

---

[1] Cranz, ' Grönland,' p. 257.

[2] Rochefort, ' Iles Antilles,' p. 429.

[3] Loubere, ' Siam,' vol. i. p. 458 ; Bastian, ' Oestl. Asien,' vol. iii. p. 259 ;
see p. 278.

[4] Diog. Laert. x. 67-8 ; see Serv. ad. Æn. iv. 654.

[5] Irenæus contra Hæres. v. 7, 1 ; see Origen, De Princep. ii. 3, 2.

[6] Tertull. De Anima, 9.

[7] Hampole, ' Ayenbite of Inwyt.'

[8] Wuttke, ' Volksaberglaube,' pp. 216, 226.

doctrine ever more distinctly stated than by a modern spiritualistic writer, who observes that 'a spirit is no immaterial substance ; on the contrary, the spiritual organization is composed of matter . . . . in a very high state of refinement and attenuation.'[1]

Among rude races, the original conception of the human soul seems to have been that of ethereality, or vaporous materiality, which has held so large a place in human thought ever since. In fact, the later metaphysical notion of immateriality could scarcely have conveyed any meaning to a savage. It is moreover to be noticed that, as to the whole nature and action of apparitional souls, the lower philosophy escapes various difficulties which down to modern times have perplexed metaphysicians and theologians of the civilized world. Considering the thin ethereal body of the soul to be itself sufficient and suitable for visibility, movement, and speech, the primitive animists required no additional hypotheses to account for these manifestations ; they had no place for theories such as detailed by Calmet, as that immaterial souls have their own vaporous bodies, or occasionally have such vaporous bodies provided for them by supernatural means to enable them to appear as spectres, or that they possess the power of condensing the circumambient air into phantom-like bodies to invest themselves in, or of forming from it vocal instruments.[2] It appears to have been within systematic schools of civilized philosophy that the transcendental definitions of the immaterial soul were obtained, by abstraction from the primitive conception of the ethereal-material soul, so as to reduce it from a physical to a metaphysical entity.

Departing from the body at the time of death, the soul or spirit is considered set free to linger near the tomb, to wander on earth or flit in the air, or to travel to the proper region of spirits—the world beyond the grave. The principal conceptions of the lower psychology as to a Future

[1] A. J. Davis, ' Philosophy of Spiritual Intercourse,' New York, 1851, p. 49.
[2] Calmet, vol. i. ch. xli. &c.

Life will be considered in the following chapters, but for
the present purpose of investigating the theory of souls in
general, it will be well to enter here upon one department
of the subject. Men do not stop short at the persuasion
that death releases the soul to a free and active existence,
but they quite logically proceed to assist nature, by slaying
men in order to liberate their souls for ghostly uses. Thus
there arises one of the most widespread, distinct, and intelligible rites of animistic religion—that of funeral human
sacrifice for the service of the dead. When a man of rank
dies and his soul departs to its own place, wherever and
whatever that place may be, it is a rational inference of
early philosophy that the souls of attendants, slaves, and
wives, put to death at his funeral, will make the same
journey and continue their service in the next life, and the
argument is frequently stretched further, to include the
souls of new victims sacrificed in order that they may enter
upon the same ghostly servitude. It will appear from the
ethnography of this rite that it is not strongly marked in
the very lowest levels of culture, but that, arising in the
lower barbaric stage, it develops itself in the higher, and
thenceforth continues or dwindles in survival.

Of the murderous practices to which this opinion leads,
remarkably distinct accounts may be cited from among
tribes of the Indian Archipelago. The following account is
given of the funerals of great men among the rude Kayans
of Borneo :—' Slaves are killed in order that they may
follow the deceased and attend upon him. Before they are
killed the relations who surround them enjoin them to take
great care of their master when they join him, to watch and
shampoo him when he is indisposed, to be always near him,
and to obey all his behests. The female relatives of the
deceased then take a spear and slightly wound the victims,
after which the males spear them to death.' Again, the
opinion of the Idaan is ' that all whom they kill in this
world shall attend them as slaves after death. This notion
of future interest in the destruction of the human species is

a great impediment to an intercourse with them, as murder goes farther than present advantage or resentment. From the same principle they will purchase a slave, guilty of any capital crime, at fourfold his value, that they may be his executioners.' With the same idea is connected the ferocious custom of ' head-hunting,' so prevalent among the Dayaks before Rajah Brooke's time. They considered that the owner of every human head they could procure would serve them in the next world, where, indeed, a man's rank would be according to his number of heads in this. They would continue the mourning for a dead man till a head was brought in, to provide him with a slave to accompany him to the ' habitation of souls ; ' a father who lost his child would go out and kill the first man he met, as a funeral ceremony ; a young man might not marry till he had procured a head, and some tribes would bury with a dead man the first head he had taken, together with spears, cloth, rice, and betel. Waylaying and murdering men for their heads became, in fact, the Dayaks' national sport, and they remarked ' the white men read books, we hunt for heads instead.'[1] Of such rites in the Pacific islands, the most hideously purposeful accounts reach us from the Fiji group. Till lately, a main part of the ceremony of a great man's funeral was the strangling of wives, friends, and slaves, for the distinct purpose of attending him into the world of spirits. Ordinarily the first victim was the wife of the deceased, and more than one if he had several, and their corpses, oiled as for a feast, clothed with new fringed girdles, with heads dressed and ornamented, and vermilion and turmeric powder spread on their faces and bosoms, were laid by the side of the dead warrior. Associates and inferior attendants were likewise slain, and these bodies

---

[1] ' Journ. Ind. Archip.' vol. ii. p. 359 ; vol. iii. pp. 104, 556 ; Earl, ' Eastern Seas,' p. 266 ; St. John, ' Far East,' vol. i. pp. 52, 73, 79, 119 ; Mundy, ' Narr. from Brooke's Journals,' p. 203. Heads were taken as funeral offerings by the Garos of N. E. India, Eliot in ' As. Res.' vol. iii. p. 28, Dalton, ' Descr. Ethnol. of Bengal,' p. 67 ; see also pp. 46-7 (Kukis).

were spoken of as ' grass for bedding the grave.' When
Ra Mbithi, the pride of Somosomo, was lost at sea, seven-
teen of his wives were killed ; and after the news of the
massacre of the Namena people, in 1839, eighty women
were strangled to accompany the spirits of their murdered
husbands. Such sacrifices took place under the same pressure of public opinion which kept up the widow-burning in
modern India. The Fijian widow was worked upon by her
relatives with all the pressure of persuasion and of menace ;
she understood well that life to her henceforth would mean
a wretched existence of neglect, disgrace, and destitution ;
and tyrannous custom, as hard to struggle against in the
savage as in the civilized world, drove her to the grave.
Thus, far from resisting, she became importunate for death,
and the new life to come, and till public opinion reached a
more enlightened state, the missionaries often used their
influence in vain to save from the strangling-cord some wife
whom they could have rescued, but who herself refused to
live. / So repugnant to the native mind was the idea of
a chieftain going unattended into the other world, that
the missionaries' prohibition of the cherished custom was
one reason of the popular dislike to Christianity. / Many of
the nominal Christians, when once a chief of theirs was shot
from an ambush, esteemed it most fortunate that a stray
shot at the same time killed a young man at a distance
from him, and thus provided a companion for the spirit
of the slain chief.[1]

In America, the funeral human sacrifice makes its characteristic appearance. A good example may be taken from
among the Osages, whose habit was sometimes to plant in
the cairn raised over a corpse a pole with an enemy's scalp
hanging to the top. Their notion was that by taking an
enemy and suspending his scalp over the grave of a deceased
friend, the spirit of the victim became subjected to the spirit

[1] T. Williams, ' Fiji,' vol. i. pp. 188-204 ; Mariner, ' Tonga Is.' vol. ii.
p. 220. For New Zealand accounts, see R. Taylor, ' New Zealand,' pp. 218,
227 ; Polack, ' New Zealanders,' vol. i. pp. 66, 78, 116.

of the buried warrior in the land of spirits. Hence the last and best service that could be performed for a deceased relative was to take an enemy's life, and thus transmit it by his scalp.[1] The correspondence of this idea with that just mentioned among the Dayaks is very striking. With a similar intention, the Caribs would slay on the dead master's grave any of his slaves they could lay hands on.[2] Among the native peoples risen to considerably higher grades of social and political life, these practices were not suppressed but exaggerated, in the ghastly sacrifices of warriors, slaves, and wives, who departed to continue their duteous offices at the funeral of the chief or monarch in Central America[3] and Mexico,[4] in Bogota[5] and Peru.[6] It is interesting to notice, in somewhat favourable contrast with these customs of comparatively cultured American nations, the practice of certain rude tribes of the North-West. The Quakeolths, for instance, did not actually sacrifice the widow, but they made her rest her head on her husband's corpse while it was being burned, until at last she was dragged more dead than alive from the flames ; if she recovered, she collected her husband's ashes and carried them about with her for three years, during which any levity or deficiency of grief would render her an outcast. This looks like a mitigated survival from an earlier custom of actual widow-burning.[7]

Of such funeral rites, carried out to the death, graphic

[1] J. M'Coy, ' Hist. of Baptist Indian Missions,' p. 360 ; Waitz, vol. iii. p. 200.

[2] Rochefort, ' Iles Antilles,' pp. 429, 512 ; see also J. G. Müller, pp. 174, 222.

[3] Oviedo, ' Hist. de las Indias,' lib. xxix. c. 31 ; Charlevoix, ' Nouv. Fr.' vol. vi. p. 178 (Natchez); Waitz, vol. iii. p. 219. See Brinton, ' Myths of New World,' p. 239.

[4] Brasseur, ' Mexique,' vol. iii. p. 573.

[5] Piedrahita, ' Nuevo Reyno de Granada,' part i. lib. i. c. 3.

[6] Cieza de Leon, p. 161 ; Rivero and Tschudi, ' Peruv. Ant.' p. 200 ; Prescott, ' Peru,' vol. i. p. 29. See statements as to effigies, J. G. Müller, p. 379.

[7] Simpson, ' Journey,' vol. i. p. 190 ; similar practice among Takulli or Carrier Ind., Waitz, vol. iii. p. 200.

and horrid descriptions are recorded in the countries across Africa—East, Central, and West. A headman of the Wadoe is buried sitting in a shallow pit, and with the corpse a male and female slave alive, he with a bill-hook in his hand to cut fuel for his lord in the death-world, she seated on a little stool with the dead chief's head in her lap. A chief of Unyamwezi is entombed in a vaulted pit, sitting on a low stool with a bow in his right hand, and provided with a pot of native beer ; with him are shut in alive three women slaves, and the ceremony is concluded with a libation of beer on the earth heaped up above them all. The same idea which in Guinea makes it common for the living to send messages by the dying to the dead, is developed in Ashanti and Dahome into a monstrous system of massacre. The King of Dahome must enter Deadland with a ghostly court of hundreds of wives, eunuchs, singers, drummers, and soldiers. Nor is this all. Captain Burton thus describes the yearly 'Customs:'—'They periodically supply the departed monarch with fresh attendants in the shadowy world. For unhappily these murderous scenes are an expression, lamentably mistaken but perfectly sincere, of the liveliest filial piety.' Even this annual slaughter must be supplemented by almost daily murder :—' Whatever action, however trivial, is performed by the King, it must dutifully be reported to his sire in the shadowy realm. A victim, almost always a war-captive, is chosen ; the message is delivered to him, an intoxicating draught of rum follows it, and he is dispatched to Hades in the best of humours.'[1] In southern districts of Africa, accounts of the same class begin in Congo and Angola with the recorded slaying of the dead man's favourite wives, to live with him in the other world, a practice still in vogue among the Chevas of the Zambesi district, and formerly known among the Maravis ; while the funeral sacrifice of attendants with a chief is a

[1] Burton, ' Central Afr.' vol. i. p. 124 ; vol. ii. p. 25 ; ' Dahome,' vol. ii. p. 18, &c. ; ' Tr. Eth. Soc.' vol. iii. p. 403 ; J. L. Wilson, ' W. Afr.' pp. 203, 219, 394. See also H. Rowley, ' Mission to Central Africa,' p. 229.

thing of the past among the Barotse, as among the Zulus, who yet have not forgotten the days when the chief's servants and attendant warriors were cast into the fire which had consumed his body, that they might go with him, and prepare things beforehand, and get food for him.[1]

If now we turn to the records of Asia and Europe, we shall find the sacrifice of attendants for the dead widely prevalent in both continents in old times, while in the east its course may be traced continuing onward to our own day. The two Mohammedans who travelled in Southern Asia in the ninth century relate that on the accession of certain kings a quantity of rice is prepared, which is eaten by some three or four hundred men, who present themselves voluntarily to share it, thereby undertaking to burn themselves at the monarch's death. With this corresponds Marco Polo's thirteenth-century account in Southern India of the king of Maabar's guard of horsemen, who, when he dies and his body is burnt, throw themselves into the fire to do him service in the next world.[2] In the seventeenth century the practice is described as still prevailing in Japan, where, on the death of a nobleman, from ten to thirty of his servants put themselves to death by the ' hara kari,' or ripping-up, having indeed engaged during his lifetime, by the solemn compact of drinking wine together, to give their bodies to their lord at his death. Yet already in ancient times such funeral sacrifices were passing into survival, when the servants who followed their master in death were replaced by clay images set up at the tomb.[3] Among the Ossetes of the Caucasus, an interesting relic of widow-sacrifice is still kept up : the dead man's widow and his saddle-horse are led thrice round the grave, and no man may marry the

[1] Cavazzi, ' Ist. Descr. de' tre Regni Congo, Matamba, et Angola,' Bologna, 1687, lib. i. 264 ; Waitz, vol. ii. pp. 419-21 ; Callaway, ' Religion of Amazulu,' p. 212.

[2] Renaudot, ' Acc. by two Mohammedan Travellers,' London, 1733, p. 81 ; and in Pinkerton, vol. vii. p. 215 ; Marco Polo, book iii. chap. xx. ; and in Pinkerton, vol. vii. p. 162.

[3] Caron, ' Japan,' ibid., p. 622 ; Siebold, ' Nippon,' v. p. 22.

widow or mount the horse thus devoted.[1] In China, legend preserves the memory of the ancient funeral human sacrifice. The brother of Chin Yang, a disciple of Confucius, died, and his widow and steward wished to bury some living persons with him, to serve him in the regions below. Thereupon the sage suggested that the proper victims would be the widow and steward themselves, but this not precisely meeting their views, the matter dropped, and the deceased was interred without attendants. This story at least shows the rite to have been not only known but understood in China long ago. In modern China, the suicide of widows to accompany their husbands is a recognized practice, sometimes even performed in public. Moreover, the ceremonies of providing sedan-bearers and an umbrella-bearer for the dead, and sending mounted horsemen to announce beforehand his arrival to the authorities of Hades, although these bearers and messengers are only made of paper and burnt, seem to represent survivals of a more murderous reality.[2]

The Aryan race gives striking examples of the rite of funeral human sacrifice in its sternest shape, whether in history or in myth, that records as truly as history the manners of old days.[3] The episodes of the Trojan captives laid with the horses and hounds on the funeral pile of Patroklos, and of Evadne throwing herself into the funeral pile of her husband, and Pausanias's narrative of the suicide of the three Messenian widows, are among its Greek representatives.[4] In Scandinavian myth, Baldr is burnt with his

---

[1] ' Journ. Ind. Archip.' new series, vol ii. p. 374.

[2] Legge, ' Confucius,' p. 119 ; Doolittle, ' Chinese,' vol. i. pp. 108, 174, 192. The practice of attacking or killing all persons met by a funeral procession is perhaps generally connected with funeral human sacrifice ; any one met on the road by the funeral of a Mongol prince was slain and ordered to go as escort ; in the Kimbunda country, any one who meets a royal funeral procession is put to death with the other victims at the grave (Magyar, ' Süd. Afrika,' p. 353) ; see also Mariner, ' Tonga Is.' vol. i. p. 403 ; Cook, ' First Voy.' vol. i. pp. 146, 236 (Tahiti).

[3] Jakob Grimm, ' Verbrennen der Leichen,' contains an instructive collection of references and citations.

[4] Homer, Il. xxiii. 175 ; Eurip. Suppl. ; Pausanias, iv. 2.

dwarf foot-page, his horse and saddle ; Brynhild lies on the pile by her beloved Sigurd, and men and maids follow after them on the hell-way.[1] The Gauls in Cæsar's time burned at the dead man's sumptuous funeral whatever was dear to him, animals also, and much-loved slaves and clients.[2] Old mentions of Slavonic heathendom describe the burning of the dead with clothing and weapons, horses and hounds, with faithful servants, and above all, with wives. Thus St. Boniface says that ' the Wends keep matrimonial love with so great zeal, that the wife may refuse to survive her husband, and she is held praiseworthy among women who slays herself by her own hand, that she may be burnt on one pyre with her lord.'[3] This Aryan rite of widow-sacrifice has not only an ethnographic and antiquarian interest, but even a place in modern politics. In Brahmanic India the widow of a Hindu of the Brahman or the Kshatriya caste was burnt on the funeral pile with her husband, as a *satî* or ' good woman,' which word has passed into English as *suttee*. Mentioned in classic and mediæval times, the practice was in full vigour at the beginning of the last century.[4] Often one dead husband took many wives with him. Some went willingly and gaily to the new life, many were driven by force of custom, by fear of disgrace, by family persuasion, by priestly threats and promises, by sheer violence. When the rite was suppressed under modern British rule, the priesthood resisted to the uttermost, appealing to the Veda, as sanctioning the ordinance, and demanding that the foreign rulers should respect it. Yet in fact, as Prof. H. H. Wilson proved, the priests had actually falsified their sacred Veda in support of a rite enjoined by long and inveterate prejudice, but not by the traditional standards of Hindu faith. The ancient Brah-

---

[1] Edda, ' Gylfaginning,' 49; ' Brynhildarqvitha,' &c.

[2] Cæsar. Bell. Gall. vi. 19.

[3] Hanusch, ' Slaw. Myth.' p. 145.

[4] Strabo, xv. 1, 62 ; Cic. Tusc. Disp. v. 27, 78 ; Diod. Sic. xvii. 91 ; xix. 33, &c. ; Grimm, ' Verbrennen,' p. 261 ; Renaudot, ' Two Mohammedans,' p. 4 ; and in Pinkerton, vol. vii. p. 194. See Buchanan, ibid. pp. 675, 682 ; Ward, ' Hindoos,' vol. ii. pp. 298-312.

manic funeral rites have been minutely detailed from the
Sanskrit authorities in an essay by Prof. Max Müller.
Their directions are that the widow is to be set on the
funeral pile with her husband's corpse, and if he be a warrior his bow is to be placed there too. But then a brother-
in-law or adopted child or old servant is to lead the widow
down again at the summons, ' Rise, woman, come to the
world of life ; thou sleepest nigh unto him whose life is
gone. Come to us. Thou hast thus fulfilled thy duties of
a wife to the husband who once took thy hand, and made
thee a mother.' The bow, however, is to be broken and
thrown back upon the pile, and the dead man's sacrificial
instruments are to be laid with him and really consumed.
While admitting that the modern ordinance of Suttee-
burning is a corrupt departure from the early Brahmanic ritual, we may nevertheless find reason to consider
the practice as not a new invention by the later Hindu
priesthood, but as the revival, under congenial influences,
of an ancient Aryan rite belonging originally to a period
even earlier than the Veda. The ancient authorized ceremony looks as though, in a primitive form of the rite,
the widow had been actually sent with the dead, for
which real sacrifice a humaner law substituted a mere
pretence. This view is supported by the existence of
an old and express prohibition of the wife being sacrificed, a prohibition seemingly directed against a real custom, ' to follow the dead husband is prohibited, so says the
law of the Brahmans. With regard to the other castes this
law for women may be or may not be.' [1] To treat the
Hindu widow-burning as a case of survival and revival
seems to me most in accordance with a general ethnographic
view of the subject. Widow-sacrifice is found in various
regions of the world under a low state of civilization, and

[1] H. H. Wilson, ' On the supposed Vaidik authority for the Burning of
Hindu Widows,' in ' Journ. Roy. As. Soc.' vol. xvi. (1854) p. 201 ; in his
'Works,' vol. ii. p. 270. Max Müller, 'Todtenbestattung bei den Brahmanen,' in ' Zeitschr. der Deutsch. Morgenl. Ges.' vol. ix. ; ' Chips,' vol. ii.
p. 34.

this fits with the hypothesis of its having belonged to the Aryan race while yet in an early and barbarous condition. Thus the prevalence of a rite of suttee like that of modern India among ancient Aryan nations settled in Europe, Greeks, Scandinavians, Germans, Slaves, may be simply accounted for by direct inheritance from the remote common antiquity of them all. If this theory be sound, it will follow that ancient as the Vedic ordinances may be, they represent in this matter a reform and a reaction against a yet more ancient barbaric rite of widow-sacrifice, which they prohibited in fact, but yet kept up in symbol. The history of religion displays but too plainly the proneness of mankind to relapse, in spite of reformation, into the lower and darker condition of the past. Stronger and more tenacious than even Vedic authority, the hideous custom of the suttee may have outlived an attempt to suppress it in early Brahmanic times, and the English rulers, in abolishing it, may have abolished a relic not merely of degenerate Hinduism, but of the far more remotely ancient savagery out of which the Aryan civilization had grown.

In now passing from the consideration of the souls of men to that of the souls of the lower animals, we have first to inform ourselves as to the savage man's idea, which is very different from the civilized man's, of the nature of these lower animals. A remarkable group of observances customary among rude tribes will bring this distinction sharply into view. Savages talk quite seriously to beasts alive or dead as they would to men alive or dead, offer them homage, ask pardon when it is their painful duty to hunt and kill them. A North American Indian will reason with a horse as if rational. Some will spare the rattlesnake, fearing the vengeance of its spirit if slain ; others will salute the creature reverently, bid it welcome as a friend from the land of spirits, sprinkle a pinch of tobacco on its head for an offering, catch it by the tail and dispatch it with extreme dexterity, and carry off its skin as a trophy. If an Indian is attacked and torn by a bear, it is that the beast fell upon him intentionally in anger, perhaps to revenge the hurt done to another bear. When a bear is killed, they will beg pardon of him, or even make him condone the offence by smoking the peace-pipe with his murderers, who put the pipe in his mouth and blow down it, begging his spirit not to take revenge.[1] So in Africa, the Kafirs will hunt the elephant, begging him not to tread on them and kill them, and when he is dead they will assure him that they did not kill him on purpose, and they will bury his trunk, for the elephant is a mighty chief, and his trunk is his hand that he may hurt withal. The Congo people will even avenge such a murder by a pretended attack on the hunters who did the deed.[2] Such customs are common among the lower Asiatic tribes. The Stiens of Kambodia ask pardon of the beast they have killed ;[3] the Ainos of Yesso kill the bear, offer obeisance and salutation to him, and cut up his carcase.[4] The Koriaks, if they have slain a bear or wolf, will flay him, dress one of their people in the skin, and dance round him, chanting excuses that they did not do it, and especially laying the blame on a Russian. But if it is a fox, they take his skin, wrap his dead body in hay, and sneering tell him to go to his own people and say what famous hospitality he has had, and how they gave him a new coat instead of his old one.[5] The Samoyeds excuse themselves to the slain bear, telling him it was the Russians who did it, and that a Russian knife will cut him up.[6] The Goldi will set up the slain bear, call him ' my lord ' and do ironical homage to him, or taking him alive will fatten him in a cage, call him ' son ' and ' brother,' and kill and eat him as a sacrifice at a solemn festival.[7] In Borneo,

---

[1] Schoolcraft, ' Indian Tribes,' part i. p. 543 ; part iii. pp. 229, 520 ; Waitz, vol. iii. pp. 191-3.

[2] Klemm, ' Cultur-Gesch.' vol. iii. pp. 355, 364 ; Waitz, vol. ii. p. 178.

[3] Mouhot, ' Indo-China,' vol. i. p. 252.

[4] Wood in ' Tr. Eth. Soc.' vol. iv. p. 36.

[5] Bastian, ' Mensch,' vol. iii. p. 26.

[6] De Brosses, ' Dieux Fétiches,' p. 61.

[7] Ravenstein, ' Amur,' p. 382 ; T. W. Atkinson, p. 483.

the Dayaks, when they have caught an alligator with a baited hook and rope, address him with respect and soothing till they have his legs fast, and then mocking call him ' rajah ' and ' grandfather.'[1] Thus when the savage gets over his fears, he still keeps up in ironical merriment the reverence which had its origin in trembling sincerity. Even now the Norse hunter will say with horror of a bear that will attack man, that he can be ' no Christian bear.'

The sense of an absolute psychical distinction between man and beast, so prevalent in the civilized world, is hardly to be found among the lower races. Men to whom the cries of beasts and birds seem like human language, and their actions guided as it were by human thought, logically enough allow the existence of souls to beasts, birds, and reptiles, as to men. The lower psychology cannot but recognize in beasts the very characteristics which it attributes to the human soul, namely, the phenomena of life and death, will and judgment, and the phantom seen in vision or in dream. As for believers, savage or civilized, in the great doctrine of metempsychosis, these not only consider that an animal may have a soul, but that this soul may have inhabited a human being, and thus the creature may be in fact their own ancestor or once familiar friend. A line of facts, arranged as waymarks along the course of civilization, will serve to indicate the history of opinion from savagery onward, as to the souls of animals during life and after death. North American Indians held every animal to have its spirit, and these spirits their future life ; the soul of the Canadian dog went to serve his master in the other world ; among the Sioux, the prerogative of having four souls was not confined to man, but belonged also to the bear, the most human of animals.[2] The Greenlanders considered that a sick human soul might be replaced by the sorcerer with a fresh healthy soul of a hare, a reindeer, or a young

[1] St. John, ' Far East,' vol. ii. p. 253 (Dayaks).
[2] Charlevoix, ' Nouvelle France,' vol. vi. p. 78 ; Sagard, ' Hist. du Canada,' p. 497 ; Schoolcraft, ' Indian Tribes,' part iii. p. 229.

child.[1] Maori tale-tellers have heard of the road by which the spirits of dogs descend to Reinga, the Hades of the departed ; the Hovas of Madagascar know that the ghosts of beasts and men, dwelling in a great mountain in the south called Ambondrombe, come out occasionally to walk among the tombs or execution-places of criminals.[2] The Kamchadals held that every creature, even the smallest fly, would live again in the under-world.[3] The Kukis of Assam think that the ghost of every animal a Kuki kills in the chase or for the feast will belong to him in the next life, even as the enemy he slays in the field will then become his slave. The Karens apply the doctrine of the spirit or personal life-phantom, which is apt to wander from the body and thus suffer injury, equally to men and to animals.[4] The Zulus say the cattle they kill come to life again, and become the property of the dwellers in the world beneath.[5] The Siamese butcher, when in defiance of the very principles of his Buddhism he slaughters an ox, before he kills the creature has at least the grace to beseech its spirit to seek a happier abode.[6] In connexion with such transmigration, Pythagorean and Platonic philosophy gives to the lower animals undying souls, while other classic opinion may recognize in beasts only an inferior order of soul, only the ' anima ' but not the human ' animus ' besides. Thus Juvenal :

' Principio indulsit communis conditor illis
    Tantùm animas ; nobis animum quoque. . . .'[7]

Through the middle ages, controversy as to the psychology of brutes has lasted on into our own times, ranging between

[1] Cranz, ' Grönland,' p. 257.
[2] Taylor, ' New Zealand,' p. 271 ; Ellis, ' Madagascar,' vol. i. p. 429.
[3] Steller, ' Kamtschatka,' p. 269.
[4] Stewart, ' Notes on Northern Cachar,' in ' Journ. As. Soc. Bengal,' vol. xxiv. p. 632 ; Cross, ' Karens,' l.c. ; Mason, ' Karens,' l.c.
[5] Callaway, ' Zulu Tales,' vol. i. p. 317.
[6] Low in ' Journ. Ind. Archip.' vol. i. p. 426. See Meiners, vol. i. p. 220 ; vol. ii. p. 791.
[7] Juvenal, Sat. xv. 148.

two extremes; on the one the theory of Descartes which
reduced animals to mere machines, on the other what Mr.
Alger defines as ' the faith that animals have immaterial
and deathless souls.' Among modern speculations may be
instanced that of Wesley, who thought that in the next life
animals will be raised even above their bodily and mental
state at the creation, ' the horridness of their appearance
will be exchanged for their primæval beauty,' and it even
may be that they will be made what men are now, creatures
capable of religion. Adam Clarke's argument for the future
life of animals rests on abstract justice: whereas they did
not sin, but yet are involved in the sufferings of sinful man,
and cannot have in the present state the happiness designed
for them, it is reasonable that they must have it in another.[1]
Although, however, the primitive belief in the souls of
animals still survives to some extent in serious philosophy,
it is obvious that the tendency of educated opinion on the
question whether brutes have soul, as distinguished from
life and mind, has for ages been in a negative and sceptical
direction. The doctrine has fallen from its once high
estate. It belonged originally to real, though rude science.
It has now sunk to become a favourite topic in that mild
speculative talk which still does duty so largely as intellectual conversation, and even then its propounders defend
it with a lurking consciousness of its being after all a piece
of sentimental nonsense.

Animals being thus considered in the primitive psychology to have souls like human beings, it follows as the
simplest matter of course that tribes who kill wives and
slaves, to dispatch their souls on errands of duty with

---

[1] Alger, ' Future Life,' p. 632, and see ' Bibliography,' appendix ii. ;
Wesley, ' Sermon on Rom. viii. 19-22 ;' Adam Clarke, ' Commentary,' on
same text. This, by the way, is the converse view to Bellarmine's, who so
patiently let the fleas bite him, saying, ' We shall have heaven to reward us
for our sufferings, but these poor creatures have nothing but the enjoyment
of the present life.'—Bayle ' Biog. Dic.' The argument in Butler's
' Analogy,' part i. ch. i. puts the evidence for souls of brutes on much the
same footing as that for souls of men.

their departed lords, may also kill animals in order that
their spirits may do such service as is proper to them.
The Pawnee warrior's horse is slain on his grave to be
ready for him to mount again, and the Comanche's best
horses are buried with his favourite weapons and his
pipe, all alike to be used in the distant happy hunting-
grounds.[1]   In South America not only do such rites
occur, but they reach a practically disastrous extreme.
Patagonian tribes, says D'Orbigny, believe in another
life, where they are to enjoy perfect happiness, therefore
they bury with the deceased his arms and ornaments,
and even kill on his tomb all the animals which belonged
to him, that he may find them in the abode of bliss ; and
this opposes an insurmountable barrier to all civilization,
by preventing them from accumulating property and fixing
their habitations.[2]   Not only do Pope's now hackneyed
lines express a real motive with which the Indian's
dog is buried with him, but on the North American continent the spirit of the dog has another remarkable office
to perform.   Certain Esquimaux, as Cranz relates, would
lay a dog's head in a child's grave, that the soul of the dog,
who is everywhere at home, might guide the helpless infant
to the land of souls.   In accordance with this, Captain
Scoresby in Jameson's Land found a dog's skull in a small
grave, probably a child's.   Again, in the distant region of
the Aztecs, one of the principal funeral ceremonies was to
slaughter a techichi, or native dog ; it was burnt or buried
with the corpse, with a cotton thread fastened to its neck,
and its office was to convey the deceased across the deep
waters of Chiuhnahuapan, on the way to the Land of the
Dead.[3]   The dead Buraet's favourite horse, led saddled to
the grave, killed, and flung in, may serve for a Tatar

---

[1] Schoolcraft, ' Indian Tribes,' part i. pp. 237, 262 ; part ii. p. 68.

[2] D'Orbigny, 'L'Homme Américain,' vol. i. p. 196; vol. ii. pp. 23, 78 ;
Falkner, ' Patagonia,' p. 118 ; Musters, ' Patagonians,' p. 178.

[3] Egede, 'Greenland,' p. 152; Cranz, p. 301; see Nilsson, p. 140. Torquemada, ' Monarquia Indiana,' xiii. ch. 47 ; Clavigero, ' Messico,' vol. ii.
pp. 94-6.

example.[1]   In Tonquin, even wild animals have been customarily drowned at funeral ceremonies of princes, to be at the service of the departed in the next world.[2]   Among Semitic tribes, an instance of the custom may be found in the Arab sacrifice of a camel on the grave, for the dead man's spirit to ride upon.[3]   Among the nations of the Aryan race in Europe, the prevalence of such rites is deep, wide, and full of purpose.   Thus, warriors were provided in death with horses and housings, with hounds and falcons. Customs thus described in chronicle and legend, are vouched for in our own time by the opening of old barbaric burial-places.   How clear a relic of savage meaning lies here may be judged from a Livonian account as late as the fourteenth century, which relates how men and women slaves, sheep and oxen, with other things, were burnt with the dead, who, it was believed, would reach some region of the living, and find there, with the multitude of cattle and slaves, a country of life and happiness.[4]   As usual, these rites may be traced onward in survival.   The Mongols, who formerly slaughtered camels and horses at their owner's burial, have been induced to replace the actual sacrifice by a gift of the cattle to the Lamas.[5]   The Hindus offer a black cow to the Brahmans, in order to secure their passage across the Vaitaranî, the river of death, and will often die grasping the cow's tail as if to swim across in herdsman's fashion, holding on to a cow.[6]   It is mentioned as a belief in Northern Europe that he who has given a cow to the poor will find a cow to take

[1] Georgi, ' Reise im Russ. R.' vol. i. p. 312.

[2] Baron, ' Tonquin,' in Pinkerton, vol. ix. p. 704.

[3] W. G. Palgrave, ' Arabia,' vol. i. p. 10 ; Bastian, ' Mensch,' vol. ii. p. 334; Waitz, vol. ii. p. 519 (Gallas).

[4] Grimm, ' Verbrennen der Leichen.'   A curious correspondence in the practice of cutting off a fowl's head as a funeral rite is to be noticed among the Yorubas of W. Africa (Burton, ' W. and W.' p. 220), Chuwashes of Siberia (Castrén, ' Finn. Myth.' p. 120), old Russians (Grimm, ' Verbrennen,' p. 254).

[5] Bastian, ' Mensch,' vol. ii. p. 335.

[6] Colebrooke, ' Essays,' vol. i. p. 177; Ward, ' Hindoos,' vol. ii. pp. 62, 284, 331.

him over the bridge of the dead, and a custom of leading a cow in the funeral procession is said to have been kept up to modern times.[1] All these rites probably belong together as connected with ancient funeral sacrifice, and the survival of the custom of sacrificing the warrior's horse at his tomb is yet more striking. Saint-Foix long ago put the French evidence very forcibly. Mentioning the horse led at the funeral of Charles VI., with the four valets-de-pied in black, and bareheaded, holding the corners of its caparison, he recalls the horses and servants killed and buried with præ-Christian kings. And that his readers may not think this an extraordinary idea, he brings forward the records of property and horses being presented at the offertory in Paris, in 1329, of Edward III. presenting horses at King John's funeral in London, and of the funeral service for Bertrand Duguesclin, at St. Denis, in 1389, when horses were offered, the Bishop of Auxerre laid his hand on their heads, and they were afterwards compounded for.[2] Germany retained the actual sacrifice within the memory of living men. A cavalry general, Count Friedrich Kasimir Boos von Waldeck, was buried at Treves in 1781 according to the forms of the Teutonic Order ; his horse was led in the procession, and the coffin having been lowered into the grave the horse was killed and thrown in upon it.[3] This was, perhaps, the last occasion when such a sacrifice was consummated in solemn form in Europe. But that pathetic incident of a soldier's funeral, the leading of the saddled and bridled charger in the mournful procession, keeps up to this day a lingering reminiscence of the grim religious rite now passed away.

Plants, partaking with animals the phenomena of life and death, health and sickness, not unnaturally have some kind of soul ascribed to them. In fact, the notion of a vegetable

[1] Mannhardt, ' Götterwelt der Deutschen, &c.' vol. i. p. 319.
[2] Saint-Foix, ' Œuvres,' Maestricht, 1778, vol. iv. p. 150.
[3] Chr. von Stramberg, ' Rheinischer Antiquarius,' I. vol. i., Coblence, 1851, p. 203 ; J. M. Kemble, ' Horæ Ferales,' p. 66.

soul, common to plants and to the higher organisms possessing an animal soul in addition, was familiar to mediæval
philosophy, and is not yet forgotten by naturalists. But in
the lower ranges of culture, at least within one wide district
of the world, the souls of plants are much more fully
identified with the souls of animals. The Society Islanders
seem to have attributed ' varua,' i.e. surviving soul or
spirit, not to men only but to animals and plants.[1] The
Dayaks of Borneo not only consider men and animals to
have a spirit or living principle, whose departure from the
body causes sickness and eventually death, but they also
give to the rice its ' samangat padi,' or ' spirit of the
paddy,' and they hold feasts to retain this soul securely,
lest the crop should decay.[2] The Karens say that plants as
well as men and animals have their ' là ' (' kelah '), and
the spirit of sickly rice is here also called back like a human
spirit considered to have left the body. Their formulas for
the purpose have even been written down, and this is part
of one :—' O come, rice kelah, come. Come to the field.
Come to the rice. . . . . Come from the West. Come
from the East. From the throat of the bird, from the maw
of the ape, from the throat of the elephant. . . . .
From all granaries come. O rice kelah, come to the rice.'[3]
There is reason to think that the doctrine of the spirits of
plants lay deep in the intellectual history of South-East
Asia, but was in great measure superseded under Buddhist
influence. The Buddhist books show that in the early days
of their religion, it was matter of controversy whether trees
had souls, and therefore whether they might lawfully be
injured. Orthodox Buddhism decided against the tree-
souls, and consequently against the scruple to harm them,
declaring trees to have no mind or sentient principle,

---

[1] Moerenhout, ' Voy. Aux Iles du Grand Océan,' vol. i. p. 430.
[2] St. John ' Far East,' vol. i. p. 187.
[3] Mason, ' Karens,' in ' Journ. As. Soc. Bengal,' 1865, part ii. p. 202 ; Cross
in ' Journ. Amer. Oriental Soc.' vol. iv. p. 309. See comparison of Siamese
and Malay ideas ; Low in ' Journ. Ind. Archip.' vol. i. p. 340.

though admitting that certain dewas or spirits do reside in
the body of trees, and speak from within them. Buddhists
also relate that a heterodox sect kept up the early doctrine
of the actual animate life of trees, in connexion with which
may be remembered Marco Polo's somewhat doubtful statement as to certain austere Indians objecting to green herbs
for such a reason, and some other passages from later
writers. The subject of the spirits of plants is an obscure
one, whether from the lower races not having definite
opinions, or from our not finding it easy to trace them.[1]
The evidence from funeral sacrifices, so valuable as to most
departments of early psychology, fails us here, from plants
not being thought suitable to send for the service of the
dead.[2] Yet, as we shall see more fully elsewhere, there are
two topics which bear closely on the matter. On the one
hand, the doctrine of transmigration widely and clearly recognises the idea of trees or smaller plants being animated
by human souls; on the other, the belief in tree-spirits and
the practice of tree-worship involve notions more or less
closely coinciding with that of tree-souls, as when the
classic hamadryad dies with her tree, or when the Talein
of South-East Asia, considering every tree to have a demon
or spirit, offers prayers before he cuts one down.

Thus far the details of the lower animistic philosophy
are not very unfamiliar to modern students. The primitive
view of the souls of men and beasts, as asserted or acted on
in the lower and middle levels of culture, so far belongs to
current civilized thought, that those who hold the doctrine
to be false, and the practices based upon it futile, can
nevertheless understand and sympathise with the lower
nations to whom they are matters of the most sober and
serious conviction. Nor is even the notion of a separable
spirit or soul as the cause of life in plants too incongruous

[1] Hardy, ' Manual of Budhism,' pp. 291, 443 ; Bastian, ' Oestl. Asien,' vol.
ii. p. 184 ; Marco Polo, book iii. ch. xxii. (compare various readings);
Meiners, vol. i. p. 215 ; vol. ii. p. 799.
[2] Malay evidence has since been noticed by Wilken, ' Het Animisme bij
den Volken van den Indischen Archipel.' p. 104. [Note to 3rd edition.]

with ordinary ideas to be readily appreciable. But the theory of souls in the lower culture stretches beyond this limit, to take in a conception much stranger to modern thought. Certain high savage races distinctly hold, and a large proportion of other savage and barbarian races make a more or less close approach to, a theory of separable and surviving souls or spirits belonging to stocks and stones, weapons, boats, food, clothes, ornaments, and other objects which to us are not merely soulless but lifeless.

Yet, strange as such a notion may seem to us at first sight, if we place ourselves by an effort in the intellectual position of an uncultured tribe, and examine the theory of object-souls from their point of view, we shall hardly pronounce it irrational. In discussing the origin of myth, some account has been already given of the primitive stage of thought in which personality and life are ascribed not to men and beasts only, but to things. It has been shown how what we call inanimate objects—rivers, stones, trees, weapons, and so forth—are treated as living intelligent beings, talked to, propitiated, punished for the harm they do. Hume, whose ' Natural History of Religion' is perhaps more than any other work the source of modern opinions as to the development of religion, comments on the influence of this personifying stage of thought. ' There is an universal tendency among mankind to conceive all beings like themselves, and to transfer to every object those qualities with which they are familiarly acquainted, and of which they are intimately conscious. . . . . The *unknown causes*, which continually employ their thought, appearing always in the same aspect, are all apprehended to be of the same kind or species. Nor is it long before we ascribe to them thought and reason, and passion, and sometimes even the limbs and figures of men, in order to bring them nearer to a resemblance with ourselves.' Auguste Comte has ventured to bring such a state of thought under terms of strict definition in his conception of the primary mental condition of mankind—a state of ' pure fetishism, constantly characterized by the free and direct exercise of our primitive tendency to conceive all external bodies soever, natural or artificial, as animated by a life essentially analogous to our own, with mere differences of intensity.'[1] Our comprehension of the lower stages of mental culture depends much on the thoroughness with which we can appreciate this primitive, childlike conception, and in this our best guide may be the memory of our own childish days. He who recollects when there was still personality to him in posts and sticks, chairs, and toys, may well understand how the infant philosophy of mankind could extend the notion of vitality to what modern science only recognises as lifeless things; thus one main part of the lower animistic doctrine as to souls of objects is accounted for. The doctrine requires for its full conception of a soul not only life, but also a phantom or apparitional spirit ; this development, however, follows without difficulty, for the evidence of dreams and visions applies to the spirits of objects in much the same manner as to human ghosts. Everyone who has seen visions while light-headed in fever, everyone who has ever dreamt a dream, has seen the phantoms of objects as well as of persons. How then can we charge the savage with far-fetched absurdity for taking into his philosophy and religion an opinion which rests on the very evidence of his senses? The notion is implicitly recognized in his accounts of ghosts, which do not come naked, but clothed, and even armed ; of course there must be spirits of garments and weapons, seeing that the spirits of men come bearing them. It will indeed place savage philosophy in no unfavourable light, if we compare this extreme animistic development of it with the popular opinion still surviving in civilized countries, as to ghosts and the nature of the human soul as connected with them. When the ghost of Hamlet's father appeared armed cap-a-pe,

' Such was the very armour he had on,
When he the ambitious Norway combated.'

[1] Hume, ' Nat. Hist. of Rel.' sec. ii. ; Comte, 'Philosophie Positive,' vol. v. p. 30.

And thus it is a habitual feature of the ghost-stories of the civilized, as of the savage world, that the ghost comes dressed, and even dressed in well-known clothing worn in life. Hearing as well as sight testifies to the phantoms of objects : the clanking of ghostly chains and the rustling of ghostly dresses are described in the literature of apparitions. Now by the savage theory, according to which the ghost and his clothes are alike real and objective, and by the modern scientific theory, according to which both ghost and garment are alike imaginary and subjective, the facts of apparitions are rationally met. But the modern vulgar who ignore or repudiate the notion of ghosts of things, while retaining the notion of ghosts of persons, have fallen into a hybrid state of opinion which has neither the logic of the savage nor of the civilized philosopher.

Among the lower races of mankind, three have been observed to hold most explicitly and distinctly the doctrine of object-souls. These are the Algonquin tribes, extending over a great district of North America, the islanders of the Fijian group, and the Karens of Burma. Among the Indians of North America, Father Charlevoix wrote, souls are, as it were, the shadows and the animated images of the body, and it is by a consequence of this principle that they believe everything to be animate in the universe. This missionary was especially conversant with the Algonquins, and it was among one of their tribes, the Ojibwas, that Keating noticed the opinion that not only men and beasts have souls, but inorganic things, such as kettles, &c., have in them a similar essence. In the same district Father Le Jeune had described, in the seventeenth century, the belief that the souls, not only of men and animals, but of hatchets and kettles, had to cross the water to the Great Village, out where the sun sets.[1] In interesting correspondence with

---

[1] Charlevoix, vol. vi. p. 74 ; Keating, ' Long's Exp.' vol. ii. p. 154 ; Le Jeune, ' Nouvelle France,' p. 59 ; also Waitz, vol. iii. p. 199 ; Gregg, ' Commerce of Prairies,' vol. ii. p. 244 ; see Addison's No. 56 of the ' Spectator.'

this quaint thought is Mariner's description of the Fiji doctrine—' If an animal or a plant die, its soul immediately
goes to Bolotoo ; if a stone or any other substance is
broken, immortality is equally its reward ; nay, artificial
bodies have equal good luck with men, and hogs, and yams.
If an axe or a chisel is worn out or broken up, away flies its
soul for the service of the gods. If a house is taken down
or any way destroyed, its immortal part will find a situation
on the plains of Bolotoo ; and, to confirm this doctrine,
the Fiji people can show you a sort of natural well, or deep
hole in the ground, at one of their islands, across the bottom
of which runs a stream of water, in which you may clearly
perceive the souls of men and women, beasts and plants, of
stocks and stones, canoes and houses, and of all the broken
utensils of this frail world, swimming, or rather tumbling
along one over the other pell-mell into the regions of immortality.' A full generation later the Rev. Thomas
Williams, while remarking that the escape of brutes and
lifeless substances to the spirit-land of Mbulu does not receive universal credit among the Fijians, nevertheless confirms the older account of it :—' Those who profess to have
seen the souls of canoes, houses, plants, pots, or any artificial bodies, swimming with other relics of this frail world
on the stream of the Kauvandra well, which bears them
into the regions of immortality, believe this doctrine as a
matter of course ; and so do those who have seen the foot-
marks left about the same well by the ghosts of dogs, pigs,
&c.'[1] The theory among the Karens is stated by the Rev.
E. B. Cross, as follows :—' Every object is supposed to
have its " kelah." Axes and knives, as well as trees and
plants, are supposed to have their separate "kelahs."' 'The
Karen, with his axe and cleaver, may build his house, cut
his rice, and conduct his affairs, after death as before.'[2]

[1] Mariner, 'Tonga Is.' vol. ii. p. 129 ; Williams, 'Fiji,' vol. i. p. 242.
Similar ideas in Tahiti, Cook's 3rd Voy. vol. ii. p. 166.
[2] Cross, l.c. pp. 309, 313 ; Mason, l.c. p. 202. Compare Meiners, vol. i.
p. 144 ; Castrén, 'Finn. Myth.' pp. 161-3.

As so many races perform funeral sacrifices of men and animals, in order to dispatch their souls for the service of the soul of the deceased, so tribes who hold this doctrine of object-souls very rationally sacrifice objects, in order to transmit these souls. Among the Algonquin tribes, the sacrifice of objects for the dead was a habitual rite, as when we read of a warrior's corpse being buried with musket and war-club, calumet and war-paint, and a public address being made to the body at burial concerning his future path ; while in like manner a woman would be buried with her paddle and kettle, and the carrying-strap for the everlasting burden of her heavily-laden life. That the purpose of such offerings is the transmission of the object's spirit or phantom to the possession of the man's is explicitly stated as early as 1623 by Father Lallemant ; when the Indians buried kettles, furs, &c., with the dead, they said that the bodies of the things remained, but their souls went to the dead who used them. The whole idea is graphically illustrated in the following Ojibwa tradition or myth. Gitchi Gauzini was a chief who lived on the shores of Lake Superior, and once, after a few days' illness, he seemed to die. He had been a skilful hunter, and had desired that a fine gun which he possessed should be buried with him when he died. But some of his friends not thinking him really dead, his body was not buried; his widow watched him for four days, he came back to life, and told his story. After death, he said, his ghost travelled on the broad road of the dead toward the happy land, passing over great plains of luxuriant herbage, seeing beautiful groves, and hearing the songs of innumerable birds, till at last, from the summit of a hill, he caught sight of the distant city of the dead, far across an intermediate space, partly veiled in mist, and spangled with glittering lakes and streams. He came in view of herds of stately deer and moose, and other game, which with little fear walked near his path. But he had no gun, and re-membering how he had requested his friends to put his gun in his grave, he turned back to go and fetch it. Then he

met face to face the train of men, women, and children who
were travelling toward the city of the dead. They were
heavily laden with guns, pipes, kettles, meats, and other
articles ; women were carrying basket-work and painted
paddles, and little boys had their ornamented clubs and
their bows and arrows, the presents of their friends. Refusing a gun which an overburdened traveller offered him,
the ghost of Gitchi Gauzini travelled back in quest of his
own, and at last reached the place where he had died.
There he could see only a great fire before and around him,
and finding the flames barring his passage on every side, he
made a desperate leap through, and awoke from his trance.
Having concluded his story, he gave his auditors this
counsel, that they should no longer deposit so many
burdensome things with the dead, delaying them on their
journey to the place of repose, so that almost everyone he
met complained bitterly. It would be wiser, he said, only
to put such things in the grave as the deceased was particularly attached to, or made a formal request to have
deposited with him.[1]

With purpose no less distinct, when a dead Fijian chief
is laid out oiled and painted and dressed as in life, a heavy
club is placed ready near his right hand, which holds one
or more of the much-prized carved ' whale's tooth ' ornaments. The club is to serve for defence against the
adversaries who await his soul on the road to Mbulu, seeking to slay and eat him. We hear of a Fijian taking a
club from a companion's grave, and remarking in explanation to a missionary who stood by, ' The ghost of the club
has gone with him.' The purpose of thé whale's tooth is
this ; on the road to the land of the dead, near the solitary
hill of Takiveleyawa, there stands a ghostly pandanus-tree,
and the spirit of the dead man is to throw the spirit of the
whale's tooth at this tree, having struck which he is to
ascend the hill and await the coming of the spirits of his

[1] Schoolcraft, ' Indian Tribes,' part ii. p. 68 ; ' Algec Res.' vol. ii. p. 128 ;
Lallemant in ' Rel. des Jésuites dans la Nouvelle France,' 1626, p. 3.

strangled wives.[1] The funeral rites of the Karens complete the present group. They kept up what seems a clear survival from actual human and animal sacrifice, fastening up near an important person's grave a slave and a pony; these invariably released themselves, and the slave became henceforth a free man. Moreover, the practice of placing food, implements and utensils, and valuables of gold and silver, near the remains of the deceased, was general among them.[2]

Now the sacrifice of property for the dead is one of the great religious rites of the world; are we then justified in asserting that all men who abandon or destroy property as a funeral ceremony believe the articles to have spirits, which spirits are transmitted to the deceased? Not so; it is notorious that there are people who recognize no such theory but who nevertheless deposit offerings with the dead. Affectionate fancy or symbolism, a horror of the association of death leading the survivors to get rid of anything that even suggests the dreadful thought, a desire to abandon the dead man's property, an idea that the hovering ghost may take pleasure in or make use of the gifts left for him, all these are or may be efficient motives.[3] Yet, having made full

---

[1] Williams, 'Fiji,' vol. i. pp. 188, 243, 246; Alger, p. 82; Seemann, 'Viti,' p. 229.

[2] 'Journ. Ind. Archip.' new series, vol. ii. p. 421.

[3] For some cases in which horror or abnegation are assigned as motives for abandonment of the dead man's property, see Humboldt and Bonpland, vol. v. p. 626; Dalton in 'Journ. As. Soc. Bengal,' 1866, part ii. p. 191, &c.; Earl, 'Papuans,' p. 108; Callaway, 'Rel. of Amazulu,' p. 13; Egede, 'Greenland,' p. 151; Cranz, p. 301; Loskiel, 'Ind. N. A.' part i. p. 64, but see p. 76. The destruction or abandonment of the whole property of the dead may plausibly, whether justly or not, be explained by horror or abnegation; but these motives do not generally apply to cases where only part of the property is sacrificed, or new objects are provided expressly, and here the service of the dead seems the reasonable motive. Thus, at the funeral of a Garo girl, earthen vessels were broken as they were thrown in above the buried ashes. 'They said, the spirit of the girl would not benefit by them if they were given unbroken, but for her the fragments would unite again.' (Dalton, 'Descriptive Ethnology of Bengal,' p. 67.) The mere fact of breaking or destruction of objects at funerals does not carry its own explanation, for it is equally applicable to sentimental abandonment and to practical transmission of the spirit of the object, as a man is killed to liberate his soul.

allowance for all this, we shall find good reason to judge
that many other peoples, though they may never have stated
the theory of object-souls in the same explicit way as the
Algonquins, Fijians, and Karens, have recognized it with
more or less distinctness. It has given me the more confidence in this opinion to find it held, under proper reservation, by Mr. W. R. Alger, an American investigator, who
in a treatise entitled ' A Critical History of the Doctrine of
a Future Life' has discussed the ethnography of his subject with remarkable learning and sagacity. ' The barbarian
brain,' he writes, ' seems to have been generally impreg-
nated with the feeling that everything else has a ghost as
well as man. . . . The custom of burning or burying things
with the dead probably arose, in some cases at least, from
the supposition that every object has its *manes*.'[1] It will
be desirable briefly to examine further the subject of funeral
offerings, as bearing on this interesting question of early
psychology.

A wide survey of funeral sacrifices over the world will
plainly show one of their most usual motives to be a more

For good cases of the breaking of vessels and utensils given to the dead, see
' Journ. Ind. Archip.' vol. i. p. 325 (Mintira); Grey, ' Australia,' vol. i.
p. 322 ; G. F. Moore, ' Vocab. W. Australia,' p. 13 (Australians) ; Markham
in ' Tr. Eth. Soc.' vol. iii. p. 188 (Ticunas); St John, vol. i. p. 68 (Dayaks) ;
Ellis, ' Madagascar,' vol. i. p. 254 ; Schoolcraft, ' Indian Tribes,' part i.
p. 84 (Appalachicola) ; D. Wilson, ' Prehistoric Man,' vol. ii. p. 196 (N. A. I.
and ancient graves in England). Cases of formal sacrifice where objects
are offered to the dead and taken away again, are generally doubtful as to
motive ; see Spix and Martius, vol. i. p. 383 ; Martius, vol. i. p. 485 (Brazilian
Tribes) ; Moffat, ' S. Africa,' p. 308 (Bechuanas) ; ' Journ. Ind. Archip.' vol.
iii. p. 149 (Kayans).

[1] Alger, ' Future Life,' p. 81. He treats, however (p. 76), as intentionally
symbolic the rite of the Winnebagos, who light fires on the grave to provide night after night camp-fires for the soul on its far journey (Schoolcraft,
' Ind. Tr.' vol. iv. p. 55 ; the idea is introduced in Longfellow's ' Hiawatha,'
xix.). I agree with Dr. Brinton (' Myths of New World,' p. 241) that to
look for recondite symbolic meaning in these simple childish rites is unreasonable. There was a similar Aztec rite (Clavigero, vol. ii. p. 94). The
Mintira light fires on the grave for the spirit to warm itself at (' Journ. Ind.
Archip.' vol. i. p. 325*, see p. 271, and compare Martius, vol. i. p. 491). So
Australians will light a fire near their camp at night for the ghost of some
lately dead relative to sit by (Millett, ' Australian Parsonage,' p. 76.

or less defined notion of benefiting the deceased, whether out of kindness to him or from fear of his displeasure. How such an intention may have taken this practical shape we can perhaps vaguely guess, familiar as we are with a state of mind out of which funeral sacrifices could naturally have sprung. The man is dead, but it is still possible to fancy him alive, to take his cold hand, to speak to him, to place his chair at the table, to bury suggestive mementoes in his coffin, to throw flowers into his grave, to hang wreaths of everlastings on his tomb. The Cid may be set on Babieca with his sword Tizona in his hand, and carried out to do battle as of old against the unbeliever ; the dead king's meal may be carried in to him in state, although the chamberlain must announce that the king does not dine to-day. Such child-like ignoring of death, such childlike make-believe that the dead can still do as heretofore, may well have led the savage to bury with his kinsman the weapons, clothes, and orna-ments that he used in life, to try to feed the corpse, to put a cigar in the mouth of the skull before its final burial, to lay playthings in the infant's grave. But one thought be-yond would carry this dim blind fancy into the range of logical reasoning. Granted that the man is dead and his soul gone out of him, then the way to provide that departed soul with food or clothes or weapons is to bury or burn them with the body, for whatever happens to the man may be taken to happen to the objects that lie beside him and share his fate, while the precise way in which the transmission takes place may be left undecided. It is possible that the funeral sacrifice customary among mankind may have rested at first, and may to some extent still rest, on vague thoughts and imaginations like these, as yet fitted into no more definite and elaborate philosophic theory.

There are, however, two great groups of cases of funeral sacrifice, which so logically lead up to or involve the notion of souls or spirits of objects, that the sacrificer himself could hardly answer otherwise a point-blank question as to their meaning. The first group is that in which those who sacrifice men and beasts with the intention of conveying their souls to the other world, also sacrifice lifeless things indiscriminately with them. The second group is that in which the phantoms of the objects sacrificed are traced distinctly into the possession of the human phantom.

The Caribs, holding that after decease man's soul found its way to the land of the dead, sacrificed slaves on a chief's grave to serve him in the new life, and for the same purpose buried dogs with him, and also weapons.[1] The Guinea negroes, at the funeral of a great man, killed several wives and slaves to serve him in the other world, and put fine clothes, gold fetishes, coral, beads, and other valuables, into the coffin, to be used there too.[2] When the New Zealand chief had slaves killed at his death for his service, and the mourning family gave his chief widow a rope to hang herself with in the woods and so rejoin her husband,[3] it is not easy to discern here a motive different from that which induced them at the same time to provide the dead man also with his weapons. Nor can an intellectual line well be drawn between the intentions with which the Tunguz has buried with him his horse, his bow and arrows, his smoking apparatus and kettle. In the typical description which Herodotus gives of the funeral of the ancient Scythian chiefs, the miscellaneous contents of the burial-mound, the strangled wife and household servants, the horses, the choice articles of property, the golden vessels, fairly represent the indiscriminate purpose which actuated the barbaric sacrifice of creatures and things.[4] So in old Europe, the warrior with his sword and spear, the horse with his saddle, the hunter's hound and hawk and his bow and arrow, the wife with her gay clothes and jewels, lie together in the burial-mound. Their common purpose has become one of the most undisputed inferences of Archæology.

[1] J. G. Müller, ' Amer. Urrelig.' p. 222, see 420.
[2] Bosman, ' Guinea,' in Pinkerton, vol. xvi. p. 430.
[3] Polack, ' M. of New Zealanders,' vol. ii. pp. 66, 78, 116, 127.
[4] Georgi, ' Russ. R.' vol. i. p. 266 ; Herodot. iv. 71, see note in Rawlin-son's Tr. &c. &c.

As for what becomes of the objects sacrificed for the dead there are on record the most distinct statements taken from the sacrificers themselves. Although the objects rot in the grave or are consumed on the pile, they nevertheless come in some way into the possession of the disembodied souls they are intended for. Not the material things themselves, but phantasmal shapes corresponding to them, are carried by the souls of the dead on their far journey beyond the grave, or are used in the world of spirits; while sometimes the phantoms of the dead appear to the living, bearing property which they have received by sacrifice, or demanding something that has been withheld. The Australian will take his weapons with him to his paradise.[1] A Tasmanian, asked the reason of a spear being deposited in a native's grave, replied ' To fight with when he is alseep.'[2] Many Greenlanders thought that the kayak and arrows and tools laid by a man's grave, the knife and sewing implements laid by a woman's, would be used in the next world.[3] The instruments buried with the Sioux are for him to make a living with hereafter ; the paints provided for the dead Iroquois were to enable him to appear decently in the other world.[4] The Aztec's water-bottle was to serve him on the journey to Mictlan, the land of the dead ; the bonfire of garments and baskets and spoils of war was intended to send them with him, and somehow to protect him against the bitter wind ; the offerings to the warrior's manes on earth would reach him on the heavenly plains.[5] Among the old Peruvians, a dead prince's wives would hang themselves in order to continue in his service, and many of his attendants would be buried in his fields or places of favourite resort, in order that his soul, passing

---

[1] Oldfield in ' Tr. Eth. Soc.' vol. iii. pp. 228, 245.

[2] Bonwick, ' Tasmanians,' p. 97.

[3] Cranz, ' Grönland,' pp. 263, 301.

[4] Schoolcraft, ' Indian Tribes,' part iv. pp. 55. 65 ; J. G. Müller, ' Amer. Urrel.' pp. 88, 287.

[5] Sahagun, book iii. App. in Kingsborough, ' Antiquities of Mexico,' vol. vii. ; Clavigero, vol. ii. p. 94 ; Brasseur, vol. iii. pp. 497, 569.

through those places, might take their souls along with him for future service. In perfect consistency with these strong animistic notions, the Peruvians declared that their reason for sacrifice of property to the dead was that they ' have seen, or thought they saw, those who have long been dead walking, adorned with the things that were buried with them, and accompanied by their wives who had been buried alive.'[1]

As definite an implication of the spirit or phantom of an object appears in a recent account from Madagascar, where things are buried to become in some way useful to the dead. When King Radama died, it was reported and firmly believed that his ghost was seen one night in the garden of his country seat, dressed in óne of the uniforms which had been buried with him, and riding one of the best horses killed opposite his tomb.[2] Turanian tribes of North Asia avow that the motive of their funeral offerings of horses and sledges, clothes and axes and kettles, flint and steel and tinder, meat and butter, is to provide the dead for his journey to the land of souls, and for his life there.[3] Among the Esths of Northern Europe, the dead starts properly equipped on his ghostly journey with needle and thread, hairbrush and soap, bread and brandy and coin ; a toy, if it is a child. And so full a consciousness of practical meaning survived till lately, that now and then a soul would come back at night to reproach its relations with not having provided properly for it, but left it in distress.[4] To turn from these now Europeanized Tatars to a rude race of the Eastern Archipelago, among the Orang Binua of Sambawa there prevails this curious law of inheritance; not only does each surviving relative, father, mother, son, brother, and so forth,

[1] Cieza de Leon, p. 161 ; Rivero and Tschudi, ' Peruvian Antiquities,' pp. 186, 200.

[2] Ellis, ' Hist. of Madagascar,' vol. i. pp. 254, 429 ; see Flacourt, p. 60.

[3] Castrén, ' Finn. Myth.' p. 118 ; J. Billings, ' Exp. to N. Russia,' p. 129 ; see ' Samoiedia ' in Pinkerton, vol. i. p. 532, and Leems, ' Lapland,' ibid. p. 484.

[4] Boecler, ' Ehsten Gebraüche,' p. 69.

take his or her proper share, but the deceased inherits one share from himself, which is devoted to his use by eating the animals at the funeral feast, burning everything else that will burn, and burying the remainder.[1] In Cochin China, the common people object to celebrating their feast of the dead on the same day with the upper classes, for this excellent reason, that the aristocratic souls might make the servant souls carry home their presents for them. These people employ all the resources of their civilization to perform with the more lavish extravagance the savage funeral sacrifices. Here are details from an account published in 1849 of the funeral of a late king of Cochin China. ' When the corpse of Thien Tri was deposited in the coffin, there were also deposited in it many things for the use of the deceased in the other world, such as his crown, turbans, clothes of all descriptions, gold, silver, and other precious articles, rice and other provisions.' Meals were set out near the coffin, and there was a framed piece of damask with woollen characters, the abode of one of the souls of the defunct. In the tomb, an enclosed edifice of stone, the childless wives of the deceased were to be perpetually shut up to guard the sepulchre, 'and prepare daily the food and other things of which they think the deceased has need in the other life.' At the time of the deposit of the coffin in a cavern behind the tomb building, there were burnt there great piles of boats, stages, and everything used in the funeral, ' and moreover of all the objects which had been in use by the king during his lifetime, of chessmen, musical instruments, fans, boxes, parasols, mats, fillets, carriages, &c., &c., and likewise a horse and an elephant of wood and pasteboard.' ' Some months after the funeral, at two different times, there were constructed in a forest near a pagoda two magnificent palaces of wood with rich furnishings, in all things similar to the palace which the defunct monarch had inhabited. Each palace was composed of twenty rooms, and the most scrupulous attention was given

[1] ' Journ. Ind. Archip.' vol. ii. p. 691 ; see vol. i. pp. 297, 349.

in order that nothing might be awanting necessary for a palace, and these palaces were burned with great pomp, and it is thus that immense riches have been given to the flames from the foolish belief that it would serve the dead in the other world.'[1]

Though the custom is found among the Beduins of arraying the dead with turban, girdle, and sword, yet funeral offerings for the service of the dead are by no means conspicuous among Semitic nations. The mention of the rite by Ezekiel, while showing a full sense of its meaning, characterizes it as not Israelite, but Gentile : ' The mighty fallen of the uncircumcised, which are gone down to Hades with weapons of war, and they have laid their swords under their heads.'[2] Among the Aryan nations, on the contrary, such funeral offerings are known to have prevailed widely and of old, while for picturesqueness of rite and definiteness of purpose they can scarcely be surpassed even among savages. Why the Brahman's sacrificial instruments are to be burnt with him on the funeral pile, appears from this line of the Veda recited at the ceremony: 'Yadâ gachchâtyasunîtimetâmathâ devânâm vasanîrbhavâti,'—' When he cometh unto that life, faithfully will he do the service of the gods.'[3] Lucian is sarcastic, but scarcely unfair, in his comments on the Greek funeral rites, speaking of those who slew horses and slave-girls and cupbearers, and burned or buried clothes and ornaments, as for use and service in the world below ; of the meat amd drink offerings on the tombs which serve to feed the bodiless shades in Hades ; of the splendid garments and the garlands of the dead, that they might not suffer cold upon the road, nor be seen naked by Kerberos. For Kerberos was intended the honey-cake deposited with the dead ; and the obolus

[1] Bastian. ' Psychologie,' p. 89 ; ' Journ. Ind. Archip.' vol. iii. p. 337. For other instances, see Bastian, ' Mensch,' vol. ii. p. 332, &c. ; Alger, ' Future Life,' part ii.

[2] Klemm, ' C. G.' vol. iv. p. 159 ; Ezek. xxxii. 27.

[3] Max Müller, ' Todtenbestattung der Brahmanen,' in D. M. Z. vol. ix. pp. vii.-xiv.

placed in the mouth was the toll for Charon, save at
Hermione in Argolis, where men thought there was a
short descent to Hades, and therefore provided the dead
with no coin for the grim ferryman. How such ideas could
be realized, may be seen in the story of Eukrates, whose
dead wife appeared to him to demand one of her golden
sandals, which had been dropped underneath the chest, and
so not burnt for her with the rest of her wardrobe ; or in
the story of Periander, whose dead wife Melissa refused to
give him an oracular response, for she was shivering and
naked, because the garments buried with her had not been
burnt, and so were of no use, wherefore Periander plundered
the Corinthian women of their best clothes, which he burned
in a great trench with prayer, and now obtained his answer.[1]
The ancient Gauls were led, by their belief in another life,
to burn and bury with the dead things suited to the living ;
nor is the record improbable that they transferred to the
world below the repayment of loans, for even in modern
centuries the Japanese would borrow money in this life, to
be repaid with heavy interest in the next.[2] The souls of the
Norse dead took with them from their earthly home servants
and horses, boats and ferry-money, clothes and weapons.
Thus, in death as in life, they journeyed, following the long
dark ' hell-way ' (helvegr). The ' hell-shoon ' (helskô)
were bound upon the dead man's feet for the toilsome
journey ; and when King Harald was slain in the battle of
Bravalla, they drove his war-chariot, with the corpse upon it
into the great burial-mound, and there they killed the horse,
and King Hring gave his own saddle beside, that the fallen
chief might ride or drive to Walhalla, as it pleased him.[3]
Lastly, in the Lithuanian and old Prussian district, where
Aryan heathendom held its place in Europe so firmly and so

---

[1] Lucian. De Luctu, 9, &c. ; Philopseudes, 27 ; Strabo, viii. 6, 12 ; Herodot. v. 92 ; Smith's ' Dic. Gr. and Rom. Ant.' art. ' funus.'

[2] Valer. Max. ii. ; Mela, iii. 2. Froius (1565) in Maffei, ' Histor. In-
dicarum,' lib. iv.

[3] Grimm, ' Verbrennen der Leichen,' pp. 232, &c., 247, &c. ; ' Deutsche
Myth.' pp. 795-800.

late, accounts of funeral sacrifice of men, and beasts, and
things, date on even beyond the middle ages. Even as they
thought that men would live again in the resurrection rich
or poor, noble or peasant, as on earth, so ' they believed
that the things burned would rise again with them, and serve
them as before.' Among these people lived the Kriwe Kri-
weito, the great priest, whose house was on the high steep
mountain Anafielas. All the souls of their dead must
clamber up this mountain, wherefore they burned with them
claws of bears and lynxes for their help. All the souls
must pass through the Kriwe's house, and he could describe
to the surviving relatives of each the clothes, and horse, and
weapons he had seen him come with, and even show, for
greater certainty, some mark made with lance or other
instrument by the passing soul.[1] Such examples of funeral
rites show a common ceremony, and to a great degree a
common purpose, obtaining from savagery through barbarism, and even into the higher civilization. Now could
we have required from all these races a distinct answer to
the question, whether they believed in spirits of all things,
from men and beasts down to spears and cloaks, sticks
and stones, it is likely that we might have often received
the same acknowledgment of fully developed animism
which stands on record in North America, Polynesia, and
Burma. Failing such direct testimony, it is at least justifiable to say that the lower culture, by practically dealing
with object-souls, goes far towards acknowledging their
existence.

Before quitting the discussion of funeral offerings for
transmission to the dead, the custom must be traced to its
final decay. It is apt not to die out suddenly, but to leave
surviving remnants, more or less dwindled in form and
changed in meaning. The Kanowits of Borneo talk of

[1] Dusburg, ' Chronicon Prussiæ,' iii. c. v. ; Hanusch, ' Slaw. Myth.' pp.
898, 415 (Anafielas is the glass-mountain of Slavonic and German myth,
see Grimm, ' D. M.' p. 796). Compare statement in St. Clair and Brophy,
' Bulgaria,' p. 61 ; as to food transmitted to dead in other world, with more
probable explanation, p. 77.

setting a man's property adrift for use in the next world, and even go so far as to lay out his valuables by the bier, but in fact they only commit to the frail canoe a few old things not worth plundering.[1] So in North America, the funeral sacrifice of the Winnebagos has come down to burying a pipe and tobacco with the dead, and sometimes a club in a warrior's grave, while the goods brought and hung up at the burial-place are no longer left there, but the survivors gamble for them.[2] The Santals of Bengal put two vessels, one for rice and the other for water, on the dead man's couch, with a few rupees, to enable him to appease the demons on the threshold of the shadowy world, but when the funeral pile is ready these things are removed.[3] The fanciful art of replacing costly offerings by worthless imitations is at this day worked out into the quaintest devices in China. As the men and horses dispatched by fire for the service of the dead are but paper figures, so offerings of clothes and money may be represented likewise. The imitations of Spanish pillar-dollars in pasteboard covered with tinfoil, the sheets of tinfoil-paper which stand for silver money, and if coloured yellow for gold, are consumed in such quantities that the sham becomes a serious reality, for the manufacture of mock-money is the trade of thousands of women and children in a Chinese city. In a similar way trunks full of property are forwarded in the care of the newly deceased, to friends who are gone before. Pretty paper houses, ' replete with every luxury,' as our auctioneers say, are burnt for the dead Chinaman to live in hereafter, and the paper keys are burnt also, that he may unfasten the paper locks of the paper chests that hold the ingots of gold-paper and silver-paper, which are to be realized as current gold and silver in the other world, an idea which, however, does not prevent the careful survivors from

[1] St. John, ' Far East,' vol. i. pp. 54, 68. Compare Bosman, ' Guinea,' in Pinkerton, vol. xvi. p. 430.

[2] Schoolcraft, ' Indian Tribes,' part iv. p. 54.

[3] Hunter, ' Rural Bengal,' p. 210.

collecting the ashes to re-extract the tin from them in this.[1]
Again, when the modern Hindu offers to his dead parent
funeral cakes with flowers and betel, he presents a woollen
yarn which he lays across the cake, and naming the deceased
says, ' May this apparel, made of woollen yarn, be acceptable to thee.'[2]   Such facts as these suggest a symbolic
meaning in the practically useless offerings which Sir John
Lubbock groups together—the little models of kayaks and
spears in Esquimaux graves, the models of objects in
Egyptian tombs, and the flimsy unserviceable jewelry
buried with the Etruscan dead.[3]

Just as people in Borneo, after they had become Mohammedans, still kept up the rite of burying provisions for the
dead man's journey, as a mark of respect,[4] so the rite of
interring funeral offerings survived in Christian Europe.
The ancient Greek burial of the dead with the obolus in his
mouth for Charon's toll is represented in the modern Greek
world, where Charon and the funeral coin are both familiar.
As the old Prussians furnished the dead with spending-
money to buy refreshment on his weary journey, so to this
day German peasants bury a corpse with money in his mouth
or hand, a fourpenny-piece or so.   Similar little funeral
offerings of coin are recorded in the folklore books elsewhere in Europe.[5]   Christian funeral offerings of this kind
are mostly trifling in value, and doubtful as to the meaning
with which they were kept up.   The early Christians retained the heathen custom of placing in the tomb such
things as articles of the toilette and children's playthings ;
modern Greeks would place oars on a shipman's grave, and

[1] Davis, ' Chinese,' vol. i. p. 276 ; Doolittle, vol. i. p. 193 ; vol. ii. p. 275 ;
Bastian, ' Mensch,' vol. ii. p. 334 ; see Marco Polo, book ii. ch. lxviii.
[2] Colebrooke, ' Essays,' vol. i. pp. 161, 169.
[3] Lubbock, ' Prehistoric Times,' p. 142 ; Wilkinson, ' Ancient Eg.' vol. ii.
p. 319.
[4] Beeckmann, ' Voy. to Borneo,' in Pinkerton, vol. xi. p. 110.
[5] Politis, 'Neohellen. Mythologia,' vol. i. part i. p. 266; Hartknoch, 'Alt.
und Neues Preussen,' part i. p. 181 ; Grimm, ' D. M.' pp. 791-5 ; Wuttke,
'Deutsche Volksaberglaube,' p. 212 ; Rochholz, 'Deutscher Glaube,' &c.
vol. i. p. 187, &c. ; Maury, ' Magie,' &c. p. 158 (France).

other such tokens for other crafts; the beautiful classic rite of scattering flowers over the dead still holds its place in Europe.[1] Whatever may have been the thoughts which first prompted these kindly ceremonies, they were thoughts belonging to far præ-Christian ages. The change of sacrifice from its early significance is shown among the Hindus, who have turned it to account for purposes of priestcraft : he who gives water or shoes to a Brahman will find water to refresh him, and shoes to wear, on the journey to the next world, while the gift of a present house will secure him a future palace.[2] In interesting correspondence with this, is a transition from pagan to Christian folklore in our own land. The Lyke-Wake Dirge, the not yet forgotten funeral chant of the North Country, tells, like some savage or barbaric legend, of the passage over the Bridge of Death and the dreadful journey to the other world. But though the ghostly traveller's feet are still shod with the old Norseman's hell-shoon, he gains them no longer by funeral offering, but by his own charity in life :—

' This a nighte, this a nighte
  Every night and alle ;
Fire and fleet and candle-light,
  And Christe receive thy saule.

When thou from hence away are paste
  Every night and alle ;
To Whinny-moor thou comes at laste,
  And Christe receive thy saule.

If ever thou gave either hosen or shoon,
  Every night and alle ;
Sit thee down and put them on,
  And Christe receive thy saule.

But if hosen nor shoon thou never gave neean,
  Every night and alle ;
The Whinnes shall prick thee to the bare beean,
  And Christe receive thy saule.

[1] Maitland, ' Church in the Catacombs,' p. 137 ; Forbes Leslie, vol. ii. p. 502 ; Meiners, vol. ii. p. 750 ; Brand, ' Pop. Ant.' vol. ii. p. 307.
[2] Ward, ' Hindoos,' vol. ii. p. 284.

From Whinny-moore when thou may passe,
　　Every night and alle ;
To Brig o' Dread thou comes at laste,
　　And Christe receive thy saule.

From Brig o' Dread when thou are paste,
　　Every night and alle ;
To Purgatory Fire thou comes at laste,
　　And Christe receive thy saule.

If ever thou gave either milke or drink,
　　Every night and alle ;
The fire shall never make thee shrinke,
　　And Christe receive thy saule.

But if milk nor drink thou never gave neean,
　　Every night and alle ;
The fire shall burn thee to the bare beean
　　And Christe receive thy saule.'[1]

What reader, unacquainted with the old doctrine of offerings for the dead, could realize the meaning of its remnants
thus lingering in peasants' minds ? The survivals from
ancient funeral ceremony may here again serve as warnings
against attempting to explain relics of intellectual antiquity by viewing them from the changed level of modern
opinion.

Having thus surveyed at large the theory of spirits or
souls of objects, it remains to point out what, to general
students, may seem the most important consideration belonging to it, namely, its close relation to one of the most

---

[1] From the collated and annotated text in J. C. Atkinson, ' Glossary of
Cleveland Dialect,' p. 595 (a= one, neean= none, beean= bone). Other
versions in Scott, ' Minstrelsy of the Scottish Border,' vol. ii. p. 367 ; Kelly,
' Indo-European Folk-lore,' p. 115 ; Brand, ' Pop. Ant.' vol. ii. p. 275.
Two verses have perhaps been lost between the fifth and sixth. J. C. A.
reads ' meate ' in vv. 7 and 8 ; the usual reading ' milke ' is retained here.
The sense of these two verses may be that the liquor sacrificed in life will
quench the fire: an idea parallel to that known to folklore, that he who
gave bread in his lifetime will find it after death ready for him to cast
into the hellhound's jaws (Mannhardt, ' Götterwelt der Deutschen and
Nordischen Völker,' p. 319), a sop to Cerberus.

influential doctrines of civilized philosophy. The savage thinker, though occupying himself so much with the phenomena of life, sleep, disease, and death, seems to have taken for granted, as a matter of course, the ordinary operations of his own mind. It hardly occurred to him to think about the machinery of thinking. Metaphysics is a study which first assumes clear shape at a comparatively high level of intellectual culture. The metaphysical philosophy of thought taught in our modern European lecture-rooms is historically traced back to the speculative psychology of classic Greece. Now one doctrine which there comes into view is especially associated with the name of Democritus, the philosopher of Abdera, in the fifth century B.C. When Democritus propounded the great problem of metaphysics, ' How do we perceive external things ? '—thus making, as Lewes says, an era in the history of philosophy,—he put forth, in answer to the question, a theory of thought. He explained the fact of perception by declaring that things are always throwing off images (εἴδωλα) of themselves, which images, assimilating to themselves the surrounding air, enter a recipient soul, and are thus perceived. Now, supposing Democritus to have been really the originator of this famed theory of ideas, how far is he to be considered its inventor ? Writers on the history of philosophy are accustomed to treat the doctrine as actually made by the philosophical school which taught it. Yet the evidence here brought forward shows it to be really the savage doctrine of object-souls, turned to a new purpose as a method of explaining the phenomena of thought. Nor is the correspondence a mere coincidence, for at this point of junction between classic religion and classic philosophy the traces of historical continuity may be still discerned. To say that Democritus was an ancient Greek is to say that from his childhood he had looked on at the funeral ceremonies of his country, beholding the funeral sacrifices of garments and jewels and money and food and drink, rites which his mother and his nurse could tell him were performed in order that the phantasmal images of these objects might pass into the possession of forms shadowy like themselves, the souls of dead men. Thus Democritus, seeking a solution of his great problem of the nature of thought, found it by simply decanting into his metaphysics a surviving doctrine of primitive savage animism. This thought of the phantoms or souls of things, if simply modified to form a philosophical theory of perception, would then and there become his doctrine of Ideas. Nor does even this fully represent the closeness of union which connects the savage doctrine of flitting object-souls with the Epicurean philosophy. Lucretius actually makes the theory of film-like images of things (simulacra, membranæ) account both for the apparitions which come to men in dreams, and the images which impress their minds in thinking. So unbroken is the continuity of philosophic speculation from savage to cultured thought. Such are the debts which civilized philosophy owes to primitive animism.

The doctrine of ideas, thus developed in the classic world, has, indeed, by no means held its course thenceforth unchanged through metaphysics, but has undergone transition somewhat like that of the doctrine of the soul itself. Ideas, fined down to the abstract forms or species of material objects, and applied to other than visible qualities, have at last come merely to denote subjects of thought. Yet to this day the old theory has not utterly died out, and the retention of the significant term ' idea ' (ἰδέα, visible form) is accompanied by a similar retention of original meaning. It is still one of the tasks of the metaphysician to display and refute the old notion of ideas as being real images, and to replace it by more abstract conceptions. It is a striking instance that Dugald Stewart can cite from the works of Sir Isaac Newton the following distinct recognition of ' sensible species:' ' Is not the sensorium of animals, the place where the sentient substance is present; and to which the sensible species of things are brought, thr ouh the nerves and brain, that there they may be perceived by the mind present in that place ? ' Again, Dr. Reid states the original theory of ideas, while declaring that he conceives it ' to have no solid foundation, though it has been adopted very generally by philosophers. . . . This notion of our perceiving external objects, not immediately, but in certain images or species of them conveyed by the senses, seems to be the most ancient philosophical hypothesis we have on the subject of perception, and to have, with small variations, retained its authority to this day.' Granted that Dr. Reid exaggerated the extent to which metaphysicians have kept up the notion of ideas as real images of things, few will deny that it does linger much in modern minds, and that people who talk of ideas do often, in some hazy metaphorical way, think of sensible images.[1] One of the shrewdest things ever said about either ideas or ghosts was Bishop Berkeley's retort upon Halley, who bantered him about his idealism. The bishop claimed the mathematician as an idealist also, his ' ultimate ratios ' being ghosts of departed quantities, appearing when the terms that produced them vanished.

It remains to sum up in few words the doctrine of souls, in the various phases it has assumed from first to last among mankind. In the attempt to trace its main course through the successive grades of man's intellectual history, the evidence seems to accord best with a theory of its development, somewhat to the following effect. At the lowest levels of culture of which we have clear knowledge, the notion of a ghost-soul animating man while in the body, and appearing in dream and vision out of the body, is found deeply ingrained. There is no reason to think that this belief was learnt by savage tribes from contact with higher races, nor that it is a relic of higher culture from which the savage tribes have degenerated ; for what is here treated as the

---

[1] Lewes, ' Biographical History of Philosophy,' Democritus (and see his remarks on Reid) ; Lucretius, lib. iv. ; ' Early Hist. of Mankind,' p. 8 ; Stewart, ' Philosophy of Human Mind,' vol i. chap. i. sec. 2 ; Reid, ' Essays,' ii. chaps. iv. xiv. ; see Thos. Browne, ' Philosophy of the Mind,' lect. 27.

primitive animistic doctrine is thoroughly at home among savages, who appear to hold it on the very evidence of their senses, interpreted on the biological principle which seems to them most reasonable. We may now and then hear the savage doctrines and practices concerning souls claimed as relics of a high religious culture pervading the primæval race of man. They are said to be traces of remote ancestral religion, kept up in scanty and perverted memory by tribes degraded from a nobler state. It is easy to see that such an explanation of some few facts, sundered from their connexion with the general array, may seem plausible to certain minds. But a large view of the subject can hardly leave such argument in possession. The animism of savages stands for and by itself ; it explains its own origin. The animism of civilized men, while more appropriate to advanced knowledge, is in great measure only explicable as a developed product of the older and ruder system. It is the doctrines and rites of the lower races which are, according to their philosophy, results of point-blank natural evidence and acts of straightforward practical purpose. It is the doctrines and rites of the higher races which show survival of the old in the midst of the new, modification of the old to bring it into conformity with the new, abandonment of the old because it is no longer compatible with the new. Let us see at a glance in what general relation the doctrine of souls among savage tribes stands to the doctrine of souls among barbaric and cultured nations. Among races within the limits of savagery, the general doctrine of souls is found worked out with remarkable breadth and consistency. The souls of animals are recognized by a natural extension from the theory of human souls ; the souls of trees and plants follow in some vague partial way ; and the souls of inanimate objects expand the general category to its extremest boundary. Thenceforth, as we explore human thought onward from savage into barbarian and civilized life, we find a state of theory more conformed to positive science, but in itself less complete and consistent. Far on into civilization, men still act as though in some half-meant way they believed in souls or ghosts of objects, while nevertheless their knowledge of physical science is beyond so crude a philosophy. As to the doctrine of souls of plants, fragmentary evidence of the history of its breaking down in Asia has reached us. In our own day and country, the notion of souls of beasts is to be seen dying out. Animism, indeed, seems to be drawing in its outposts, and concentrating itself on its first and main position, the doctrine of the human soul. This doctrine has undergone extreme modification in the course of culture. It has outlived the almost total loss of one great argument attached to it,—the objective reality of apparitional souls or ghosts seen in dreams and visions. The soul has given up its ethereal substance, and become an immaterial entity, ' the shadow of a shade.' Its theory is becoming separated from the investigations of biology and mental science, which now discuss the phenomena of life and thought, the senses and the intellect, the emotions and the will, on a ground-work of pure experience. There has arisen an intellectual product whose very existence is of the deepest significance, a ' psychology ' which has no longer anything to do with ' soul.' The soul's place in modern thought is in the metaphysics of religion, and its especial office there is that of furnishing an intellectual side to the religious doctrine of the future life. Such are the alterations which have differenced the fundamental animistic belief in its course through successive periods of the world's culture. Yet it is evident that, notwithstanding all this profound change, the conception of the human soul is, as to its most essential nature, continuous from the philosophy of the savage thinker to that of the modern professor of theology. Its definition has remained from the first that of an animating, separable, surviving entity, the vehicle of individual personal existence. The theory of the soul is one principal part of a system of religious philosophy which unites, in an unbroken line of mental connexion, the savage fetish-worshipper and the civilized Christian. The divisions which have separated the great religions of the world into intolerant and hostile sects are for the most part superficial in comparison with the deepest of all religious schisms, that which divides Animism from Materialism.

CHAPTER XII

ANIMISM (*continued*)

Doctrine of Soul's Existence after Death; its main divisions, Transmigration and Future Life—Transmigration of Souls: re-birth in Human and Animal Bodies, transference to Plants and Objects—Resurrection of Body: scarcely held in savage religion—Future Life: a general if not universal doctrine of low races—Continued existence, rather thàn Immortality; second death of Soul—Ghost of Dead remains on earth, especially if corpse unburied; its attachment to bodily remains—Feasts of the Dead.

HAVING thus traced upward from the lower levels of culture the opinions of mankind as to the souls, spirits, ghosts, or phantoms, considered to belong to men, to the lower animals, to plants, and to things, we are now prepared to investigate one of the great religious doctrines of the world, the belief in the soul's continued existence in a Life after Death. Here let us once more call to mind the consideration which cannot be too strongly put forward, that the doctrine of a Future Life as held by the lower races is the all but necessary outcome of savage Animism. The evidence that the lower races believe the figures of the dead seen in dreams and visions to be their surviving souls, not only goes far to account for the comparative universality of their belief in the continued existence of the soul after the death of the body, but it gives the key to many of their speculations on the nature of this existence, speculations rational enough from the savage point of view, though apt to seem far-fetched absurdities to moderns in their much changed intellectual condition. The belief in a Future Life falls into two main divisions. Closely connected and even largely overlapping one another, both world-wide in their distribution, both ranging back in time to periods of unknown antiquity, both deeply rooted in the lowest strata of human life which lie open to our observation, these two doctrines have in the modern world passed into wonderfully different conditions. The one is the theory of the Transmigration of Souls, which has indeed risen from its lower stages to establish itself among the huge religious communities of Asia, great in history, enormous even in present mass, yet arrested and as it seems henceforth unprogressive in development ; but the more highly educated world has rejected the ancient belief, and it now only survives in Europe in dwindling remnants. Far different has been the history of the other doctrine, that of the independent existence of the personal soul after the death of the body, in a Future Life. Passing onward through change after change in the condition of the human race, modified and renewed in its long ethnic course, this great belief may be traced from its crude and primitive manifestations among savage races to its establishment in the heart of modern religion, where the faith in a future existence forms at once an inducement to goodness, a sustaining hope through suffering and across the fear of death, and an answer to the perplexed problem of the allotment of happiness and misery in this present world, by the expectation of another world to set this right.

In investigating the doctrine of Transmigration, it will be well first to trace its position among the lower races, and afterwards to follow its developments, so far as they extend in the higher civilization. The temporary migration of souls into material substances, from human bodies down to morsels of wood and stone, is a most important part of the lower psychology. But it does not relate to the continued existence of the soul after death, and may be more conveniently treated of elsewhere, in connexion with such subjects as dæmoniacal possession and fetish-worship. We are here concerned with the more permanent tenancy of souls for successive lives in successive bodies.

Permanent transition, new birth, or re-incarnation of human souls in other human bodies, is especially considered to take place by the soul of a deceased person animating the body of an infant. It is recorded by Brebeuf that the Hurons, when little children died, would bury them by the wayside, that their souls might enter into mothers passing by, and so be born again.[1] In North-West America, among the Tacullis, we hear of direct transfusion of soul by the medicine-man, who, putting his hands on the breast of the dying or dead, then holds them over the head of a relative and blows through them ; the next child born to this recipient of the departed soul is animated by it, and takes the rank and name of the deceased.[2] The Nutka Indians not without ingenuity accounted for the existence of a distant tribe speaking the same language as themselves, by declaring them to be the spirits of their dead.[3] In Greenland, where the wretched custom of abandoning and even plundering widows and orphans was tending to bring the whole race to extinction, a helpless widow would seek to persuade some father that the soul of a dead child of his had passed into a living child of hers, or *vice versâ*, thus gaining for herself a new relative and protector.[4] It is mostly ancestral or kindred souls that are thought to enter into children, and this kind of transmigration is therefore from the savage point of view a highly philosophical theory, accounting as it does so well for the general resemblance between parents and children, and even for the more special

---

[1] Brebeuf in ' Rel. des Jés. dans la Nouvelle France,' 1636, p. 130 ; Charlevoix, ' Nouvelle France,' vol. vi. p. 75. See Brinton, p. 253.

[2] Waitz, vol. iii. p. 195, see p. 213. Morse, ' Report on Indian Affairs,' p. 345.

[3] Mayne, ' British Columbia,' p. 181.

[4] Cranz, 'Grönland,' pp. 248, 258, see p. 212. See also Turner, 'Polynesia,' p 353 ; Meiners, vol. ii. p. 793.

phenomena of atavism. In North-West America, among the Koloshes, the mother sees in a dream the deceased relative whose transmitted soul will give his likeness to the child ;[1] and in Vancouver's Island in 1860 a lad was much regarded by the Indians because he had a mark like the scar of a gun-shot wound on his hip, it being believed that a chief dead some four generations before, who had such a mark, had returned.[2] In Old Calabar, if a mother loses a child, and another is born soon after, she thinks the departed one to have come back.[3] The Wanika consider that the soul of a dead ancestor animates a child, and this is why it resembles its father or mother ;[4] in Guinea a child bearing a strong resemblance, physical or mental, to a dead relative, is supposed to have inherited his soul ;[5] and the Yorubas, greeting a new-born infant with the salutation, ' Thou art come ! ' look for signs to show what ancestral soul has returned among them.[6] Among the Khonds of Orissa, births are celebrated by a feast on the seventh day, and the priest, divining by dropping rice-grains in a cup of water, and judging from observations made on the person of the infant, determines which of his progenitors has reappeared, and the child generally at least among the northern tribes receives the name of that ancestor.[7] In Europe the Lapps repeat an instructive animistic idea just noticed in America ; the future mother was told in a dream what name to give her child, this message being usually given by the very spirit of the deceased ancestor, who was about to be incarnate in her.[8] Among the lower races generally the

[1] Bastian, ' Psychologie,' p. 28.

[2] Bastian, ' Zur vergl. Psychologie,' in Lazarus and Steinthal's ' Zeitschrift,' vol. v. p. 160, &c., also Papuas and other races.

[3] Burton, ' W. & W. fr. W. Afr.' p. 376.

[4] Krapf, ' E. Afr.' p. 201.

[5] J. L. Wilson, 'W. Afr.' p. 210; see also R. Clarke, 'Sierra Leone, p. 159.

[6] Bastian, l. c.

[7] Macpherson, p. 72 ; also Tickell in ' Journ. As. Soc. Bengal,' vol. ix. pp. 793, &c. ; Dalton in ' Tr. Eth. Soc.' vol. vi. p. 22 (similar rite of Mundas and Oraons).

[8] Klemm, ' C. G.' vol. iii. p 77 ; K. Leems, ' Lapper,' c. xiv.

renewal of old family names by giving them to new-born children may always be suspected of involving some such thought. The following is a curious pair of instances from the two halves of the globe. The New Zealand priest would repeat to the infant a long list of names of its ancestors, fixing upon that name which the child by sneezing or crying when it was uttered, was considered to select for itself ; while the Cheremiss in Russia would shake the baby till it cried, and then repeat names to it, till it chose itself one by leaving off crying.[1]

The belief in the new human birth of the departed soul, which has even led West African negroes to commit suicide when in distant slavery, that they may revive in their own land, in fact amounts among several of the lower races to a distinct doctrine of an earthly resurrection. One of the most remarkable forms which this belief assumes is when dark-skinned races, wanting some reasonable theory to account for the appearance among them of human creatures of a new strange sort, the white men, and struck with their pallid deathly hue combined with powers that seem those of superhuman spiritual beings, have determined that the manes of their dead must have come back in this wondrous shape. The aborigines of Australia have expressed this theory in the simple formula, ' Blackfellow tumble down, jump up Whitefellow.' Thus a native who was hanged years ago at Melbourne expressed in his last moments the hopeful belief that he would jump up Whitefellow, and have lots of sixpences. The doctrine has been current among them since early days of European intercourse, and in accordance with it they habitually regarded the Englishmen as their own deceased kindred, come back to their country from an attachment to it in a former life. Real or imagined likeness completed the delusion, as when

[1] R. Taylor, ' New Zealand,' p. 284; see Shortland, ' Traditions,' p. 145; Turner, ' Polynesia,' p. 353; Bastian, ' Mensch,' vol. ii. p. 279; see also p. 276 (Samoyeds). Compare Charlevoix, ' Nouvelle France,' vol. v. p. 426; Steller, ' Kamtschatka,' p. 353; Kracheninnikow, ii. 117. See Plath, ' Rel. der alten Chinesen,' ii. p. 98.

Sir George Grey was hugged and wept over by an old woman who found in him a son she had lost, or when a convict, recognized as a deceased relative, was endowed anew with the land he had possessed during his former life. A similar theory may be traced northward by the Torres Islands to New Caledonia, where the natives thought the white men to be the spirits of the dead who bring sickness, and assigned this as their reason for wishing to kill white men.[1] In Africa, again, the belief is found among the Western negroes that they will rise again white, and the Bari of the White Nile, believing in the resurrection of the dead on earth, considered the first white people they saw as departed spirits thus come back.[2]

Next, the lower psychology, drawing no definite line of demarcation between souls of men and of beasts, can at least admit without difficulty the transmission of human souls into the bodies of the lower animals. A series of examples from among the native tribes of America will serve well to show the various ways in which such ideas are worked out. The Ahts of Vancouver's Island consider the living man's soul able to enter into other bodies of men and animals, going in and out like the inhabitant of a house. In old times, they say, men existed in the forms of birds, beasts, and fishes, or these had the spirits of the Indians in their bodies ; some think that after death they will pass again into the bodies of the animals they occupied in this former state.[3] In an Indian district of North-West

---

[1] Grey, ' Australia,' vol. i. p. 301, vol. ii. p. 363 [native's accusation against some foreign sailors who had assaulted him, ' *djanga* Taal-wurt kyle-gut bomb-gur,'—' one of the dead struck Taal-wurt under the ear,' &c. The word *djanga*=the dead, the spirits of deceased persons (see Grey, 'Vocab. of S. W. Australia '), had come to be the usual term for a European]. Lang, ' Queensland,' pp. 34, 336 ; Bonwick, ' Tasmanians,' p. 183 ; Scherzer, ' Voy. of Novara,' vol. iii. p. 34 ; Bastian, ' Psychologie,' p. 222, ' Mensch,' vol. iii. pp. 362-3, and in Lazarus and Steinthal's ' Zeitschrift,' l. c. ; Turner, ' Polynesia,' p. 424.

[2] Römer, 'Guinea,' p. 85 ; Brun-Rollet, ' Nil Blanc,' &c. p. 234.

[3] Sproat, 'Savage Life,' ch. xviii., xix., xxi. Souls of the dead appear in dreams, either in human or animal forms, p. 174. See also Brinton, p. 145.

California, we find natives believing the spirits of their dead to enter into bears, and travellers have heard of a tribe begging the life of a wrinkle-faced old she grizzly bear as the recipient of the soul of some particular grandam, whom they fancied the creature to resemble.[1] So, among the Esquimaux, a traveller noticed a widow who was living for conscience' sake upon birds, and would not touch walrus-meat, which the angekok had forbidden her for a time, because her late husband had entered into a walrus.[2] Among other North American tribes, we hear of the Pow-hatans refraining from doing harm to certain small wood-birds which received the souls of their chiefs;[3] of Huron souls turning into turtle-doves after the burial of their bones at the Feast of the Dead;[4] of that pathetic funeral rite of the Iroquois, the setting free a bird on the evening of burial, to carry away the soul.[5] In Mexico, the Tlascalans thought that after death the souls of nobles would animate beautiful singing birds, while plebeians passed into weasels and beetles and such like vile creatures.[6] So, in Brazil, the Içannas say that the souls of the brave will become beautiful birds, feeding on pleasant fruits, but cowards will be turned into reptiles.[7] Among the Abipones we hear of certain little ducks which fly in flocks at night, uttering a mournful hiss, and which fancy associates with the souls of the dead;[8] while in Popayan it is said that doves were not killed, as inspired by departed souls.[9] Lastly, transmigration into brutes is also a received doctrine in South America as when a missionary heard a Chiriquane woman of western

[1] Schoolcraft, 'Indian Tribes,' part iii. p. 113.
[2] Hayes, 'Arctic Boat Journey,' p. 198.
[3] Brinton, 'Myths of New World,' p. 102.
[4] Brebeuf in 'Rel. des Jés.' 1636, p. 104.
[5] Morgan, 'Iroquois,' p. 174.
[6] Clavigero, 'Messico,' vol. ii. p. 5.
[7] Martius, 'Ethnog. Amer.' vol. i. p. 602; Markham in 'Tr. Eth. Soc.' vol. iii. p. 195.
[8] Dobrizhoffer, 'Abipones,' vol. ii. pp. 74, 270.
[9] Coreal in Brinton, l. c. See also J. G. Müller, pp. 139 (Natchez), 223 (Caribs), 402 (Peru).

Brazil say of a fox, ' May not that be the spirit of my dead daughter ? ' [1]

In Africa, again, mention is made of the Maravi thinking that the souls of bad men became jackals, and of good men snakes.[2] The Zulus, while admitting that a man may turn into a wasp or lizard, work out in the fullest way the idea of the dead becoming snakes, a creature whose change of skin has so often been associated with the thought of resurrection and immortality. It is especially certain green or brown harmless snakes, which come gently and fearlessly into houses, which are considered to be ' amatongo ' or ancestors, and therefore are treated respectfully, and have offerings of food given them. In two ways, the dead man who has become a snake can still be recognized ; if the creature is one-eyed, or has a scar or some other mark, it is recognized as the ' itongo ' of a man who was thus marked in life ; but if he had no mark the ' itongo ' appears in human shape in dreams, thus revealing the personality of the snake.[3] In Guinea, monkeys found near a graveyard are supposed to be animated by the spirits of the dead, and in certain localities monkeys, crocodiles, and snakes, being thought men in metempsychosis, are held sacred.[4] It is to be borne in mind that notions of this kind may form in barbaric psychology but a portion of the wide doctrine of the soul's future existence. For a conspicuous instance of this, let us take the system of the Gold-Coast negroes. They believe that the ' kla ' or ' kra,' the vital soul, becomes at death a ' sisa ' or ghost, which can remain in the house with the body, plague the living, and cause sickness, till it departs or is driven by the sorcerer to the bank of the River Volta, where the ghosts build themselves houses and dwell. But they can and do come back from

---

[1] Chomé in ' Lettres Edif.' vol. viii. ; see also Martius, vol. i. p. 446.
[2] Waitz, vol. ii. p. 419 (Maravi).
[3] Callaway, ' Rel. of Amazulu,' p. 196, &c. ; Arbousset and Daumas, p. 237.
[4] J. L. Wilson, ' W. Afr.' pp. 210, 218. See also Brun-Rollet, pp. 200, 234 ; Meiners, vol. i. p. 211.

this Land of Souls. They can be born again as souls in new human bodies, and a soul who was poor before will now be rich. Many will not come back as men, but will become animals. To an African mother who has lost her child, it is a consolation to say, ' He will come again.'[1]

In higher levels of culture, the theory of re-embodiment of the soul appears in strong and varied development. Though seemingly not received by the early Aryans, the doctrine of migration was adopted and adapted by Hindu philosophy, and forms an integral part of that great system common to Brahmanism and Buddhism, wherein successive births or existences are believed to carry on the consequences of past and prepare the antecedents of future life. To the Hindu the body is but the temporary receptacle of the soul, which, ' bound in the chains of deeds ' and ' eating the fruits of past actions,' promotes or degrades itself along a series of embodiments in plant, beast, man, deity. Thus all creatures differ rather in degree than kind, all are akin to man, an elephant or ape or worm may once have been human, and may become human again, a pariah or barbarian is at once low-caste among men and high-caste among brutes. Through such bodies migrate the sinful souls which desire has drawn down from primal purity into gross material being ; the world where they do penance for the guilt incurred in past existences is a huge reformatory, and life is the long grievous process of developing evil into good. The rules are set forth in the book of Manu how souls endowed with the quality of goodness acquire divine nature, while souls governed by passion take up the human state, and souls sunk in darkness are degraded to brutes. Thus the range of migration stretches downward from gods and saints, through holy ascetics, Brahmans, nymphs, kings, counsellors, to actors, drunkards, birds, dancers, cheats, elephants, horses, Sudras, barbarians, wild beasts, snakes, worms, insects, and inert things. Obscure as the relation mostly is between the crime and its punishment in a new

[1] Steinhauser in ' Mag. der Evang. Miss.' Basel, 1856, No. 2, p. 135.

life, there may be discerned through the code of penal
transmigration an attempt at appropriateness of penalty,
and an intention to punish the sinner wherein he sinned.
For faults committed in a previous existence men are
afflicted with deformities, the stealer of food shall be
dyspeptic, the scandal-monger shall have foul breath, the
horse-stealer shall go lame, and in consequence of their
deeds men shall be born idiots, blind, deaf and dumb, mis-
shaped, and thus despised of good men. After expiation of
their wickedness in the hells of torment, the murderer of a
Brahman may pass into a wild beast or pariah ; he who
adulterously dishonours his guru or spiritual father shall
be a hundred times re-born as grass, a bush, a creeper, a
carrion bird, a beast of prey ; the cruel shall become bloodthirsty beasts ; stealers of grain and meat shall turn into
rats and vultures ; the thief who took dyed garments,
kitchen-herbs, or perfumes, shall become accordingly a red
partridge, a peacock, or a musk-rat. In short, ' in whatever disposition of mind a man accomplishes such and such
an act, he shall reap the fruit in a body endowed with such
and such a quality.'[1] The recognition of plants as possible
receptacles of the transmigrating spirit well illustrates the
conception of souls of plants. The idea is one known to
lower races in a district of the world which has been under
Hindu influence. Thus we hear among the Dayaks of
Borneo of the human soul entering the trunks of trees,
where it may be seen damp and blood-like, but no longer
personal and sentient, or of its being re-born from an animal
which has eaten of the bark, flower, or fruit ;[2] and the
Santals of Bengal are said to fancy that uncharitable men
and childless women are eaten eternally by worms and
snakes, while the good enter into fruit-bearing trees.[3]
But it is an open question how far these and the Hindu

[1] Manu, xi. xii. Ward, ' Hindoos,' vol. i. p. 164, vol. ii. pp. 215, 347-52.
[2] St. John, ' Far East,' vol. i. p. 181 ; Perelaer, ' Ethnog, Beschr. der
Dajaks,' p. 17.
[3] Hunter, ' Rural Bengal,' p. 210. See also Shaw in ' As. Res.' vol. iv.
p. 46 (Rajmahal tribes).

ideas of vegetable transmigration can be considered as independent. A curious commentary on the Hindu working out of the conception of plant-souls is to be found in a passage in a 17th-century work, which describes certain Brahmans of the Coromandel Coast as eating fruits, but being careful not to pull the plants up by the roots, lest they should dislodge a soul ; but few, it is remarked, are so scrupulous as this, and the consideration has occurred to them that souls in roots and herbs are most vile and abject bodies, so that if dislodged they may become better off by entering into the bodies of men or beasts.[1] Moreover, the Brahmanic doctrine of souls transmigrating into inert things has in like manner a bearing on the savage theory of object-souls.[2]

Buddhism, like the Brahmanism from which it seceded, habitually recognized transmigration between superhuman and human beings and the lower animals, and in an exceptional way recognized a degradation even into a plant or a thing. How the Buddhist mind elaborated the doctrine of metempsychosis, may be seen in the endless legends of Gautama himself undergoing his 550 births, suffering pain and misery through countless ages to gain the power of freeing sentient beings from the misery inherent in all existence. Four times he became Maha Brahma, twenty times the dewa Sekra, and many times or few he passed through such stages as a hermit, a king, a rich man, a slave, a potter, a gambler, a curer of snake bites, an ape, an elephant, a bull, a serpent, a snipe, a fish, a frog, the dewa or genius of a tree. At last, when he became the supreme Buddha, his mind, like a vessel overflowing with honey, overflowed with the ambrosia of truth, and he proclaimed his triumph over life :—

[1] Abraham Roger, ' La Porte Ouverte,' Amst. 1670, p. 107.
[2] Manu, xii. 9 : ' çarîrajâih karmmadoshaih yâti sthâvaratâm narah '— ' for crimes done in the body, the man goes to the inert (motionless) state;' xii. 42, 'sthâvarâh krimakîtâçcha matsyâh sarpâh sakachhapâh paçavaçcha mrigaschaiva jaghanyâ tâmasî gatih '—' inert (motionless) things, worms and insects, fish, serpents, tortoises and beasts and deer also are the last dark form.'

> ' Painful are repeated births.
> O house-builder ! I have seen thee,
> Thou canst not build again a house for me.
> Thy rafters are broken
> Thy roof-timbers are shattered.
> My mind is detached,
> I have attained to the extinction of desire.'

Whether the Buddhists receive the full Hindu doctrine of the migration of the individual soul from birth to birth, or whether they refine away into metaphysical subtleties the notion of continued personality, they do consistently and systematically hold that a man's life in former existences is the cause of his now being what he is, while at this moment he is accumulating merit or demerit whose result will determine his fate in future lives.   Memory, it is true, fails generally to recall these past births, but memory, as we know, stops short of the beginning even of this present life. When King Bimsara's feet were burned and rubbed with salt by command of his cruel son that he might not walk, why was this torture inflicted on a man so holy ?   Because in a previous birth he had walked near a dagoba with his slippers on, and had trodden on a priest's carpet without washing his feet.   A man may be prosperous for a time on account of the merit he has received in former births, but if he does not continue to keep the precepts, his next birth will be in one of the hells, he will then be born in this world as a beast, afterwards as a preta or sprite ; a proud man may be born again ugly with large lips, or as a demon or a worm.   The Buddhist theory of ' karma ' or ' action,' which controls the destiny of all sentient beings, not by judicial reward and punishment, but by the inflexible result of cause into effect, wherein the present is ever determined by the past in an unbroken line of causation, is indeed one of the world's most remarkable developments of ethical speculation.[1]

[1] Köppen, 'Religion des Buddha,' vol. i. pp. 35, 289, &c., 318; Barthélemy Saint-Hilaire, ' Le Bouddha et sa Religion,' p. 122 ; Hardy, ' Manual of Budhism,' pp. 98, &c., 180, 318, 445, &c.

Within the classic world, the ancient Egyptians were described as maintaining a doctrine of migration, whether by successive embodiments of the immortal soul through creatures of earth, sea, and air, and back again to man, or by the simpler judicial penalty which sent back the wicked dead to earth as unclean beasts.[1] The pictures and hieroglyphic sentences of the Book of the Dead, however, do not afford the necessary confirmation for these statements, even the mystic transformations of the soul not being of the nature of transmigrations. Thus it seems that the theological centre whence the doctrine of moral metempsychosis may have spread over the ancient cultured religions, must be sought elsewhere than in Egypt. In Greek philosophy, great teachers stood forth to proclaim the doctrine in a highly developed form. Plato had mythic knowledge to convey of souls entering such new incarnations as their glimpse of real existence had made them fit for, from the body of a philosopher or a lover down to the body of a tyrant and usurper; of souls transmigrating into beasts and rising again to man according to the lives they led ; of birds that were light-minded souls ; of oysters suffering in banishment the penalty of utter ignorance. Pythagoras is made to illustrate in his own person his doctrine of metempsychosis, by recognizing where it hung in Here's temple the shield he had carried in a former birth, when he was that Euphorbos whom Menelaos slew at the siege of Troy. Afterwards he was Hermotimos, the Klazomenian prophet whose funeral rites were so prematurely celebrated while his soul was out, and after that, as Lucian tells the story, his prophetic soul passed into the body of a cock. Mikyllos asks this cock to tell him about Troy—were things there really as Homer said ? But the cock replies, ' How should Homer have known, O Mikyllos? When the Trojan war was going on, he was a camel in Baktria ! '[2]

[1] Herod. ii. 123, see Rawlinson's Tr. ; Plutarch. De Iside 31, 72 ; Wilkinson, ' Ancient Eg.' vol. ii. ch. xvi.

[2] Plat. Phædo, Timæus, Phædrus, Repub.; Diog. Laert. Empedokles xii.;

In the later Jewish philosophy, the Kabbalists took up the doctrine of migration, the *gilgul* or ' rolling on ' of souls, and maintained it by that characteristic method of Biblical interpretation which it is good to hold up from time to time for a warning to the mystical interpreters of our own day. The soul of Adam passed into David, and shall pass into the Messiah, for are not these initials in the very name of Ad(a)m, and does not Ezekiel say that ' my servant David shall be their prince for ever.' Cain's soul passed into Jethro, and Abel's into Moses, and therefore it was that Jethro gave Moses his daughter to wife. Souls migrate into beasts and birds and vermin, for is not Jehovah ' the lord of the spirits of all flesh ' ? and he who has done one sin beyond his good works shall pass into a brute. He who gives a Jew unclean meat to eat, his soul shall enter into a leaf, blown to and fro by the wind ; ' for ye shall be as an oak whose leaf fadeth ; ' and he who speaks ill words, his soul shall pass into a dumb stone, as did Nabal's, ' and he became a stone.'[1] Within the range of Christian influence the Manichæans appear as the most remarkable exponents of the metempsychosis. We hear of their ideas of sinners' souls transmigrating into beasts, the viler according to their crimes ; that he who kills a fowl or rat will become a fowl or rat himself ; that souls can pass into plants rooted in the ground, which thus have not only life but sense ; that the souls of reapers pass into beans and barley, to be cut down in their turn, and thus the elect were careful to explain to the bread when they ate it, that it was not they who reaped the corn it was made of ; that the souls of the auditors, that is, the spiritually low commonalty who lived a married life, would pass into melons and cucumbers, to finish their purification by being eaten by the elect. But these details come to us from the accounts of bitter theological adversaries, and

Pindar. Olymp. ii. antistr. 4 ; Ovid. Metam. xv. 160 ; Lucian. Somn. 17, &c. Philostr. Vit. Apollon. Tyan. See also Meyer's Conversations-Lexicon, art. ' Seelenwanderung.' For re-birth in old Scandinavia, see Helgakvidha, iii., in ' Edda.'

[1] Eisenmenger, part ii. p. 23, &c.

the question is, how much of them did the Manichæans really and soberly believe ? Allowing for exaggeration and constructive imputation, there is some reason to consider the account at least founded on fact. The Manichæans appear to have recognized a wandering of imperfect souls, whether or not their composite religion may with its Zarathustrian and Christian elements have also absorbed in so Indian a shape the doctrine of purification of souls by migration into animals and plants.[1] In later times, the doctrine of metempsychosis has been again and again noticed in a district of South-Western Asia. William of Ruysbroek speaks of the notion of souls passing from body to body as general among the mediæval Nestorians, even a somewhat intelligent priest consulting him as to the souls of brutes, whether they could find refuge elsewhere so as not to be compelled to labour after death. Rabbi Benjamin of Tudela records in the 12th century of the Druses of Mount Hermon : ' They say that the soul of a virtuous man is transferred to the body of a new-born child, whereas that of the vicious transmigrates into a dog, or some other animal.' Such ideas indeed, seem not yet extinct in the modern Druse nation. Among the Nassairi, also, transmigration is believed in as a penance and purification : we hear of migration of unbelievers into camels, asses, dogs, or sheep, of disobedient Nassairi into Jews, Sunnis, or Christians, of the faithful into new bodies of their own people, a few such changes of ' shirt ' (i.e. body), bringing them to enter paradise or become stars.[2] An instance of the belief within the limits of modern Christian Europe may be found among the Bulgarians, whose superstition is that Turks who have never eaten pork in life will become wild boars after death. A

[1] Beausobre, 'Hist. de Manichée,' &c., vol. i. pp. 245-6, vol. ii. pp. 496-9; G. Flügel, ' Mani.' See Augustin. Contra Faust. ; De Hæres. ; De Quantitate Animæ.
[2] Gul. de Rubruquis in ' Rec. des Voy. Soc. de Géographie de Paris,' vol. iv. p. 356. Benjamin of Tudela, ed. and tr. by Asher, Hebrew 22, Eng. p. 62. Niebuhr, ' Reisebeschr. nach Arabien,' &c., vol. ii. pp. 438-443 ; Meiners, vol. ii. p. 796.

party assembled to feast on a boar has been known to throw it all away, for the meat jumped off the spit into the fire, and a piece of cotton was found in the ears, which the wise man decided to be a piece of the ci-devant Turk's turban.[1] Such cases, however, are exceptional. Metempsychosis never became one of the great doctrines of Christendom, though not unknown in mediæval scholasticism, and though maintained by an eccentric theologian here and there into our own times. It would be strange were it not so. It is in the very nature of the development of religion that speculations of the earlier culture should dwindle to survivals, yet be again and again revived. Doctrines transmigrate, if souls do not ; and metempsychosis, wandering along the course of ages, came at last to animate the souls of Fourier and Soame Jenyns.[2]

Thus we have traced the theory of metempsychosis in stage after stage of the world's civilization, scattered among the native races of America and Africa, established in the Asiatic nations, especially where elaborated by the Hindu mind into its system of ethical philosophy, rising and falling in classic and mediæval Europe, and lingering at last in the modern world as an intellectual crotchet, of little account but to the ethnographer who notes it down as an item of

[1] St. Clair and Brophy, ' Bulgaria,' p. 57. Compare the tenets of the Russian sect of Dukhobortzi, in Haxthausen, ' Russian Empire,' vol. i. p. 288, &c.

[2] Since the first publication of the above remark, M. Louis Figuier has supplied a perfect modern instance by his book, entitled ' Le Lendemain de la Mort,' translated into English as 'The Day after Death: Our Future Life according to Science.' His attempt to revive the ancient belief, and to connect it with the evolution-theory of modern naturalists, is carried out with more than Buddhist elaborateness. Body is the habitat of soul, which goes out when a man dies, as one forsakes a burning house. In the course of development, a soul may migrate through bodies stage after stage, zoophyte and oyster, grasshopper and eagle, crocodile and dog, till it arrives at man, thence ascending to become one of the superhuman beings or angels who dwell in the planetary ether, and thence to a still higher state, the secret of whose nature M. Figuier does not endeavour to penetrate, ' because our means of investigation fail at this point.' The ultimate destiny of the more glorified being is the Sun ; the pure spirits who form its mass of burning gases, pour out germs and life to start the course of planetary existence. (Note to 2nd edition.)

evidence for his continuity of culture. What, we may well ask, was the original cause and motive of the doctrine of transmigration? Something may be said in answer, though not at all enough for full explanation. The theory that ancestral souls return, thus imparting their own likeness of mind and body to their descendants and kindred, has been already mentioned and commended as in itself a very reasonable and philosophical hypothesis, accounting for the phenomenon of family likeness going on from generation to generation. But why should it have been imagined that men's souls could inhabit the bodies of beasts and birds? As has been already pointed out, savages not unreasonably consider the lower animals to have souls like their own, and this state of mind makes the idea of a man's soul transmigrating into a beast's body at least seem possible. But it does not actually suggest the idea. The view stated in a previous chapter as to the origin of the conception of soul in general, may perhaps help us here. As it seems that the first conception of souls may have been that of the souls of men, this being afterwards extended by analogy to the souls of animals, plants, &c., so it may seem that the original idea of transmigration was the straightforward and reasonable one of human souls being re-born in new human bodies, where they are recognized by family likenesses in successive generations. This notion may have been afterwards extended to take in re-birth in bodies of animals, &c. There are some well-marked savage ideas which will fit with such a course of thought. The half-human features and actions and characters of animals are watched with wondering sympathy by the savage, as by the child. The beast is the very incarnation of familiar qualities of man; and such names as lion, bear, fox, owl, parrot, viper, worm, when we apply them as epithets to men, condense into a word some leading feature of a human life. Consistently with this, we see in looking over details of savage transmigration that the creatures often have an evident fitness to the character of the human beings whose souls are to pass into them, so that the savage

philosopher's fancy of transferred souls offered something
like an explanation of the likeness between beast and man.
This comes more clearly into view among the more civilized
races who have worked out the idea of transmigration into
ethical schemes of retribution, where the appropriateness of
the creatures chosen is almost as manifest to the modern
critic as it could have been to the ancient believer. Perhaps the most graphic restoration of the state of mind in
which the theological doctrine of metempsychosis was
worked out in long-past ages, may be found in the writings
of a modern theologian whose spiritualism often follows to
the extreme the intellectual tracks of the lower races. In
the spiritual world, says Emanuel Swedenborg, such persons
as have opened themselves for the admission of the devil
and acquired the nature of beasts, becoming foxes in cunning, &c., appear also at a distance in the proper shape of
such beasts as they represent in disposition.[1] Lastly, one of
the most notable points about the theory of transmigration
is its close bearing upon a thought which lies very deep in
the history of philosophy, the development-theory of
organic life in successive stages. An elevation from the
vegetable to the lower animal life, and thence onward
through the higher animals to man, to say nothing of
superhuman beings, does not here require even a succession
of distinct individuals, but is brought by the theory of
metempsychosis within the compass of the successive
vegetable and animal lives of a single being.

Here a few words may be said on a subject which cannot
be left out of sight, connecting as it does the two great
branches of the doctrine of future existence, but which it
is difficult to handle in definite terms, and much more to
trace historically by comparing the views of lower and
higher races. This is the doctrine of a bodily renewal or

---

[1] Swedenborg, 'The True Christian Religion,' 13. Compare the notion
attributed to the followers of Basilides the Gnostic, of men whose souls are
affected by spirits or dispositions as of wolf, ape, lion, or bear, wherefore
their souls bear the properties of these, and imitate their deeds (Clem.
Alex. Stromat. ii. c. 20).

resurrection. To the philosophy of the lower races it is by no means necessary that the surviving soul should be provided with a new body, for it seems itself to be of a filmy or vaporous corporeal nature, capable of carrying on an independent existence like other corporeal creatures. Savage descriptions of the next world are often such absolute copies of this, that it is scarcely possible to say whether the dead are or are not thought of as having bodies like the living ; and a few pieces of evidence of this class are hardly enough to prove the lower races to hold original and distinct doctrines of corporeal resurrection.[1] Again, attention must be given to the practice, so common among low and high races, of preserving relics of the dead, from mere morsels of bone up to whole mummified bodies. It is well known that the departed soul is often thought apt to revisit the remains of the body, as is seen in the well-known pictures of the Egyptian funeral ritual. But the preservation of these remains, even where it thus involves a permanent connexion between body and soul, does not necessarily approach more closely to a bodily resurrection.[2] In discussing the closely allied doctrine of metempsychosis, I have described the theory of the soul's transmigration into a new human body as asserting in fact an earthly resurrection. From the same point of view, a bodily resurrection in Heaven or Hades is technically a transmigration of the soul. This is plain among the higher races, in whose religion these doctrines take at once clearer definition and more practical import. There are some distinct mentions of bodily resurrection in the Rig Veda : the dead is spoken of as glorified, putting on his body (tanu) ; and it is even promised that the pious man shall be born in the next world with his entire body (sarvatanû). In Brah-

[1] See J. G. Müller, ' Amer. Urrel.' p. 208 (Caribs) ; but compare Rochefort, p. 429. Steller, ' Kamtschatka,' p. 269 ; Castrén, ' Finnische Mythologie,' p. 119.
[2] For Egyptian evidence see the funeral papyri and translations of the ' Book of the Dead.' Compare Brinton, ' Myths of New World,' p. 254, &c.

minism and Buddhism, the re-births of souls in bodies to inhabit heavens and hells are simply included as particular cases of transmigration. The doctrine of the resurrection appears far back in the religion of Persia, and is thence supposed to have passed into late Jewish belief.[1] In early Christianity, the conception of bodily resurrection is developed with especial strength and fulness in the Pauline doctrine. For an explicit interpretation of this doctrine, such as commended itself to the minds of later theologians, it is instructive to cite the remarkable passage of Origen, where he speaks of ' corporeal matter, of which matter, in whatever quality placed, the soul always has use, now indeed carnal, but afterwards indeed subtler and purer, which is called spiritual.'[2]

Passing from these metaphysical doctrines of civilized theology, we now take up a series of beliefs higher in practical moment, and more clearly conceived in savage thought. There may well have been, and there may still be, low races destitute of any belief in a Future State. Nevertheless, prudent ethnographers must often doubt accounts of such, for this reason, that the savage who declares that the dead live no more, may merely mean to say that they are dead. When the East African is asked what becomes of his buried ancestors, the ' old people,' he can reply that ' they are ended,' yet at the same time he fully admits that their ghosts survive.[3] In an account of the religious ideas of the Zulus, taken down from a native, it is explicitly stated that Unkulunkulu the Old-Old-One said that people ' were to die and never rise again,' and that he allowed them to ' die and rise no more.'[4] Knowing so thoroughly as we now do the theology of the Zulus, whose ghosts not only survive in

---

[1] Aryan evidence in ' Rig-Veda,' x. 14, 8 ; xi. 1, 8 ; Manu, xii. 16-22 ; Max Müller, ' Todtenbestattung,' pp. xii. xiv. ; ' Chips,' vol. i. p. 47 ; Muir in ' Journ. As. Soc. Bengal,' vol. i. 1865, p. 306 ; Spiegel, 'Avesta'; Haug, ' Essays on the Parsis.'

[2] Origen, De Princip. ii. 3, 2 : ' materiæ corporalis, cujus materiæ anima usum semper habet, in qualibet qualitate positæ, nunc quidem carnali, postmodum vero subtiliori et puriori, quæ spiritalis appellatur.'

[3] Burton, ' Central Africa,' vol. ii. p. 345.

[4] Callaway, ' Rel. of Amazulu,' p. 84.

the under-world, but are the very deities of the living, we can put the proper sense to these expressions. But without such information, we might have mistaken them for denials of the soul's existence after death. This objection may even apply to one of the most formal denials of a future life ever placed on record among an uncultured race, a poem of the Dinka tribe of the White Nile, concerning Dendid the Creator :—

' On the day when Dendid made all things,
  He made the sun ;
And the sun comes forth, goes down, and comes again :
  He made the moon ;
And the moon comes forth, goes down, and comes again :
  He made the stars ;
And the stars come forth, go down, and come again :
  He made man ;
And man comes forth, goes down into the ground, and comes no more.'

It is to be remarked, however, that the close neighbours of these Dinka, the Bari, believe that the dead do return to live again on earth, and the question arises whether it is the doctrine of bodily resurrection, or the doctrine of the surviving ghost-soul, that the Dinka poem denies. The missionary Kaufmann says that the Dinka do not believe the immortality of the soul, that they think it but a breath, and with death all is over ; Brun-Rollet's contrary authority goes to prove that they do believe in another life ; both leave it an open question whether they recognize the existence of surviving ghosts.[1]

Looking at the religion of the lower races as a whole, we shall at least not be ill-advised in taking as one of its general and principal elements the doctrine of the soul's Future Life. But here it is needful to explain, to limit, and to reserve, lest modern theological ideas should lead us to misconstrue more primitive beliefs. In such enquiries the

---

[1] Kaufmann, ' Schilderungen aus Centralafrika,' p. 124 ; G. Lejean in ' Rev. des Deux Mondes,' Apr. 1, 1860, p. 760 ; see Brun-Rollet, ' Nil Blanc,' pp. 100, 234. A dialogue by the missionary Beltrame (1859-60), in Mitterutzner, ' Dinka-Sprache,' p. 57, ascribes to the Dinkas ideas of heaven and hell, which, however, show Christian influence.

phrase ' immortality of the soul ' is to be avoided as misleading. It is doubtful how far the lower psychology enter-
tains at all an absolute conception of immortality, for past
and future fade soon into utter vagueness as the savage mind
quits the present to explore them, the measure of months
and years breaks down even within the narrow span of
human life, and the survivor's thought of the soul of the
departed dwindles and disappears with the personal memory
that kept it alive. The doctrine of the surviving soul may
indeed be treated as common to all known races, though its
acceptance is not unanimous. In savage as in civilized life,
dull and careless natures ignore a world to come as too far
off, while sceptical intellects are apt to reject its belief as
wanting proof. There are even statements on record of
whole classes being formally excluded from future life.
This may be a matter of social pride. In the Tonga Islands,
according to Mariner, it was held that the chiefs and nobles
would live hereafter in the happy island of Bolotu, but that
the souls of the common people would die with their bodies.
So Captain John Smith relates as to the belief of the
Virginians, that the chiefs went after death beyond the
sunset mountains, there to dance and sing with their pre-
decessors, ' but the common people they suppose shall not
live after death.' In the record of a missionary examination of the Nicaraguans, they are made to state their belief
that if a man lived well, his soul would ascend to dwell
among the gods, but if ill it would perish with the body,
and there would be an end of it.[1] None of these accounts,
however, agree with what is known of the religion of
kindred peoples, Polynesian, Algonquin, or Aztec. But
granted that the soul survives the death of the body,
instance after instance from the records of the lower
culture shows this soul to be regarded as a mortal
being, liable like the body itself to accident and death.
The Greenlanders pitied the poor souls who must pass
in winter or in storm the dreadful mountain where

[1] Mariner, ' Tonga Is.' vol. ii. p. 136 ; John Smith, ' Descr. of Virginia,'
33 ; Oviedo, ' Nicaragua,' p. 50. The reference to the Laos in Meiners,
vol. ii. p. 760, is worthless.

the dead descend to reach the other world, for then a soul is like to come to harm, and die the other death where there is nothing left, and this is to them the dolefullest thing of all.[1] Thus the Fijians tell of the fight which the ghost of a departed warrior must wage with the soul-killing Samu and his brethren; this is the contest for which the dead man is armed by burying the war-club with his corpse, and if he conquers, the way is open for him to the judgment-seat of Ndengei, but if he is wounded, his doom is to wander among the mountains, and if killed in the encounter he is cooked and eaten by Samu and his brethren. But the souls of unmarried Fijians will not even survive to stand this wager of battle ; such try in vain to steal at low water round to the edge of the reef past the rocks where Nangananga, destroyer of wifeless souls, sits laughing at their hopeless efforts, and asking them if they think the tide will never flow again, till at last the rising flood drives the shivering ghosts to the beach, and Nangananga dashes them in pieces on the great black stone, as one shatters rotten firewood.[2] Such, again, were the tales told by the Guinea negroes of the life or death of departed souls. Either the great priest before whom they must appear after death would judge them, sending the good in peace to a happy place, but killing the wicked a second time with the club that stands ready before his dwelling ; or else the departed shall be judged by their god at the river of death, to be gently wafted by him to a pleasant land if they have kept feasts and oaths and abstained from forbidden meats, but if not, to be plunged into the river by the god, and thus drowned and buried in eternal oblivion.[3] Even common water can drown a negro ghost, if we may believe the missionary Cavazzi's story of the Matamba widows being ducked in the river or pond to drown off the

[1] Cranz, Grönland,' p. 259.

[2] Williams, ' Fiji,' vol. i. p. 244. See ' Journ. Ind. Archip.' vol. iii. p. 113 (Dayaks). Compare wasting and death of souls in depths of Hades, Taylor, ' New Zealand,' p. 232.

[3] Bosman, ' Guinea ' in Pinkerton, vol. xvi. p. 401. See also Waitz, ' Anthropologie,' vol. ii. p. 191 (W. Afr.) ; Callaway, ' Rel. of Amazulu,' p. 355.

souls of their departed husbands, who might still be hanging about them, clinging closest to the best-loved wives.
After this ceremony, they went and married again.[1] From
such details it appears that the conception of some souls
suffering extinction at death or dying a second death, a
thought still as heretofore familiar to speculative theology,
is not unknown in the lower culture.

The soul, as recognized in the philosophy of the lower
races, may be defined as an ethereal surviving being, conceptions of which preceded and led up to the more transcendental theory of the immaterial and immortal soul,
which forms part of the theology of higher nations. It is
principally the ethereal surviving soul of early culture that
has now to be studied in the religions of savages and barbarians and the folk-lore of the civilized world. That this
soul should be looked on as surviving beyond death is a
matter scarcely needing elaborate argument. Plain experience is there to teach it to every savage ; his friend or
his enemy is dead, yet still in dream or open vision he sees
the spectral form which is to his philosophy a real objective
being, carrying personality as it carries likeness. This
thought of the soul's continued existence is, however, but
the gateway into a complex region of belief. The doctrines
which, separate or compounded, make up the scheme of
future existence among particular tribes, are principally
these : the theories of lingering, wandering, and returning
ghosts, and of souls dwelling on or below or above the earth
in a spirit-world, where existence is modelled upon the
earthly life, or raised to higher glory, or placed under reversed conditions, and lastly, the belief in a division between
happiness and misery of departed souls, by a retribution for
deeds done in life, determined in a judgment after death.

‘ All argument is against it ; but all belief is for it,’ said
Dr. Johnson of the apparition of departed spirits. The
doctrine that ghost-souls of the dead hover among the

[1] Cavazzi, ‘ Congo, Matamba, et Angola,’ lib. i. p. 270. See also Liebrecht
in ‘ Zeitschr. für Ethnologie,’ vol. v. p. 96 (Tartary, Scandinavia, Greece).

living is indeed rooted in the lowest levels of savage culture, extends through barbaric life almost without a break, and survives largely and deeply in the midst of civilization. From the myriad details of travellers, missionaries, historians, theologians, spiritualists, it may be laid down as an admitted opinion, as wide in distribution as it is natural in thought, that the two chief hunting-grounds of the departed soul are the scenes of its fleshly life and the burial place of its body. As in North America the Chickasaws believed that the spirits of the dead in their bodily shape moved about among the living in great joy; as the Aleutian islanders fancied the souls of the departed walking unseen among their kindred, and accompanying them in their journeys by sea and land; as Africans think that souls of the dead dwell in their midst, and eat with them at meal times; as Chinese pay their respects to kindred spirits present in the hall of ancestors;[1] so multitudes in Europe and America live in an atmosphere that swarms with ghostly shapes—spirits of the dead, who sit over against the mystic by his midnight fire, rap and write in spirit-circles, and peep over girls' shoulders as they scare themselves into hysterics with ghost-stories. Almost throughout the vast range of animistic religion, we shall find the souls of the departed hospitably entertained by the survivors on set occasions, and manes-worship, so deep and strong among the faiths of the world, recognizes with a reverence not without fear and trembling those ancestral spirits which, powerful for good or ill, manifest their presence among mankind. Nevertheless death and life dwell but ill together, and from savagery onward there is recorded many a device by which the survivors have sought to rid themselves of household ghosts. Though the unhappy savage custom of deserting houses after a decease may often be connected with other causes, such as horror or abnegation of all things belonging to the dead, there are cases where it

---

[1] Schoolcraft, 'Indian Tribes,' part i. p. 310; Bastian, 'Psychologie,' pp. 111, 193; Doolittle, 'Chinese,' vol. i. p. 235.

appears that the place is simply abandoned to the ghost. In Old Calabar it was customary for the son to leave his fathers' house to decay, but after two years he might re-build it, the ghost being thought by that time to have departed;[1] the Hottentots abandoned the dead man's house, and were said to avoid entering it lest the ghost should be within;[2] the Yakuts let the hut fall in ruins where any one had expired, thinking it the habitation of demons;[3] the Karens were said to destroy their villages to escape the dangerous neighbourhood of departed souls.[4] Such proceedings, however, scarcely extend beyond the limits of barbarism, and only a feeble survival of the old thought lingers on into civilization, where from time to time a haunted house is left to fall in ruins, abandoned to a ghostly tenant who cannot keep it in repair.   But even in the lowest culture we find flesh holding its own against spirit, and at higher stages the householder rids himself with little scruple of an unwelcome inmate.   The Green-landers would carry the dead out by the window, not by the door, while an old woman, waving a firebrand behind, cried ' piklerrukpok ! ' i.e., ' there is nothing more to be had here !';[5] the Hottentots removed the dead from the hut by an opening broken out on purpose, to prevent him from finding the way back ;[6] the Siamese, with the same inten-tion, break an opening through the house wall to carry the coffin through, and then hurry it at full speed thrice round the house ;[7] in Russia the Chuwashes fling a red-hot stone

[1] Bastian, ' Mensch,' vol. ii. p. 323.
[2] Kolben, p. 579.
[3] Billings, p. 125.
[4] Bastian, 'Oestl. Asien.' vol. i. p. 145;   Cross, l.c., p. 311.   For other cases of desertion of dwellings after a death, possibly for the same motive, see Bourien, ' Tribes of Malay Pen.' in ' Tr. Eth. Soc.' vol. iii. p. 82 ; Polack, ' M. of New Zealanders,' vol. i. pp. 204, 216 ; Steller, ' Kamtschatka,' p. 271. But the Todas say that the buffaloes slaughtered and the hut burnt at the funeral are transferred to the spirit of the deceased in the next world ; Shortt in ' Tr. Eth. Soc.' vol. vii. p. 247. See Waitz, vol. iii. p. 199.
[5] Egede, ' Greenland,' p. 152 ; Cranz, p. 300.
[6] Bastian, ' Mensch,' vol. ii. p. 323 ; see pp. 329, 363.
[7] Bowring, ' Siam,' vol. i. p. 122 ; Bastian, ' Oestl. Asien.' vol. iii. p. 258.

after the corpse is carried out, for an obstacle to bar the soul from coming back;[1] so Brandenburg peasants pour out a pail of water at the door after the coffin, to prevent the ghost from walking ; and Pomeranian mourners returning from the churchyard leave behind the straw from the hearse that the wandering soul may rest there, and not come back so far as home.[2]   In the ancient and mediæval world, men habitually invoked supernatural aid beyond such material shifts as these, calling in the priest to lay or banish intruding ghosts, nor is this branch of the exorcist's art even yet forgotten.   There is, and always has been, a prevalent feeling that disembodied souls, especially such as have suffered a violent or untimely death, are baneful and malicious beings.   As Meiners suggests in his ' History of Religions,' they were driven unwillingly from their bodies, and have carried into their new existence an angry longing for revenge.   No wonder that mankind should so generally agree that if the souls of the dead must linger in the world at all, their fitting abode should be not the haunts of the living but the resting-places of the dead.

After all, it scarcely seems to the lower animistic philosophy that the connexion between body and soul is utterly broken by death.   Various wants may keep the soul from its desired rest, and among the chief of these is when its mortal remains have not had the funeral rites.   Hence the deep-lying belief that the ghosts of such will walk.   Among some Australian tribes the ' ingna,' or evil spirits, human in shape, but with long tails and long upright ears, are mostly souls of departed natives, whose bodies were left to lie unburied or whose death the avenger of blood did not expiate, and thus they have to prowl on the face of the earth, and about the place of death, with no gratification

---

[1] Castrén, ' Finn. Myth.' p. 120.

[2] Wuttke, ' Volksaberglaube,' pp. 213-17.   Other cases of taking out the dead by a gap made on purpose : Arbousset and Daumas, p. 502 (Bushmen) ; Magyar, p. 351 (Kimbunda) ; Moffat, p. 307 (Bechuanas) ; Waitz, vol. iii. p. 199 (Ojibwas) ;—their motive is probably that the ghost may not find its way back by the door.

but to harm the living.[1]   In New Zealand, the ideas were
to be found that the souls of the dead were apt to linger
near the bodies, and that the spirits of men left unburied
or killed in battle and eaten, would wander; and the bringing such malignant souls to dwell within the sacred burial-
enclosure was a task for the priest to accomplish with his
charms.[2] Among the Iroquois of North America the spirit
also stays near the body for a time, and ' unless the rites
of burial were performed, it was believed that the spirits of
the dead hovered for a time upon the earth, in a state of
great unhappiness.   Hence their extreme solicitude to procure the bodies of the slain in battle.'[3]   Among Brazilian
tribes, the wandering shadows of the dead are said to be
considered unresting till burial.[4]   In Turanian regions of
North Asia, the spirits of the dead who have no resting-
place in earth are thought of as lingering above ground,
especially where their dust remains.[5] South Asia has such
beliefs : the Karens say that the ghosts who wander on
earth are not the spirits of those who go to Plu, the land
of the dead, but of infants, of such as died by violence, of
the wicked, and of those who by accident have not been
buried or burned;[6] the Siamese fear as unkindly spirits the
souls of such as died a violent death or were not buried
with the proper rites, and who desiring expiation, invisibly
terrify their descendants.[7] Nowhere in the world had
such thoughts a stronger hold than in classic antiquity,
where it was the most sacred of duties to give the body
its funeral rites, that the shade should not flit moaning
near the gates of Hades, nor wander in the dismal crowd

---

[1] Oldfield in ' Tr. Eth. Soc.' vol. iii. pp. 228, 236, 245.
[2] Taylor, ' New Zealand,' p. 221 ; Schirren, p. 91 ; see Turner, ' Polynesia,'
p. 233.
[3] Morgan, ' League of Iroquois,' p. 174.
[4] J. G. Müller, p. 286.
[5] Castrén, ' Finn. Myth.' p. 126.
[6] Cross in ' Journ. Amer. Or. Soc.' vol. iv. p. 309 ; Mason in ' Journ. As.
Soc. Bengal,' 1865, part ii. p. 203. See also J. Anderson, ' Exp. to W.
Yunnan,' pp. 126, 131 (Shans).
[7] Bastian, ' Psychologie,' pp. 51, 99-101.

along the banks of Acheron.[1]   An Australian or a Karen
would have taken in the full significance of the fatal
accusation against the Athenian commanders, that they
abandoned the bodies of their dead in the sea-fight of
Arginousai.   The thought is not unknown to Slavonic
folk-lore : ' Ha ! with the shriek the spirit flutters from
the mouth, flies up to the tree, from tree to tree, hither
and thither till the dead is burned.'[2]   In mediæval
Europe the classic stories of ghosts that haunt the living
till laid by rites of burial pass here and there into new
legends, where, under a changed dispensation, the doleful
wanderer now asks Christian burial in consecrated earth.[3]
It is needless to give here elaborate details of the world-
wide thought that when the corpse is buried, exposed,
burned, or otherwise disposed of after the accepted custom
of the land, the ghost accompanies its relics.   The soul
stays near the Polynesian or the American Indian burial-
place ; it dwells among the twigs and listens joyfully to the
singing birds in the trees where Siberian tribes suspend
their dead ; it lingers by the Samoyed's scaffolded coffin ;
it haunts the Dayak's place of burial or burning; it inhabits
the little soul-hut above the Malagasy grave, or the Peruvian house of sun-dried bricks ;   it is deposited in the
Roman tomb (animamque sepulchro condimus) ;   it comes
back for judgment into the body of the later Israelite and
the Moslem ;   it inhabits, as a divine ancestral spirit, the
palace-tombs of the old classic and new Asiatic world ; it is
kept down by the huge cairn raised over Antar's body lest
his mighty spirit should burst forth, by the iron nails with
which the Cheremiss secures the corpse in its coffin, by the
stake that pins down the suicide's body at the four-cross
way.   And through all the changes of religious thought
from first to last in the course of human history, the hover-

---

[1] Lucian. De Luctu. See Pauly, ' Real. Encyclop.' and Smith, ' Dic. of
Gr. and Rom. Ant.' s.v. ' inferi.'
[2] Hanusch, ' Slaw. Myth.' p. 277.
[3] Calmet, vol. ii. ch. xxxvi. ; Brand, vol. iii. p. 67.

ing ghosts of the dead make the midnight burial-ground a place where men's flesh creeps with terror. Not to discuss here the general subject of funeral rites of mankind, of which only part of the multifarious details are directly relevant to the present purpose, a custom may be selected which is admirably adapted for the study of animistic religion, at once from the clear conception it gives of the belief in disembodied souls present among the living, and from the distinct line of ethnographic continuity in which it may be traced onward from the lower to the higher culture. This is the custom of Feasts of the Dead.

Among the funeral offerings described in the last chapter of which the purpose more or less distinctly appears to be that the departed soul shall take them away in some ghostly or ideal manner, or that they shall by some means be conveyed to him in his distant spirit-home, there are given supplies of food and drink. But the feasts of the dead with which we are now concerned are given on a different principle ; they are, so to speak, to be consumed on the premises. They are set out in some proper place, especially near the tombs or in the dwelling-houses, and there the souls of the dead come and satisfy themselves. In North America, among Algonquins who held that one of a man's two souls abides with the body after death, the provisions brought to the grave were intended for the nourishment of this soul ; tribes would make offerings to ancestors of part of any dainty food, and an Indian who fell by accident into the fire would believe that the spirits of his ancestors pushed him in for neglecting to make due offerings.[1] The minds of the Hurons were filled with fancies not less lifelike than this. It seemed to them that the dead man's soul, in his proper human figure, walked in front of the corpse as they carried it to the burial-ground, there to dwell till the great feast of the dead ; but meanwhile it would come and walk by night in the village, and eat the remnants in the kettles,

[1] Charlevoix, 'Nouvelle France,' vol. vi. p. 75 ; Schoolcraft, 'Indian Tribes,' part i. pp. 39, 83 ; part iv. p. 65 ; Tanner's 'Narr.' p. 293.

wherefore some would not eat of these, nor touch the food
at funeral feasts—though some indeed would eat all.[1]   In
Madagascar, the elegant little upper chamber in King
Radama's mausoleum was furnished with a table and two
chairs, and a bottle of wine, a bottle of water, and two
tumblers were placed there conformably with the ideas
entertained by most of the natives, that the ghost of the
departed monarch might occasionally visit the resting-place
of his body, meet with the spirit of his father, and partake
of what he was known to be fond of in his lifetime.[2]   The
Wanika of East Africa set a coco-nut shell full of rice and
tembo near the grave for the ' koma ' or shade, which
cannot exist without food and drink.[3]   In West Africa the
Efik cook food and leave it on the table in the little shed
or ' devil-house ' near the grave, and thither not only the
spirit of the deceased, but the spirits of the slaves sacrificed
at his funeral, come to partake of it.[4]   Farther south, in the
Congo district, the custom has been described of making a
channel into the tomb to the head or mouth of the corpse,
whereby to send down month by month the offerings of
food and drink.[5]

Among rude Asiatic tribes, the Bodo of North-East India
thus celebrate the last funeral rites. The friends repair to
the grave, and the nearest of kin to the deceased, taking an
individual's usual portion of food and drink, solemnly presents it to the dead with these words, ' Take and eat, heretofore you have eaten and drunk with us, you can do so no
more ; you were one of us, you can be so no longer ; we
come no more to you, come you not to us.' Thereupon each
of the party breaks off a bracelet of thread put on his wrist
for this purpose, and casts it on the grave, a speaking symbol of breaking the bond of fellowship, and ' next the party

[1] Brebeuf in ' Rel. des Jés.' 1636, p. 104.
[2] Ellis, 'Madagascar,' vol. i. pp. 253, 364. See Taylor, 'New Zealand,' p. 220.
[3] Krapf, ' E. Afr.' p. 150.
[4] T. J. Hutchinson, p. 206.
[5] Cavazzi, ' Congo, &c.' lib. i. p. 264. So in ancient Greece, Lucian.
Charon, 22.

proceed to the river and bathe, and having thus lustrated themselves, they repair to the banquet and eat, drink, and make merry as though they never were to die.'[1] With more continuance of affection, Naga tribes of Assam celebrate their funeral feasts month by month, laying food and drink on the graves of the departed.[2] In the same region of the world, the Kol tribes of Chota Nagpur are remarkable for their pathetic reverence for their dead. When a Ho or Munda has been burned on the funeral pile, collected morsels of his bones are carried in procession with a solemn, ghostly, sliding step, keeping time to the deep-sounding drum, and when the old woman who carries the bones on her bamboo tray lowers it from time to time, then girls who carry pitchers and brass vessels mournfully reverse them to show that they are empty ; thus the remains are taken to visit every house in the village, and every dwelling of a friend or relative for miles, and the inmates come out to mourn and praise the goodness of the departed ; the bones are carried to all the dead man's favourite haunts, to the fields he cultivated, to the grove he planted, to the threshing-floor where he worked, to the village dance-room where he made merry.   At last they are taken to the grave, and buried in an earthen vase upon a store of food, covered with one of those huge stone slabs which European visitors wonder at in the districts of the aborigines in India.   Besides these, monumental stones are set up outside the village to the memory of men of note ; they are fixed on an earthen plinth, where the ghost, resting in its walks among the living, is supposed to sit shaded by the pillar.   The Kheriahs have collections of these monuments in the little enclosures round their houses, and offerings and libations are constantly made at them.   With what feelings such rites are celebrated may be judged from this Ho dirge :—

' We never scolded you ; never wronged you ;
   Come to us back !

[1] Hodgson, ' Abor. of India,' p. 180.   [2] ' Journ. Ind. Archip.' vol. ii. p. 235.

We ever loved and cherished you ; and have lived long together
  Under the same roof ;
  Desert it not now !
The rainy nights, and the cold blowing days, are coming on ;
  Do not wander here !
Do not stand by the burnt ashes ; come to us again !
You cannot find shelter under the peepul, when the rain comes down.
The saul will not shield you from the cold bitter wind.
  Come to your home !
It is swept for you, and clean ; and we are there who loved you ever ;
And there is rice put for you ; and water ;
  Come home, come home, come to us again ! '

Among the Kol tribes this kindly hospitality to ancestral
souls passes on into the belief and ceremony of full manes-
worship : votive offerings are made to the ' old folks ' when
their descendants go on a journey, and when there is sickness in the family it is generally they who are first propitiated.[1]   Among Turanian races, the Chuwash put food
and napkins on the grave, saying, ' Rise at night and eat
your fill, and there ye have napkins to wipe your mouths ! '
while the Cheremiss simply said, ' That is for you, ye dead,
there ye have food and drink ! '   In this Tatar region we
hear of offerings continued year after year, and even of
messengers sent back by a horde to carry offerings to the
tombs of their forefathers in the old land whence they had
emigrated.[2]

Details of this ancient rite are to be traced from the level
of these rude races far upward in civilization.   South-East
Asia is full of it, and the Chinese may stand as its representative.   He keeps his coffined parent for years, serving
him with meals as if alive.   He summons ancestral souls
with prayer and beat of drum to feed on the meat and drink
set out on special days when they are thought to return
home.   He even gives entertainments for the benefit of

[1] Tickell in ' Journ. As. Soc. Bengal,' vol. ix. p. 795 ; Dalton, ibid. 1866,
part ii. p. 153, &c. ; and in ' Tr. Eth. Soc.' vol. vi. p. 1, &c. ; Latham,
' Descr. Eth.' vol. ii. p. 415, &c.
[2] Bastian, ' Psychologie,' p. 62 ; Castrén, ' Finn. Myth.' p. 121.

destitute and unfortunate souls in the lower regions, such as those of lepers and beggars. Lanterns are lighted to show them the way, a feast is spread for them, and with characteristic fancy, some victuals are left over for any blind or feeble spirits who may be late, and a pail of gruel is provided for headless souls, with spoons for them to put it down their throats with. Such proceedings culminate in the so-called Universal Rescue, now and then celebrated, when a little house is built for the expected visitors, with separate accommodation and bath-rooms for male and female ghosts.[1] The ancient Egyptian would set out his provision of cakes and trussed ducks on reed scaffolds in the tomb, or would even keep the mummy in the house to be present as a guest at the feast, σύνδειπνον καὶ συμπότην ἐποιήσατο, as Lucian says.[2] The Hindu, as of old, offers to the dead the funeral cakes, places before the door the earthen vessels of water for him to bathe in, of milk for him to drink, and celebrates at new and full moon the solemn presentation of rice-cakes made with ghee, with its attendant ceremonies so important for the soul's release from its twelvemonth's sojourn with Yama in Hades, and its transition to the Heaven of the Pitaras, the Fathers.[3] In the classic world such rites were represented by funeral feasts and oblations of food.[4]

In Christian times there manifests itself that interesting kind of survival which, keeping up the old ceremony in form, has adapted its motive to new thoughts and feelings. The classic funeral oblations became Christian, the silicernium was succeeded by the feast held at the martyr's tomb. Faustus inveighs against the Christians for carrying on the ancient rites : ' Their sacrifices indeed ye have turned into love-feasts, their idols into martyrs whom with like vows ye

---

[1] Doolittle, ' Chinese,' vol. i. p. 173, &c. ; vol. ii. p. 91, &c. ; Meiners, vol. i. p. 306.

[2] Wilkinson, ' Ancient Eg.' vol. ii. p. 362 ; Lucian. De Luctu, 21.

[3] Manu, iii. ; Colebrooke, ' Essays,' vol. i. p. 161, &c. ; Pictet, ' Origines Indo-Europ.' part ii. p. 600 ; Ward, ' Hindoos,' vol. ii. p. 332.

[4] Pauly, ' Real-Encyclop.' s.v. ' funus ' ; Smith's ' Dic.' s.v. ' funus.' See Meiners, vol. i. pp. 305-19.

worship ; ye appease the shades of the dead with wine and meals, ye celebrate the Gentiles' solemn days with them, such as calends and solstices,—of their life certainly ye have changed nought,'[1] and so forth. The story of Monica shows how the custom of laying food on the tomb for the manes passed into the ceremony, like to it in form, of setting food and drink to be sanctified by the sepulchre of a Christian saint. Saint-Foix, who wrote in the time of Louis XIV., has left us an account of the ceremonial after the death of a King of France, during the forty days before the funeral when his wax effigy lay in state. They continued to serve him at meal-times as though still alive, the officers laid the table, and brought the dishes, the maître d'hôtel handed the napkin to the highest lord present to be presented to the king, a prelate blessed the table, the basins of water were handed to the royal arm-chair, the cup was served in its due course, and grace was said in the accustomed manner,, save that there was added to it the De Profundis.[2] Spaniards still offer bread and wine on the tombs of those they love, on the anniversary of their decease.[3] The conservative Eastern Church still holds to ancient rite. The funeral feast is served in Russia, with its tables for the beggars, laden with fish pasties and bowls of shchi and jugs of kvas, its more delicate dinner for friends and priests, its incense and chants of 'everlasting remembrance'; and even the repetition of the festival on the ninth, and twentieth, and fortieth day are not forgotten. The offerings of saucers of kutiya or kolyvo are still made in the church ; this used to be of parboiled wheat and was deposited over the body, it is now made of boiled rice and raisins, sweetened with honey. In their usual mystic fashion, the Orthodox Christians now explain away into symbolism this remnant of primitive offering to the dead : the honey is heavenly sweetness, the

[1] Augustin. contra Faustum, xx. 4 ; De Civ. Dei, viii. 27 ; conf. vi. 2. See Beausobre, vol. ii. pp. 633, 685 ; Bingham, xx. c. 7.

[2] Saint-Foix, ' Essais Historiques sur Paris,' in ' Œuvres,' vol. iv. p. 147, &c.

[3] Lady Herbert, ' Impressions of Spain,' p. 8.

shrivelled raisins will be full beauteous grapes, the grain typifies the resurrection, ' that which thou sowest is not quickened except it die.'[1]

In the calendar of many a people, differing widely as they may in race and civilization, there are to be found special yearly festivals of the dead. Their rites are much the same as those performed on other days for individuals ; their season differs in different districts, but seems to have particular associations with harvest-time and the fall of the year, and with the year's end as reckoned at midwinter or in early spring.[2] The Karens make their annual offerings to the dead in the ' month of shades,' that is, December ;[3] the Kocch of North Bengal every year at harvest-home offer fruits and a fowl to deceased parents ;[4] the Barea of East Africa celebrate in November the feast of Thiyot, at once a feast of general peace and merry-making, of thanksgiving for the harvest, and of memorial for the deceased, for each of whom a little pot-full of beer is set out two days, to be drunk at last by the survivors ;[5] in West Africa we hear of the feast of the dead at the time of yam-harvest ;[6] at the end of the year the Haitian negroes take food to the graves for the shades to eat, ' manger zombi,' as they say.[7] The Roman Feralia and Lemuralia were held in February

---

[1] H. C. Romanoff, ' Rites and Customs of Greco-Russian Church,' p. 249 ; Ralston, ' Songs of the Russian People,' pp. 135, 320 ; St. Clair and Brophy, ' Bulgaria,' p. 77 ; Brand, ' Pop. Ant.' vol. i. p. 115.

[2] Beside the accounts of annual festivals of the dead cited here, see the following :—Santos, ' Ethiopia,' in Pinkerton, vol. xvi. p. 685 (Sept.) ; Brasseur, ' Mexique,' vol. iii. pp. 23, 522, 528 (Aug., Oct., Nov.) ; Rivero and Tschudi, ' Peru,' p. 134 (Peruvian feast dated as Nov. 2 in coincidence with All Souls', but this reckoning is vitiated by confusion of seasons of N. and S. hemisphere, see J. G. Müller, p. 389 ; moreover, the Peruvian feast may have been originally held at a different date, and transferred, as happened elsewhere, to the Spanish All Souls') ; Doolittle, ' Chinese,' vol. ii. pp. 44, 62 (esp. Apr.) ; Caron, ' Japan,' in Pinkerton, vol. vii. p. 629 (Aug.).

[3] Mason, ' Karens,' l. c. p. 238.

[4] Hodgson, ' Abor. of India,' p. 147.

[5] Munzinger, ' Ostafr. Stud.' p. 473.

[6] Waitz, vol. ii. p. 194.

[7] G. D'Alaux in ' Rev. des Deux Mondes,' May 15, 1852, p. 76.

and May.[1] In the last five or ten days of their year the
Zoroastrians hold their feasts for departed relatives, when
souls come back to the world to visit the living, and receive
from them offerings of food and clothing.[2] The custom of
setting empty seats at the St. John's Eve feast, for the
departed souls of kinsfolk, is said to have lasted on in
Europe to the seventeenth century. Spring is the season
of the time-honoured Slavonic rite of laying food on the
graves of the dead. The Bulgarians hold a feast in the
cemetery on Palm Sunday, and, after much eating and
drinking, leave the remains upon the graves of their friends,
who, they are persuaded, will eat them during the night.
In Russia such scenes may still be watched on the two
appointed days called Parents' Days. The higher classes
have let the rite sink to prayer at the graves of lost relatives, and giving alms to the beggars who flock to the
cemeteries. But the people still 'howl' for the dead, and
set out on their graves a handkerchief for a tablecloth, with
gingerbread, eggs, curd-tarts, and even vodka, on it ; when
the weeping is over, they eat up the food, especially commemorating the dead in Russian manner by partaking of
his favourite dainty, and if he were fond of a glass, the
vodka is sipped with the ejaculation, ' The Kingdom of
Heaven be his ! He loved a drink, the deceased ! '[3] When
Odilo, Abbot of Cluny, at the end of the tenth century, instituted the celebration of All Souls' Day (November 2),[4]

[1] Ovid. Fast. ii. 533 ; v. 420.

[2] Spiegel, ' Avesta,' vol. ii. p. ci. ; Alger, p. 137.

[3] Hanusch, ' Slaw. Myth.' pp. 374, 408 ; St. Clair and Brophy, ' Bulgaria,'
p. 77 ; Romanoff, ' Greco-Roman Church,' p. 255.

[4] Petrus Damianus, ' Vita S. Odilonis,' in the Bollandist ' Acta Sanctorum,'
Jan. 1, has the quaint legend attached to the new ordinance. An island
hermit dwelt near a volcano, where souls of the wicked were tormented in
the flames. The holy man heard the officiating demons lament that their
daily task of new torture was interfered with by the prayers and alms of
devout persons leagued against them to save souls, and especially they
complained of the Monks of Cluny. Thereupon the hermit sent a message
to Abbot Odilo, who carried out the work to the efficacy of which he had
received such perfect spiritual testimony, by decreeing that November 2, the
day after All Saints', should be set apart for services for the departed.

he set on foot one of those revivals which have so often
given the past a new lease of life. The Western Church at
large took up the practice, and round it there naturally
gathered surviving remnants of the primitive rite of banquets to the dead. The accusation against the early Christians, that they appeased the shades of the dead with feasts
like the Gentiles, would not be beside the mark now, fifteen
hundred years later. On the eve of All Souls' begins,
within the limits of Christendom, a commemoration of the
dead which combines some touches of pathetic imagination
with relics of savage animism scarcely to be surpassed in
Africa or the South Sea Islands. In Italy the day is given
to feasting and drinking in honour of the dead, while skulls
and skeletons in sugar and paste form appropriate children's
toys. In Tyrol, the poor souls released from purgatory fire
for the night may come and smear their burns with the
melted fat of the ' soul light ' on the hearth, or cakes are
left for them on the table, and the room is kept warm for
their comfort. Even in Paris the souls of the departed
come to partake of the food of the living. In Brittany the
crowd pours into the churchyard at evening, to kneel bareheaded at the graves of dead kinsfolk, to fill the hollow of
the tombstone with holy water, or to pour libations of milk
upon it. All night the church bells clang, and sometimes
a solemn procession of the clergy goes round to bless the
graves. In no household that night is the cloth removed,
for the supper must be left for the souls to come and take
their part, nor must the fire be put out, where they will
come to warm themselves. And at last, as the inmates
retire to rest, there is heard at the door a doleful chant—it
is the souls, who, borrowing the voices of the parish poor,
have come to ask the prayers of the living.[1]

If we ask how the spirits of the dead are in general sup-

---

[1] Bastian, 'Mensch,' vol. ii. p. 336. Meiners, vol. i. p. 316; vol. ii. p. 290.
Wuttke, ' Deutsche Volksaberglaube,' p. 216. Cortet, ' Fêtes Religieuses,'
p. 233 ; ' Westminster Rev.' Jan. 1860 ; Hersart de la Villemarqué, ' Chants
de la Bretagne,' vol. ii. p. 307.

posed to feed on the viands set before them, we come upon difficult questions, which will be met with again in discussing the theory of sacrifice. Even where the thought is certainly that the departed soul eats, this thought may be very indefinite, with far less of practical intention in it than of childish make-believe. Now and then, however, the sacrificers themselves offer closer definitions of their meaning. The idea of the ghost actually devouring the material food is not unexampled. Thus, in North America, Algonquin Indians considered that the shadow-like souls of the dead can still eat and drink, often even telling Father Le Jeune that they had found in the morning meat gnawed in the night by the souls. More recently, we read that some Potawatomis will leave off providing the supply of food at the grave if it lies long untouched, it being concluded that the dead no longer wants it, but has found a rich hunting-ground in the other world.[1] In Africa, again, Father Cavazzi records of the Congo people furnishing their dead with supplies of provisions, that they could not be persuaded that souls did not consume material food.[2] In Europe the Esths, offering food for the dead on All Souls', are said to have rejoiced if they found in the morning that any of it was gone.[3] A less gross conception is that the soul con-

---

[1] Le Jeune in ' Rel. des Jés.' 1634, p. 16 ; Waitz, vol. iii. p. 195.

[2] Cavazzi, ' Congo,' &c., book i. 265.

[3] Grimm, ' D. M.' p. 865, but not so in the account of the Feast of the Dead in Boecler, ' Ehsten Abergl. Gebr.' (ed. Kreutzwald), p. 89. Compare Martius, ' Ethnog. Amer.' vol. i. p. 345 (Gês). The following passage from a spiritualist journal, ' The Medium,' Feb. 9, 1872, shows this primitive notion curiously surviving in modern England. ' Every time we sat at dinner, we had not only spirit-voices calling to us, but spirit-hands touching us ; and last evening, as it was his farewell, they gave us a special manifestation, un-asked for and unlooked for. He sitting at the right hand of me, a vacant chair opposite to him began moving, and, in answer to whether it would have some dinner, said " Yes." I then asked it to select what it would take, when it chose *croquets des pommes de terre* (a French way of dressing potatoes, about three inches long and two wide. I will send you one that you may see it). I was desired to put this on the chair, either in a tablespoon or on a plate. I placed it in a tablespoon, thinking that probably the plate might be broken. In a few seconds I was told that it was eaten, and looking, found the half of it gone, with the marks showing the teeth.' (Note to 2nd ed.)

sumes the steam or savour of the food, or its essence or spirit. It is said to have been with such purpose that the Maoris placed food by the dead man's side, and some also with him in the grave.[1] The idea is well displayed among the natives in Mexican districts, where the souls who came to the annual feast are described as hovering over and smelling the food set out for them, or sucking out its nutritive quality.[2] The Hindu entreats the manes to quaff the sweet essence of the offered food ; thinking on them, he slowly sets the dish of rice before the Brahmans, and while they silently eat the hot food, the ancestral spirits take their part of the feast.[3] At the old Slavonic meals for the dead, we read of the survivors sitting in silence and throwing morsels under the table, fancying that they could hear the spirits rustle, and see them feed on the smell and steam of the viands. One account describes the mourners at the funeral banquet inviting in the departed soul thought to be standing outside the door, and every guest throwing morsels and pouring drink under the table, for him to refresh himself. What lay on the ground was not picked up, but was left for friendless and kinless souls. When the meal was over, the priest rose from table, swept out the house, and hunted out the souls of the dead ' like fleas,' with these words, ' Ye have eaten and drunken, souls, now go, now go ! '[4] Many travellers have described the imagination with which the Chinese make such offerings. It is that the spirits of the dead consume the impalpable essence of the food, leaving behind its coarse material substance, wherefore the dutiful sacrificers, having set out sumptuous feasts for ancestral souls, allow them a proper time to satisfy their appetite, and then fall to themselves.[5] The Jesuit Father Christoforo Borri suggestively translates the native idea into his own scholastic phraseology. In Cochin China,

[1] Taylor, ' New Zealand,' p. 220, see 104.
[2] Brasseur, ' Mexique,' vol. iii. p. 24.
[3] Colebrooke, ' Essays,' vol. i. p. 163, &c. ; Manu. iii.
[4] Hanusch, ' Slaw. Myth.' p. 408 ; Hartknoch, ' Preussen,' part i. p. 187.
[5] Doolittle, ' Chinese,' vol. ii. pp. 33, 48 ; Meiners, vol. i. p. 318.

according to him, people believed ' that the souls of the dead have need of corporeal sustenance and maintenance, wherefore several times a year, according to their custom, they make splendid and sumptuous banquets, children to their deceased parents, husbands to their wives, friends to their friends, waiting a long while for the dead guest to come and sit down at table to eat.' The missionaries argued against this proceeding, but were met by ridicule of their ignorance, and the reply ' that there were two things in the food, one the substance, and the other the accidents of quantity, quality, smell, taste, and the like. The immaterial souls of the dead, taking for themselves the substance of the food, which being immaterial is food suited to the incorporeal soul, left only in the dishes the accidents which corporeal senses perceive ; for this the dead had no need of corporeal instruments, as we have said.' Thereupon the Jesuit proceeds to remark, as to the prospect of conversion of these people, ' it may be judged from the distinction they make between the accidents and the substance of the food which they prepare for the dead,' that it will not be very difficult to prove to them the mystery of the Eucharist.[1] Now to peoples among whom prevails the rite of feasts of the dead, whether they offer the food in mere symbolic pretence, or whether they consider the souls really to feed on it in this spiritual way (as well as in the cases inextricably mixed up with these, where the offering is spiritually conveyed away to the world of spirits), it can be of little consequence what becomes of the gross material food. When the Kafir sorcerer, in cases of sickness, declares that the shades of ancestors demand a particular cow, the beast is slaughtered and left shut up for a time for the shades to eat, or for its spirit to go to the land of shades, and then is taken out to be eaten by the sacrificers.[2] So, in more civilized Japan, when the survivors have placed

---

[1] Borri, ' Relatione della Nuova Missione della Comp. di Giesu,' Rome, 1631, p. 208 ; and in Pinkerton, vol. ix. p. 822, &c.

[2] Grout, ' Zulu Land,' p. 140 ; see Callaway, ' Rel. of Amazulu,' p. 11.

their offering of unboiled rice and water in a hollow made
for the purpose in a stone of the tomb, it seems to them
no matter that the poor or the birds really carry off the
grain.[1]

Such rites as these are especially exposed to dwindle in
survival. The offerings of meals and feasts to the dead
may be traced at their last stage into mere traditional
ceremonies, at most tokens of affectionate remembrance of
the dead, or works of charity to the living. The Roman
Feralia in Ovid's time were a striking example of such
transition, for while the idea was recognized that the ghosts
fed upon the offerings, ' nunc posito pascitur umbra cibo,'
yet there were but ' parva munera,' fruits and grains of
salt, and corn soaked in wine, set out for their meal in the
middle of the road. ' Little the manes ask, the pious
thought stands instead of the rich gift, for Styx holds no
greedy gods : '—

> ' Parva petunt manes. Pietas pro divite grata est
>   Munere. Non avidos Styx habet ima deos.
> Tegula porrectis satis est velata coronis,
>   Et sparsae fruges, parcaque mica salis,
> Inque mero mollita ceres, violaeque solutae :
>   Haec habeat media testa relicta via.
> Nec majora veto. Sed et his placabilis umbra est.'[2]

Still farther back, in old Chinese history, Confucius had
been called on to give an opinion as to the sacrifices to the
dead. Maintainer of all ancient rites as he was, he stringently kept up this, ' he sacrificed to the dead as if they were
present,' but when he was asked if the dead had knowledge
of what was done or no, he declined to answer the question ;
for if he replied yes, then dutiful descendants would injure their substance by sacrifices, and if no, then undutiful
children would leave their parents unburied. The evasion
was characteristic of the teacher who expressed his theory
of worship in this maxim, ' to give oneself earnestly to the

---

[1] Caron, ' Japan,' vol. vii. p. 629 ; see Turpin, ' Siam,' ibid. vol. ix. p. 590.
[2] Ovid. Fast. ii. 533.

duties due to men, and, while respecting spiritual beings, to keep aloof from them, may be called wisdom.' It is said that in our own time the Taepings have made a step beyond Confucius ; they have forbidden the sacrifices to the spirits of the dead, yet keep up the rite of visiting their tombs on the customary day, for prayer and the renewal of vows.[1] How funeral offerings may pass into commemorative banquets and feasts to the poor, has been shown already. If we seek in England for vestiges of the old rite of funeral sacrifice, we may find a lingering survival into modern centuries, doles of bread and drink given to the poor at funerals, and 'soul-mass cakes' which peasant girls perhaps to this day beg for at farmhouses with the traditional formula,

> ' Soul, soul, for a soul cake,
> Pray you, mistress, a soul cake.'[2]

Were it not for our knowledge of the intermediate stages through which these fragments of old custom have come down, it would seem far-fetched indeed to trace their origin back to the savage and barbaric times of the institution of feasts of departed souls.

[1] Legge, ' Confucius,' pp. 101-2, 130 ; Bunsen, ' God in History,' p. 271.
[2] Brand, ' Pop. Ant.' vol. i. p. 392, vol. ii. p. 289.

CHAPTER XIII

ANIMISM (*continued*)

Journey of the Soul to the Land of the Dead—Visits by the Living to the Regions of Departed Souls—Connexion of such legends with myths of Sunset : the Land of the Dead thus imagined as in the West—Realization of current religious ideas, whether of savage or civilized theology, in narratives of visits to the Regions of Souls—Localization of the Future Life—Distant earthly region : Earthly Paradise, Isles of the Blest—Subterranean Hades or Sheol—Sun, Moon, Stars—Heaven—Historical course of belief as to such localization—Nature of Future Life—Continuance-theory, apparently original, belongs especially to the lower races—Transitional theories—Retribution-theory, apparently derived, belongs especially to the higher races—Doctrine of Moral Retribution as developed in the higher culture—Survey of Doctrine of Future State, from savage to civilized stages—Its practical effect on the sentiment and conduct of Mankind.

THE departure of the dead man's soul from the world of living men, its journey to the distant land of spirits, the life it will lead in its new home, are topics on which the lower races for the most part hold explicit doctrines. When these fall under the inspection of a modern ethnographer, he treats them as myths ; often to a high degree intelligible and rational in their origin, consistent and regular in their structure, but not the less myths. Few subjects have aroused the savage poet's mind to such bold and vivid imagery as the thought of the hereafter. Yet also a survey of its details among mankind displays in the midst of variety a regular recurrence of episode which brings the ever-recurring question, how far is this correspondence due to transmission of the same thought from tribe to tribe, and how far to similar but independent development in distant lands ?

From the savage state up into the midst of civilization,

the comparison may be carried through. Low races and
high, in region after region, can point out the very spot
whence the flitting souls start to travel toward their new
home. At the extreme western cape of Vanua Levu, a calm
and solemn place of cliff and forest, the souls of the Fijian
dead embark for the judgement-seat of Ndengei, and thither
the living come in pilgrimage, thinking to see their ghosts
and gods.[1] The Baperi of South Africa will venture to
creep a little way into their cavern of Marimatlé, whence
men and animals came forth into the world, and whither
souls return at death.[2] In Mexico the cavern of Chalcha-
tongo led to the plains of paradise, and the Aztec name of
Mictlan, 'Land of the Dead,' now Mitla, keeps up the
remembrance of another subterranean temple which opened
the way to the sojourn of the blessed.[3] How naturally a
dreary place, fit rather for the dead than the living, suggests
the thought of an entrance to the land of the departed,
is seen in the fictitious travels known under the name of
Sir John Mandevill, where the description of the Vale Peri-
lous, adapted from the terrible valley which Friar Odoric
had seen full of corpses and heard resound with strange
noise of drums, has this appropriate ending : ' This vale es
full of deuilles and all way has bene ; and men saise in that
cuntree that thare es ane entree to hell.'[4] In more genuine
folklore, North German peasants still remember on the
banks of the swampy Drömling the place of access to the
land of departed souls.[5] To us Englishmen the shores of
lake Avernus, trodden daily by our tourists, are more
familiar than the Irish analogue of the place, Lough Derg,
with its cavern entrance of St. Patrick's Purgatory leading
down to the awful world below. The mass of mystic details

---

[1] Williams, ' Fiji,' vol. i. p. 239 ; Seemann, ' Viti,' p. 398.

[2] Arbousset and Daumas, p. 347 ; Casalis, p. 247.

[3] Brasseur, ' Mexique,' vol. iii. p. 20, &c.

[4] See ' The Buke of John Mandeuill,' 31, edited by Geo. F. Warner,
published by the Roxburghe Club, 1889 ; Yule, ' Cathay,' Hakluyt Soc.
[Note to 3rd ed.]

[5] Wuttke, ' Volksaberglaube,' p. 215. Other cases in Bastian, ' Mensch,'
vol. ii. pp. 58, 369, &c.

need not be repeated here of the soul's dread journey by caverns and rocky paths and weary plains, over steep and slippery mountains, by frail bark or giddy bridge across gulfs or rushing rivers, abiding the fierce onset of the soul-destroyer or the doom of the stern guardian of the other world. But before describing the spirit-world which is the end of the soul's journey, let us see what the proof is which sustains the belief in both. The lower races claim to hold their doctrines of the future life on strong tradition, direct revelation, and even personal experience. To them the land of souls is a discovered country, from whose bourne many a traveller returns.

Among the legendary visits to the world beyond the grave, there are some that seem pure myth, without a touch of real personal history. Ojibwa, the eponymic hero of his North American tribe, as one of his many exploits descended to the subterranean world of departed spirits, and came up again to earth.[1] When the Kamchadals were asked how they knew so well what happens to men after death, they could answer with their legend of Haetsh the first man. He died and went down into the world below, and a long while after came up again to his former dwelling, and there, standing above by the smoke-hole, he talked down to his kindred in the house and told them about the life to come ; it was then that his two daughters whom he had left below followed him in anger and smote him so that he died a second time, and now he is chief in the lower world, and receives the Italmen when they die and rise anew.[2] Thus, again, in the great Finnish epic, the Kalewala, one great episode is Wainamoinen's visit to the land of the dead. Seeking the last charm-words to build his boat, the hero travelled with quick steps week after week through bush and wood till he came to the Tuonela river, and saw before him the island of Tuoni the god of death. Loudly he called to Tuoni's daughter to bring the ferry-boat across :—

[1] Schoolcraft, ' Algic Res.' vol. ii. pp. 32, 64, and see ante, vol. i. p. 312.
[2] Steller, ' Kamtschatka,' p. 271 ; Klemm, ' C. G.' vol. ii. p. 312.

' She, the virgin of Manala,
  She, the washer of the clothing,
  She, the wringer of the linen,
  By the river of Tuonela,
  In the under-world Manala,
  Spake in words, and this their meaning,
  This their answer to the hearer :—
  " Forth the boat shall come from hither,
  When the reason thou hast given
  That hath brought thee to Manala,
  Neither slain by any sickness,
  Nor by Death dragged from the living,
  Nor destroyed by other ending." '

Wainamoinen replies with lying reasons. Iron brought him,
he says, but Tuoni's daughter answers that no blood drips
from his garment ; Fire brought him, he says, but she
answers that his locks are unsinged, and at last he tells his
real mission.   Then she ferries him over, and Tuonetar the
hostess brings him beer in the two-eared jug, but Wainamoinen can see the frogs and worms within and will not
drink, for it was not to drain Manala's beer-jug he had
come.   He lay in the bed of Tuoni, and meanwhile they
spread the hundred nets of iron and copper across the river
that he might not escape ; but he turned into a reed in the
swamp, and as a snake crept through the meshes :—

' Tuoni's son with hooked fingers
  Iron-pointed hooked fingers
  Went to draw his nets at morning—
  Salmon-trout he found a hundred,
  Thousands of the little fishes,
  But he found no Wainamoinen,
  Not the old friend of the billows.
  Then the ancient Wainamoinen,
  Come from out of Tuoni's kingdom,
  Spake in words, and this their meaning,
  This their answer to the hearer :—
  " Never mayst thou, God of goodness,
  Never suffer such another
  Who of self-will goes to Mana,
  Thrusts his way to Tuoni's kingdom.

Many they who travel thither,
Few who thence have found the home-way,
From the houses of Tuoni
From the dwellings of Manala." ' [1]

It is enough to name the familiar classic analogues of these mythic visits to Hades,—the descent of Dionysos to bring back Semele, of Orpheus to bring back his beloved Eurydike, of Herakles to fetch up the three-headed Kerberos at the command of his master Eurystheus ; above all, the voyage of Odysseus to the ends of the deep-flowing Ocean, to the clouded city of Kimmerian men, where shining Helios looks not down with his rays, and deadly night stretches always over wretched mortals,—thence they passed along the banks to the entrance of the land where the shades of the departed, quickened for a while by the taste of sacrificial blood, talked with the hero and showed him the regions of their dismal home. [2]

The scene of the descent into Hades is in very deed enacted day by day before our eyes, as it was before the eyes of the ancient myth-maker, who watched the sun descend to the dark under-world, and return at dawn to the land of living men.   These heroic legends lie in close-knit connexion with episodes of solar myth.   It is by the simplest poetic adaptation of the Sun's daily life, typifying Man's life in dawning beauty, in mid-day glory, in evening death, that mythic fancy even fixed the belief in the religions of the world, that the Land of Departed Souls lies in the Far West or the World Below.   How deeply the myth of the Sunset has entered into the doctrine of men concerning a Future State, how the West and the Under-World have become by mere imaginative analogy Regions of the Dead, how the quaint day-dreams of savage poets may pass into

[1] Kalewala, Rune xvi. ; see Schiefner's German Translation, and Castrén, ' Finn. Myth.' pp. 128, 134.   A Slavonic myth in Hanusch, p. 412.

[2] Homer. Odyss. xi.   On the vivification of ghosts by sacrifice of blood, and on libations of milk and blood, see Meiners, vol. i. p. 315, vol. ii. p. 89 ; J. G. Müller, p. 85 ; Rochholz, ' Deutscher Glaube und Brauch,' vol. i. p. 1, &c.

honoured dogmas of classic sages and modern divines,—all this the crowd of details here cited from the wide range of culture stand to prove.

Moreover, visits from or to the dead are matters of personal experience and personal testimony. When in dream or vision the seer beholds the spirits of the departed, they give him tidings from the other world, or he may even rise and travel thither himself, and return to tell the living what he has seen among the dead. It is sometimes as if the traveller's material body went to visit a distant land, and sometimes all we are told is that the man's self went, but whether in body or in spirit is a mere detail of which the story keeps no record. Mostly, however, it is the seer's soul which goes forth, leaving his body behind in ecstasy, sleep, coma, or death. Some of these stories, as we trace them on from savage into civilized times, are no doubt given in good faith by the visionary himself, while others are imitations of these genuine accounts.[1] Now such visions are naturally apt to reproduce the thoughts with which the seer's mind was already furnished. Every idea once lodged in the mind of a savage, a barbarian, or an enthusiast, is ready thus to be brought back to him from without. It is a vicious circle ; what he believes he therefore sees, and what he sees he therefore believes. Beholding the reflexion of his own mind like a child looking at itself in a glass, he humbly receives the teaching of his second self. The Red Indian visits his happy hunting-grounds, the Tongan his shadowy island of Bolotu, the Greek enters Hades and looks on the Elysian Fields, the Christian beholds the heights of Heaven and the depths of Hell.

Among the North American Indians, and especially the Algonquin tribes, accounts are not unusual of men whose spirits, travelling in dreams or in the hallucinations of extreme illness to the land of the dead, have returned to reanimate their bodies, and tell what they have seen.

[1] See for example, various details in Bastian, ' Mensch,' vol. ii. pp. 369-75, &c.

Their experiences have been in great measure what they were taught in early childhood to expect, the journey along the path of the dead, the monstrous strawberry at which the jebi-ug or ghosts refresh themselves, but which turns to red rock at the touch of their spoons, the bark offered them for dried meat and great puff-balls for squashes, the river of the dead with its snake-bridge or swinging log, the great dog standing on the other side, the villages of the dead beyond.[1] The Zulus of our own day tell of men who have gone down by holes in the ground into the under-world, where mountains and rivers and all things are as here above, and where a man may find his kindred, for the dead live in their villages, and may be seen milking their cattle, which are the cattle killed on earth and come to life anew. The Zulu Umpengula, who told one of these stories to Dr. Callaway, remembered when he was a boy seeing an ugly little hairy man called Uncama, who once, chasing a porcupine that ate his mealies, followed it down a hole in the ground into the land of the dead. When he came back to his home on earth he found that he had been given up for dead himself, his wife had duly burnt and buried his mats and blankets and vessels, and the wondering people at sight of him again shouted the funeral dirge. Of this Zulu Dante it used to be continually said, ' There is the man who went to the underground people.'[2] One of the most characteristic of these savage narratives is from New Zealand. This story, which has an especial interest from the reminiscence it contains of the gigantic extinct Moa, and which may be repeated at some length as an illustration of the minute detail and lifelike reality which such visionary legends assume in barbaric life, was told to Mr. Shortland by a servant of his named Te Wharewera. An aunt of this

---

[1] See vol. i. p. 481 ; also below, p. 52, note. Tanner's ' Narr.' p. 290 ; Schoolcraft, ' Indian Tribes,' part iii. p. 233 ; Keating, vol. ii. p. 154 ; Loskiel, part i. p. 35 ; Smith, ' Virginia,' in Pinkerton, vol. xiii. p. 14. See Cranz, ' Grönland,' p. 269.

[2] Callaway, 'Zulu Tales,' vol. i. pp. 316-20.

man died in a solitary hut near the banks of Lake Rotorua. Being a lady of rank she was left in her hut, the door and windows were made fast, and the dwelling was abandoned, as her death had made it tapu. But a day or two after, Te Wharewera with some others paddling in a canoe near the place at early morning saw a figure on the shore beckoning to them. It was the aunt come to life again, but weak and cold and famished. When sufficiently restored by their timely help, she told her story. Leaving her body, her spirit had taken flight toward the North Cape, and arrived at the entrance of Reigna. There, holding on by the stem of the creeping akeake-plant, she descended the precipice, and found herself on the sandy beach of a river. Looking round, she espied in the distance an enormous bird, taller than a man, coming towards her with rapid strides. This terrible object so frightened her, that her first thought was to try to return up the steep cliff; but seeing an old man paddling a small canoe towards her she ran to meet him, and so escaped the bird. When she had been safely ferried across she asked the old Charon, mentioning the name of her family, where the spirits of her kindred dwelt. Following the path the old man pointed out, she was surprised to find it just such a path as she had been used to on earth ; the aspect of the country, the trees, shrubs, and plants were all familiar to her. She reached the village and among the crowd assembled there she found her father and many near relations ; they saluted her, and welcomed her with the wailing chant which Maoris always address to people met after long absence. But when her father had asked about his living relatives, and especially about her own child, he told her she must go back to earth, for no one was left to take care of his grandchild. By his orders she refused to touch the food that the dead people offered her, and in spite of their efforts to detain her, her father got her safely into the canoe, crossed with her, and parting gave her from under his cloak two enormous sweet potatoes to plant at home for his grandchild's especial eating. But as she began

to climb the precipice again, two pursuing infant spirits
pulled her back, and she only escaped by flinging the roots
at them, which they stopped to eat, while she scaled the
rock by help of the akeake-stem, till she reached the earth
and flew back to where she had left her body. On returning to life she found herself in darkness, and what had
passed seemed as a dream, till she perceived that she was
deserted and the door fast, and concluded that she had
really died and come to life again. When morning dawned,
a faint light entered by the crevices of the shut-up house,
and she saw on the floor near her a calabash partly full of
red ochre mixed with water ; this she eagerly drained to
the dregs, and then feeling a little stronger, succeeded in
opening the door and crawling down to the beach, where
her friends soon after found her. Those who listened to
her tale firmly believed the reality of her adventures, but it
was much regretted that she had not brought back at least
one of the huge sweet-potatoes, as evidence of her visit to
the land of spirits.[1] Races of North Asia[2] and West Africa[3]
have in like manner their explorers of the world beyond
the grave.

Classic literature continues the series. Lucian's graphic

---

[1] Shortland, ' Traditions of New Zealand,' p. 150 ; R. Taylor, ' New
Zealand,' p. 423. The idea, of which the classic representative belongs to
the myth of Persephone, that the living who tastes the food of the dead
may not return, and which is so clearly stated in this Maori story, appears
again among the Sioux of North America. Ahak-tah (' Male Elk ') seems
to die, but after two days comes down from the funeral-scaffold where his
body had been laid, and tells his tale. His soul had travelled by the path of
braves through the beautiful land of great trees and gay loud-singing birds,
till he reached the river, and saw the homes of the spirits of his forefathers
on the shore beyond. Swimming across, he entered the nearest house, where
he found his uncle sitting in a corner. Very hungry, he noticed some wild
rice in a bark dish. ' I asked my uncle for some rice to eat, but he did not
give it to me. Had I eaten of the food for spirits, I never should have
returned to earth.' Eastman, ' Dacotah,' p. 177.

[2] Castrén, ' Finn. Myth.' p. 139, &c.

[3] Bosman,' ' Guinea,' Letter 19, in Pinkerton, vol. xvi. p. 501 ; Burton,
' Dahome,' vol. ii. p. 158. For modern visits to hell and heaven by Christianized negro visionaries in America, see Macrae, ' Americans at Home,'
vol. ii. p. 91.

tales represent the belief of their age, if not of their author. His Eukrates looks down the chasm into Hades, and sees the dead reclining on the asphodel in companies of kinsfolk and friends ; among them he recognizes Sokrates with his bald head and pot-belly, and also his own father, dressed in the clothes he was buried in. Then Kleodemos caps this story with his own, how when he was sick, on the seventh day when his fever was burning like a furnace, every one left him, and the doors were shut. Then there stood before him an all-beauteous youth in a white garment, who led him through a chasm into Hades, as he knew by seeing Tantalos and Tityos and Sisyphos ; and bringing him to the court of judgement, where were Aiakos and the Fates and the Erinyes, the youth set him before Pluto the King, who sat reading the names of those whose day of life was over. But Pluto was angry, and said to the guide, ' This one's thread is not run out, that he should depart, but bring me Demylos the coppersmith, for he is living beyond the spindle.' So Kleodemos came back to himself free from his fever and announced that Demylos, who was a sick neighbour, would die ; and accordingly a little while after there was heard the cry of the mourners wailing for him.[1] Plutarch's stories, told more seriously, are yet one in type with the mocking Lucian's. The wicked, pleasure-seeking Thespesios lies three days as dead, and revives to tell his vision of the world below. One Antyllos was sick, and seemed to the doctors to retain no trace of life ; till, waking without sign of insanity, he declared that he had been indeed dead, but was ordered back to life, those who brought him being severely chidden by their lord, and sent to fetch Nikander instead, a well-known currier, who was accordingly taken with a fever, and died on the third day.[2] Such stories, old and new, are current among the Hindus at this day. A certain man's soul, for instance, is carried to the

[1] Lucian. Philopseudes, c. 17-28.
[2] Plutarch. De Sera Numinis Vindicta, xxii. ; and in Euseb. Præp. Evang. xi. 36.

realm of Yama by mistake for a namesake, and is sent back in haste to regain his body before it is burnt ; but in the meanwhile he has a glimpse of the hideous punishments of the wicked, and of the glorious life of those who had mortified the flesh on earth, and of suttee-widows now sitting in happiness by their husbands.[1] Mutatis mutandis these tales reappear in Christian mythology, as when Gregory the Great records that a certain nobleman named Stephen died, who was taken to the region of Hades, and saw many things he had heard before but not believed ; but when he was set before the ruler there presiding, he sent him back, saying that it was this Stephen's neighbour— Stephen the smith—whom he had commanded to be brought ; and accordingly the one returned to life, and the other died.[2]

The thought of human visitors revealing the mysteries of the world beyond the grave, which indeed took no slight hold on Christian belief, attached itself in a remarkable way to the doctrine of Christ's descent into Hades. This dogma had so strongly established itself by the end of the 4th century, that Augustine could ask, ' Quis nisi infidelis negaverit fuisse apud inferos Christum ? '[3]   A distinct statement of the dogma was afterwards introduced into the symbol commonly called the ' Apostles' Creed : ' ' Descendit ad inferos,' ' Descendit ad inferna,' He descended into hell.'[4]   The Descent into Hades, which had the theological use of providing a theory of salvation applicable to the saints of the old covenant, imprisoned in the limbo of the fathers, is narrated in full in the apocryphal Gospel of Nicodemus, and is made there to rest upon a legend which belongs to the present group of human visits to the other world.   It is related that two sons of Simeon,

---

[1] Ward, ' Hindoos,' vol. ii. p. 63.

[2] Gregor. Dial. iv. 36. See Calmet, vol. ii. ch. 49.

[3] Augustin. Epist. clxiv. 2.

[4] See Pearson, ' Exposition of the Creed ; ' Bingham, ' Ant. Ch. Ch.' book x. ch. iii.   Art. iii. of the Church of England was reduced to its present state by Archbp. Parker's revision.

named Charinus and Leucius, rose from their tombs at the Resurrection, and went about silently and prayerfully among men, till Annas and Caiaphas brought them into the synagogue, and charged them to tell of their raising from the dead. Then, making the sign of the cross upon their tongues, the two asked for parchment and wrote their record. They had been set with all their fathers in the depths of Hades, when on a sudden there appeared the colour of the sun like gold, and a purple royal light shining on them ; then the patriarchs and prophets, from Adam to Simeon and John the Baptist, rejoicing proclaimed the coming of the light and the fulfilment of the prophecies ; Satan and Hades wrangled in strife together ; in vain the brazen gates were shut with their iron bars, for the summons came to open the gates that the king of glory may come in, who hath broken the gates of brass and cut the bars of iron in sunder ; then the mighty Lord broke the fetters and visited them who sat in darkness and the shadow of death ; Adam and his righteous children were delivered from Hades, and led into the glorious grace of Paradise.[1]

Dante, elaborating in the 'Divina Commedia' the conceptions of paradise, purgatory, and hell familiar to the actual belief of his age, describes them once more in the guise of a living visitor to the land of the dead. Echoes in mediæval legend of such exploring expeditions to the world below still linger faintly in the popular belief of Europe. It has been thus with St. Patrick's Purgatory,[2] the cavern in the island of Lough Derg, in the county Donegal, which even in the seventeenth century O'Sullevan could describe first and foremost in his ' Catholic History ' as ' the greatest of all memorable things of Ireland.' Mediæval visits to the other world were often made in the

---

[1] Codex Apocr. N. T. Evang. Nicod. ed. Giles. ' Apocryphal Gospels,' &c. tr. by A. Walker ; ' Gospel of Nicodemus.' The Greek and Latin texts differ much.

[2] The following details mostly from T. Wright, ' St. Patrick's Purgatory ' (an elaborate critical dissertation on the mediæval legends of visits to the other world).

spirit. But like Ulysses, Wainamoinen, and Dante, men could here make the journey in body, as did Sir Owain and the monk Gilbert. When the pilgrim had spent fifteen days in prayer and fasting in the church, and had been led with litanies and sprinkling of holy water to the entrance of the purgatory, and the last warnings of the monks had failed to turn him from his venture, the door was closed upon him, and if found next morning, he could tell the events of his awful journey—how he crossed the narrow bridge that spans the river of death, how he saw the hideous torments of hell, and approached the joys of paradise. Sir Owain, one of King Stephen's knights, went thither in penance for his life of violence and rapine, and this was one of the scenes he beheld in purgatory :—

> ' There come develes other mony mo,
>   And badde the knygth with hem to go,
>   And ladde him into a fowle contreye,
>   Where ever was nygth and never day,
>   For hit was derke and wonther colde :
>   Yette was there never man so bolde,
>   Hadde he never so mony clothes on,
>   But he wolde be colde as ony stone.
>   Wynde herde he none blowe,
>   But faste hit frese bothe hye and lowe.
>   They browgte him to a felde full brode,
>   Overe suche another never he yode,
>   For of the lengthe none ende he knewe
>   Thereover algate he moste nowe.
>   As he wente he herde a crye,
>   He wondered what hit was, and why,
>   He syg ther men and wymmen also
>   That lowde cryed, for hem was woo.
>   They leyen thykke on every londe,
>   Faste nayled bothe fote and honde
>   With nayles glowyng alle of brasse :
>   They ete the erthe so wo hem was ;
>   Here face was nayled to the grownde.
>   " Spare," they cryde, " a lytylle stounde."
>   The develes wolde hem not spare :
>   To hem peyne they thowgte yare.'

When Owain had seen the other fields of punishment, with their fiery serpents and toads, and the fires where sinners were hung up by their offending members, and roasted on spits, and basted with molten metal, and turned about on a great wheel of fire, and when he had passed the Devil's Mouth over the awful bridge, he reached the fair white glassy wall of the Earthly Paradise, reaching upward and upward, and saw before him the beautiful gate, whence issued a ravishing perfume. Then he soon forgot his pains and sorrows.

> ' As he stode, and was so fayne,
>   Hym thowgth ther come hym agayne
>   A swyde fayr processyoun
>   Of alle manere menne of relygyoun,
>   Fayre vestementes they hadde on,
>   So ryche syg he never none.
>   Myche joye hym thowgte to se
>   Bysshopes yn here dygnité ;
>   Ilkone wente other be and be,
>   Every man yn his degré.
>   He syg ther monkes and chanones,
>   And freres with newe shavene crownes ;
>   Ermytes he saw there amonge,
>   And nonnes with fulle mery songe ;
>   Persones, prestes, and vycaryes ;
>   They made fulle mery melodyes.
>   He syg ther kynges and emperoures,
>   And dukes that had casteles and toures,
>   Erles and barones fele,
>   That some tyme hadde the worldes wele.
>   Other folke he syg also,
>   Never so mony as he dede thoo.
>   Wymmen he syg ther that tyde :
>   Myche was the joye ther on every syde :
>   For alle was joye that with hem ferde,
>   And myche solempnyté he herde.'

The procession welcomed Owain, and led him about, showing him the beauties of that country :—

> ' Hyt was grene, and fulle of flowres
>   Of mony dyvers colowres ;

Hyt was grene on every syde,
As medewus are yn someres tyde.
Ther were trees growyng fulle grene
Fulle of fruyte ever more, y wene;
For ther was frwyte of mony a kynde,
Such yn the londe may no mon fynde.
Ther they have the tree of lyfe,
Theryn ys myrthe, and never stryfe;
Frwyte of wysdom also ther ys,
Of the whyche Adam and Eve dede amysse:
Other manere frwytes ther were fele,
And alle manere joye and wele.
Moche folke he syg ther dwelle,
There was no tongue that mygth hem telle;
Alle were they cloded yn ryche wede,
What cloth hit was he kowthe not rede.

.   .   .   .

There was no wronge, but ever rygth,
Ever day and nevere nygth.
They shone as brygth and more clere
Than ony sonne yn the day doth here.'

The poem, in fifteenth-century English, from which these passages are taken, is a version of the original legend of earlier date, and as such contrasts with a story really dating from early in the fifteenth century—William Staunton's descent into Purgatory, where the themes of the old sincerely-believed visionary lore are fading into moral allegory, and the traveller sees the gay gold and silver collars and girdles burning into the wearer's flesh, and the jags that men were clothed in now become adders and dragons, sucking and stinging them, and the fiends drawing down the skin of women's shoulders into pokes, and smiting into their heads with burning hammers their gay chaplets of gold and jewels turned to burning nails, and so forth. Late in this fifteenth century, St. Patrick's Purgatory fell into discredit, but even the destruction of the entrance-building, in 1479, by Papal order, did not destroy the ideal road. About 1693, an excavation on the spot brought to light a window with iron stanchions ; there was a cry for holy water to keep the spirits from breaking out from prison, and the priest smelt brimstone from the dark cavity below, which, however, unfortunately turned out to be a cellar. In still later times, the yearly pilgrimage of tens of thousands of votaries to the holy place has kept up this interesting survival from the lower culture, whereby a communication may still be traced, if not from Earth to Hades, at least from the belief of the New Zealander to that of the Irish peasant.

To study and compare the ideal regions where man has placed the abodes of departed souls is not an unprofitable task. True, geography has now mapped out into mere earth and water the space that lay beyond the narrower sea and land known to the older nations, and astronomy no longer recognizes the flat earth trodden by men as being the roof of subterranean halls, nor the sky as being a solid firmament, shutting out men's gaze from strata or spheres of empyræan regions beyond. Yet if we carry our minds back to the state of knowledge among the lower races, we shall not find it hard to understand the early conceptions as to the locality of the regions beyond the grave. They are no secrets of high knowledge made known to sages of old; they are the natural fancies which childlike ignorance would frame in any age. The regularity with which such conceptions repeat themselves over the world bears testimony to the regularity of the processes by which opinion is formed among mankind. At the same time, the student who carefully compares them will find in them a perfect illustration of an important principle, widely applicable to the general theory of the formation of human opinion. When a problem has presented itself to mankind at large, susceptible of a number of solutions about equally plausible, the result is that the several opinions thus produced will be found lying scattered in country after country. The problem here is, given the existence of souls of the dead who from time to time visit the living, where is the home of these ghosts ? Why men in one district should have preferred the earth, in another the under-world, in another the sky, as the abode of departed souls, is a question often difficult to answer. But we may at least see how again and again the question was taken in hand, and how out of the three or four available answers some peoples adopted one, some another, some several at once. Primitive theologians had all the world before them where to choose their place of rest for the departed, and they used to the full their speculative liberty.

Firstly, when the land of souls is located on the surface of the earth, there is choice of fit places among wild and cloudy precipices, in secluded valleys, in far-off plains and islands. In Borneo, Mr. St. John visited the heaven of the Idaan race, on the summit of Kina Balu, and the native guides, who feared to pass the night in this abode of spirits, showed the traveller the moss on which the souls of their ancestors fed, and the footprints of the ghostly buffaloes that followed them. On Gunung Danka, a mountain in West Java, there is such another ' Earthly Paradise.' The Sajira who dwell in the district indeed profess themselves Mohammedans, but they secretly maintain their old belief, and at death or funeral they enjoin the soul in solemn form to set aside the Moslem Allah, and to take the way to the dwelling-place of his own forefathers' souls :—

' Step up the bed of the river, and cross the neck of land,
   Where the aren trees stand in a clump, and the pinangs in a row,
   Thither direct thy steps, Laillah being set aside.'

Mr. Jonathan Rigg had lived ten years among these people, and knew them well, yet had never found out that their paradise was on this mountain. When at last he heard of it, he made the ascent, finding on the top only a few river-stones, forming one of the balai, or sacred cairns, common in the district. But the popular belief, that a tiger would devour the chiefs who permitted a violation of the sacred place, soon received the sort of confirmation which such beliefs receive everywhere, for a tiger killed two children a few days later, and the disaster was of course ascribed to Mr. Rigg's profanation.[1] The Chilians said that the soul goes westward over the sea to Gulcheman, the dwelling-place of the dead beyond the mountains ; life, some said, was all pleasure there, but others thought that part would be happy and part miserable.[2] Hidden among the mountains of Mexico lay the joyous garden-land of Tlalocan, where maize, and pumpkins, and chilis, and tomatos never failed, and where abode the souls of children sacrificed to Tlaloc, its god, and the souls of such as died by drowning or thunderstroke, or by leprosy or dropsy, or other acute disease.[3] A survival of such thought may be traced into mediæval civilization, in the legends of the Earthly Paradise, the fire-girt abode of saints not yet raised to highest bliss, localized in the utmost East of Asia, where earth stretches up towards heaven.[4] When Columbus sailed westward across the Atlantic to seek ' the new heaven and the new earth ' he had read of in Isaiah, he found them, though not as he sought. It is a quaint coincidence that he found there also, though not as he sought it, the Earthly Paradise which was another main object of his venturous quest. The Haitians described to the white men their Coaibai, the paradise of the dead, in the lovely Western valleys of their island, where the souls hidden by day among the cliffs came down at night to feed on the delicious fruit of the mamey-trees, of which the living ate but sparingly, lest the souls of their friends should want.[5]

Secondly, there are Australians who think that the spirit of the dead hovers awhile on earth and goes at last toward

---

[1] St. John, ' Far East,' vol. i. p. 278. Rigg. in ' Journ. Ind. Archip.' vol. iv. p. 119. See also Ellis, ' Polyn. Res.' vol. i. p. 397 ; Bastian, ' Oestl. Asien,' vol. i. p. 83 ; Irving, ' Astoria,' p. 142.

[2] Molina, ' Chili,' vol. ii. p. 89.

[3] Brasseur, 'Mexique,' vol. iii. p. 496; Sahagun, iii. App. c. 2, x. c. 29; Clavigero, vol. ii. p. 5.

[4] See Wright, l.c. &c. ; Alger, p. 391 ; &c.

[5] ' History of Colon,' ch. 61 ; Pet. Martyr. Dec. i. lib. ix. ; Irving, ' Life of Columbus,' vol. ii. p. 121.

the setting sun, or westward over the sea to the island of souls, the home of his fathers. Thus these rudest savages have developed two thoughts which we meet with again and again far onward in the course of culture—the thought of an island of the dead, and the thought that the world of departed souls is in the West, whither the Sun descends at evening to his daily death.[1] Among the North American Indians, when once upon a time an Algonquin hunter left his body behind and visited the land of souls in the sunny south, he saw before him beautiful trees and plants, but found he could walk right through them. Then he paddled in the canoe of white shining stone across the lake where wicked souls perish in the storm, till he reached the beautiful and happy island where there is no cold, no war, no bloodshed, but the creatures run happily about, nourished by the air they breathe.[2] Tongan legend says that, long ago, a canoe returning from Fiji was driven by stress of weather to Bolotu, the island of gods and souls lying in the ocean north-west of Tonga. That island is larger than all theirs together, full of all finest fruits and loveliest flowers, that fill the air with fragrance, and come anew the moment they are plucked ; birds of beauteous plumage are there, and hogs in plenty, all immortal save when killed for the gods to eat, and then new living ones appear immediately to fill their places. But when the hungry crew of the canoe landed, they tried in vain to pluck the shadowy bread-fruit, they walked through unresisting trees and houses, even as the souls of chiefs who met them walked unchecked through their solid bodies. Counselled to hasten home from this land of no earthly food, the men sailed to Tonga, but the deadly air of Bolotu had infected them, and they soon all died.[3]

---

[1] Stanbridge in ' Tr. Eth. Soc.' vol. i. p. 299 ; G. F. Moore, ' Vocab. W. Austr.' p. 83 ; Bonwick, ' Tasmanians,' p. 181.

[2] Schoolcraft, ' Indian Tribes,' part i. p. 321 ; see part iii. p. 229.

[3] Mariner, ' Tonga Is.' vol. ii. p. 107. See also Burton, ' W. and W. fr. W. Africa,' p. 154 (Gold Coast).

Such ideas took strong hold on classic thought, in the belief in a paradise in the Fortunate Islands of the far Western Ocean. Hesiod in the ' Works and Days ' tells of the half-gods of the Fourth Age, between the Age of Bronze and the Age of Iron. When death closed on this heroic race, Zeus granted them at the ends of Earth a life and home, apart from man and far from the immortals. There Kronos reigns over them, and they dwell careless in the Islands of the Happy, beside deep-eddying Ocean— blest heroes, for whom the grain-giving field bears, thrice blooming yearly, the honey-sweet fruit :—

"Ἔνθ· ἤτοι τοὺς μὲν θανάτου τέλος ἀμφεκάλυψε·
Τοῖς δὲ δίχ' ἀνθρώπων βίοτον καὶ ἤθε ὀπάσσας
Ζεὺς Κρονίδης κατένασσε πατὴρ ἐς πείρατα γαίης,
Τηλοῦ ἀπ' ἀθανάτων· τοῖσιν Κρόνος ἐμβασιλεύει·
Καὶ τοὶ μὲν ναίουσιν ἀκηδέα θυμὸν ἔχοντες
Ἐν μακάρων νήσοισι παρ' Ὠκεανὸν βαθυδίνην,
Ὄλβιοι ἥρωες, τοῖσιν μελιηδέα καρπὸν
Τρὶς ἔτεος θάλλοντα φέρει ζείδωρος ἄρουρα.' [1]

These Islands of the Blest, assigned as the abode of blessed spirits of the dead, came indeed to be identified with the Elysian Fields. Thus Pindar sings of steadfast souls, who through three lives on either side have endured free from injustice ; then they pass by the road of Zeus to the tower of Kronos, where the ocean breezes blow round the islands of the happy, blazing with golden flowers of land and water. Thus, also, in the famous hymn of Kallistratos in honour of Harmodios and Aristogeiton, who slew the tyrant Hipparchos :—

' Φίλταθ' 'Αρμόδι, οὔ τί πω τέθνηκας
Νήσοις δ' ἐν μακάρων σε φασὶν εἶναι,
"Ινα περ ποδώκης 'Αχιλλεύς,
Τυδείδην τε φασὶ τὸν ἐσθλὸν Διομήδεα.' [1]

This group of legends has especial interest to us Englishmen, who ourselves dwell, it seems, on such an island of the

[1] Hesiod. Opera et Dies, 165. Pindar, Olymp. ii. antistr. 4. Callistrat. Hymn. in Ilgen, Scolia Græca, 10. Strabo, iii. 2, 13 ; Plin. iv. 36.

dead. It is not that we or our country are of a more ghostly
nature than others, but the idea is geographical we are
dwellers in the region of the setting sun, the land of death.
The elaborate account by Procopius, the historian of the
Gothic War, dates from the 6th century. The island of
Brittia, according to him, lies opposite the mouths of the
Rhine, some 200 stadia off, between Britannia and Thule,
and on it dwell three populous nations, the Angles, Frisians,
and Britons. (By Brittia, it appears, he means our Great
Britain, his Britannia being the coast-land from modern
Brittany to Holland, and his Thule being Scandinavia.)
In the course of his history it seems to him needful to record
a story, mythic and dreamlike as he thinks, yet which
numberless men vouch for as having been themselves witnesses by eye and ear to its facts. This story is that the
souls of the departed are conveyed across the sea to the
island of Brittia. Along the mainland coast are many
villages, inhabited by fishermen and tillers of the soil
and traders to this island in their vessels. They are subject to the Franks, but pay no tribute, having from of old
had to do by turns the burdensome service of transporting
the souls. Those on duty for each night stay at home till
they hear a knocking at the doors, and a voice of one unseen
calling them to their work. Then without delay rising from
their beds, compelled by some unknown power they go down
to the beach, and there they see boats, not their own but
others, lying ready but empty of men. Going on board and
taking the oars, they find that by the burden of the multitude of souls embarked, the vessel lies low in the water,
gunwale under within a finger's breadth. In an hour they
are at the opposite shore, though in their own boats they
would hardly make the voyage in a night and day. When
they reach the island, the vessel becomes empty, till it is so
light that only the keel touches the waves. They see no
man on the voyage, no man at the landing, but a voice is
heard that proclaims the name and rank and parentage of
each newly arrived passenger, or if women, those of their

husbands. Traces of this remarkable legend seem to have survived, thirteen centuries later, in that endmost district of the Britannia of Procopius which still keeps the name of Bretagne. Near Raz, where the narrow promontory stretches westward into the ocean, is the ' Bay of Souls ' (boé ann anavo) ; in the commune of Plouguel the corpse is taken to the churchyard, not by the shorter road by land, but in a boat by the ' Passage de l'Enfer,' across a little arm of the sea ; and Breton folk-lore holds fast to the legend of the Curé de Braspar, whose dog leads over to Great Britain the souls of the departed, when the wheels of the soul-car are heard creaking in the air. These are but mutilated fragments, but they seem to piece together with another Keltic myth, told by Macpherson in the last century, the voyage of the boat of heroes to Flath-Innis, Noble Island, the green island home of the departed, which lies calm amid the storms far in the Western Ocean. With full reason, also, Mr. Wright traces to the situation of Ireland in the extreme West its especial association with legends of descents to the land of shades. Claudian placed at the extremity of Gaul the entrance where Ulysses found a way to Hades—

' Est locus extremum qua pandit Gallia litus,
Oceani prætentus aquis, ubi fertur Ulysses,' &c.

No wonder that this spot should have been since identified with St. Patrick's Purgatory, and that some ingenious etymologist should have found in the name of ' Ulster ' a corruption of ' Ulyssisterra,' and a commemoration of the hero's visit.[1]

Thirdly, the belief in a subterranean Hades peopled by the ghosts of the dead is quite common among the lower races. The earth is flat, say the Italmen of Kamchatka,

[1] Procop. De Bello Goth. iv. 20 ; Plut. Fragm. Comm. in Hesiod. 2 ; Grimm, ' D. M.' p. 793 ; Hersart de Villemarqué, vol. i. p. 136 ; Souvestre, ' Derniers Bretons,' p. 37 ; Jas. Macpherson, ' Introd. to Hist. of Great Britain and Ireland,' 2nd ed. London, 1772, p. 180 ; Wright, ' St. Patrick's Purgatory,' pp. 64, 129.

for if it were round, people would fall off ; it is the wrong
side of another heaven, which covers another earth below,
whither the dead will go down to their new life, and so, as
Steller says, their mundane system is like a tub with three
bottoms.[1] In North America, the Tacullis held that the
soul goes after death into the bowels of the earth, whence
it can come back in human shape to visit friends.[2] In
South America, Brazilian souls travel down to the world
below in the West, and Patagonian souls will depart to
enjoy eternal drunkenness in the caves of their ancestral
deities.[3] The New Zealander who says ' The sun has returned to Hades ' (kua hoki mai te Ra ki te Rua), simply
means that it has set. When a Samoan Islander dies, the
host of spirits that surround the house, waiting to convey
his soul away, set out with him crossing the land and
swimming the sea, to the entrance of the spirit-world.
This is at the westernmost point of the westernmost island,
Savaii, and there one may see the two circular holes or
basins where souls descend, chiefs by the bigger and
plebeians by the smaller, into the regions of the under-
world. There below is a heaven, earth, and sea, and
people with real bodies, planting, fishing, cooking, as in the
present life ; but at night their bodies become like a confused collection of fiery sparks, and in this state during the
hours of darkness they come up to revisit their former
abodes, retiring at dawn to the bush or to the lower
regions.[4] For the state of thought on this subject among
rude African tribes, it is enough to cite the Zulus, who at
death will descend to live in Hades among their ancestors,
the ' Abapansi,' the ' people underground.'[5] Among rude
Asiatic tribes, such an example may be taken from the

[1] Steller, ' Kamtschatka,' p. 269.
[2] Harmon, ' Journal,' p. 299 ; see Lewis and Clarke, p. 139 (Mandans).
[3] J. G. Müller, ' Amer. Urrelig.' pp. 140, 287 ; see Humboldt and Bonpland, ' Voy.' vol. iii. p. 132 ; Falkner, ' Patagonia,' p. 114.
[4] Taylor, ' New Zealand,' p. 232 ; Turner, ' Polynesia,' p. 235.
[5] Callaway, ' Zulu Tales,' vol. i. p. 317, &c. ; Arbousset and Daumas,
p. 474. See also Burton, ' Dahome,' vol. ii. p. 157.

Karens. They are not quite agreed where Plu, the land of
the dead, is situate ; it may be above the earth or beyond
the horizon. But the dominant and seemingly indigenous
opinion is that it is below the earth. When the sun sets on
earth, it rises in the Karen Hades, and when it sets in
Hades it rises in this world. Here, again, the familiar
belief of the European peasant is found ; the spirits of the
dead may come up from the land of shades by night, but
at daybreak must return.[1]

Such ideas, developed by uncultured races, may be followed up in various detail, through the stage of religion represented by the Mexican and Peruvian nations,[2] into higher
ranges of culture. The Roman Orcus was in the bowels of
the earth, and when the ' lapis manalis,' the stone that
closed the mouth of the world below, was moved away on
certain solemn days, the ghosts of the dead came up to the
world above, and partook of the offerings of their friends.[3]
Among the Greeks, the Land of Hades was in the world
below, nor was the thought unknown that it was the sunset
realm of the Western god (πρὸς ἑσπέρου θεοῦ). What Hades
seemed like to the popular mind, Lucian thus describes :—
' The great crowd, indeed, whom the wise call " idiots,"
believing Homer and Hesiod, and the other myth-makers
about these things, and setting up their poetry as a law,
have supposed a certain deep place under the earth, Hades,
and that it is vast, and roomy, and gloomy, and sunless,
and how thought to be lighted up so as to behold every one
within, I know not.'[4] In the ancient Egyptian doctrine of
the future life, modelled on solar myth, the region of the
departed combines the under-world and the west, Amenti ;
the dead passes the gate of the setting sun to traverse the
roads of darkness, and behold his father Osiris ; and with

[1] Mason, ' Karens,' l.c. p. 195 ; Cross, l.c. p. 313. Turanian examples
in Castrén, ' Finn. Myth.' p. 119.

[2] See below, pp. 79, 85.

[3] Festus, s.v. ' manalis,' &c.

[4] Sophocl. Œdip. Tyrann. 178 ; Lucian. De Luctu, 2. See classic details
in Pauly, ' Real-Encyclop.' art. ' inferi.'

this solar thought the Egyptian priests, representing in symbolic ceremony the scenes of the other world, carried the corpse in the sacred boat across to the burial-place, on the western side of the sacred lake.[1] So, too, the cavernous Sheol of the Israelites, the shadowy region of departed souls, lay deep below the earth. Through the great Aryan religious systems, Brahmanism, Zarathustrism, Buddhism, and onward into the range of Islam and of Christianity, subterranean hells of purgatory or punishment make the doleful contrast to heavens of light and glory.

It is, however, a point worthy of special notice that the conception of hell as a fiery abyss, so familiar to the religions of the higher civilization, is all but unknown to savage thought, so much so that if met with, its genuineness is doubtful. Captain John Smith's ' History of Virginia,' published in 1624, contains two different accounts of the Indians' doctrine of a future life. Smith's own description is of a land beyond the mountains, toward sunset, where chiefs and medicine-men in paint and feathers shall smoke, and sing, and dance with their forefathers, while the common people have no life after death, but rot in their graves. Heriot's description is of tabernacles of the gods to which the good are taken up to perpetual happiness, while the wicked are carried to ' Popogusso,' a great pit which they think to be at the furthest parts of the world where the sun sets, and there burn continually.[2] Now knowing so much as we do of the religion of the Algonquins, to whom these Virginians belonged, we may judge that while the first account is genuinely native, though perhaps not quite correctly understood, the second was borrowed by the Indians from the white men themselves. Yet even here the touch of solar myth is manifest, and the description of the fiery abyss in the region of sunset may be compared with one

[1] Birch in Bunsen's ' Egypt,' vol. v. ; Wilkinson, ' Ancient Eg.' vol. ii. p. 368 ; Alger, p. 101.
[2] Smith, ' History of Virginia,' in ' Works ' ed. by Arber ; Pinkerton, vol. xiii. pp. 14, 41 ; vol. xii. p. 604 ; see below, p. 95.

from our own country, in the Anglo-Saxon dialogue of Saturn and Solomon. ' Saga me forhwan byth seo sunne read on æfen ? Ic the secge, forthon heo locath on helle. —Tell me, why is the sun red at even ? I tell thee, because she looketh on hell '[1] To the same belief belongs another striking mythic feature. The idea of volcanos being mouths of the under-world seems not unexampled among the lower races, for we hear of certain New Zealanders casting their dead down into a crater.[2] But in connexion with the thought of a gehenna of fire and brimstone, Vesuvius, Etna, and Hecla had spiritual as well as material terrors to the mind of Christendom, for they were believed to be places of purgatory or the very mouths of the pit where the souls of the damned were cast down.[3] The Indians of Nicaragua used in old times to offer human sacrifices to their volcano Masaya, flinging the corpses into the crater, and in later years, after the conversion of the country, we hear of Christian confessors sending their penitents to climb the mountain, and (as a glimpse of hell) to look down upon the molten lava.[4]

Fourthly, in old times and new, it has come into men's minds to fix upon the sun and moon as abodes of departed souls. When we have learnt from the rude Natchez of the Mississippi and the Apalaches of Florida that the sun is the bright dwelling of departed chiefs and braves, and have traced like thoughts on into the theologies of Mexico and Peru, then we may compare these savage doctrines with Isaac Taylor's ingenious supposition in his ' Physical Theory of Another Life,'—the sun of each planetary system is the house of the higher and ultimate spiritual corporeity, and the centre of assembly to those who have passed on the planets their preliminary era of corruptible organization. Or perhaps some may prefer the Rev. Tobias Swinden's

---

[1] Thorpe, ' Analecta Anglo-Saxonica,' p. 115.
[2] Schirren, p. 151. See Taylor, ' N. Z.' p. 525.
[3] Meiners, vol. ii. p. 781 ; Maury, ' Magie,' &c. p. 170.
[4] Oviedo, ' Nicaragua,' p. 160 ; Brinton, p. 288.

book, published in the last century, and translated into French and German, which proved the sun to be hell, and its dark spots gatherings of damned souls.[1] And when in South America the Saliva Indians have pointed out the moon, their paradise where no mosquitos are, and the Guaycurus have shown it as the home of chiefs and medicine-men deceased, and the Polynesians of Tokelau in like manner have claimed it as the abode of departed kings and chiefs, then these pleasant fancies may be compared with Plutarch's description of the virtuous souls who after purification in the middle space gain their footing on the moon, and there are crowned as victors.[2] The converse notion of the moon as the seat of hell, has been elaborated in profoundest bathos by Mr. M. F. Tupper :

> ' I know thee well, O Moon, thou cavern'd realm,
> Sad Satellite, thou giant ash of death,
> Blot on God's firmament, pale home of crime,
> Scarr'd prison-house of sin, where damned souls
> Feed upon punishment. Oh, thought sublime,
> That amid night's black deeds, when evil prowls
> Through the broad world, thou, watching sinners well,
> Glarest o'er all, the wakeful eye of—Hell ! '

Skin for skin, the brown savage is not ill matched in such speculative lore with the white philosopher.

Fifthly, as Paradise on the face of the earth, and Hades beneath it where the sun goes down, are regions whose existence is asserted or not denied by savage and barbaric science, so it is with Heaven. Among the examples which display for us the real course of knowledge among mankind, and the real relation which primitive bears to later culture, the belief in the existence of a firmament is one of the most

[1] J. G. Müller, ' Amer. Urrel.' p. 138, see also 220 (Caribs), 402 (Peru), 505, 660 (Mexico) ; Brinton, ' Myths of New World,' p. 233 ; Taylor, ' Physical Theory,' ch. xvi. ; Alger, ' Future Life,' p. 590 ; see also above, p. 16, note.

[2] Humboldt and Bonpland, ' Voy.' vol. v. p. 90 ; Martius, ' Ethnog. Amer.' vol. i. p. 233 ; Turner, ' Polynesia,' p. 531 ; Plutarch. De Facie in Orbe Lunæ ; Bastian, ' Psychologie,' pp. 80, 89 (souls in stars).

instructive. It arises naturally in the minds of children
still, and in accordance with the simplest childlike thought,
the cosmologies of the North American Indians [1] and the
South Sea Islanders [2] describe their flat earth arched over
by the solid vault of heaven. Like thoughts are to be
traced on through such details as the Zulu idea that the
blue heaven is a rock encircling the earth, inside which are
the sun, moon, and stars, and outside which dwell the
people of heaven ; the modern negro's belief that there is a
firmament stretched above like a cloth or web ; the Finnish
poem which tells how Ilmarinen forged the firmament of
finest steel, and set in it the moon and stars.[3] The New
Zealander, with his notion of a solid firmament, through
which the waters can be let down on earth through a crack
or hole from the reservoir of rain above, could well explain
the passage in Herodotus concerning that place in North
Africa where, as the Libyans said, the sky is pierced, as
well as the ancient Jewish conception of a firmament of
heaven, ' strong as a molten mirror,' with its windows
through which the rain pours down in deluge from the
reservoirs above, windows which late Rabbinical literature
tells us were made by taking out two stars.[4] In nations
where the theory of the firmament prevails, accounts of
bodily journeys or spiritual ascents to heaven are in general
meant not as figure, but as fact. Among the lower races,
the tendency to localize the region of departed souls above
the sky seems less strong than that which leads them to
place their world of the dead on or below the earth's surface. Yet some well-marked descriptions of a savage

[1] See Schoolcraft, ' Indian Tribes,' part i. pp. 269, 311 ; Smith, ' Virginia,'
in Pinkerton, vol. xiii. p. 54 ; Waitz, vol. iii. p. 223 ; Squier, ' Abor. Mon.
of N. Y.' p. 156 ; Catlin, ' N. A. Ind.' vol. i. p. 180.
[2] Mariner, ' Tonga Is.' vol. ii. p. 134 ; Turner, ' Polynesia,' p. 103 ;
Taylor, ' New Zealand,' pp. 101, 114, 256.
[3] Callaway, ' Rel. of Amazulu,' p. 393 ; Burton, ' W. and W. fr. W. Afr.'
p. 454 ; Castrén, ' Finn. Myth.' p. 295.
[4] Herodot, iv. 158, see 185, and Rawlinson's note. See Smith's ' Dic. of
the Bible,' s.v. ' firmament.' Eisenmenger, part i. p. 408.

Heaven are on record, the following, and others to be cited presently. Even some Australians seem to think of going up to the clouds at death, to eat and drink, and hunt and fish as here.[1]   In North America, the Winnebagos placed their paradise in the sky, where souls travel along that ' Path of the Dead ' which we call the Milky Way ; and working out the ever-recurring solar idea, the modern Iroquois speak of the soul going upward and westward, till it comes out on the beauteous plains of heaven, with people and trees and things as on earth.[2]   In South America the Guarayos, representatives in some sort of the past condition of the Guarani race, worship Tamoi the Grandfather, the Ancient of Heaven ; he was their first ancestor, who lived among them in old days and taught them to till the ground ; then rising to heaven in the East he disappeared, having promised to be the helper of his people on earth, and to transport them, when they died, from the top of a sacred tree into another life, where they shall find their kindred and have hunting in plenty, and possess all that they possessed on earth ; therefore it is that the Guarayos adorn their dead, and burn their weapons for them, and bury them with their faces to the East, whither they are to go.[3] Among American peoples whose culture rose to a higher level than that of these savage tribes, we hear of the Peruvian Heaven, the glorious ' Upper World,' and of the temporary abode of Aztec warriors on heavenly wooded plains, where the sun shines when it is night on earth, wherefore it was a Mexican saying that the sun goes at evening to lighten the dead.[4]   What thoughts of heaven were in the minds of the old Aryan poets, this hymn from the Rig-Veda may show :—

[1] Eyre, ' Australia,' vol. ii. p. 367.
[2] Schoolcraft, ' Indian Tribes,' part iv. p. 240 (but compare part v. p. 403) ; Morgan, ' Iroquois,' p. 176 ; Sproat, ' Savage Life,' p. 209.
[3] D'Orbigny, ' L'Homme Américain,' vol. ii. pp. 319, 328 ; see Martius, vol. i. p. 485 (Jumanas).
[4] J. G. Müller, p. 403 ; Brasseur, ' Mexique,' vol. iii. p. 496 ; Kingsborough, ' Mexico,' Cod. Letellier, fol. 20.

' Where there is eternal light, in the world where the sun is placed, in that
   immortal imperishable world place me, O Soma !

Where king Vaivasvata reigns, where the secret place of heaven is, where
   these mighty waters are, there make me immortal !

Where life is free, in the third heaven of heavens, where the worlds are
   radiant, there make me immortal !

Where wishes and desires are, where the place of the bright sun is, where
   there is freedom and delight, there make me immortal !

Where there is happiness and delight, where joy and pleasure reside,
   where the desires of our desire are attained, there make me immortal ! ' [1]

In such bright vague thoughts from the poet's religion of
nature, or in cosmic schemes of ancient astronomy, with
their artificial glories of barbaric architecture exaggerated
in the skies, or in the raptures of mystic vision, or in
the calmer teaching of the theologic doctrine of a future
life, descriptions of realms of blessed souls in heaven are
to be followed through the religions of the Brahman, the
Buddhist, the Parsi, the later Jew, the Moslem, and the
Christian.

For the object, not of writing a handbook of religions,
but of tracing the relation which the religion of savages
bears to the religion of cultured nations, these details are
enough to show the general line of human thought regarding the local habitations of departed souls. It seems plain
from the most cursory inspection of these various localiza-
tions, however much we may consider them as inherited or
transmitted from people to people in the complex movements of theological history, that they are at any rate not
derived from any single religion accepted among ancient or
primæval men. They bear evident traces of independent
working out in the varied definition of the region of souls,
as on earth among men, on earth in some distant country,
below the earth, above or beyond the sky. Similar ideas
of this kind are found in different lands, but this simi-

[1] Max Müller, ' Chips,' vol. i. p. 46 ; Roth in ' Zeitschr. d. Deutsch.
Morgenl. Ges.' vol. iv. p. 427.

larity seems in large measure due to independent re-currence of thoughts so obvious. Not less is independent fancy compatible with the ever-recurring solar myth in such ideas, placing the land of Death in the land of Evening or of Night, and its entrance at the gates of Sunset. Barbaric poets of many a distant land must have gazed into the West to read the tale of Life and Death, and tell it of Man. If, however, we look more closely into the stages of intellectual history to which these theories of the Future World belong, it will appear that the assignment of the realm of departed souls to the three great regions, Earth, Hades, Heaven, has not been uniform. Firstly, the doctrine of a land of souls on Earth belongs widely and deeply to savage culture, but dwindles in the barbaric stage, and survives but feebly into the mediæval. Secondly, the doctrine of a subterranean Hades holds as large a place as this in savage belief, and has held it firmly along the course of higher religions, where, however, this under-world is looked on less and less as the proper abode of the dead, but rather as the dismal place of purgatory and hell. Lastly, the doctrine of a Heaven, floored upon a firmament, or placed in the upper air, seems in early savage belief less common than the other two, but yields to neither of them in its vigorous retention by the thought of modern nations. These local theories appear to be taken, firstly and mostly, in the most absolute literal sense, and although, under the influence of physical science, much that was once distinctly-meant philosophy has now passed among theologians into imagery and metaphor, yet at low levels of knowledge the new canons of interpre-tation find little acceptance, and even in modern Europe the rude cosmology of the lower races in no small measure retains its place.

Turning now to consider the state of the departed in these their new homes, we have to examine the definitions of the Future Life which prevail through the religions of mankind. In these doctrines there is much similarity caused by the spreading of established beliefs into new countries, and also much similarity that is beyond what such transmission can account for. So there is much variety due to local colour and circumstance, and also much variety beyond the reach of such explanation. The main causes of both similarity and variety seem to lie far deeper, in the very origin and inmost meaning of the doctrines. The details of the future life, among the lower races and upwards, are no heterogeneous mass of arbitrary fancies. Classified, they range themselves naturally round central ideas, in groups whose correspondence seems to indicate the special course of their development. Amongst the pictures into which this world has shaped its expectations of the next, two great conceptions are especially to be discerned. The one is that the future life is, as it were, a reflexion of this ; in a new world, perhaps of dreamy beauty, perhaps of ghostly gloom, men are to retain their earthly forms and their earthly conditions, to have around them their earthly friends, to possess their earthly property, to carry on their earthly occupations. The other is that the future life is a compensation for this, where men's conditions are re-allotted as the consequence, and especially as the reward or punishment, of their earthly life. The first of these two ideas we may call (with Captain Burton) the ' continuance-theory,' contrasting with it the second as the ' retribution-theory.' Separately or combined, these two doctrines are the keys of the subject, and by grouping typical examples under their two headings, it will be possible to survey systematically man's most characteristic schemes of his life beyond the grave.

To the doctrine of Continuance belongs especially the savage view of the spirit-land, that it is as the dreamland where the souls of the living so often go to visit the souls of the dead. There the soul of the dead Karen, with the souls of his axe and cleaver, builds his house and cuts his rice ; the shade of the Algonquin hunter hunts souls of beaver and elk, walking on the souls of his snow-shoes over the soul of the snow ; the fur-wrapped

Kamchadal drives his dog-sledge; the Zulu milks his
cows and drives his cattle to kraal; South American
tribes live on, whole or mutilated, healthy or sick, as
they left this world, leading their old lives, and having
their wives with them again, though indeed, as the Araucanians said, they have no more children, for they are but
souls.[1] Soul-land is dream-land in its shadowy unreal
pictures, for which, nevertheless, material reality so plainly
furnished the models, and it is dream-land also in its vivid
idealization of the soberer thoughts and feelings of waking
life,

> ' There was a time when meadow, grove, and stream,
>   The earth, and every common sight,
>   To me did seem
>   Apparell'd in celestial light,
>   The glory and the freshness of a dream.'

Well might the Mohawk Indian describe the good land of
paradise, as he had seen it in a dream. The shade of the
Ojibwa follows a wide and beaten path that leads toward the
West, he crosses a deep and rapid water, and reaching a
country full of game and all things the Indian covets, he
joins his kindred in their long lodge.[2] So, on the southern
continent, the Bolivian Yuracarés will go, all of them, to a
future life where there will be plenty of hunting, and
Brazilian forest-tribes will find a pleasant forest full of
calabash-trees and game, where the souls of the dead will
live happily in company.[3] The Greenlanders hoped that
their souls—pale, soft, disembodied forms which the living
could not grasp—would lead a life better than that of earth,
and never ceasing. It might be in heaven, reached by the

---

[1] Cross, ' Karens,' l.c. pp. 309, 313 ; Le Jeune in ' Rel. des Jés.' 1634,
p. 16 ; Steller, ' Kamtschatka,' p. 272 ; Callaway, ' Zulu Tales,' vol. i. p. 316;
Klemm, ' Cultur-Gesch.' vol. ii. pp. 310, 315 ; J. G. Müller, ' Amer. Urrel.'
pp. 139, 286.

[2] Bastian, ' Psychologie,' p. 224 ; Schoolcraft, ' Indian Tribes,' part ii.
p. 135.

[3] D'Orbigny, ' L'Homme Américain,' vol. i. p. 364 ; Spix and Martius,
' Brasilien,' vol. i. p. 383 ; De Laet, Novus Orbis, xv. 2.

rainbow, where the souls pitch their tents round the great lake rich in fish and fowl, the lake whose waters above the firmament overflowing make rain on earth, and if its banks broke, there would be another deluge. But gaining the most and best of their living from the depths of the sea, they were also apt to think the land of Torngarsuk to be below the sea or earth, and to be entered by the deep holes in the rocks. Perpetual summer is there, ever beauteous sunshine, and no night, good water and superfluity of birds and fish, seals and reindeer to be caught without difficulty, or found alive seething in a great kettle.[1] In the Kimbunda country of South-West Africa, souls live on in ' Kalunga,' the world where it is day when it is night here ; and with plenty of food and drink, and women to serve them, and hunting and dancing for pastime, they lead a life which seems a corrected edition of this.[2] On comparison of these pictures of the future life with such as have expressed the longings of more cultured nations, there appear indeed different details, but the principle is ever the same—the idealization of earthly good. The Norseman's ideal is sketched in the few broad touches which show him in Walhalla, where he and the other warriors without number ride forth arrayed each morning and hew each other on Odin's plain, till the slain have been ' chosen ' as in earthly battle, and meal-tide comes, and slayers and slain mount and ride home to feast on the everlasting boar, and drink mead and ale with the Æsir.[3] To understand the Moslem's mind, we must read the two chapters of the Koran where the Prophet describes the faithful in the garden of delights, reclining on their couches of gold and gems, served by children ever young, with bowls of liquor whose fumes will not rise into the drinkers' heads, living among the thornless lotus-trees and date-palms loaded to the ground, feasting on the fruits they love and the meat of the rarest birds, with the houris near them with beautiful black eyes, like

[1] Cranz, ' Grönland,' p. 258.   [2] Magyar, ' Süd-Afrika,' p. 336.
[3] Edda : ' Gylfaginning.'

pearls in the shell, where no idle or wicked speech is heard, but only the words ' Peace, Peace.'

> ' They who fear the judgment of God shall have two gardens.
> Which of the benefits of God will ye deny ?
> Adorned with groves.
> Which of the benefits of God will ye deny ?
> In each of them shall spring two fountains.
> Which of the benefits of God will ye deny ?
> In each of them shall grow two kinds of fruits.
> Which of the benefits of God will ye deny ?
> They shall lie on carpets brocaded with silk and embroidered with gold ;
>   the fruits of the two gardens shall be near, easy to pluck.
> Which of the benefits of God will ye deny ?
> There shall be young virgins with modest looks, unprofaned by man or
>   jinn.
> Which of the benefits of God will ye deny ?
> They are like jacinth and coral.
> Which of the benefits of God will ye deny ?
> What is the recompence of good, if not good ?
> Which of the benefits of God will ye deny ? ' &c.[1]

With these descriptions of Paradise idealized on secular life, it is interesting to compare others which bear the impress of a priestly caste, devising a heaven after their manner. We can almost see the faces of the Jewish rabbis settling their opinions about the high schools in the firmament of heaven, where Rabbi Simeon ben Yochai and the great Rabbi Eliezer teach Law and Talmud as they taught when they were here below, and masters and learners go prosing on with the weary old disputations of cross question and crooked answer that pleased their souls on earth.[2] Nor less suggestively do the Buddhist heavens reflect the minds of the ascetics who devised them. As in their thoughts sensual pleasure seemed poor and despicable in comparison with mystic inward joy, rising and rising till consciousness fades in trance, so, above their heavens of millions of years of mere divine happiness, they raised other ranges of heavens where sensual pain and pleasure cease, and enjoy-

---

[1] ' Koran,' ch. lv. lvi.
[2] Eisenmenger, ' Entdecktes Judenthum,' part i. p. 7.

ment becomes intellectual, till at a higher grade even bodily form is gone, and after the last heaven of ' Neither-consciousness-nor-unconsciousness ' there follows Nirwâna, as ecstasy passes into swoon.[1]

But the doctrine of the continuance of the soul's life has another and a gloomier side. There are conceptions of an abode of the dead characterized not so much by dreaminess as by ghostliness. The realm of shades, especially if it be a cavern underground, has seemed a dim and melancholy place to the dwellers in this ' white world,' as the Russian calls the land of the living. One description of the Hurons tells how the other world, with its hunting and fishing, its much-prized hatchets and robes and necklaces, is like this world, yet day and night the souls groan and lament.[2] Thus the region of Mictlan, the subterranean land of Hades whither the general mass of the Mexican nation, high and low, expected to descend from the natural death-bed, was an abode looked forward to with resignation, but scarcely with cheerfulness. At the funeral the survivors were bidden not to mourn too much, the dead was reminded that he had passed and suffered the labours of this life, transitory as when one warms himself in the sun, and he was bidden to have no care or anxiety to return to his kinsfolk now that he has departed for ever and aye, for his consolation must be that they too will end their labours, and go whither he has gone before.[3] Among the Basutos, where the belief in a future life in Hades is general, some imagine in this under-world valleys ever green, and herds of hornless speckled cattle owned by the dead ; but it seems more generally thought that the shades wander about in silent calm, experiencing neither joy nor sorrow. Moral retribution there is none.[4] The Hades of the West African seems no

---

[1] Hardy, ' Manual of Budhism,' pp. 5, 24 ; Köppen, ' Rel. des Buddha,' vol. i. p. 235, &c.

[2] Brebeuf in ' Rel. des Jés.' 1636, p. 105.

[3] Sahagun, ' Hist. de Nueva España,' book iii. appendix ch. i., in Kingsborough, vol. vii. ; Brasseur, vol. iii. p. 571.

[4] Casalis, ' Basutos,' pp. 247, 254.

ecstatic paradise, to judge by Captain Burton's description: ' It was said of the old Egyptians that they lived rather in Hades than upon the banks of the Nile. The Dahomans declare that this world is man's plantation, the next is his home,—a home which, however, no one visits of his own accord. They of course own no future state of rewards and punishment : there the King will be a King, and the slave a slave for ever. Ku-to-men, or Deadman's land, the Dahoman's other but not better world, is a country of ghosts, of umbræ, who, like the spirits of the nineteenth century in Europe, lead a quiet life, except when by means of mediums they are drawn into the drawing-rooms of the living.' With some such hopeless expectation the neighbours of the Dahomans, the Yorubas, judge the life to come in their simple proverb that ' A corner in this world is better than a corner in the world of spirits.'[1] The Finns, who feared the ghosts of the departed as unkind, harmful beings, fancied them dwelling with their bodies in the grave, or else, with what Castrén thinks a later philosophy, assigned them their dwelling in the subterranean Tuonela. Tuonela was like this upper earth, the sun shone there, there was no lack of land and water, wood and field, tilth and meadow, there were bears and wolves, snakes and pike, but all things were of a hurtful, dismal kind, the woods dark and swarming with wild beasts, the water black, the cornfields bearing seed of snakes' teeth, and there stern pitiless old Tuoni, and his grim wife and son with the hooked fingers with iron points, kept watch and ward over the dead lest they should escape.[2] Scarce less dismal was the classic ideal of the dark realm below, whither the shades of the dead must go to join the many gone before (ἐς πλεόνων ἱκέσθαι; penetrare ad plures ; andare tra i più). The Roman Orcus holds the pallid souls, rapacious Orcus, sparing neither good nor bad.

---

[1] Burton, ' Dahome,' vol. ii. p. 156 ; ' Tr. Eth. Soc.' vol. iii. p. 403 ; ' Wit and Wisdom from W. Afr.' pp. 280, 449 ; see J. G. Müller, p. 140.

[2] Castrén, ' Finn. Myth.' p. 126, &c. ; Kalewala, Rune xv. xvi. xlv. &c. ; Meiners, vol. ii. p. 780.

Gloomy is the Greek land of Hades, dark dwelling of the images of departed mortals, where the shades carry at once their living features and their dying wounds, and glide and cluster and whisper, and lead the shadow of a life. Like the savage hunter on his ghostly prairie, the great Orion still bears his brazen mace, still chases over the meadows of asphodel the flying beasts he slew of yore in the lonely mountains. Like the rude African of to-day, the swift-footed Achilles scorns such poor, thin, shadowy life ; rather would he serve a mean man upon earth than be lord of all the dead.

> ' Truly, oxen and goodly sheep may be taken for booty,
> Tripods, too, may be bought, and the yellow beauty of horses ;
> But from the fence of the teeth when once the soul is departed,
> Never cometh it back, regained by plunder or purchase.'[1]

Where and what was Sheol, the dwelling of the ancient Jewish dead ? Of late years the Biblical critic has no longer to depend on passages of the Old Testament for realizing its conception, so plainly is it connected with the seven-circled Irkalla of the Babylonian-Assyrian religion, the gloomy subterranean abode whence there is no return for man, though indeed the goddess Isthar passed through its seven gates, and came back to earth from her errand of saving all life from destruction. In the history of religions, few passages are more instructive than those in which the prophets of the Old Testament recognize the ancestral connexion of their own belief with the national religions of Babylon-Assyria, as united in the doctrine of a gloomy prison of ghosts, through whose gates Jew and Gentile alike must pass. Sheol (שְׁאוֹל from שָׁאַל) is, as its name implies, a cavern-ous recess, yet it is no mere surface-grave or tomb, but an under-world of awful depth : ' High as Heaven, what doest thou ? deeper than Sheol, what knowest thou ? ' Asshur and all her company, Elam and all her multitude, the

---

[1] Homer. Il. ix. 405 ; Odyss. xi. 218, 475 ; Virg. Æn. vi. 243, &c., &c.

mighty fallen of the uncircumcised, lie there. The great
king of Babylon must go down :—

'Sheol from beneath is moved because of thee, to meet thee at thy
    coming :
He rouseth for thee the mighty dead, all the great chiefs of the earth ;
He maketh to rise up from their thrones, all the kings of the nations.
All of them shall accost thee, and shall say unto thee :
Art thou, even thou too, became weak as we ? Art thou made like
    unto us ? '

To the Greek Septuagint, *Sheol* was *Hades*, and for this
the Coptic translators had their long-inherited Egyptian
name of *Amenti*, while the Vulgate renders it as *Infernus*,
the lower regions. The Gothic Ulfilas, translating the
Hades of the New Testament, could use *Halja* in its old
German sense of the dim shadowy home of the dead below
the earth ; and the corresponding word *Hell*, if this its
earlier sense be borne in mind, fairly translates Sheol
and Hades in the English version of the Old and New
Testament, though the word has become misleading to un-
educated ears by being used also in the sense of Gehenna,
the place of torment. The early Hebrew historians and
prophets, holding out neither the hope of everlasting glory
nor the fear of everlasting agony as guiding motives for
man's present life, lay down little direct doctrine of a future
state, yet their incidental mentions justify the translators
who regard Sheol as Hades. Sheol is a special locality where
dead men go to their dead ancestors : 'And Isaac gave up
the ghost, and died, and was gathered unto his people . . .
and his sons Esau and Jacob buried him.' Abraham,
though not even buried in the land of his forefathers, is thus
' gathered unto his people ; ' and Jacob has no thought of
his body being laid with Joseph's body, torn by wild beasts
in the wilderness, when he says, ' I shall go down to my
son mourning to Sheol ('εἰs ᾅδου' in the LXX., ' èpesēt
èàmenti ' in the Coptic, ' in infernum ' in the Vulgate).
The rephaim, the ' shades ' of the dead, who dwell in
Sheol, love not to be disturbed from their rest by the

necromancer; 'And Samuel said to Saul, why hast thou disquieted me to bring me up?' Yet their quiet is contrasted in a tone of sadness with the life on earth; 'Whatsoever thy hand findeth to do, do it with thy might; for there is no work, nor device, nor knowledge, nor widsom, in Sheol, whither thou goest.'[1] Such thoughts of the life of the shades below did not disappear when, in the later years of the Jewish nation, the great change in the doctrine of the future life passed in so large a measure over the Hebrew mind, their earlier thoughts of ghostly continuance giving place to the doctrines of resurrection and retribution. The ancient ideas have even held their place on into Christian thought, in pictures like that of the Limbus Patrum, the Hades where Christ descended to set free the patriarchs.

The Retribution-theory of the future life comprises in a general way the belief in different grades of future happiness, especially in different regions of the other world allotted to men according to their lives in this. This doctrine of retribution is, as we have already seen, far from universal among mankind, many races recognizing the idea of a spirit outliving the body, without considering the fate of this spirit to depend at all upon the conduct of the living man. The doctrine of retribution indeed hardly seems an original part of the doctrine of the future life. On the contrary, if we judge that men in a primitive state of culture arrived at the notion of a surviving spirit, and that some races, but by no means all, afterwards reached the further stage of recognizing a retribution for deeds done in the body, this theory will not, so far as I know, be discountenanced by facts.[2] Even among the higher savages, however, a con-

[1] Gen. xxxv. 29; xxv. 8; xxxvii. 35; Job xi. 8; Amos ix. 2; Psalm lxxxix. 48; Ezek. xxxi., xxxii.; Isaiah xiv. 9, xxxviii. 10-18; 1 Sam., xxviii. 15; Eccles. ix. 10. 'Records of the Past,' vol. i. pp. 141-9; Sayce 'Lectures on Hist. of Rel.' part ii.; Alger, 'Critical History of the Doctrine of a Future Life,' ch. viii.

[2] The doctrine of reversal, as in Kamchatka, where rich and poor will thange places in the other world (Steller, pp. 269-72), is too exceptional in che lower culture to be generalized. See Steinhauser, 'Rel. des Negers,'

nexion between man's life and his happiness or misery after
death is often held as a definite article of theology, and
thence it is to be traced onward through barbaric religions,
and into the very heart of Christianity. Yet the grounds
of good and evil in the future life are so far from uniform
among the religions of the world, that they may differ
widely within what is considered one and the same creed.
The result is more definite than the cause, the end than the
means. Men who alike look forward to a region of un-
earthly happiness beyond the grave, hope to reach that
happy land by roads so strangely different, that the path of
life which leads one nation to eternal bliss may seem to the
next the very descent into the pit. In noticing among
savage and barbaric peoples the qualifications which determine future happiness, we may with some distinctness
define these as being excellence, valour, social rank, religious ordinance. On the whole, however, in the religions
of the lower range of culture, unless where they may have
been affected by contact with higher religions, the destiny
of the man after death seems hardly to turn on judicial
reward or punishment for his moral conduct in life. Such
difference as is made between the future conditions of
different classes of souls, seems more often to belong to a
remarkable intermediate doctrine, standing between the
earlier continuance-theory and the later retribution-theory.
The idea of the next life being similar to this seems to have
developed into the idea that what gives prosperity and re-
nown here will give it also there, so that earthly conditions
carry on their contrasts into the changed world after death.
Thus a man's condition after death will be a result of,
rather than a compensation or retribution for, his condition
during life. A comparison of doctrines held at various
stages of culture may justify a tentative speculation as to
their actual sequence in history, favouring the opinion that

l. c., p. 135. A Wolof proverb is ' The more powerful one is in this world,
the more servile one will be in the next.' (Burton, ' Wit and Wisdom,'
p. 28.)

through such an intermediate stage the doctrine of simple future existence was actually developed into the doctrine of future reward and punishment, a transition which for deep import to human life has scarcely its rival in the history of religion.

The effect of earthly rank on the future life, as looked at by the lower races, brings out this intermediate stage in bold relief. Mere transfer from one life to another makes chiefs and slaves here chiefs and slaves hereafter, and this natural doctrine is very usual. But there are cases in which earthly caste is exaggerated into utter difference in the life to come. The aerial paradise of Raiatea, with its fragrant ever-blooming flowers, its throngs of youths and girls all perfection, its luxurious feasts and merrymakings, were for the privileged orders of Areois and chiefs who could pay the priests their heavy charges, but hardly for the common populace. This idea reached its height in the Tonga islands, where aristocratic souls would pass to take their earthly rank and station in the island paradise of Bolotu, while plebeian souls, if indeed they existed, would die with the plebeian bodies they dwelt in.[1] In Vancouver's Island, the Ahts fancied Quawteaht's calm sunny plenteous land in the sky as the resting-place of high chiefs, who live in one great house as the Creator's guests, while the slain in battle have another to themselves. But otherwise all Indians of low degree go deep down under the earth to the land of Chay-her, with its poor houses and no salmon and small deer, and blankets so small and thin that when the dead are buried the friends often bury blankets with them, to send them to the world below with the departed soul.[2] The expectation of royal dignity in the life after death, distinct from the fate of ordinary mortals, comes well into view among the Natchez of Louisiana, where the sun-descended royal family would in some way return to the Sun ; thus

[1] Ellis, ' Polyn. Res.' vol. i. pp. 245, 397 ; see also Turner, ' Polynesia,' p. 237 (Samoans) ; Mariner, ' Tonga Is.' vol. ii. p. 105.
[2] Sproat, ' Savage Life,' p. 209.

also in the mightier empire of Peru, where each sun-descended Inca, feeling the approach of death, announced to his assembled vassals that he was called to heaven to rest with his father the Sun.[1] But in the higher religions, the change in this respect from the doctrine of continuance to the doctrine of retribution is wonderful in its completeness. The story of that great lady who strengthened her hopes of future happiness by the assurance, ' They will think twice before they refuse a person of my condition,' is a mere jest to modern ears. Yet, like many other modern jest, it is only an archaism which in an older stage of culture had in it nothing ridiculous.

To the happy land of Torngarsuk the Great Spirit, says Cranz, only such Greenlanders came as have been valiant workers, for other ideas of virtue they have none ; such as have done great deeds, taken many whales and seals, borne much hardship, been drowned at sea, or died in childbirth.[2] Thus Charlevoix says of the Indians further south, that their claim to hunt after death on the prairies of eternal spring is to have been good hunters and warriors here. Lescarbot, speaking of the belief among the Indians of Virginia that after death the good will be at rest and the wicked in pain, remarks that their enemies are the wicked and themselves the good, so that in their opinion they are after death much at their ease, and principally when they have well defended their country and slain their enemies.[3] So Jean de Lery said of the rude Tubinambas of Brazil, they they think the souls of such as have lived virtuously, that is to say, who have well avenged themselves and eaten many of their enemies, will go behind the great mountains and dance in beautiful gardens with the souls of their fathers, but the souls of the effeminate and worthless, who

[1] ' Rec. des Voy. au Nord,' vol. v. p. 23 (Natchez) ; Garcilaso de la Vega, ' Commentarios Reales,' lib. i. c. 23, tr. by C. R. Markham ; Prescott, ' Peru,' vol. i. pp. 29, 83 ; J. G. Müller, p. 402, &c.

[2] Cranz, Grönland,' p. 259.

[3] Charlevoix, ' Nouvelle France,' vol. vi. p. 77 ; Lescarbot, ' Hist. de la Nouvelle France,' Paris, 1619, p. 679.

have not striven to defend their country, will go to Aygnan the Evil Spirit, to incessant torments.[1] More characteristic and probably more genuinely native than most of these expectations, is that of the Caribs, that the braves of their nation should go after death to happy islands, where all good fruits grow wild, there to spend their time in dancing and feasting, and to have their enemies the Arawaks for slaves ; but the cowards who feared to go to war should go to serve the Arawaks, dwelling in their waste and barren lands beyond the mountains.[2]

The fate of warriors slain in battle is the subject of two singularly contrasted theories. We have elsewhere examined the deep-lying belief that if a man's body be wounded or mutilated, his soul will arrive in the same state in the other world. Perhaps it is some such idea of the soul being injured with the body by a violent death, that leads the Mintira of the Malay Peninsula, though not believing in a future reward and punishment, to exclude from the happy paradise of ' Fruit Island ' (Pulo Bua) the souls of such as die a bloody death, condemning them to dwell on ' Red Land ' (Tana Mera), a desolate barren place, whence they must even go to the fortunate island to fetch their food.[3] In North America, the idea is mentioned among the Hurons that the souls of the slain in war live in a band apart, neither they nor suicides being admitted to the spirit-villages of their tribe. A belief ascribed to certain Indians of California may be cited here, though less as a sample of real native doctrine than to illustrate that borrowing of Christian ideas which so often spoils such evidence for ethnological purposes. They held, it is said, that Niparaya, the Great Spirit, hates war, and will have no warriors in his paradise, but that his adversary Wac, shut up for rebellion in a great cave, takes thither to himself the

Lery, ' Hist. d'un Voy. en Brésil,' p. 234 ; Coreal, ' Voi. aux Indes Occ.' i. p. 224.
Rochefort, ' Iles Antilles,' p. 430.
' Journ. Ind. Archip.' vol. i. p. 325.

slain in battle.[1] On the other hand, the thought which shows out in such bold relief in the savage mind, that courage is virtue, and battle and bloodshed the hero's noblest pursuit, leads naturally to a hope of glory for his soul when his body has been slain in fight. Such expectation was not strange in North America, to that Indian tribe, for instance, who talked of the Great Spirit walking in the moonlight on his island in Lake Superior, whither slain warriors will go to him to take their pleasure in the chace.[2] The Nicaraguans declared that men who died in their houses went underground, but the slain in war went to serve the gods in the east, where the sun comes from. This corresponds in part with a remarkable threefold contrast of the future life among their Aztec kinsfolk. Mictlan, the Hades of the general dead, and Tlalocan, the Earthly Paradise, reached by certain special and acute ways of death, have been mentioned here already. But the souls of warriors slain in battle or sacrificed as captives, and of women who died in child-birth, were transported to the heavenly plains ; there the heroes, peeping through the holes in their bucklers pierced by arrows in earthly fight, watched the Sun arise and saluted him with shout and clash of arms, and at noon the mothers received him with music and dance to escort him on his western way.[3] In such wise, to the old Norseman, to die the ' straw-death ' of sickness or old age was to go down into the dismal loathly house of Hela the Death-goddess ; if the warrior's fate on the field of battle were denied him, and death came to fetch him from a peaceful couch, yet at least he could have the scratch of the spear, Odin's mark, and so contrive to go with a blood-stained soul to the glorious Walhalla. Surely then if ever, says a

[1] Brebeuf in ' Rel. des Jés.' 1636, p. 104 ; see also Meiners, vol. ii. p. 769 ; J. G. Müller, pp. 89, 139.

[2] Chateaubriand, ' Voy. en Amérique ' (Religion).

[3] Oviedo, ' Nicaragua,' p. 22 ; Torquemada, ' Monarquia Indiana,' book xiii. c. 48 ; Sahagun, book iii. app. ch. i.-iii. in Kingsborough, vol. vii. Compare Anderson, ' Exp. to W. Yunnan,' p. 125. (Shans, good men and mothers dying in child-birth to heaven, bad men and those killed by the sword to hell.)

modern writer, the kingdom of heaven suffered violence, and the violent took it by force.[1] Thence we follow the idea onward to the battle-fields of holy war, where the soldier earned with his blood the unfading crown of martyr-dom, and Christian and Moslem were urged in mutual onset and upheld in agony by the glimpse of paradise opening to receive the slayer of the infidel.

Such ideas, current among the lower races as to the soul's future happiness or misery, do not seem, setting aside some exceptional points, to be thoughts adopted or degraded from doctrines of cultured nations. They rather belong to the intellectual stratum in which they are found. If so, we must neither ignore nor exaggerate their standing in the lower ethics. ' The good are good warriors and hunters,' said a Pawnee chief ; whereupon the author who mentions the saying remarks that this would also be the opinion of a wolf, if he could express it.[2] Nevertheless, if experience has led societies of savage men to fix on certain qualities, such as courage, skill, and industry, as being virtues, then many moralists will say that such a theory is not only ethical, but lying at the very foundation of ethics. And if these savage societies further conclude that such virtues obtain their reward in another world as in this, then their theories of future happiness and misery, destined for what they call good and bad men, may be looked on in this sense as belonging to morality, though at no high stage of development. But many or most writers, when they mention morality, assume a narrower definition of it. This must be borne in mind in appreciating what is meant by the statements of several well-qualified ethnologists, who have, in more or less degree, denied a moral character to the future retribution as con-ceived in savage religion. Mr. Ellis, describing the Society Islanders, at least gives an explicit definition. When he tried to ascertain whether they connected a person's con-

---

[1] Alger, ' Future Life,' p. 93.
[2] Brinton, ' Myths of New World,' p. 300.

dition in a future state with his disposition and conduct in this, he never could learn that they expected in the world of spirits any difference in the treatment of a kind, generous, peaceful man, and that of a cruel, parsimonious, quarrelsome one.[1] This remark, it seems to me, applies to savage religion far and wide. Dr. Brinton, commenting on the native religions of America, draws his line in a somewhat different place. Nowhere, he says, was any well-defined doctrine that moral turpitude was judged and punished in the next world. No contrast is discoverable between a place of torments and a realm of joy ; at the worst but a negative castigation awaited the liar, the coward, or the niggard.[2] Professor J. G. Müller, in his ' American Religions,' yet more pointedly denies any ' ethical meaning ' in the contrasts of the savage future life, and looks upon what he well calls its 'light-side' and 'shadow-side' not as recompensing earthly virtue and vice, but rather as carrying on earthly conditions in a new existence.[3]

The idea that admission to the happier region depends on the performance of religious rites and the giving of offerings, seems scarcely known to the lowest savages. It is worth while, however, to notice some statements which seem to mark its appearance at the level of high savagery or low barbarism. Thus in the Society Islands, though the destiny of man's spirit to the region of night or to elysium was irrespective of moral character, we hear of neglect of rites and offerings as being visited by the displeasure of deities.[4] In Florida, the belief of the Sun-worshipping people of Achalaque was thus described : those who had lived well, and well served the Sun, and given many gifts to the poor in his honour, would be happy after

[1] Ellis, ' Polyn. Res.' vol. i. p. 397 ; see also Williams, ' Fiji,' vol. i. p. 243.

[2] Brinton, p. 242, &c.

[3] J. G. Müller, ' Amer. Urrel.' pp. 87, 224. See also the opinions of Meiners, ' Gesch. der Religion,' vol. ii. p. 768 ; Wuttke, ' Gesch. des Heidenthums,' vol. i. p. 115.

[4] Ellis, l. c. ; Moerenhout, ' Voyage,' vol. i. p. 433.

death and be changed into stars, whereas the wicked would be carried to a destitute and wretched existence among mountain precipices, where fierce wild beasts have their dens.[1] According to Bosman, the souls of Guinea negroes reaching the river of death must answer to the divine judge how they have lived ; have they religiously observed the holy days dedicated to their god, have they abstained from all forbidden meats and kept their vows inviolate, they are wafted across to paradise ; but if they have sinned against these laws they are plunged in the river and there drowned for ever.[2] Such statements among peoples at these stages of culture are not frequent, and perhaps not very valid as accounts of original native doctrine. It is in the elaborate religious systems of more organized nations, in modern Brahmanism and Buddhism, and degraded forms of Christianity, that the special adaptation of the doctrine of retribution to the purposes of priestcraft and ceremonialism has become a commonplace of missionary reports.

It is well not to speak too positively on a subject so difficult and doubtful as this of the history of the belief in future retribution. Careful criticism of the evidence is above all necessary. For instance, we have to deal with several statements recorded among low races, explicitly assigning reward or punishment to men after death, according as they were good or bad in life. Here the first thing to be done is to clear up, if possible, the question whether the doctrine of retribution may have been borrowed from some more cultured neighbouring religion, as the very details often show to have been the case. Examples of direct adoption of foreign dogmas on this subject are not uncommon in the world. When among the Dayaks of Borneo it is said that a dead man becomes a spirit and lives in the jungle, or haunts the place of burial or burning, or when some distant mountain-top is pointed to as the abode of spirits of departed friends, it is hardly needful to question

[1] Rochefort, ' Iles Antilles,' p. 378.
[2] Bosman, ' Guinea,' letter x. ; in Pinkerton, vol. xvi. p. 401.

the originality of ideas so characteristically savage. But one of these Dayak tribes, burning the dead, says that ' as the smoke of the funeral pile of a good man rises, the soul ascends with it to the sky, and that the smoke from the pile of a wicked man descends, and his soul with it is borne down to the earth, and through it to the regions below.'[1] Did not this exceptional idea come into the Dayak's mind by contact with Hinduism ? In Orissa, again, Khond souls have to leap across the black unfathomable river to gain a footing on the slippery Leaping Rock, where Dinga Pennu, the judge of the dead, sits writing his register of all men's daily lives and actions, sending virtuous souls to become blessed spirits, keeping back wicked ones and sending them to suffer their penalties in new births on earth.[2] Here the striking myth of the leaping rock is perfectly savage, but the ideas of a judgment, moral retribution, and transmigration, may have come from the Hindus of the plains, as the accompanying notion of the written book unquestionably did. Dr. Mason is no doubt right in taking as the indigenous doctrine of the Karens their notion of an underworld where the ghosts of the dead live on as here, while he sets down to Hindu influence the idea of Tha-ma, the judge of the dead (the Hindu Yama), as allotting their fate according to their lives, sending those who have done deeds of merit to heaven, those who have done wickedness to hell, and keeping in Hades the neither good nor bad.[3] How the theory of moral retribution may be superposed on more primitive doctrines of the future life, comes remarkably into view in Turanian religion. Among the Lapps, Jabme-Aimo, the subterranean ' home of the dead ' below the earth, where the departed have their cattle and follow their livelihood like Lapps above, though they are richer, wiser,

[1] St. John, ' Far East,' vol. i. p. 181 ; see Mundy, ' Narrative,' vol. i. p. 332.

[2] Macpherson, p. 92.   Compare Moerenhout, l. c. (Tahiti).

[3] Mason, l. c. p. 195.   See also De Brosses, ' Nav. aux Terres Australes,' vol. ii. p. 482 (Caroline Is.).

stronger folk, and also Saivo-Aimo, a yet happier 'home of the gods,' are conceptions thoroughly in the spirit of the lower culture. But in one account the subterranean abode becomes a place of transition, where the dead stay awhile, and then with bodies renewed are taken up to the Heaven-god, or if misdoers, are flung into the abyss. Castrén is evidently right in rejecting this doctrine as not native, but due to Catholic influence. So, at the end of the 16th Rune of the Finnish Kalewala, which tells of Wainamoinen's visit to the dismal land of the dead, there is put into the hero's mouth a second speech, warning the children of men to harm not the innocent, for sad payment is in Tuoni's dwelling—the bed of evil-doers is there, with its glowing red-hot stones below and its canopy of snakes above. But the same critic condemns this moral ' tag,' as a later addition to the genuine heathen picture of Manala, the under-world of the dead.[1] Nor did Christianity scorn to borrow details from the religions it abolished. The narrative of a mediæval visit to the other world would be incomplete without its description of the awful Bridge of Death ; Acheron and Charon's bark were restored to their places in Tartarus by the visionary and the poet ; the wailing of sinful souls might be heard as they were hammered white-hot in Vulcan's smithies ; and the weighing of good and wicked souls, as we may see it figured on every Egyptian mummy-case, now passed into the charge of St. Paul and the Devil.[2]

The foregoing considerations having been duly weighed, it remains to call attention to the final problem, at what state of religious history the full theological doctrine of judicial retribution and moral compensation in a future life may have arisen. It is hard, however, to define where this development takes place even at a barbaric stage of culture. Thus among the barbaric nations of West Africa, there

[1] Castrén, ' Finn. Myth.' pp. 136, 144. See Georgi, ' Reise im Russ. Reich,' vol. i. p. 278. Compare accounts of Purgatory among the North American Indians, apparently derived from missionaries, in Morgan, ' Iroquois,' p. 169 ; Waitz, vol. iii. p. 345.

[2] See T. Wright, ' St. Patrick's Purgatory.'

appear such beliefs as that in Nuffi, that criminals who escape their punishment here will receive it in the other world ; the division of the Yoruba under-world into an upper and a lower region for the righteous and wicked ; the Kru doctrine that only the good will rejoin their ancestors in heaven ; the Oji doctrine that only the good will dwell after death in the heavenly house or city of the Deity whom they call the ' Highest.'[1] How far is all this to be taken as native conception, and how far as due to ages of Christian and Moslem intercourse, to which at any rate few will scruple to refer the last case ?

In the lower ranges of civilization, some of the most remarkable doctrines of this class are recorded in North America. Thus they appear in connexion with the fancy of a river or gulf to be passed by the departing soul on its way to the land of the dead, one of the most remarkable traits of the mythology of the world. This seems in its origin a nature-myth, connected probably with the Sun's passage across the sea into Hades, and in many of its versions it appears as a mere episode of the soul's journey without any moral sense attached to it. Brebeuf, the same early Jesuit missionary who says explicitly of the Hurons that there is no difference in their future life between the fate of the virtuous and the vicious, mentions also among them the tree-trunk that bridges the river of death ; here the dead must cross, the dog that guards it attacks some souls, and they fall. Yet in other versions this myth has a moral sense attached to it, and the passage of the heaven-gulf becomes an ordeal to separate good and wicked. To take but one instance, there is Catlin's account of the Choctaw souls journeying far westward, to whom the long slippery barkless pine-log, stretching from hill to hill, bridges over the deep and dreadful river ; the good pass safely to a beauteous Indian paradise, the wicked fall into the abyss of waters, and go the dark hungry wretched

[1] Waitz, vol. ii. pp. 171, 191 ; Bowen, ' Yoruba Lang.' p. xvi. See J. L. Wilson, p. 210.

land where they are henceforth to dwell.[1] This and many similar beliefs current in the religions of the world, which need not be particularised here, seem best explained as originally nature-myths, afterwards adapted to a religious purpose. A different conception was recorded so early as 1623, by Captain John Smith among the Massachusetts, whose name is still borne by the New England district they once inhabited : They say, at first there was no king but Kiehtan, that dwelleth far westerly above the heavens, whither all good men go when they die, and have plenty of all things. The bad men go thither also and knock at the door, but he bids them go wander in endless want and misery, for they shall not stay there.[2] Lastly, the Salish Indians of Oregon say that the good go to a happy hunting-ground of endless game, while the bad go to a place where there is eternal snow, hunger, and thirst, and are tantalised by the sight of game they cannot kill, and water they cannot drink.[3] If, now, in looking at these records, the doubts which beset them can be put aside, and the accounts of the different fates assigned to the good and wicked can be accepted as belonging to genuine native American religion and if, moreover, it be considered that the goodness and wickedness for which men are to be thus rewarded and punished are moral qualities, however undeveloped in definition, this will amount to an admission that the doctrine of moral retribution at any rate appears within the range of savage theology. Such a view, however, by no means invalidates the view here put forward as to the historical development of the doctrine, but only goes to prove at how early a stage it may have begun to take place. The general mass of evidence still remains to show the savage doctrine of the future state, as originally involving no moral retribution,

[1] Brebeuf in ' Rel. des Jés.' 1635, p. 35 ; 1636, p. 105. Catlin, ' N. A. Ind.' vol. ii. p. 127 ; Long's ' Exp.' vol. i. p. 180. See Brinton, p. 247 ; Waitz, vol. ii. p. 191, vol. iii. p. 197 ; and the collection of myths of the Heaven-Bridge and Heaven-Gulf in ' Early History of Mankind,' chap. xii.
[2] Smith, ' New England,' in Pinkerton, vol. xiii. p. 244.
[3] Wilson in ' Tr. Eth. Soc.' vol. iii. p. 303.

or arriving at this through transitional and rudimentary stages.

In strong contrast with the schemes of savage future existence, I need but set before the reader's mind a salient point here and there in the doctrine of distinct and unquestionable moral retribution, as held in religions of the higher culture. The inner mystic doctrines of ancient Egypt may perhaps never be extracted now from the pictures and hieroglyphic formulas of the ' Book of the Dead.' But the ethnographer may satisfy himself of two important points as to the place which the Egyptian view of the future life occupies in the history of religion. On the one hand, the soul's quitting and revisiting the corpse, the placing of the image in the tomb, the offering of meat and drink, the fearful journey to the regions of the departed, the renewed life like that on earth, with its houses to dwell in and fields to cultivate—all these are conceptions which connect the Egyptian religion with the religions of the ruder races of mankind. But on the other hand, the mixed ethical and ceremonial standard by which the dead are to be judged adapts these primitive and even savage thoughts to a higher social development, such as may be shown by fragments from that remarkable ' negative confession ' which the dead must make before Osiris and the forty-two judges in Amenti. ' O ye Lords of Truth ! let me know you ! . . . Rub ye away my faults. I have not privily done evil against mankind. . . . I have not told falsehoods in the tribunal of Truth. . . . I have not done any wicked thing. I have not made the labouring man do more than his task daily. . . . I have not calumniated the slave to his master. . . . I have not murdered. . . . I have not done fraud to men. I have not changed measures of the country. I have not injured the images of the gods. I have not taken scraps of the bandages of the dead. I have not committed adultery. I have not withheld milk from the mouths of sucklings. I have not hunted wild animals in the pasturages. I have not netted

sacred birds. . . . I am pure ! I am pure ! I am
pure ! ' [1]

The Vedic hymns, again, tell of endless happiness for
the good in heaven with the gods, and speak also of the
deep pit where the liars, the lawless, they who give no
sacrifice, will be cast.[2]   The rival theories of continuance
and retribution are seen in instructive coexistence in classic
Greece and Rome.   What seems the older belief holds its
ground in the realm of Hades ; that dim region of bodiless,
smoke-like ghosts remains the home of the undistinguished
crowd in the μέσος βίος, the 'middle life.'   Yet at the
same time the judgment-seat of Minos and Rhadamanthos,
the joys of Elysium for the just and good, fiery Tartarus
echoing with the wail of the wicked, represent the newer
doctrine of a moral retribution.   The idea of purgatorial
suffering, which hardly seems to have entered the minds of
the lower races, expands in immense vigour in the great
Aryan religions of Asia.   In Brahmanism and Buddhism,
the working out of good and evil actions into their necessary consequence of happiness and misery is the very key
to the philosophy of life, whether life's successive transmigrations be in animal, or human, or demon births on earth,
or in luxurious heaven-palaces of gold and jewels, or in the
agonizing hells where Oriental fancy riots in the hideous
inventory of torture—caldrons of boiling oil and liquid fire ;
black dungeons and rivers of filth ; vipers, and vultures,
and cannibals ; thorns, and spears, and red-hot pincers, and
whips of flame.   To the modern Hindu, it is true, ceremonial morality seems to take the upper hand, and the
question of happiness or misery after death turns rather
on ablutions and fasts, on sacrifices and gifts to brahmans, than on purity and beneficence of life.   Buddhism in
South East Asia, sadly degenerate from its once high

[1] Birch, Introduction to and translation of the ' Book of the Dead,' in
Bunsen, vol. v. ; Wilkinson, ' Ancient Eg.' vol. v.
[2] For references to Rig Veda see Muir, ' Sanskrit Texts,' sec. xviii. ; Max
Müller, Lecture on Vedas in ' Essays,' vol. ii.

estate, is apt to work out the doctrine of merit and de-merit into debtor and creditor accounts kept in good and bad marks from day to day ; to serve out so much tea in hot weather counts 1 to the merit-side, and putting a stop to one's women scolding for a month counts 1 like-wise, but this may be balanced by the offence of letting them keep the bowls and plates dirty for a day, which counts 1 the wrong way ; and it appears that giving wood for two coffins, which count 30 marks each, and burying four bones, at 10 marks a-piece, would just be balanced by murdering a child, which counts 100 to the bad.[1] It need hardly be said here that these two great religions of Asia must be judged rather in their records of long past ages, than in the lingering degeneration of their modern reality.

In the Khordah-Avesta, a document of the old Persian religion, the fate of good and wicked souls at death is pic-tured in a dialogue between Zarathustra (Zoroaster), and Ahura-Mazda and Anra-Mainyu (Ormuzd and Ahriman). Zarathustra asks, ' Ahura-Mazda, Heavenly, Holiest, Creator of the corporeal world, Pure ! When a pure man dies, where does his soul dwell during this night ? ' Then answers Ahura-Mazda : ' Near his head it sits down, re-citing the Gâthâ Ustavaiti, praying happiness for itself ; "Happiness be to the man who conduces to the happiness of each. May Ahura-Mazda create, ruling after his wish."' On this night the soul sees as much joyfulness as the whole living world possesses ; and so the second and the third night. When the lapse of the third night turns itself to light, then the soul of the pure man goes forward, recollecting itself by the perfume of plants. A wind blows to meet it from the mid-day regions, a sweet-scented one, more sweet-scented than the other winds, and the soul of the pure man receives it—' Whence blows this wind, the sweetest-scented which I ever have smelt with the nose ? ' Then comes to meet him

[1] ' Journ. Ind. Archip.' new ser. vol. ii. p. 210. See Bastian, ' Oestl. Asien,' vol. iii. p. 387.

his own law (his rule of life) in the figure of a maiden beautiful, shining, with shining arms, powerful, well-grown, slender, large-bosomed, with praiseworthy body, noble, with brilliant face, one of fifteen years, as fair in her growth as the fairest creatures.   Then to her speaks the soul of the pure man, asking, ' What maiden art thou whom I have seen here as the fairest of maidens in body ? '   She answers, ' I am, O youth, thy good thoughts, words, and works, thy good law, the own law of thine own body.   Thou hast made the pleasant yet pleasanter to me, the fair yet fairer, the desirable yet more desirable, the sitting in a high place sitting in a yet higher place.'   Then the soul of the pure man takes the first step and comes to the first paradise, the second and third step to the second and third paradise, the fourth step and arrives at the Eternal Lights.   To the souls speaks a pure one deceased before, asking it, ' How art thou, O pure deceased, come away from the fleshly dwellings, from the corporeal world hither to the invisible, from the perishable world hither to the imperishable.   Hail ! has it happened to thee long ? '   ' Then speaks Ahura-Mazda : " Ask not him whom thou askest, for he is come on the fearful way of trembling, the separation of body and soul.   Bring him hither of the food, of the full fatness, that is the food for a youth who thinks, speaks, and does good, who is devoted to the good law after death—that is the food for a woman who especially thinks good, speaks good, does good, the following, obedient, pure after death." '   And now Zarathustra asks, when a wicked one dies, where his soul dwells ?   He is told how, running about near the head, it utters the prayer, Ke maúm :—' Which land shall I praise, whither shall I go praying, O Ahura-Mazda ? ' In this night it sees as much unjoyfulness as the whole living world ; and so the second and the third night, and it goes at dawn to the impure place, recollecting itself by the stench. An evil-smelling wind comes towards the dead from the north, and with it the ugly hateful maiden who is his own wicked deeds, and the soul takes the fourth step into the darkness without beginning, and a wicked soul asks how long—woe to thee !—art thou come ? and the mocking Anra-Mainyu, answering in words like the words of Ahura-Mazda to the good, bids food to be brought—poison, and mixed with poison, for them who think and speak and do evil, and follow the wicked law. The Parsi of our own time, following in obscure tradition the ancient Zoroastrian faith, before he prays for forgiveness for all that he ought to have thought, and said, and done, and has not, for all that he ought not to have thought, and said, and done, and has, confesses thus his faith of the future life :—' I am wholly without doubt in the existence of the good Mazada-yaçnian faith, in the coming of the resurrection and the later body, in the stepping over the bridge Chinvat, in an invariable recompense of good deeds and their reward, and of bad deeds and their punishment.' [1]

In Jewish theology, the doctrine of future retribution appears after the Babylonish captivity, not in ambiguous terms, but as the strongly-expressed and intensely-felt religious conviction it has since remained among the children of Israel. Not long afterward, it received the sanction of Christianity.

A broad survey of the doctrine of the Future Life among the various nations of the world shows at once how difficult and how important is a systematic theory of its development. Looked at ethnographically, the general relations of the lower to the higher culture as to the belief in future existence may be defined somewhat as follows :—If we draw a line dividing civilization at the junction of savagery and barbarism—about where the Carib and New Zealander ends and the Aztec or Tatar begins, we may see clearly the difference of prevalent doctrine on either side. On the savage side, the theory of hovering ghosts is strong, re-birth in human or animal bodies is often thought of, but above all there prevails the expectation of a new life, most

[1] Spiegel, 'Avesta,' ed. Bleek, vol. iii. pp. 136, 163 ; see vol. i. pp. xviii. 90, 141 ; vol. ii. p. 68.

often located in some distant earthly region, or less commonly in the under-world or on the sky. On the cultured side, the theory of hovering ghosts continues, but tends to subside from philosophy into folklore, the theory of re-birth is elaborated into great philosophic systems, but eventually dies out under the opposition of scientific biology, while the doctrine of a new life after death maintains its place with immense power in the human mind, although the dead have been ousted by geography from any earthly district, and the regions of heaven and hell are more and more spiritualized out of definite locality into vague expressions of future happiness and misery. Again, on the savage side we find the dominant idea to be a continuance of the soul in a new existence, like the present life, or idealized and exaggerated on its model ; while on the cultured side the doctrine of judgment and moral retribution prevails with paramount, though not indeed absolute sway. What, then, has been the historical course of theological opinion, to have produced in different stages of culture these contrasted phases of doctrine ?

In some respects, theories deriving savage from more civilized ideas are tenable. In certain cases, to consider a particular savage doctrine of the future state as a fragmentary, or changed, or corrupted outcome of the religion of higher races, seems as easy as to reverse this view by taking savagery as representing the starting-point. It is open to anyone to suppose that the doctrine of transmigration among American savages and African barbarians may have been degraded from elaborate systems of metempsychosis established among philosophic nations like the Hindus ; that the North American and South African doctrine of continued existence in a subterranean world may be derived from similar beliefs held by races at the level of the ancient Greeks ; that when rude tribes in the Old or New World assign among the dead a life of happiness to some, and of misery to others, this idea may have been inherited or adopted from cultured nations holding more strongly and systematically the doctrine of retribution. In such cases the argument is to a great extent the same, whether the lower race be considered degenerate descendants of a higher nation, or whether the simpler supposition be put forward that they have adopted the ideas of some more cultured people. These views ought to have full attention, for degenerate and borrowed beliefs form no small item in the opinions of uncivilized races. Yet this kind of explanation is more adapted to meet special cases than general conditions ; it is rather suited to piecemeal treatment, than to comprehensive study, of the religions of mankind. Worked out on a large scale, it would endeavour to account for the doctrines of the savage world, as being a patchwork of fragments from various religions of high nations, transported by not easily-conceived means from their distant homes and set down in remote regions of the earth. It may be safely said that no hypothesis can account for the varied doctrines current among the lower tribes, without the admission that religious ideas have been in no small measure developed and modified in the districts where they are current.

Now this theory of development, in its fullest scope, combined with an accessory theory of degeneration and adoption, seems best to meet the general facts of the case. A hypothesis which finds the origin of the doctrine of the future life in the primitive animism of the lower races, and thence traces it along the course of religious thought, in varied developments fitted to exacter knowledge and forming part of loftier creeds, may well be maintained as in reasonable accordance with the evidence. Such a theory, as has been sufficiently shown in the foregoing chapters, affords a satisfactory explanation of the occurrence, in the midst of cultured religions, of intellectually low superstitions, such as that of offerings to the dead, and various others. These, which the development theory treats naturally as survivals from a low stage of education lingering on in a higher, are by no means so readily accounted for by the degeneration theory. There are more special arguments which favour the priority of the savage to the civilized phases of the doctrine of a future life. If savages did in general receive their views of another existence from the religious systems of cultured nations, these systems can hardly have been such as recognize the dominant doctrines of heaven and hell. For, as to the locality of the future world, savage races especially favour a view little represented in civilized belief, namely, that the life to come is in some distant earthly country. Moreover, the belief in a fiery abyss or Gehenna, which excites so intensely and lays hold so firmly of the imagination of the most ignorant men, would have been especially adapted to the minds of savages, had it come down to them by tradition from an ancestral faith. Yet, in fact, the lower races so seldom recognize such an idea, that even the few cases in which it occurs lie open to suspicion of not being purely native. The proposition that the savage doctrines descend from the more civilized seems thus to involve the improbable supposition, that tribes capable of keeping up traditions of Paradise, Heaven, or Hades, should nevertheless have forgotten or discarded a tradition of Hell. Still more important is the contrast between the continuance-theory and the retribution-theory of the future existence, in the sections of culture where they respectively predominate. On the one hand, the continuance-theory, with its ideas of a ghostly life like this, is directly vouched for by the evidence of the senses in dreams and visions of the dead, and may be claimed as part of the ' Natural Religion,' properly so called, of the lower races. On the other hand, the retribution-theory is a dogma which this evidence of apparitions could hardly set on foot, though capable of afterwards supporting it. Throughout the present study of animistic religion, it constantly comes into view that doctrines which in the lower culture are philosophical, tend in the higher to become ethical ; that what among savages is a science of nature, passes among civilized nations into a moral engine. Herein lies the distinction of deepest import between the two great theories of the soul's existence after bodily death. According to a development theory of culture, the savage, unethical doctrine of continuance would be taken as the more primitive, succeeded in higher civilization by the ethical doctrine of retribution. Now this theory of the course of religion in the distant and obscure past is conformable with experience of its actual history, so far as this lies within our knowledge. Whether we compare the early Greek with the later Greek, the early Jew with the later Jew, the ruder races of the world in their older condition with the same races as affected by the three missionary religions of Buddhism, Mohammedanism, Christianity, the testimony of history vouches for the like transition towards ethical dogma.

In conclusion, though theological argument on the actual validity of doctrines relating to the future life can have no place here, it will be well not to pass by without further remark one great practical question which lies fairly within the province of Ethnography. How, in the various stages of culture, has the character and conduct of the living been affected by the thought of a life to come ? If we take the savage beliefs as a starting-point, it will appear that these belong rather to speculative philosophy than to practical rule of life. The lower races hold opinions as to a future state because they think them true, but it is not surprising that men who take so little thought of a contingency three days off, should receive little practical impulse from vague anticipations of a life beyond the grave. Setting aside the consideration of possible races devoid of all thought of a future existence, there unquestionably has been and is a great mass of mankind whose lives are scarcely affected by such expectations of another life as they do hold. The doctrine of continuance, making death as it were a mere journey into a new country, can have little direct action on men's conduct, though indirectly it has indeed an enormous and disastrous influence on society, leading as it does to the slaughter of wives and slaves, and the destruction of property, for the use of the dead in the next world. If this world to come be thought a happier region, the looking forward to it makes men more willing to risk their lives in battle, promotes the habit of despatching the sick and aged into a better life, and encourages suicide when life is very hateful here. When the half-way house between continuance and retribution is reached, and the idea prevails that the manly virtues which give rank and wealth and honour here will lead hereafter to yet brighter glory, then this belief must add new force to the earthly motives which make bold warriors and mighty chiefs. But among men who expect to become hovering ghosts at death, or to depart to some gloomy land of shades, such expectation strengthens the natural horror and hatred of dissolution. They tend toward the state of mind frequent among modern Africans, whose thought of death is that he shall drink no more rum, wear no more fine clothes, have no more wives. The negro of our own day would feel to the utmost the sense of those lines in the beginning of the Iliad, which describe the heroes' ' souls ' being cast down to Hades, but ' themselves ' left a prey to dogs and carrion birds.

Rising to the level of the higher races, we mark the thought of future existence taking a larger and larger place in the convictions of religion, the expectation of a judgment after death gaining in intensity and becoming, what it scarcely seems to the savage, a real motive in life. Yet this change is not to be measured as proceeding throughout in any direct proportion with the development of culture. The doctrine of the future life has hardly taken deeper and stronger root in the higher than in the middle levels of civilization. In the language of ancient Egypt, it is the dead who are emphatically called the ' living,' for their life is everlasting, whether in the world of the departed, or nearer home in the tomb, the ' eternal dwelling.' The Moslem says that men sleep in life and wake in death ; the Hindu likens the body which a soul has quitted to the bed he rises from in the morning. The story of the ancient

Getæ, who wept at births and laughed at funerals, embodies an idea of the relation of this life to the next which comes to the surface again and again in the history of religion, nowhere perhaps touched in with a lighter hand than in the Arabian Nights' tale where Abdallah of the Sea indignantly breaks off his friendship with Abdallah of the Land, when he hears that the dwellers on the land do not feast and sing when one of them dies, like the dwellers in the sea, but mourn and weep and tear their garments. Such thoughts lead on into the morbid asceticism that culminates in the life of the Buddhist saint, eating his food with loathing from the alms-bowl that he carries as though it held medicine, wrapping himself in grave-clothes from the cemetery, or putting on his disfigured robe as though it were a bandage to cover a sore, whose looking forward is to death for deliverance from the misery of life, whose dreamiest hope is that after an inconceivable series of successive existences he may find in utter dissolution and not-being a refuge even from heaven.

The belief in future retribution has been indeed a powerful engine in shaping the life of nations. Powerful both for good and evil, it has been made the servant-of-all-work of many faiths. Priesthoods have used it unscrupulously for their professional ends, to gain wealth and power for their own caste, to stop intellectual and social progress beyond the barriers of their consecrated systems. On the banks of the river of death, a band of priests has stood for ages to bar the passage against all poor souls who cannot satisfy their demands for ceremonies, and formulas, and fees. This is the dark side of the picture. On the bright side, as we study the moral standards of the higher nations, and see how the hopes and fears of the life to come have been brought to enforce their teachings, it is plain that through most widely differing religions the doctrine of future judgment has been made to further goodness and to check wickedness, according to the shifting rules by which men have divided right from wrong. The philosophic schools

which from classic times onward have rejected the belief in
a future existence, appear to have come back by a new road
to the very starting-point which perhaps the rudest races of
men never quitted. At least this seems true as regards the
doctrine of future retribution, which is alike absent from
the belief of classes of men at the two extremes of culture.
How far the moral standard of life may have been adjusted
throughout the higher races with reference to a life hereafter, is a problem difficult of solution, so largely do unbelievers in this second life share ethical principles which
have been more or less shaped under its influence. Men
who live for one world or for two, have high motives of
virtue in common ; the noble self-respect which impels them
to the life they feel worthy of them ; the love of goodness
for its own sake and for its immediate results ; and beyond
this, the desire to do good that shall survive the doer, who
will not indeed be in the land of the living to see his work,
but who can yet discount his expectations into some measure
of present satisfaction. Yet he who believes that his thread
of life will be severed once and for ever by the fatal shears,
well knows that he wants a purpose and a joy in life, which
belong to him who looks for a life to come. Few men feel
real contentment in the expectation of vanishing out of conscious existence, henceforth, like the great Buddha, to exist
only in their works. To remain incarnate in the memory of
friends is something. A few great spirits may enjoy in the
reverence of future ages a thousand years or so of ' subjective immortality ; ' though as for mankind at large, the
individual's personal interest hardly extends beyond those
who have lived in his time, while his own memory scarce
outlives the third and fourth generation. But over and
above these secular motives, the belief in immortality
extends its powerful influence through life, and culminates
at the last hour, when, setting aside the very evidence of
their senses, the mourners smile through their tears, and
say it is not death but life.

CHAPTER XIV

ANIMISM (*continued*)

Animism, expanding from the Doctrine of Souls to the wider Doctrine of
  Spirits, becomes a complete Philosophy of Natural Religion—Definition
  of Spirits similar to and apparently modelled on that of Souls—Transition stage : classes of Souls passing into good and evil Demons—Manes-
  Worship—Doctrine of Embodiment of Spirits in human, animal, vegetable, and inert bodies—Demoniacal Possession and Obsession as causes
  of Disease and Oracle-inspiration—Fetishism—Disease-spirits embodied
  —Ghost attached to remains of Corpse—Fetish produced by a Spirit
  embodied in, attached to, or operating through, an Object—Analogues
  of Fetish-doctrine in Modern Science—Stock-and-Stone Worship—
  Idolatry—Survival of Animistic Phraseology in modern Language—
  Decline of Animistic theory of Nature.

THE general scheme of Animism, of which the doctrine of
souls hitherto discussed forms part, thence expands to complete the full general philosophy of Natural Religion among
mankind. Conformably with that early childlike philosophy
in which human life seems the direct key to the understanding of nature at large, the savage theory of the universe
refers its phenomena in general to the wilful action of pervading personal spirits. It was no spontaneous fancy, but
the reasonable inference that effects are due to causes, which
led the rude men of old days to people with such ethereal
phantoms their own homes and haunts, and the vast earth
and sky beyond. Spirits are simply personified causes. As
men's ordinary life and actions were held to be caused by
souls, so the happy or disastrous events which affect mankind, as well as the manifold physical operations of the

outer-world, were accounted for as caused by soul-like beings, spirits whose essential similarity of origin is evident through all their wondrous variety of power and function. Much that the primitive animistic view thus explains, has been indeed given over by more advanced education to the 'metaphysical' and 'positive' stages of thought. Yet animism is still plainly to be traced onward from the intellectual state of the lower races, along the course of the higher culture, whether its doctrines have been continued and modified into the accepted philosophy of religion, or whether they have dwindled into mere survivals in popular superstition. Though all I here undertake is to sketch in outline such features of this spiritualistic philosophy as I can see plainly enough to draw at all, scarcely attempting to clear away the haze that covers great parts of the subject, yet even so much as I venture on is a hard task, made yet harder by the responsibility attaching to it. For it appears that to follow the course of animism on from its more primitive stages, is to account for much of mediæval and modern opinion whose meaning and reason could hardly be comprehended without the aid of a development-theory of culture, taking in the various processes of new formation, abolition, survival, and revival. Thus even the despised ideas of savage races become a practically important topic to the modern world, for here, as usual, whatever bears on the origin of philosophic opinion, bears also on its validity.

At this point of the investigation, we come fully into sight of the principle which has been all along implied in the use of the word Animism, in a sense beyond its narrower meaning of the doctrine of souls. By using it to express the doctrine of spirits generally, it is practically asserted that the idea of souls, demons, deities, and any other classes of spiritual beings, are conceptions of similar nature throughout, the conceptions of souls being the original ones of the series. It was best, from this point of view, to begin with a careful study of souls, which are the spirits proper to men,

animals, and things, before extending the survey of the
spirit-world to its fullest range. If it be admitted that souls
and other spiritual beings are conceived of as essentially
similar in their nature, it may be reasonably argued that the
class of conceptions based on evidence most direct and
accessible to ancient men, is the earlier and fundamental
class. To grant this, is in effect to agree that the doctrine
of souls, founded on the natural perceptions of primitive
man, gave rise to the doctrine of spirits, which extends
and modifies its general theory for new purposes, but in
developments less authenticated and consistent, more fanciful and far-fetched. It seems as though the conception of
a human soul, when once attained to by man, served as a
type or model on which he framed not only his ideas of
other souls of lower grade, but also his ideas of spiritual
beings in general, from the tiniest elf that sports in the long
grass up to the heavenly Creator and Ruler of the world,
the Great Spirit.

The doctrines of the lower races fully justify us in classing
their spiritual beings in general as similar in nature to the
souls of men. It will be incidentally shown here, again
and again, that souls have the same qualities attributed to
them as other spirits, are treated in like fashion, and pass
without distinct breaks into every part of the general
spiritual definition. The similar nature of soul and other
spirit is, in fact, one of the commonplaces of animism, from
its rudest to its most cultured stages. It ranges from the
native New Zealanders' and West Indians' conceptions of
the ' atua ' and the ' cemi,' beings which require special
definition to show whether they are human souls or demons
or deities of some other class,[1] and so onward to the declaration of Philo Judæus, that souls, demons, and angels
differ indeed in name, but are in reality one,[2] and to the
state of mind of the modern Roman Catholic priest, who is

[1] See Taylor, ' New Zealand,' p. 134 ; J. G. Müller, ' Amerikanische Urre-
ligionen,' p. 171.
[2] Philo Jud. de Gigantibus, iv.

cautioned in the rubric concerning the examination of a possessed patient, not to believe the demon if he pretends to be the soul of some saint or deceased person, or a good angel (neque ei credatur, si dæmon simularet se esse animam alicujus Sancti, vel defuncti, vel Angelum bonum).[1] Nothing can bring more broadly into view the similar nature of souls and other spiritual beings than the existence of a full transitional series of ideas. Souls of dead men are in fact considered as actually forming one of the most important classes of demons and deities.

It is quite usual for savage tribes to live in terror of the souls of the dead as harmful spirits. Thus Australians have been known to consider the ghosts of the unburied dead as becoming malignant demons.[2] New Zealanders have supposed the souls of their dead to become so changed in nature as to be malignant to their nearest and dearest friends in life;[3] the Caribs said that, of man's various souls, some go to the seashore and capsize boats, others to the forest to be evil spirits;[4] among the Sioux Indians the fear of a ghost's vengeance has been found to act as a check on murder;[5] of some tribes in Central Africa it may be said that their main religious doctrine is the belief in ghosts, and that the main characteristic of these ghosts is to do harm to the living.[6] The Patagonians lived in terror of the souls of their wizards, which become evil demons after death;[7] Turanian tribes of North Asia fear their shamans even more when dead than when alive, for they become a special class of spirits who are the hurtfullest in all nature, and who among the Mongols plague the living on

---

[1] Rituale Romanum : De Exorcizandis Obsessis a Dæmonio.

[2] Oldfield, ' Abor. of Australia' in ' Tr. Eth. Soc.' vol. iii. p. 236. See Bonwick, ' Tasmanians,' p. 181.

[3] Taylor, ' New Zealand,' p. 104.

[4] Rochefort, ' Iles Antilles,' p. 429.

[5] Schoolcraft, ' Indian Tribes,' part ii. p. 195 ; M. Eastman, ' Dahcotah,' p. 72.

[6] Burton, ' Central Afr.' vol. ii. p. 344 ; Schlegel, ' Ewe-Sprache,' p. xxv.

[7] Falkner, ' Patagonia,' p. 116 ; but cf. Musters, p. 180.

purpose to make them bring offerings.[1] In China it is held that the multitudes of wretched destitute spirits in the world below, such as souls of lepers and beggars, can sorely annoy the living ; therefore at certain times they are to be appeased with offerings of food, scant and beggarly ; and a man who feels unwell, or fears a mishap in business, will prudently have some mock-clothing and mock-money burnt for these ' gentlemen of the lower regions.'[2] Notions of this sort are widely prevalent in Indo-China and India ; whole orders of demons there were formerly human souls, especially of people left unburied or slain by plague or violence, of bachelors or of women who died in childbirth, and who henceforth wreak their vengeance on the living. They may, however, be propitiated by temples and offerings, and thus have become in fact a regular class of local deities.[3] Among them may be counted the diabolic soul of a certain wicked British officer, whom native worshippers in the Tinnevelly district still propitiate by offering at his grave the brandy and cheroots he loved in life.[4] India even carried theory into practice by an actual manufacture of demons, as witness the two following accounts. A certain brahman, on whose lands a kshatriya raja had built a house, ripped himself up in revenge, and became a demon of the kind called brahmadasyu, who has been ever since the terror of the whole country, and is the most common village deity in Kharakpur.[5] Toward the close of the last century there were two brahmans, out of whose house a man had wrongfully, as they thought, taken forty rupees ; whereupon one of the brahmans proceeded to cut off his own mother's

[1] Castrén, ' Finn. Myth,' p. 122.
[2] Doolittle, ' Chinese,' vol. i. p. 206.
[3] Bastian, ' Oestl. Asien,' vol. ii. pp. 129, 416 ; vol. iii. pp. 29, 257, 278 ; ' Psychologie,' pp. 77, 99 ; Cross, ' Karens,' l.c. p. 316 ; Elliot in ' Journ. Eth. Soc.' vol. i. p. 115 ; Buchanan, ' Mysore, &c.,' in Pinkerton, vol. viii. p. 677.
[4] Shortt, ' Tribes of India,' in ' Tr. Eth. Soc.' vol. vii. p. 192 ; Tinling, ' Tour round India,' p. 19.
[5] Bastian, ' Psychologie,' p. 101.

head, with the professed view, entertained by both mother and son, that her spirit, excited by the beating of a large drum during forty days, might haunt, torment, and pursue to death the taker of their money and those concerned with him. Declaring with her last words that she would blast the thief, the spiteful hag deliberately gave up her life to take ghostly vengeance for those forty rupees.[1] By instances like these it appears that we may trace up from the psychology of the lower races the familiar ancient and modern European tales of baleful ghost-demons. The old fear even now continues to vouch for the old belief.

Happily for man's anticipation of death, and for the treatment of the sick and aged, thoughts of horror and hatred do not preponderate in ideas of deified ancestors, who are regarded on the whole as kindly patron spirits, at least to their own kinsfolk and worshippers. Manes-worship is one of the great branches of the religion of mankind. Its principles are not difficult to understand, for they plainly keep up the social relations of the living world. The dead ancestor, now passed into a deity, simply goes on protecting his own family and receiving suit and service from them as of old ; the dead chief still watches over his own tribe, still holds his authority by helping friends and harming enemies, still rewards the right and sharply punishes the wrong. It will be enough to show by a few characteristic examples the general position of manes-worship among mankind, from the lower culture upward.[2] In the two Americas it appears not unfrequently, from the low savage level of the Brazilian Camacans, to the somewhat higher stage of northern Indian tribes whom we hear of as praying to the spirits of their forefathers for good weather or luck in hunting, and fancying when an Indian falls into the fire that the ancestral spirits pushed him in to punish

[1] Sir J. Shore in ' Asiatic Res.' vol. iv. p. 331.
[2] For some collections of details of manes-worship, see Meiners, ' Geschichte der Religionen,' vol. i. book 3 ; Bastian, ' Mensch,' vol. ii. pp. 402-11 ; ' Psychologie,' pp. 72-114.

neglect of the customary gifts, while the Natchez of Louisiana are said to have even gone so far as to build temples
for dead men.[1] Turning to the dark races of the Pacific,
we find the Tasmanians laying their sick round a corpse
on the funeral pile, that the dead might come in the night
and take out the devils that caused the diseases ; it is asserted in a general way of the natives, that they believed
most implicitly in the return of the spirits of their departed
friends or relations to bless or injure them as the case might
be.[2] In Tanna, the gods are spirits of departed ancestors,
aged chiefs becoming deities after death, presiding over the
growth of yams and fruit trees, and receiving from the
islanders prayer and offerings of first fruits.[3] Nor are the
fairer Polynesians behind in this respect. Below the great
mythological gods of Tonga and New Zealand, the souls of
chiefs and warriors form a lower but active and powerful
order of deities, who in the Tongan paradise intercede for
man's benefit with the higher deities, who direct the Maori
war parties on the march, hover over them and give them
courage in the fight, and, watching jealously their own
tribes and families, punish any violation of the sacred laws
of tapu.[4] Thence we trace the doctrine into the Malay
islands, where the souls of deceased ancestors are looked
to for prosperity in life and help in distress.[5] In Madagascar, the worship of the spirits of the dead is remarkably
associated with the Vazimbas, the aborigines of the island,
who are said still to survive as a distinct race in the interior, and whose peculiar graves testify to their former occu-
pancy of other districts. These graves, small in size, and
distinguished by a cairn and an upright stone slab or altar,

[1] J. G. Müller, ' Amer. Urrel.' pp. 73, 173, 209, 261 ; Schoolcraft, ' Indian
Tribes,' part i. p. 39, part iii. p. 237 ; Waitz, ' Anthropologie,' vol. iii. pp. 191,
204.

[2] Backhouse, ' Australia,' p. 105 ; Bonwick, ' Tasmanians,' p. 182.

[3] Turner, ' Polynesia,' p. 88.

[4] Mariner, ' Tonga Is.' vol. ii. p. 104 ; S. S. Farmer, p. 126 ; Shortland,
' Trads. of N. Z.' p. 81 ; Taylor, ' New Zealand,' p. 108.

[5] J. R. Forster, ' Observations,' p. 604 ; Marsden, ' Sumatra,' p. 258 ;
' Journ. Ind. Archip.' vol. ii. p. 234.

are places which the Malagasy regard with equal fear and veneration, and their faces become sad and serious when they even pass near. To take a stone or pluck a twig from one of these graves, to stumble against one in the dark, would be resented by the angry Vazimba inflicting disease, or coming in the night to carry off the offender to the region of ghosts. The Malagasy is thus enabled to account for every otherwise unaccountable ailment by his having knowingly or unknowingly given offence to some Vazimba. They are not indeed always malevolent, they may be placable or implacable, or partake of both characters. Thus it comes to pass, that at the altar-slab which long ago some rude native family set up for commemoration or dutiful offering of food to a dead kinsman, a barbaric supplanting race now comes to smear the burnt fat of sacrifice, and set up the heads of poultry and sheep and the horns of bullocks, that the mysterious tenant may be kind, not cruel, with his superhuman powers.[1]

On the continent of Africa, manes-worship appears with extremest definiteness and strength. Thus Zulu warriors, aided by the ' amatongo,' the spirits of their ancestors, conquer in the battle ; but if the dead turn their backs on the living, the living fall in the fight, to become ancestral spirits in their turn. In anger the ' itongo ' seizes a living man's body and inflicts disease and death ; in beneficence he gives health, and cattle, and corn, and all men wish. Even the little children and old women, of small account in life, become at death spirits having much power, the infants for kindness, the crones for malice. But it is especially the head of each family who receives the worship of his kin. Why it is naturally and reasonably so, a Zulu thus explains. ' Although they worship the many Amatongo of their tribe, making a great fence around them for their protection ; yet their father is far before all others when they worship the Amatongo. Their father is a great

---

[1] Ellis, ' Madagascar,' vol. i. pp. 123, 423. As to the connexion of the Vazimbas with the Mazimba of East Africa, see Waitz, vol. ii. pp. 360, 426.

treasure to them even when he is dead. And those of his
children who are already grown up know him thoroughly,
his gentleness, and his bravery.' ' Black people do not
worship all Amatongo indifferently, that is, all the dead of
their tribe. Speaking generally, the head of each house is
worshipped by the children of that house ; for they do not
know the ancients who are dead, nor their laud-giving
names, nor their names. But their father whom they knew
is the head by whom they begin and end in their prayer,
for they know him best, and his love for his children ; they
remember his kindness to them whilst he was living ; they
compare his treatment of them whilst he was living, support themselves by it, and say, " He will still treat us in the
same way now he is dead. We do not know why he should
regard others besides us ; he will regard us only." '[1] It will
be seen in another place how the Zulu follows up the doctrine of divine ancestors till he reaches a first ancestor of
man and creator of the world, the primæval Unkulunkulu.
In West Africa, manes-worship displays in contrast its two
special types. On the one hand, we see the North Guinea
negroes transferring the souls of the dead, according to
their lives, to the rank of good and evil spirits, and if evil
worshipping them the more zealously, as fear is to their
minds a stronger impulse than love. On the other hand,
in Southern Guinea, we see the deep respect paid to the
aged during life, passing into worship when death has
raised them to yet higher influence. There the living bring
to the images of the dead food and drink, and even a small
portion of their profits gained in trade ; they look especially
to dead relatives for help in the trials of life, and ' it is no
uncommon thing to see large groups of men and women, in
times of peril or distress, assembled along the brow of some
commanding eminence, or along the skirts of some dense

[1] Callaway, ' Religious System of Amazulu,' part ii. ; see also Arbousset
and Daumas, p. 469; Casalis, ' Basutos,' pp. 248-54; Waitz, ' Anthropologie,' vol. ii. pp. 411, 419 ; Magyar, ' Reisen in Süd-Afrika,' pp. 21, 335
(Congo) ; Cavazzi, ' Congo,' lib. i.

forest, calling in the most piteous and touching tones upon the spirits of their ancestors.'[1]

In Asia, manes-worship comes to the surface in all directions. The rude Veddas of Ceylon believe in the guardianship of the spirits of the dead ; these, they say, are ' ever watchful, coming to them in sickness, visiting them in dreams, giving them flesh when hunting;' and in every calamity and want they call for aid on the ' kindred spirits,' and especially the shades of departed children, the ' infant spirits.'[2] Among non-Hindu tribes of India, whose religions more or less represent præ-Brahmanic and præ-Buddhistic conditions, wide and deep traces appear of an ancient and surviving cultus of ancestors.[3] Among Turanian tribes spread over the northern regions of the Old World, a similar state of things may be instanced from the Mongols, worshipping as good deities the princely souls of Genghis Khan's family, at whose head stands the divine Genghis himself.[4] Nor have nations of the higher Asiatic culture generally rejected the time-honoured rite. In Japan the ' Way of the Kami,' better known to foreigners as the Sin-tu religion, is one of the officially recognized faiths, and in it there is still kept up in hut and palace the religion of the rude old mountain-tribes of the land, who worshipped their divine ancestors, the Kami, and prayed to them for help and blessing. To the time of these ancient Kami, say the modern Japanese, the rude stone implements belong which are found in the ground in Japan as elsewhere: to modern ethnologists, however, these bear witness not of divine but savage parentage.[5] In Siam the lower orders scruple to

[1] J. L. Wilson, ' W. Afr.' pp. 217, 388-93. See Waitz, vol. ii. pp. 181, 194.

[2] Bailey in ' Tr. Eth. Soc.' vol. ii. p. 301. Compare Taylor, ' New Zealand,' p. 153.

[3] Buchanan, ' Mysore,' in Pinkerton, vol. viii. pp. 674-7. See Macpherson, ' India,' p. 95 (Khonds) ; Hunter, ' Rural Bengal,' p. 183 (Santals).

[4] Castrén, ' Finn. Myth.' p. 122 ; Bastian, ' Psychologie,' p. 90. See Palgrave, ' Arabia,' vol. i. p. 373.

[5] Siebold, ' Nippon,' vol. i. p. 3, vol. ii. p. 51 ; Kempfer, ' Japan,' in Pinkerton, vol. vii. pp. 672, 680, 723, 755.

worship the great gods, lest through ignorance they should blunder in the complex ritual ; they prefer to pray to the ' theparak,' a lower class of deities among whom the souls of great men take their places at death.[1]　In China, as every one knows, ancestor-worship is the dominant religion of the land, and interesting problems are opened out to the Western mind by the spectacle of a great people who for thousands of years have been thus seeking the living among the dead.　Nowhere is the connexion between parental authority and conservatism more graphically shown.　The worship of ancestors, begun during their life, is not interrupted but intensified when death makes them deities.　The Chinese, prostrate bodily and mentally before the memorial tablets that contain the souls of his ancestors, little thinks that he is all the while proving to mankind how vast a power unlimited filial obedience, prohibiting change from ancestral institutions, may exert in stopping the advance of civilization.　The thought of the souls of the dead as sharing the happiness and glory of their descendants is one which widely pervades the world, but most such ideas would seem vague and weak to the Chinese, who will try hard for honour in his competitive examination with the special motive of glorifying his dead ancestors, and whose titles of rank will raise his deceased father and grandfather a grade above himself, as though, with us, Zachary Macaulay and Copley the painter should now have viscounts' coronets officially placed on their tombstones.　As so often happens, what is jest to one people is sober sense to another.　There are 300 millions of Chinese who would hardly see a joke in Charles Lamb reviling the stupid age that would not read him, and declaring that he would write for antiquity.　Had he been a Chinese himself, he might have written his book in all seriousness for the benefit of his great-great-grandfather.　Among the Chinese, manes-worship is no rite of mere affection.　The living want the help of the ancestral spirits, who reward virtue and punish vice : ' The exalted

[1] Bastian, ' Oestl. Asien,' vol. iii. p. 250.

ancestor will bring thee, O Prince, much good ! '—' Ancestors and fathers will abandon you and give you up, and come not to help, and ye will die.' If no help comes in time of need, the Chinese will reproach his ancestor, or even come to doubt his existence. Thus in a Chinese ode the sufferers in a dreadful drought cry, ' Heu-tsi cannot or will not help. . . . Our ancestors have surely perished. . . . Father, mother, ancestors, how could you calmly bear this ? ' Nor does manes-worship stop short with direct family ties ; it is naturally developed to produce, by deification of the heroic dead, a series of superior gods to whom worship is given by the public at large. Thus, according to legend, the War-god or Military Sage was once in human life a distinguished soldier, the Mechanics' god was a skilful workman and inventor of tools, the Swine-god was a hog-breeder who lost his pigs and died of sorrow, and the Gamblers' god, a desperate gamester who lost his all and died of want, is represented by a hideous image called a ' devil gambling for cash,' and in this shape receives the prayers and offerings of confirmed gamblers, his votaries. The spirits of San-kea Ta-te, and Chang-yuen-sze go to partake of the offerings set out in their temples, returning flushed and florid from their meal ; and the spirit of Confucius is present in the temple, where twice a year the Emperor does sacrifice to him.[1]

The Hindu unites in some degree with the Chinese as to ancestor-worship, and especially as to the necessity of having a son by blood or adoption, who shall offer the proper sacrifices to him after death. ' May there be born in our lineage,' the manes are supposed to say, ' a man to offer to us, on the thirteenth day of the moon, rice boiled in milk, honey and ghee.' Offerings made to the divine manes, the ' pitaras ' (patres, fathers) as they are called, preceded and followed by offerings to the greater deities, give to the worshipper merit

---

[1] Plath, ' Religion der alten Chinesen,' part i. p. 65, part ii. p. 89 ; Doolittle, ' Chinese,' vol. i. pp. vi. viii. ; vol. ii. p. 373 ; ' Journ. Ind. Archip.' New Ser. vol. ii. p. 363 ; Legge, ' Confucius,' p. 92.

and happiness.[1] In classic Europe, apotheosis lies part within the limits of myth, where it was applied to fabled ancestors, and part within the limits of actual history, as where Julius and Augustus shared its honours with the vile Domitian and Commodus. The most special representatives of ancestor-worship in Europe were perhaps the ancient Romans, whose word ' manes ' has become the recognized name for ancestral deities in modern civilized language ; they embodied them as images, set them up as household patrons, gratified them with offerings and solemn homage, and counting them as or among the infernal gods, inscribed on tombs D. M., ' Diis Manibus.'[2] The occurrence of this D. M. in Christian epitaphs is an often-noticed case of religious survival.

Although full ancestor-worship is not practised in modern Christendom, there remains even now within its limits a well-marked worship of the dead. A crowd of saints, who were once men and women, now form an order of inferior deities, active in the affairs of men and receiving from them reverence and prayer, thus coming strictly under the definition of manes. This Christian cultus of the dead, belonging in principle to the older manes-worship, was adapted to answer another purpose in the course of religious transition in Europe. The local gods, the patron gods of particular ranks and crafts, the gods from whom men sought special help in special needs, were too near and dear to the inmost heart of præ-Christian Europe to be done away with without substitutes. It proved easier to replace them by saints who could undertake their particular professions, and even succeed them in their sacred dwellings. The system of spiritual division of labour was in time worked out with wonderful minuteness in the vast array of professional saints, among whom the most familiar to modern English ears are St. Cecilia, patroness of musicians ; St. Luke, patron

[1] Manu, book iii.
[2] Details in Pauly, ' Real-Encyclop.' s.v. 'inferi ' ; Smith's ' Dic. of Gr. and Rom. Biog. and Myth.' ; Meiners, Hartung, &c.

of painters ; St. Peter, of fishmongers ; St. Valentine, of lovers ; St. Sebastian, of archers ; St. Crispin, of cobblers ; St. Hubert, who cures the bite of mad dogs ; St. Vitus, who delivers madmen and sufferers from the disease which bears his name ; St. Fiacre, whose name is now less known by his shrine than by the hackney-coaches called after him in the seventeenth century. Not to dwell here minutely on an often-treated topic, it will be enough to touch on two particular points. First, as to the direct historical succession of the Christian saint to the heathen deity, the following are two very perfect illustrations. It is well known that Romulus, mindful of his own adventurous infancy, became after death a Roman deity propitious to the health and safety of young children, so that nurses and mothers would carry sickly infants to present them in his little round temple at the foot of the Palatine. In after ages the temple was replaced by the church of St. Theodorus, and there Dr. Conyers Middleton, who drew public attention to its curious history, used to look in and see ten or a dozen women, each with a sick child in her lap, sitting in silent reverence before the altar of the saint. The ceremony of blessing children, especially after vaccination, may still be seen there on Thursday mornings.[1] Again, Sts. Cosmas and Damianus, according to Maury, owe their recognized office to a similar curious train of events. They were martyrs who suffered under Diocletian, at Ægææ in Cilicia. Now this place was celebrated for the worship of Æsculapius, in whose temple incubation, i.e. sleeping for oracular dreams, was practised. It seems as though the idea was transferred on the spot to the two local saints, for we next hear of them as appearing in a dream to the Emperor Justinian, when he was ill at Byzantium. They cured him, he built them a temple, their cultus spread far and wide, and they frequently appeared to the sick to show them what they should do. Legend settled that Cosmas and Damianus were physicians while they lived on earth,

[1] Middleton, ' Letter from Rome ' ; Murray's 'Handbook of Rome.'

and at any rate they are patron-saints of the profession of medicine to this day.[1] Second, as to the actual state of hagiolatry in modern Europe, it is obvious on a broad view that it is declining among the educated classes. Yet modern examples may be brought forward to show ideas as extreme as those which prevailed more widely a thousand years ago. In the Church of the Jesuit College at Rome lies buried St. Aloysius Gonzaga, on whose festival it is customary especially for the college students to write letters to him, which are placed on his gaily decorated and illuminated altar, and afterwards burnt unopened. The miraculous answering of these letters is vouched for in an English book of 1870. To the same year belongs an English tract commemorating a late miraculous cure. An Italian lady afflicted with a tumour and incipient cancer of the breast was exhorted by a Jesuit priest to recommend herself to the Blessed John Berchmans, a pious Jesuit novice from Belgium, who died in 1621, and was beatified in 1865. Her adviser procured for her 'three small packets of dust gathered from the coffin of this saintly innocent, a little cross made of the boards of the room the blessed youth occupied, as well as some portion of the wadding in which his venerable head was wrapped.' During nine days' devotion the patient accordingly invoked the Blessed John, swallowed small portions of his dust in water, and at last pressed the cross to her breast so vehemently that she was seized with sickness, went to sleep, and awoke without a symptom of the complaint. And when Dr. Panegrossi the physician beheld the incredible cure, and heard that the patient had addressed herself to the Blessed Berchmans, he bowed his head, saying, ' When such physicians interfere, *we* have nothing more to say !'[2] To sum up the whole

[1] L. F. Alfred Maury, ' Magie, &c.,' p. 249 ; ' Acta Sanctorum,' 27 Sep. ; Gregor. Turon. De Gloria Martyr, i. 98.

[2] J. R. Beste, ' Nowadays at Home and Abroad,' London, 1870, vol. ii. p. 44 ; ' A New Miracle at Rome ; being an Account of a Miraculous Cure, &c., &c.,' London (Washbourne), 1870.

history of manes-worship, it is plain that in our time the dead still receive worship from far the larger half of mankind, and it may have been much the same ever since the remote periods of primitive culture in which the religion of the manes probably took its rise.

It has now been seen that the theory of souls recognizes them as capable either of independent existence, or of inhabiting human, animal, or other bodies. On the principle here maintained, that the general theory of spirits is modelled on the theory of souls, we shall be able to account for several important branches of the lower philosophy of religion, which without such explanation may appear in great measure obscure or absurd. Like souls, other spirits are supposed able either to exist and act flitting free about the world, or to become incorporate for more or less time in solid bodies. It will be well at once to get a secure grasp of this theory of Embodiment, for without it we shall be stopped every moment by a difficulty in understanding the nature of spirits, as defined in the lower animism. The theory of embodiment serves several highly important purposes in savage and barbarian philosophy. On the one hand it provides an explanation of the phenomena of morbid exaltation and derangement, especially as connected with abnormal utterance, and this view is so far extended as to produce an almost general doctrine of disease. On the other hand, it enables the savage either to ' lay ' a hurtful spirit in some foreign body, and so get rid of it, or to carry about a useful spirit for his service in a material object, to set it up as a deity for worship in the body of an animal, or in a block or stone or image or other thing, which contains the spirit as a vessel contains a fluid : this is the key to strict fetishism, and in no small measure to idolatry. In briefly considering these various branches of the Embodiment-theory, there may be conveniently included certain groups of cases often impossible to distinguish apart. These cases belong theoretically rather to obsession than possession, the spirits not actually inhabiting the bodies, but hanging or hovering about them and affecting them from the outside.

As in normal conditions the man's soul, inhabiting his body, is held to give it life, to think, speak, and act through it, so an adaptation of the self-same principle explains abnormal conditions of body or mind, by considering the new symptoms as due to the operation of a second soul-like being, a strange spirit. The possessed man, tossed and shaken in fever, pained and wrenched as though some live creature were tearing or twisting him within, pining as though it were devouring his vitals day by day, rationally finds a personal spiritual cause for his sufferings. In hideous dreams he may even sometimes see the very ghost or nightmare-fiend that plagues him. Especially when the mysterious unseen power throws him helpless on the ground, jerks and writhes him in convulsions, makes him leap upon the bystanders with a giant's strength and a wild beast's ferocity, impels him, with distorted face and frantic gesture, and voice not his own nor seemingly even human, to pour forth wild incoherent raving, or with thought and eloquence beyond his sober faculties to command, to counsel, to foretell—such a one seems to those who watch him, and even to himself, to have become the mere instrument of a spirit which has seized him or entered into him, a possessing demon in whose personality the patient believes so implicitly that he often imagines a personal name for it, which it can declare when it speaks in its own voice and character through his organs of speech; at last, quitting the medium's spent and jaded body, the intruding spirit departs as it came. This is the savage theory of dæmoniacal possession and obsession, which has been for ages, and still remains, the dominant theory of disease and inspiration among the lower races. It is obviously based on an animistic interpretation, most genuine and rational in its proper place in man's intellectual history, of the actual symptoms of the cases. The general doctrine of disease-spirits and oracle-spirits appears to have its earliest, broadest, and most consistent position within the limits of savagery. When we have gained a clear idea of it in this its original home, we shall be able to trace it along from grade to grade of civilization, breaking away piecemeal under the influence of new medical theories, yet sometimes expanding in revival, and at least in lingering survival holding its place into the midst of our modern life. The possession-theory is not merely known to us by the statements of those who describe diseases in accordance with it. Disease being accounted for by attack of spirits, it naturally follows that to get rid of these spirits is the proper means of cure. Thus the practices of the exorcist appear side by side with the doctrine of possession, from its first appearance in savagery to its survival in modern civilization; and nothing could display more vividly the conception of a disease or a mental affection as caused by a personal spiritual being than the proceedings of the exorcist who talks to it, coaxes or threatens it, makes offerings to it, entices or drives it out of the patient's body, and induces it to take up its abode in some other. That the two great effects ascribed to such spiritual influence in obsession and possession, namely, the infliction of ailments and the inspiration of oracles, are not only mixed up together but often run into absolute coincidence, accords with the view that both results are referred to one common cause. Also that the intruding or invading spirit may be either a human soul or may belong to some other class in the spiritual hierarchy, countenances the opinion that the possession-theory is derived from, and indeed modelled on, the ordinary theory of the soul acting on the body. In illustrating the doctrine by typical examples from the enormous mass of available details, it will hardly be possible to discriminate among the operating spirits, between those which are souls and those which are demons, nor to draw an exact line between obsession by a demon outside and possession by a demon inside, nor between the condition of the demon-tormented patient and the demon-actuated doctor, seer, or priest. In a word, the confusion of these conceptions in the savage mind only fairly represents their intimate connexion in the Possession-theory itself.

In the Australian-Tasmanian district, disease and death are ascribed to more or less defined spiritual influences ; descriptions of a demon working a sorcerer's wicked will by coming slyly behind his victim and hitting him with his club on the back of his neck, and of a dead man's ghost angered by having his name uttered, and creeping up into the utterer's body to consume his liver, are indeed peculiarly graphic details of savage animism.[1] The theory of disease-spirits is well stated in its extreme form among the Mintira, a low race of the Malay peninsula. Their ' hantu ' or spirits have among their functions that of causing ailments ; thus the ' hantu kalumbahan ' causes small-pox ; the ' hantu kamang' brings on inflammation and swellings in the hands and feet ; when a person is wounded, the ' hantu pari ' fastens on the wound and sucks, and this is the cause of the blood flowing. And thus, as the describer says, ' To enumerate the remainder of the hantus would be merely to convert the name of every species of disease known to the Mintira into a proper one. If any new disease appeared, it would be ascribed to a hantu bearing the same name.'[2] It will help us to an idea of the distinct personality which the disease-demon has in the minds of the lower races, to notice the Orang Laut of this district placing thorns and brush in the paths leading to a part where small-pox had broken out, to keep the demons off ; just as the Khonds of Orissa try with thorns, and ditches, and stinking oil poured on the ground, to barricade the paths to their hamlets against the goddess of small-pox, Jugah Pennu.[3] Among the Dayaks of Borneo, ' to have been smitten by a spirit ' is to be ill ; sickness may be caused

---

[1] Oldfield in ' Tr. Eth. Soc.' vol. iii. p. 235 ; see Grey, ' Australia,' vol. ii. p. 337. Bonwick, 'Tasmanians,' pp. 183, 195.

[2] ' Journ. Ind. Archip.' vol. i. p. 307.

[3] Bastian, ' Psychologie,' p. 204 ; ' Mensch,' vol. ii. p. 73, see p. 125 (Battas); Macpherson, 'India,' p. 370. See also Mason, 'Karens,' l. c. p. 201.

by invisible spirits inflicting invisible wounds with invisible spears, or entering men's bodies and driving out their souls, or lodging in their hearts and making them raving mad. In the Indian Archipelago, the personal semi-human nature of the disease-spirits is clearly acknowledged by appeasing them with feasts and dances and offerings of food set out for them away in the woods, to induce them to quit their victims, or by sending tiny proas to sea with offerings, that spirits which have taken up their abode in sick men's bowels may embark and not come back.[1] The animistic theory of disease is strongly marked in Polynesia, where every sickness is ascribed to spiritual action of deities, brought on by the offerings of enemies, or by the victim's violation of the laws of tapu. Thus in New Zealand each ailment is caused by a spirit, particularly an infant or un-developed human spirit, which sent into the patient's body gnaws and feeds inside ; and the exorcist, finding the path by which such a disease-spirit came from below to feed on the vitals of a sick relative, will persuade it by a charm to get upon a flax-stalk and set off home. We hear, too, of an idea of the parts of the body—forehead, breast, stomach, feet, &c.—being apportioned each to a deity who inflicts aches and pains and ailments there.[2] So in the Samoan group, when a man was near death, people were anxious to part on good terms with him, feeling assured that if he died with angry feelings towards any one, he would certainly return and bring calamity on that person or some one closely allied to him. This was considered a frequent source of disease and death, the spirit of a departed member of the family returning and taking up his abode in the head, chest, or stomach of a living man, and so causing sickness and death. If a man died suddenly, it was thought that he was

---

[1] 'Journ. Ind. Archip.' vol. iii. p. 110, vol. iv. p. 194; St. John, 'Far East,' vol. i. pp. 71, 87 ; Beeckman in Pinkerton, vol. ix. p. 133 ; Meiners, vol. i. p. 278. See also Doolittle, 'Chinese,' vol. i. p. 159.

[2] Shortland, 'Trads. of N. Z.' pp. 97, 114, 125 ; Taylor, 'New Zealand,' pp. 48, 137.

eaten by the spirit that took him ; and though the soul of
one thus devoured would go to the common spirit-land of
the departed, yet it would have no power of speech there,
and if questioned could but beat its breast. It completes
this account to notice that the disease-inflicting souls of the
departed were the same which possessed the living under
more favourable circumstances, coming to talk through a
certain member of the family, prophesying future events,
and giving directions as to family affairs.[1] Farther east, in
the Georgian and Society Islands, evil demons are sent to
scratch and tear people into convulsions and hysterics, to
torment poor wretches as with barbed hooks, or to twist and
knot inside them till they die writhing in agony. But madmen are to be treated with great respect, as entered by
a god, and idiots owe the kindness with which they are
appeased and coaxed to the belief in their superhuman
inspiration.[2] Here, and elsewhere in the lower culture,
the old real belief has survived which has passed into a
jest of civilized men in the famous phrase of the ' inspired
idiot.'

American ethnography carries on the record of rude races
ascribing disease to the action of evil spirits. Thus the
Dacotas believe that the spirits punish them for misconduct,
especially for neglecting to make feasts for the dead ; these
spirits have the power to send the spirit of something, as
of a bear, deer, turtle, fish, tree, stone, worm, or deceased
person, which entering the patient causes disease ; the
medicine-man's cure consists in reciting charms over him,
singing ' He-le-li-lah, &c.,' to the accompaniment of a
gourd-rattle with beads inside, ceremonially shooting a
symbolic bark representation of the intruding creature,
sucking over the seat of pain to get the spirit out, and

---

[1] Turner, ' Polynesia,' p. 236.

[2] Ellis, ' Polyn. Res.' vol. i. pp. 363, 395, &c., vol. ii. pp. 193, 274 ;
Cook, ' 3rd Voy.' vol. iii. p. 131. Details of the superhuman character
ascribed to weak or deranged persons among other races, in Schoolcraft,
part iv. p. 49 ; Martius, vol i. p. 633 ; Meiners, vol. i. p. 323 ; Waitz, vol. ii.
p. 181.

firing guns at it as it is supposed to be escaping.[1] Such
processes were in full vogue in the West Indies in the time
of Columbus, when Friar Roman Pane put on record his
quaint account of the native sorcerer pulling the disease off
the patient's legs (as one pulls off a pair of trousers), going
out of doors to blow it away, and bidding it begone to the
mountain or the sea ; the performance concluding with the
regular sucking-cure and the pretended extraction of some
stone or bit of flesh, or such thing, which the patient is
assured that his patron-spirit or deity (cemi) put into him
to cause the disease, in punishment for neglect to build him
a temple or honour him with prayer or offerings of goods.[2]
Patagonians considered sickness as caused by a spirit entering the patient's body ; ' they believe every sick person to
be possessed of an evil demon ; hence their physicians
always carry a drum with figures of devils painted on it,
which they strike at the beds of sick persons to drive out
from the body the evil demon which causes the disorder.'[3]
In Africa, according to the philosophy of the Basutos and
the Zulus, the causes of disease are the ghosts of the dead,
come to draw the living to themselves, or to compel them
to sacrifice meat-offerings. They are recognized by the
diviners, or by the patient himself, who sees in dreams the
departed spirit come to torment him. Congo tribes in like
manner consider the souls of the dead, passed into the ranks
of powerful spirits, to cause disease and death among mankind. Thus, in both these districts, medicine becomes an
almost entirely religious matter of propitiatory sacrifice
and prayer addressed to the disease-inflicting manes. The

---

[1] Schoolcraft, ' Indian Tribes,' part i. p. 250, part ii. pp. 179, 199,
part iii. p. 498 ; M. Eastman, ' Dahcotah,' pp. xxiii. 34, 41, 72. See also
Gregg, ' Commerce of Prairies,' vol. ii. p. 297 (Comanches) ; Morgan,
' Iroquois,' p. 163 ; Sproat, p. 174 (Ahts) ; Egede, ' Greenland,' p. 186 ;
Cranz, p. 269.

[2] Roman Pane, xix. in ' Life of Colon ' ; in Pinkerton, vol. xii. p. 87.

[3] D'Orbigny, ' L'Homme Américain,' vol. ii. pp. 73, 168 ; Musters,
' Patagonians,' p. 180. Se also J. G. Müller, pp. 207, 231 (Caribs) ; Spix
and Martius, ' Brasilien,' vol. i. p. 70 ; Martius, ' Ethnog. Amer.' vol. i. p. 646
(Marcusis).

Barolong give a kind of worship to deranged persons, as
being under the direct influence of a deity ; while in East
Africa the explanation of madness and idiocy is simple
and typical—' he has fiends.'[1] Negroes of West Africa, on
the supposition that an attack of illness has been caused
by some spiritual being, can ascertain to their satisfaction
what manner of spirit has done it, and why. The patient
may have neglected his ' wong ' or fetish-spirit, who has
therefore made him ill ; or it may be his own ' kla ' or
personal guardian-spirit, who on being summoned explains
that he has not been treated respectfully enough, &c. ; or
it may be a ' sisa ' or ghost of some dead man, who has
taken this means of making known that he wants perhaps
a gold ornament that was left behind when he died.[2] Of
course, the means of cure will then be to satisfy the demands
of the spirit. Another aspect of the negro doctrine of
disease-spirits is displayed in the following description from
Guinea, by the Rev. J. L. Wilson, the missionary :—' Demoniacal possessions are common, and the feats performed
by those who are supposed to be under such influence are
certainly not unlike those described in the New Testament.
Frantic gestures, convulsions, foaming at the mouth, feats
of supernatural strength, furious ravings, bodily lacerations,
gnashing of teeth, and other things of a similar character,
may be witnessed in most of the cases which are supposed
to be under diabolical influence.'[3] The remark several
times made by travellers is no doubt true, that the spiritualistic theory of disease has tended strongly to prevent
progress in the medical art among the lower races. Thus
among the Bodo and Dhimal of North-East India, who
ascribe all diseases to a deity tormenting the patient for
some impiety or neglect, the exorcists divine the offended

[1] Casalis, ' Basutos,' p. 247 ; Callaway, ' Rel. of Amazulu,' p. 147, &c. ;
Magyar, ' Süd-Afrika,' p. 21, &c. ; Burton, ' Central Afr.' vol. ii. pp. 320,
354 ; Steere in ' Journ. Anthrop. Inst.' vol. i. 1871, p. cxlvii.
[2] Steinhauser, ' Religion des Negers,' in ' Magaz. der Evang. Missions und
Bibel-Gesellschaften,' Basel, 1856, No. 2, p. 139.
3 J. L. Wilson, ' W. Afr.' pp. 217, 388.

god and appease him with the promised sacrifice of a hog ;
these exorcists are a class of priests, and the people have
no other doctors.[1] Where the world-wide doctrine of
disease-demons has held sway, men's minds, full of spells
and ceremonies, have scarce had room for thought of drugs
and regimen.

The cases in which disease-possession passes into oracle-
possession are especially connected with hysterical, convulsive, and epileptic affections. Mr. Backhouse describes a
Tasmanian native sorcerer, ' affected with fits of spasmodic
contraction of the muscles of one breast,which he attributes,
as they do all other diseases, to the devil ' ; this malady
served to prove his inspiration to his people.[2] When Dr.
Mason was preaching near a village of heathen Pwo, a man
fell down in an epileptic fit, his familiar spirit having come
over him to forbid the people to listen to the missionary,
and he sang out his denunciations like one frantic. This
man was afterwards converted, and told the missionary that
' he could not account for his former exercises, but that it
certainly appeared to him as though a spirit spoke, and he
must tell what was communicated.' In this Karen district
flourishes the native ' wee ' or prophet, whose business is
to work himself into the state in which he can see departed
spirits, visit their distant home, and even recall them to the
body, thus raising the dead ; these wees are nervous excit-
able men, such as would become mediums, and in giving
oracles they go into actual convulsions.[3] Dr. Callaway's
details of the state of the Zulu diviners are singularly instructive. Their symptoms are ascribed to possession by
' amatongo ' or ancestral spirits ; the disease is common,
from some it departs of its own accord, others have the
ghost laid which causes it, and others let the affection take
its course and become professional diviners, whose powers
of finding hidden things and giving apparently inaccessible

[1] Hodgson, ' Abor. of India,' pp. 163, 170.
[2] Backhouse, ' Australia,' p. 103.
[3] Mason, ' Burmah,' p. 107, &c. Cross, l.c. p. 305.

information are vouched for by native witnesses, who at the
same time are not blind to their tricks and their failures.
The most perfect description is that of a hysterical visionary, who had ' the disease which precedes the power to
divine.' This man describes that well-known symptom of
hysteria, the heavy weight creeping up within him to his
shoulders, his vivid dreams, his waking visions of objects
that are not there when he approaches, the songs that come
to him without learning, the sensation of flying in the air.
This man was ' of a family who are very sensitive, and become doctors.'[1] Persons whose constitutional unsoundness
induces morbid manifestations are indeed marked out by
nature to become seers and sorcerers. Among the Patagonians, patients seized with falling sickness or St. Vitus's
dance were at once selected for magicians, as chosen by the
demons themselves who possessed, distorted, and convulsed
them.[2] Among Siberian tribes, the shamans select children
liable to convulsions as suitable to be brought up to the
profession, which is apt to become hereditary with the
epileptic tendencies it belongs to.[3] Thus, even in the lower
culture, a class of sickly brooding enthusiasts begin to have
that power over the minds of their lustier fellows, which
they have kept in so remarkable a way through the course
of history.

Morbid oracular manifestations are habitually excited on
purpose, and moreover the professional sorcerer commonly
exaggerates or wholly feigns them. In the more genuine
manifestations the medium may be so intensely wrought
upon by the idea that a possessing spirit is speaking from
within him, that he may not only give this spirit's name and
speak in its character, but possibly may in good faith alter
his voice to suit the spiritual utterance. This gift of spirit-
utterance, which belongs to ' ventriloquism ' in the ancient
and proper sense of the term, of course lapses into sheer

[1] Callaway, ' Religion of Amazulu,' pp. 183, &c., 259, &c.
[2] Falkner, ' Patagonia,' p. 116. See also Rochefort, ' Iles Antilles,' p. 418 (Caribs).
[3] Georgi, ' Reise im Russ. Reich,' vol. i. p. 280 ; Meiners, vol. ii. p. 488.

trickery. But that the phenomena should be thus artificially excited or dishonestly counterfeited, rather confirms than alters the present argument. Real or simulated, the details of oracle-possession alike illustrate popular belief. The Patagonian wizard begins his performance with drumming and rattling till the real or pretended epileptic fit comes on by the demon entering him, who then answers questions from within him with a faint and mournful voice.[1] In Southern India and Ceylon the so-called ' devil-dancers ' have to work themselves into paroxysms, to gain the inspiration whereby they profess to cure their patients.[2] So, with furious dancing to the music and chanting of the attendants, the Bodo priest brings on the fit of maniacal inspiration in which the deity fills him and gives oracles through him.[3] In Kamchatka the female shamans, when Billukai came down into them in a thunderstorm, would prophesy ; or, receiving spirits with a cry of ' hush ! ' their teeth chattered as in fever, and they were ready to divine.[4] Among the Singpho of South-East Asia, when the ' natzo ' or conjurer is sent for to a sick patient, he calls on his ' nat ' or demon, the soul of a deceased foreign prince, who descends into him and gives the required answers.[5] In the Pacific Islands, spirits of the dead would enter for a time the body of a living man, inspiring him to declare future events, or to execute some commission from the higher deities. The symptoms of oracular possession among savages have been especially well described in this region of the world. The Fijian priest sits looking steadfastly at a whale's tooth ornament, amid dead silence. In a few minutes he trembles, slight twitchings of face and limbs come on, which increase to strong convulsions, with swelling of the veins, murmurs and sobs. Now the god has entered

[1] Falkner, l.c.
[2] Caldwell, ' Dravidian Languages,' App. ; Latham, vol. ii. p. 469.
[3] Hodgson, ' Abor. of India,' p. 172.
[4] Steller, ' Kamtschatka,' p. 278.
[5] Bastian, ' Oestl. Asien,' vol. ii. p. 328, see vol. iii. p. 201, ' Psychologie,' p. 139. See also Römer, ' Guinea,' p. 59.

him, and with eyes rolling and protruding, unnatural voice, pale face and livid lips, sweat streaming from every pore, and the whole aspect of a furious madman, he gives the divine answer, and then, the symptoms subsiding, he looks round with a vacant stare, and the deity returns to the land of spirits. In the Sandwich Islands, where the god Oro thus gave his oracles, his priest ceased to act or speak as a voluntary agent, but with his limbs convulsed, his features distorted and terrific, his eyes wild and strained, he would roll on the ground foaming at the mouth, and reveal the will of the possessing god in shrill cries and sounds violent and indistinct, which the attending priests duly interpreted to the people. In Tahiti, it was often noticed that men who in the natural state showed neither ability nor eloquence, would in such convulsive delirium burst forth into earnest lofty declamation, declaring the will and answers of the gods, and prophesying future events, in well-knit harangues full of the poetic figure and metaphor of the professional orator. But when the fit was over, and sober reason returned, the prophet's gifts were gone.[1] Lastly, the accounts of oracular possession in Africa show the primitive ventriloquist in perfect types of morbid knavery. In Sofala, after a king's funeral, his soul would enter into a sorcerer, and speaking in the familiar tones that all the bystanders recognized, would give counsel to the new monarch how to govern his people.[2] About a century ago, a negro fetish-woman of Guinea is thus described in the act of answering an enquirer who has come to consult her. She is crouching on the earth, with her head between her knees and her hands up to her face, till, becoming inspired by the fetish, she snorts and foams and gasps. Then the suppliant may put his question, ' Will my friend or brother get well of this sickness ? '—' What shall I give thee to set him free from his sickness ? ' and so

[1] Ellis, ' Polyn. Res.' vol. i. pp. 352, 373 ; Moerenhout, ' Voyage,' vol. i. p. 479 ; Mariner, ' Tonga Islands,' vol. i. p. 105 ; Williams, ' Fiji,' vol. i. p. 373. [2] Dos Santos, ' Ethiopia,' in Pinkerton, vol. xvi. p. 686,

forth. Then the fetish-woman answers in a thin, whistling voice, and with the old-fashioned idioms of generations past ; and thus the suppliant receives his command, perhaps to kill a white cock and put him at a four-cross way, or tie him up for the fetish to come and fetch him, or perhaps merely to drive a dozen wooden pegs into the ground, so to bury his friend's disease with them.[1]

The details of demoniacal possession among barbaric and civilized nations need no elaborate description, so simply do they continue the savage cases.[2] But the state of things we notice here agrees with the conclusion that the possession-theory belongs originally to the lower culture, and is gradually superseded by higher medical knowledge. Surveying its course through the middle and higher civilization, we shall notice first a tendency to limit it to certain peculiar and severe affections, especially connected with mental disorder, such as epilepsy, hysteria, delirium, idiocy, madness ; and after this a tendency to abandon it altogether, in consequence of the persistent opposition of the medical faculty. Among the nations of South-East Asia, obsession and possessions by demons is strong at least in popular belief. The Chinese attacked with dizziness, or loss of the use of his limbs, or other unaccountable disease, knows that he has been influenced by a malignant demon, or punished for some offence by a deity whose name he will mention, or affected by his wife of a former existence, whose spirit has after a long search discovered him. Exorcism of course exists, and when the evil spirit or influence is expelled, it is especially apt to enter some person standing near ; hence the common saying, ' idle spectators should not be present at an exorcism.' Divination by possessed mediums is usual in China : among such is the professional woman who sits at a table in contemplation, till the soul of a deceased person from whom

[1] Römer, ' Guinea,' p. 57. See also Steinhauser, l.c. pp. 132, 139 ; J. B. Schlegel, ' Ewe-Sprache,' p. xvi.

[2] Details from Tatar races in Castrén, ' Finn. Myth.' pp. 164, 173, &c. ; Bastian, ' Psychologie,' p. 90 ; from Abyssinia in Parkyns, ' Life in A.,' ch. xxxiii.

communication is desired enters her body and talks through
her to the living ; also the man into whom a deity is brought
by invocations and mesmeric passes, when, assuming the
divine figure and attitude, he pronounces the oracle.[1] In
Burma, the fever-demon of the jungle seizes trespassers on
his domain, and shakes them in ague till he is exorcised,
while falls and apoplectic fits are the work of other spirits.
The dancing of women by demoniacal possession is treated
by the doctor covering their heads with a garment, and
thrashing them soundly with a stick, the demon and not the
patient being considered to feel the blows ; the possessing
spirit may be prevented from escaping by a knotted and
charmed cord hung round the bewitched person's neck, and
when a sufficient beating has induced it to speak by the
patient's voice and declare its name and business, it may
either be allowed to depart, or the doctor tramples on the
patient's stomach till the demon is stamped to death.   For
an example of invocation and offerings, one characteristic
story told by Dr. Bastian will suffice.   A Bengali cook was
seized with an apoplectic fit, which his Burmese wife declared
was but a just retribution, for the godless fellow had gone
day after day to market to buy pounds and pounds of meat,
yet in spite of her remonstrances would never give a morsel
to the patron-spirit of the town ; as a good wife, however,
she now did her best for her suffering husband, placing near
him little heaps of coloured rice for the 'nat,' and putting
on his fingers rings with prayers addressed to the same
offended being—' Oh ride him not ! '—' Ah let him go ! '
—'Grip him not so hard ! '—' Thou shalt have rice!'—
' Ah, how good that tastes ! '   How explicitly Buddhism
recognizes such ideas, may be judged from one of the questions officially put to candidates for admission as monks or
talapoins—' Art thou afflicted by madness or the other ills
caused by giants, witches, or evil demons of the forest and
mountain ? '[2]   Within our own domain of British India,

[1] Doolittle, ' Chinese,' vol. i. p. 143, vol. ii. pp. 110, 320.
[2] Bastian, ' Oestl. Asien,' vol. ii. pp. 103, 152, 381, 418, vol. iii. p. 247,

the possession-theory and the rite of exorcism belonging to it may be perfectly studied to this day. There the doctrine of sudden ailment or nervous disease being due to a blast or possession by a ' bhut,' or being, that is, a demon, is recognized as of old ; there the old witch who has possessed a man and made him sick or deranged, will answer spiritually out of his body and say who she is and where she lives ; there the frenzied demoniac may be seen raving, writhing, tearing, bursting his bonds, till, subdued by the exorcist, his fury subsides, he stares and sighs, falls helpless to the ground, and comes to himself ; and there the deities caused by excitement, singing, and incense to enter into men's bodies, manifest their presence with the usual hysterical or epileptic symptoms, and speaking in their own divine name and personality, deliver oracles by the vocal organs of the inspired medium.[1]

In the Ancient Babylonian-Assyrian texts, the exorcism-formulas show the doctrine \of disease-demons in full development, and similar opinions were current in ancient Greece and Rome, to whose languages indeed our own owes the technical terms of the subject, such as ' demoniac ' and ' exorcist.' Homer's sick men racked with pain are tormented by a hateful demon ($\sigma\tau\upsilon\gamma\epsilon\rho\grave{o}s$ $\delta\acute{\epsilon}$ $o\acute{\iota}$ $\acute{\epsilon}\chi\rho\alpha\epsilon$ $\delta\alpha\acute{\iota}\mu\omega\nu$). ' Epilepsy ' ($\acute{\epsilon}\pi\acute{\iota}\lambda\eta\psi\iota s$) was, as its name imports, the ' seizure ' of the patient by a superhuman agent : the agent being more exactly defined in ' nympholepsy,' the state of being seized or possessed by a nymph, i.e., rapt or entranced ($\nu\upsilon\mu\phi\acute{o}\lambda\eta\pi\tau os$, lymphatus). The causation of mental derangement and delirious utterance by spiritual possession was an accepted tenet of Greek philosophy. To be insane was simply to have an evil spirit, as when Sokrates said of those who denied demonic or spiritual knowledge, that they

&c. See also Bowring, ' Siam,' vol. i. p. 139 ; ' Journ. Ind. Archip.' vol. iv. p. 507, vol. vi. p. 614 ; Turpin, in Pinkerton, vol. ix. p. 761 ; Kempfer, ' Japan,' *ibid.* vol. vii. pp. 701, 730, &c.

[1] Ward, ' Hindoos,' vol. i. p. 155, vol. ii. p. 183 ; Roberts, ' Oriental Illustrations of the Scriptures,' p. 529 ; Bastian, ' Psychologie,' pp. 164, 184-7. Sanskrit paiçâcha-graha= demon-seizure, possession. Ancient evidence in Pictet, ' Origines Indo-Europ.' part ii. ch. v.

themselves were demoniac (δαιμονᾶν ἔφη), and Alexander ascribed to the influence of offended Dionysos the ungovernable drunken fury in which he killed his friend Kleitos ; raving madness was obsession or possession by an evil demon (κακοδαιμονία). So the Romans called madmen ' larvati,' ' larvarum pleni,' full of ghosts. Patients possessed by demons stared and foamed, and the spirits spoke from within them by their voices. The craft of the exorcist was well known. As for oracular possession, its theory and practice remained in fullest vigour through the classic world, scarce altered from the times of lowest barbarism. Could a South Sea Islander have gone to Delphi to watch the convulsive struggles of the Pythia, and listen to her raving, shrieking utterances, he would have needed no explanation whatever of a rite so absolutely in conformity with his own savage philosophy.[1]

The Jewish doctrine of possession[2] at no time in its long course exercised a direct influence on the opinion of the civilized world comparable to that produced by the mentions of demoniacal possession in the New Testament. It is needless to quote here even a selection from the familiar passages of the Gospels and Acts which display the manner in which certain described symptoms were currently accounted for in public opinion. Regarding these documents from an ethnographic point of view, it need only be said that they prove, incidentally but absolutely, that Jews and Christians at that time held the doctrine which had prevailed for ages before, and continued to prevail for ages after, referring to possession and obsession by spirits the symptoms of mania, epilepsy, dumbness, delirious and oracular utterance, and other morbid conditions, mental and bodily.[3] Modern missionary works, such as have been cited

---

[1] Homer. Odyss. v. 396, x. 64 ; Plat. Phædr. Tim. &c. ; Pausan. iv. 27, 2 ; Xen. Mem. I. i. 9 ; Plutarch. Vit. Alex. ; De Orac. Def. ; Lucian. Philopseudes ; Petron. Arbiter, Sat. ; &c., &c.

[2] Joseph. Ant. Jud. viii. 2, 5. Eisenmenger, ' Entdecktes Judenthum,' part ii. p. 454. See Maury, p. 290.

[3] Matth. ix. 32, xi. 18, xii. 22, xvii. 15 ; Mark, i. 23, ix. 17 ; Luke, iv.

here, give the most striking evidence of the correspondence of these demoniac symptoms with such as may still be observed among uncivilized races. During the early centuries of Christianity, demoniacal possession indeed becomes peculiarly conspicuous, perhaps not from unusual prevalence of the animistic theory of disease, but simply because a period of intense religious excitement brought it more than usually into requisition. Ancient ecclesiastical records describe, under the well-known names of ' dæmoniacs ' (δαιμονιζόμενοι), ' possessed ' (κατεχόμενοι), ' energumens ' (ἐνεργούμενοι), the class of persons whose bodies are seized or possessed by an evil spirit ; such attacks being frequently attended with great commotions and vexations and disturbances of the body, occasioning sometimes frenzy and madness, sometimes epileptic fits, and other violent tossings and contortions. These energumens formed a recognized part of an early Christian congregation, a standing-place apart being assigned to them in the church. The church indeed seems to have been the principal habitation of these afflicted creatures, they were occupied out of service-time in such work as sweeping, daily food was provided for them, and they were under the charge of a special order of clergy, the exorcists, whose religious function was to cast out devils by prayer and adjuration and laying on of hands. As to the usual symptoms of possession, Justin, Tertullian, Chrysostom, Cyril, Minucius, Cyprian, and other early Fathers, give copious descriptions of demons entering into the bodies of men, disordering their health and minds, driving them to wander among the tombs, forcing them to writhe and wallow and rave and foam, howling and declaring their own diabolical names by the patients' voices, but when overcome by conjuration or by blows administered to their victims, quitting the bodies they had entered, and acknowledging the pagan deities to be but devils.[1]

33, 39, vii. 33, viii. 27, ix. 39, xiii. 11 ; John, x. 20 ; Acts, xvi. 16, xix. 13 ; &c.

[1] For general evidence see Bingham, ' Antiquities of Christian Church,'

On a subject so familiar to educated readers I may be excused from citing at length a vast mass of documents, barbaric in nature and only more or less civilized in circumstance, to illustrate the continuance of the doctrine of possession and the rite of exorcism through the middle ages and into modern times. A few salient examples will suffice. For a type of medical details, we may instance the recipes in the ' Early English Leechdoms ' : a cake of the ' thost ' of a white hound baked with meal is to be taken against the attack by dwarves (i.e. convulsions) ; a drink of herbs worked up off clear ale with the aid of garlic, holy water, and singing of masses, is to be drunk by a fiend-sick patient out of a church bell. Philosophical argument may be followed in the dissertations of the ' Malleus Maleficarum,' concerning demons substantially inhabiting men and causing illness in them, enquiries which may be pursued under the auspices of Glanvil in the ' Saducismus Triumphatus.' Historical anecdote bears record of the convulsive clairvoyant demon who possessed Nicola Aubry, and under the Bishop of Laon's exorcism testified in an edifying manner to the falsity of Calvinism ; of Charles VI. of France, who was possessed, and whose demon a certain priest tried in vain to transfer into the bodies of twelve men who were chained up to receive it ; of the German woman at Elbingerode who in a fit of toothache wished the devil might enter into her teeth, and who was possessed by six demons accordingly, which gave their names as Schalk der Wahrheit, Wirk, Widerkraut, Myrrha, Knip, Stüp ; of George Lukins of Yatton, whom seven devils threw into fits and talked and sang and barked out of, and who was delivered by a solemn exorcism by seven clergymen at the Temple Church at Bristol in the year 1788.[1] A strong

book iii. ch. iv. ; Calmet, ' Dissertation sur les Esprits ' ; Maury, ' Magie,' &c. ; Lecky, ' Hist. of Rationalism.' Among particular passages are Tertull. Apolog. 23 ; De Spectaculis, 26 ; Chrysostom. Homil. xxviii. in Matth. iv. ; Cyril. Hierosol. Catech. xvi. 16 ; Minuc. Fel. Octavius. xxi. ; Concil. Carthag. iv. ; &c.. &c.

[1] Details in Cockayne, ' Leechdoms, &c., of Early England,' vol. i. p. 365,

sense of the permanence of the ancient doctrine may be
gained from accounts of the state of public opinion in
Europe, from Greece and Italy to France, where within the
last century derangement and hysteria were still popularly
ascribed to possession and treated by exorcism, just as in
the dark ages.[1] In the year 1861, at Morzine, at the south
of the Lake of Geneva, there might be seen in full fury an
epidemic of diabolical possession worthy of a Red Indian
settlement or a negro kingdom of West Africa, an outburst
which the exorcisms of a superstitious priest had so aggra-
vated that there were a hundred and ten raving demoniacs
in that single village.[2] The following is from a letter
written in 1862 by Mgr. Anouilh, a French missionary-
bishop in China. ' Le croiriez-vous? dix villages se sont
convertis. Le diable est furieux et fait les cent coups. Il y
a eu, pendant les quinze jours que je viens de prêcher, cinq
ou six possessions. Nos catéchumènes avec l'eau bénite
chassent les diables, guérissent les malades. J'ai vu des
choses merveilleuses. Le diable m'est d'un grand secours
pour convertir les païens. Comme au temps de Notre-
Seigneur, quoique père du mensonge, il ne peut s'empêcher
de dire la vérité. Voyez ce pauvre possédé faisant mille
contorsions et disant à grands cris : ' Pourquoi prêches-tu
la vraie religion ? Je ne puis souffrir que tu m'enlèves mes
disciples.'—' Comment t'appelles-tu ? ' lui demande le caté-
chiste. Après quelques refus: ' Je suis l'envoyé de Lucifer '
—' Combien êtes-vous ? '—' Nous sommes vingt-deux.'
' L'eau bénite et le signe de la croix ont délivré ce possédé.'[3]
To conclude the series with a modern spiritualistic instance,

vol. ii. p. 137, 355 ; Sprenger, ' Malleus Maleficarum,' part ii.; Calmet,
' Dissertation,' vol. i. ch. xxiv.; Horst, ' Zauber-Bibliothek ' ; Bastian,
' Mensch,' vol. ii. p. 557, &c.; ' Psychologie,' p. 115, &c. ; Voltaire,
' Questions sur l'Encyclopédie,' art., ' Superstition ' ; ' Encyclopædia Britan-
nica,' 5th ed. art. ' Possession.'

[1] See Maury, ' Magie,' &c., part ii. ch. ii.

[2] A. Constans, ' Rel. sur une Epidémie d'Hystéro-Démonopathie, en 1861.'
2nd ed. Paris, 1863. For descriptions of such outbreaks, among the North
American Indians, see Le Jeune in ' Rel. des Jés. dans la Nouvelle France,'
1639 ; Brinton, p. 275 ; and in Guinea, see J.L.Wilson,'Western Africa,' p. 217.

[3] Gaume,'L'Eau Bénite au Dix-Neuvième Siècle,' 3rd ed.Paris,1866, p.353.

one of those where the mediums feel themselves entered and acted though by a spirit other than their own soul. The Rev. Mr. West of Philadelphia describes how a certain possessed medium went through the sword exercise, and fell down senseless ; when he came to himself again, the spirit within him declared itself to be the soul of a deceased ancestor of the minister's, who had fought and died in the American War.[1] We in England now hardly hear of demoniacal possession except as a historical doctrine of divines. We have discarded from religious services the solemn ceremony of casting out devils from the bodies of the possessed, a rite to this day officially retained in the Rituals of the Greek and Roman Churches. Cases of diabolical influence alleged from time to time among ourselves are little noticed except by newspaper paragraphs on superstition and imposture. If, however, we desire to understand the doctrine of possession, its origin and influence in the world, we must look beyond countries where public opinion has passed into this stage, and must study the demoniac theory as it still prevails in lower and lowest levels of culture.

It has to be thoroughly understood that the changed aspect of the subject in modern opinion is not due to disappearance of the actual manifestations which early philosophy attributed to demoniacal influence. Hysteria and epilepsy, delirium and mania, and such like bodily and mental derangement, still exist. Not only do they still exist, but among the lower races, and in superstitious districts among the higher, they are still explained and treated as of old. It is not too much to assert that the doctrine of demoniacal possession is kept up, substantially the same theory to account for substantially the same facts, by half the human race, who thus stand as consistent representatives of their forefathers back into primitive antiquity. It is in the civilized world, under the influence of the medical doctrines which have been developing since classic times, that the early animistic theory of these morbid phenomena has been

[1] West, in ' Spiritual Telegraph,' cited by Bastian.

gradually superseded by views more in accordance with modern science, to the great gain of our health and happiness. The transition which has taken place in the famous insane colony of Gheel in Belgium is typical. In old days, the lunatics were carried there in crowds to be exorcised from their demons at the church of St. Dymphna ; to Gheel they still go, but the physician reigns in the stead of the exorcist. Yet wherever, in times old or new, demoniacal influences are brought forward to account for affections which scientific physicians now explain on a different principle, care must be taken not to misjudge the ancient doctrine and its place in history. As belonging to the lower culture it is a perfectly rational philosophical theory to account for certain pathological facts. But just as mechanical astronomy gradually superseded the animistic astronomy of the lower races, so biological pathology gradually supersedes animistic pathology, the immediate operation of personal spiritual beings in both cases giving place to the operation of natural processes.

We now pass to the consideration of another great branch of the lower religion of the world, a development of the same principles of spiritual operation with which we have become familiar in the study of the possession-theory. This is the doctrine of Fetishism. Centuries ago, the Portuguese in West Africa, noticing the veneration paid by the negroes to certain objects, such as trees, fish, plants, idols, pebbles, claws of beasts, sticks and so forth, very fairly compared these objects to the amulets or talismans with which they were themselves familiar, and called them *feitiço* or ' charm,' a word derived from Latin *factitius*, in the sense of ' magically artful.' Modern French and English adopted this word from the Portuguese as *fétiche*, *fetish*, although curiously enough both languages had already possessed the word for ages in a different sense, Old French *faitis*, ' well made, beautiful,' which Old English adopted as *fetys*, ' well made, neat.' It occurs in the commonest of all quotations from Chaucer :

'And Frensch sche spak ful faire and *fetysly*,
Aftur the scole of Stratford atte Bowe,
For Frensch of Parys was to hire unknowe.'

The President de Brosses, a most original thinker of the
18th century, struck by the descriptions of the African worship of material and terrestrial objects, introduced the word
Fétichisme as a general descriptive term,[1] and since then it
has obtained great currency by Comte's use of it to denote
a general theory of primitive religion, in which external
objects are regarded as animated by a life analogous to
man's. It seems to me, however, more convenient to use
the word Animism for the doctrine of spirits in general, and
to confine the word Fetishism to that subordinate department
which it properly belongs to, namely, the doctrine of spirits
embodied in, or attached to, or conveying influence through,
certain material objects. Fetishism will be taken as including the worship of ' stocks and stones,' and thence it
passes by an imperceptible gradation into Idolatry.

Any object whatsoever may be a fetish. Of course, among
the endless multitude of objects, not as we should say
physically active, but to which ignorant men ascribe mysterious power, we are not to apply indiscriminately the idea
of their being considered vessels or vehicles or instruments
of spiritual beings. They may be mere signs or tokens set
up to represent ideal notions or ideal beings, as fingers or
sticks are set up to represent numbers. Or they may be
symbolic charms working by imagined conveyance of their
special properties, as an iron ring to give firmness, or a
kite's foot to give swift flight. Or they may be merely regarded in some undefined way as wondrous ornaments or
curiosities. The tendency runs through all human nature
to collect and admire objects remarkable in beauty, form,
quality, or scarceness. The shelves of ethnological museums
show heaps of the objects which the lower races treasure up

---

[1] (C. de Brosses.) ' Du culte des dieux fétiches ou Parallèle de l'ancienne
Religion de l'Egypte avec la religion actuelle de Nigritie.' 1760. [De
Brosses supposed the word *fétiche* connected with *chose fée*, *fatum*.]

and hang about their persons—teeth and claws, roots and berries, shells and stones, and the like. Now fetishes are in great measure selected from among such things as these, and the principle of their attraction for savage minds is clearly the same which still guides the superstitious peasant in collecting curious trifles ' for luck.' The principle is one which retains its force in far higher ranges of culture than the peasant's. Compare the Ostyak's veneration for any peculiar little stone he has picked up, with the Chinese love of collecting curious varieties of tortoise-shell, or an old-fashioned English conchologist's delight in a reversed shell. The turn of mind which in a Gold-Coast negro would manifest itself in a museum of monstrous and most potent fetishes, might impel an Englishman to collect scarce postage-stamps or queer walking-sticks. In the love of abnormal curiosities there shows itself a craving for the marvellous, an endeavour to get free from the tedious sense of law and uniformity in nature. As to the lower races, were evidence more plentiful as to the exact meaning they attach to objects which they treat with mysterious respect, it would very likely appear more often and more certainly than it does now, that these objects seem to them connected with the action of spirits, so as to be, in the strict sense in which the word is here used, real fetishes. But this must not be taken for granted. To class an object as a fetish, demands explicit statement that a spirit is considered as embodied in it or acting through it or communicating by it, or at least that the people it belongs to do habitually think this of such objects ; or it must be shown that the object is treated as having personal consciousness and power, is talked with, worshipped, prayed to, sacrificed to, petted or ill-treated with reference to its past or future behaviour to its votaries. In the instances now selected, it will be seen that in one way or another they more or less satisfy such conditions. In investigating the exact significance of fetishes in use among men, savage or more civilized, the peculiar difficulty is to know whether the effect of the object is thought due to a whole personal spirit embodied in or attached to it, or to some less definable influence exerted through it. In some cases this point is made clear, but in many it remains doubtful.

It will help us to a clearer conception of the nature of a fetish, to glance at a curious group of nations which connect a disease at once with spiritual influence, and with the presence of some material object. They are a set of illustrations of the savage principle, that a disease or an actual disease-spirit may exist embodied in a stick or stone or such-like material object. Among the natives of Australia, one hears of the sorcerers extracting from their own bodies by passes and manipulations a magical essence called ' boylya,' which they can make to enter the patient's body like pieces of quartz, which causes pain there and consumes the flesh, and may be magically extracted either as invisible or in the form of a bit of quartz. Even the spirit of the waters, ' nguk-wonga,' which had caused an attack of erysipelas in a boy's leg (he had been bathing too long when heated) is declared to have been extracted by the conjurers from the affected part in the shape of a sharp stone.[1] The Caribs, who very distinctly referred diseases to the action of hostile demons or deities, had a similar sorcerer's process of extracting thorns or splinters from the affected part as the peccant causes, and it is said that in the Antilles morsels of stone and bone so extracted were wrapped up in cotton by the women, as protective fetishes in childbirth.[2] The Malagasy, considering all diseases as inflicted by an evil spirit, consult a diviner, whose method is often to remove the disease by means of a ' faditra ; ' this is some object, such as a little grass, ashes, a sheep, a pumpkin, the water the patient has rinsed his mouth with, or what not, and when the priest has counted on it the evils

[1] Grey, ' Australia,' vol. ii. p. 337 ; Eyre, ' Australia,' vol. ii. p. 362 ; Oldfield in ' Tr. Eth. Soc.' vol. iii. p. 235, &c.; G. F. Moore, ' Vocab. of S. W. Austr.' pp. 18, 98, 103. See Bonwick, ' Tasmanians,' p. 195.

[2] Rochefort, ' Iles Antilles,' pp. 419, 508 ; J. G. Müller, pp. 173, 207, 217.

that may injure the patient, and charged the faditra to take
them away for ever, it is thrown away, and the malady with
it.[1]   Among those strong believers in disease-spirits, the
Dayaks of Borneo, the priest, waving and jingling charms
over the affected part of the patient, pretends to extract
stones, splinters, and bits of rag, which he declares are
spirits ; of such evil spirits he will occasionally bring half-
a-dozen out of a man's stomach, and as he is paid a fee of
six gallons of rice for each, he is probably disposed (like a
chiropodist under similar circumstances) to extract a good
many.[2]   The most instructive accounts of this kind are
those which reach us from Africa.   Dr. Callaway has taken
down at length a Zulu account of the method of stopping
out disease caused by spirits of the dead.   If a widow is
troubled by her late husband's ghost coming and talking to
her night after night as though still alive, till her health is
affected and she begins to waste away, they find a ' nyanga '
or sorcerer who can bar out the disease.   He bids her not
lose the spittle collected in her mouth while she is dreaming, and gives her medicine to chew when she wakes.   Then
he goes with her to lay the ' itongo,' or ghost ; perhaps
he shuts it up in a bulb of the inkomfe plant, making a
hole in the side of this, putting in the medicine and the
dream-spittle, closing the hole with a stopper, and re-
planting the bulb.   Leaving the place, he charges her not
to look back till she gets home.   Thus the dream is barred ;
it may still come occasionally, but no longer infests the
woman ;   the doctor prevails over the dead man as regards
that dream.   In other cases the cure of a sick man attacked
by the ancestral spirits may be effected with some of his
blood put into a hole in an anthill by the doctor, who closes
the hole with a stone, and departs without looking back ;   or
the patient may be scarified over the painful place, and the
blood put into the mouth of a frog, caught for the purpose
and carried back.   So the disease is barred out from the

---

[1] Ellis, ' Madagascar,' vol. i. pp. 221, 232, 422.
[2] St. John, ' Far East,' vol. i. p. 211, see 72.

man.[1] In West Africa, a case in point is the practice of transferring a sick man's ailment to a live fowl, which is set free with it, and if any one catches the fowl, the disease goes to him.[2] Captain Burton's account from Central Africa is as follows. Disease being possession by a spirit or ghost, the 'mganga' or sorcerer has to expel it, the principal remedies being drumming, dancing, and drinking, till at last the spirit is enticed from the body of the patient into some inanimate article, technically called a 'keti' or stool for it. This may be an ornament, such as a peculiar bead or a leopard's claw, or it may be a nail or rag, which by being driven into or hung to a 'devil's tree' has the effect of laying the disease-spirit. Or disease-spirits may be extracted by chants, one departing at the end of each stave, when a little painted stick made for it is flung on the ground, and some patients may have as many as a dozen ghosts extracted, for here also the fee is so much apiece.[3] In Siam, the Laos sorcerer can send his 'phi phob' or demon into a victim's body, where it turns into a fleshy or leathery lump, and causes disease ending in death.[4] Thus, on the one hand, the spirit-theory of disease is seen to be connected with that sorcerer's practice prevalent among the lower races, of pretending to extract objects from the patient's body, such as stones, bones, balls of hair, &c., which are declared to be causes of disease conveyed by magical means into him ; of this proceeding I have given a detailed account elsewhere, under the name of the 'sucking-cure.'[5] On the other hand, there appears among the lower races that well-known conception of a disease or evil influence as an individual being, which may be not merely conveyed by an infected object (though this of course may have much to do with the idea), but may be

[1] Callaway, 'Religion of Amazulu,' p. 314.
[2] Steinhauser, l.c. p. 141. See also Steere, 'East Afr. Tribes,' in ' Journ. Anthrop. Soc.' vol. i. p. cxlviii.
[3] Burton, 'Central Africa,' vol. ii. p. 352. See 'Sindh,' p. 177.
[4] Bastian, 'Oestl. Asien,' vol. iii. p. 275.
[5] 'Early Hist. of Mankind,' ch. x. See Bastian, 'Mensch,' vol. ii. p. 116, &c.

removed by actual transfer from the patient into some other animal or object. Thus Pliny informs us how pains in the stomach may be cured by transmitting the ailment from the patient's body into a puppy or duck, which will probably die of it;[1] it is considered baneful to a Hindu woman to be a man's third wife, wherefore the precaution is taken of first betrothing him to a tree, which dies in her stead;[2] after the birth of a Chinese baby, its father's trousers are hung in the room wrong side up, that all evil influences may enter into them instead of into the child.[3] Modern folklore still cherishes such ideas. The ethnographer may still study in the ' white witchcraft ' of European peasants the arts of curing a man's fever or headache by transferring it to a crawfish or a bird, or of getting rid of ague or gout or warts by giving them to a willow, elder, fir, or ash-tree, with suitable charms, ' Goe morgen, olde, ick geef oe de Kolde,' ' Goden Abend, Herr Fleder, hier bring ick mien Feber, ick bind em di an und gah davan,' ' Ash-tree, ashen tree, pray buy this wart of me,' and so forth ; or of nailing or plugging an ailment into a tree-trunk, or conveying it away by some of the patient's hair or nail-parings or some such thing, and so burying it. Looking at these proceedings from a moral point of view, the practice of transferring the ailment to a knot or a lock of hair and burying it is the most harmless, but another device is a very pattern of wicked selfishness. In England, warts may be touched each with a pebble, and the pebbles in a bag left on the road to church, to give up their ailments to the unlucky finder ; in Germany, a plaister from a sore may be left at a cross-way to transfer the disease to a passer-by ; I am told on medical authority that the bunches of flowers which children offer to travellers in Southern Europe are sometimes intended for the ungracious purpose of sending some disease away from their homes.[4] One case of this

---

[1] Plin. xxx. 14, 20. Cardan, ' De Var. Rerum,' cap. xliii.
[2] Ward, ' Hindoos,' vol. i. p. 134, vol. ii. p. 247.
[3] Doolittle, ' Chinese,' vol. i. p. 122.
[4] Grimm, ' D. M.' pp. 1118-23 ; Wuttke, ' Volksaberglaube,' pp. 155-70 ;

group, mentioned to me by Mr. Spottiswoode, is particularly interesting. In Thuringia it is considered that a string of rowan-berries, a rag, or any small article, touched by a sick person and then hung on a bush beside some forest path, imparts the malady to any person who may touch this article in passing, and frees the sick person from the disease. This gives great probability to Captain Burton's suggestion that the rags, locks of hair, and what not, hung on trees near sacred places by the superstitious from Mexico to India and from Ethiopia to Ireland, are deposited there as actual receptacles of disease ; the African ' devil's trees ' and the sacred trees of Sindh, hung with rags through which votaries have transferred their complaints, being typical cases of a practice surviving in lands of higher culture.

The spirits which enter or otherwise attach themselves to objects may be human souls. Indeed one of the most natural cases of the fetish-theory is when a soul inhabits or haunts what is left of its former body. It is plain enough that by a simple association of ideas the dead person is imagined to keep up a connexion with his remains. Thus we read of the Mandan women going year after year to take food to the skulls of their dead kinsfolk, and sitting by the hour to chat and jest in their most endearing strain with the relics of a husband or child ;[1] thus the Guinea negroes, who keep the bones of parents in chests, will go to talk with them in the little huts which serve for their tombs.[2] And thus, from the savage who keeps and carries with his household property the cleaned bones of his forefathers,[3] to

Brand, ' Pop. Ant.' vol. ii. p. 375, vol. iii. p. 286 ; Halliwell, ' Pop. Rhymes,' p. 208 ; R. Hunt, ' Pop. Romances,' 2nd Series, p. 211 ; Hylten-Cavallius, ' Wärend och Wirdarne,' vol. i. p. 173. It is said, however, that rags fastened on trees by Gypsies, which passers-by avoid with horror as having diseases thus banned into them, are only signs left for the information of fellow vagrants ; Liebich, ' Die Zigeuner,' p. 96.

[1] Catlin, ' N. A. Indians,' vol. i. p. 90.
[2] J. L. Wilson, ' W. Africa,' p. 394.
[3] Meiners, ' Gesch. der Rel.' vol. i. p. 305 ; J. G. Müller, p. 209.

the mourner among ourselves who goes to weep at the grave
of one beloved, imagination keeps together the personality
and the relics of the dead. Here, then, is a course of
thought open to the animistic thinker, leading him on from
fancied association to a belief in the real presence of a
spiritual being in a material object. Thus there is no
difficulty in understanding how the Karens thought the
spirits of the dead might come back from the other world
to reanimate their bodies;[1] nor how the Marian islanders
should have kept the dried bodies of their dead ancestors
in their huts as household gods, and even expected them to
give oracles out of their skulls;[2] nor how the soul of a
dead Carib might be thought to abide in one of his bones,
taken from the grave and carefully wrapped in cotton, in
which state it could answer questions, and even bewitch an
enemy if a morsel of his property were wrapped up with it;[3]
nor how the dead Santal should be sent to his fathers by the
ceremony of committing to the sacred river morsels of his
skull from the funeral-pile.[4] Such ideas are of great interest
in studying the burial rites of mankind, especially the habit
of keeping relics of the dead as vehicles of superhuman
power, and of even preserving the whole body as a mummy,
as in Peru and Egypt. The conception of such human
relics becoming fetishes, inhabited or at least acted through
by the souls which formerly belonged to them, will give a
rational explanation of much relic-worship otherwise
obscure.

A further stretch of imagination enables the lower races
to associate the souls of the dead with mere objects, a
practice which may have had its origin in the merest childish make-believe, but which would lead a thorough savage
animist straight on to the conception of the soul entering

[1] Mason, Karens, l.c. p. 231.

[2] Meiners, vol. ii. pp. 721-3.

[3] Rochefort, ' Iles Antilles,' p. 418. See Martius, ' Ethnog. Amer.' vol. i.
p. 485 (Yumanas swallow ashes of deceased with liquor, that he may live
again in them).

[4] Hunter, ' Rural Bengal,' p. 210. See Bastian, ' Psychologie,' p. 73 ;
J. G. Müller, ' Amer. Urrel.' pp. 209, 262, 289, 401, 419.

the object as a body. Mr. Darwin saw two Malay women
in Keeling Island who held a wooden spoon dressed in
clothes like a doll ; this spoon had been carried to the grave
of a dead man, and becoming inspired at full moon, in fact
lunatic, it danced about convulsively like a table or a hat
at a modern spirit-séance.[1] Among the Salish Indians of
Oregon, the conjurers bring back men's lost souls as little
stones or bones or splinters, and pretend to pass them down
through the tops of their heads into their hearts, but great
care must be taken to remove the spirits of any dead
people that may be in the lot, for the patient receiving one
would die.[2] There are indigenous Kol tribes of India who
work out this idea curiously in bringing back the soul of a
deceased man into the house after the funeral, apparently
to be worshipped as a household spirit ; while some catch
the spirit re-embodied in a fowl or fish, the Binjwar of Rae-
pore bring it home in a pot of water, and the Bunjia in a
pot of flour.[3] The Chinese hold such theories with extreme
distinctness, considering one of a man's three spirits to take
up its abode in the ancestral tablet, where it receives
messages and worship from the survivors ; while the long
keeping of the dead man's gilt and lacquered coffin, and the
reverence and offerings continued at the tomb, are connected
with the thought of a spirit lingering about the corpse.
Consistent with these quaint ideas are ceremonies in vogue
in China, of bringing home in a cock (live or artificial) the
spirit of a man deceased in a distant place, and of enticing
into a sick man's coat the departing spirit which has already
left his body, and so conveying it back.[4] Tatar folklore
illustrates the idea of soul-embodiment in the quaint but
intelligible story of the demon-giant who could not be slain,
for he did not keep his soul in his body, but in a twelve-

[1] Darwin, ' Journal,' p. 458.
[2] Bastian, ' Mensch,' vol. ii. p. 320.
[3] ' Report of Jubbulpore Ethnological Committee,' Nagpore, 1868, part i.
p. 5.
[4] Doolittle, ' Chinese,' vol. i. pp. 151, 207, 214, vol. ii. p. 401 ; see Plath,
' Religion der alten Chinesen,' part i. p. 59, part ii. p. 101,

headed snake carried in a bag on his horse's back ; the hero
finds out the secret and kills the snake, and then the giant
dies too. This tale is curious, as very likely indicating the
original sense of a well-known group of stories in European
folklore, the Scandinavian one, for instance, where the giant
cannot be made an end of, because he keeps his heart not
in his body, but in a duck's egg in a well far away ; at last
the young champion finds the egg and crushes it, and the
giant bursts.[1] Following the notion of soul-embodiment
into civilized times, we learn that ' A ghost may be laid for
any term less than an hundred years, and in any place or
body, full or empty ; as, a solid oak—the pommel of a sword
—a barrel of beer, if a yeoman or simple gentleman—or a
pipe of wine, if an esquire or a justice.' This is from
Grose's bantering description in the 18th century of the art
of ' laying ' ghosts,[2] and it is one of the many good instances
of articles of serious savage belief surviving as jests among
civilized men.

Thus other spiritual beings, roaming free about the world,
find fetish-objects to act through, to embody themselves in,
to present them visibly to their votaries. It is extremely
difficult to draw a distinct line of separation between the
two prevailing sets of ideas relating to spiritual action
through what we call inanimate objects. Theoretically we
can distinguish the notion of the object acting as it were by
the will and force of its own proper soul or spirit, from the
notion of some foreign spirit entering its substance or acting on it from without, and so using it as a body or instrument. But in practice these conceptions blend almost
inextricably. This state of things is again a confirmation
of the theory of animism here advanced, which treats both
sets of ideas as similar developments of the same original

---

[1] Castrén, ' Finn. Myth.' p. 187 ; Dasent, ' Norse Tales,' p. 69 ; Lane,
' Thousand and One Nights,' vol. iii. p. 316 ; Grimm, ' D. M.' p. 1033.
See also Bastian, ' Psychologie,' p. 213. Eisenmenger, ' Judenthum,' part
ii. p. 39.

[2] Brand, ' Pop. Ant.' vol. iii. p. 72.

idea, that of the human soul, so that they may well shade imperceptibly into one another. To depend on some typical descriptions of fetishism and its allied doctrines in different grades of culture, is a safer mode of treatment than to attempt too accurate a general definition.

There is a quaint story, dating from the time of Columbus, which shows what mysterious personality and power rude tribes could attach to lifeless matter. The cacique Hatuey, it is related, heard by his spies in Hispaniola that the Spaniards were coming to Cuba. So he called his people together, and talked to them of the Spaniards—how they persecuted the natives of the islands, and how they did such things for the sake of a great lord whom they much desired and loved. Then, taking out a basket with gold in it, he said, ' Ye see here their lord whom they serve and go after ; and, as ye have heard, they are coming hither to seek this lord. Therefore let us make him a feast, that when they come he may tell them not to do us harm.' So they danced and sang from night to morning before the gold-basket, and then the cacique told them not to keep the Christian's lord anywhere, for if they kept him in their very bowels they would have to bring him out ; so he bade them cast him to the bottom of the river, and this they did.[1] If this story be thought too good to be true, at any rate it does not exaggerate authentic savage ideas. The ' maraca ' or cere-monial rattle, used by certain rude Brazilian tribes, was an eminent fetish. It was a calabash with a handle and a hole for a mouth, and stones inside ; yet to its votaries it seemed no mere rattle, but the receptacle of a spirit that spoke from it when shaken ; therefore the Indians set up their maracas, talked to them, set food and drink and burned incense be-fore them, held annual feasts in their honour, and would even go to war with their neighbours to satisfy the rattle-spirits' demand for human victims.[2] Among the North American Indians, the fetish-theory seems involved in that

[1] Herrera, ' Hist. de las Indias Occidentales,' Dec. i. ix. 3.
[2] Lery, Brésil, p. 249 ; J. G. Müller, pp. 210, 262.

remarkable and general proceeding known as getting ' medicine.' Each youth obtains in a vision or dream a sight of his medicine, and considering how thoroughly the idea prevails that the forms seen in visions and dreams are spirits, this of itself shows the animistic nature of the matter. The medicine thus seen may be an animal, or part of one, such as skin or claws, feather or shell, or such a thing as a plant, a stone, a knife, a pipe ; this object he must obtain, and thenceforward through life it becomes his protector. Considered as a vehicle or receptacle of a spirit, its fetish-nature is shown in many ways ; its owner will do homage to it, make feasts in its honour, sacrifice horses, dogs, and other valuable objects to it or its spirit, fast to appease it if offended, have it burned with him to conduct him as a guardian-spirit to the happy hunting-grounds. Beside these special protective objects, the Indians, especially the medicine-men (the word is French, ' médecin,' applied to these native doctors or conjurers, and since stretched to take in all that concerns their art), use multitudes of other fetishes as means of spiritual influence.[1] Among the Turanian tribes of Northern Asia, where Castrén describes the idea of spirits contained in material objects, to which they belong, and wherein they dwell in the same incomprehensible way as the souls in a man's body, we may notice the Ostyak's worship of objects of scarce or peculiar quality, and also the connexion of the shamans or sorcerers with fetish-objects, as where the Tatars consider the innumerable rags and tags, bells and bits of iron, that adorn the shaman's magic costume, to contain spirits helpful to their owner in his magic craft.[2] John Bell, in his journey across Asia in 1719, relates a story which well illustrates Mongol ideas as to the action of self-moving objects. A certain Russian merchant told him that once some pieces of damask

---

[1] Schoolcraft, ' Indian Tribes '; Waitz, vol. iii.; Catlin, 'N. A. Ind.' vol. i. p. 36 ; Keating, ' Narrative,' vol. i. p. 421 ; J. G. Müller, p. 74, &c. See Cranz, ' Grönland,' p. 274.

[2] Castrén, ' Finn. Myth.' pp. 162, 221, 230 ; Meiners, vol. i. p. 170.

were stolen out of his tent. He complained, and the Kutuchtu Lama ordered the proper steps to be taken to find out the thief. One of the Lamas took a bench with four feet, and after turning it several times in different directions, at last it pointed directly to the tent where the stolen goods lay concealed. The Lama now mounted astride the bench, and soon carried it, or, as was commonly believed, it carried him, to the very tent, where he ordered the damask to be produced. The demand was directly complied with : for it is vain in such cases to offer any excuse.[1]

A more recent account from Central Africa may be placed as a pendant to this Asiatic account of divination by a fetish-object. The Rev. H. Rowley says of the Manganja, that they believed the medicine-men could impart a power for good or evil to objects either animate or inanimate, which objects the people feared,though they did not worship them. This missionary once saw this art employed to detect the thief who had stolen some corn. The people assembled round a large fig-tree. The magician, a wild-looking man, produced two sticks, like our broomsticks, which after mysterious manipulation and gibberish he delivered to four young men, two holding each stick. A zebra-tail and a calabash-rattle were given to a young man and a boy. The medicine-man rolled himself about in hideous fashion, and chanted an unceasing incantation ; the bearers of the tail and rattle went round the stick-holders, and shook these implements over their heads. After a while the men with the sticks had spasmodic twitchings of the arms and legs, these increased nearly to convulsions, they foamed at the mouth, their eyes seemed starting from their heads, they realized to the full the idea of demoniacal possession. According to the native notion, it was the sticks which were possessed primarily, and through them the men, who could hardly hold them. The sticks whirled and dragged the men round and round like mad, through bush and thorny shrub, and over every obstacle, nothing stopped them, their bodies

[1] Bell, in Pinkerton, vol. vii. p. 357.

were torn and bleeding ; at last they came back to the
assembly, whirled round again, and rushed down the path
to fall panting and exhausted in the hut of one of a chief's
wives, the sticks rolling to her very feet, denouncing her as
the thief. She denied it, but the medicine-man answered,
' The spirit has declared her guilty, the spirit never lies.'
However, the ' muavi ' or ordeal-poison was administered
to a cock, as deputy for the woman ; the bird threw it up,
and she was acquitted.[1]

Fetishism in the lower civilization is thus by no means
confined to the West African negro with whom we specially
associate the term. Yet, what with its being in fact extremely prevalent there, and what with the attention of
foreign observers having been particularly drawn to it, the
accounts from West Africa are certainly the fullest and
most minute on record. The late Professor Waitz's
generalization of the principle involved in these is much to
the purpose. He thus describes the negro's conception
of his fetish. ' According to his view, a spirit dwells or can
dwell in every sensible object, and often a very great and
mighty one in an insignificant thing. This spirit he does
not consider as bound fast and unchangeably to the corporeal
thing it dwells in, but it has only its usual or principal
abode in it. The negro indeed in his conception not un-
commonly separates the spirit from the sensible object
which it inhabits, he even sometimes contrasts the one with
the other, but most usually combines the two as forming a
whole, and this whole is (as the Europeans call it) the
" fetish," the object of his religious worship.' Some further particulars will show how this principle is worked out.
Fetishes (native names for them are ' grigri,' ' juju,'
&c.) may be mere curious mysterious objects that strike a
negro's fancy, or they may be consecrated or affected by
a priest or fetish-man ; the theory of their influence is that
they belong to or are made effectual by a spirit or demon
yet they have to stand the test of experience, and if they

[1] H. Rowley, ' Universities' Mission to Central Africa,' p. 217.

fail to bring their owner luck and safety, he discards them for some more powerful medium. The fetish can see and hear and understand and act, its possessor worships it, talks familiarly with it as a dear and faithful friend, pours libations of rum over it, and in times of danger calls loudly and earnestly on it as if to wake up its spirit and energy. To give an idea of the sort of things which are chosen as fetishes, and of the manner in which they are associated with spiritual influences, Römer's account from Guinea about a century ago may serve. In the fetish-house, he says, there hang or lie thousands of rubbishy trifles, a pot with red earth and a cock's feather stuck in it, pegs wound over with yarn, red parrots' feathers, men's hair, and so forth. The principal thing in the hut is the stool for the fetish to sit on, and the mattress for him to rest on, the mattress being no bigger than a man's hand and the stool in proportion, and there is a little bottle of brandy always ready for him. Here the word fetish is used as it often is, to denote the spirit which dwells in this rudimentary temple, but we see that the innumerable quaint trifles which we call fetishes were associated with the deity in his house. Römer once peeped in at an open door, and found an old negro caboceer sitting amid twenty thousand fetishes in his private fetish-museum, thus performing his devotions. The old man told him he did not know the hundredth part of the use they had been to him ; his ancestors and he had collected them, each had done some service. The visitor took up a stone about as big as a hen's egg, and its owner told its history. He was once going out on important business, but crossing the threshold he trod on this stone and hurt himself. Ha ha ! thought he, art thou here ? So he took the stone, and it helped him through his undertaking for days. In our own time, West Africa is still a world of fetishes. The traveller finds them on every path, at every ford, on every house-door, they hang as amulets round every man's neck, they guard against sickness or inflict it if neglected, they bring rain, they fill the sea with fishes

willing to swim into the fisherman's net, they catch and
punish thieves, they give their owner a bold heart and con-
found his enemies, there is nothing that the fetish cannot
do or undo, if it be but the right fetish. Thus the one-
sided logic of the barbarian, making the most of all that fits
and glossing over all that fails, has shaped a universal
fetish-philosophy of the events of life. So strong is the
pervading influence, that the European in Africa is apt to
catch it from the negro, and himself, as the saying is,
' become black.' Thus even yet some traveller, watching
a white companion asleep, may catch a glimpse of some
claw or bone or such-like sorcerer's trash secretly fastened
round his neck.[1]

European life, lastly, shows well-marked traces of the
ancient doctrine of spirits or mysterious influences inhabiting objects. Thus a mediæval devil might go into an old
sow, a straw, a barleycorn, or a willow-tree. A spirit might
be carried about in a solid receptacle for use :—

> ' Besides in glistering glasses fayre, or else in christall cleare,
> They sprightes enclose.'

Modern peasant folklore knows that spirits must have some
animal body or other object to dwell in, a feather, a bag, a
bush, for instance. The Tyrolese object to using grass for
toothpicks because of the demons that may have taken up
their abode in the straws. The Bulgarians hold it a great
sin not to fumigate the flour when it is brought from the
mill (particularly if the mill be kept by a Turk) in order to
prevent the devil from entering into it.[2] Amulets are still
carried in the most civilized countries of the world, by the

---

[1] Waitz, ' Anthropologie,' vol. ii. p. 174; Römer, ' Guinea,' p. 56, &c. ;
J. L. Wilson, ' West Africa,' pp. 135, 211-6, 275, 338 ; Burton, ' Wit and
Wisdom from W. Afr.' pp. 174, 455 ; Steinhauser, l.c. p. 134 ; Bosman,
' Guinea,' in Pinkerton, vol. xvi. p. 397 ; Meiners, ' Gesch. der Relig.' vol. i.
p. 173. See also Ellis, ' Madagascar,' vol. i. p. 396 ; Flacourt, ' Madag.'
p. 191.
[2] Brand, ' Popular Antiquities,' vol. iii. p. 255, &c. Bastian, ' Psychologie,'
p. 171. Wuttke, ' Deutsche Volksaberglaube,' pp. 75-95, 225, &c. St. Clair
and Brophy, ' Bulgaria,' p. 46.

ignorant and superstitious with real savage faith in their mysterious virtues, by the more enlightened in quaint survival from the past. The mental and physical phenomena of what is now called ' table-turning ' belong to a class of proceedings which have here been shown to be familiar to the lower races, and accounted for by them on a theory of extra-human influence which is in the most extreme sense spiritualistic.

In giving its place in the history of mental development to the doctrine of the lower races as to embodiment in or penetration of an object by a spirit or an influence, there is no slight interest in comparing it with theories familiar to the philosophy of cultured nations. Thus Bishop Berkeley remarks on the obscure expressions of those who have described the relation of power to the objects which exert it. He cites Torricelli as likening matter to an enchanted vase of Circe serving as a receptacle of force, and declaring that power and impulse are such subtle abstracts and refined quintessences, that they cannot be enclosed in any other vessels but the inmost materiality of natural solids ; also Leibnitz as comparing active primitive power to soul or substantial form. Thus, says Berkeley, must even the greatest men, when they give way to abstraction, have recourse to words having no certain signification, and indeed mere scholastic shadows.[1] We may fairly add that such passages show the civilized metaphysician falling back on such primitive conceptions as still occupy the minds of the rude natives of Siberia and Guinea. To go yet farther, I will venture to assert that the scientific conceptions current in my own schoolboy days, of heat and electricity as invisible fluids passing in and out of solid bodies, are ideas which reproduce with extreme closeness the special doctrine of Fetishism.

Under the general heading of Fetishism, but for convenience' sake separately, may be considered the worship of ' stocks and stones.' Such objects, if merely used as

[1] Berkeley, ' Concerning Motion,' in ' Works,' vol. ii. p. 86.

altars, are not of the nature of fetishes, and it is first necessary to ascertain that worship is actually addressed to them. Then arises the difficult question, are the stocks and stones set up as mere ideal representatives of deities, or are these deities considered as physically connected with them, embodied in them, hovering about them, acting through them ? In other words, are they only symbols, or have they passed in the minds of their votaries into real fetishes ? The conceptions of the worshippers are sometimes in this respect explicitly stated, may sometimes be fairly inferred from the circumstances, and are often doubtful.

Among the lower races of America, the Dacotas would pick up a round boulder, paint it, and then, addressing it as grandfather, make offerings to it and pray to it to deliver them from danger;[1] in the West India Islands, mention is made of three stones to which the natives paid great devotion—one was profitable for the crops, another for women to be delivered without pain, the third for sunshine and rain when they were wanted;[2] and we hear of Brazilian tribes setting up stakes in the ground, and making offerings before them to appease their deities or demons.[3] Stone-worship held an important place in the midst of the comparatively high culture of Peru, where not only was reverence given to especial curious pebbles and the like, but stones were placed to represent the penates of households and the patron-deities of villages. It is related by Montesinos that when the worship of a certain sacred stone was given up, a parrot flew from it into another stone, to which adoration was paid : and though this author is not of good credit, he can hardly have invented a story which, as we shall see, so curiously coincides with the Polynesian idea of a bird conveying to and from an idol the spirit which embodies itself in it.[4]

[1] Schoolcraft, ' Indian Tribes,' part ii. p. 196, part iii. p. 229.
[2] Herrera, ' Indias Occidentales,' dec. i. iii. 3.
[3] De Laet, Novus Orbis, xv. 2.
[4] Garcilaso de la Vega, ' Commentarios Reales,' i. 9 ; J. G. Müller, pp. 263, 311, 371, 387 ; Waitz, vol. iv. p. 454 ; see below, p. 175.

In Africa, stock-and-stone worship is found among the Damaras of the South, whose ancestors are represented at the sacrificial feasts by stakes cut from trees or bushes consecrated to them, to which stakes the meat is first offered;[1] among the Dinkas of the White Nile, where the missionaries saw an old woman in her hut offering the first of her food and drink before a short thick staff planted in the ground, that the demon might not hurt her;[2] among the Gallas of Abyssinia, a people with a well-marked doctrine of deities, and who are known to worship stones and logs, but not idols.[3] In the island of Sambawa, the Orang Dongo attribute all supernatural or incomprehensible force to the sun, moon, trees, &c., but especially to stones, and when troubled by accident or disease, they carry offerings to certain stones to implore the favour of their genius or dewa.[4] Similar ideas are to be traced through the Pacific islands, both among the lighter and the darker races. Thus in the Society Islands, rude logs or fragments of basalt columns, clothed in native cloth and anointed with oil, received adoration and sacrifice as divinely powerful by virtue of the atua or deity which had filled them.[5] So in the New Hebrides worship was given to water-worn pebbles,[6] while Fijian gods and goddesses had their abodes or shrines in black stones like smooth round milestones, and there received their offerings of food.[7] The curiously anthropomorphic idea of stones being husbands and wives, and even having children, is familiar to the Fijians as it is to the Peruvians and the Lapps.

The Turanian tribes of North Asia display stock-and-stone worship in full sense and vigour. Not only were

---

[1] Hahn, 'Gramm. des Hereró,' s.v. 'omu-makisina.'
[2] Kaufmann, 'Central-Afrika,' (White Nile), p. 131.
[3] Waitz, vol. ii. pp. 518, 523.
[4] Zollinger in 'Journ. Ind. Archip.' vol. ii. p. 692.
[5] Ellis, 'Polyn. Res.' vol. i. p. 337. See also Ellis, 'Madagascar,' vol. i. p. 399.
[6] Turner, 'Polynesia,' pp. 347, 526.
[7] Williams, 'Fiji,' vol. i. p. 220; Seemann, 'Viti,' pp. 66, 89.

stones, especially curious ones and such as were like men or animals, objects of veneration, but we learn that they were venerated because mighty spirits dwelt in them. The Samoyed travelling ark-sledge, with its two deities, one with a stone head, the other a mere black stone, both dressed in green robes with red lappets, and both smeared with sacrificial blood, may serve as a type of stone-worship. And as for the Ostyaks, had the famous King Log presented himself among them, they would without more ado have wrapped his sacred person in rags, and set him up for worship on a mountain-top or in the forest.[1] The frequent stock-and-stone worship of modern India belongs especially to races non-Hindu or part-Hindu in race and culture. Among such may serve as examples the bamboo which stands for the Bodo goddess Mainou, and for her receives the annual hog, and the monthly eggs offered by the women;[2] the stone under the great cotton-tree of every Khond village, shrine of Nadzu Pennu the village deity;[3] the clod or stone under a tree, which in Behar will represent the deified soul of some dead personage who receives worship and inspires oracles there;[4] the stone kept in every house by the Bakadâra and Betadâra, which represents their god Bûta, whom they induce by sacrifice to restrain the demon-souls of the dead from troubling them;[5] the two rude stones placed under a shed among the Shanars of Tinnevelly, by the medium of which the great god and goddess receive sacrifice, but which are thrown away or neglected when done with.[6] The remarkable groups of standing-stones in India are, in many cases at least, set up for each stone to represent

---

[1] Castrén, ' Finn. Myth.' p. 193, &c., 204, &c. ; ' Voyages au Nord,' vol. viii. pp. 103, 410; Klemm, ' C. G.' vol. iii. p. 120. See also Steller, ' Kamtschatka,' pp. 265, 276.

[2] Hodgson, ' Abor. of India,' p. 174. See also Macrae in ' As. Res.' vol. vii. p. 196; Dalton, ' Kols,' in ' Tr. Eth. Soc.' vol. vi. p. 33.

[3] Macpherson, ' India,' pp. 103, 358.

[4] Bastian, ' Psychologie,' p. 177. See also Shortt, ' Tribes of Neilgherries,' in ' Tr. Eth. Soc.' vol. vii. p. 281.

[5] Elliot in ' Journ. Eth. Soc.' vol. i. 1869, p. 115.

[6] Buchanan, ' Mysore,' in Pinkerton, vol. vii. p. 739.

or embody a deity. Mr. Hislop remarks that in every part of Southern India, four or five stones may often be seen in the ryot's field, placed in a row and daubed with red paint, which they consider as guardians of the field and call the five Pândus ; he reasonably takes these Hindu names to have superseded more ancient native appellations. In the Indian groups it is a usual practice to daub each stone with red paint, forming as it were a great blood-spot where the face would be if it were a shaped idol.[1] In India, moreover, the rites of stone-worship are not unexampled among the Hindus proper. Shashtî, protectress of children, receives worship, vows, and offerings, especially from women ; yet they provide her with no idol or temple, but her proper representative is a rough stone as big as a man's head, smeared with red paint and set at the foot of the sacred vata-tree. Even Siva is worshipped as a stone, especially that Siva who will afflict a child with epileptic fits, and then, speaking by its voice, will announce that he is Panchânana the Five-faced, and is punishing the child for insulting his image ; to this Siva, in the form of a clay idol or of a stone beneath a sacred tree, there are offered not only flowers and fruits, but also bloody sacrifices.[2]

This stone-worship among the Hindus seems a survival of a rite belonging originally to a low civilization, probably a rite of the rude indigenes of the land, whose religion, largely incorporated into the religion of the Aryan invaders, has contributed so much to form the Hinduism of to-day. It is especially interesting to survey the stock-and-stone worship of the lower culture, for it enables us to explain by the theory of survival the appearance in the Old World, in the very midst of classic doctrine and classic art, of the

[1] Elliot in ' Journ. Eth. Soc.' vol. i. pp. 96, 115, 125. Lubbock, ' Origin of Civilization,' p. 222. Forbes Leslie, ' Early Races of Scotland,' vol. ii. p. 462, &c. Prof. Liebrecht, in ' Ztschr. für Ethnologie,' vol. v. p. 100, compares the field-protecting Priapos-hermes of ancient Italy, daubed with minium.

[2] Ward, 'Hindoos,' vol. ii. pp. 142, 182, &c., see 221. See also Latham, 'Descr. Eth.' vol. ii. p. 239. (Siah-push, stone offered to the representative of deity.)

worship of the same rude objects, whose veneration no doubt dated from remote barbaric antiquity. As Mr. Grote says, speaking of Greek worship, ' The primitive memorial erected to a god did not even pretend to be an image, but was often nothing more than a pillar, a board, a shapeless stone or a post, receiving care and decoration from the neighbourhood, as well as worship.' Such were the log that stood for Artemis in Euboea, the stake that represented Pallas Athene, ' sine effigie rudis palus, et informe lignum,' the unwrought stone (λίθος ἀργός) at Hyettos which ' after the ancient manner ' represented Herakles, the thirty such stones which the Pharæans in like archaic fashion worshipped for the gods, and that one which received such honour in Bœotian festivals as representing the Thespian Eros. Theophrastus, in the 4th century B.C., depicts the superstitious Greek passing the anointed stones in the streets, taking out his phial and pouring oil on them, falling on his knees to adore, and going his way. Six centuries later, Arnobius could describe from his own heathen life the state of mind of the stock-and-stone worshipper, telling how when he saw one of the stones anointed with oil, he accosted it in flattering words, and asked benefits from the senseless thing as though it contained a present power.[1] The ancient and graphic passage in the book of Isaiah well marks stone-worship within the range of the Semitic race :

> ' Among the smooth stones of the valley is thy portion :
> They, they are thy lot :
> Even to them hast thou poured a drink-offering,
> Hast thou offered a meat-offering.'[2]

Long afterwards, among the local deities which Mohammed

[1] Grote, ' Hist. of Greece,' vol. iv. p. 132 ; Welcker, ' Griechische Götter-lehre,' vol. i. p. 220. Meiners, vol. i. p. 150, &c. Details esp. in Pausanias ; Theophrast. Charact. xvi. ; Tacit. Hist. ii. 3 ; Arnobius, Adv. Gent. ; Tertullianus ; Clemens Alexandr.

[2] Is. lvii. 6. The first line, ' behhalkey-nahhal hhĕlkech,' turns on the pun on hhlk = smooth (stone), and also lot or portion ; a double sense probably connected with the use of smooth pebbles for casting lots.

found in Arabia, and which Dr. Sprenger thinks he even acknowledged as divine during a moment when he well-nigh broke down in his career, were Manah and Lât, the one a rock, the other a stone or a stone idol ; while the veneration of the black stone of the Kaaba, which Captain Burton thinks an aërolite, was undoubtedly a local rite which the Prophet transplanted into his new religion, where it flourishes to this day.[1] The curious passage in Sanchoniathon which speaks of the Heaven-god forming the ' bætyls, animated stones ' (θεὸς Οὐρανὸς Βαιτύλια, λίθους ἐμψύχους, μηχανησάμενος) perhaps refers to meteorites or supposed thunderbolts fallen from the clouds. To the old Phœnician religion, which made so deep a contact with the Jewish world on the one side and the Greek and Roman on the other, there belonged the stone pillars of Baal and the wooden ashera-posts, but how far these objects were of the character of altars, symbols, or fetishes, is a riddle.[2] We may still say with Tacitus, describing the conical pillar which stood instead of an image to represent the Paphian Venus—' et ratio in obscuro.'

There are accounts of formal Christian prohibitions of stone-worship in France and England, reaching on into the early middle ages,[3] which show this barbaric cultus as then distinctly lingering in popular religion. Coupling this fact with the accounts of the groups of standing-stones set up to represent deities in South India, a corresponding explanation has been suggested in Europe. Are the menhirs, cromlechs, &c., idols, and circles and lines of idols, worshipped by remotely ancient dwellers in the land as representatives or embodiments of their gods ? The question at least deserves consideration, although the ideas with which

[1] Sprenger, ' Mohammad,' vol. ii. p. 7, &c. Burton, ' El Medinah,' &c., vol. ii. p. 157.

[2] Euseb. Præp. Evang. i. 10. Deut. xii. 3 ; Micah v. 13, &c. Movers, ' Phönizier,' vol. i. pp. 105, 569, and see index, ' Säule,' &c. See De Brosses, ' Dieux Fétiches,' p. 135 (considers bætyl=beth-el, &c.).

[3] For references see Ducange s.v. ' petra ' ; Leslie, ' Early Races of Scotland,' vol. i. p. 256.

stone-worship is carried on by different races are multifarious, and the analogy may be misleading. It is remarkable to what late times full and genuine stone-worship has
survived in Europe. In certain mountain districts of
Norway, up to the end of the last century, the peasants
used to preserve round stones, washed them every Thursday
evening (which seems to show some connection with Thor),
smeared them with butter before the fire, laid them in the
seat of honour on fresh straw, and at certain times of the
year steeped them in ale, that they might bring luck and
comfort to the house.[1] In an account dating from 1851,
the islanders of Inniskea, off Mayo, are declared to have a
stone carefully wrapped in flannel, which is brought out
and worshipped at certain periods, and when a storm arises
it is supplicated to send a wreck on the coast.[2] No savage
ever showed more clearly by his treatment of a fetish that
he considered it a personal being, than did these Nor-
wegians and Irishmen. The ethnographic argument from
the existence of stock-and-stone worship among so many
nations of comparatively high culture seems to me of great
weight as bearing on religious development among mankind.
To imagine that peoples skilled in carving wood and stone,
and using these arts habitually in making idols, should
have gone out of their way to invent a practice of worshipping logs and pebbles, is not a likely theory. But on the
other hand, when it is considered how such a rude object
serves to uncultured men as a divine image or receptacle,
there is nothing strange in its being a relic of early barbarism holding its place against more artistic models
through ages of advancing civilization, by virtue of the
traditional sanctity which belongs to survival from remote
antiquity.

[1] Nilsson, ' Primitive Inhabitants of Scandinavia,' p. 241. See also
Meiners, vol. ii. p. 671 (speaking stones in Norway, &c.).
[2] Earl of Roden, ' Progress of Reformation in Ireland,' London, 1851,
p. 51. Sir J. E. Tennent in ' Notes and Queries,' Feb. 7, 1852. See Borlase,
' Antiquities of Cornwall,' Oxford, 1754, book iii. ch. 2.

By a scarcely perceptible transition, we pass to Idolatry. A few chips or scratches or daubs of paint suffice to convert the rude post or stone into an idol. Difficulties which complicate the study of stock-and-stone worship disappear in the worship of even the rudest of unequivocal images, which can no longer be mere altars, and if symbols must at least be symbols of a personal being. Idolatry occupies a remarkable district in the history of religion. It hardly belongs to the lowest savagery, which simply seems not to have attained to it, and it hardly belongs to the highest civilization, which has discarded it. Its place is intermediate, ranging from the higher savagery where it first clearly appears, to the middle civilization where it reaches its extreme development, and thenceforward its continuance is in dwindling survival and sometimes expanding revival. The position thus outlined is, however, very difficult to map exactly. Idolatry does not seem to come in uniformly among the higher savages ; it belongs, for instance, fully to the Society Islanders, but not to the Tongans and Fijians. Among higher nations, its presence or absence does not necessarily agree with particular national affinities or levels of culture—compare the idol-worshipping Hindu with his ethnic kinsman the idol-hating Parsi, or the idolatrous Phœnician with his ethnic kinsman the Israelite, among whose people the incidental relapse into the proscribed image-worship was a memory of disgrace. Moreover, its tendency to revive is ethnographically embarrassing. The ancient Vedic religion seems not to recognize idolatry, yet the modern Brahmans, professed followers of Vedic doctrine, are among the greatest idolators of the world. Early Christianity by no means abrogated the Jewish law against image-worship, yet image-worship became and still remains widely spread and deeply rooted in Christendom.

Of Idolatry, so far as its nature is symbolic or representative, I have given some account elsewhere.[1] The old and

---

[1] ' Early Hist. of Mankind,' chap. vi.

greatest difficulty in investigating the general subject is
this, that an image may be, even to two votaries kneeling
side by side before it, two utterly different things ; to the
one it may be only a symbol, a portrait, a memento; while
to the other it is an intelligent and active being, by virtue
of a life or spirit dwelling in it or acting through it.   In
both cases Image-worship is connected with the belief in
spiritual beings, and is in fact a subordinate development
of animism.   But it is only so far as the image approxi-
mates to the nature of a material body provided for a spirit,
that Idolatry comes properly into connexion with Fetishism.
It is from this point of view that it is proposed to examine
here its purpose and its place in history.   An idol, so far as
it belongs to the theory of spirit-embodiment, must combine
the characters of portrait and fetish.   Bearing this in mind,
and noticing how far the idol is looked on as in some way
itself an energetic object, or as the very receptacle enshrin-
ing a spiritual god, let us proceed to judge how far, along
the course of civilization, the idea of the image itself exert-
ing power or being personally animate has prevailed in the
mind of the idolater.

As to the actual origin of idolatry, it need not be
supposed that the earliest idols made by man seemed to
their maker living or even active things.   It is quite likely
that the primary intention of the image was simply to
serve as a sign or representative of some soul or deity, and
certainly this original character is more or less maintained
in the world through the long history of image-worship.
At a stage succeeding this original condition, it may be
argued, the tendency to identify the symbol and the
symbolized, a tendency so strong among children and the
ignorant everywhere, led to the idol being treated as a
living powerful being, and thence even to explicit doctrines
as to the manner of its energy or animation.   It is, then,
in this secondary stage, where the once merely representative image is passing into the active image-fetish,
that we are particularly concerned to understand it.

Here it is reasonable to judge the idolater by his distinct
actions and beliefs. A line of illustrative examples will
carry the personality of the idol through grade after
grade of civilization. Among the lower races, such
thoughts are displayed by the Kurile islander throwing
his idol into the sea to calm the storm ; by the negro who
feeds ancestral images and brings them a share of his
trade profits, but will beat an idol or fling it into the fire if
it cannot give him luck or preserve him from sickness ; by
famous idols of Madagascar, of which one goes about of
himself or guides his bearers, and another answers when
spoken to—at least, they did this till they were ignominiously
found out a few years ago. Among Tatar peoples of North
Asia and Europe, conceptions of this class are illustrated
by the Ostyak, who clothes his puppet and feeds it with
broth, but if it brings him no sport will try the effect of a
good thrashing on it, after which he will clothe and feed it
again ; by the Lapps, who fancied their uncouth images
could go about at will ; or the Esths, who wondered that
their idols did not bleed when Dieterich the Christian priest
hewed them down. Among high Asiatic nations, what
could be more anthropomorphic than the rites of modern
Hinduism, the dances of the nautch-girls before the idols,
the taking out of Jagannath in procession to pay visits, the
spinning of tops before Krishna to amuse him ? Buddhism
is a religion in its principles little favourable to idolatry.
Yet, from setting up portrait-statues of Gautama and other
saints, there developed itself the full worship of images, and
even of images with hidden joints and cavities, which moved
and spoke as in our own middle ages. In China, we read
stories of worshippers abusing some idol that has failed in
its duty. ' How now,' they say, ' you dog of a spirit ; we
have given you an abode in a splendid temple, we gild you
and feed you and fumigate you with incense, and yet you
are so ungrateful that you won't listen to our prayers ! ' So
they drag him in the dirt, and then, if they get what they
want, it is but to clean him and set him up again, with

apologies and promises of a new coat of gilding. There is what appears a genuine story of a Chinaman who had paid an idol priest to cure his daughter, but she died ; whereupon the swindled worshipper brought an action at law against the god, who for his fraud was banished from the province. The classic instances, again, are perfect—the dressing and anointing of statues, feeding them with delicacies and diverting them with raree-shows, summoning them as witnesses ; the story of the Arkadian youths coming back from a bad day's hunting and revenging themselves by scourging and pricking Pan's statue, and the companion tale of the image which fell upon the man who ill-treated it ; the Tyrians chaining the statue of the Sun-god that he might not abandon their city ; Augustus chastising in effigy the ill-behaved Neptune ; Apollo's statue that moved when it would give an oracle ; and the rest of the images which brandished weapons, or wept, or sweated, to prove their supernatural powers. Such ideas continued to hold their place in Christendom, as was natural, considering how directly the holy image or picture took the place of the household god or the mightier idol of the temple. The Russian boor covering up the saint's picture that it may not see him do wrong ; the Mingrelian borrowing a successful neighbour's saint when his own crop fails, or when about to perjure himself choosing for the witness of his deceitful oath a saint of mild countenance and merciful repute ; the peasant of Southern Europe, alternately coaxing and trampling on his special saint-fetish, and ducking the Virgin or St. Peter for rain ; the winking and weeping images that are worked, even at this day, to the greater glory of God, or rather to the greater shame of Man—these are but the extreme instances of the worshipper's endowment of the sacred image with a life and personality modelled on his own.[1]

[1] For general collections of evidence, see especially Meiners, ' Geschichte der Religionen,' vol. i. books i. and v. ; Bastian, ' Mensch,' vol. ii. ; Waitz, ' Anthropologie ;' De Brosses, ' Dieux Fétiches,' &c. Particular details in

The appearance of idolatry at a grade above the lowest of known human culture, and its development in extent and elaborateness under higher conditions of civilization, are well displayed among the native races of America. 'Conspicuous by its absence' among many of the lower tribes, image-worship comes plainly into view toward the upper levels of savagery, as where, for instance, Brazilian native tribes set up in their huts, or in the recesses of the forest, their pygmy heaven-descended figures of wax or wood;[1] or where the Mandans, howling and whining, made their prayers before puppets of grass and skins; or where the spiritual beings of the Algonquins (manitu) or the Hurons (oki) were represented by, and in language identified with, the carved wooden heads or more complete images to which worship and sacrifice were offered. Among the Virginians and other of the more cultured Southern tribes, these idols even had temples to dwell in.[2] The discoverers of the New World found idolatry an accepted institution among the islanders of the West Indies. These strong animists are recorded to have carved their little images in the shapes in which they believed the spirits themselves to have appeared to them; and some human figures bore the names of ancestors in memory of them. The images of such 'cemi' or spirits, some animal, but most of human type, were found by thousands; and it is even declared that an island near Hayti had a population of idol-makers, who especially made images of nocturnal spectres. The spirit could be conveyed with the image, both were called 'cemi,' and in the local accounts of sacrifices, oracles, and miracles, the deity and the idol are mixed together in a way which at least shows the extreme closeness of their connexion in the native

J. L. Wilson, 'W. Afr.' p. 393; Ellis, 'Madagascar,' vol. i. p. 395; Castrén, 'Finnische Mythologie,' p. 193, &c.; Ward, 'Hindoos,' vol. ii.; Köppen, 'Rel. des Buddha,' vol. i. p. 493, &c.; Grote, 'Hist. of Greece.'

[1] J. G. Müller, 'Amer. Urrelig.' p. 263; Meiners, vol. i. p. 163.

[2] Loskiel, 'Ind. of N. A.' vol. i. p. 39. Smith, 'Virginia,' in Pinkerton, vol. xiii. p. 14. Waitz, vol. iii. p. 203; J. G. Müller, pp. 95-8, 128.

mind.[1] If we pass to the far higher culture of Peru, we find idols in full reverence, some of them complete figures, but the great deities of Sun and Moon figured by discs with human countenances, like those which to this day represent them in symbol among ourselves. As for the conquered neighbouring tribes brought under the dominion of the Incas, their idols were carried, half trophies and half hostages, to Cuzco, to rank among the inferior deities of the Peruvian Pantheon.[2] In Mexico, idolatry had attained to its full barbaric development. As in the Aztec mind the world swarmed with spiritual deities, so their material representatives, the idols, stood in the houses at the corners of the streets, on every hill and rock, to receive from passers-by some little offering—a nosegay, a whiff of incense, a drop or two of blood; while in the temples more huge and elaborate images enjoyed the dances and processions in their honour, were fed by the bloody sacrifice of men and beasts, and received the tribute and reverence paid to the great national gods.[3] Up to a certain point, such evidence bears upon the present question. We learn that the native races of the New World had idols, that those idols in some sort represented ancestral souls and other deities, and for them received adoration and sacrifice. But whether the native ideas of the connexion of spirit and image were obscure, or whether the foreign observers did not get at these ideas, or partly for both reasons, there is a general want of express statement how far the idols of America remained mere symbols or portraits, or how far they had come to be considered the animated bodies of the gods.

It is not always thus, however. In the island regions of

[1] Fernando Colombo, 'Vita del Amm. Cristoforo Colombo,' Venice, 1571, p. 127, &c.; and 'Life of Colon,' in Pinkerton, vol. xii. p. 84. Herrera, dec. i. iii. 3. Rochefort, 'Iles Antilles,' pp. 421-4. Waitz, vol. iii. p. 384; J. G. Müller, pp. 171-6, 182, 210, 232.
[2] Prescott, ' Peru,' vol. i. pp. 71, 89; Waitz, vol. iv. p. 458; J. G. Müller, pp. 322, 371.
[3] Brasseur, 'Mexique,' vol. iii. p. 486; Waitz, vol. iv. p. 148; J. G. Müller, p. 642.

the Southern Hemisphere, while image-worship scarcely appears among the Andaman islanders, Tasmanians, or Australians, and is absent or rare in various Papuan and Polynesian districts, it prevails among the majority of the island tribes who have attained to middle and high savage levels. In Polynesian islands, where the meaning of the native idolatry has been carefully examined, it is found to rest on the most absolute theory of spirit-embodiment. Thus, New-Zealanders set up memorial idols of deceased persons near the burial-place, talking affectionately to them as if still alive, and casting garments to them when they passed by, also they preserve in their houses small carved wooden images, each dedicated to the spirit of an ancestor. It is distinctly held that such an atua or ancestral deity enters into the substance of an image in order to hold converse with the living. A priest can by repeating charms cause the spirit to enter into the idol, which he will even jerk by a string round its neck to arrest its attention ; it is the same atua or spirit which will at times enter not the image but the priest himself, throw him into convulsions, and deliver oracles through him ; while it is quite understood that the images themselves are not objects of worship, nor do they possess in themselves any virtue, but derive their sacredness from being the temporary abodes of spirits.[1] In the Society Islands, it was noticed in Captain Cook's exploration that the carved wooden images at burial-places were not considered mere memorials, but abodes into which the souls of the departed retired. In Mr. Ellis's account of the Polynesian idolatry, relating as it seems especially to this group, the sacred objects might be either mere stocks and stones, or carved wooden images, from six or eight feet long down to as many inches. Some of these were to represent ' tii,' divine manes or spirits of the dead, while others were to represent ' tu,' or deities of higher rank and power. At certain seasons, or in answer to the prayers of the priests, these spiritual beings entered into the idols,

[1] Shortland, ' Trads. of N. Z.' &c., p. 83 ; Taylor, pp. 171, 183, 212.

which then became very powerful, but when the spirit departed, the idol remained only a sacred object. A god often came to and passed from an image in the body of a bird, and spiritual influence could be transmitted from an idol by imparting it by contact to certain valued kinds of feathers, which could be carried away in this ' inhabited ' state, and thus exert power elsewhere, and transfer it to new idols. Here then we have the similarity of souls to other spirits shown by the similar way in which both become embodied in images, just as these same people consider both to enter into human bodies. And we have the pure fetish, which here is a feather or a log or stone, brought together with the more elaborate carved idol, all under one common principle of spirit-embodiment.[1] In Borneo, notwithstanding the Moslem prohibition of idolatry, not only do images remain in use, but the doctrine of spirit-embodiment is distinctly applied to them. Among the tribes of Western Sarawak the priestesses have made for them rude figures of birds, which none but they may touch. These are supposed to become inhabited by spirits, and at the great harvest feasts are hung up in bunches of ten or twenty in the long common room, carefully veiled with coloured handkerchiefs. Again, among some Dayak tribes, they will make rude figures of a naked man and woman, and place these opposite to one another on the path to the farms. On their heads are head-dresses of bark, by their sides is the betel-nut basket, and in their hands a short wooden spear. These figures are said to be inhabited each by a spirit who prevents inimical influences from passing on to the farms, and likewise from the farms to the village, and evil betide the profane wretch who lifts his hand against them—violent fever and sickness would be sure to follow.[2]

West Africa naturally applies its familiar fetish-doctrine

[1] J. R. Forster, ' Obs. during Voyage,' London, 1778, p. 534, &c. ; Ellis, ' Polyn. Res.' vol. i. p. 281, &c., 323, &c. See also Earl, ' Papuans,' p. 84 ; Bastian, ' Psychologie,' p. 78 (Nias).

[2] St. John, ' Far East,' vol. i. p. 198.

of spirit-embodiment to images or idols. How an image may be considered a receptacle for a spirit, is well shown here by the straw and rag figures of men and beasts made in Calabar at the great triennial purification, for the expelled spirits to take refuge in, whereupon they are got rid of over the border.[1] As to positive idols, nothing could be more explicit than the Gold-Coast account of certain wooden figures called 'amagai,' which are specially treated by a 'wong-man' or priest, and have a 'wong' or deity in connexion with them; so close is the connexion conceived between spirit and image, that the idol is itself called 'wong.'[2] So in the Ewe district, the same 'edro' or deity who inspires the priest is also present in the idol, and 'edro' signifies both god and idol.[3] Waitz sums up the principles of West African idolatry in a distinct theory of embodiment, as follows : ' The god himself is invisible, but the devotional feeling and especially the lively fancy of the negro demands a visible object to which worship may be directed. He wishes really and sensibly to behold the god, and seeks to shape in wood or clay the conception he has formed of him. Now if the priest, whom the god himself at times inspires and takes possession of, consecrates this figure to him, the idea has only to follow that the god may in consequence be pleased to take up his abode in the figure, to which he may be specially invited by the consecration, and thus image-worship is seen to be comprehensible enough. Denham found that even to take a man's portrait was dangerous and caused mistrust, from the fear that a part of the living man's soul might be conveyed by magic into the artificial figure. The idols are not, as Bosman thinks, deputies of the gods, but merely objects in which the god loves to place himself, and which at the same time display him in sensible presence to his adorers. The

[1] Hutchinson in ' Tr. Eth. Soc.' vol. i. p. 336 ; see Bastian, ' Psychologie,' p. 172.

[2] Steinhauser, in ' Magaz. der Evang. Missionen,' Basel, 1856, No. 2, p. 131.

[3] Schlegel, ' Ewe-Sprache,' p. xvi.

god is also by no means bound fast to his dwelling in the image, he goes out and in, or rather is present in it sometimes with more and sometimes with less intensity.'[1]

Castrén's wide and careful researches among the rude Turanian tribes of North Asia led him to form a similar conception of the origin and nature of their idolatry. The idols of these people are uncouth objects, often mere stones or logs with some sort of human countenance, or sometimes more finished images, even of metal ; some are large, some mere dolls ; they belong to individuals, or families, or tribes ; they may be kept in the yurts for private use, or set up in sacred groves or on the steppes or near the hunting and fishing places they preside over, or they may even have special temple-houses ; some open-air gods are left naked, not to spoil good clothes, but others under cover are decked out with all an Ostyak's or Samoyed's wealth of scarlet cloths and costly furs, necklaces and trinkets ; and lastly, to the idols are made rich offerings of food, clothes, furs, kettles, pipes, and the rest of the inventory of Siberian nomade riches. Now these idols are not to be taken as mere symbols or portraits of deities, but the worshippers mostly imagine that the deity dwells in the image or, so to speak, is embodied in it, whereby the idol becomes a real god capable of giving health and prosperity to man. On the one hand, the deity becomes serviceable to the worshipper by being thus contained and kept for his use, and on the other hand, the god profits by receiving richer offerings, failing which it would depart from its receptacle. We even hear of numerous spirits being contained in one image, and flying off at the death of the shaman who owned it. In Buddhist Tibet, as in West Africa, the practice of conjuring into puppets the demons which molest men is a recognized rite ; while in Siam the making of clay puppets to be exposed on trees or by the roadside, or set adrift with food-

[1] Waitz, ' Anthropologie,' vol. ii. p. 183 ; Denham, ' Travels,' vol. i. p. 113 ; Römer, ' Guinea ' ; Bosman, ' Guinea,' in Pinkerton, vol. xvi. See also Livingstone, ' S. Afr.' p. 282 (Balonda).

offerings in baskets, is a recognized manner of expelling disease-spirits.[1] In the image-worship of modern India, there crop up traces of the embodiment-theory. It is possible for the intelligent Hindu to attach as little real personality to a divine image, as to the man of straw which he makes in order to celebrate the funeral rites of a relative whose body cannot be recovered. He can even protest against being treated as an idolater at all, declaring the images of his gods to be but symbols, bringing to his mind thoughts of the real deities, as a portrait reminds one of a friend no longer to be seen in the body. Yet in the popular religion of his country, what could be more in conformity with the fetish-theory than the practice of making temporary hollow clay idols by tens of thousands, which receive no veneration for themselves, and only become objects of worship when the officiating brahman has invited the deity to dwell in the image, performing the ceremony of the ' adhivâsa ' or inhabitation, after which he puts in the eyes and the ' prâna,' i.e., breath, life, or soul.[2]

Nowhere, perhaps, in the wide history of religion, can we find definitions more full and absolute of the theory of deities actually animating their images, than in those passages from early Christian writers which describe the nature and operation of the heathen idols. Arnobius introduces the heathen as declaring that it is not the bronze or gold and silver material they consider to be gods, but they worship in them those beings which sacred dedication introduces, and causes to inhabit the artificial images.[3] Augustine cites as follows the opinions attributed to Hermes Trismegistus. This Egyptian, he tells us, considers some gods as made by the highest Deity, and some by men ; ' he asserts the visible and tangible images to be as it were bodies of

[1] Castrén, ' Finn. Myth,' p. 193, &c.; Bastian, ' Psych.' p. 34, 208, ' Oestl. Asien,' vol. iii. pp. 293, 486. See ' Journ. Ind. Archip.' vol. ii. p. 350 (Chinese).

[2] Max Müller, ' Chips,' vol. i. p. xvii.; ' Ward, 'Hindoos,' vol. i. p. 198, vol. ii. pp. xxxv. 164, 234, 292, 485.

[3] Arnobius Adversus Gentes, vi. 17-19.

gods, for there are within them certain invited spirits, of some avail for doing harm or for fulfilling certain desires of those who pay them divine honours and rites of worship. By a certain art to connect these invisible spirits with visible objects of corporeal matter, that such may be as it were animated bodies, effigies dedicate and subservient to the spirits—this is what he calls making gods, and men have received this great and wondrous power.' And further, this Trismegistus is made to speak of 'statues animated with sense and full of spirit, doing so great things ; statues prescient of the future, and predicting it by lots, by priests, by dreams, and by many other ways.'[1] This idea, as accepted by the early Christians themselves, with the qualification that the spiritual beings inhabiting the idols were not beneficent deities but devils, is explicitly stated by Minucius Felix, in a passage in the ' Octavius,' which gives an instructive account of the aministic philosophy of Christianity towards the beginning of the third century : ' Thus these impure spirits or demons, as shown by the magi, by the philosophers, and by Plato, are concealed by consecration in statues and images, and by their afflatus obtain the authority as of a present deity when at times they inspire priests, inhabit temples, occasionally animate the filaments of the entrails, govern the flight of birds, guide the falling of lots, give oracles enveloped in many falsehoods . . . also secretly creeping into (men's) bodies as thin spirits, they feign diseases, terrify minds, distort limbs, in order to compel men to their worship; that fattening on the steam of altars or their offered victims from the flocks, they may seem to have cured the ailments which they had constrained. And these are the madmen whom ye see rush forth into

---

[1] Augustinus ' De Civ. Dei,' viii. 23 : ' at ille visibilia et contrectabilia simulacra, velut corpora deorum esse asserit ; inesse autem his quosdam spiritus invitatos, &c. . . . . Hos ergo spiritus invisibiles per artem quandam visibilibus rebus corporalis materiæ copulare, ut sint quasi animata corpora, illis spiritibus dicata et subdita simulacra, &c. See also Tertullianus De Spectaculis, xii. : ' In mortuorum autem idolis dæmonia consistunt, &c.'

public places ; and the very priests without the temple thus
go mad, thus rave, thus whirl about. . . . All these
things most of you know, how the very demons confess of
themselves, so often as they are expelled by us from the
patients' bodies with torments of word and fires of prayer.
Saturn himself, and Serapis, and Jupiter, and whatsoever
demons ye worship, overcome by pain declare what they
are ; nor surely do they lie concerning their iniquity, above
all when several of you are present. Believe these witnesses, confessing the truth of themselves, that they are
demons. For adjured by the true and only God, they
shudder reluctant in the wretched bodies ; and either they
issue forth at once, or vanish gradually, according as the
faith of the patient aids, or the grace of the curer
favours.'[1]

The strangeness with which such words now fall upon
our ears is full of significance. It is one symptom of that
vast quiet change which has come over animistic philosophy
in the modern educated world. Whole orders of spiritual
beings, worshipped in polytheistic religion, and degraded
in early Christendom to real but evil demons, have since
passed from objective to subjective existence, have faded
from the Spiritual into the Ideal. By the operation of
similar intellectual changes, the general theory of spirit-
embodiment, having fulfilled the great work it had for ages
to do in religion and philosophy, has now dwindled within
the limits of the educated world to near its vanishing-point.
The doctrines of Disease-possession and Oracle-possession,
once integral parts of the higher philosophy, and still maintaining a vigorous existence in the lower culture, seem to
be dying out within the influence of the higher into dogmatic survival, conscious metaphor, and popular superstition. The doctrine of spirit-embodiment in objects,
Fetishism, now scarcely appears outside barbaric regions

---

[1] Marcus Minucius Felix, Octavius, cap. xxvii. : ' Isti igitur impuri
spiritus, dæmones, ut ostensum a magis, a philosophis, et a Platone sub
statuis et imaginibus consecrati delitescunt, &c.'

save in the peasant folklore which keeps it up amongst us with so many other remnants of barbaric thought. And the like theory of spiritual influence as applied to Idolatry, though still to be studied among savages and barbarians, and on record in past ages of the civilized world, has perished so utterly amongst ourselves, that few but students are aware of its ever having existed.

To bring home to our minds the vastness of the intellectual tract which separates modern from savage philosophy, and to enable us to look back along the path where step by step the mind's journey was made, it will serve us to glance over the landmarks which language to this day keeps standing. Our modern languages reach back through the middle ages to classic and barbaric times, where in this matter the transition from the crudest primæval animism is quite manifest. We keep in daily use, and turn to modern meaning, old words and idioms which carry us home to the philosophy of ancient days. We talk of ' genius ' still, but with thought how changed. The genius of Augustus was a tutelary demon, to be sworn by and to receive offerings on an altar as a deity. In modern English, Shakspere, Newton, or Wellington, is said to be led and prompted by his genius, but that genius is a shrivelled philosophic metaphor. So the word ' spirit ' and its kindred terms keep up with wondrous pertinacity the traces which connect the thought of the savage with its hereditary successor, the thought of the philosopher. Barbaric philosophy retains as real what civilized language has reduced to simile. The Siamese is made drunk with the demon of the arrack that possesses the drinker, while we with so different sense still extract the ' spirit of wine.'[1] Look at the saying ascribed to Pythagoras, and mentioned by Porphyry. ' The sound indeed which is given by striking brass, is the voice of a certain demon contained in that brass.' These might have been the representative words of some savage animistic

[1] Bastian, ' Oestl. Asien,' vol. ii. p. 455. See Spiegel, ' Avesta,' vol. ii. p. 54.

philosopher; but with the changed meaning brought by centuries of philosophizing, Oken hit upon a definition almost identical in form, that ' What sounds, announces its spirit' (' Was tönt, gibt seinen Geist kund ').[1] What the savage would have meant, or Porphyry after him did mean, was that the brass was actually animated by a spirit of the brass apart from its matter, but when a modern philosopher takes up the old phrase, all he means is the qualities of the brass. As in other animistic phrases of thought and feeling such as ' animal spirits,' or being in ' good and bad spirits,' the term only recalls with an effort the long-past philosophy which it once expressed. The modern theory of the mind considers it capable of performing even exalted and unusual functions without the intervention of prompting or exciting demons ; yet the old recognition of such beings crops up here and there in phrases which adapt animistic ideas to commonplaces of human disposition, as when a man is still said to be animated by a patriotic spirit, or possessed by a spirit of disobedience. In old times the ἐγγαστρίμυθος, or ' ventriloquus ' was really held to have a spirit rumbling or talking from inside his body, as when Eurykles the soothsayer was inspired by such a familiar ; or when a certain Patriarch mentioning a demon heard to speak out of a man's belly, remarks on the worthy place it had chosen to dwell in. In the time of Hippokrates, the giving of oracular responses by such ventriloquism was practised by certain women as a profession. To this day in China one may get an oracular response from a spirit apparently talking out of a medium's stomach, for a fee of about twopence-halfpenny. How changed a philosophy it marks, that among ourselves the word ' ventriloquist ' should have sunk to its present meaning.[2] Nor is that

---

[1] Porphyr. de Vita Pythagoræ. Oken, ' Lehrbuch der Naturphilosophie,' 2753.

[2] Suidas, s.v. ἐγγαστρίμυθος; Isidor. Gloss. s.v. 'præcantatores'; Bastian, ' Mensch,' vol. ii. p. 578. Maury, ' Magie,' &c. p. 269. Doolittle, ' Chinese,' vol. ii. p. 115.

change less significant which, starting with the conception of a man being really ἔνθεος, possessed by a deity within him, carries on a metamorphosed relic of this thorough animistic thought, from ἐνθουσιασμός to 'enthusiasm.' With all this, let it not be supposed that such change of opinion in the educated world has come about through wanton incredulity or decay of the religious temperament. Its source is the alteration in natural science, assigning new causes for the operations of nature and the events of life. The theory of the immediate action of personal spirits has here, as so widely elsewhere, given place to ideas of force and law. No indwelling deity now regulates the life of the burning sun, no guardian angels drive the stars across the arching firmament, the divine Ganges is water flowing down into the sea to evaporate into cloud and descend again in rain. No deity simmers in the boiling pot, no presiding spirits dwell in the volcano, no howling demon shrieks from the mouth of the lunatic. There was a period of human thought when the whole universe seemed actuated by spiritual life. For our knowledge of our own history, it is deeply interesting that there should remain rude races yet living under the philosophy which we have so far passed from, since Physics, Chemistry, Biology, have seized whole provinces of the ancient Animism, setting force for life and law for will.

ANIMISM (*continued*)

WE have now to enter on the final topic of the investigation of Animism, by completing the classified survey of
spiritual beings in general, from the myriad souls, elves,
fairies, genii, conceived as filling their multifarious offices in
man's life and the world's, up to the deities who reign, few
and mighty, over the spiritual hierarchy. In spite of endless diversity of detail, the general principles of this investigation seem comparatively easy of access to the enquirer,
if he will use the two keys which the foregoing studies
supply : first, that spiritual beings are modelled by man on
his primary conception of his own human soul, and second,
that their purpose is to explain nature on the primitive
childlike theory that it is truly and throughout ' Animated
Nature.' If, as the poet says, ' Felix qui potuit rerum
cognoscere causas,' then rude tribes of ancient men had
within them this source of happiness, that they could
explain to their own content the causes of things. For to

them spiritual beings, elves and gnomes, ghosts and manes, demons and deities, were the living personal causes of universal life. ' The first men found everything easy, the mysteries of nature were not so hidden from them as from us,' said Jacob Böhme the mystic. True, we may well answer, if these primitive men believed in that animistic philosophy of nature which even now survives in the savage mind. They could ascribe to kind or hostile spirits all good and evil of their own lives, and all striking operations of nature ; they lived in familiar intercourse with the living and powerful souls of their dead ancestors, with the spirits of the stream and grove, plain and mountain, they knew well the living mighty Sun pouring his beams of light and heat upon them, the living mighty Sea dashing her fierce billows on the shore, the great personal Heaven and Earth protecting and producing all things. For as the human body was held to live and act by virtue of its own inhabiting spirit-soul, so the operations of the world seemed to be carried on by the influence of other spirits. And thus Animism, starting as a philosophy of human life, extended and expanded itself till it became a philosophy of nature at large.

To the minds of the lower races it seems that all nature is possessed, pervaded, crowded, with spiritual beings. In seeking by a few types to give an idea of this conception of pervading Spirits in its savage and barbaric stage, it is not indeed possible to draw an absolute line of separation between spirits occupied in affecting for good and ill the life of Man, and spirits specially concerned in carrying on the operations of Nature. In fact these two classes of spiritual beings blend into one another as inextricably as do the original animistic doctrines they are based on. As, however, the spirits considered directly to affect the life and fortune of Man lie closest to the centre of the animistic scheme, it is well to give them precedence. The description and function of these beings extend upwards from among the rudest human tribes. Milligan writes of the Tasmanians : ' They were polytheists ; that is, they believed in guardian angels or spirits, and in a plurality of powerful but generally evil-disposed beings, inhabiting crevices and caverns of rocky mountains, and making temporary abode in hollow trees and solitary valleys ; of these a few were supposed to be of great power, while to the majority were imputed much of the nature and attributes of the goblins and elves of our native land.'[1] Oldfield writes of the aborigines of Australia, ' The number of supernatural beings, feared if not loved, that they acknowledge, is exceedingly great ; for not only are the heavens peopled with such, but the whole face of the country swarms with them ; every thicket, most watering-places, and all rocky places abound with evil spirits. In like manner, every natural phenomenon is believed to be the work of demons, none of which seem of a benign nature, one and all apparently striving to do all imaginable mischief to the poor black fellow.'[2] It must be indeed an unhappy race among whom such a demonology could shape itself, and it is a relief to find that other people of low culture, while recognizing the same spiritual world swarming about them, do not hold its main attribute to be spite against themselves. Among the Algonquin Indians of North America, School-craft finds the very groundwork of their religion in the belief ' that the whole visible and invisible creation is animated with various orders of malignant or benign spirits, who preside over the daily affairs and over the final destinies of men.'[3] Among the Khonds of Orissa, Mac-pherson describes the greater gods and tribal manes, and below these the order of minor and local deities : ' They are the tutelary gods of every spot on earth, having power over the functions of nature which operate there, and over everything relating to human life in it. Their number is

---

[1] F. R. Nixon, ' Cruise of the Beacon ' ; Bonwick, p. 182.

[2] Oldfield in ' Tr. Eth. Soc.' vol. iii. p. 228.

[3] Schoolcraft, ' Algic Res.' vol. i. p. 41. ' Indian Tribes,' vol. iii. p. 327. Waitz, vol. iii. p. 191. See also J. G. Müller, p. 175. (Antilles Islanders) ; Brasseur, ' Mexique,' vol. iii. p. 482.

unlimited. They fill all nature, in which no power or object, from the sea to the clods of the field, is without its deity. They are the guardians of hills, groves, streams, fountains, paths, and hamlets, and are cognizant of every human action, want, and interest in the locality, where they preside.'[1] Describing the animistic mythology of the Turanian tribes of Asia and Europe, Castrén has said that every land, mountain, rock, river, brook, spring, tree, or whatsoever it may be, has a spirit for an inhabitant ; the spirits of the trees and stones, of the lakes and brooks, hear with pleasure the wild man's pious prayers and accept his offerings.[2] Such are the conceptions of the Guinea negro, who finds the abodes of his good and evil spirits in great rocks, hollow trees, mountains, deep rivers, dense groves, echoing caverns, and who passing silently by these sacred places leaves some offering, if it be but a leaf or a shell picked up on the beach.[3] Such are examples which not unfairly picture the belief of the lower races in a world of spirits on earth, and such descriptions apply to the state of men's minds along the course of civilization.

The doctrine of ancient philosophers such as Philo[4] and Iamblichus,[5] of spiritual beings swarming through the atmosphere we breathe, was carried on and developed in special directions in the discussions concerning the nature and functions of the world-pervading host of angels and devils, in the writings of the early Christian Fathers.[6] Theologians of modern centuries have for the most part seen reason to reduce within comparatively narrow limits the action ascribed to external spiritual beings on mankind ;

[1] Macpherson, ' India,' p. 90. See also Cross, ' Karens,' in ' Journ. Amer. Or. Soc.' vol. iv. p. 315 ; Williams, ' Fiji,' vol. i. p. 239.
[2] Castrén, ' Finn. Myth.' p. 114, 182, &c.
[3] J. L. Wilson, ' W. Afr.' p. 218, 388 ; Waitz, vol. ii. p. 171.
[4] Philo, De Gigant. I. iv.
[5] Iamblichus, ii.
[6] Collected passages in Calmet, ' Diss. sur les Esprits ' ; Horst, ' Zauber-Bibliothek,' vol. ii. p. 263, &c. ; vol. vi. p. 49, &c. ; see Migne's Dictionaries.

yet there are some who retain to the full the angelology and demonology of Origen and Tertullian. These two views may be well contrasted by setting side by side the judgments of two ecclesiastics of the Roman Church, as to the belief in pervading demons prevalent in uncivilized countries. The celebrated commentator, Dom Calmet, lays down in the most explicit terms the doctrine of angels and demons, as a matter of dogmatic theology. But he is less inclined to receive unquestioned the narratives of particular manifestations in the mediæval and modern world. He mentions indeed the testimony of Louis Vivez, that in the newly discovered countries of America, nothing is more common than to see spirits which appear at noonday, not only in the country but in towns and villages, speaking, commanding, sometimes even striking men ; and the account by Olaus Magnus of the spectres or spirits seen in Sweden and Norway, Finland and Lapland, which do wonderful things, some even serving men as domestics and driving the cattle out to pasture. But what Calmet remarks on these stories, is that the greater ignorance prevails in a country, the more superstitition reigns there.[1] It seems that in our own day, however, the tendency is to encourage less sceptical views. Monsignor Gaume's book on ' Holy Water,' which not long since received the special and formal approval of Pius IX., appears ' at an epoch when the millions of evil angels which surround us are more enterprising than ever ; ' and here Olaus Magnus' story of the demons infesting Northern Europe is not only cited but corroborated.[2] On the whole, the survey of the doctrine of pervading spirits through all the grades of culture is a remarkable display of intellectual continuity. Most justly does Ellis the missionary, depicting the South Sea Islanders' world crowded with its innumerable pervading spirits, point out the closeness of correspondence here between doctrines of the savage and the

---

[1] Calmet, ' Dissertation sur les Esprits,' vol. i. ch. xlviii.
[2] Gaume, ' L'Eau Bénite au XIXme Siècle,' pp. 295, 341.

civilized animist, expressed as both may be in Milton's
familiar lines :—

> ' Millions of spiritual creatures walk the earth,
> Unseen, both when we wake, and when we sleep.' [1]

As with souls, so with other spirits, man's most distinct
and direct intercourse is had where they become actually
present to his senses in dreams and visions. The belief
that such phantoms are real and personal spirits, suggested
and maintained as it is by the direct evidence of the senses
of sight, touch, and hearing, is naturally an opinion usual
in savage philosophy, and indeed elsewhere, long and ob-
stinately resisting the attacks of the later scientific doctrine.
The demon Koin strives to throttle the dreaming Australian; [2] the evil ' na ' crouches on the stomach of the
Karen; [3] the North American Indian, gorged with feasting,
is visited by nocturnal spirits; [4] the Caribs, subject to
hideous dreams, often woke declaring that the demon
Maboya had beaten them in their sleep, and they could
still feel the pain. [5] These demons are the very elves
and nightmares that to this day in benighted districts of
Europe ride and throttle the snoring peasant, and whose
names, not forgotten among the educated, have only
made the transition from belief to jest. [6] A not less distinct product of the savage animistic theory of dreams
as real visits from personal spiritual beings, lasted on
without a shift or break into the belief of mediæval
Christendom. This is the doctrine of the incubi and
succubi, those male and female nocturnal demons which
consort sexually with men and women. We may set out

[1] Ellis, ' Polyn. Res.' vol. i. p. 331.
[2] Backhouse, ' Australia,' p. 555 ; Grey, ' Australia,' vol. ii. p. 337.
[3] Mason, ' Karens,' l.c. p. 211.
[4] Schoolcraft, ' Indian Tribes,' part iii. p. 226.
[5] Rochefort, ' Antilles,' p. 419.
[6] Grimm, ' D. M.' p. 1193 ; Hanusch, ' Slaw. Myth.' p. 332 ; St. Clair
and Brophy, ' Bulgaria,' p. 59 ; Wuttke, ' Volksaberglaube,' p. 122 ; Bastian,
' Psychologie,' p. 103 ; Brand, vol. iii. p. 279.   The *mare* in *nightmare*
means spirit, elf, or nymph ; compare Anglo-Sax. *wudumære* (wood-mare)
=echo.

with their descriptions among the islanders of the Antilles, where they are the ghosts of the dead, vanishing when clutched;[1] in New Zealand, where ancestral deities ' form attachments with females and pay them repeated visits,' while in the Samoan Islands such intercourse of mischievious inferior gods caused ' many supernatural conceptions;'[2] and in Lapland, where details of this last extreme class have also been placed on record.[3] From these lower grades of culture the idea may be followed onward. Formal rites are specified in the Hindu Tantra, which enable a man to obtain a companion-nymph by worshipping her and repeating her name by night in a cemetery.[4] Augustine, in an instructive passage, states the popular notions of the visits of incubi, vouched for, he tells us, by testimony of such quantity and quality that it may seem impudence to deny it ; yet he is careful not to commit himself to a positive belief in such spirits.[5] Later theologians were less cautious, and grave argumentation on nocturnal intercourse with incubi and succubi was carried on till, at the height of mediæval civilization, it is found accepted in full belief by ecclesiastics and lawyers. Nor is it to be counted as an ugly but harmless superstition, when for example it is set forth in the Bull of Pope Innocent VIII. in 1484, as an

---

[1] ' Vita del Amm. Christoforo Colombo,' ch. xiii. ; and ' Life of Colon,' in Pinkerton, vol. xii. p. 84.

[2] Taylor, ' New Zealand,' pp. 149, 389. Mariner, ' Tonga Is.' vol. ii. p. 119.

[3] Högström, ' Lapmark,' ch. xi.

[4] Ward, ' Hindoos,' vol. ii. p. 151. See also Borri, ' Cochin-China,' in Pinkerton, vol. ix. p. 823.

[5] Augustin. ' De Civ. Dei,' xv. 23 : ' Et quoniam creberrima fama est, multique se expertos, vel ab eis qui experti essent, de quorum fide dubitandum non esset, audisse confirmant, Silvanos et Faunos, quos vulgo incubos vocant, improbos sæpe extitisse mulieribus, et earum appetisse ac peregisse concubitum; et quosdam dæmones, quos Dusios Galli nuncupant, hanc assidue immunditiam et tentare et efficere ; plures talesque asseverant, ut hoc negare impudentiæ videatur ; non hinc aliquid audeo definire, utrum aliqui spiritus . . . possint etiam hanc pati libidinem ; ut . . . . sentientibus feminibus misceantur.' See also Grimm, ' D. M.' pp. 449, 479; Hanusch, ' Slaw. Myth.' p. 332 ; Cockayne, ' Leechdoms of Early England,' vol. i. p. xxxviii., vol. ii. p. 345.

accepted accusation against 'many persons of both sexes, forgetful of their own salvation, and falling away from the Catholic faith.' The practical outcome of this belief is known to students who have traced the consequence of the Papal Bull in the legal manual of the witchcraft tribunals, drawn up by the three appointed Inquisitors, the infamous Malleus Maleficarum ; and have followed the results of this again into those dreadful records which relate in their bald matter-of-fact phraseology the confessions of the crime of diabolic intercourse, wrung from the wretched victims worked on by threat and persuasion in the intervals of the rack, till enough evidence was accumulated for clear judgment, and sentence of the stake.[1] I need not dwell on the mingled obscenity and horror of these details, which here only have their bearing on the history of animism. But it will aid the ethnographer to understand the relation of modern to savage philosophy, if he will read Richard Burton's seriously believing account in the ' Anatomy of Melancholy,' where he concludes with acquiescence in a declaration lately made by Lipsius, that on the showing of daily narratives and judicial sentences, in no age had these lecherous demons appeared in such numbers as in his own time—and this was about A.D. 1600.[2]

In connexion with the nightmare and the incubus, another variety of nocturnal demon requires notice, the vampire. Inasmuch as certain patients are seen becoming day by day, without apparent cause, thin, weak, and bloodless, savage animism is called upon to produce a satisfactory explanation, and does so in the doctrine that there exist certain demons which eat out the souls or hearts or suck the blood of their victims. The Polynesians said that it was the

[1] The ' Malleus Maleficarum ' was published about 1489. See on the general subject, Horst, ' Zauber-Bibliothek,' vol. vi. ; Ennemoser, ' Magic,' vol. ii. ; Maury, ' Magie,' &c. p. 256 ; Lecky, ' Hist. of Rationalism,' vol. i.
[2] Burton, ' Anatomy of Melancholy,' iii. 2. ' Unum dixero, non opinari me ullo retro ævo tantam copiam Satyrorum, et salacium istorum Geniorum se ostendisse, quantum nunc quotidianæ narrationes, et judiciales sententiæ proferunt.'

departed souls (tii) which quitted the graves and grave-idols to creep by night into the houses, and devour the heart and entrails of the sleepers, and these died.[1] The Karens tell of the ' kephu,' which is a wizard's stomach going forth in the shape of a head and entrails, to devour the souls of men, and they die.[2] The Mintira of the Malay Peninsula have their ' hantu penyadin ; ' he is a water-demon, with a dog's head and an alligator's mouth, who sucks blood from men's thumbs and great toes, and they die.[3] It is in Slavonia and Hungary that the demon blood-suckers have their principal abode, and to this district belongs their special name of *vampire*, Polish *upior*, Russian *upir*. There is a whole literature of hideous vampire-stories, which the student will find elaborately discussed in Calmet. The shortest way of treating the belief is to refer it directly to the principles of savage animism. We shall see that most of its details fall into their places at once, and that vampires are not mere creations of groundless fancy, but causes conceived in spiritual form to account for specific facts of wasting disease. As to their nature and physical action, there are two principal theories, but both keep close to the original animistic idea of spiritual beings, and consider these demons to be human souls. The first theory is that the soul of a living man, often a sorcerer, leaves its proper body asleep and goes forth, perhaps in the visible form of a straw or fluff of down, slips through keyholes and attacks its sleeping victim. If the sleeper should wake in time to clutch this tiny soul-embodiment, he may through it have his revenge by maltreating or destroying its bodily owner. Some say these ' mury ' come by night to men, sit upon their breasts and suck their blood, while others think it is only children's blood they suck, they being to grown people mere nightmares. Here we have the actual phenomenon of nightmare, adapted to a particular purpose. The second

[1] J. R. Forster, ' Observations during Voyage round World,' p. 543.
[2] Cross, ' Karens,' l.c. p. 312.
[3] ' Journ. Ind. Archip.' vol. i. p. 307.

theory is that the soul of a dead man goes out from its buried corpse and sucks the blood of living men. The victim becomes thin, languid, and bloodless, falls into a rapid decline and dies. Here again is actual experience, but a new fancy is developed to complete the idea. The corpse thus supplied by its returning soul with blood, is imagined to remain unnaturally fresh and supple and ruddy; and accordingly the means of detecting a vampire is to open his grave, where the reanimated corpse may be found to bleed when cut, and even to move and shriek. One way to lay a vampire is to stake down the corpse (as with suicides and with the same intention); but the more effectual plan is to behead and burn it. This is the substance of the doctrine of vampires. Still, as one order of demons is apt to blend into others, the vampire-legends are much mixed with other animistic folklore. Vampires appear in the character of the poltergeist or knocker, as causing those disturbances in houses which modern spiritualism refers in like manner to souls of the departed. Such was the ghost of a certain surly peasant who came out of his grave in the island of Mycone in 1700, after he had been buried but two days; he came into the houses, upset the furniture, put the lamps out, and carried on his tricks till the whole population went wild with terror. Tournefort happened to be there and was present at the exhumation; his account is curious evidence of the way an excited mob could persuade themselves, without the least foundation of fact, that the body was warm and its blood red. Again, the blood-sucker is very generally described under the Slavonic names of werewolf (wilkodlak, brukolaka, &c.); the descriptions of the two creatures are inextricably mixed up, and a man whose eyebrows meet, as if his soul were taking flight like a butterfly, to enter some other body, may be marked by this sign either as a werewolf or a vampire. A modern account of vampirism in Bulgaria well illustrates the nature of spirits as conceived in such beliefs as these. A sorcerer armed with a saint's picture will hunt

a vampire into a bottle containing some of the filthy food
that the demon loves ; as soon as he is fairly inside he is
corked down, the bottle is thrown into the fire, and the
vampire disappears for ever.[1]

As to the savage visionary and the phantoms he beholds,
the Greenlander preparing for the profession of sorcerer
may stand as type, when, rapt in contemplation in his
desert solitude, emaciated by fasting and disordered by fits,
he sees before him scenes with figures of men and animals,
which he believes to be spirits. Thus it is interesting to
read the descriptions by Zulu converts of the dreadful
creatures which they see in moments of intense religious
exaltation, the snake with great eyes and very fearful, the
leopard creeping stealthily, the enemy approaching with his
long assagai in his hand—these coming one after another
to the place where the man has gone to pray in secret, and
striving to frighten him from his knees.[2] Thus the visionary
temptations of the Hindu ascetic and the mediæval saint are
happening in our own day, though their place is now rather
in the medical handbook than in the record of miracle.
Like the disease-demons and the oracle-demons, these
spiritual groups have their origin not in fancy, but in real
phenomena interpreted on animistic principles.

In the dark especially, harmful spirits swarm. Round
native Australian encampments, Sir George Grey used to
see the bush dotted with little moving points of fire; these
were the firesticks carried by the old women sent to look
after the young ones, but who dared not quit the firelight
without a brand to protect them from the evil spirits.[3] So
South American Indians would carry brands or torches for
fear of evil demons when they ventured into the dark.[4]

[1] J. V. Grohmann, ' Aberglaüben aus Böhmen,' &c., p. 24 ; Calmet, ' Diss.
sur les Esprits,' vol. ii.; Grimm, 'D.M.' p. 1048, &c.; St. Clair and Brophy,
' Bulgaria,' p. 49 ; see Ralston, ' Songs of Russian People,' p. 409.

[2] Cranz, ' Grönland,' p. 268. Callaway, ' Rel. of Amazulu,' p. 246, &c.

[3] Grey, ' Australia,' vol. ii. p. 302. See also Bonwick, ' Tasmanians,'
p. 180.

[4] Southey, ' Brazil,' part i. p. 238. See also Rochefort, p. 418 ; J. G.

Tribes of the Malay Peninsula light fires near a mother at childbirth, to scare away the evil spirits.[1] Such notions extend to higher levels of civilization. In Southern India, where for fear of pervading spirits only pressing need will induce a man to go abroad after sundown, the unlucky wight who has to venture into the dark will carry a fire-brand to keep off the spectral foes. Even in broad day-light, the Hindu lights lamps to keep off the demons,[2] a ceremony which is to be noticed again at a Chinese wed-ding.[3] In Europe, the details of the use of fire to drive off demons and witches are minute and explicit. The ancient Norse colonists in Iceland carried fire round the lands they intended to occupy, to expel the evil spirits. Such ideas have brought into existence a whole group of Scandinavian customs, still remembered in the country, but dying out in practice. Till a child is baptized, the fire must never be let out, lest the trolls should be able to steal the infant; a live coal must be cast after the mother as she goes to be churched, to prevent the trolls from carrying her off bodily or bewitching her ; a live coal is to be thrown after a troll-wife or witch as she quits a house, and so forth.[4] Into modern times, the people of the Hebrides continued to protect the mother and child from evil spirits, by carrying fire round them.[5] In modern Bulgaria, on the Feast of St. Demetrius, lighted candles are placed in the stables and the wood-shed, to prevent evil spirits from entering into

---

Müller, p. 273 (Caribs) ; Cranz, ' Grönland,' p. 301 ; Schoolcraft, ' Indian Tribes,' part iii. p. 140.

[1] ' Journ. Ind. Archip.' vol. i. pp. 270, 298 ; vol. ii. ' N. S.' p. 117.

[2] Roberts, ' Oriental Illustrations,' p. 531 ; Colebrook in ' As. Res.' vol. vii. p. 274.

[3] Doolittle, ' Chinese,' vol. i. p. 77.

[4] Hylten-Cavallius, ' Wärend och Wirdarne,' vol. i. p. 191 ; Atkinson, ' Glossary of Cleveland Dial.' p. 597. [Prof. Liebrecht, in ' Zeitschrift für Ethnologie,' vol. v. 1873, p. 99, adds comparison of the still usual German custom of keeping a light burning in the lying-in room till the child is baptized (Wuttke, 2nd ed. No. 583), and the similar ancient Roman practice whence the goddess Candelifera had her name (note to 2nd. ed.).]

[5] Martin, ' Western Islands,' in Pinkerton, vol. iii. p. 612.

the domestic animals.[1] Nor did this ancient idea remain a mere lingering notion of peasant folklore. Its adoption by the Church is obvious in the ceremonial benediction of candles in the Roman Ritual : ' Ut quibuscumque locis accensæ, sive positæ fuerint, discedant principes tenebrarum, et contremiscant, et fugiant pavidi cum omnibus ministris suis ab habitationibus illis, &c.' The metrical translation of Naogeorgus shows perfectly the retention of primitive animistic ideas in the middle ages :—

> '. . . . a wondrous force and might
> Doth in these candels lie, which if at any time they light,
> They sure beleve that neyther storm or tempest dare abide,
> Nor thunder in the skies be heard, nor any devil's spide,
> Nor fearefull sprightes that walke by night, nor hurts of frost or
> haile.'[2]

Animals stare and startle when we see no cause ; is it that they see spirits invisible to man ? Thus the Greenlander says that the seals and wildfowl are scared by spectres, which no human eye but the sorcerer's can behold ;[3] and thus the Khonds hold that their flitting ethereal gods, invisible to man, are seen by beasts.[4] The thought holds no small place in the folklore of the world. Telemachos could not discern Athene standing near him, for not to all do the gods visibly appear ; but Odysseus saw her, and the dogs, and they did not bark, but with low whine slunk across the dwelling to the further side.[5] So in old Scandinavia, the dogs could see Hela the deathgoddess move unseen by men ;[6] so Jew and Moslem, hearing the dogs howl, know that they have seen the Angel of Death come on his awful errand;[7] while the

---

[1] St. Clair and Brophy, ' Bulgaria,' p. 44.

[2] Rituale Romanum ; Benedictio Candelarum. Brand, ' Popular Antiquities,' vol. i. p. 46.

[3] Cranz, ' Grönland,' p. 267, see 296.

[4] Macpherson, ' India,' p. 100.

[5] Homer, Odyss, xvi. 160.

[6] Grimm, ' D. M.' p. 632.

[7] Eisenmenger, ' Judenthum,' part i. p. 872. Lane, ' Thousand and One Nights,' vol. ii. p. 56.

beliefs that animals see spirits, and that a dog's melancholy howl means death somewhere near, are still familiar to our own popular superstition.

Another means by which men may detect the presence of invisible spirits, is to adopt the thief-catcher's well-known device of strewing ashes. According to the ideas of a certain stage of animism, a spirit is considered substantial enough to leave a footprint. The following instances relate sometimes to souls, sometimes to other beings. The Philippine islanders expected the dead to return on the third day to his dwelling, wherefore they set a vessel of water for him to wash himself clean from the grave-mould, and strewed ashes to see footprints.[1] A more elaborate rite forms part of the funeral customs of the Hos of North-East India. On the evening of a death, the near relatives perform the ceremony of calling the dead. Boiled rice and a pot of water are placed in an inner room, and ashes sprinkled from thence to the threshold. Two relatives go to the place where the body was burnt, and walk round it beating ploughshares and chanting a plaintive dirge to call the spirit home ; while two others watch the rice and water to see if they are disturbed, and look for the spirit-footsteps in the ashes. If a sign appears, it is received with shivering horror and weeping, the mourners outside coming in to join. Till the survivors are thus satisfied of the spirit's return, the rite must be repeated.[2] In Yucatan there is mention of the custom of leaving a child alone at night in a place strewn with ashes ; if the footprint of an animal were found next morning, this animal was the guardian deity of the child.[3] Beside this may be placed the Aztec ceremony at the second festival of the Sun-god Tezcatlipoca, when they sprinkled maize-flour before his sanctuary, and his

[1] Bastian, ' Psychologie,' p. 162. Other localities in ' Journ. Ind. Archip.' vol. iv. p. 333.

[2] Tickell in ' Journ. As. Soc. Bengal,' vol. ix. p. 795. The dirge is given above, p. 32.

[3] De Brosses, ' Dieux Fétiches,' p. 46.

high-priest watched till he beheld the divine footprints, and then shouted to announce, ' Our great god is come.' [1] Among such rites in the Old World, the Talmud contains a salient instance ; there are a great multitude of devils, it is said; and he who will be aware of them let him take sifted ashes and strew them by his bed, and in the early morning he shall see as it were marks of cocks' feet.[2] This is an idea that has widely spread in the modern world, as where in German folklore the little ' earth-men ' make footprints like a duck's or goose's in the strewn ashes. Other marks, too, betoken the passage of spirit-visitors ; [3] and as for ghosts, our own superstition is among the most striking of the series. On St. Mark's Eve, ashes are to be sifted over the hearth, and the foot-prints will be seen of any one who is to die within the year ; many a mischievous wight has made a superstitious family miserable by slily coming down stairs and marking the print of some one's shoe.[4] Such details as these may justify us in thinking that the lower races are apt to ascribe to spirits in general that kind of ethereal materiality which we have seen they attribute to souls. Explicit statements on the subject are scarce till we reach the level of early Christian theology. The ideas of Tertullian and Origen, as to the thin yet not immaterial substance of angels and demons, probably represent the conceptions of primitive animism far more clearly than the doctrine which Calmet lays down with the weight of theological dogma, that angels, demons, and disembodied souls are pure im-material spirit ; but that when by divine permission spirits appear, act, speak, walk, eat, they must produce tangible bodies by either condensing the air, or substituting

---

[1] Clavigero, ' Messico,' vol. ii. p. 79.

[2] Tractat. Berachoth.

[3] Grimm, ' D. M.' pp. 420, 1117 ; St. Clair and Brophy, ' Bulgaria,' p. 54. See also Bastian, ' Mensch,' vol. ii. p. 325 ; Tschudi, ' Peru,' vol. ii. p. 355.

[4] Brand, ' Popular Antiquities,' vol. i. p. 193. See Boecler, ' Ehsten Abergl.' p. 73.

other terrestrial solid bodies capable of performing these functions.[1]

No wonder that men should attack such material beings by material means, and even sometimes try to rid themselves by a general clearance from the legion of ethereal beings hovering around them. As the Australians annually drive from their midst the accumulated ghosts of the last year's dead, so the Gold Coast negroes from time to time turn out with clubs and torches to drive the evil spirits from their towns ; rushing about and beating the air with frantic howling, they drive the demons into the woods, and then come home and sleep more easily, and for a while afterwards enjoy better health.[2] When a baby was born in a Kalmuk horde, the neighbours would rush about crying and brandishing cudgels about the tents, to drive off the harmful spirits who might hurt mother and child.[3] Keeping up a closely allied idea in modern Europe, the Bohemians at Pentecost, and the Tyrolese on Walpurgisnacht, hunt the witches, invisible and imaginary, out of house and stall.[4]

Closely allied to the doctrine of souls, and almost rivalling it in the permanence with which it has held its place through all the grades of animism, is the doctrine of patron, guardian, or familiar spirits. These are beings specially attached to individual men, soul-like in their nature, and sometimes considered as actually being human souls. These beings have, like all others of the spiritual world as originally conceived, their reason and purpose. The special functions which they perform are twofold. First, while man's own proper soul serves him for the ordinary purposes of life and thought, there are times when powers

---

[1] Tertullian, De Carne Christi, vi. ; Adv. Marcion, ii. ; Origen, De Princip. i. 7. See Horst, l.c. Calmet, ' Dissertation,' vol. i. ch. xlvi.

[2] J. L. Wilson, ' W. Afr.' p. 217. See Bosman, ' Guinea,' in Pinkerton, vol. xvi. p. 402.

[3] Pallas, ' Reisen,' vol. i. p. 360.

[4] Grimm, ' D. M.' p. 1212 ; Wuttke, ' Volksaberglaube,' p. 119 ; see Hyltén-Cavallius, part i. p. 178 (Sweden).

and impressions out of the course of the mind's normal
action, and words that seem spoken to him by a voice from
without, messages of mysterious knowledge, of counsel or
warning, seem to indicate the intervention of as it were a
second superior soul, a familiar demon. And as enthusiasts, seers, sorcerers, are the men whose minds most
often show such conditions, so to these classes more than
to others the informing and controlling patron-spirits are
attached. Second, while the common expected events of
daily life pass unnoticed as in the regular course of things,
such events as seem to fall out with especial reference to
an individual, demand an intervening agent ; and thus the
decisions, discoveries, and deliverances, which civilized
men variously ascribe to their own judgment, to luck, and
to special interposition of Providence, are accounted for
in the lower culture by the action of the patron-spirit or
guardian-genius. Not to crowd examples from all the districts of animism to which this doctrine belongs, let us
follow it by a few illustrations from the lower grades of
savagery upward. Among the Watchandis of Australia, it
is held that when a warrior slays his first man, the spirit of
the dead enters the slayer's body and becomes his 'woo-
rie' or warning spirit; taking up its abode near his liver,
it informs him by a scratching or tickling sensation of the
approach of danger.[1] In Tasmania, Dr. Milligan heard
a native ascribe his deliverance from an accident to the
preserving care of his deceased father's spirit, his guardian
angel.[2] That the most important act of the North
American Indian's religion is to obtain his individual
patron genius or deity, is well known. Among the Esquimaux, the sorcerer qualifies for his profession by getting a
' torngak ' or spirit which will henceforth be his familiar
demon, and this spirit may be the soul of a deceased
parent.[3] In Chili, as to guardian spirits, it has been re-

---

[1] Oldfield, ' Abor. of Australia,' in ' Tr. Eth. Soc.' vol. iii. p. 240.
[2] Bonwick, ' Tasmanians,' p. 182.
[3] Cranz, ' Grönland,' p. 268 ; Egede, p. 187.

marked that every Araucanian imagines he has one in his service ; ' I keep my amchi-malghen (guardian nymph) still,' being a common expression when they succeed in any undertaking.[1] The Caribs display the doctrine well in both its general and special forms. On the one hand, there is a guardian deity for each man, which accompanies his soul to the next life ; on the other hand, each sorcerer has his familiar demon, which he evokes in mysterious darkness by chants and tobacco-smoke ; and when several sorcerers call up their familiars together, the consequence is apt to be a quarrel among the demons, and a fight.[2] In Africa, the negro has his guardian spirit—how far identified with what Europeans call soul or conscience, it may be hard to determine ; but he certainly looks upon it as a being separate from himself, for he summons it by sorcery, builds a little fetish-hut for it by the wayside, rewards and propitiates it by libations of liquor and bits of food.[3] In Asia, the Mongols, each with his patron genius,[4] and the Laos sorcerers who can send their familiar spirits into others' bodies to cause disease,[5] are examples equally to the purpose.

Among the Aryan nations of Northern Europe,[6] the old doctrine of man's guardian spirit may be traced, and in classic Greece and Rome it renews with philosophic eloquence and cultured custom the ideas of the Australian and the African. The thought of the spiritual guide and protector of the individual man is happily defined by Menander, who calls the attendant genius, which each man has from the hour of birth, the good mystagogue (i.e. the novice's guide to the mysteries) of this life.

[1] Molina, ' Chili,' vol. ii. p. 86.

[2] Rochefort, ' Iles Antilles,' pp. 416, 429 ; J. G. Müller, ' Amer. Urrel.' pp. 171, 217.

[3] Waitz, vol. ii. p. 182 ; J. L. Wilson, ' W. Afr.' p. 387 ; Steinhauser, l.c. p. 134. Compare Callaway, p. 327, &c.

[4] Bastian, ' Psychologie,' p. 77.

[5] Bastian, ' Oestl. Asien,' vol. iii. p. 275.

[6] Grimm, ' D. M.' p. 829 ; Rochholz, ' Deutscher Glaube,' part i. p. 92 ; Hanusch, ' Slaw. Myth.' p. 247.

Ἅπαντι δαίμων ἀνδρὶ συμπαρίσταται
Εὐθὺς γενομένῳ μυσταγωγὸς τοῦ βίου.
Ἀγαθός· κακὸν γὰρ δαίμον' οὐ νομιστέον
Εἶναι τὸν βίον βλάπτοντα χρηστόν.   Πάντα γὰρ
Δεῖ ἀγαθὸν εἶναι τὸν Θεόν.

The divine warning voice which Sokrates used to hear, is a
salient example of the mental impressions leading to the
belief in guardian spirits.[1]   In the Roman world, the
doctrine came to be accepted as a philosophy of human
life.   Each man had his ' genius natalis,' associated with
him from birth to death, influencing his action and his fate,
standing represented by its proper image as a lar among
the household gods ; and at weddings and joyous times,
and especially on the anniversary of the birthday when
genius and man began their united career, worship was
paid with song and dance to the divine image, adorned with
garlands, and propitiated with incense and libations of
wine.   The demon or genius was, as it were, the man's
companion soul, a second spiritual ego.   The Egyptian
astrologer warned Antonius to keep far from the young
Octavius, ' for thy demon,' said he, ' is in fear of his ; '
and truly in after years that genius of Augustus had become an imperial deity, by whom Romans swore solemn
oaths, not to be broken.[2]   The doctrine which could thus
personify the character and fate of the individual man,
proved capable of a yet further development.   Converting
into animistic entities the inmost operations of the human
mind, a dualistic philosophy conceived as attached to every
mortal a good and an evil genius, whose efforts through life
drew him backward and forward toward virtue and vice,
happiness and misery.   It was the kakodaimōn of Brutus

[1] Menander, 205, in Clement. Stromat. ; Xenophon, Memor. Socr. ;
Plato, Apol. Socr. &c. See Plotin. Ennead. iii. 4 ; Porphyr. Plotin.
[2] Paulus Diaconus : 'Genium appellant Deum, qui vim obtineret rerum
omnium generandarum.' Censorin. de Die Natali, 3 : ' Eundem esse genium
et larem, multi veteres memoriæ prodiderunt.' Tibull. Eleg. i. 2, 7 ; Ovid.
Trist. iii. 13, 18, v. 5, 10 ; Horat. Epist. ii. 1, 140, Od. iv. 11, 7. Appian.
de Bellis Parth. p. 156. Tertullian, Apol. xxiii.

which appeared to him by night in his tent : ' I am thy evil genius,' it said, ' we meet again at Philippi.'[1]

As we study the shapes which the attendant spirits of the individual man assumed in early and mediæval Christendom, it is plain that the good and evil angels contending for man from birth to death, the guardian angel watching and protecting him, the familiar spirit giving occult knowledge or serving with magic art, continue in principle, and even in detail, the philosophy of earlier culture. Such beings even take visible form. St. Francisca had a familiar angel, not merely that domestic one that is given as a guardian to every man, but this was as it were a boy of nine years old, with a face more splendid than the sun, clad in a little white tunic ; it was in after years that there came to her a second angel, with a column of splendour rising to the sky, and three golden palm-branches in his hands. Or such attendant beings, though invisible, make their presence evident by their actions, as in Calmet's account of that Cistercian monk whose familiar genius waited on him, and used to get his chamber ready when he was coming back from the country, so that people knew when to expect him home.[2] There is a pleasant quaintness in Luther's remark concerning guardian angels, that a prince must have a greater, stronger, wiser angel than a count, and a count than a common man.[3] Bishop Bull, in one of his vigorous sermons, thus sums up a learned argument : ' I cannot but judge it highly probable, that every faithful person at least hath his particular good *Genius* or *Angel*, appointed by God over him, as the Guardian and Guide of his Life.' But he

---

[1] Serv. in Virg. Æn. vi. 743 : ' Cum nascimur, duos genios sortimur : unus hortatur ad bona, alter depravat ad mala, quibus assistentibus post mortem aut asserimur in meliorem vitam, aut condemnamur in deteriorem.' Horat. Epist. ii. 187 ; Valer. Max. i. 7 ; Plutarch, Brutus. See Pauly, ' Real-Encyclop. ; ' Smith's ' Dic. of Biog. & Myth.' s.v. ' genius.'

[2] Acta Sanctorum Bolland. : S. Francisca Romana ix. Mart. Calmet, ' Dissertation,' ch. iv. xxx. ; Bastian, ' Mensch,' vol. ii. pp. 140, 347, vol. iii. p. 10 ; Wright, ' St. Patrick's Purgatory,' p. 33.

[3] Rochholz, p. 93.

will not insist on the belief, provided that the general
ministry of angels be accepted.[1] Swedenborg will go beyond
this. ' Every man,' he says, ' is attended by an associate
spirit ; for without such an associate, a man would be inca-
pable of thinking analytically, rationally, and spiritually.'[2]
Yet in the modern educated world at large, this group of
beliefs has passed into the stage of survival. The conception of the good and evil genius contending for man through
life, indeed, perhaps never had much beyond the idealistic
meaning which art and poetry still give it. The traveller
in France may hear in our own day the peasant's salutation, ' Bonjour à vous et à votre compagnie ! ' (i.e. your
guardian angel).[3] But at the birthday festivals of English
children, how few are even aware of the historical sequence,
plain as it is, from the rites of the classic natal genius and
the mediæval natal saint ! Among us, the doctrine of
guardian angels is to be found in commentaries, and may
be sometimes mentioned in the pulpit ; but the once distant
conception of a present guardian spirit, acting on each
individual man and interfering with circumstances on his
behalf, has all but lost its old reality. The familiar demon
which gave occult knowledge and did wicked work for the
magician, and sucked blood from miserable hags by witch-
teats, was two centuries ago as real to the popular mind as
the alembic or the black cat with which it was associated.
Now, it has been cast down to the limbo of unhallowed
superstitions.

To turn from Man to Nature. General mention has been
made already of the local spirits which belong to mountain
and rock and valley, to well and stream and lake, in brief
to those natural objects and places which in early ages
aroused the savage mind to mythological ideas, such as
modern poets in their altered intellectual atmosphere strive

---

[1] Bull, ' Sermons,' 2nd ed. London, 1714, vol. ii. p. 506.
[2] Swedenborg, ' True Christian Religion,' p. 380. See also A. J. Davis,
' Philosophy of Spiritual Intercourse,' p. 38.
[3] D. Monnier, ' Traditions Populaires,' p. 7.

to reproduce. In discussing these imaginary beings, it is above all things needful to bring our minds into sympathy with the lower philosophy. Here we must seek to realize to the utmost the definition of the Nature-Spirits, to understand with what distinct and full conviction savage philosophy believes in their reality, to discern how, as living causes, they can fill their places and do their daily work in the natural philosophy of primæval man. Seeing how the Iroquois at their festivals could thank the invisible aids or good spirits, and with them the trees, shrubs, and plants, the springs and streams, the fire and wind, the sun, moon, and stars—in a word, every object that ministered to their wants—we may judge what real personality they attached to the myriad spirits which gave animated life to the world around them.[1] The Gold Coast negro's generic name for a fetish-spirit is 'wong;' these aerial beings dwell in temple-huts and consume sacrifices, enter into and inspire their priests, cause health and sickness among men, and execute the behests of the mighty Heaven-god. But part or all of them are connected with material objects, and the negro can say, ' In this river, or tree, or amulet, there is a wong.' But he more usually says, ' This river, or tree, or amulet is a wong.' Thus among the wongs of the land are rivers, lakes, and springs, districts of land, termite-hills, trees, crocodiles, apes, snakes, elephants, birds.[2] In a word, his conceptions of animating souls and presiding spirits as efficient causes of all nature are two groups of ideas which we may well find it hard to distinguish, for the sufficient reason that they are but varying developments of the same fundamental animism.

In the doctrine of nature-spirits among nations which have reached a higher grade of culture, are found at once traces of such primitive thought, and of its change under

---

[1] L. H. Morgan, ' Iroquois,' p. 64. Brebeuf in ' Rel. des Jés.' 1636, p. 107. See Schoolcraft, ' Tribes,' vol. iii. p. 337.

[2] Steinhauser, ' Religion des Negers,' in ' Magazin der Evang. Missionen,' Basel, 1856 ; No. 2, p. 127, &c.

new intellectual conditions. Knowing the thoughts of rude
Turanian tribes of Siberia as to pervading spirits of nature,
we are prepared to look for remodelled ideas of the same
class among a nation whose religion shows plain traces of
evolution from the low Turanian stage. The archaic system of manes-worship and nature-worship, which survives
as the state religion of China, fully recognizes the worship
of the numberless spirits which pervade the universe. The
belief in their personality is vouched for by the sacrifices
offered to them. ' One must sacrifice to the spirits,' says
Confucius, ' as though they were present at the sacrifice.'
At the same time, spirits were conceived as embodied in
material objects. Confucius says, again : ' The action of
the spirits, how perfect is it ! Thou perceivest it, and
yet seest it not ! Incorporated or immembered in things,
they cannot quit them. They cause men, clean and pure
and better clothed, to bring them sacrifice. Many, many,
are there of them, as the broad sea, as though they were
above and right and left.' Here are traces of such a primitive doctrine of personal and embodied nature-spirits as is
still at home in the religion of rude Siberian hordes. But
it was natural that Chinese philosophers should find means
of refining into mere ideality these ruder animistic creations. Spirit (shin), they tell us, is the fine or tender part
in all the ten thousand things ; all that is extraordinary or
supernatural is called spirit; the unsearchable of the male
and female principles is called spirit ; he who knows the
way of passing away and coming to be, he knows the working of spirit.[1]

The classic Greeks had inherited from their barbaric ancestors a doctrine of the universe essentially similar to that
of the North American Indian, the West African, and the
Siberian. We know, more intimately than the heathen
religion of our own land, the ancient Greek scheme of
nature-spirits impelling and directing by their personal
power and will the functions of the universe, the ancient

[1] Plath, ' Religion der alten Chinesen,' part i. p. 44.

Greek religion of nature, developed by imagination, adorned
by poetry, and consecrated by faith.   History records for
our instruction, how out of the midst of this splendid and
honoured creed there were evolved the germs of the new
philosophy.   Led by minuter insight and stricter reason,
thoughtful Greeks began the piecemeal supersession of the
archaic scheme, and set in movement the transformation of
animistic into physical science, which thence pervaded the
whole cultured world.   Such, in brief, is the history of
the doctrine of nature-spirits from first to last.   Let us
endeavour, by classifying some of its principal special
groups, to understand its place in the history of the human
intellect.

What causes volcanos ?   The Australians account for
volcanic rocks by the tradition that the sulky underground
' ingna ' or demons made great fires and threw up red-hot
stones.[1] The Kamchadals say that just as they themselves
warm up their winter-houses, so the ' kamuli ' or moun-
tain-spirits heat up the mountains in which they dwell, and
fling the brands out of the chimney.[2] The Nicaraguans
offered human sacrifices to Masaya or Popogatepec (Smok-
ing-Mountain), by throwing the bodies into the crater.
It seems as though it were a controlling deity, not the
mountain itself, that they worshipped ; for one reads of the
chiefs going to the crater, whence a hideous old naked
woman came out and gave them counsel and oracle ; at the
edge were placed earthen vessels of food to please her, or
to appease her when there was a storm or earthquake.[3]
Thus animism provided a theory of volcanoes, and so it was
likewise with whirlpools and rocks.   In the Vei country in
West Africa, there is a dangerous rock on the Mafa river,
which is never passed without offering a tribute to the
spirit of the flood—a leaf of tobacco, a handful of rice, or

[1] Oldfield, ' Abor. of Austr.' in ' Tr. Eth. Soc.' vol. iii. p. 232.
[2] Steller, ' Kamtschatka,' pp. 47, 265.
[3] Oviedo, ' Nicaragua,' in Ternaux-Compans, part xiv. pp. 132, 160. Compare Catlin, ' N. A. Ind.' vol. ii. p. 169.

a drink of rum.[1]   An early missionary account of a rock-
demon worshipped by the Huron Indians will show with
what absolute personality savages can conceive such a being.
In the hollow of a certain sacred rock, it is related, dwells
an ' oki ' or spirit who can give success to travellers,
wherefore they put tobacco into one of the cracks, and pray
thus : ' Demon who dwellest in this place, behold tobacco
I present to thee ; help us, keep us from shipwreck, defend
us against our enemies, and vouchsafe that when we have
made a good trade, we may return safe and sound to our
village.'   Father Marquette relates how, travelling on a
river in the then little known region of North America, he
was told of a dreadful place to which the canoe was just
drawing near, where dwells a demon waiting to devour such
as dare to approach ; this terrific manitu proved on arrival
to be some high rocks in the bend of the river, against
which the current runs violently.[2]   Thus the missionary
found in living belief among the savage Indians the very
thought which had so long before passed into the classic
tale of Skylla and Charybdis.

In those moments of the civilized man's life when he
casts off hard dull science, and returns to childhood's
fancy, the world-old book of animated nature is open to
him anew.   Then the well-worn thoughts come back fresh
to him, of the stream's life that is so like his own ; once
more he can see the rill leap down the hillside like a child,
to wander playing among the flowers ; or can follow it as,
grown to a river, it rushes through a mountain gorge,
henceforth in sluggish strength to carry heavy burdens
across the plain.   In all that water does, the poet's fancy
can discern its personality of life.   It gives fish to the
fisher, and crops to the husbandman ; it swells in fury
and lays waste the land ; it grips the bather with chill

---

[1] Creswick, ' Veys,' in ' Tr. Eth. Soc.' vol. vi. p. 359. See Du Chaillu,
' Ashango-land,' p. 106.

[2] Brebeuf in ' Rel. des Jés.' 1636, p. 108. Long's Exp. vol. i. p. 46. See
Loskiel, ' Indians of N. A.' part i. p. 45.

and cramp, and holds with inexorable grasp its drowning victim :[1]

> " Tweed said to Till,
>   ' What gars ye rin sae still ? '
> Till said to Tweed,
>   ' Though ye rin wi' speed,
> And I rin slaw,
>   Yet, where ye drown ae man,
> I drown twa.' "

What ethnography has to teach of that great element of the religion of mankind, the worship of well and lake, brook and river, is simply this—that what is poetry to us was philosophy to early man ; that to his mind water acted not by laws of force, but by life and will ; that the water-spirits of primæval mythology are as souls which cause the water's rush and rest, its kindness and its cruelty ; that lastly man finds, in the beings which with such power can work him weal and woe, deities with a wider influence over his life, deities to be feared and loved, to be prayed to and praised and propitiated with sacrificial gifts.

In Australia, special water-demons infest pools and watering-places. In the native theory of disease and death, no personage is more prominent than the water-spirit, which afflicts those who go into unlawful pools or bathe at unlawful times, the creature which causes women to pine and die, and whose very presence is death to the beholder, save to the native doctors, who may visit the water-spirit's subaqueous abode and return with bleared eyes and wet clothes to tell the wonders of their stay.[2] It would seem that creatures with such attributes come naturally into the category of spiritual beings, but in such stories as that of the bunyip living in the lakes

[1] For details of the belief in water-spirits as the cause of drowning, see ante, vol. i. p. 109.

[2] Oldfield in ' Tr. Eth. Soc.' vol. iii. p. 328 ; Eyre, vol. ii. p. 362 ; Grey, vol. ii. p. 339 ; Bastian, ' Vorstellungen von Wasser und Feuer,' in ' Zeitschrift für Ethnologie,' vol. i. (contains a general collection of details as to water-worship).

and rivers and seen floating as big as a calf, which carries off native women to his retreat below the waters, there appears that confusion between the spiritual water-demon and the material water-monster, which runs on into the midst of European mythology in such conceptions as that of the water-kelpie and the sea-serpent.[1] America gives cases of other principal animistic ideas concerning water. The water has its own spirits, writes Cranz, among the Greenlanders, so when they come to an untried spring, an angekok or the oldest man must drink first, to free it from a harmful spirit.[2] ' Who makes this river flow ? ' asks the Algonquin hunter in a medicine-song, and his answer is, ' The spirit, he makes this river flow.' In any great river, or lake, or cascade, there dwell such spirits, looked upon as mighty manitus. Thus Carver mentions the habit of the Red Indians, when they reached the shores of Lake Superior or the banks of the Mississippi, or any other great body of water, to present to the spirit who resides there some kind of offering ; this he saw done by a Winnebago chief who went with him to the Falls of St. Anthony. Franklin saw a similar sacrifice made by an Indian, whose wife had been afflicted with sickness by the water-spirits, and who accordingly to appease them tied up in a small bundle a knife and a piece of tobacco and some other trifling articles, and committed them to the rapids.[3] On the river-bank, the Peruvians would scoop up a handful of water and drink it, praying the river-deity to let them cross or to give them fish, and they threw maize into the stream as a propitiatory offering ; even to this day the Indians of the Cordilleras perform the ceremonial sip before they will pass a river on foot or horseback.[4] Africa displays well the

[1] Compare John Morgan, ' Life of William Buckley ' ; Bonwick, p. 203 ; Taylor, ' New Zealand,' p. 48, with Forbes Leslie, Brand, &c.

[2] Cranz, ' Grönland,' p. 267.

[3] Tanner, ' Narr.' p. 341 ; Carver, ' Travels,' p. 383 ; Franklin, ' Journey to Polar Sea,' vol. ii. p. 245 ; Lubbock, ' Origin of Civilization,' pp. 213-20 (contains details as to water-worship); see Brinton, p. 124.

[4] Rivero and Tschudi, ' Peruvian Ant.' p. 161 ; Garcilaso de la Vega,

rites of water-worship. In the East, among the Wanika, every spring has its spirit, to which oblations are made ; in the West, in the Akra district, lakes, ponds, and rivers received worship as local deities. In the South, among the Kafirs, streams are venerated as personal beings, or the abodes of personal deities, as when a man crossing a river will ask leave of its spirit, or having crossed will throw in a stone ; or when the dwellers by a stream will sacrifice a beast to it in time of drought, or, warned by illness in the tribe that their river is angry, will cast into it a few hand-fuls of millet or the entrails of a slaughtered ox.[1] Not less strongly marked are such ideas among the Tatar races of the North. Thus the Ostyaks venerate the river Ob, and when fish is scanty will hang a stone about a reindeer's neck and cast it in for a sacrifice. Among the Buraets, who are professing Buddhists, the old worship may still be seen at the picturesque little mountain lake of Ikeougoun, where they come to the wooden temple on the shore to offer sacri-fices of milk and butter and the fat of the animals which they burn on the altars. So across in Northern Europe, almost every Esthonian village has its sacred sacrificial spring. The Esths could at times even see the churl with blue and yellow stockings rise from the holy brook Wöh-handa, no doubt that same spirit of the brook to whom in older days there were sacrificed beasts and little children ; in newer times, when a German landowner dared to build a mill and dishonour the sacred water, there came bad seasons that lasted year after year, and the country people burned down the abominable thing.[2] As for the water-worship prevailing among non-Aryan indigenes of British India, it

---

' Comm. Real.' i. 10. See also J. G. Müller, ' Amer. Urrelig.' pp. 258, 260, 282.

[1] Krapf, ' E. Afr.' p. 198 ; Steinhauser, l.c. p. 131 ; Villault in Astley, vol. i. p. 668 ; Backhouse, ' Afr.' p. 230 ; Callaway, ' Zulu Tales,' vol. i. p. 90 ; Bastian, l.c.

[2] Castrén, ' Vorlesungen über die Altaischen Völker,' p. 114. ' Finn. Myth.' p. 70. Atkinson, ' Siberia,' p. 444. Boecler, ' Ehsten Aberglaüb. Gebräuche,' ed. Kreutzwald, p. 6.

seems to reach its climax among the Bodo and Dhimal of
the North-East, tribes to whom the local rivers are the local
deities,[1] so that men worship according to their water-sheds,
and the map is a pantheon.

Nor is such reverence strange to Aryan nations. To the
modern Hindu, looking as he still does on a river as a living
personal being to be adored and sworn by, the Ganges is no
solitary water deity, but only the first and most familiar of
the long list of sacred streams.[2] Turn to the classic world,
and we but find the beliefs and rites of a lower barbaric
culture holding their place, consecrated by venerable antiquity and glorified by new poetry and art. To the great
Olympian assembly in the halls of cloud-compelling Zeus,
came the Rivers, all save Ocean, and thither came the
nymphs who dwell in lovely groves and at the springs of
streams, and in the grassy meads ; and they sate upon the
polished seats :—

> ' Οὔτε τις οὖν Ποταμῶν ἀπέην, νόσφ' Ὠκεανοῖο,
> Οὔτ' ἄρα Νυμφάων ταί τ' ἄλσεα καλὰ νέμονται,
> Καὶ πηγὰς ποταμῶν, καὶ πίσεα ποιήεντα.
> Ἐλθόντες δ' ἐς δῶμα Διὸς νεφεληγερέταο,
> Ξεστῆς αἰθούσῃσιν ἐφίζανον, ἃς Διὶ πατρὶ
> «Ηφαιστος ποίησεν ἰδυίῃσι πραπίδεσσιν.'

Even against Hephaistos the Fire-god, a River-god dared
to stand opposed, deep-eddying Xanthos, called of men
Skamandros. He rushed down to overwhelm Achilles and
bury him in sand and slime, and though Hephaistos prevailed against him with his flames, and forced him, with the
fish skurrying hither and thither in his boiling waves and
the willows scorched upon his banks, to rush on no more
but stand, yet at the word of white-armed Here, that it was
not fit for mortals' sake to handle so roughly an immortal
god, Hephaistos quenched his furious fire, and the returning
flood sped again along his channel :—

---

[1] Hodgson, 'Abor. of India,' p. 164; Hunter, 'Rural Bengal.' p. 184.
See also Lubbock, l.c.; Forbes Leslie, 'Early Races of Scotland,' vol. i.
p. 163, vol. ii. p. 497.
[2] Ward, 'Hindoos,' vol. ii. p. 206, &c.

'"Ηφαιστε, σχέο, τέκνον ἀγακλέες· οὐ γὰρ ἔοικεν
'Αθάνατον θεὸν ὧδε βροτῶν ἕνεκα στυφελίζειν.
"Ὡς ἔφαθ'· "Ηφαιστος δὲ κατέσβεσε θεσπιδαὲς πῦρ·
"Αψορρον δ' ἄρα κῦμα κατέσσυτο καλὰ ῥέεθρα.'

To beings thus conceived in personal divinity, full worship was given. Odysseus invokes the river of Scheria ;
Skamandros had his priest and Spercheios his grove ; and
sacrifice was done to the rival of Herakles, the river-god
Acheloos, eldest of the three thousand river-children of
old Okeanos.[1] Through the ages of the classic world,
the river-gods and the water-nymphs held their places,
till within the bounds of Christendom they came to be
classed with ideal beings like them in the mythology of the
northern nations, the kindly sprites to whom offerings were
given at springs and lakes, and the treacherous nixes who
entice men to a watery death. In times of transition, the
new Christian authorities made protest against the old
worship, passing laws to forbid adoration and sacrifice
to fountains—as when Duke Bretislav forbade the still
half-pagan country folk of Bohemia to offer libations and
sacrifice victims at springs,[2] and in England Ecgbert's
Poenitentiale proscribed the like rites, 'if any man vow
or bring his offerings to any well,' 'if one hold his
vigils at any well.'[3] But the old veneration was too strong
to be put down, and with a varnish of Christianity and sometimes the substitution of a saint's name, water-worship has
held its own to our day. The Bohemians will go to pray
on the river-bank where a man has been drowned, and
there they will cast in an offering, a loaf of new bread and
a pair of wax-candles. On Christmas Eve they will put

[1] Homer, Il. xx. xxi. See Gladstone, ' Juventus Mundi,' pp. 190, 345,
&c., &c.
[2] Cosmas, book iii. p. 197, ' superstitiosas institutiones, quas villani adhuc
semipagani in Pentecosten tertia sive quarta feria observabant offerentes
libamina super fontes mactabant victimas et dæmonibus immolabant.'
[3] Poenitentiale Ecgberti, ii. 22, 'gif hwilc man his ælmessan gehâte oththe
bringe to hwilcon wylle ;' iv. 19, ' gif hwâ his wæccan æt ænigum wylle
hæbbe.' Grimm, ' D. M.' p. 549, &c. See Hyltén-Cavallius, ' Wärend och
Wirdarne,' part i. pp. 131, 171 (Sweden).

a spoonful of each dish on a plate, and after supper throw the food into the well, with an appointed formula, somewhat thus :—

> ' House-father gives thee greeting,
> Thee by me entreating :
> Springlet, share our feast of Yule,
> But give us water to the full ;
> When the land is plagued with drought,
> Drive it with thy well-spring out.' [1]

It well shows the unchanged survival of savage thought in modern peasants' minds, to find still in Slavonic lands the very same fear of drinking a harmful spirit in the water, that has been noticed among the Esquimaux. It is a sin for a Bulgarian not to throw some water out of every bucket brought from the fountain; some elemental spirit might be floating on the surface, and if not thrown out, might take up his abode in the house, or enter into the body of some one drinking from the vessel. [2] Elsewhere in Europe, the list of still existing water-rites may be extended. The ancient lake-offerings of the South of France seem not yet forgotten in La Lozère, the Bretons venerate as of old their sacred springs, and Scotland and Ireland can show in parish after parish the sites and even the actual survivals of such observance at the holy wells. Perhaps Welshmen no longer offer cocks and hens to St. Tecla at her sacred well and church of Llandegla, but Cornish folk still drop into the old holy-wells offerings of pins, nails, and rags, expecting from their waters cure for disease, and omens from their bubbles as to health and marriage. [3]

The spirits of the tree and grove no less deserve our

[1] Grohmann, ' Aberglauben aus Böhmen und Mähren,' p. 43, &c Hanusch, ' Slaw. Myth.' p. 291, &c. Ralston, ' Songs of Russian People,' p. 139, &c.

[2] St. Clair and Brophy, ' Bulgaria,' p. 46. Similar ideas in Grohmann, p. 44. Eisenmenger, ' Entd. Judenthum,' part i. p. 426.

[3] Maury, ' Magie,' &c., p. 158. Brand, ' Pop. Ant.' vol. ii. p. 366, &c. Hunt, ' Pop. Rom. 2nd Series,' p. 40, &c. Forbes Leslie, ' Early Races of Scotland,' vol. i. p. 156, &c.

study for their illustrations of man's primitive animistic theory of nature. This is remarkably displayed in that stage of thought where the individual tree is regarded as a conscious personal being, and as such receives adoration and sacrifice. Whether such a tree is looked on as inhabited, like a man, by its own proper life or soul, or as possessed, like a fetish, by some other spirit which has entered it and uses it for a body, is often hard to determine. Shelley's lines well express a doubting conception familiar to old barbaric thought—

> ' Whether the sensitive plant, or that
> Which within its boughs like a spirit sat
> Ere its outward form had known decay,
> Now felt this change, I cannot say.'

But this vagueness is yet again a proof of the principle which I have confidently put forward here, that the conceptions of the inherent soul and of the embodied spirit are but modifications of one and the same deep-lying animistic thought. The Mintira of the Malay Peninsula believe in ' hantu kayu,' i.e. ' tree-spirits,' or ' tree-demons,' which frequent every species of tree, and afflict men with diseases ; some trees are noted for the malignity of their demons.[1] Among the Dayaks of Borneo, certain trees possessed by spirits must not be cut down ; if a missionary ventured to fell one, any death that happened afterwards would naturally be set down to this crime.[2] The belief of certain Malays of Sumatra is expressly stated, that certain venerable trees are the residence, or rather the material frame, of spirits of the woods.[3] In the Tonga Islands, we hear of natives laying offerings at the foot of particular trees, with the idea of their being inhabited by spirits.[4] So in America, the Ojibwa medicine-man has heard the tree utter its complaint

---

[1] ' Journ. Ind. Archip.' vol. i. p. 307.
[2] Beeker, ' Dyaks,' in ' Journ. Ind. Archip.' vol. iii. p. 111.
[3] Marsden, ' Sumatra,' p. 301.
[4] S. S. Farmer, ' Tonga,' p. 127.

when wantonly cut down.[1] A curious and suggestive description bearing on this point is given in Friar Roman Pane's account of the religion of the Antilles islanders, drawn up by order of Columbus.   Certain trees, he declares, were believed to send for sorcerers, to whom they gave orders how to shape their trunks into idols, and these ' cemi ' being then installed in temple-huts, received prayer and inspired their priests with oracles.[2] Africa shows as well-defined examples. The negro woodman cuts down certain trees in fear of the anger of their inhabiting demons, but he finds his way out of the difficulty by a sacrifice to his own good genius, or, when he is giving the first cuts to the great asorin-tree, and its indwelling spirit comes out to chase him, he cunningly drops palm-oil on the ground, and makes his escape while the spirit is licking it up.[3] A negro was once worshiping a tree with an offering of food, when some one pointed out to him that the tree did not eat ; the negro answered, ' O the tree is not fetish, the fetish is a spirit and invisible, but he has descended into this tree. Certainly he cannot devour our bodily food, but he enjoys its spiritual part and leaves behind the bodily which we see.'[4] Tree-worship is largely prevalent in Africa, and much of it may be of this fully animistic kind ; as where in Whidah Bosman says that ' the trees, which are the gods of the second rank of this country, are only prayed to and presented with offerings in time of sickness, more especially fevers, in order to restore the patients to health;'[5] or where in Abyssinia the Gallas made pilgrimage from all quarters to their sacred tree Wodanabe on the banks of the Hawash, worshipping it and praying to it for riches, health, life, and every blessing.[6]

[1] Bastian, ' Der Baum in vergleichender Ethnologie,' in Lazarus and Steinthal's ' Zeitschrift für Völkerpsychologie,' &c., vol. v. 1868.

[2] Chr. Colombo, ch. xix. ; and in Pinkerton, vol. xii. p. 87.

[3] Burton, ' W. & W. fr. W. Afr.' pp. 205, 243.

[4] Waitz, vol. ii. p. 188.

[5] Bosman, letter 19, and in Pinkerton, vol. xvi. p. 500.

[6] Krapf, ' E. Afr.' p. 77 ; Prichard, ' N. H. of Man,' p. 290 ; Waitz, vol. ii. p. 518. See also Merolla, ' Congo,' in Pinkerton, vol. xvi. p. 236.

The position of tree-worship in Southern Asia in relation to Buddhism is of particular interest. To this day there are districts of this region, Buddhist or under strong Buddhist influence, where tree-worship is still displayed with absolute clearness of theory and practice. Here in legend a dryad is a being capable of marriage with a human hero, while in actual fact a tree-deity is considered human enough to be pleased with dolls set up to swing in the branches. The Talein of Burmah, before they cut down a tree, offer prayers to its ' kaluk ' (*i.q.*, ' kelah '), its inhabiting spirit or soul. The Siamese offer cakes and rice to the takhien-tree before they fell it, and believe the inhabiting nymphs or mothers of trees to pass into guardian-spirits of the boats built of their wood, so that they actually go on offering sacrifice to them in this their new condition.[1] These people have indeed little to learn from any other race, however savage, of the principles of the lower animism. The question now arises, did such tree-worship belong to the local religions among which Buddhism established itself ? There is strong evidence that this was the case. Philosophic Buddhism, as known to us by its theological books, does not include trees among sentient beings possessing mind, but it goes so far as to acknowledge the existence of the ' dewa ' or genius of a tree. Buddha, it is related, told a story of a tree crying out to the brahman carpenter who was going to cut it down, ' I have a word to say, hear my word ! ' but then the teacher goes on to explain that it was not really the tree that spoke, but a dewa dwelling in it. Buddha himself was a tree-genius forty-three times in the course of his transmigrations. Legend says that during one such existence, a certain brahman used to pray for protection to the tree which Buddha was attached to ; but the transformed teacher reproved the tree-worshipper for thus

[1] Bastian, ' Oestl. Asien,' vol. ii. pp. 457, 461, vol. iii. pp. 187, 251, 289, 497. For details of tree-worship from other Asiatic districts, see Ainsworth, ' Yezidis,' in ' Tr. Eth. Soc.' vol. i. p. 23 ; Jno. Wilson, ' Parsi Religion,' p. 262.

addressing himself to a senseless thing which hears and knows nothing.[1] As for the famous Bo tree, its miraculous glories are not confined to the ancient Buddhist annals ; for its surviving descendant, grown from the branch of the parent tree sent by King Asoka from India to Ceylon in the 3rd century B.C., to this day receives the worship of the pilgrims who come by thousands to do it honour, and offer prayer before it. Beyond these hints and relics of the old worship, however, Mr. Fergusson's recent investigations, published in his ' Tree and Serpent Worship,' have brought to light an ancient state of things which the ortho-dox Buddhist literature gives little idea of. It appears from the sculptures of the Sanchi tope in Central India, that in the Buddhism of about the 1st century A.D., sacred trees had no small place as objects of authorized worship. It is especially notable that the representatives of indigenous race and religion in India, the Nagas, characterized by their tutelary snakes issuing from their backs between their shoulders and curving over their heads, and other tribes actually drawn as human apes, are seen adoring the divine tree in the midst of unquestionable Buddhist surroundings.[2] Tree-worship, even now well marked among the indigenous tribes of India, was obviously not abolished on the Buddhist conversion. The new philosophic religion seems to have amalgamated, as new religions ever do, with older native thoughts and rites. And it is quite consistent with the habits of the Buddhist theologians and hagiologists, that when tree-worship was suppressed, they should have slurred over the fact of its former prevalence, and should even have used the recollection of it as a gibe against the hostile Brahmans.

Conceptions like those of the lower races in character, and rivalling them in vivacity, belong to the mythology of Greece and Rome. The classic thought of the tree in-habited by a deity and uttering oracles, is like that of

---

[1] Hardy, ' Manual of Budhism,' pp. 100, 443.
[2] Fergusson, ' Tree and Serpent Worship,' pl. xxiv. xxvi. &c.

other regions. Thus the sacred palm of Negra in Yemen, whose demon was propitiated by prayer and sacrifice to give oracular response,[1] or the tall oaks inhabited by the gods, where old Slavonic people used to ask questions and hear the answers,[2] have their analogue in the prophetic oak of Dodona, wherein dwelt the deity, ʽ ναῖεν δ᾽ ἐνὶ πυθμένι φηγοῦ.᾽[3] The Homeric hymn to Aphrodite tells of the tree-nymphs, long-lived yet not immortal— they grow with their high-topped leafy pines and oaks upon the mountains, but when the lot of death draws nigh, and the lovely trees are sapless, and the bark rots away and the branches fall, then their spirits depart from the light of the sun :—

> ʽ Νύμφαι μιν θρέψουσιν ὀρεσκῷοι βαθύκολποι,
> αἵ τόδε ναιετάουσιν ὄρος μέγα τε ζάθεόν τε·
> αἵ ῥ᾽ οὔτε θνητοῖς οὔτ᾽ ἀθανάτοισιν ἕπονται·
> δηρὸν μὲν ζώουσι καὶ ἄμβροτον εἶδαρ ἔδουσι,
> καί τε μετ᾽ ἀθανάτοισι καλὸν χορὸν ἐρρώσαντο.
> τῇσι δὲ Σειληνοί τε καὶ εὔσκοπος Ἀργειφόντης
> μίσγοντ᾽ ἐν φιλότητι μυχῷ σπείων ἐροέντων.
> τῇσι δ᾽ ἅμ᾽ ἢ ἐλάται ἠὲ δρύες ὑψικάρηνοι
> γεινομένῃσιν ἔφυσαν ἐπὶ χθονὶ βωτιανείρῃ,
> καλαί, τηλεθάουσαι, ἐν οὔρεσιν ὑψηλοῖσιν·
>
> . . . .
>
> ἀλλ᾽ ὅτε κεν δὴ μοῖρα παρεστήκῃ θανάτοιο,
> ἀζάνεται μὲν πρῶτον ἐπὶ χθονὶ δένδρεα καλά,
> φλοιὸς δ᾽ ἀμφιπεριφθινύθει, πίπτουσι δ᾽ ἀπ᾽ ὄζοι,
> τῶν δὲ θ᾽ ὁμοῦ ψυχὴ λείπει φάος ἠελίοιο.᾽[4]

The hamadryad's life is bound to her tree, she is hurt when it is wounded, she cries when the axe threatens, she dies with the fallen trunk :—

> ʽ Non sine hamadryadis fato cadit arborea trabs.᾽[5]

How personal a creature the tree-nymph was to the classic mind, is shown in legends like that of Paraibios,

---

[1] Tabary in Bastian, l.c. p. 295.
[2] Hartknoch, ʽ Alt. und Neues Preussen,᾽ part i. ch. v.
[3] See Pauly, ʽ Real-Encyclopedie.᾽ Homer. Odyss. xiv. 327, xix. 296.
[4] Hymn. Homer. Aphrod. 257.
[5] Ausonii Idyll. De Histor. 7.

whose father, regardless of the hamadryad's entreaties, cut down her ancient trunk, and in himself and in his off-spring suffered her dire vengeance.[1] The ethnographic student finds a curious interest in transformation-myths like Ovid's, keeping up as they do vestiges of philosophy of archaic type—Daphne turned into the laurel that Apollo honours for her sake, the sorrowing sisters of Phaethon changing into trees, yet still dropping blood and crying for mercy when their shoots are torn.[2] Such episodes mediæval poetry could still adapt, as in the pathless infernal forest whose knotted dusk-leaved trees revealed their human animation to the Florentine when he plucked a twig,

> ' Allor porsi la mano un poco avante,
> E colsi un ramoscel da un gran pruno :
> E' l tronco suo gridò : Perchè mi schiante ? '[3]

or the myrtle to which Ruggiero tied his hippogriff, who tugged at the poor trunk till it murmured and oped its mouth, and with doleful voice told that it was Astolfo, enchanted by the wicked Alcina among her other lovers,

> ' D' entrar o in fera o in fonte o in legno o in sasso.'[4]

If these seem to us now conceits over quaint for beauty, we need not scruple to say so. They are not of Dante and Ariosto, they are sham antiques from classic models. And if even the classic originals have become unpleasing, we need not perhaps reproach ourselves with decline of poetic taste. We have lost something, and the loss has spoiled our appreciation of many an old poetic theme, yet it is not always our sense of the beautiful that has dwindled, but the old animistic philosophy of nature that is gone from us, dissipating from such fancies their meaning, and with

[1] Apollon. Rhod. Argonautica, ii. 476. See Welcker, ' Griech. Götterl.' vol. iii. p. 57.

[2] Ovid. Metamm. i. 452, ii. 345, xi. 67.

[3] Dante, ' Divina Commedia,' ' Inferno,' canto xiii.

[4] Ariosto, ' Orlando Furioso,' canto vi.

their meaning their loveliness. Still, if we look for living men to whom trees are, as they were to our distant fore-fathers, the habitations and embodiments of spirits, we shall not look in vain. The peasant folklore of Europe still knows of willows that bleed and weep and speak when hewn, of the fairy maiden that sits within the fir-tree, of that old tree in Rugaard forest that must not be felled, for an elf dwells within, of that old tree on the Heinzenberg near Zell, which uttered its complaint when the woodman cut it down, for in it was Our Lady, whose chapel now stands upon the spot.[1] One may still look on where Fran-conian damsels go to a tree on St. Thomas's Day, knock thrice solemnly, and listen for the indwelling spirit to give answer by raps from within, what manner of husbands they are to have.[2]

In the remarkable document of mythic cosmogony, pre-served by Eusebius under the alleged authorship of the Phœnician Sanchoniathon, is the following passage : 'But these first men consecrated the plants of the earth, and judged them gods, and worshipped the things upon which they themselves lived and their posterity, and all before them, and (to these) they made libations and sacrifices.'[3] From examples such as have been here reviewed, it seems that direct and absolute tree-worship of this kind may in-deed lie very wide and deep in the early history of religion. But the whole tree-cultus of the world must by no means be thrown indiscriminately into this one category. It is only on such distinct evidence as has been here put forward, that a sacred tree may be taken as having a spirit em-bodied in or attached to it. Beyond this limit, there is a wider range of animistic conceptions connected with tree and forest worship. The tree may be the spirit's perch or shelter or favourite haunt. Under this definition come the

---

[1] Grimm, ' D. M.' p. 615, &c. Bastian, ' Der Baum,' l.c. p. 297 ; Hanusch, ' Slaw. Myth.' p. 313.

[2] Wuttke, ' Volksaberglaube,' p. 57, see 183.

[3] Euseb. ' Præp. Evang.' i. 10.

trees hung with objects which are the receptacles of disease-spirits. As places of spiritual resort, there is no real distinction between the sacred tree and the sacred grove. The tree may serve as a scaffold or altar, at once convenient and conspicuous, where offerings can be set out for some spiritual being, who may be a tree-spirit, or perhaps the local deity, living there just as a man might do who had his hut and owned his plot of land around. The shelter of some single tree, or the solemn seclusion of a forest grove, is a place of worship set apart by nature, of some tribes the only temple, of many tribes perhaps the earliest. Lastly, the tree may be merely a sacred object patronized by or associated with or symbolizing some divinity, often one of those which we shall presently notice as presiding over a whole species of trees or other things. How all these conceptions, from actual embodiment or local residence or visit of a demon or deity, down to mere ideal association, can blend together, how hard it often is to distinguish them, and yet how in spite of this confusion they conform to the animistic theology in which all have their essential principles, a few examples will show better than any theoretical comment.[1] Take the groups of malicious wood-fiends so obviously devised to account for the mysterious influences that beset the forest wanderer. In the Australian bush, demons whistle in the branches, and stooping with outstretched arms sneak among the trunks to seize the wayfarer ; the lame demon leads astray the hunter in the Brazilian forest ; the Karen crossing a fever-haunted jungle shudders in the grip of the spiteful ' phi,' and runs to lay an offering by the tree he rested under last, from whose boughs the malaria-fiend came down upon him ; the negro of Senegambia seeks to pacify the long-haired tree-demons that send diseases ; the terrific cry of the wood-demon is heard in the Finland

[1] Further details as to tree-worship in Bastian, ' Der Baum,' &c., here cited ; Lubbock, ' Origin of Civilization,' p. 206, &c. ; Fergusson, ' Tree and Serpent Worship,' &c.

forest ; the baleful shapes of terror that glide at night through our own woodland are familiar still to peasant and poet.[1] The North American Indians of the Far West, entering the defiles of the Black Mountains of Nebraska, will often hang offerings on the trees or place them on the rocks, to propitiate the spirits and procure good weather and hunting.[2] In South America, Mr. Darwin describes the Indians offering their adorations by loud shouts when they came in sight of the sacred tree standing solitary on a high part of the Pampas, a landmark visible from afar. To this tree were hanging by threads numberless offerings such as cigars, bread, meat, pieces of cloth, &c., down to the mere thread pulled from his poncho by the poor wayfarer who had nothing better to give. Men would pour libations of spirits and maté into a certain hole, and smoke upwards to gratify Walleechu, and all around lay the bleached bones of the horses slaughtered as sacrifices. All Indians made their offerings here, that their horses might not tire, and that they themselves might prosper. Mr. Darwin reasonably judges on this evidence that it was to the deity Walleechu that the worship was paid, the sacred tree being only his altar ; but he mentions that the Gauchos think the Indians consider the tree as the god itself, a good example of the misunderstanding possible in such cases.[3] The New Zealanders would hang an offering of food or a lock of hair on a branch at a landing place, or near remarkable rocks or trees would throw a bunch of rushes as an offering to the spirit dwelling there.[4] The Dayaks fasten rags of their clothes on trees at cross roads, fearing for their health if they neglect the custom ;[5] the Macassar man halting to eat in the forest will put a morsel of rice or fish on a leaf, and lay it on a stone or stump.[6] The divinities of African tribes

---

[1] Bastian, ' Der Baum,' l.c. &c.
[2] Irving, ' Astoria,' vol. ii. ch. viii.
[3] Darwin, ' Journal,' p. 68.
[4] Polack, ' New Z.' vol. ii. p. 6 ; Taylor, p. 171, see 99.
[5] St. John, ' Far East,' vol. i. p. 89.
[6] Wallace, ' Eastern Archipelago,' vol. i. p. 338.

may dwell in trees remarkable for size and age, or inhabit sacred groves where the priest alone may enter.[1] Trees treated as idols by the Congo people, who put calabashes of palm wine at their feet in case they should be thirsty,[2] and amongst West African negro tribes farther north, trees hung with rags by the passers-by, and the great baobabs pegged to hang offerings to, and serving as shrines before which sheep are sacrificed,[3] display well the rites of tree sacrifice, though leaving undefined the precise relation conceived between deity and tree.

The forest theology that befits a race of hunters is dominant still among Turanian tribes of Siberia, as of old it was across to Lapland. Full well these tribes know the gods of the forest. The Yakuts hang on any remarkably fine tree iron, brass, and other trinkets ; they choose a green spot shaded by a tree for their spring sacrifice of horses and oxen, whose heads are set up in the boughs ; they chant their extemporised songs to the Spirit of the Forest, and hang for him on the branches of the trees along the roadside offerings of horsehair, emblems of their most valued possession. A clump of larches on a Siberian steppe, a grove in the recesses of a forest, is the sanctuary of a Turanian tribe. Gaily-decked idols in their warm fur-coats, each set up beneath its great tree swathed with cloth or tinplate, endless reindeer-hides and peltry hanging to the trees around, kettles and spoons and snuff-horns and household valuables strewn as offerings before the gods—such is the description of a Siberian holy grove, at the stage when the contact of foreign civilization has begun by ornamenting the rude old ceremonial it must end by abolishing.[4] A race ethnologically allied to these tribes, though risen to higher culture, kept up remarkable relics of tree-worship in Northern Europe. In Esthonian districts, during the last

---

[1] Prichard, ' Nat. Hist. of Man,' p. 531.

[2] Merolla in Pinkerton, vol. xvi. p. 236.

[3] Lubbock, p. 193 ; Bastian, l.c. ; Park, ' Travels,' vol. i. pp. 64, 106.

[4] Castrén, ' Finn. Myth.' p. 86, &c., 191, &c. ; Latham, ' Descr. Eth.' vol. i. p. 363 ; Simpson, ' Journey,' vol. ii. p. 261.

century, the traveller might often see the sacred tree, generally an ancient lime, oak, or ash, standing inviolate in a sheltered spot near the dwelling-house, and old memories are handed down of the time when the first blood of a slaughtered beast was sprinkled on its roots, that the cattle might prosper, or when an offering was laid beneath the holy linden, on the stone where the worshipper knelt on his bare knees, moving from east to west and back, which stone he kissed thrice when he had said, ' Receive the food as an ofiering!' It may well have been an indwelling tree-deity for whom this worship was intended, for folklore shows that the Esths recognized such a conception with the utmost distinctness ; they have a tale of the tree-elf who appeared in personal shape outside his crooked birch-tree, whence he could be summoned by three knocks on the trunk and the inquiry, ' Is the crooked one at home ? ' But also it may have been the Wood-Father or Tree-King, or some other deity, who received sacrifice and answered prayer beneath his sacred tree, as in a temple.[1] If, again, we glance at the tree-and-grove worship of the non-Aryan indigenous tribes of British India, we shall gather clear and instructive hints of its inner significance. In the courtyard of a Bodo house is planted the sacred ' sij ' or euphorbia of Batho, the national god, to whom under this representation the ' deoshi ' or priest offers prayer and kills a pig.[2] When the Khonds settle a new village, the sacred cotton-tree must be planted with solemn rites, and beneath it is placed the stone which enshrines the village deity.[3] Nowhere, perhaps, in the world in these modern days is the original meaning of the sacred grove more picturesquely shown than among the Mundas of Chota-Nagpur, in whose settlements a sacred grove of sal-trees, a remnant of the primæval forest spared by the woodman's axe, is left as a home for the

---

[1] Boecler, ' Ehsten Abergläubische Gebräuche,' &c., ed. Kreutzwald, pp. 2, 112, 146.
[2] Hodgson, ' Abor. of India,' pp. 165, 173.
[3] Macpherson, p. 61.

spirits, and in this hallowed place offerings to the gods are made.[1]

Here, then, among the lower races, is surely evidence enough to put on their true historic footing the rites of tree and grove which are found flourishing or surviving within the range of Semitic or Aryan culture. Mentions in the Old Testament record the Canaanitish Ashera-worship, the sacrifice under every green tree, the incense rising beneath oak and willow and shady terebinth, rites whose obstinate revival proves how deeply they were rooted in the old religion of the land.[2] The evidence of these Biblical passages is corroborated by other evidence from Semitic regions, as in the lines by Silius Italicus which mention the prayer and sacrifice in the Numidian holy groves, and the records of the council of Carthage which show that in the 5th century, an age after Augustine's time, it was still needful to urge that the relics of idolatry in trees and groves should be done away.[3] From the more precise descriptions which lie within the range of Aryan descent and influence, examples may be drawn to illustrate every class of belief and rite of the forest. Modern Hinduism is so largely derived from the religions of the non-Aryan indigenes, that we may fairly explain thus a considerable part of the tree-worship of modern India, as where in the Birbhûm district of Bengal a great annual pilgrimage is made to a shrine in a jungle, to give offerings of rice and money and sacrifice animals to a certain ghost who dwells in a bela-tree.[4] In thoroughly Hindu districts may be seen the pippala (Ficus religiosa) planted as the village tree, the ' chaityataru ' of Sanskrit

[1] Dalton, ' Kols,' in ' Tr. Eth. Soc.' vol. vi. p. 34. Bastian, ' Oestl. Asien.' vol. i. p. 134, vol. iii. p. 252.

[2] Deut. xii. 3 ; xvi. 21. Judges vi. 25. 1 Kings xiv. 23 ; xv. 13 ; xviii. 19. 2 Kings xvii. 10 ; xxiii. 4. Is. lvii. 5. Jerem. xvii. 2. Ezek. vi. 13 ; xx. 28. Hos. iv. 13, &c., &c.

[3] Sil. Ital. Punica, iii. 675, 690. Harduin, Acta Conciliorum, vol. i. For further evidence as to Semitic tree-and-grove worship, see Movers, ' Phönizier,' vol. i. p. 560, &c.

[4] Hunter, ' Rural Bengal,' pp. 131, 194.

literature, while the Hindu in private life plants the banyan and other trees and worships them with divine honours.[1] Greek and Roman mythology give perfect types not only of the beings attached to individual trees, but of the dryads, fauns, and satyrs living and roaming in the forest—creatures whose analogues are our own elves and fairies of the woods. Above these graceful fantastic beings are the higher deities who have trees for shrines and groves for temples. Witness the description in Ovid's story of Erisichthon :—

> ' And Ceres' grove he ravaged with the axe,
>   They say, and shame with iron the ancient glades.
>   There stood a mighty oak of age-long strength,
>   Festooned with garlands, bearing on its trunk
>   Memorial tablets, proofs of helpful vows.
>   Beneath, the dryads led their festive dance,
>   And circled hand-in-hand the giant bole.'[2]

In more prosaic fashion, Cato instructs the woodman how to gain indemnity for thinning a holy grove ; he must offer a hog in sacrifice with this prayer, 'Be thou god or goddess to whom this grove is sacred, permit me, by the expiation of this pig, and in order to restrain the overgrowth of this wood, &c., &c.'[3] Slavonic lands had their groves where burned the everlasting fire of Piorun the Heaven-god ; the old Prussians venerated the holy oak of Romowe, with its drapery and images of the gods, standing in the midst of the sacred inviolate forest where no twig might be broken nor beast slain; and so on down to the elder-tree beneath which Pushkait was worshipped with offerings of bread and beer.[4] The Keltic Heaven-god, whose image was a mighty oak, the white-robed Druids climbing the sacred tree to cut the mistletoe, and sacrificing

---

[1] Boehtlingk and Roth, s.v. ' chaityataru.' Ward, ' Hindoos,' vol. ii. p. 204.

[2] Ovid. Metamm. viii. 741.

[3] Cato de Re Rustica, 139 ; Plin. xvii. 47.

[4] Hanusch, 'Slaw. Myth.' pp. 98, 229. Hartknoch, part i. ch. v. vii.; Grimm, ' D. M.' p. 67.

the two white bulls beneath, are types from another national group.[1] Teutonic descriptions begin with Tacitus, ' Lucos ac nemora consecrant, deorumque nominibus adpellant secretum illud, quod sola reverentia vident,' and the curious passage which describes the Semnones entering the sacred grove in bonds, a homage to the deity that dwelt there; many a century after, the Swedes were still holding solemn sacrifice and hanging the carcases of the slaughtered beasts in the grove hard by the temple of Upsal.[2] With Christianity comes a crusade against the holy trees and groves. Boniface hews down in the presence of the priest the huge oak of the Hessian Heaven-god, and builds of the timber a chapel to St. Peter. Amator expostulated with the hunters who hung the heads of wild beasts to the boughs of the sacred pear-tree of Auxerre, ' Hoc opus idololatriæ culturæ est, non christianæ elegantissimæ disciplinæ ; ' but this mild persuasion not availing, he chopped it down and burned it. In spite of all such efforts, the old religion of the tree and grove survived in Europe often in most pristine form. Within the last two hundred years, there were old men in Gothland who would ' go to pray under a great tree, as their forefathers had done in their time ; ' and to this day the sacrificial rite of pouring milk and beer over the roots of trees is said to be kept up on out-of-the-way Swedish farms.[3] In Russia, the Lyeshy or wood-demon still protects the birds and beasts in his domain, and drives his flocks of field-mice and squirrels from forest to forest, when we should say they are migrating. The hunter's luck depends on his treatment of the forest-spirit, wherefore he will leave him as a sacrifice the first game he kills, or some smaller offering of bread or salted pancake on a stump. Or if one falls ill on returning from the forest, it is known that this is the Lyeshy's doing, so

[1] Maxim. Tyr. viii. ; Plin. xvi. 95.
[2] Tacit. Germania, 9, 39, &c. ; Grimm, ' D. M.' p. 66.
[3] Hyltén-Cavallius, ' Wärend och Wirdarne,' part i. p. 142.

the patient carries to the wood some bread and salt in a clean rag, and leaving it with a prayer, comes home cured.[1] Names like *Holyoake* and *Holywood* record our own old memories of the holy trees and groves, memories long lingering in the tenacious peasant mind ; and it was a great and sacred *linden*-tree with three stems, standing in the parish of Hvitaryd in South Sweden, which with curious fitness gave a name to the family of *Linnæus*. Lastly, Jakob Grimm even ventures to connect historically the ancient sacred inviolate wood with the later royal forest, an ethnological argument which would begin with the savage adoring the Spirit of the Forest, and end with the modern landowner preserving his pheasants.[2]

To the modern educated world, few phenomena of the lower civilization seem more pitiable than the spectacle of a man worshipping a beast. We have learnt the lessons of Natural History at last thoroughly enough to recognize our superiority to our ' younger brothers,' as the Red Indians call them, the creatures whom it is our place not to adore but to understand and use. By men at lower levels of culture, however, the inferior animals are viewed with a very different eye. For various motives, they have become objects of veneration ranking among the most important in the lower ranges of religion. Yet I must here speak shortly and slightly of Animal-worship, not as wanting in interest, but as over-abounding in difficulty. Wishing rather to bring general principles into view than to mass uninterpreted facts, all I can satisfactorily do is to give some select examples from the various groups of evidence, so as at once to display the more striking features of the subject, and to trace the ancient ideas upward from the savage level far into the higher civilization.

First and foremost, uncultured man seems capable of simply worshipping a beast as beast, looking on it as possessed of power, courage, cunning, beyond his own, and

[1] Ralston, ' Songs of Russian People,' p. 153, see 238.
[2] Grimm, 'D. M.' p. 62, &c.

animated like a man by a soul which continues to exist after
bodily death, powerful as ever for good and harm. Then
this idea blends with the thought of the creature as being
an incarnate deity, seeing, hearing, and acting even at a
distance, and continuing its power after the death of the
animal body to which the divine spirit was attached. Thus
the Kamchadals, in their simple veneration of all things
that could do them harm or good, worshipped the whales
that could overturn their boats, and the bears and wolves
of whom they stood in fear. The beasts, they thought,
could understand their language, and therefore they abstained from calling them by their names when they met
them, but propitiated them with certain appointed formulas.[1]
Tribes of Peru, says Garcilaso de la Vega, worshipped the
fish and vicuñas that provided them food, the monkeys for
their cunning, the sparrowhawks for their keen sight. The
tiger and the bear were to them ferocious deities, and mankind, mere strangers and intruders in the land, might well
adore these beings, its old inhabitants and lords.[2] How,
indeed, can one wonder that in direct and simple awe, the
Philippine islanders, when they saw an alligator, should
have prayed him with great tenderness to do them no harm,
and to this end offered him of whatever they had in their
boats, casting it into the water.[3] Such rites display at
least a partial truth in the famous apophthegm which attributes to fear the origin of religion : ' Primos in orbe deos
fecit timor.'[4] In discussing the question of the souls of
animals in a previous chapter, instances were adduced of
men seeking to appease by apologetic phrase and rite the
animals they killed.[5] It is instructive to observe how
naturally such personal intercourse between man and animal
may pass into full worship, when the creature is powerful

---

[1] Steller, 'Kamtschatka,' p. 276.
[2] Garcilaso de la Vega, ' Comentarios Reales,' i. ch. ix. &c.
[3] Marsden, ' Sumatra,' p. 303.
[4] Petron. Arb. Fragm. ; Statius, iii. Theb. 661.
[5] See ante, ch. xi.

or dangerous enough to claim it. When the Stiêns of Kambodia asked pardon of the beast they killed, and offered sacrifice in expiation, they expressly did so through fear lest the creature's disembodied soul should come and torment them.[1]   Yet, strange to say, even the worship of the animal as divine does not prevent the propitiatory ceremony from passing into utter mockery.   Thus Charlevoix describes North American Indians who, when they had killed a bear, would set up its head painted with many colours, and offer it homage and praise while they performed the painful duty of feasting on its body.[2]   So among the Ainos, the indigenes of Yesso, the bear is a great divinity.   It is true they slay him when they can, but while they are cutting him up they salute him with obeisances and fair speeches, and set up his head outside the house to preserve them from misfortune.[3]   In Siberia, the Yakuts worship the bear in common with the spirits of the forest, bowing toward his favourite haunts with appropriate phrases of prose and verse, in praise of the bravery and generosity of their ' beloved uncle.'   Their kindred the Ostyaks swear in the Russian courts of law on a bear's head, for the bear, they say, is all-knowing, and will slay them if they lie. This idea actually serves the people as a philosophical, though one would say rather superfluous, explanation of a whole class of accidents :   when a hunter is killed by a bear, it is considered that he must at some time have forsworn himself, and now has met his doom.   Yet these Ostyaks, when they have overcome and slain their deity, will stuff its skin with hay, kick it, spit on it, insult and mock it till they have satiated their hatred and revenge, and are ready to set it up in a yurt as an object of worship.[4]

Whether an animal be worshipped as the receptacle or

---

[1] Mouhot, ' Indo-China,' vol. i. p. 252.

[2] Charlevoix, ' Nouvelle France,' vol. v. p. 443.

[3] W. M. Wood in ' Tr. Eth. Soc.' vol. iv. p. 36.

[4] Simpson, ' Journey,' vol. ii. p. 269 ; Erman, ' Siberia,' vol. i. p. 492 ; Latham, ' Descr. Eth.' vol. i. p. 456 ; ' Journ. Ind. Archip.' vol. iv. p. 590.

incarnation of an indwelling divine soul or other deity, or as one of the myriad representatives of the presiding god of its class, the case is included under and explained by the general theory of fetish-worship already discussed. Evidence which displays these two conceptions and their blending is singularly perfect in the islands of the Pacific. In the Georgian group, certain herons, kingfishers, and woodpeckers were held sacred and fed on the sacrifices, with the distinct view that the deities were embodied in the birds, and in this form came to eat the offered food and give the oracular responses by their cries.[1] The Tongans never killed certain birds, or the shark, whale, &c., as being sacred shrines in which gods were in the habit of visiting earth ; and if they chanced in sailing to pass near a whale they would offer scented oil or kava to him.[2] In the Fiji Islands, certain birds, fish, plants, and some men, were supposed to have deities closely connected with or residing in them. Thus the hawk, fowl, eel, shark, and nearly every other animal became the shrine of some deity, which the worshipper of that deity might not eat, so that some were even tabued from eating human flesh, the shrine of their god being a man. Ndengei, the dull and otiose supreme deity, had his shrine or incarnation in the serpent.[3] Every Samoan islander had his tutelary deity or ' aitu,' appearing in some animal, an eel, shark, dog, turtle, &c., which species became his fetish, not to be slighted or injured or eaten, an offence which the deity would avenge by entering the sinner's body and generating his proper incarnation within him till he died.[4] The ' atua ' of the New Zealander, corresponding with this in name, is a divine ancestral soul, and is also apt to appear in the body of an animal.[5] If we pass to Sumatra, we shall find that the veneration paid by the Malays to the tiger, and their habit of apologizing to it

[1] Ellis, ' Polyn. Res.' vol. i. p. 336.
[2] Farmer, ' Tonga,' p. 126 ; Mariner, vol. ii. p. 106.
[3] Williams, ' Fiji,' vol. i. p. 217, &c.
[4] Turner, ' Polynesia,' p. 238.
[5] Shortland, ' Trads. of N. Z.' ch. iv.

when a trap is laid, is connected with the idea of tigers being animated by the souls of departed men.[1] In other districts of the world, one of the most important cases connected with these is the worship paid by the North American Indian to his medicine-animal, of which he kills one specimen to preserve its skin, which thenceforth receives adoration and grants protection as a fetish.[2] In South Africa, as has been already mentioned, the Zulus hold that divine ancestral shades are embodied in certain tame and harmless snakes, whom their human kinsfolk receive with kindly respect and propitiate with food.[3] In West Africa, monkeys near a grave-yard are supposed to be animated by the spirits of the dead, and the general theory of sacred and worshipped crocodiles, snakes, birds, bats, elephants, hyænas, leopards, &c., is divided between the two great departments of the fetish-theory, in some cases the creature being the actual embodiment or personation of the spirit, and in other cases sacred to it or under its protection.[4] Hardly any region of the world displays so perfectly as this the worship of serpents as fetish-animals endowed with high spiritual qualities, to kill one of whom would be an offence unpardonable. For a single description of negro ophiolatry, may be cited Bosman's description from Whydah in the Bight of Benin; here the highest order of deities were a kind of snakes which swarm in the villages, reigned over by that huge chief monster, uppermost and greatest and as it were the grandfather of all, who dwelt in his snake-house beneath a lofty tree, and there received the royal offerings of meat and drink, cattle and money and stuffs. So heartfelt was the veneration of the snakes, that the Dutchmen made it a

---

[1] Marsden, ' Sumatra,' p. 292.

[2] Loskiel, ' Ind. of N. A.' part i. p. 40 ; Catlin, ' N. A. Ind.' vol. i. p. 36 ; Schoolcraft, ' Tribes,' part i. p. 34, part v. p. 652 ; Waitz, vol. iii. p. 190.

[3] See ante, p. 8 ; Callaway, ' Rel. of Amazulu,' p. 196.

[4] Steinhauser, ' Religion des Negers,' l.c. p. 133. J. L. Wilson, ' W. Afr.' pp. 210, 218. Schlegel, ' Ewe-Sprache,' p. xv.

means of clearing their warehouses of tiresome visitors ; as Bosman says, ' If we are ever tired with the natives of this country, and would fain be rid of them, we need only speak ill of the snake, at which they immediately stop their ears and run out of doors.'[1] Lastly, among the Tatar tribes of Siberia, Castrén finds the explanation of the veneration which the nomade pays to certain animals, in a distinct fetish-theory which he thus sums up : ' Can he also contrive to propitiate the snake, bear, wolf, swan, and various other birds of the air and beasts of the field, he has in them good protectors, for in them are hidden mighty spirits.'[2]

In the lower levels of civilization the social institution known as Totemism is of frequent occurrence. Its anthropological importance was especially brought into notice by J. F. McLennan, whose views as to an early totem-period of society have much influenced opinion since his time.[3] The totemic tribe is divided into clans, the members of each clan connecting themselves with, calling themselves by the name of, and even deriving their mythic pedigree from some animal, plant, or thing, but most often an animal ; these totem-clans are exogamous, marriage not being permissible within the clan, while permissible or obligatory between clan and clan. Thus among the Ojibwa Indians of North America, the names of such clan-animals, Bear, Wolf, Tortoise, Deer, Rabbit, &c., served to designate the intermarrying clans into which the tribes were divided, Indians being actually spoken of as bears, wolves, &c., and the figures of these animals indicating their clans in the native picture-writing. The Ojibwa word for such a clan-name has passed into English in the form ' totem,' and thus has become an accepted term among anthropologists to denote

---

[1] Bosman, ' Guinea,' letter 19 ; in Pinkerton, vol. xvi. p. 499. See Burton, ' Dahome,' ch. iv., xvii. An account of the Vaudoux serpent-worship still carried on among the negroes of Hayti, in ' Lippincott's Magazine,' Philadelphia, March, 1870.

[2] Castrén, ' Finn. Myth.' p. 196, see 228.

[3] J. F. McLennan in 'Fortnightly Review,' 1869-70 ; reprinted in 'Studies in Ancient History,' 2nd Series, pp. 117, 491,

similar clan-names customary over the world, this system of dividing tribes being called Totemism. Unfortunately for the study of the subject, John Long, the trader interpreter who introduced the Ojibwa word totem into Europe in 1791, does not seem to have grasped its meaning in the native law of marriage and clanship, but to have confused the totem-animal of the clan with the patron or guardian animal of the individual hunter, his manitu or ' medicine.'[1] Even when the North American totem-clans came to be better understood as social institutions regulating marriage, the notion of the guardian spirit still clung to them. Sir George Grey, who knew of the American totem-clans from the ' Archæologia Americana,' put on record in 1841 a list of exogamous classes in West Australia, and mentioned the opinion frequently given by the natives as to the origin of these class-names, that they were derived from some animal or vegetable being very common in the district which the family inhabited, so that the name of this animal or vegetable came to be applied to the family. This seems so far valuable evidence, but Grey was evidently led by John Long's mistaken statement, which he quotes, to fall himself into the same confusion between the tribal name and the patron animal or vegetable, the 'kobong' of his natives, which he regarded as a tribal totem.[2] In Mr. J. G. Frazer's valuable collection of information on totemism,[3] the use of the self-contradictory term 'individual totem' has unfortunately tended to perpetuate this confusion. In the present state of the problem of totemism, it would be premature to discuss at length its development and purpose. Mention may however be made of observations which tend to place it on a new footing, as being distinctly related to the transmigration of souls. In Melanesia men

[1] John Long, ' Voyages and Travels of an Indian Interpreter,' London, 1791, p. 86. See pp. 233, 411 of present volume.
[2] Grey, ' Journals of Expeditions in N. W. & W. Australia,' vol. ii. pp. 225-9 ; ' Archæologia Americana,' vol. ii. p. 109.
[3] J. G. Frazer, ' Totemism,' p. 53 ; ' Golden Bough,' 2nd ed. vol. iii. pp. 419, 423.

may say that after death they will reappear for instance as sharks or bananas, and the family will acknowledge the kinship by feeding the sharks and abstaining from the bananas. It is not unreasonable that Dr. Codrington should suggest such practices as throwing light on the origin of totemism.[1] The late investigations of Spencer and Gillen, conducted with scrupulous care in an almost untouched district of Central Australia, show totemism in the Arunta tribe, not as the means of regulating the intermarriage of clans, but as based on a native theory of the ancestry of the race, as descended from the Alcheringa, quasi-human animal or vegetable ancestors, whose souls are still reborn in human form in successive generations.[2] This careful and definite account may be the starting-point of a new study. Savages would be alive to the absurdity of naming clans after animals in order to indicate a prohibition of marrying-in, opposed to the habit of the animals themselves. Indeed, it seems more likely that such animal-names may have commonly belonged to inbred clans, before the rule of exogamy was developed. At present the plainest fact as to Totemism is its historical position as shown by its immense geographical distribution. Its presence in North America and Australia has been noticed. It extends its organization through the forest-region of South America from Guyana to Patagonia. North-ward of Australia it is to be traced among the more un-changed of the Malay populations, who underneath foreign influence still keep remains of a totemic system like that of the American tribes. Thence we follow the totem-clan into India, when it appears among non-Aryan hill-tribes such as the Oraons and Mundas, who have clans named after Eel, Hawk, Heron, and so on, and must not kill or eat these creatures. North of the Himalaya it appears among Mon-goloid tribes in their native low cultured state, such as the Yakuts with their intermarrying totem-clans Swan, Raven,

[1] Codrington, 'Melanesians,' pp. 32-3, 170.
[2] Spencer and Gillen, 'Native Tribes of Central Australia,' 1899, pp. 73, 121.

and the like. In Africa totemism appears in the Bantu district up to the West Coast. For example, the Bechuana are divided into Bakuena, men of the crocodile; Batlapi, of the fish; Balaung, of the lion; Bamorara, of the wild vine. A man does not eat his tribe-animal, or clothe himself in its skin, and if he must kill it as hurtful, the lion for instance, he asks pardon of it, and purifies himself from the sacrilege. These few instances illustrate the generalization that totemism in its complete form belongs to the savage and early barbaric stages of culture, only partial remains or survivals of it having lasted into the civilized period. Though appearing in all other quarters of the globe, it is interesting to notice that there is no distinct case of totemism found or recorded in Europe.[1]

The three motives of animal-worship which have been described, viz., direct worship of the animal for itself, in-direct worship of it as a fetish acted through by a deity, and veneration for it as a totem or representative of a tribe-ancestor, no doubt account in no small measure for the phenomena of Zoolatry among the lower races, due allow-ance being also made for the effects of myth and symbolism, of which we may gain frequent glimpses. Notwithstanding the obscurity and complexity of the subject, a survey of Animal-worship as a whole may yet justify an ethnographic view of its place in the history of civilization. If we turn from its appearances among the less cultured races to notice the shapes in which it has held its place among peoples advanced to the stage of national organization and stereo-typed religion, we shall find a reasonable cause for its new position in the theory of development and survival, whereby ideas at first belonging to savage theology have in part con-tinued to spread and solidify in their original manner, while in part they have been changed to accommodate them to more advanced ideas, or have been defended from the attacks of reason by being set up as sacred mysteries. Ancient Egypt

[1] General references in J. F. McLennan, ' Studies in Ancient History ; ' J. G. Frazer, ' Totemism.'

was a land of sacred cats and jackals and hawks, whose
mummies are among us to this day, but the reason of whose
worship was a subject too sacred for the Father of History
to discuss. Egyptian animal-worship seems to show, in a
double line, traces of a savage ancestry extending into ages
lying far behind even the remote antiquity of the Pyramids.
Deities patronising special sacred animals, incarnate in
their bodies, or represented in their figures, have nowhere
better examples than the divine bull-dynasty of Apis,
the sacred hawks caged and fed in the temple of Horus,
Thoth and his cynocephalus and ibis, Hathor the cow
and Sebek the crocodile. Moreover, the local character
of many of the sacred creatures, worshipped in certain
nomes yet killed and eaten with impunity elsewhere,
fits remarkably with that character of tribe-fetishes and
deified totems with which Mr. McLennan's argument is
concerned. See the men of Oxyrynchos reverencing and
sparing the fish oxyrynchos, and those of Latopolis likewise worshipping the latos. At Apollinopolis men hated
crocodiles and never lost a chance of killing them, while
the people of the Arsinoite nome dressed geese and fish for
these sacred creatures, adorned them with necklaces and
bracelets, and mummified them sumptuously when they
died.[1] In the modern world the most civilized people
among whom animal-worship vigorously survives, lie within
the range of Brahmanism, where the sacred animal, the
deity incarnate in an animal or invested with or symbolized
by its shape, may to this day be studied in clear example.
The sacred cow is not merely to be spared, she is as a deity
worshipped in annual ceremony, daily perambulated and
bowed to by the pious Hindu, who offers her fresh grass
and flowers ; Hanuman the monkey-god has his temples
and his idols, and in him Siva is incarnate, as Durga is in
the jackal ; the wise Ganesa wears the elephant's head ;

---

[1] Herod. ii. ; Plutarch, De Iside & Osiride ; Strabo, xvii. 1 ; Wilkinson,
' Ancient Eg.,' edited by Birch, vol. iii. ; Bunsen, 2nd Edition, with notes
by Birch, vol. i.

the divine king of birds, Garuda, is Vishnu's vehicle ; the forms of fish, and boar, and tortoise, were assumed in those avatar-legends of Vishnu which are at the intellectual level of the Red Indian myths they so curiously resemble.[1] The conceptions which underlie the Hindu creed of divine animals were not ill displayed by that Hindu who, being shown the pictures of Matthew, Mark, Luke, and John with their respective man, lion, ox, and eagle, explained these quite naturally and satisfactorily as the avatars or vehicles of the four evangelists.

In Animal-worship, some of the most remarkable cases of development and survival belong to a class from which striking instances have already been taken. Serpent-worship unfortunately fell years ago into the hands of speculative writers, who mixed it up with occult philosophies, Druidical mysteries, and that portentous nonsense called the ' Arkite Symbolism,' till now sober students hear the very name of Ophiolatry with a shiver. Yet it is in itself a rational and instructive subject of inquiry, especially notable for its width of range in mythology and religion. We may set out among the lower races, with such accounts as those of the Red Indian's reverence to the rattlesnake, as grandfather and king of snakes, as a divine protector able to give fair winds or cause tempests;[2] or of the worship of great snakes among the tribes of Peru before they received the religion of the Incas, as to whom an old author says, ' They adore the demon when he presents himself to them in the figure of some beast or serpent, and talks with them.'[3] Thenceforth such examples of direct Ophiolatry may be traced on into classic and barbaric Europe ; the great serpent which defended the citadel of Athens and enjoyed its monthly honey-cakes;[4] the Roman genius loci appearing in the form of the snake (Nullus enim locus sine

[1] Ward, ' Hindoos,' vol. ii. p. 195, &c.
[2] Schoolcraft, part iii. p. 231 ; Brinton, p. 108, &c.
[3] Garcilaso de la Vega, ' Comentarios Reales,' i. 9.
[4] Herodot. viii. 41.

genio est, qui per anguem plerumque ostenditur);[1] the old
Prussian serpent-worship and offering of food to the
household snakes;[2] the golden viper adored by the Lom-
bards, till Barbatus got it in his hands and the goldsmiths
made it into paten and chalice.[3] To this day, Europe has
not forgotten in nursery tales or more serious belief the
snake that comes with its golden crown and drinks milk out
of the child's porringer ; the house-snake, tame and kindly
but seldom seen, that cares for the cows and the children
and gives omens of a death in the family ; the pair of
household snakes which have a mystic connexion of life
and death with the husband and housewife themselves.[4]
Serpent-worship, apparently of the directest sort, was prominent in the indigenous religions of Southern Asia. It
now even appears to have maintained no mean place in
early Indian Buddhism, for the sculptures of the Sanchi
tope show scenes of adoration of the five-headed snake-
deity in his temple, performed by a race of serpent-wor-
shippers, figuratively represented with snakes growing from
their shoulders, and whose raja himself has a five-headed
snake arching hood-wise over his head. Here, moreover,
the totem-theory comes into contact with ophiolatry. The
Sanskrit name of the snake, ' nâga,' becomes also the
accepted designation of its adorers, and thus mythological
interpretation has to reduce to reasonable sense legends of
serpent-races who turn out to be simply serpent-worship-
pers, tribes who have from the divine reptiles at once their
generic name of Nâgas, and with it their imagined ancestral
descent from serpents.[5] In different ways, these Nâga
tribes of South Asia are on the one hand analogues of the

---

[1] Servius ad Æn. v. 95.

[2] Hartknoch, ' Preussen,' part i. pp. 143, 162.

[3] Grimm, ' D. M.' p. 648.

[4] Grimm, ' D. M.' p. 650. Rochholz, ' Deutscher Glaube,' &c., vol. i. p. 146.
Monnier, ' Traditions Populaires,' p. 644. Grohmann, ' Aberglauben aus
Böhmen,' &c., p. 78. Ralston, ' Songs of Russian People,' p. 175.

[5] Fergusson ' Tree and Serpent Worship,' p. 55, &c., pl. xxiv. McLennan
l.c. p. 563, &c.

Snake Indians of America, and on the other of the Ophio-
genes or Serpent-race of the Troad, kindred of the vipers
whose bite they could cure by touch, and descendants of an
ancient hero transformed into a snake.[1]

Serpents hold a prominent place in the religions of the
world, as the incarnations, shrines, or symbols of high
deities. Such were the rattlesnake worshipped in the
Natchez temple of the Sun, and the snake belonging in
name and figure to the Aztec deity Quetzalcoatl;[2] the
snake as worshipped still by the Slave Coast negro, not for
itself but for its indwelling deity;[3] the snake kept and fed
with milk in the temple of the old Slavonic god Potrimpos;[4]
the serpent-symbol of the healing deity Asklepios, who
abode in or manifested himself through the huge tame
snakes kept in his temples[5] (it is doubtful whether this had
any original connexion with the adoption of the snake, from
its renewal by casting its old slough, as the accepted emblem
of new life or immortality in later symbolism) ; and lastly,
the Phœnician serpent with its tail in its mouth, symbol of
the world and of the Heaven-god Taaut, in its original
meaning perhaps a mythic world-snake like the Scandinavian Midgard-worm, but in the changed fancy of later ages
adapted into an emblem of eternity.[6] It scarcely seems
proved that savage races, in all their mystic contemplations
of the serpent, ever developed out of their own minds the
idea, to us so familiar, of adopting it as a personification of
evil.[7] In ancient times, we may ascribe this character perhaps to the monster whose well-known form is to be seen
on the mummy-cases, the Apophis-serpent of the Egyptian

---

[1] Strabo, xiii. 1, 14.
[2] J. G. Müller, ' Amer. Urrel.' pp. 62, 585.
[3] J. B. Schlegel, ' Ewe-Sprache,' p. xiv.
[4] Hanusch, ' Slaw. Myth.' p. 217.
[5] Pausan. ii. 28 ; Ælian. xvi. 39. See Welcker, ' Griech. Götterl.' vol. ii.
p. 734.
[6] Macrob. Saturnal. i. 9. Movers, ' Phönizier,' vol. i. p. 500.
[7] Details such as in Schoolcraft, ' Ind. Tribes,' part i. pp. 38, 414, may be
ascribed to Christian intercourse. See Brinton, p. 121.

Hades;[1] and it unequivocally belongs to the destroying serpent of the Zarathustrians, Azhi Dahâka,[2] a figure which
bears so remarkable a relation to that of the Semitic serpent
of Eden, which may possibly stand in historical connexion
with it. A wondrous blending of the ancient rites of Ophiolatry with mystic conceptions of Gnosticism appears in the
cultus which tradition (in truth or slander) declares the semi-
Christian sect of Ophites to have rendered to their tame
snake, enticing it out of its chest to coil round the sacra-
mental bread, and worshipping it as representing the great
king from heaven who in the beginning gave to the man
and woman the knowledge of the mysteries.[3] Thus the
extreme types of religious veneration, from the soberest
matter-of-fact to the dreamiest mysticism, find their places
in the worship of animals.[4]

Hitherto in the study of animistic doctrine, our attention
has been turned especially to those minor spirits whose
functions concern the closer and narrower detail of man's
life and its surroundings. In passing thence to the consideration of divine beings whose functions have a wider
scope, the transition may be well made through a special
group. An acute remark of Auguste Comte's calls attention
to an important process of theological thought, which we
may here endeavour to bring as clearly as possible before
our minds. In his ' Philosophie Positive,' he defines deities
proper as differing by their general and abstract character
from pure fetishes (i.e., animated objects), the humble
fetish governing but a single object from which it is
inseparable, while the gods administer a special order
of phenomena at once in different bodies. When, he con-

---

[1] Lepsius, ' Todtenbuch,' and Birch's transl. in Bunsen's ' Egypt,' vol. v.

[2] Spiegel, ' Avesta,' vol. i. p. 66, vol. iii. p. lix.

[3] Epiphan. Adv. Hæres. xxxvii. Tertullian. De Præscript. contra
Hæreticos, 47.

[4] Further collections of evidence relating to Zoolatry in general may be
found in Bastian, ' Das Thier in seiner mythologischen Bedeutung,' in
Bastian and Hartmann's ' Zeitschrift für Ethnologie,' vol. i. ; Meiners,
' Geschichte der Religionen,' vol. i.

tinues, the similar vegetation of the different oaks of a
forest led to a theological generalization from their common
phenomena, the abstract being thus produced was no longer
the fetish of a single tree, but became the god of the forest;
here, then, is the intellectual passage from fetishism to
polytheism, reduced to the inevitable preponderance of
specific over individual ideas.[1] Now this observation of
Comte's may be more immediately applied to a class of
divine beings which may be accurately called species-deities.
It is highly suggestive to study the crude attempts of barbaric theology to account for the uniformity observed in
large classes of objects, by making this generalization from
individual to specific ideas. To explain the existence of
what we call a species, they would refer it to a common
ancestral stock, or to an original archetype, or to a species-
deity, or they combined these conceptions. For such speculations, classes of plants and animals offered perhaps an
early and certainly an easy subject. The uniformity of each
kind not only suggested a common parentage, but also the
notion that creatures so wanting in individuality, with
qualities so measured out as it were by line and rule, might
not be independent arbitrary agents, but mere copies from
a common model, or mere instruments used by controlling
deities. Thus in Polynesia, as has been just mentioned,
certain species of animals were considered as incarnations
of certain deities, and among the Samoans it appears that
the question as to the individuality of such creatures was
actually asked and answered. If, for instance, a village
god were accustomed to appear as an owl, and one of his
votaries found a dead owl by the roadside, he would mourn
over the sacred bird and bury it with much ceremony, but
the god himself would not be thought to be dead, for he
remains incarnate in all existing owls.[2] According to
Father Geronimo Boscana, the Acagchemen tribe of Upper
California furnish a curious parallel to this notion. They

[1] Comte, ' Philosophie Positive,' vol. v. p. 101.
[2] Turner, ' Polynesia,' p. 242.

worshipped the ' panes ' bird, which seems to have been an eagle or vulture, and each year, in the temple of each village, one of them was solemnly killed without shedding blood, and the body burned. Yet the natives maintained and believed that it was the same individual bird they sacrificed each year, and more than this, that the same bird was slain by each of the villages.[1] Among the comparatively cultured Peruvians, Acosta describes another theory of celestial archetypes. Speaking of star-deities, he says that shepherds venerated a certain star called Sheep, another star called Tiger protected men from tigers, &c. : ' And generally, of all the animals and birds there are on the earth, they believed that a like one lived in heaven, in whose charge were their procreation and increase, and thus they accounted of divers stars, such as that they call Chacana, and Topatorca, and Mamana, and Mizco, and Miquiquiray, and other such, so that in a manner it appears that they were drawing towards the dogma of the Platonic ideas.'[2] The North American Indians also have speculated as to the common ancestors or deities of species. One missionary notes down their idea as he found it in 1634. ' They say, moreover, that all the animals of each species have an elder brother, who is as it were the principle and origin of all the individuals, and this elder brother is marvellously great and powerful. The elder brother of the beavers, they told me, is perhaps as large as our cabin.' Another early account is that each species of animals has its archetype in the land of souls; there exists, for example, a manitu or archetype of all oxen, which animates all oxen.[3] Here, again, occurs a noteworthy correspondence with the ideas of a distant race. In Buyán, the island paradise of Russian myth, there

[1] Brinton, ' Myths of New World,' p. 105.
[2] Acosta, ' Historia de las Indias,' book v. c. iv. ; Rivero & Tschudi, pp. 161, 179 ; J. G. Müller, p. 365.
[3] Le Jeune in ' Rel. des Jés. dans la Nouvelle France,' 1634, p. 13. Lafitau, ' Mœurs des Sauvages,' vol. i. p. 370. See also Waitz, vol. iii. p. 194 ; Schoolcraft, part iii. p. 327.

are to be found the Snake older than all snakes, and the prophetic Raven, elder brother of all ravens, and the Bird, the largest and oldest of all birds, with iron beak and copper claws, and the Mother of Bees, eldest among bees.[1] Morgan's comparatively modern account of the Iroquois mentions their belief in a spirit of each species of trees and plants, as of oak, hemlock, maple, whortleberry, raspberry, spearmint, tobacco ; most objects of nature being thus under the care of protecting spirits.[2] The doctrine of such species-deities is perhaps nowhere more definitely stated than by Castrén in his ' Finnish Mythology.' In his description of the Siberian nature-worship, the lowest level is exemplified by the Samoyeds, whose direct worship of natural objects for themselves may perhaps indicate the original religious condition of the whole Turanian race. But the doctrine of the comparatively cultured heathen Finns was at a different stage. Here every object in nature has a ' haltia,' a guardian deity or genius, a being which was its creator and thenceforth became attached to it. These deities or genii are, however, not bound to each single transitory object, but are free personal beings which have movement, form, body, and soul. Their existence in no wise depends on the existence of the individual objects, for although no object in nature is without its guardian deity, this deity extends to the whole race or species. This ash-tree, this stone, this house, has indeed its particular ' haltia,' yet these same ' haltiat ' concern themselves with other ash-trees, stones, and houses, of which the individuals may perish, but their presiding genii live on in the species.[3] It seems as though some similar view ran through the doctrine of more civilized races, as in the well-known

---

[1] Ralston, ' Songs of the Russian People,' p. 375. The Slavonic myth of Buyán with its dripping oak and the snake Garafena lying beneath, is obviously connected with the Scandinavian myth of the dripping ash, Yggdrasill, the snake Nidhögg below, and the two Swans of the Urdhar-fount, parents of all swans.

[2] Morgan, ' Iroquois,' p. 162.

[3] Castrén, ' Finn. Myth.' pp. 106, 160, 189, &c.

Egyptian and Greek examples where whole species of animals, plants, or things, stand as symbolic of, and as protected by, particular deities. The thought appears with
most perfect clearness in the Rabbinical philosophy which
apportions to each of the 2100 species, of plants for instance, a presiding angel in heaven, and assigns this as the
motive of the Levitical prohibition of mixtures among animals and plants.[1] The interesting likeness pointed out by
Father Acosta between these crude theological conceptions
and the civilized philosophical conceptions which have replaced them, was again brought into view in the last century
by the President De Brosses, in comparing the Red Indians'
archetypes of species with the Platonic archetypal ideas.[2]
As for animals and plants, the desire of naturalists to ascend
to primal unity to some extent finds satisfaction in a theory
tracing each species to an origin in a single pair. And
though this is out of the question with inanimate objects,
our language seems in suggestive metaphor to lay hold on
the same thought, when we say of a dozen similar swords,
or garments, or chairs, that they have the same *pattern*
(patronus, as it were father), whereby they were shaped
from their *matter* (materia, or mother substance).

[1] Eisenmenger, ' Judenthum,' part ii. p. 376 ; Bastian, ' Mensch,' vol. iii.
p. 194.
[2] De Brosses, ' Dieux Fétiches,' p. 58.

CHAPTER XVI

ANIMISM (*continued*)

Higher Deities of Polytheism—Human characteristics applied to Deity—
Lords of Spiritual Hierarchy—Polytheism : its course of development
in lower and higher Culture—Principles of its investigation ; classification of Deities according to central conceptions of their significance
and function—Heaven-god—Rain-god—Thunder-god—Wind-gods—
Earth-god—Water-god—Sea-god—Fire-god—Sun-god—Moon-god.

SURVEYING the religions of the world and studying the
descriptions of deity among race after race, we may recur
to old polemical terms in order to define a dominant idea of
theology at large. Man so habitually ascribes to his deities
human shape, human passions, human nature, that we may
declare him an Anthropomorphite, an Anthropopathite, and
(to complete the series) an Anthropophysite. In this state
of religious thought, prevailing as it does through so immense a range among mankind, one of the strongest con-
firmations may be found of the theory here advanced concerning the development of Animism. This theory that
the conception of the human soul is the very ' fons et
origo ' of the conceptions of spirit and deity in general,
has been already vouched for by the fact of human souls
being held to pass into the characters of good and evil
demons, and to ascend to the rank of deities. But beyond
this, as we consider the nature of the great gods of the
nations, in whom the vastest functions of the universe are
vested, it will still be apparent that these mighty deities are
modelled on human souls, that in great measure their feeling
and sympathy, their character and habit, their will and
action, even their material and form, display throughout
their adaptations, exaggerations and distortions, charac-

teristics shaped upon those of the human spirit. The key
to investigation of the Dii Majorum Gentium of the world
is the reflex of humanity, and as we behold their figures in
their proper districts of theology, memory ever brings back
the Psalmist's words, ' Thou thoughtest I was altogether
as thyself.'

The higher deities of Polytheism have their places in the
general animistic system of mankind. Among nation after
nation it is still clear how, man being the type of deity,
human society and government became the model on which
divine society and government were shaped. As chiefs
and kings are among men, so are the great gods among
the lesser spirits. They differ from the souls and minor
spiritual beings which we have as yet chiefly considered,
but the difference is rather of rank than of nature. They
are personal spirits, reigning over personal spirits. Above
the disembodied souls and manes, the local genii of rocks
and fountains and trees, the host of good and evil demons,
and the rest of the spiritual commonality, stand these
mightier deities, whose influence is less confined to local or
individual interests, and who, as it pleases them, can act
directly within their vast domain, or control and operate
through the lower beings of their kind, their servants,
agents, or mediators. The great gods of Polytheism,
numerous and elaborately defined in the theology of the
cultured world, do not however make their earliest appearance there. In the religions of the lower races their
principal types were already cast, and thenceforward, for
many an age of progressing or relapsing culture, it became
the work of poet and priest, legend-monger and historian,
theologian and philosopher, to develop and renew, to degrade and abolish, the mighty lords of the Pantheon.

With little exception, wherever a savage or barbaric system of religion is thoroughly described, great gods make
their appearance in the spiritual world as distinctly as
chiefs in the human tribe. In the lists, it is true, there are
set down great deities, good or evil, who probably came

in from modern Christian missionary teaching, or otherwise by contact with foreign religions. It is often difficult
to distinguish from these the true local gods, animistic
figures of native meaning and origin. Among the following polytheistic systems, examples may be found of such
combinations, with the complex theological problems
they suggest. Among the Australians, above the swarming souls, nature-spirits, demons, there stand out mythic
figures of higher divinity ; Nguk-wonga, the Spirit of
the Waters ; Biam, who gives ceremonial songs and
causes disease, and is perhaps the same as Baiame the
creator ; Nambajandi and Warrugura, lords of heaven and
the nether world.[1] In South America, if we look into the
theology of the Manaos (whose name is well known in the
famous legend of El Dorado and the golden city of Manoa),
we see Mauari and Saraua, who may be called the Good
and Evil Spirit, and beside the latter the two Gamainhas,
Spirits of the Waters and the Forest.[2] In North America
the description of a solemn Algonquin sacrifice introduces
a list of twelve dominant manitus or gods; first the Great
Manitu in heaven, then the Sun, Moon, Earth, Fire, Water,
the House-god, the Indian corn, and the four Winds or
Cardinal Points.[3] The Polynesian's crowd of manes, and
the lower ranks of deities of earth, sea, and air, stand below
the great gods of Peace and War, Oro and Tane the national
deities of Tahiti and Huahine, Raitubu the Sky-producer,
Hina who aided in the work of forming the world, her
father Taaroa, the uncreate Creator who dwells in Heaven.[4]
Among the Land Dayaks of Borneo, the commonalty of
spirits consists of the souls of the departed, and of such
beings as dwell in the noble old forests on the tops of lofty
hills, or such as hover about villages and devour the stores
of rice; above these are Tapa, creator and preserver of man,

[1] Eyre, ' Australia,' vol. ii. p. 362 ; Oldfield in ' Tr. Eth. Soc.' vol. iii.
p. 228 ; Lang, ' Queensland,' p. 444.
[2] Martius, ' Ethnog. Amer.' vol. i. p. 583.
[3] Loskiel, ' Ind. of N. America,' part i. p. 43.
[4] Ellis, ' Polyn. Res.' vol. i. p. 322.

and Iang, who taught the Dayaks their religion, Jirong, whose function is the birth and death of men, and Tenabi, who made, and still causes to flourish, the earth and all things therein save the human race.[1] In West Africa, an example may be taken from the theology of the Slave Coast, a systematic scheme of all nature as moved and quickened by spirits, kindly or hostile to mankind. These spirits dwell in field and wood, mountain and valley; they live in air and water; multitudes of them have been human souls, such ghosts hover about the graves and near the living, and have influence with the under-gods, whom they worship; among these 'edrŏ' are the patron-deities of men and families and tribes ; through these subordinate beings works the highest god, Mawu. The missionary who describes this negro hierarchy quite simply sees in it Satan and his Angels.[2] In Asia, the Samoyed's little spirits that are bound to his little fetishes, and the little elves of wood and stream, have greater beings above them, the Forest-Spirit, the River-Spirit, the Sun and Moon, the Evil Spirit and the Good Spirit above all.[3] The countless host of the local gods of the Khonds pervade the world, rule the functions of nature, and control the life of men, and these have their chiefs; above them rank the deified souls of men who have become tutelary gods of tribes ; above these are the six great gods, the Rain-god, the goddess of Firstfruits, the god of Increase, the god of Hunting, the iron god of War, the god of Boundaries, with which group stands also the Judge of the Dead, and above all other gods, the Sun-god and Creator Boora Pennu, and his wife the mighty Earth-goddess, Tari Pennu.[4] The Spanish conquerors found in Mexico a complex and systematic hierarchy of spiritual beings ; numberless were the little deities who had their worship in house and lane,

[1] St. John, ' Far East,' vol. i. p. 180.
[2] J. B. Schlegel, ' Schlüssel zur Ewe Sprache,' p. xii. ; compare Bowen, 'Yoruba Lang.' in 'Smithsonian Contrib.' vol. i. p. xvi.
[3] Samoiedia, in Pinkerton, vol. i. p. 531.
[4] Macpherson, p. 84, &c.

grove and temple, and from these the worshipper could pass to gods of flowers or of pulque, of hunters and gold-smiths, and then to the great deities of the nation and the world, the figures which the mythologist knows so well, Centeotl the Earth-goddess, Tlaloc the Water-god, Huit-zilopochtli the War-god, Mictlanteuctli the Lord of Hades, Tonatiuh and Metztli the Sun and Moon.[1] Thus, starting from the theology of savage tribes, the student arrives at the polytheistic hierarchies of the Aryan nations. In ancient Greece, the cloud-compelling Heaven-god reigns over such deities as the god of War and the goddess of Love, the Sun-god and the Moon-goddess, the Fire-god and the ruler of the Under-world, the Winds and Rivers, the nymphs of wood and well and forest.[2] In modern India, Brahma-Vishnu-Siva reign pre-eminent over a series of divinities, heterogeneous and often obscure in nature, but among whom stand out in clear meaning and purpose such figures as Indra of Heaven and Sûrya of the Sun, Agni of the Fire, Pavana of the Winds and Varuna of the Waters, Yama lord of the Under-world, Kâma god of Love and Kârttikeya of War, Panchânana who gives epilepsy and Manasâ who preserves from snake-bites, the divine Rivers, and below these the ranks of nymphs, elves, demons, minis-tering spirits, of heaven and earth—Gandharvas, Apsaras, Siddhas, Asuras, Bhûtas, Râkshasas.[3]

The systematic comparison of polytheistic religions has been of late years worked with admirable results. These have been due to the adoption of comparatively exact methods, as where the ancient Aryan deities of the Veda have been brought into connexion with those of the Homeric poems, in some cases as clearly as where we Englishmen can study in the Scandinavian Edda the old gods of our own race, whose names stand in local names on the map of England, and serve as counters to reckon our days of the

[1] Clavigero, ' Messico,' vol. ii. ch. i.
[2] Gladstone, ' Juventus Mundi,' ch. vii. &c.
[3] Ward, ' Hindoos,' vol. ii.

week. Yet it need scarcely be said that to compare in full
detail the deities even of closely connected nations, and a
fortiori those of tribes not united in language and history,
is still a difficult and unsatisfactory task. The old-fashioned
identifications of the gods and heroes of different nations
admitted most illusory evidence. Some had little more
ground than similar-sounding names, as when the Hindu
Brahma and Prajâpati were discovered to be the Hebrew
Abraham and Japhet, and when even Sir William Jones
identified Woden with Buddha. With not much more
stringency, it is still often taken as matter of course that
the Keltic Beal, whose bealtines correspond with a whole
class of bonfire-customs among several branches of the Aryan
race, is the Bel or the Baal of the Semitic cultus. Unfortunately, classical scholarship at the Renaissance started
the subject on an unsound footing, by accepting the Greek
deities with the mystified shapes and perverted names they
had assumed in Latin literature. That there was a partial
soundness in such comparisons, as in identifying Zeus and
Jupiter, Hestia and Vesta, made the plan all the more misleading when Kronos came to figure as Saturn, Poseidon
as Neptune, Athene as Minerva. To judge by example of
the possible results of comparative theology worked on such
principles, Thoth being identified with Hermes, Hermes
with Mercury, and Mercury with Woden, there comes to
pass the absurd transition from the Egyptian ibis-headed
divine scribe of the gods, to the Teutonic heaven-dwelling
driver of the raging tempest. It is not in this loose fashion
that the mental processes are to be sought out, which led
nations to arrange so similarly and yet so diversely their
array of deities.

A twofold perplexity besets the soberest investigator on
this ground, caused by the modification of deities by development at home and adoption from abroad. Even among
the lower races, gods of long traditional legend and worship
acquire a mixed and complex personality. The mythologist
who seeks to ascertain the precise definition of the Red

Indian Michabu in his various characters of Heaven-god and Water-god, Creator of the Earth and first ancestor of Man, or who examines the personality of the Polynesian Maui in his relation to Sun, lord of Heaven or Hades, first Man, and South Sea Island hero, will sympathize with the Semitic or Aryan student bewildered among the heterogeneous attributes of Baal and Astarte, Herakles and Athene. Sir William Jones scarcely overstated the perplexity of the problem in the following remarkable forecast delivered more than a century ago, in the first anniversary discourse before the Asiatic Society of Bengal, at a time when glimpses of the relation of the Hindu to the Greek Pantheon were opening into a new broad view of comparative theology in his mind. ' We must not be surprised,' he says, ' at finding, on a close examination, that the characters of all the Pagan deities, male and female, melt into each other and at last into one or two ; for it seems a well-founded opinion, that the whole crowd of gods and goddesses in ancient Rome, and modern Váránes [Benares] mean only the powers of nature, and principally those of the Sun, expressed in a variety of ways and by a multitude of fanciful names.' As to the travelling of gods from country to country, and the changes they are apt to suffer on the road, we may judge by examples of what has happened within our knowledge. It is not merely that one nation borrows a god from another with its proper figure and attributes and rites, as where in Rome the worshipper of the Sun might take his choice whether he would adore in the temple of the Greek Apollo, the Egyptian Osiris, the Persian Mithra, or the Syrian Elagabalus. The intercourse of races can produce quainter results than this. Any Orientalist will appreciate the wonderful hotchpot of Hindu and Arabic language and religion in the following details, noted down among rude tribes of the Malay Peninsula. We hear of Jin Bumi the Earth-god (Arabic jin = demon, Sanskrit bhûmi = earth) ; incense is burnt to Jewajewa (Sanskrit dewa = god) who intercedes with Pirman the

supreme invisible deity above the sky (Brahma ?) ; the
Moslem Allah Táala, with his wife Nabi Mahamad (Prophet
Mohammed), appear in the Hinduized characters of creator
and destroyer of all things; and while the spirits worshipped
in stones are called by the Hindu term of ' dewa ' or deity,
Moslem conversion has so far influenced the mind of the
stone-worshipper, that he will give to his sacred boulder
the title of a Prophet Mohammed.[1] If we would have examples nearer home, we may trace the evil demon Aeshma
Daeva of the ancient Persian religion becoming the Asmo-
deus of the book of Tobit, afterwards to find a place in the
devilry of the middle ages, and to end his career as the
Diable Boiteux of Le Sage. Even the Aztec war-god
Huitzilopochtli may be found figuring as the demon Vizli-
puzli in the popular drama of Doctor Faustus.

In ethnographic comparisons of the religions of mankind,
unless there is evidence of direct relation between gods belonging to two peoples, the safe and reasonable principle is
to limit the identification of deities to the attributes they
have in common. Thus it is proper to compare the Dendid
of the White Nile with the Aryan Indra, in so far as both
are Heaven-gods and Rain-gods; the Aztec Tonatiuh with
the Greek Apollo, in so far as both are Sun-gods ; the
Australian Baiame with the Scandinavian Thor, in so far
as both are Thunder-gods. The present purpose of displaying Polytheism as a department of Animism does not
require that elaborate comparison of systems which would
be in place in a manual of the religions of the world. The
great gods may be scientifically ranged and treated according to their fundamental ideas, the strongly-marked and
intelligible conceptions which, under names often obscure
and personalities often mixed and mystified, they stand to
represent. It is enough to show the similarity of principle
on which the theologic mind of the lower races shaped
those old familiar types of deity, with which our first
acquaintance was gained in the pantheon of classic mytho-

[1] ' Journ. Ind. Archip.' vol. i. pp. 33, 255, 275, 338, vol. ii. p. 692.

logy. It will be observed that not all, but the principal
figures, belong to strict Nature-worship. These may be
here first surveyed. They are Heaven and Earth, Rain
and Thunder, Water and Sea, Fire and Sun and Moon,
worshipped either directly for themselves, or as animated
by their special deities, or these deities are more fully set
apart and adored in anthropomorphic shape—a group of
conceptions distinctly and throughout based on the principles of savage fetishism. True, the great Nature-gods are
huge in strength and far-reaching in influence, but this is
because the natural objects they belong to are immense
in size or range of action, pre-eminent and predominant
among lesser fetishes, though still fetishes themselves.

In the religion of the North American Indians, the
Heaven-god displays perfectly the gradual blending of the
material sky itself with its personal deity. In the early
times of French colonization, Father Brebeuf mentions the
Hurons addressing themselves to the earth, rivers, lakes,
and dangerous rocks, but above all to heaven, believing
that it is all animated, and some powerful demon dwells
therein. He describes them as speaking directly to
heaven by its personal name ' Aronhiaté ! ' Thus when
they throw tobacco into the fire as sacrifice, if it is
Heaven they address, they say ' Aronhiaté ! (Heaven !)
behold my sacrifice, have pity on me, aid me ! ' They
have recourse to Heaven in almost all their necessities,
and respect this great body above all creatures, remarking
in it particularly something divine. They imagine in the
sky an ' oki,' i.e. demon or power, which rules the seasons
of the year and controls the winds and waves. They
dread its anger, calling it to witness when they make
some important promise or treaty, saying, Heaven hears
what we do this day, and fearing chastisement should
their word be broken. One of their renowned sorcerers
said, Heaven will be angry if men mock him ; when
they cry every day to Heaven, Aronhiaté ! yet give him
nothing, he will avenge himself. Etymology again suggests

the divine sky as the inner meaning of the Iroquois supreme deity, Taronhiawagon the 'sky-comer' or 'sky-holder,' who had his festival about the winter solstice, who brought the ancestral race out of the mountain, taught them hunting, marriage, and religion, gave them corn and beans, squashes and potatoes and tobacco, and guided them on their migrations as they spread over the land. Among the North American tribes, not only does the conception of the personal divine Heaven thus seem the fundamental idea of the Heaven-god, but it may expand under Christian influence into a yet more general thought of divinity in the Great Spirit in Heaven.[1] In South Africa, the Zulus speak of the Heaven as a person, ascribing to it the power of exercising a will, and they also speak of a Lord of Heaven, whose wrath they deprecate during a thunderstorm. In the native legends of the Zulu princess in the country of the Half-Men, the captive maiden expostulates personally with the Sky, for only acting in an ordinary way, and not in the way she wishes, to destroy her enemies :—

> 'Listen, yon heaven. Attend ; mayoya, listen.
> Listen, heaven. It does not thunder with loud thunder.
> It thunders in an undertone. What is it doing ?
> It thunders to produce rain and change of season.'

Thereupon the clouds gather tumultuously ; the princess sings again and it thunders terribly, and the Heaven kills the Half-Men round about her, but she is left unharmed.[2] West Africa is another district where the Heaven-god reigns, in whose attributes may be traced the transition from the direct conception of the personal sky to that of the supreme creative deity. Thus in Bonny, one word serves for god, heaven, cloud ; and in Aquapim, Yankupong is at once the highest god and the weather. Of this latter deity, the

---

[1] Brebeuf in 'Rel. des Jés.,' 1636, p. 107; Lafitau, 'Mœurs des Sauvages Amériquains,' vol. i. p. 132. Schoolcraft, 'Iroquois,' p. 36, &c. 237. Brinton, 'Myths of New World,' pp. 48, 172. J. G. Müller, 'Amer. Urrelig.' p. 119.

[2] Callaway, 'Zulu Tales,' vol. i. p. 203.

Nyankupon of the Oji nation, it is remarked by Riis, ' The idea of him as a supreme spirit is obscure and uncertain, and often confounded with the visible heavens or sky, the upper world (sorro) which lies beyond human reach ; and hence the same word is used also for heavens, sky, and even for rain and thunder.'[1] The same transition from the divine sky to its anthropomorphic deity shows out in the theology of the Tatar tribes. The rude Samoyed's mind scarcely if at all separates the visible personal Heaven from the divinity united with it under one and the same name, Num. Among the more cultured Finns, the cosmic attributes of the Heaven-god, Ukko the Old One, display the same original nature ; he is the ancient of Heaven, the father of Heaven, the bearer of the Firmament, the god of the Air, the dweller on the Clouds, the Cloud-driver, the shepherd of the Cloud-lambs.[2] So far as the evidence of language, and document, and ceremony, can preserve the record of remotely ancient thought, China shows in the highest deity of the state religion a like theologic development. Tien, Heaven, is in personal shape the Shang-ti or Upper Emperor, the Lord of the Universe. The Chinese books may idealize this supreme divinity ; they may say that his command is fate, that he rewards the good and punishes the wicked, that he loves and protects the people beneath him, that he manifests himself through events, that he is a spirit full of insight, penetrating, fearful, majestic. Yet they cannot refine him so utterly away into an abstract celestial deity, but that language and history still recognize him as what he was in the beginning, Tien, Heaven.[3]

[1] Waitz, ' Anthropologie,' vol. ii. p. 168, &c. ; Burton, ' W. & W. fr. W. Afr.' p. 76.

[2] Castrén, ' Finn. Myth.' p. 7, &c.

[3] Plath, ' Religion und Cultus der alten Chinesen,' part i. p. 18, &c. ; part ii. p. 32; Doolittle, 'Chinese,' vol. ii. p. 396. See Max Müller, ' Lectures,' 2nd S. p. 437; Legge, 'Confucius,' p. 100. For further evidence as to savage and barbaric worship of the Heaven as Supreme Deity, see chap. xvii.

With such evidence perfectly accords the history of the
Heaven-god among our Indo-European race. This being,
adored in ancient Aryan religion, was—

> ' . . . . the whole circle of the heavens, for him
> A sensitive existence, and a God,
> With lifted hands invoked, and songs of praise.'

The evidence of language to this effect has been set
forth with extreme clearness by Professor Max Müller. In
the first stage, the Sanskrit Dyu (Dyaus), the bright sky,
is taken in a sense so direct that it expresses the idea of
day, and the storms are spoken of as going about in it; while
Greek and Latin rival this distinctness in such terms as
ἔνδιος, 'in the open air,' εὔδιος, 'well-skyed, calm,' sub
divo, ' in the open air,' sub Jove frigido, ' under the cold
sky,' and that graphic description by Ennius of the bright
firmament, Jove whom all invoke :—

> ' Aspice hoc sublime candens, quem invocant omnes Jovem.'

In the second stage, Dyaus pitar, Heaven-father, stands in
the Veda as consort of Prithivî mâtar, Earth-mother, ranked
high or highest among the bright gods. To the Greek he
is Ζεὺς πατήρ, the Heaven-father, Zeus the All-seer, the
Cloud-compeller, King of Gods and Men. As Max Müller
writes : ' There was nothing that could be told of the sky
that was not in some form or other ascribed to Zeus. It
was Zeus who rained, who thundered, who snowed, who
hailed, who sent the lightning, who gathered the clouds,
who let loose the winds, who held the rainbow. It is Zeus
who orders the days and nights, the months, seasons, and
years. It is he who watches over the fields, who sends rich
harvests, and who tends the flocks. Like the sky, Zeus
dwells on the highest mountains; like the sky, Zeus em-
braces the earth ; like the sky, Zeus is eternal, unchanging,
the highest god. For good and for evil, Zeus the sky and
Zeus the god are wedded together in the Greek mind, language triumphing over thought, tradition over religion.'
The same Aryan Heaven-father is Jupiter, in that original

name and nature which he bore in Rome long before they arrayed him in the borrowed garments of Greek myth, and adapted him to the ideas of classic philosophy.[1] Thus, in nation after nation, took place the great religious development by which the Father-Heaven became the Father in Heaven.

The Rain-god is most often the Heaven-god exercising a special function, though sometimes taking a more distinctl y individual form, or blending in characteristics with a general Water-god. In East Central Africa, the spirit of an old chief dwelling on a cloudy mountain-top may receive the worship of his votaries and send down the refreshing showers in answer to their prayers ; among the Damaras the highest deity is Omakuru the Rain-giver, who dwells in the far North ; while to the negro of West Africa the Heaven-god is the rain-giver, and may pass in name into the rain itself.[2] Pachacamac, the Peruvian world-creator, has set the Rain-goddess to pour waters over the land, and send down hail and snow.[3] The Aztec Tlaloc was no doubt originally a Heaven-god, for he holds the thunder and lightning, but he has taken especially the attributes of Water-god and Rain-god ; and so in Nicaragua the Rain-god Quiateot (Aztec quiahuitl = rain, teotl = god) to whom children were sacrificed to bring rain, shows his larger celestial nature by being also sender of thunder and lightning.[4] The Rain-god of the Khonds is Pidzu Pennu, whom the priests and elders propitiate with eggs and arrack and rice and a sheep, and invoke with quaintly pathetic prayers. They tell him how, if he will not give water, the

[1] Max Müller, ' Lectures,' 2nd Series, p. 425 ; Grimm, ' D. M.' ch. ix.; Cicero, De Natura Deorum, iii. 4. Connexion of the Sanskrit Dyu with the Scandinavian Tyr and the Anglo Saxon Tiw is perhaps rather of etymology than definition.

[2] Duff Macdonald, ' Africana,' vol. i. p. 60 (E. Centr. Afr.). Waitz, ' Anthropologie,' vol. ii. p. 169 (W. Afr.) p. 416.(Damaras).

[3] Markham, ' Quichua Gr. and Dic.' p. 9 ; J. G. Müller, ' Amer. Urrel.' pp. 318, 368.

[4] Ibid. pp. 496-9 ; Oviedo, ' Nicaragua,' pp. 40, 72.

land must remain unploughed, the seed will rot in the ground, they and their children and cattle will die of want, the deer and the wild hog will seek other haunts, and then of what avail will it be for the Rain-god to relent, how little any gift of water will avail, when there shall be left neither man, nor cattle, nor seed ; so let him, resting on the sky, pour waters down upon them through his sieve, till the deer are drowned out of the forest and take refuge in the houses, till the soil of the mountains is washed into the valleys, till the cooking-pots burst with the force of the swelling rice, till the beasts gather so plentifully in the green and favoured land, that men's axes shall be blunted with cutting up the game.[1] With perfect meteorological fitness, the Kol tribes of Bengal consider their great deity Marang Buru, Great Mountain, to be the Rain-god. Marang Buru, one of the most conspicuous hills of the plateau near Lodmah in Chota-Nagpur, is the diety himself or his dwelling. Before the rains come on, the women climb the hill, led by the wives of the pahans, with girls drumming, to carry offerings of milk and bel-leaves, which are put on the flat rock at the top. Then the wives of the pahans kneel with loosened hair and invoke the deity, beseeching him to give the crops seasonable rain. They shake their heads violently as they reiterate this prayer, till they work themselves into a frenzy, and the movement becomes involuntary. They go on thus wildly gesticulating, till a cloud is seen ; then they rise, take the drums, and dance the kurrun on the rock, till Marang Buru's response to their prayer is heard in the distant rumbling of thunder, and they go home rejoicing. They must go fasting to the mount, and stay there till there is ' a sound of abundance of rain,' when they get them down to eat and drink. It is said that the rain always comes before evening, but the old women appear to choose their own moment for beginning the fast.[2] It was to Ukko the

---

[1] Macpherson, ' India,' pp. 89, 355.
[2] Dalton, ' Kols,' in ' Tr. Eth. Soc.' vol. vi. p. 34. Compare I Kings xviii.

Heaven-god, that in old days the Finn turned with such prayers :—

> ' Ukko, thou, O God above us
> Thou, O Father in the heavens,
> Thou who rulest in the cloud-land,
> And the little cloud-lambs leadest,
> Send us down the rain from heaven,
> Make the clouds to drop with honey,
> Let the drooping corn look upward,
> Let the grain with plenty rustle.'[1]

Quite like this were the classic conceptions of Ζεὺς ὑέτιος Jupiter Pluvius. They are typified in the famous Athenian prayer recorded by Marcus Aurelius, ' Rain, rain, O dear Zeus, on the plough-lands of the Athenians, and the plains ! '[2] and in Petronius Arbiter's complaint of the irreligion of his times, that now no one thinks heaven is heaven, no one keeps a fast, no one cares a hair for Jove, but all men with closed eyes reckon up their goods. Aforetime the ladies walked up the hill in their stoles with bare feet and loosened hair and pure minds, and entreated Jove for water ; then all at once it rained bucketsfull, then or never, and they all went home wet as drowned rats.[3] In later ages, when drought parched the fields of the mediæval husbandman, he transferred to other patrons the functions of the Rain-god, and with procession and litany sought help from St. Peter or St. James, or, with more of mythological consistency, from the Queen of Heaven. As for ourselves, we have lived to see the time when men shrink from addressing even to Supreme Deity the old customary rain-prayers, for the rainfall is passing from the region of the supernatural, to join the tides and seasons in the realm of physical science.

---

[1] Castrén, ' Finn. Myth.' p. 36 ; Kalewala, Rune ii. 317.

[2] Marc. Antonin. v. 7. 'Εὐχὴ Ἀθηναίων, ὗσον, ὗσον, ὦ φίλε Ζεῦ, κατὰ τῆς ἀρούρας τῶν Ἀθηναίων καὶ τῶν πεδίων.'

[3] Petron. Arbiter. Sat. xliv. 'Antea stolatæ ibant nudis pedibus in clivum, passis capillis, mentibus puris, et Jovem aquam exorabant. Itaque statim urceatim pluebat : aut tunc aut nunquam ; et omnes redibant udi tanquam mures.' See Grimm, ' D. M.' p. 160.

The place of the Thunder-god in polytheistic religion is similar to that of the Rain-god, in many cases even to entire coincidence. But his character is rather of wrath than of beneficence, a character which we have half lost the power to realize, since the agonizing terror of the thunderstorm which appals savage minds has dwindled away in ours, now that we behold in it not the manifestation of divine wrath, but the restoration of electric equilibrium. North American tribes, as the Mandans, heard in the thunder and saw in the lightning the clapping wings and flashing eyes of that awful heaven-bird which belongs to, or even is, the Great Manitu himself.[1] The Dacotas could show at a place called Thunder-tracks, near the source of the St. Peter's River, the footprints of the thunder-bird five and twenty miles apart. It is to be noticed that these Sioux, among their varied fancies about thunder-birds and the like, give unusually well a key to the great thunderbolt-myth which recurs in so many lands. They consider the lightning entering the ground to scatter there in all directions thunderbolt-stones, which are flints, &c., their reason for this notion being the very rational one, that these siliceous stones actually produce a flash when struck.[2] In an account of certain Carib deities, who were men and are now stars, occurs the name of Savacou, who was changed into a great bird ; he is captain of the hurricane and thunder, he blows fire through a tube and that is lightning, he gives the great rain. Rochefort describes the effect of a thunderstorm on the partly Europeanized Caribs of the West Indies two centuries ago. When they perceive its approach, he says, they quickly betake themselves to their cabins, and range themselves in the kitchen on their little seats near the fire ; hiding their faces and leaning their heads in their hands and on their knees, they fall to weeping and lamenting in their jargon ' Maboya mouche fache contre Caraïbe,' i.e.,

[1] Pr. Max v. Wied, ' N. Amer.' vol. ii. pp. 152, 223 ; J. G. Müller, p. 120 ; Waitz, vol. iii. p. 179.

[2] Keating, 'Narr.' vol. i. p. 407; Eastman, 'Dahcotah,' p. 71 ; Brinton, p. 150, &c. ; see M'Coy, ' Baptist Indian Missions,' p. 363.

Maboya (the evil demon) is very angry with the Caribs. This they say also when there comes a hurricane, not leaving off this dismal exercise till it is over, and there is no end to their astonishment that the Christians on these occasions manifest no such affliction and fear.[1] The Tupi tribes of Brazil are an example of a race among whom the Thunder or the Thunderer, Tupan, flapping his celestial wings and flashing with celestial light, was developed into the very representative of highest deity, whose name still stands among their Christian descendants as the equivalent of God.[2] In Peru, a mighty and far-worshipped deity was Catequil the Thunder-god, child of the Heaven-god, he who set free the Indian race from out of the ground by turning it up with his golden spade, he who in thunder-flash and clap hurls from his sling the small round smooth thunderstones, treasured in the villages as fire-fetishes and charms to kindle the flames of love. How distinct in personality and high in rank was the Thunder and Lightning (Chuqui yllayllapa) in the religion of the Incas, may be judged from his huaca or fetish-idol standing on the bench beside the idols of the Creator and the Sun at the great Solar festival in Cuzco, when the beasts to be sacrificed were led round them, and the priests prayed thus : ' O Creator, and Sun, and Thunder, be for ever young ! do not grow old. Let all things be at peace ! let the people multiply, and their food, and let all other things continue to increase.'[3]

In Africa, we may contrast the Zulu, who perceives in thunder and lightning the direct action of Heaven or Heaven's lord, with the Yoruba, who assigns them not to Olorun the Lord of Heaven, but to a lower deity, Shango the Thunder-god, whom they call also Dzakuta the Stone-caster, for it is he who (as among so many other peoples

[1] De la Borde, ' Caraïbes,' p. 530 ; Rochefort, ' Iles Antilles,' p. 431.
[2] De Laet, ' Novus Orbis,' xv. 2. Waitz, vol. iii. p. 417 ; J. G. Müller, p. 270 ; also 421 (thunderstorms by anger of Sun, in Cumana, &c.).
[3] Brinton, p. 153 ; Herrera, ' Indias Occidentales,' Dec., v. 4. J. G. Müller p. 327. ' Rites and Laws of the Yncas,' tr. & ed. by C. R. Markham, p. 16, see 81 ; Prescott, ' Peru,' vol. i. p. 86.

who have forgotten their Stone Age) flings down from
heaven the stone hatchets which are found in the ground,
and preserved as sacred objects.[1] In the religion of the
Kamchadals, Billukai, the hem of whose garment is the
rainbow, dwells in the clouds with many spirits, and sends
thunder and lightning and rain.[2] Among the Ossetes of the
Caucasus the Thunderer is Ilya, in whose name mytholo-
gists trace a Christian tradition of Elijah, whose fiery
chariot seems indeed to have been elsewhere identified with
that of the Thunder-god, while the highest peak of Ægina,
once the seat of Pan-hellenic Zeus, is now called Mount
St. Elias. Among certain Moslem schismatics, it is even
the historical Ali, cousin of Mohammed, who is enthroned
in the clouds, where the thunder is his voice, and the lightning the lash wherewith he smites the wicked.[3] Among the
Turanian or Tatar race, the European branch shows most
distinctly the figure of the Thunder-god. To the Lapps,
Tiermes appears to have been the Heaven-god, especially
conceived as Aija the Thunder-god ; of old they thought
the Thunder (Aija) to be a living being, hovering in the air
and hearkening to the talk of men, smiting such as spoke
of him in an unseemly way; or, as some said, the Thunder-
god is the foe of sorcerers, whom he drives from heaven
and smites, and then it is that men hear in thunder-peals
the hurtling of his arrows, as he speeds them from his
bow, the Rainbow. In Finnish poetry, likewise, Ukko
the Heaven-god is portrayed with such attributes. The
Runes call him Thunderer, he speaks through the clouds,
his fiery shirt is the lurid storm-cloud, men talk of his stones
and his hammer, he flashes his fiery sword and it lightens,
or he draws his mighty rainbow, Ukko's bow, to shoot his
fiery copper arrows, wherewith men would invoke him to

---

[1] Bowen, ' Yoruba Lang.' p. xvi. in ' Smithsonian Contr.' vol. i. See
Burton, ' Dahome,' vol. ii. p. 142. Details as to thunder-axes, &c., in ' Early
Hist. of Mankind,' ch. viii.

[2] Steller, ' Kamtschatka,' p. 266.

[3] Klemm, ' C. G.' vol. iv. p. 85. (Ossetes, &c.) See Welcker, vol. i. p. 170 ;
Grimm, ' D. M.' p. 158. Bastian, ' Mensch.' vol. ii. p. 423 (Ali-sect.).

smite their enemies. Or when it is dark in his heavenly house he strikes fire, and that is lightning. To this day the Finlanders call a thunderstorm an ' ukko,' or an ' ukkonen,' that is, ' a little ukko,' and when it lightens they say, ' There is Ukko striking fire ! '[1]

What is the Aryan conception of the Thunder-god, but a poetic elaboration of thoughts inherited from the savage state through which the primitive Aryans had passed ? The Hindu Thunder-god is the Heaven-god Indra, Indra's bow is the rainbow, Indra hurls the thunderbolts, he smites his enemies, he smites the dragon-clouds, and the rain pours down on earth, and the sun shines forth again. The Veda is full of Indra's glories : ' Now will I sing the feats of Indra, which he of the thunderbolt did of old. He smote Ahi, then he poured forth the waters ; he divided the rivers of the mountains. He smote Ahi by the mountain ; Tvashtar forged for him the glorious bolt.'—' Whet, O strong Indra, the heavy strong red weapon against the enemies ! ' —' May the axe (the thunderbolt) appear with the light ; may the red one blaze forth bright with splendour ! '— ' When Indra hurls again and again his thunderbolt, then they believe in the brilliant god.' Nor is Indra merely a great god in the ancient Vedic pantheon, he is the very patron-deity of the invading Aryan race in India, to whose help they look in their conflicts with the dark-skinned tribes of the land. ' Destroying the Dasyus, Indra protected the Aryan colour '—' Indra protected in battle the Aryan worshipper, he subdued the lawless for Manu, he conquered the black skin.'[2] This Hindu Indra is the offspring of Dyaus the Heaven. But in the Greek religion, Zeus is himself Zeus Kerauneios, the wielder of the thunderbolt, and thunders from the cloud-capped tops of Ida or Olympos. In like manner the Jupiter Capitolinus of Rome is himself Jupiter Tonans :

[1] Castrén, ' Finn. Myth.' p. 39, &c.
[2] ' Rig-Veda,' i. 32. 1, 55. 5, 130. 8, 165 ; iij. 34. 9 ; vi. 20 ; x. 44. 9, 89, 9. Max Müller, ' Lectures,' 2nd S. p. 427 ; ' Chips,' vol. i. p. 42, vol. ii. p. 323. See Muir, ' Sanskrit Texts.'

'Ad penetrale Numæ, Capitolinumque Tonantem.'[1]

Thus, also, it was in accurate language that the old Slavonic nations were described as adoring Jupiter Tonans as their highest god. He was the cloud-dwelling Heaven-god, his weapon the thunder-bolt, the lightning-flash, his name Perun the Smiter (Perkun, Perkunas). In the Lithuanian district, the thunder itself is Perkun ; in past times the peasant would cry when he heard the thunder peal ' Dewe Perkune apsaugog mus !—God Perkun spare us ! ' and to this day he says, ' Perkunas gravja !—Perkun is thundering ! ' or ' Wezzajs barrahs !—the Old One growls ! '[2] The old German and Scandinavian theology made Thunder, Donar, Thor, a special deity to rule the clouds and rain, and hurl his crushing hammer theough the air. He reigned high in the Saxon heaven, till the days came when the Christian convert had to renounce him in solemn form, ' ec forsacho Thunare !—I forsake Thunder ! ' Now, his survival is for the most part in mere verbal form, in the etymology of such names as Donnersberg, Thorwaldsen, Thursday.[3]

In the polytheism of the lower as of the higher races, the Wind-gods are no unknown figures. The Winds themselves, and especially the Four Winds in their four regions, take name and shape as personal divinities, while some deity of wider range, a Wind-god, Storm-god, Air-god, or the mighty Heaven-god himself, may stand as compeller or controller of breeze and gale and tempest. We have already taken as examples from the Algonquin mythology of North America the four winds whose native legends have been versified in ' Hiawatha ; ' Mudjekeewis the West Wind, Father of the Winds of Heaven, and his children, Wabun the East Wind, the morning-bringer, the lazy Shawondasse the South Wind, the wild and cruel North

---

[1] Homer. Il. viii. 170, xvii. 595.   Ovid. Fast. ii. 69.   See Welcker, ' Griech. Götterl.' vol. ii. p. 194.

[2] Hanusch, ' Slaw. Myth.' p. 257.

[3] Grimm, ' Deutsche Myth.' ch. viii. Edda ; Gylfaginning, 21, 44.

Wind, the fierce Kabibonokka. Viewed in their religious aspect, these mighty beings correspond with four of the great manitus sacrificed to among the Delawares, the West, South, East, and North ; while the Iroquois acknowledged a deity of larger grasp, Gäoh, the Spirit of the Winds, who holds them prisoned in the mountains in the Home of the Winds.[1] The Polynesian Wind-gods are thus described by Ellis : ' The chief of these were Veromatautoru and Tairibu, brother and sister to the children of Taaroa, their dwelling was near the great rock, which was the foundation of the world. Hurricanes, tempests, and all destructive winds, were supposed to be confined within them, and were employed by them to punish such as neglected the worship of the gods. In stormy weather their compassion was sought by the tempest-driven mariner at sea, or the friends of such on shore. Liberal presents, it was supposed, would at any time purchase a calm. If the first failed, subsequent ones were certain of success. The same means were resorted to for procuring a storm, but with less certainty. Whenever the inhabitants of one island heard of invasion from those of another, they immediately carried large offerings to these deities, and besought them to destroy by tempest the hostile fleet whenever it might put to sea. Some of the most intelligent people still think evil spirits had formerly great power over the winds, as they say there have been no such fearful storms since they abolished idolatry, as there were before.' Or, again, the great deity Maui adds a new complication to his enigmatic solar-celestial character by appearing as a Wind-God. In Tahiti he was identified with the East Wind ; in New Zealand he holds all the winds but the west in his hands, or he imprisons them with great stones rolled to the mouths of their caves, save the West Wind

[1] Schoolcraft, ' Algic Res.' vol. i. p. 139, vol. ii. p. 214 ; Loskiel, part i. p. 43 ; Waitz, vol. iii. p. 190. Morgan, ' Iroquois,' p. 157 ; J. G. Müller, p. 56. Further American evidence in Brinton, ' Myths of New World,' pp. 50, 74 ; Cranz, ' Grönland,' p. 267 (Sillagiksartok, Weather-spirit) ; De la Borde, ' Caraïbes,' p. 530 (Carib Star Curumon, makes the billows and upsets canoes).

which he cannot catch or prison, so that it almost always blows.[1] To the Kamchadal, it is Billukai the Heaven-god who comes down and drives his sledge on earth, and men see his traces in the wind-drifted snow.[2] To the Finn, while there are traces of subordinate Wind-gods in his mythology, the great ruler of wind and storm is Ukko the Heaven-god ;[3] while the Esth looked rather to Tuule-ema, Wind's Mother, and when the gale shrieks he will still say ' Wind's mother wails, who knows what mothers shall wail next.'[4] Such instances from Allophylian mythology[5] show types which are found developed in full vigour by the Aryan races. In the Vedic hymns, the Storm Gods, the Maruts, borne along with the fury of the boisterous winds, with the rain-clouds distribute showers over the earth, make darkness during the day, rend the trees and devour the forests like wild elephants.[6] No effort of the Red Indian's personifying fancy in the tales of the dancing Pauppuk-keewis the Whirlwind, or that fierce and shifty hero, Manabozho the North-West Wind, can more than match the description in the Iliad, of Achilles calling on Boreas and Zephyros with libations and vows of sacrifice, to blow into a blaze the funeral pyre of Patroklos—

> '. . . . his prayer
> Swift Iris heard, and bore it to the Winds.
> They in the hall of gusty Zephyrus
> Were gathered round the feast ; in haste appearing,
> Swift Iris on the stony threshold stood.
> They saw, and rising all, besought her each
> To sit beside him ; she with their requests
> Refused compliance, and addressed them thus,' &c.

---

[1] Ellis, ' Polyn. Res.' vol. i. p. 329 (compare with the Maori Tempest-god Tawhirimatea, Grey, ' Polyn. Myth.' p. 5); Schirren, ' Wandersage der Neuseeländer,' &c. p. 85 ; Yate, ' New Zealand,' p. 144. See also Mariner, ' Tonga Is.' vol. ii. p. 115.

[2] Steller, ' Kamschatka,' p. 266.

[3] Castrén, ' Finn. Myth.' pp. 37, 68.

[4] Boecler, pp. 106, 147.

[5] See also Klemm, ' Cultur-Gesch.' vol. iv. p. 85 (Circassian Water-god and Wind-god).

[6] Muir, ' Sanskrit Texts,' vol. v. p. 150

Æolus with the winds imprisoned in his cave has the office of the Red Indian Spirit of the Winds, and of the Polynesian Maui. With quaint adaptation to nature-myth and even to moral parable, the Harpies, the Storm-gusts that whirl and snatch and dash and smirch with eddying dust-clouds, become the loathsome bird-monsters sent to hover over the table of Phineus to claw and defile his dainty viands.[1] If we are to choose an Aryan Storm-god for ideal grandeur, we must seek him in

> '. . . . the hall where Runic Odin
> Howls his war-song to the gale.'

Jakob Grimm has defined Odin or Woden as ' the all-penetrating creative and formative power.' But such abstract conceptions can hardly be ascribed to his barbaric worshippers. As little may his real nature be discovered among the legends which degrade him to a historical king of Northern men, an ' Othinus rex.' See the All-father sitting cloud-mantled on his heaven-seat, overlooking the deeds of men, and we may discern in him the attributes of the Heaven-god. Hear the peasant say of the raging tempest, that it is ' Odin faring by ; ' trace the mythological transition from Woden's tempest to the ' Wütende Heer,' the ' Wild Huntsman ' of our own grand storm-myth, and we shall recognize the old Teutonic deity in his function of cloud-compeller, of Tempest-god.[2] The ' rude Carinthian boor ' can show a relic from a yet more primitive stage of mental history, when he sets up a wooden bowl of various meats on a tree before his house, to fodder the wind that it may do no harm. In Swabia, Tyrol, and the Upper Palatinate, when the storm rages, they will fling a spoonful or a handful of meal in the face of the gale, with this formula in the last-named district, ' Da Wind, hast du Mehl für dein Kind, aber aufhören musst du ! '[3]

[1] Homer. Il. xxiii. 192, Odyss. xx. 66, 77 ; Apollon. Rhod. Argonautica ; Apollodor. i. 9. 21 ; Virg. Æn. i. 56 ; Welcker, ' Griech. Götterl.' vol. i. p. 707, vol. iii. p. 67.
[2] Grimm, ' Deutsche Myth.' pp. 121, 871.
[3] Wuttke, ' Deutsche Volksabergl.' p. 86.

The Earth-deity takes an important place in polytheistic religion. The Algonquins would sing medicine-songs to Mesukkummik Okwi, the Earth, the Great-Grandmother of all. In her charge (and she must be ever at home in her lodge) are left the animals whose flesh and skins are man's food and clothing, and the roots and medicines of sovereign power to heal sickness and kill game in time of hunger ; therefore good Indians never dig up the roots of which their medicines are made, without depositing an offering in the earth for Mesukkummik Okwi.[1] In the list of fetish-deities of Peruvian tribes, the Earth, adored as Mamapacha, Mother Earth, took high subordinate rank below Sun and Moon in the pantheon of the Incas, and at harvest-time ground corn and libations of chicha were offered to her that she might grant a good harvest.[2] Her rank is similar in the Aquapim theology of West Africa ; first the Highest God in the firmament, then the Earth as universal mother, then the fetish. The negro, offering his libation before some great undertaking, thus calls upon the triad : ' Creator, come drink ! Earth, come drink ! Bosumbra, come drink ! '[3]

Among the indigenes of India, the Bygah tribes of Seonee show a well-marked worship of the Earth. They call her ' Mother Earth ' or Dhurteemah, and before praying or eating their food, which is looked on always as a daily sacrifice, they invariably offer some of it to the earth, before using the name of any other god.[4] Of all religions of the world, perhaps that of the Khonds of Orissa gives the Earth-goddess her most remarkable place and function. Boora Pennu or Bella Pennu, the Light-god or Sun-god, created Tari Pennu the Earth-goddess for his

---

[1] Tanner's ' Narrative,' p. 193 ; Loskiel, l.c. See also Rochefort, ' Iles Antilles,' p. 414 ; J. G. Müller, p. 178 (Antilles).

[2] Garcilaso de la Vega, ' Commentarios Reales,' i. 10 ; Rivero & Tschudi, p. 161 ; J. G. Müller, p. 369.

[3] Waitz, ' Anthropologie,' vol. ii. p. 170.

[4] ' Report of Ethnological Committee, Jubbulpore Exhibition,' 1866-7. Nagpore, 1868, part ii. p. 54.

consort, and from them were born the other great gods. But strife arose between the mighty parents, and it became the wife's work to thwart the good creation of her husband, and to cause all physical and moral ill. Thus to the Sun-worshipping sect she stands abhorred on the bad eminence of the Evil Deity. But her own sect, the Earth-worshipping sect, seem to hold ideas of her nature which are more primitive and genuine. The functions which they ascribe to her, and the rites with which they propitiate her, display her as the Earth-mother, raised by an intensely agricultural race to an extreme height of divinity. It was she who with drops of her blood made the soft muddy ground harden into firm earth ; thus men learnt to offer human victims, and the whole earth became firm ; the pastures and ploughed fields came into use, and there were cattle and sheep and poultry for man's service ; hunting began, and there were iron and ploughshares and harrows and axes, and the juice of the palm-tree ; and love arose between the sons and daughters of the people, making new households, and society with its relations of father and mother, and wife and child, and the bonds between ruler and subject. It was the Khond Earth-goddess who was propitiated with those hideous sacrifices, the suppression of which is matter of recent Indian history. With dances and drunken orgies, and a mystery play to explain in dramatic dialogue the purpose of the rite, the priest offered Tari Pennu her sacrifice, and prayed for children and cattle and poultry and brazen pots and all wealth ; every man and woman wished a wish, and they tore the slave-victim piecemeal, and spread the morsels over the fields they were to fertilize.[1] In Northern Asia, also, among the Tatar races, the office of the Earth-deity is strongly and widely marked. Thus in the nature-worship of the Tunguz and Buraets, Earth stands among the greater divinities. It is especially interesting to notice among the Finns a transition like that just observed from the god

[1] Macpherson, ' India,' chap. vi.

Heaven to the Heaven-god. In the designation of **Maa-emä**, Earth-mother, given to the earth itself, there may be traced survival from the stage of direct nature-worship, while the passage to the conception of a divine being inhabiting and ruling the material substance, is marked by the use of the name Maan emo, Earth's mother, for the ancient sub-terranean goddess whom men would ask to make the grass shoot thick and the thousandfold ears mount high, or might even entreat to rise in person out of the earth to give them strength. The analogy of other mythologies agrees with the definition of the divine pair who reign in Finn theology: as Ukko the Grandfather is the Heaven-god, so his spouse Akka the Grandmother is the Earth-goddess.[1] Thus in the ancient nature-worship of China, the personal Earth holds a place below the Heaven. Tien and Tu are closely associated in the national rites, and the idea of the pair as universal parents, if not an original conception in Chinese theology, is at any rate developed in Chinese classic symbolism. Heaven and Earth receive their solemn sacrifices not at the hands of common mortals but of the Son of Heaven, the Emperor, and his great vassals and mandarins. Yet their adoration is national ; they are wor-shipped by the people who offer incense to them on the hill-tops at their autumn festival, they are adored by suc-cessful candidates in competitive examination ; and, espe-cially and appropriately, the prostration of bride and bridegroom before the father and mother of all things, the ' worshipping of Heaven and Earth,' is the all-important ceremony of a Chinese marriage.[2]

The Vedic hymns commemorate the goddess Prithivî, the broad Earth, and in their ancient strophes the modern Brahmans still pray for benefits to mother Earth and father Heaven, side by side :—

---

[1] Georgi, ' Reise im Russ. Reich,' vol. i. pp. 275, 317. Castrén, ' Finn. Myth,' p. 86, &c.

[2] Plath, ' Religion der alten Chinesen,' part i. pp. 36, 73, part ii. p. 32. Doolittle, ' Chinese,' vol. i. pp. 86, 354, 413, vol. ii. pp. 67, 380, 455.

'Tanno Vâto mayobhu vâtu bheshajam tanmâtâ Prithivî tatpitâ Dyauh.'[1]

Greek religion shows a transition to have taken place like that among the Turanian tribes, for the older simpler nature-deity Gaia, Γῆ πάντων μήτηρ, Earth the All-Mother, seems to have faded into the more anthropomorphic Dēmētēr, Earth-Mother, whose eternal fire burned in Mantinēa, and whose temples stood far and wide over the land which she made kindly to the Greek husbandman.[2] The Romans acknowledged her plain identity as Terra Mater, Ops Mater.[3] Tacitus could rightly recognize this deity of his own land among German tribes, worshippers of ' Nerthum (or, Hertham), id est Terram matrem,' Mother Earth, whose holy grove stood in an ocean isle, whose chariot drawn by cows passed through the land making a season of peace and joy, till the goddess, satiated with mortal conversation, was taken back by her priest to her temple, and the chariot and garments and even the goddess herself were washed in a secret lake, which forthwith swallowed up the ministering slaves—' hence a mysterious terror and sacred ignorance, what that should be which only the doomed to perish might behold.'[4] If in these modern days we seek in Europe traces of Earth-worship, we may find them in curiously distinct survival in Germany, if no longer in the Christmas food-offerings buried in and for the earth up to early in this century,[5] at any rate among Gypsy hordes. Dewel, the great god in heaven (dewa, deus), is rather feared than loved by these weatherbeaten outcasts, for he harms them on their wanderings with his thunder and lightning, his snow and rain, and his stars interfere with their dark doings. Therefore they curse him foully when misfortune falls on them, and when a child dies, they say that Dewel has eaten it. But Earth, Mother of all good,

---

[1] ' Rig-Veda,' i. 89. 4, &c., &c.
[2] Welcker, ' Griech. Götterl.' vol. i. p. 385, &c.
[3] Varro de Ling. Lat. iv.
[4] Tacit. Germania, 40. Grimm, ' Deutsche Myth.' p. 229, &c.
[5] Wuttke, ' Deutsche Volksabergl.' p. 87.

self-existing from the beginning, is to them holy, so holy
that they take heed never to let the drinking-cup touch
the ground, for it would become too sacred to be used by
men.[1]

Water-worship, as has been seen, may be classified as a
special department of religion. It by no means follows,
however, that savage water-worshippers should necessarily
have generalized their ideas, and passed beyond their particular water-deities to arrive at the conception of a general
deity presiding over water as an element. Divine springs,
streams, and lakes, water-spirits, deities concerned with the
clouds and rain, are frequent, and many details of them are
cited here, but I have not succeeded in finding among the
lower races any divinity whose attributes, fairly criticized,
will show him or her to be an original and absolute elemental Water-god. Among the deities of the Dakotas,
Unktahe the fish-god of the waters is a master-spirit of
sorcery and religion, the rival even of the mighty Thunder-
bird.[2] In the Mexican pantheon, Tlaloc god of rain and
waters, fertilizer of earth and lord of paradise, whose wife
is Chalchihuitlicue, Emerald-Skirt, dwells among the
mountain-tops where the clouds gather and pour down the
streams.[3] Yet neither of these mythic beings approaches
the generality of conception that belongs to full elemental
deity, and even the Greek Nēreus, though by his name he
should be the very personification of water ($\nu\eta\rho\acute{o}\varsigma$), seems
too exclusively marine in his home and family to be cited
as the Water-god. Nor is the reason of this hard to find.
It is an extreme stretch of the power of theological generalization to bring water in its myriad forms under one
divinity, though each individual body of water, even the
smallest stream or lake, can have its personal individuality
or indwelling spirit.

---

[1] Liebich, 'Die Zigeuner,' pp. 30, 84.
[2] Schoolcraft, 'Indian Tribes,' part iii. p. 485 ; Eastman, 'Dahcotah,'
pp. i. 118, 161.
[3] Clavigero, vol. ii. p. 14.

Islanders and coast-dwellers indeed live face to face with mighty water-deities, the divine Sea and the great Sea-gods. What the sea may seem to an uncultured man who first beholds it, we may learn among the Lampongs of Sumatra : ' The inland people of that country are said to pay a kind of adoration to the sea, and to make to it an offering of cakes and sweetmeats on their beholding it for the first time, deprecating its power of doing them mischief.'[1] The higher stage of such doctrine is where the sea, no longer itself personal, is considered as ruled by indwelling spirits. Thus Tuaraatai and Ruahatu, principal among marine deities of Polynesia, send the sharks to execute their vengeance. Hiro descends to the depths of the ocean and dwells among the monsters, they lull him to sleep in a cavern, the Wind-god profits by his absence to raise a violent storm to destroy the boats in which Hiro's friends are sailing, but, roused by a friendly spirit-messenger, the Sea-god rises to the surface and quells the tempest.[2] This South Sea Island myth might well have been in the Odyssey. We may point to the Guinea Coast as a barbaric region where Sea-worship survives in its extremest form. It appears from Bosman's account, about 1700, that in the religion of Whydah, the Sea ranked only as younger brother in the three divine orders, below the Serpents and Trees. But at present, as appears from Captain Burton's evidence, the religion of Whydah extends through Dahome, and the divine Sea has risen in rank. ' The youngest brother of the triad is Hu, the ocean or sea. Formerly it was subject to chastisement, like the Hellespont, if idle or useless. The Huno, or ocean priest, is now considered the highest of all, a fetish king, at Whydah, where he has 500 wives. At stated times he repairs to the beach, begs ' Agbwe,' the . . . ocean god, not to be boisterous, and throws in rice and corn, oil and beans, cloth, cowries, and other valuables. . . . At times the king sends as an ocean sacrifice

---

[1] Marsden, ' Sumatra,' p. 301 ; see also 303 (Tagals).
[2] Ellis, ' Polyn. Res.' vol. i. p. 328.

from Agbome a man carried in a hammock, with the dress, the stool, and the umbrella of a caboceer ; a canoe takes him out to sea, where he is thrown to the sharks.'[1] While in these descriptions the individual divine personality of the sea is so well marked, an account of the closely related Slave Coast religion states that a great god dwells in the sea, and it is to him, not to the sea itself, that offerings are cast in.[2] In South America the idea of the divine Sea is clearly marked in the Peruvian worship of Mamacocha, Mother Sea, giver of food to men.[3] Eastern Asia, both in its stages of lower and higher civilization, contributes members to the divine group. In Kamchatka, Mitgk the Great Spirit of the Sea, fish-like himself, sends the fish up the rivers.[4] Japan deifies separately on land and at sea the lords of the waters ; Midsuno Kami, the Water-god, is worshipped during the rainy season; Jebisu, the Sea-god, is younger brother of the Sun.[5]

Among barbaric races we thus find two conceptions current, the personal divine Sea and the anthropomorphic Sea-god. These represent two stages of development of one idea—the view of the natural object as itself an animated being, and the separation of its animating fetish-soul as a distinct spiritual deity. To follow the enquiry into classic times shows the same distinction as strongly marked. When Kleomenes marched down to Thyrea, having slaughtered a bull to the sea ($\sigma\phi\alpha\gamma\iota\alpha\sigma\acute{\alpha}\mu\epsilon\nu\sigma\varsigma$ $\delta\acute{\epsilon}$ $\tau\hat{\eta}$ $\theta\alpha\lambda\acute{\alpha}\sigma\sigma\eta$ $\tau\alpha\hat{\nu}\rho\sigma\nu$) he embarked his army in ships for the Tirynthian land and Nauplia.[6] Cicero makes Cotta remark to Balbus that ' our generals, embarking on the sea, have been accustomed to immolate a victim to the waves,' and he goes on to argue,

---

[1] Bosman, ' Guinea,' letter xix. ; in Pinkerton, vol. xvi. p. 494. Burton, 'Dahome,' vol. ii. p. 141. See also below, chap. xviii. (sacrifice).

[2] Schlegel, ' Ewe Sprache,' p. xiv.

[3] Garcilaso de la Vega, ' Commentarios Reales,' i. 10, vi. 17 ; Rivero & Tschudi, ' Peru,' p. 161.

[4] Steller, ' Kamtschatka,' p. 265.

[5] Siebold, ' Nippon,' part v. p. 9.

[6] Herod. vi. 76.

not unfairly, that if the Earth herself is a goddess, what is
she other than Tellus, and 'if the Earth, the Sea too,
whom thou saidst to be Neptune.'¹ Here is direct nature-
worship in its extremest sense of fetish-worship. But in
the anthropomorphic stage appear that dim præ-Olympian
figure of Nēreus the Old Man of the Sea, father of the Ne-
reids in their ocean caves, and the Homeric Poseidōn the
Earth-shaker, who stables his coursers in his cave in the
Ægean deeps, who harnesses the gold-maned steeds to his
chariot and drives through the dividing waves, while the
subject sea-beasts come up at the passing of their lord, a
king so little bound to the element he governs, that he can
come from the brine to sit in the midst of the gods in the
assembly on Olympos, and ask the will of Zeus.²

Fire-worship brings into view again, though under different aspects and with different results, the problems presented by water-worship. The real and absolute worship
of fire falls into two great divisions, the first belonging
rather to fetishism, the second to polytheism proper, and
the two apparently representing an earlier and later stage of
theological ideas. The first is the rude barbarian's adoration of the actual flame which he watches writhing, roaring,
devouring like a live animal ; the second belongs to an advanced generalization, that any individual fire is a manifestation of one general elemental being- the Fire-god.
Unfortunately, evidence of the exact meaning of fire-worship
among the lower races is scanty, while the transition from
fetishism to polytheism seems a gradual process of which
the stages elude close definition. Moreover, it must be
borne in mind that rites performed with fire are, though
often, yet by no means necessarily, due to worship of the
fire itself. Authors who have indiscriminately mixed up
such rites as the new fire, the perpetual fire, the passing

¹ Cicero, De Natura Deorum, iii. 20.
² Homer, Il. i. 538, xiii. 18, xx. 13. Welcker, 'Griech. Götterl.' vol. i.
p. 616 (Nereus), p. 622 (Poseidon). Cox, 'Mythology of Aryan Nations,'
vol. ii. ch. vi.

through the fire, classing them as acts of fire-worship, without proper evidence as to their meaning in any particular
case, have added to the perplexity of a subject not too easy
to deal with, even under strict precautions. Two sources
or error are especially to be noted. On the one hand, fire
happens to be a usual means whereby sacrifices are transmitted to departed souls and deities in general ; and on the
other hand, the ceremonies of earthly fire-worship are habitually and naturally transferred to celestial fire-worship in
the religion of the Sun.

It may best serve the present purpose to carry a line of
some of the best-defined facts which seems to bear on fire-
worship proper, from savagery on into the higher culture.
In the last century, Loskiel, a missionary among the North
American Indians, remarks that ' In great danger, an
Indian has been observed to lie prostrate on his face, and
throwing a handful of tobacco into the fire, to call aloud, as
in an agony of distress, " There, take and smoke, be paci-
fied, and don't hurt me." ' Of course this may have been
a mere sacrifice transmitted to some other spiritual being
through fire, but we have in this region explicit statements
as to a distinct fire-deity. The Delawares, it appears from
the same author, acknowledged the Fire-manitu, first parent
of all Indian nations, and celebrated a yearly festival in his
honour, when twelve manitus, animal and vegetable, attended him as subordinate deities.[1] In North-West America,
in Washington Irving's account of the Chinooks and other
Columbia River Tribes, mention is made of the spirit which
inhabits fire. Powerful both for evil and good, and seemingly rather evil than good in nature, this being must be
kept in good humour by frequent offerings. The Fire-spirit
has great influence with the winged aërial supreme deity,
wherefore the Indians implore him to be their interpreter,
to procure them success in hunting and fishing, fleet horses,
obedient wives, and male children.[2] In the elaborately

[1] Loskiel, ' Ind. of N. A.' part i. pp. 41, 45. See also J. G. Müller, p. 55.
[2] Irving, ' Astoria,' vol. ii. ch. xxii.

systematic religion of Mexico, there appears in his proper place a Fire-god, closely related to the Sun-god in character, but keeping well marked his proper identity. His name was Xiuhteuctli, Fire-lord, and they called him likewise Huehueteotl, the old god. Great honour was paid to this god Fire, who gives them heat, and bakes their cakes, and roasts their meat. Therefore at every meal the first morsel and libation were cast into the fire, and every day the deity had incense burnt to him. Twice in the year were held his solemn festivals. At the first, a felled tree was set up in his honour, and the sacrificers danced round his fire with the human victims, whom afterwards they cast into a great fire, only to drag them out half roasted for the priests to complete the sacrifice. The second was distinguished by the rite of the new fire, so well known in connexion with solar worship ; the friction-fire was solemnly made before the image of Xiuhteuctli in his sanctuary in the court of the great teocalli, and the game brought in at the great hunt which began the festival was cooked at the sacred fire for the banquets that ended it.[1] Polynesia well knows from the mythological point of view Mahuika the Fire-god, who keeps the volcano-fire on his subterranean hearth, whither Maui goes down (as the Sun into the Underworld) to bring up fire for man ; but in the South Sea islands there is scarcely a trace of actual rites of fire-worship.[2] In West Africa, among the gods of Dahome is Zo the fire-fetish ; a pot of fire is placed in a room, and sacrifice is offered to it, that fire may ' live ' there, and not go forth to destroy the house.[3]

Asia is a region where distinct fire-worship may be peculiarly well traced through the range of lower and higher civilization. The rude Kamchadals, worshipping all things

[1] Torquemada, ' Monarquia Indiana,' vi. c. 28, x. c. 22, 30 ; Brasseur, ' Mexique,' vol. iii. pp. 492, 522, 536.
[2] Schirren, ' Wandersage der Neuseeländer,' &c., p. 32 ; Turner, ' Polynesia,' pp. 252, 527.
[3] Burton, ' Dahome,' vol. ii. p. 148 ; Schlegel, ' Ewe Sprache,' p. xv.

that did them harm or good, worshipped the fire, offering
to it noses of foxes and other game, so that one might tell
by looking at furs whether they had been taken by baptized
or heathen hunters.[1] The Ainos of Yesso worship Abe kamui
the Fire-deity as the benefactor of men, the messenger to
the other gods, the purifier who heals the sick.[2] Turanian
tribes likewise hold fire a sacred element, many Tunguz, Mongol, and Turk tribes sacrifice to Fire, and some clans will not
eat meat without first throwing a morsel upon the hearth.
The following passage is from a Mongol wedding-song to
the personified Fire, ' Mother Ut, Queen of Fire, thou who
art made from the elm that grows on the mountain-tops of
Changgai-Chan and Burchatu-Chan, thou who didst come
forth when heaven and earth divided, didst come forth from
the footsteps of Mother Earth, and wast formed by the
King of Gods. Mother Ut, whose father is the hard steel,
whose mother is the flint, whose ancestors are the elm-trees,
whose shining reaches to the sky and pervades the earth.
Goddess Ut, we bring thee yellow oil for offering, and a
white wether with yellow head, thou who hast a manly son,
a beauteous daughter-in-law, bright daughters. To thee,
Mother Ut, who ever lookest upward, we bring brandy in
bowls, and fat in both hands. Give prosperity to the
King's son (the bridegroom), to the King's daughter (the
bride), and to all the people ! '[3] As an analogue to
Hephaistos the Greek divine smith, may stand the Circassian Fire-god, Tleps, patron of metal-workers, and the
peasants whom he has provided with plough and hoe.[4]

Among the most ancient cultured nations of the Old
World, Egyptians, Babylonians, Assyrians, accounts of fire-
worship are absent, or so scanty and obscure that their

---

[1] Steller, ' Kamtschatka,' p. 276.
[2] Batchelor in ' Tr. As. Soc. Japan,' vols. x. xvi.
[3] Castrén, ' Finn. Myth.' p. 57; Billings, ' N. Russia,' p. 123 (Yakuts);
Bastian, ' Vorstellungen von Wasser und Feuer,' in ' Zeitschr. für Ethnologie,' vol. i. p. 383 (Mongols).
[4] Klemm, ' Cultur-Gesch.' vol. vi. p. 85 (Circassia). Welcker, vol. i.
p. 663.

study is more valuable in compiling the history than in elucidating the principles of religion.[1] For this scientific purpose, the more full and minute documents of Aryan religion can give a better answer. In various forms and under several names, the Fire-god is known. Nowhere does he carry his personality more distinctly than under his Sanskrit name of Agni, a word which keeps its quality, though not his divinity, in the Latin ' ignis.' The name of Agni is the first word of the first hymn of the Rig-Veda : ' Agnim île puro-hitaṁ yajnasya devaṁ ritvijaṁ !—Agni I entreat, divine appointed priest of sacrifice ! ' The sacrifices which Agni receives go to the gods, he is the mouth of the gods, but he is no lowly minister, as it is said in another hymn :

' No god indeed, no mortal is beyond the might of thee, the mighty one, with the Maruts come hither, O Agni ! '

Such the mighty Agni is among the gods, yet he comes within the peasant's cottage to be protector of the domestic hearth. His worship has survived the transformation of the ancient patriarchal Vedic religion of nature into the priest-ridden Hinduism of our own day. In India there may yet be found the so-called Fire-priests (Agnihotri) who perform according to Vedic rite the sacrifices entitling the worshippers to heavenly life. The sacred fire-drill for churning the new fire by friction of wood (arani) is used so that Agni still is new-born of the twirling fire-sticks, and receives the melted butter of the sacrifice.[2] Among the records of fire-worship in Asia, is the account of Jonas Hanways's ' Travels,' dating from about 1740, of the everlasting fire at the burning wells near Baku, on the Caspian. At the sacred spot stood several ancient stone temples, mostly arched vaults 10 to 15 feet high. One little temple was

[1] See ' Records of the Past,' vol. iii. p. 137, vol. ix. p. 143 ; Sayce, ' Lectures on Rel. of Ancient Babylonians,' p. 170. For accounts of Semitic fire-worship, see Movers, ' Phönizier,' vol. i. p. 327, &c., 337, &c., 401.

[2] ' Rig-Veda,' i. 1. 1, 19. 2, iii. 1. 18, &c. ; Max Müller, vol. i. p. 39 ; Ward, ' Hindoos,' vol. ii. p. 53. Haug, ' Essays on Parsis,' iv. ; ' Early Hist. of Mankind,' p. 255.

still used for worship, near the altar of which, about
three feet high, a large hollow cane conveyed the gas up
from the ground, burning at the mouth with a blue flame.
Here were generally forty or fifty poor devotees, come on
pilgrimage from their country to make expiation for themselves and others, and subsisting on wild celery, &c. These
pilgrims are described as marking their foreheads with
saffron, and having great veneration for a red cow ; they
wore little clothing, and the holiest of them kept one arm
on their heads, or continued unmoved in some other posture; they are described as Ghebers, or Gours, the usual
Moslem term for Fire-worshippers.[1]

In general, this name of Ghebers is applied to the
Zoroastrians or Parsis, whom a modern European would all
but surely point to if asked to instance a modern race of
Fire-worshippers. Classical accounts of the Persian religion set down fire-worship as part and parcel of it ; the
Magi, it is recorded, hold the gods to be Fire and Earth
and Water ; and again, the Persians reckon the Fire to be
a god ($\theta\epsilon o\phi o\rho o\hat{v}\sigma\iota\nu$).[2] On the testimony of the old religious
books of the Parsis themselves, Fire, as the greatest Ized,
as giver of increase and health, as craving for wood and
scents and fat, seems to take the distinctest divine personality. Their doctrine that Ardebehist, the presiding
angel or spirit of fire, is adored, but not the material object
he belongs to, is a perfect instance of the development of
the idea of an elemental divinity from that of an animated
fetish. When, driven by Moslem persecution from Persia,
Parsi exiles landed in Gujarat, they described their religion in an official document as being the worship of Agni
or Fire, thus claiming for themselves a place among recognized Hindu sects.[3] In modern times, though for the most
part the Parsis have found toleration and prosperity in

---

[1] Hanway, ' Journal of Travels,' London, 1753, vol. i. ch. lvii.

[2] Diog. Lært. Procem. ii. 6. Sextus Empiricus adv. Physicos, ix. ; Strabo,
xv. 3, 13.

[3] John Wilson, ' The Parsi Religion,' ch. iv. ; ' Avesta,' tr. by Spiegel,
Yaçna, i. lxi.

India, yet an oppressed remnant of the race still keeps up the everlasting fires at Yezd and Kirman, in their old Persian land. The modern Parsis, as in Strabo's time, scruple to defile the fire or blow it with their breath, they abstain from smoking out of regard not to themselves but to the sacred element, and they keep up consecrated ever-burning fires before which they do worship. Nevertheless, Prof. Max Müller is able to say of the Parsis of our own day: ' The so-called Fire-worshippers certainly do not worship the fire, and they naturally object to a name which seems to place them on a level with mere idolators. All they admit is, that in their youth they are taught to face some luminous object while worshipping God, and that they regard the fire, like other great natural phenomena, as an emblem of the Divine power. But they assure us that they never ask assistance or blessings from an unintelligent material object, nor is it even considered necessary to turn the face to any emblem whatever in praying to Ormuzd '[1] Now, admitting this view of fire-worship as true of the more intelligent Parsis, and leaving aside the question how far among the more ignorant this symbolism may blend (as in such cases is usual) into actual adoration, we may ask what is the history of ceremonies which thus imitate, yet are not, fire-worship. The ethnographic answer is clear and instructive. The Parsi is the descendant of a race in this respect represented by the modern Hindu, a race who did simply and actually worship Fire. Fire-worship still forms a link historically connecting the Vedic with the Zoroastrian ritual ; for the Agnishtoma or praise of Agni the Fire, where four goats are to be sacrificed and burnt, is represented by the Yajishn ceremony, where the Parsi priests are now content to put some hair of an ox in a vessel and show in to the Fire. But the development of the more philosophic Zarathustrian doctrines has led to a result common in the history of religion, that the ancient distinctly

[1] Max Müller, ' Chips,' vol. i. p. 169. Haug, ' Essays on Parsis,' p. 281.

meant rite has dwindled to a symbol, to be preserved with changed sense in a new theology.

Somewhat of the same kind may have taken place among the European race who seem in some respects the closest relatives of the old Persians. Slavonic history possibly keeps up some trace of direct and absolute fire-worship, as where in Bohemia the Pagans are described as worshipping fires, groves, trees, stones. But though the Lithuanians and Old Prussians and Russians are among the nations whose especial rite it was to keep up sacred everlasting fires, yet it seems that their fire-rites were in the symbolic stage, ceremonies of their great celestial-solar religion, rather than acts of direct worship to a Fire-god.[1] Classical religion, on the other hand, brings prominently into view the special deities of fire. Hēphaistos, Vulcan, the divine metallurgist who had his temples on Ætna and Lipari, stands in especial connexion with the subterranean volcanic fire, and combines the nature of the Polynesian Mahuika and the Circassian Tleps. The Greek Hestia, the divine hearth, the ever-virgin venerable goddess, to whom Zeus gave fair office instead of wedlock, sits in the midst of the house, receiving fat :—

> ' Τῇ δὲ πατὴρ Ζεὺς δῶκε καλὸν γέρας ἀντὶ γάμοιο,
> Καί τε μέσῳ οἴκῳ κατ' ἄρ' ἕζετο πῖαρ ἑλοῦσα.'

In the high halls of gods and men she has her everlasting seat, and without her are no banquets among mortals, for to Hestia first and last is poured the honey-sweet wine :—

> ' Ἑστίη, ἡ πάντων ἐν δώμασιν ὑψηλοῖσιν
> Ἀθανάτων τε θεῶν χαμαὶ ἐρχομένων τ' ἀνθρώπων
> Ἕδρην ἀΐδιον ἔλαχε, πρεσβηΐδα τιμὴν,
> Καλὸν ἔχουσα γέρας καὶ τίμιον· οὐ γὰρ ἄτερ σοῦ
> Εἰλαπίναι θνητοῖσιν, ἵν' οὐ πρώτῃ πυμάτῃ τε
> Ἑστίῃ ἀρχόμενος σπένδει μελιηδέα οἶνον.' [2]

In Greek civil life, Hestia sat in house and assembly as

---

[1] Hanusch, ' Slaw. Myth.' pp. 88, 98.

[2] Homer. Hymn. Aphrod. 29, Hestia 1. Welcker, ' Griech. Götterl.' vol. ii. pp. 686, 691.

representative of domestic and social order. Like her in name and origin, but not altogether in development, is Vesta with her ancient Roman cultus, and her retinue of virgins to keep up her pure eternal fire in her temple, needing no image, for she herself dwelt within :—

> ' Esse diu stultus Vestæ simulacra putavi :
> Mox didici curvo nulla subesse tholo.
> Ignis inextinctus templo celatur in illo.
> Effigiem nullam Vesta nec ignis habet.' [1]

The last lingering relics of fire-worship in Europe reach us, as usual, both through Turanian and Aryan channels of folklore. The Esthonian bride consecrates her new hearth and home by an offering of money cast into the fire, or laid on the oven for Tule-ema, Fire-mother.[2] The Carinthian peasant will ' fodder ' the fire to make it kindly, and throw lard or dripping to it, that it may not burn his house. To the Bohemian it is a godless thing to spit into the fire, ' God's fire ' as he calls it. It is not right to throw away the crumbs after a meal, for they belong to the fire. Of every kind of dish some should be given to the fire, and if some runs over it is wrong to scold, for it belongs to the fire. It is because these rites are now so neglected that harmful fires so often break out.[3]

What the Sea is to Water-worship, in some measure the Sun is to Fire-worship. From the doctrines and rites of earthly fire, various and ambiguous in character, generalized from many phenomena, applied to many purposes, we pass to the religion of heavenly fire, whose great deity has a perfect definiteness from his embodiment in one great individual fetish, the Sun.

Rivalling in power and glory the all-encompassing Heaven, the Sun moves eminent among the deities of nature, no mere cosmic globe affecting distant material worlds by force

---

[1] Ovid. Fast. vi. 295.
[2] Boecler, ' Ehsten Abergl.' p. 29, &c.
[3] Wuttke, ' Volksabergl.' p. 86. Grohmann, ' Aberglauben aus Böhmen,' p. 41.

in the guise of light and heat and gravity, but a living reigning Lord :—

> ' O thou, that with surpassing glory crown'd,
> Look'st from thy sole dominion like the God
> Of this new world.'

It is no exaggeration to say, with Sir William Jones, that one great fountain of all idoltary in the four quarters of the globe was the veneration paid by men to the sun : it is no more than an exaggeration to say with Mr. Helps of the sun-worship in Peru, that it was inevitable. Sun-worship is by no means universal among the lower races of mankind, but manifests itself in the upper levels of savage religion in districts far and wide over the earth, often assuming the prominence which it keeps and develops in the faiths of the barbaric world. Why some races are sun-worshippers and others not, is indeed too hard a question to answer in general terms. Yet one important reason is obvious, that the Sun is not so evidently the god of wild hunters and fishers, as of the tillers of the soil, who watch him day by day giving or taking away their wealth and their very life. On the geographical significance of sun-worship, D'Orbigny has made a remark, suggestive if not altogether sound, connecting the worship of the sun not so much with the torrid regions where his glaring heat oppresses man all day long, and drives him to the shade for refuge, as with climates where his presence is welcomed for his life-giving heat, and nature chills at his departure. Thus while the low sultry forests of South America show little prominence of Sun-worship, this is the dominant organized cultus of the high table-lands of Peru and Cundinamarca.[1] The theory is ingenious, and if not carried too far may often be supported. We may well compare the feelings with which the sun-worshipping Massagetæ of Tartary must have sacrificed their horses to the deity who freed them from the miseries of winter, with the thoughts of men in those burn-

---

[1] D'Orbigny, ' L'Homme Américain,' vol. i. p. 242.

ing lands of Central Africa where, as Sir Samuel Baker
says, ' the rising of the sun is always dreaded . . . the sun
is regarded as the common enemy,' words which recall
Herodotus' old description of the Atlantes or Atarantes who
dwelt in the interior of Africa, who cursed the sun at his
rising, and abused him with shameful epithets for afflicting
them with his burning heat, them and their land.[1]

The details of Sun-worship among the native races of
America give an epitome of its development among mankind at large. Among many of the ruder tribes of the
northern continent, the Sun is looked upon as one of the
great deities, as representative of the greatest deity, or as
that greatest deity himself. Indian chiefs of Hudson's Bay
smoked thrice to the rising sun. In Vancouver Island men
pray in time of need to the sun as he mounts toward the
zenith. Among the Delawares the sun received sacrifice as
second among the twelve great manitus : the Virginians
bowed before him with uplifted hands and eyes as he rose
and set ; the Pottawatomis would climb sometimes at sunrise on their huts, to kneel and offer to the luminary a mess
of Indian corn ; his likeness is found representing the
Great Manitu in Algonquin picture-writings. Father Hennepin, whose name is well known to geologists as the
earliest visitor to the Falls of Niagara, about 1678, gives
an account of the native tribes, Sioux and others, of this
far-west region. He describes them as venerating the Sun,
' which they recognize, though only in appearance, as the
Maker and Preserver of all things ; ' to him first they offer
the calumet when they light it, and to him they often
present the best and most delicate of their game in the lodge
of the chief, ' who profits more by it than the Sun.' The
Creeks regarded the Sun as symbol or minister of the Great
Spirit, sending toward him the first puff of the calumet at
treaties, and bowing reverently toward him in confirming
their council talk or haranguing their warriors to battle.[2]

---

[1] Herod. i. 216, iv. 184. Baker, ' Albert Nyanza,' vol. i. p. 144.
[2] Waitz, ' Anthropologie,' vol. iii. p. 181 (Hudson's B., Pottawatomies),

Among the rude Botocudos of Brazil, the idea of the Sun
as the great good deity seems not unknown ; the Araucanians are described as bringing offerings to him as highest
deity ; the Puelches as ascribing to the sun, and praying to
him for, all good things they possess or desire ; the Diaguitas of Tucuman as having temples dedicated to the Sun,
whom they adored, and to whom they consecrated birds'
feathers, which they then brought back to their cabins, and
sprinkled from time to time with the blood of animals.[1]

Such accounts of Sun-worship appearing in the lower
native culture of America, may be taken to represent its
first stage. It is on the whole within distinctly higher culture that its second stage appears, where it has attained to
full development of ritual and appurtenance, and become in
some cases even the central doctrine of national religion
and statecraft. Sun-worship had reached this level among
the Natchez of Louisiana, with whom various other tribes of
this district stood in close relation. Every morning at sunrise the great Sun-chief stood at the house-door facing the
east, shouted and prostrated himself thrice, and smoked
first toward the sun, and then toward the other three
quarters. The Sun-temple was a circular hut some thirty
feet across and dome-roofed : here in the midst was kept up
the everlasting fire, here prayer was offered thrice daily, and
here were kept images and fetishes and the bones of dead
chiefs. The Natchez government was a solar hierarchy.
At its head stood the great chief, called the Sun or the

---

205 (Virginians). J. G. Müller, ' Amer. Urrel.' p. 117 (Delawares, Sioux,
Mingos, &c.). Sproat, ' Ind. of Vancouver's I.' in ' Tr. Eth. Soc.' vol. v.
p. 253. Loskiel, ' Ind. of N. A.' part i. p. 43 (Delawares). Hennepin, ' Voyage
dans l'Amérique,' p. 302 (Sioux), &c. Bartram, ' Creek and Cherokee Ind.'
in ' Tr. Amer. Eth. Soc.' vol. iii. part i. pp. 20, 26 ; see also Schoolcraft,
' Ind. Tribes,' part ii. p. 127 (Comanches, &c.) ; Morgan, ' Iroquois,' p. 164 ;
Gregg, vol. ii. p. 238 (Shawnees) ; but compare the remarks of Brinton,
' Myths of New World,' p. 141.

[1] Martius, ' Ethnog. Amer.' vol. i. p. 327 (Botocudos). Waitz, vol. iii.
p. 518 (Araucanians). Dobrizhoffer, vol. ii. p. 89 (Puelches). Charlevoix,
' Hist. du Paraguay,' vol. i. p. 331 (Diaguitas). J. G. Müller, p. 255
(Botocudos, Aucas, Diaguitas).

Sun's brother, high priest and despot over his people. By his side stood his sister or nearest female relative, the female chief who of all women was alone permitted to enter the Sun-temple. Her son, after the custom of female succession common among the lower races, would succeed to the primacy and chiefship ; and the solar family took to themselves wives and husbands from the plebeian order, who were their inferiors in life, and were slain to follow them as attendants in death.[1] Another nation of sun-worshippers were the Apalaches of Florida, whose daily service was to salute the Sun at their doors as he rose and set. The Sun, they said, had built his own conical mountain of Olaimi, with its spiral path leading to the cave-temple, in the east side. Here, at the four solar festivals, the worshippers saluted the rising sun with chants and incense as his rays entered the sanctuary, and again when at midday the sunlight poured down upon the altar through the hole or shaft pierced for this purpose in the rocky vault of the cave ; through this passage the sun-birds, the tonatzuli, were let fly up sunward as messengers, and the ceremony was over.[2] Day by day, in the temples of Mexico, the rising sun was welcomed with blast of horns, and incense, and offering of a little of the officiators' own blood drawn from their ears, and a sacrifice of quails. Saying, the Sun has risen, we know not how he will fulfil his course nor whether misfortune will happen, they prayed to him—' Our Lord, do your office prosperously.' In distinct and absolute personality, the divine Sun in Aztec theology was Tonatiuh, whose huge pyramid-mound stands on the plain of Teotihuacan, a witness of his worship for future ages. Beyond this, the religion of Mexico, in its complex system or congeries of great gods, such as results from the mixture and alliance of the deities of several nations, shows the solar element rooted deeply and widely in other personages of its divine mythology, and attributes

[1] Charlevoix, ' Nouvelle France,' vol. vi. p. 172 ; Waitz, vol. iii. p. 217.
[2] Rochefort, ' Iles Antilles,' book ii. ch. viii.

especially to the Sun the title of Teotl, God.[1] Again, the high plateau of Bogota in New Granada was the seat of the semi-civilized Chibchas or Muyscas, of whose mythology and religion the leading ideas were given by the Sun. The Sun was the great deity to whom the human sacrifices were offered, and especially the holiest sacrifice, the blood of a pure captive youth daubed on a rock on a mountain-top for the rising sun to shine on. In native Muysca legend, the mythic civilizer of the land, the teacher of agriculture, the founder of the theocracy and institutor of sun-worship, is a figure in whom we cannot fail to discern the personal Sun himself.[2] It is thus, lastly, in the far more celebrated native theocracy to the south. In the royal religion of Peru, the Sun was at once ancestor and founder of the dynasty of Incas, who reigned as his representatives and almost in his person, who took wives from the convent of virgins of the Sun, and whose descendants were the solar race, the ruling aristocracy. The Sun's innumerable flocks of llamas grazed on the mountains, and his fields were tilled in the valleys, his temples stood throughout the land, and first among them the ' Place of Gold ' in Cuzco, where his new fire was kindled at the annual solar festival of Raymi, and where his splendid golden disc with human countenance looked forth to receive the first rays of its divine original. Sun-worship was ancient in Peru, but it was the Incas who made it the great state religion, imposing it wherever their wide conquests reached, till it became the central idea of Peruvian life.[3]

---

[1] Torquemada, ' Monarquia Indiana,' ix. c. 34 ; Sahagun, ' Hist. de Nueva España,' ii. App. in Kingsborough, ' Antiquities of Mexico ; ' Waitz, vol. iv. p. 138 ; J. G. Müller, p. 474, &c. ; Brasseur, ' Mexique,' vol. iii. p. 487 ; Tylor, ' Mexico,' p. 141.

[2] Piedrahita, ' Hist. Gen. de las Conquistas del Nuevo Reyno de Granada,' Antwerp, 1688 : part i. book i. c. iii. iv. ; Humboldt, ' Vues des Cordillères ; ' Waitz, vol. iv. p. 352, &c. ; J. G. Müller, p. 432, &c.

[3] Garcilaso de la Vega, ' Commentarios Reales,' lib. i. c. 15, &c., iii. c. 20 ; v. c. 2, 6 ; ' Rites and Laws of the Yncas,' tr. & ed. by C. R. Markham, (Hakluyt Soc., 1873) p. 84 ; Prescott, ' Peru,' book i. ch. iii. ; Waitz, vol. iv. p. 447, &c. ; J. G. Müller, p. 362, &c.

The culture of the Old World never surpassed this highest range of Sun-worship in the New.

In Australia and Polynesia the place of the solar god or hero is rather in myth than in religion. In Africa, though found in some districts,[1] Sun-worship is not very conspicuous out of Egypt. In tracing its Old World development, we begin among the ruder Allophylian tribes of Asia, and end among the great polytheistic nations. The northeast quarter of India shows the doctrine well defined among the indigenous stocks. The Bodo and Dhimal place the Sun in the pantheon as an elemental god, though in practical rank below the sacred rivers.[2] The Kol tribes of Bengal, Mundas, Oraons, Santals, know and worship as supreme, Sing-bonga, the Sun-god ; to him some tribes offer white animals in token of his purity, and while not regarding him as author of sickness or calamity, they will resort to him when other divine aid breaks down in sorest need.[3] Among the Khonds, Bura Pennu the Light-god, or Bella Pennu the Sun-god, is creator of all things in heaven and earth, and great first cause of good. As such, he is worshipped by his own sect above the ranks of minor deities whom he brought into being to carry out the details of the universal work.[4] The Tatar tribes with much unanimity recognize as a great god the Sun, whose figure may be seen beside the Moon's on their magic drums, from Siberia to Lapland. Castrén, the ethnologist, speaking of the Samoyed expression for heaven or deity in general (jilibeambaertje), tells an anecdote from his travels, which gives a lively idea of the thorough simple nature-religion still possible to the wanderers of the steppes. ' A Samoyed woman,' he says, ' told me it was her habit every morning and evening to step out of her tent and bow down before the sun ; in the morning

---

[1] Meiners, ' Gesch. der Rel.' vol. i. p. 383. Burton, ' Central Afr.' vol ii.. p. 346 ; ' Dahome,' vol. ii. p. 147.

[2] Hodgson, ' Abor. of India,' pp. 167, 175 (Bodos, &c.).

[3] Dalton, ' Kols,' in ' Tr. Eth. Soc.' vol. vi. p. 33 (Oraons, &c.) ; Hunter, ' Annals of Rural Bengal,' p. 184 (Santals).

[4] Macpherson, ' India,' p. 84, &c. (Khonds).

saying, ' When thou Jilibeambaertje risest, I too rise from my bed!' in the evening, ' When thou Jilibeambaertje sinkest down, I too get me to rest ! ' The woman brought this as a proof of her assertion that even among the Samoyeds they said their morning and evening prayers, but she added with pity that ' there were also among them wild people who never sent up a prayer to God.' Mongol hordes may still be met with whose shamans invoke the Sun, and throw milk up into the air as an offering to him, while the Karagas Tatars would bring to him as a sacrifice the head and heart of bear or stag. Tunguz, Ostyaks, Woguls, worship him in a character blending with that of their highest deity and Heaven-god ; while among the Lapps, Baiwe the Sun, though a mighty deity, stood in rank below Tiermes the Thunder-god, and the great celestial ruler who had come to bear the Norwegian name of Storjunkare.[1]

In direct personal nature-worship like that of Siberian nomades of our day, the solar cultus of the ancient pastoral Aryans had its source. The Vedic bards sing of the great god Sûrya, knower of beings, the all-revealer before whom the stars depart with the nights like thieves. We approach Sûrya (they say) shining god among the gods, light most glorious. He shines on the eight regions, the three worlds, the seven rivers ; the golden-handed Savitar, all-seeing, goes between heaven and earth. To him they pray, ' On thy ancient paths, O Savitar, dustless, well made, in the air, on those good-going paths this day preserve us and bless us, O God ! ' Modern Hinduism is full of the ancient Sun-worship, in offerings and prostrations, in daily rites and appointed festivals, and it is Savitar the Sun who is invoked in the ' gâyatrî,' the time-honoured formula repeated day by day since long-past ages by every Brahman : 'Tat Savitur varenyam bhargo devasya dhîmahi

[1] Castrén, ' Finn. Myth.' pp. 16, 51, &c. Meiners, l.c. Georgi, ' Reise im Russ. Reich.' vol. i. pp. 275, 317. Klemm, ' Cultur-Geschichte,' vol. iii. p. 87. Sun-Worship in Japan, Siebold, ' Nippon,' part v. p. 9. For further evidence as to savage and barbaric worship of the Sun as Supreme Deity, see chap. xvii.

dhiyo yo nah prakodayât.—Let us meditate on the desirable
light of the divine Sun ; may he rouse our minds ! ' Every
morning the Brahman worships the sun, standing on one
foot and resting the other against his ankle or heel, looking
towards the east, holding his hands open before him in a
hollow form, and repeating to himself these prayers : ' The
rays of light announce the splendid fiery sun, beautifully
rising to illumine the universe.'—' He rises, wonderful, the
eye of the sun, of water, and of fire, collective power of
gods ; he fills heaven, earth, and sky with his luminous net ;
he is the soul of all that is fixed or locomotive.'—' That
eye, supremely beneficial, rises pure from the east ; may we
see him a hundred years ; may we live a hundred years ;
may we hear a hundred years.'—' May we, preserved by
the divine power, contemplating heaven above the region of
darkness, approach the deity, most splendid of luminaries!'[1]
A Vedic celestial deity, Mitra the Friend, came to be developed in the Persian religion into that great ruling divinity
of light, the victorious Mithra, lord of life and head of all
created beings. The ancient Persian Mihr-Yasht invokes
him in the character of the sun-light, Mithra with wide
pastures, whom the lords of the regions praise at early dawn,
who as the first heavenly Yazata rises over Hara-berezaiti
before the sun, the immortal with swift steeds, who first
with golden form seizes the fair summits, then surrounds
the whole Aryan region. Mithra came to be regarded as
the very Sun, as where Dionysos addresses the Tyrian Bel,
'εἴτε σὺ Μίθρης Ἥλιος Βαβυλῶνος.' His worship spread
from the East across the Roman empire, and in Europe he
takes rank among the great solar gods absolutely identified
with the personal Sun, as in this inscription on a Roman
altar dating from Trajan's time—' Deo Soli Mithræ.'[2]

---

[1] ' Rig-Veda,' i. 35, 50 ; iii. 62, 10. Max Müller, ' Lectures,' 2nd Ser.
pp. 378, 411 ; ' Chips,' vol. i. p. 19. Colebrooke, ' Essays,' vol. i. pp. 30, 133.
Ward, ' Hindoos,' vol. ii. p. 42.

[2] ' Khordah-Avesta,' xxvi. in Avesta tr. by Spiegel, vol. iii. ; M. Haug,
' Essays on Parsis.' Strabo, xv. 3, 13. Nonnus, xl. 400. Movers, ' Phönizier,'
vol. i. p. 180 : ' ' Ἡλίῳ Μίθρᾳ ἀνικήτῳ ' ; ' Διὸς ἀνικήτου ' Ἡλίου.'

The earlier Sun-worship of Europe, upon which this new Oriental variety was intruded, in certain of its developments shows the same clear personality. The Greek Helios, to whom horses were sacrificed on the mountain-top of Taugetos, was that same personal Sun to whom Sokrates, when he had staid rapt in thought till daybreak, offered a prayer before he departed (ἔπειτ᾽ ᾤχετ᾽ ἀπιὼν προσευξάμενος τῷ ἡλίῳ).[1] Cæsar devotes to the German theology of his time three lines of his Commentaries. They reckon in the number of the gods, he says, those only whom they perceive and whose benefits they openly enjoy, Sun and Vulcan and Moon, the rest they know not even by report.[2] It is true that Cæsar's short summary does no justice to the real number and quality of the deities of the German pantheon, yet his forcible description of nature-worship in its most primitive stage may probably be true of the direct adoration of the sun and moon, and possibly of fire. On the other hand, European sun-worship leads into the most perplexing problems of mythology. Well might Cicero exclaim, ' How many suns are set forth by the theologians ! '[3] The modern student who shall undertake to discriminate among the Sun-gods of European lands, to separate the solar and non-solar elements of the Greek Apollo and Herakles, or of the Slavonic Swatowit, has a task before him complicate with that all but hopeless difficulty which besets the study of myth, the moment that the clue of direct comparison with nature falls away.

The religion of ancient Egypt is one of which we know much, yet little—much of its temples, rites, names of deities, liturgical formulas, but little of the esoteric religious ideas which lay hidden within these outer manifestations. Yet it is clear that central solar conceptions as it

[1] Plat. Sympos. xxxvi. See Welcker, ' Griech. Götterlehre,' vol. i. pp. 400, 412.
[2] Cæsar de Bello Gallico, vi. 21 : ' Deorum numero eos solos ducunt, quos cernunt et quorum aperte opibus juvantur, Solem et Vulcanum et Lunam, reliquos ne fama quidem acceperunt.'
[3] Cicero de Natura Deorum, iii. 21.

were radiate through the Egyptian theology. Ra, who traverses in his boat the upper and lower regions of the universe, is the Sun himself in plain cosmic personality. And to take two obvious instances of solar characters in other deities, Osiris the manifester of good and truth, who dies by the powers of darkness and becomes judge of the dead in the west-land of Amenti, is solar in his divine nature, as is also his son Horus, smiter of the monster Set.[1] In the religions of the Semitic race, the place of the Sun is marked through a long range of centuries. The warning to the Israelites lest they should worship and serve sun, moon, and stars, and the mention of Josiah taking away the horses that the Kings of Judah had given to the sun, and burning the chariots of the sun with fire,[2] agree with the place given in other Semitic religions to the Sun-god, Shamas of Assyria, or Baal, even expressly qualified as Baal-Shemesh or Lord Sun. Syrian religion, like Persian, introduced a new phase of Sun-worship into Rome, the cultus of Elagabal, and the vile priest emperor who bore this divine name made it more intelligible to classic ears as Heliogabalus.[3] Eusebius is a late writer as regards Semitic religion, but with such facts as these before us we need not withhold our confidence from him when he describes the Phœnicians and Egyptians as holding Sun, Moon, and Stars to be gods, sole causes of the generation and destruction of all things.[4]

The widely spread and deeply rooted religion of the Sun naturally offered strenuous resistance to the invasion of Christianity, and it was one of the great signs of the religious change of the civilized world when Constantine, that ardent votary of the Sun, abandoned the faith of Apollo for that of Christ. Amalgamation even proved possible

---

[1] See Wilkinson, 'Ancient Egyptians'; Renouf, 'Religion of Ancient Egypt.'

[2] Deut. iv. 19, xvii. 3; 2 Kings xxiii. 11.

[3] Movers, 'Phönizier,' vol. i. pp. 162, 180, &c. Lamprid. Heliogabal. i.

[4] Euseb. Præparat. Evang. i. 6.

between the doctrines of Sabæism and Christianity, and in and near Armenia a sect of Sun-worshippers have lasted on into modern times under the profession of Jacobite Christians ;[1] a parallel case within the limits of Mohammedanism being that of Beduin Arabs who still continue the old adoration of the rising sun, in spite of the Prophet's expressed command not to bow before the sun or moon, and in spite of the good Moslem's dictum, that ' the sun rises between the devil's horns.'[2] Actual worship of the sun in Christendom soon shrank to the stage of survival. In Lucian's time the Greeks kissed their hands as an act of worship to the rising sun ; and Tertullian had still to complain of many Christians that with an affectation of adoring the heavenly bodies they would move their lips toward the sunrise (Sed et plerique vestrum affectatione aliquando et cœlestia adorandi ad solis ortum labia vibratis).[3] In the 5th century, Leo the Great complains of certain Christians who, before entering the Basilica of St. Peter, or from the top of a hill, would turn and bow to the rising sun ; this comes, he says, partly of ignorance and partly of the spirit of paganism.[4] To this day, in the Upper Palatinate, the peasant takes off his hat to the rising sun ; and in Pomerania, the fever-stricken patient is to pray thrice turning toward the sun at sunrise, ' Dear Sun, come soon down, and take the seventy-seven fevers from me. In the name of God the Father, &c.'[5]

For the most part, the ancient rites of solar worship are represented in modern Christendom in two ways ; by the ceremonies connected with turning to the east, of which an account is given in an ensuing chapter under the heading of Orientation ; and in the continuance of the great sun-

---

[1] Neander, ' Church History,' vol. vi. p. 341. Carsten Niebuhr, ' Reisebeschr.' vol. ii. p. 396.

[2] Palgrave, ' Arabia,' vol. i. p. 9 ; vol. ii. p. 258. See Koran, xli. 37.

[3] Tertullian. Apolog. adv. Gentes, xvi. See Lucian. de Saltat. xvii. ; compare Job. xxxi. 26.

[4] Leo. I. Serm. viii. in Natal. Dom.

[5] Wuttke, ' Volksaberglaube,' p. 150.

festivals, countenanced by or incorporated in Christianity. Spring-tide, reckoned by so many peoples as New-Year, has in great measure had its solar characteristics transferred to the Paschal festival. The Easter bonfires with which the North German hills used to be ablaze mile after mile, are not altogether given up by local custom. On Easter morning in Saxony and Bradenburg, the peasants still climb the hill-tops before dawn, to see the rising sun give his three joyful leaps, as our forefathers used to do in England in the days when Sir Thomas Browne so quaintly apologized for declaring that ' the sun doth not dance on Easter Day.' The solar rite of the New Fire, adopted by the Roman Church as a Paschal ceremony, may still be witnessed in Europe, with its solemn curfew on Easter Eve, and the ceremonial striking of the new holy fire. On Easter Eve, under the solemn auspices of the Greek Church, a mob of howling fanatics crush and trample to death the victims who faint and fall in their struggles to approach the most shameless imposture of modern Christendom, the miraculous fire from heaven which descends into the Holy Sepulchre.[1] Two other Christian festivals have not merely had solar rites transferred to them, but seem distinctly themselves of solar origin. The Roman winter-solstice festival, as celebrated on December 25 (VIII. Kal. Jan.) in connexion with the worship of the Sun-god Mithra, appears to have been instituted in this special form after the Eastern campaign of Aurelian A.D. 273, and to this festival the day owes its apposite name of Birthday of the Unconquered Sun, ' Dies Natalis Solis invicti.' With full symbolic appropriateness, though not with historical justification, the day was adopted in the Western Church, where it appears to have been generally introduced by the 4th century, and whence in time it passed to the Eastern Church, as the solemn anniversary of the birth of Christ,

---

[1] Grimm, ' Deutsche Myth.' p. 581, &c. Wuttke, pp. 17, 93. Brand, Pop. Ant.' vol. i. p. 157, &c. ' Early Hist. of Mankind,' p. 260. Murray's Handbook for Syria and Palestine,' 1868, p. 162.

the Christian Dies Natalis, Christmas Day. Attempts have been made to ratify this date as matter of history, but no valid nor even consistent early Christian tradition vouches for it. The real solar origin of the festival is clear from the writings of the Fathers after its institution. In religious symbolism of the material and spiritual sun, Augustine and Gregory of Nyassa discourse on the glowing light and dwindling darkness that follow the Nativity, while Leo the Great, among whose people the earlier solar meaning of the festival evidently remained in strong remembrance, rebukes in a sermon the pestiferous persuasion, as he calls it, that this solemn day is to be honoured not for the birth of Christ, but for the rising, as they say, of the new sun.[1] As for modern memory of the sun-rites of mid-winter, Europe recognizes Christmas as a primitive solar festival by bonfires which our ' yule-log,' the ' souche de Noël,' still keeps in mind; while the adaptation of ancient solar thought to Christian allegory is as plain as ever in the Christmas service chant, ' Sol novus oritur.'[2] The solar Christmas festival has its pendant at Midsummer. The summer solstice was the great season of fire-festivals throughout Europe, of bonfires on the heights, of dancing round and leaping through the fires, of sending blazing fire-wheels to roll down from the hills into the valleys in sign of the sun's descending course. These ancient rites attached themselves in Christendom to St. John's Eve.[3] It seems as though the same train of symbolism which had adapted the mid-winter festival to the Nativity, may have suggested the dedication of the midsummer festival to John the Baptist, in clear allusion to his words, ' He must increase, but I must decrease.'

[1] See Pauly, ' Real-Encyclop.' s.v. ' Sol ; ' Petavius, ' Juliani Imp. Opera,' 290-2, 277. Bingham, ' Antiquities of Christian Church,' book xx. ch. iv. ; Neander, ' Church Hist.' vol. iii. p. 437 ; Beausobre, ' Hist. de Manichée,' vol. ii. p. 691 ; Gibbon, ch. xxii. ; Creuzer, ' Symbolik,' vol. i. p. 761, &c.

[2] Grimm, ' D. M.' pp. 593, 1223. Brand, ' Popular Antiquities,' vol. i. p. 467. Monnier, ' Traditions Populaires,' p. 188.

[3] Grimm, ' D. M.' p. 583 ; Brand, vol. i. p. 298 ; Wuttke, pp. 14, 140. Beausobre, l.c.

Moon-worship, naturally ranking below Sun-worship in importance, ranges through nearly the same district of culture. There are remarkable cases in which the Moon is recognized as a great deity by tribes who take less account, or none at all, of the Sun. The rude savages of Brazil seem especially to worship or respect the moon, by which they regulate their time and festivals, and draw their omens. They would lift up their hands to the moon with wonder-struck exclamations of teh ! teh ! they would have children smoked by the sorcerers to preserve them from moon-given sickness, or the women would hold up their babes to the luminary. The Botocudos are said to give the highest rank among the heavenly bodies to Taru the Moon, as causing thunder and lightning and the failure of vegetables and fruits, and as even sometimes falling to the earth, whereby many men die.[1] An old account of the Caribs describes them as esteeming the Moon more than the Sun, and at new moon coming out of their houses crying ' Behold the Moon ! '[2] The Ahts of Vancouver's Island, it is stated, worship the Sun and Moon, particularly the full moon and the sun ascending to the zenith. Regarding the Moon as husband and the Sun as wife, their prayers are more generally addressed to the Moon as the superior deity ; he is the highest object of their worship, and they speak of him as ' looking down upon the earth in answer to prayer, and seeing everybody.'[3] With a somewhat different turn of mythic fancy, the Hurons seems to have considered Ataentsic the Moon as maker of the earth and man, and grandmother of Iouskeha the Sun, with whom she governs the world.[4] In Africa, Moon-worship is prominent in an immense district where Sun-worship is unknown or insignificant. Among south-central tribes, men will watch for the

[1] Spix and Martius, ' Reise in Brasilien,' vol. i. pp. 377, 381 ; Martius, ' Ethnog. Amer.' vol. i. p. 327 ; Pr. Max. v. Wied, vol. ii. p. 58 ; J. G. Müller, pp. 218, 254 ; also Musters, ' Patagonians,' pp. 58, 179.

[2] De la Borde, ' Caraibes,' p. 525.

[3] Sproat, ' Savage Life,' p. 206 ; ' Tr. Eth. Soc.' vol. v. p. 253.

[4] Brebeuf in ' Rel. des Jés.' 1635, p. 34.

first glimpses of the new Moon, which they hail with shouts of kua ! and vociferate prayers to it ; on such an occasion Dr. Livingstone's Makololo prayed, ' Let our journey with the white man be prosperous ! ' &c.[1] These people keep holiday at new-moon, as indeed in many countries her worship is connected with the settlement of periodic festival. Negro tribes seem almost universally to greet the new Moon, whether in delight or disgust. The Guinea people fling themselves about with droll gestures, and pretend to throw firebrands at it ; the Ashango men behold it with superstitious fear ; the Fetu negroes jumped thrice into the air with hands together and gave thanks.[2] The Congo people fell on their knees, or stood and clapped their hands, crying, ' So may I renew my life as thou art renewed ! '[3] The Hottentots are described early in the last century as dancing and singing all night at new and full moon, calling the Moon the Great Captain, and crying to him ' Be greeted ! ' ' Let us get much honey ! ' ' May our cattle get much to eat and give much milk ! ' With the same thought as that just noticed in the district north-west of them, the Hottentots connect the Moon in legend with that fatal message sent to Man, which ought to have promised to the human race a moon-like renewal of life, but which was perverted into a doom of death like that of the beast who brought it.[4]

The more usual status of the Moon in the religions of the world is, as nature suggests, that of a subordinate companion deity to the Sun, such a position as is acknowledged in the precedence of Sunday to Monday. Their various mutual relations as brother and sister, husband and wife, have already been noticed here as matter of mythology. As wide-lying rude races who place them thus side by side in their theology, it is enough to mention the Delawares of

[1] Livingstone, ' S. Afr.' p. 235 ; Waitz, vol. ii. pp. 175, 342.
[2] Römer, ' Guinea,' p. 84 ; Du Chaillu, ' Ashango-land,' p. 428 ; see Purchas, vol. v. p. 766. Müller, ' Fetu,' p. 47.
[3] Merolla, ' Congo,' in Pinkerton, vol. xvi. p. 273.
[4] Kolbe, ' Beschryving van de Kaap de Goede Hoop,' part i. xxix. See ante, vol. i. p. 355.

North America,[1] the Ainos of Yesso,[2] the Bodos of North-East-India,[3] the Tunguz of Siberia.[4]   This is the state of things which continues at higher levels of systematic civilization.   Beside the Mexican Tonatiuh the Sun, Metztli the Moon had a smaller pyramid and temple;[5] in Bogota, the Moon, identified in local myth with the Evil Deity, had her place and figure in the temple beside the Sun her husband;[6] the Peruvian Mother-Moon, Mama-Quilla, had her silver disc-face to match the golden one of her brother and husband the Sun, whose companion she had been in the legendary civilizing of the land.[7]   In the ancient Kami-religion of Japan, the supreme Sun-god ranks high above the Moon-god, who was worshipped under the form of a fox.[8]   Among the historic nations of the Old World, documents of Semitic culture show Sun and Moon side by side. For one, we may take the Jewish law, to stone with stones till they died the man or woman who 'hath gone and served other gods, and worshipped them, either the sun, or moon, or any of the host of heaven.'   For another, let us glance over the curious record of the treaty-oath between Philip of Macedon and the general of the Carthaginian and Libyan army, which so well shows how the original identity of nature-deities may be forgotten in their different local shapes, so that the same divinity may come twice or even three times over in as many national names and forms. Herakles and Apollo stand in company with the personal Sun, and as well as the personal Moon is to be seen the 'Carthaginian deity,' whom there is reason to look on as Astarte, a goddess latterly of lunar nature.   This is the list of deities invoked: 'Before Zeus and Hera and

[1] Loskiel, ' Ind. of N. A.' part i. p. 43.
[2] Bickmore, ' Ainos,' in ' Tr. Eth. Soc.' vol. vii. p. 20.
[3] Hodgson, ' Abor. of India,' p. 167.
[4] Georgi, ' Reise im Russ. R.' vol. i. p. 275.
[5] Clavigero, ' Messico,' vol. ii. pp. 9, 35 ; Tylor, ' Mexico,' l.c.
[6] Waitz, vol. iv. p. 362.
[7] Garcilaso de la Vega, ' Commentarios Reales,' iii. 21.
[8] Siebold, ' Nippon,' part v. p. 9.

Apollo; before the goddess of the Carthaginians (δαίμονος Καρχηδονίων) and Herakles and Iolaos; before Ares, Triton, Poseidon; before the gods who fought with the armies, and Sun and Moon and Earth; before the rivers and meadows and waters; before all the gods who rule Macedonia and the rest of Greece; before all the gods who were at the war, they who have presided over this oath.'[1] When Lucian visited the famous temple of Hierapolis in Syria, he saw the images of the other gods, ' but only of the Sun and Moon they show no images.' And when he asked why, they told him that the forms of other gods were not seen by all, but Sun and Moon are altogether clear, and all men see them.[2] In Egyptian theology, not to discuss other divine beings to whom a lunar nature has been ascribed, it is at least certain that Khonsu is the Moon in absolute personal divinity.[3] In Aryan theology, the personal Moon stands as Selēnē beside the more anthropomorphic forms of Hekatē and Artemis,[4] as Luna beside the less understood Lucina, and Diana with her borrowed attributes,[5] while our Teutonic forefathers were content with his plain name of Moon.[6] As for lunar survivals in the higher religions, they are much like the solar. Monotheist as he is, the Moslem still claps his hands at sight of the new moon, and says a prayer.[7] In Europe in the 15th century it was matter of complaint that some still adored the new moon with bended knee, or hood or hat removed, and to this day we may still see a hat raised or a curtsey dropped to her, half in conservatism and half in jest. It is with reference to silver as the lunar metal, that money is turned

---

[1] Deuteron. xvii. 3; Polyb. vii. 9; see Movers, ' Phönizier,' pp. 159, 536, 605.

[2] Lucian. de Syria Dea, iv. 34.

[3] Wilkinson, ' Ancient Egyptians,' ed. by Birch, vol. iii. p. 174. See Plutarch. Is. et Osir.

[4] Welcker, ' Griech. Götterl.' vol. i. p. 550, &c.

[5] Cic. de Nat. Deor. ii. 27.

[6] Grimm, ' D. M.' ch. xxii.

[7] Akerblad, ' Lettre à Italinsky.' Burton, ' Central Afr.' vol. ii. p. 346. Mungo Park, ' Travels,' in ' Pinkerton,' vol. xvi. p. 875.

when the act of adoration is performed, while practical peasant wit dwells on the ill-luck of having no piece of silver when the new moon is first seen.[1]

Thus, in tracing the development of Nature-Worship, it appears that though Fire, Air, Earth, and Water are not yet among the lower races systematized into a quaternion of elements, their adoration, with that of Sun and Moon, shows already arising in primitive culture the familiar types of those great divinities, who received their further development in the higher Polytheism.

[1] Grimm, ' D. M.' pp. 29, 667 ; Brand, vol. iii. p. 146 ; Forbes Leslie, ' Early Races of Scotland,' vol. i. p. 136.

CHAPTER XVII

ANIMISM (*continued*)

Polytheism comprises a class of Great Deities, ruling the course of Nature
and the life of Man—Childbirth-god—Agriculture-god—War-god—God
of the Dead—First Man as Divine Ancestor—Dualism; its rudimentary and unethical nature among low races; its development through
the course of culture—Good and Evil Deity—Doctrine of Divine
Supremacy, distinct from, while tending towards, the doctrine of
Monotheism—Idea of a Highest or Supreme Diety evolved in various
forms; its place as completion of the Polytheistic system and outcome of the Animistic philosophy; its continuance and development
among higher nations—General survey of Animism as a Philosophy of Religion—Recapitulation of the theory advanced as to its
development through successive stages of culture; its primary phases
best represented among the lower races, while survivals of these among
the higher races mark the transition from savage through barbaric to
civilized faiths—Transition of Animism in the History of Religion;
its earlier and later stages as a Philosophy of the Universe; its later
stages as the principle of a Moral Institution.

POLYTHEISM acknowledges, beside great fetish-deities like
Heaven and Earth, Sun and Moon, another class of great
gods whose importance lies not in visible presence, but
in the performance of certain great offices in the course
of Nature and the life of Man. The lower races can
furnish themselves with such deities, either by giving the
recognized gods special duties to perform, or by attributing
these functions to beings invented in divine personality for
the purpose. The creation of such divinities is however
carried to a much greater extent in the complex systems of
the higher polytheism. For a compact group of examples
showing to what different ideas men will resort for a deity
to answer a special end, let us take the deity presiding over

Childbirth. In the West Indies, a special divinity occupied with this function took rank as one of the great indigenous fetish-gods;[1] in the Samoan group, the household god of the father's or mother's family was appealed to;[2] in Peru the Moon takes to this office,[3] and the same natural idea recurs in Mexico;[4] in Esthonian religion the productive Earth-mother appropriately becomes patroness of human birth;[5] in the classic theology of Greece and Italy, the divine spouse of the Heaven-king, Hēra,[6] Juno,[7] favours and protects on earth marriage and the birth of children ; and to conclude the list, the Chinese work out the problem from the manes-worshipper's point of view, for the goddess whom they call 'Mother' and propitiate with many a ceremony and sacrifice to save and prosper their children, is held to have been in human life a skilful midwife.[8]

The deity of Agriculture may be a cosmic being affecting the weather and the soil, or a mythic giver of plants and teacher of their cultivation and use. Thus among the Iroquois, Heno the Thunder, who rides through the heavens on the clouds, who splits the forest-trees with the thunder-bolt-stones he hurls at his enemies, who gathers the clouds and pours out the warm rains, was fitly chosen as patron of husbandry, invoked at seed-time and harvest, and called Grandfather by his children the Indians.[9] It is interesting to notice again on the southern continent the working out of this idea in the Tupan of Brazilian tribes; Thunder and Lightning, it is recorded, they call Tupan, considering themselves to owe to him their hoes and the profitable art of tillage, and therefore acknowledging him as a deity.[10]

---

[1] Herrera, 'Indias Occidentales,' Dec. i. 3, 3 ; J. G. Müller, 'Amer. Urrel.' pp. 175, 221.

[2] Turner, 'Polynesia,' p. 174.

[3] Rivero and Tschudi, 'Peru,' p. 160.

[4] Kingsborough, 'Mexico,' vol. v. p. 179.

[5] Castrén, 'Finn. Myth.' p. 89.

[6] Welcker, 'Griech. Götterl.' vol. i. p. 371.

[7] Ovid. Fast. ii. 449.

[8] Doolittle, 'Chinese,' vol. i. p. 264.   [9] Morgan, 'Iroquois,' p. 158.

[10] De Laet, 'Novus Orbis,' xv. 2 ; Waitz, vol. iii. p. 417 ; Brinton, pp. 152, 185 ; J. G. Müller, p. 271, &c.

Among the Guarani race, Tamoi the Ancient of Heaven
had no less rightful claim, in his character of heaven-god,
to be venerated as the divine teacher of agriculture to his
people.[1] In Mexico, Centeotl the Grain-goddess received
homage and offerings at her two great festivals, and took
care of the growth and keeping of the corn.[2] In Polynesia,
we hear in the Society Islands of Ofanu the god of husbandry, in the Tonga Islands of Alo Alo the fanner, god of
wind and weather, bearing office as god of harvest, and
receiving his offering of yams when he had ripened them.[3]
A picturesque figure from barbaric Asia is Pheebee Yau, the
Ceres of the Karens, who sits on a stump and watches the
growing and ripening corn, to fill the granaries of the frugal
and industrious.[4] The Khonds worship at the same shrine,
a stone or tree near the village, both Būrbi Pennu the goddess of new vegetation, and Pidzu Pennu the rain-god.[5]
Among Finns and Esths it is the Earth-mother who appropriately undertakes the task of bringing forth the fruits.[6]
And so among the Greeks it is the same being, Dēmētēr the
Earth-mother, who performs this function, while the Roman
Ceres who is confused with her is rather, as in Mexico, a
goddess of grain and fruit.[7]

The War-god is another being wanted among the lower
races, and formed or adapted accordingly. Areskove the
Iroquois War-god seems to be himself the great celestial
deity; for his pleasant food they slaughtered human victims,
that he might give them victory over their enemies ; as a
pleasant sight for him they tortured the war-captives ; on
him the war-chief called in solemn council, and the warriors,
shouting his name, rushed into the battle he was surveying

[1] D'Orbigny, ' L'Homme Américain,' vol. ii. p. 319.
[2] Clavigero, ' Messico,' vol. ii. pp. 16, 68, 75.
[3] Ellis, ' Polyn. Res.' vol. i. p. 333. Mariner, ' Tonga Is.' vol. ii. p. 115.
[4] Cross, in ' Journ. Amer. Oriental Soc.' vol. iv. p. 316 ; Mason, p. 215.
[5] Macpherson, ' India,' pp. 91, 355.
[6] Castrén, ' Finn. Myth.' p. 89.
[7] Welcker, ' Griech. Götterl.' vol. ii. p. 467. Cox, ' Mythology of Aryan
Nations,' vol ii. p. 308.

from on high. Canadian Indians before the fight would
look toward the sun, or addressed the Great Spirit as god of
war ; Floridan Indians prayed to the Sun before their wars.[1]
Araucanians of Chili entreated Pillan the Thunder-god
that he would scatter their enemies, and thanked him
amidst their cups after a victory.[2] The very name of Mexico
seems derived from Mexitli, the national War-god, identical or identified with the hideous gory Huitzilopochtli.
Not to attempt a general solution of the enigmatic nature
of this inextricable compound parthenogenetic deity, we
may notice the association of his principal festival with
the winter-solstice, when his paste idol was shot through
with an arrow, and being thus killed, was divided into
morsels and eaten, wherefore the ceremony was called
the teoqualo or ' god-eating.' This and other details tend
to show Huitzilopochtli as originally a nature-deity,
whose life and death were connected with the year's,
while his functions of War-god may be of later addition.[3]
Polynesia is a region where quite an assortment of war-
gods may be collected. Such, to take but one example,
was Tairi, war-god of King Kamehameha of the Sandwich
Islands, whose hideous image, covered with red feathers,
shark-toothed, mother-of-pearl-eyed, with helmet-crest of
human hair, was carried into battle by his special priest,
distorting his own face into hideous grins, and uttering
terrific yells which were considered to proceed from the
god.[4] Two examples from Asia may show what different
original conceptions may serve to shape such deities as
these upon. The Khond War-god, who entered into all
weapons, so that from instruments of peace they became
weapons of war, who gave edge to the axe and point
to the arrow, is the very personified spirit of tribal war,

---

[1] J. G. Müller, ' Amer. Urrel.' pp. 141, 271, 274, 591, &c.
[2] Dobrizhoffer, ' Abipones,' vol. ii. p. 90.
[3] Clavigero, ' Messico,' vol. ii. pp. 17, 81.
[4] Ellis, ' Polyn. Res.' vol. i. p. 326 ; vol. iv. p. 158. See also Mariner,
onga Is.' vol. ii. p. 112 ; Williams, ' Fiji,' vol. i. p. 218.

his token is the relic of iron and the iron weapons buried in his sacred grove which stands near each group of hamlets, and his name is Loha Pennu or Iron-god.[1] The Chinese War-god, Kuang Tä, on the other hand, is an ancient military ghost ; he was a distinguished officer, as well as a ' faithful and honest courtier,' who flourished during the wars of the Han dynasty, and emperors since then have delighted to honour him by adding to his usual title more and more honorary distinctions.[2] Looking at these selections from the army of War-gods of the different regions of the world, we may well leave their classic analogues, Arēs and Mars, as beings whose warlike function we recognize, but not so easily their original nature.[3]

It would be easy, going through the religious systems of Polynesia and Mexico, Greece and Rome, India and China, to give the names and offices of a long list of divinities, patrons of hunting and fishing, carpentering and weaving, and so forth. But studying here rather the continuity of polytheistic ideas than the analysis of polytheistic divinities, it is needless to proceed farther in the comparison of these deities of special function, as recognized to some extent in the lower civilization, before their elaborate development became one of the great features of the higher.

The great polytheistic deities we have been examining, concerned as they are with the earthly course of nature and human life, are gods of the living. But even in savage levels man began to feel an intellectual need of a God of the Dead, to reign over the souls of men in the next life, and this necessity has been supplied in various ways. Of the deities set up as lords of Deadman's Land, some are beings whose original meaning is obscure. Some are distinctly nature-deities appointed to this office, often for local reasons, as happening to belong to the regions where the dead take

[1] Macpherson, ' India,' pp. 90, 360.
[2] Doolittle, ' Chinese,' vol. i. p. 267.
[3] Welcker, ' Griech. Götterl.' vol. i. p. 413. Cox, ' Myth. of Aryan N.,' vol. ii. pp. 254, 311.

up their abode. Some, again, are as distinctly the deified
souls of men. The two first classes may be briefly instanced
together in America, where the light-side and shadow-side
(as Dr. J. G. Müller well calls them) of the conception of a
future life are broadly contrasted in the definitions of the
Lord of the Dead. Among the Northern Indians this may
be Tarenyawagon the Heaven-God, identified with the Great
Spirit, who receives good warriors in his happy hunting-
grounds, or his grandmother, the Death-goddess Atahentsic.[1]
In Brazil, the Under-world-god, who places good warriors
and sorcerers in Paradise, contrasts with Aygnan the evil
deity who takes base and cowardly Tupi souls,[2] much as
the Mexican Tlaloc, Water-god and lord of the earthly
paradise, contrasts with Mictlanteuctli, ruler of the dismal
dead-land in the shades below.[3] In Peru there has been
placed on record a belief that the departed spirits went to
be with the Creator and Teacher of the World—' Bring us
too near to thee . . . that we may be fortunate, being near
to thee, O Uira-cocha ! ' There are also statements as to
an under-world of shades, the land of the demon Supay.[4]
Accounts of this class must often be suspected of giving
ideas mis-stated under European influence, or actually
adopted from Europeans, but there is in some a look of
untouched genuineness. Thus in Polynesia, the idea of a
Devil borrowed from colonists or missionaries may be suspected in such a figure as the evil deity Wiro, chief of
Reigna, the New Zealander's western world of departed
souls. But few conceptions of deity are more quaintly
original than that of the Samoan deity Saveasiuleo, at once

---

[1] J. G. Müller, ' Amer. Urrel.' pp. 137, &c., 272, 286, &c., 500, &c. See
Sproat, p. 213 (Ahts), cited ante, p. 85. Chay-her signifies not only the
world below, but Death personified as a boneless greybeard who wanders at
night stealing men's souls away.

[2] Lery, ' Bresil,' p. 234.

[3] Clavigero, vol. ii. pp. 14, 17 ; Brasseur, ' Mexique,' vol. iii. p. 495.

[4] ' Rites and Laws of Yncas,' tr. and ed. by C. R. Markham, pp. 32, 48
(prayer from MS. communication by C. R. M.); Garcilaso de la Vega, lib. ii.
c. 2, 7 ; Brinton, ' Myths of New World,' p. 251.

ruler of destinies of war and other affairs of men and chief of the subterranean Bulotū, with the human upper half of his body reclining in his great house in company with the spirits of departed chiefs, while his tail or extremity stretches far away into the sea, in the shape of an eel or serpent. Under a name corresponding dialectically (Siuleo = Hikuleo), this composite being reappears in the kindred myths of the neighbouring group, the Tonga Islands. The Tongan Hikuleo has his home in the spirit-land of Bulotū, here conceived as out in the far western sea. Here we are told the use of his tail. His body goes away on journeys, but his tail remains watching in Bulotū, and thus he is aware of what goes on in more places than one. Hikuleo used to carry off the first-born sons of Tongan chiefs, to people his island of the blest, and he so thinned the ranks of the living that at last the other gods were moved to compassion. Tangaloa and Maui seized Hikuleo, passed a strong chain round him, and fastened one end to heaven and the other to earth. Another god of the dead, of well-marked native type, is the Rarotongan Tiki, an ancestral deity as in New Zealand, to whose long house, a place of unceasing joys, the dead are to find their way.[1] Among Turanian tribes, there are Samoyeds who believe in a deity called 'A,' dwelling in impenetrable darkness, sending disease and death to men and reindeer, and ruling over a crowd of spirits which are manes of the dead. Tatars tell of the nine Irle-Chans, who in their gloomy subterranean kingdom not only rule over souls of the dead, but have at their command a multitude of ministering spirits, visible and invisible. In the gloomy under-world of the Finns reigns Mana or Tuoni, a being whose nature is worked out by personification from the dismal dead-land or death itself.[2] Much the

---

[1] Turner, 'Polynesia,' p. 237; Farmer, 'Tonga,' p. 126. Yate, 'New Zealand,' p. 140; J. Williams, 'Missionary Enterprise,' p. 145. See Schirren, 'Wandersagen der Neuseeländer,' p. 89; Williams, 'Fiji,' vol. i. p. 246.

[2] Castrén, 'Finn. Myth.' pp. 128, 147, 155; Waitz, vol. ii. p. 171 (Africa).

same may be said of the Greek Aidēs, Hades, and the Scandinavian Hel, whose names, perhaps not so much by confusion as with a sense of their latent significance, have become identified in language with the doleful abodes over which a personifying fancy set them to preside.[1] As appropriately, though working out a different idea, the ancient Egyptians conceived their great solar deity to rule in the regions of his western under-world—Osiris is Lord of the Dead in Amenti.[2]

In the world's assembly of great gods, an important place must be filled up by the manes-worshipper in logical development of his special system. The theory of family manes, carried back to tribal gods, leads to the recognition of superior deities of the nature of Divine Ancestor or First Man, and it is of course reasonable that such a being, if recognized, should sometimes fill the place of lord of the dead, whose ancestral chief he is. There is an anecdote among the Mandans told by Prince Maximilian von Wied, which brings into view conceptions lying in the deepest recesses of savage religion, the idea of the divine first ancestor, the mythic connexion of the sun's death and descent into the under-world, with the like fate of man and the nature of the spiritual intercourse between man's own soul and his deity. The First Man, it is said, promised the Mandans to be their helper in time of need, and then departed into the West. It came to pass that the Mandans were attacked by foes. One Mandan would send a bird to the great ancestor to ask for help, but no bird could fly so far. Another thought a look would reach him, but the hills walled him in. Then said a third, thought must be the safest way to reach the First Man. He wrapped himself in his buffalo-robe, fell down, and spoke, ' I think—I have thought—I come back.' Throwing off the fur, he was bathed in sweat. The divine helper he had called on in his

---

[1] Welcker, ' Griech. Götterl.' vol. i. p. 395 ; Roscher, s.v. ' Hades.' Grimm, ' Deutsch. Myth.' p. 288.
[2] Brugsch, ' Religion der alten Aegypter ' ; ' Book of Dead.'

distress appeared.[1] There is instructive variety in the ways
in which the lower American races work out the conception
of the divine forefather. The Mingo tribes revere and
make offerings to the First Man, he who was saved at the
great deluge, as a powerful deity under the Master of Life,
or even as identified with him ; some Mississippi Indians
said that the First Man ascended into heaven, and thunders
there ; among the Dog-ribs, he was creator of sun and
moon ;[2] Tamoi, the grandfather and ancient of heaven of
the Guaranis, was their first ancestor, who dwelt among
them and taught them to till the soil, and rose to heaven in
the east, promising to succour them on earth, and at death
to carry them from the sacred tree into a new life where
they should all meet again, and have much hunting.[3]

Polynesia, again, has thoroughly worked the theory of
divine ancestors into the native system of multiform and
blending nature-deities. Men are sprung from the divine
Maui, whom Europeans have therefore called the ' Adam
of New Zealand,' or from the Rarotongan Tiki, who seems
his equivalent (Mauitiki), and who again is the Tii of
the Society Islands ; it is, however, the son of Tii who
precisely represents a Polynesian Adam, for his name is
Taata, i.e., Man, and he is the ancestor of the human race.
There is perhaps also reason to identify Maui and the First
Man with Akea, first King of Hawaii, who at his earthly
death descended to rule over his dark subterranean kingdom,
where his subjects are the dead who recline under the
spreading kou-trees, and drink of the infernal rivers, and
feed on lizards and butterflies.[4] In the mythology of Kamchatka, the relation between the Creator and the First Man
is one not of identity but of parentage. Among the sons of

---

[1] Pr. Max. v. Wied, ' N. Amerika,' vol. ii. p. 157.
[2] J. G. Müller, ' Amer. Urrel.' pp. 133, &c., 228, 255. Catlin, ' N. A. Ind.'
vol. i. pp. 159, 177 ; Pr. Max v. Wied, vol. ii. pp. 149, &c. Compare Sproat,
' Savage Life,' p. 179 (Quawteaht the Great Spirit is also First Man).
[3] D'Orbigny, ' L'Homme Américain,' vol. ii. p. 319.
[4] Schirren,' ' Wandersagen der Neuseeländer,' p. 64, &c., 88, &c. Ellis,
' Polyn. Res.' vol. i. p. 111, vol. iv. pp. 145, 366.

Kutka the Creator is Haetsh the First Man, who dwelt on earth, and died, and descended into Hades to be chief of the under-world ; there he receives the dead and new-risen Kamchadals, to continue a life like that of earth in his pleasant subterranean land where mildness and plenty prevail, as they did in the regions above in the old days when the Creator was still on earth.[1] Among all the lower races who have reasoned out this divine ancestor, none excel those consistent manes-worshippers, the Zulus. Their worship of the manes of the dead has not only made the clan-ancestors of a few generations back into tribal deities (Unkulunkulu), but beyond these, too far off and too little known for actual worship, yet recognized as the original race-deity and identified with the Creator, stands the First Man, he who ' broke off in the beginning,' the Old-Old-One, the great Unkulunkulu. While the Zulu's most intense religious emotions are turned to the ghosts of the departed, while he sacrifices his beloved oxen and prays with agonising entreaty to his grandfather, and carries his tribal worship back to those ancestral deities whose praise-giving names are still remembered, the First Man is beyond the reach of such rites. ' At first we saw that we were made by Unkulunkulu. But when we were ill we did not worship him, nor ask anything of him. We worshipped those whom we had seen with our eyes, their death and their life among us. . . . . Unkulunkulu had no longer a son who could worship him ; there was no going back to the beginning, for people increased, and were scattered abroad, and each house had its own connections ; there was no one who said, " For my part I am of the house of Unkulunkulu." ' Nay more, the Zulus who would not dare to affront an ' idhlozi,' a common ghost, that might be angry and kill them, have come to make open mock of the name of the great first ancestor. When the grown-up people wish to talk privately or eat something by themselves, it is the regular thing to send the children out to

[1] Steller, ' Kamtschatka,' p. 271.

call at the top of their voices for Unkulunkulu. ' The name of Unkulunkulu has no respect paid to it among black men ; for his house no longer exists. It is now like the name of a very old crone, who has no power to do even a little thing for herself, but sits continually where she sat in the morning till the sun sets. And the children make sport of her, for she cannot catch them and flog them, but only talk with her mouth. Just so is the name of Un-kulunkulu when all the children are told to go and call him. He is now a means of making sport of children.'[1]

In Aryan religion, the divinities just described give us analogues for the Hindu Yama, throughout his threefold nature as First Man, as solar God of Hades, as Judge of the Dead. Professor Max Müller thus suggests his origin, which may indeed be inferred from his being called the child of Vivasvat, himself the Sun : ' The sun, conceived as setting or dying every day, was the first who had trodden the path of life from East to West—the first mortal—the first to show us the way when our course is run, and our sun sets in the far West. Thither the fathers followed Yama ; there they sit with him rejoicing, and thither we too shall go when his messengers (day and night) have found us out. . . . . Yama is said to have crossed the rapid waters, to have shown the way to many, to have first known the path on which our fathers crossed over.' It is a perfectly consistent myth-formation, that the solar Yama should become the first of mortals who died and discovered the way to the other world, who guides other man thither and assembles them in a home which is secured to them for ever. As representative of death, Yama had even in early Aryan times his aspects of terror, and in later Indian theo-logy he becomes not only the Lord but the awful Judge of the Dead, whom some modern Hindus are said to worship alone of all the gods, alleging that their future state is to be determined only by Yama, and that they have nothing therefore to hope or fear from any beside him. In these

[1] Callaway, ' Religion of Amazulu,' pp. 1-104.

days, Hindu and Parsi in Bombay are learning from scholars in Europe the ancient connexion of their long antagonistic faiths, and have to hear that Yama son of Visavat sitting on his awful judgment-seat of the dead, to reward the good and punish the wicked with hideous tortures, and Yima son of Vivanhâo who in primæval days reigned over his happy deathless kingdom of good Zarathustrian men, are but two figures developed in the course of ages out of one and the same Aryan nature-myth.[1] Within the limits of Jewish, Christian, and Moslem theology, the First Man scarcely occupies more than a place of precedence among the human race in Hades or in Heaven, not the high office of Lord of the Dead. Yet that tendency to deify an ideal ancestor, which we observe to act so strongly on lower races, has taken effect also here. The Rabbinical Adam is a gigantic being reaching from earth to heaven, for the definition of whose stature Rabbi Eliezer cites Deuteronomy iv. 32, ' God made man (Adam) upon the earth, and from one end of heaven to the other.'[2] It is one of the familiar episodes of the Koran, how the angels were bidden to bow down before Adam, the regent of Allah upon earth, and how Eblis (Diabolus) swelling with pride, refused the act of adoration.[3] Among the Gnostic sect of the Valentinians, Adam the primal man in whom the Deity had revealed himself, stood as earthly representative of the Demiurge, and was even counted among the Æons.[4]

The figures of the great deities of Polytheism, thus traced in outline according to the determining idea on which each is shaped, seem to show that conceptions originating under rude and primitive conditions of human thought and passing thence into the range of higher culture,

---

[1] ' Rig-Veda,' x. 'Atharva-Veda,' xviii. Max Müller, ' Lectures,' 2nd Ser. p. 514. Muir, ' Yama,' &c., in ' Journ. As. Soc. N. S.' vol. i. 1865. Roth in ' Ztschr. Deutsch. Morgenl. G.' vol. iv. p. 426. Ward, ' Hindoos,' vol. ii. p. 60. Avesta : ' Vendidad,' ii. Pictet, ' Origines Indo-Europ.' part ii. p. 621.

[2] Eisenmenger, part i. p. 365.

[3] Koran, ii. 28, vii. 10, &c.

[4] Neander, ' Hist. of Chr.' vol. ii. pp. 81, 109, 174.

may suffer in the course of ages the most various fates, to be expanded, elaborated, transformed, or abandoned. Yet the philosophy of modern ages still to a remarkable degree follows the primitive courses of savage thought, even as the highways of our land so often follow the unchanging tracks of barbaric roads. Let us endeavour timidly and circumspectly to trace onward from savage times the courses of vast and pregnant generalization which tend towards the two greatest of the world's schemes of religious doctrine, the systems of Dualism and Monotheism.

Rudimentary forms of Dualism, the antagonism of a Good and Evil Deity, are well known among the lower races of mankind. The investigation of these savage and barbaric doctrines, however, is a task demanding peculiar caution. The Europeans in contact with these rude tribes since their discovery, themselves for the most part holding strongly dualistic forms of Christianity, to the extent of practically subjecting the world to the contending influences of armies of good and evil spirits under the antagonistic control of God and Devil, were liable on the one hand tomis take and exaggerate savage ideas in this direction, so that their records of native religion can only be accepted with reserve, while on the other hand there is no doubt that dualistic ideas have been largely introduced and developed among the savages themselves, under this same European influence. For instance, among the natives of Australia, we hear of the great deity Nambajandi who dwells in his heavenly paradise, where the happy shades of black men feast and dance and sing for evermore ; over against him stands the great evil being Warrūgūra, who dwells in the nethermost regions, who causes the great calamities which befall mankind, and whom the natives represent with horns and tail, although no horned beast is indigenous in the land.[1] There may be more or less native substratum in all this, but the hints borrowed from popular Christian ideas are unmistake-

[1] Oldfield in ' Tr. Eth. Soc.' vol. iii. p. 228. See also Eyre, vol. ii. p. 356 ; Lang, ' Queensland,' p. 444.

able. Thus also, among the North American Indians, the native religion was modified under the influence of ideas borrowed from the white men, and there arose a full dualistic scheme, of which Loskiel, a Moravian missionary conversant especially with Algonquin and Iroquois tribes, gives the following suggestive particulars, dating from 1794. ' They (the Indians) first received in modern times through the Europeans the idea of the Devil, the Prince of Darkness. They consider him as a very mighty spirit, who can only do evil, and therefore call him the Evil One. Thus they now believe in a great good and a great evil spirit ; to the one they ascribe all good, and to the other all evil. About thirty years ago, a remarkable change took place in the religious opinions of the Indians. Some preachers of their own nation pretended to have received revelations from above, to have travelled into heaven, and conversed with God. They gave different accounts of their journey to heaven, but all agreed in this, that no one could arrive there without great danger ; for the road runs close by the gates of hell. There the Devil lies in ambush, and snatches at every one who is going to God. Now those who have passed by this dangerous place unhurt, come first to the Son of God, and from him to God himself, from whom they pretend to have received a commandment, to instruct the Indians in the way to heaven. By them the Indians were informed that heaven was the dwelling of God, and hell that of the Devil. Some of these preachers had not indeed reached the dwelling of God, but professed to have approached near enough to hear the cocks in heaven crow, or to see the smoke of the chimneys in heaven, &c., &c.'[1]

Such unequivocal proofs that savage tribes can adopt and work into the midst of their native beliefs the European doctrine of the Good and Evil Spirit, must induce us to criticize keenly all recorded accounts of the religion of un-

[1] Loskiel, ' Gesch.. der Mission unter den Ind. in Nord-Amer.' part i. ch. 3.

cultured tribes, lest we should mistake the confused reflexion of Christendom for the indigenous theology of Australia or Canada. It is the more needful to bring this state of things into the clearest light, in order that the religion of the lower tribes may be placed in its proper relation to the religion of the higher nations. Genuine savage faiths do in fact bring to our view what seem to be rudimentary forms of ideas which underlie dualistic theological schemes among higher nations. It is certain that even among rude savage hordes, native thought has already turned toward the deep problem of good and evil. Their crude though earnest speculation has already tried to solve the great mystery which still resists the efforts of moralists and theologians. But as in general the animistic doctrine of the lower races is not yet an ethical institution, but a philosophy of man and nature, so savage dualism is not yet a theory of abstract moral principles, but a theory of pleasure or pain, profit or loss, affecting the individual man, his family, or at the utmost stretch, his people. This narrow and rudimentary distinction between good and evil was not unfairly stated by the savage who explained that if anybody took away his wife, that would be bad, but if he himself took someone's else, that would be good. Now by the savage or barbarian mind, the spiritual beings which by their personal action account for the events of life and the operations of nature, are apt to be regarded as kindly or hostile, sometimes or always, like the human beings on whose type they are so obviously modelled. In such a case, we may well judge by the safe analogy of disembodied human souls, and it appears that these are habitually regarded as sometimes friends and sometimes foes of the living. Nothing could be more conclusive in this respect than an account of the three days' battle between two factions of Zulu ghosts for the life of a man and wife whom the one spiritual party desired to destroy and the other to save ; the defending spirits prevailed, dug up the bewitched charm-bags which had been buried to cause sympathetic disease, and flung these objects into the midst of the assembly of the people watching in silence, just as the spirits now fling real flowers at a table-rapping séance.[1] For spirits less closely belonging to the definition of ghosts, may be taken Rochefort's remarks in the 17th century as to the two sorts of spirits, good and bad, recognized by the Caribs of the West Indies. This writer declares that their good spirits or divinities are in fact so many demons who seduce them and keep them enchained in their damnable servitude ; but nevertheless, he says, the people themselves do distinguish them from their evil spirits.[2] Nor can we pronounce this distinction of theirs unreasonable, learning from other authorities that it was the office of some of these spirits to attend men as familiar genii, and of others to inflict diseases. After the numerous details which have incidentally been cited in the present volumes, it will be needless to offer farther proof that spiritual beings are really conceived by savages and barbarians as ranged in antagonistic ranks as good and evil, i.e., friendly and hostile to themselves. The interesting enquiry on which it is here desirable to collect evidence, is this : how far are the doctrines of the higher nations anticipated in principle among the lower tribes, in the assignment of the conduct of the universe to two mighty hostile beings, in whom the contending powers of good and evil are personified, the Good Deity and the Evil Deity, each the head and ruler of a spiritual host like-minded ? The true answer seems to be that savage belief displays to us the primitive conceptions which, when developed in systematic form and attached to ethical meaning, take their place in religious systems of which the Zoroastrian is the type.

First, when in district after district two special deities with special native names are contrasted in native religion as the Good and Evil Deity, it is in some cases easier to explain these beings as native at least in origin, than to suppose that foreign intercourse should have exerted the

---

[1] Callaway, ' Rel. of Amazulu,' p. 348.
[2] Rochefort, ' Iles Antilles,' p. 416. See J. G. Müller, p. 207.

consistent and far-reaching influence needed to introduce them. Second, when the deities in question are actually polytheistic gods, such as Sun, Moon, Heaven, Earth, considered as of good or evil, i.e., favourable or unfavourable aspect, this looks like native development, not innovation derived from a foreign religion ignoring such divinities. Third, when it is held that the Good Deity is remote and otiose, but the Evil Deity present and active, and worship is therefore directed especially to the propitiation of the hostile principle, we have here a conception which appears native in the lower culture, rather than derived from the higher culture to which it is unfamiliar and even hateful. Now Dualism, as prevailing among the lower races, will be seen in a considerable degree to assert its originality by satisfying one or more of these conditions.

There have been recorded among the Indians of North America a group of mythic beliefs, which display the fundamental idea of dualism in the very act of germinating in savage religion. Yet the examination of these myths leads us first to destructive criticism of a picturesque but not ancient member of the series. An ethnologist, asked to point out the most striking savage dualistic legend of the world, would be likely to name the celebrated Iroquois myth of the Twin Brethren. The current version of this legend is that set down in 1825 by the Christian chief of the Tuscaroras, David Cusick, as the belief of his people. Among the ancients, he relates, there were two worlds, the lower world in darkness and possessed by monsters, the upper world inhabited by mankind. A woman near her travail sank from this upper region to the dark world below. She alighted on a Tortoise, prepared to receive her with a little earth on his back, which Tortoise became an island. The celestial mother bore twin sons into the dark world, and died. The tortoise increased to a great island, and the twins grew up. One was of gentle disposition, and was called Enigorio, the Good Mind, the other was of insolent character, and was named Enigonhahetgea, the Bad Mind.

The Good Mind, not contented to remain in darkness, wished to create a great light; the Bad Mind desired that the world should remain in its natural state. The Good Mind took his dead mother's head and made it the sun, and of a remnant of her body he made the moon. These were to give light to the day and to the night. Also he created many spots of light, now stars : these were to regulate the days, nights, seasons, years. Where the light came upon the dark world, the monsters were displeased, and hid themselves in the depths, lest man should find them. The Good Mind continued the creation, formed many creeks and rivers on the Great Island, created small and great beasts to inhabit the forests, and fishes to inhabit the waters. When he had made the universe, he doubted concerning beings to possess the Great Island. He formed two images of the dust of the ground in his own likeness, male and female, and by breathing into their nostrils gave them living souls, and named them Ea-gwe-howe, that is ' real people ; ' and he gave the Great Island all the animals of game for their maintenance ; he appointed thunder to water the earth by frequent rains ; the island became fruitful, and vegetation afforded to the animals subsistence. The Bad Mind went throughout the island and made high mountains and waterfalls and great steeps, and created reptiles injurious to mankind ; but the Good Mind restored the island to its former condition. The Bad Mind made two clay images in the form of man, but while he was giving them existence they became apes ; and so on. The Good Mind accomplished the works of creation, notwithstanding the imaginations of the Bad Mind were continually evil ; thus he attempted to enclose all the animals of game in the earth away from mankind, but his brother set them free, and traces of them were made on the rocks near the cave where they were shut in. At last the brethren came to single combat for the mastery of the universe. The Good Mind falsely persuaded the Bad Mind that whipping with flags would destroy his own life, but he himself used the

deer-horns, the instrument of death. After a two days'
fight, the Good Mind slew his brother and crushed him in
the earth ; and the last words of the Bad Mind were that
he would have equal power over men's souls after death,
then he sank down to eternal doom and became the Evil
Spirit. The Good Mind visited the people, and then retired
from the earth.[1]

This is a graphic tale. Its versions of the cosmic myth
of the World-Tortoise, and its apparent philosophical myth
of fossil footprints, have much mythological interest. But
its Biblical copying extends to the very phraseology, and
only partial genuineness can be allowed to its main theme.
Dr. Brinton has shown from early American writers how
much dualistic fancy has sprung up since the times of first
intercourse between natives and white men. When this
legend is compared with the earlier version given by Father
Brebeuf, missionary to the Hurons in 1636, we find its
whole complexion altered ; the moral dualism banishes ;
the names of Good and Bad Mind do not appear ; it is the
story of Ioskeha the White One, with his brother Tawiscara
the Dark One, and we at once perceive that Christian influence in the course of two centuries had given the tale a
meaning foreign to its real intent. Yet to go back to the
earliest sources and examine this myth of the White One
and the Dark One, proves it to be itself a perfect example of
the rise of primitive dualism in the savage mind. Father
Brebeuf's story is as follows : Ataentsic the Moon fell
from heaven on earth, and bore two sons, Taouiscaron and
Iouskeha, who being grown up quarrelled ; judge, he says,
if there be not in this a touch of the death of Abel. They
came to combat, but with very different weapons. Iouskeha
had a stag-horn, Taouiscaron contented himself with some
wild-rose berries, persuading himself that as soon as he
should thus smite his brother, he would fall dead at his

[1] Schoolcraft, ' Indian Tribes,' part v. p. 632; see part i. p. 316, part
vi. p. 166; ' Iroquois,' p. 36, see 237; Brinton, ' Myths of New World,'
p. 63.

feet ; but it fell out quite otherwise than he had promised himself, and Iouskeha struck him so heavy a blow in the side that the blood gushed forth in streams. The poor wretch fled, and from his blood which fell upon the land came the flints which the savages still call Taouiscara, from the victim's name. From this we see it to be true that the original myth of the two brothers, the White One and the Dark One, had no moral element. It seems mere nature-myth, the contest between Day and Night, for the Hurons knew that Iouskeha was the Sun, even as his mother or grandmother Aataentsic was the Moon. Yet in the contrast between these two, the Huron mind had already come to the rudimentary contrast of the Good and Evil Deity. Iouskeha the Sun, it is expressly said, seemed to the Indians their benefactor ; their kettle would not boil were it not for him ; it was he who learnt from the Tortoise the art of making fire ; without him they would have no luck in hunting ; it is he who makes the corn to grow. Iouskeha the Sun takes care for the living and all things concerning life, and therefore, says the missionary, they say he is good. But Aataentsic the Moon, the creatress of earth and man, makes men die and has charge of their departed souls, and they say she is evil. The Sun and Moon dwell together in their cabin at the end of the earth, and thither it was that the Indians made the mythic journey of which various episodes have been more than once cited here ; true to their respective characters, the Sun receives the travellers kindly and saves them from the harm the beauteous but hurtful Moon would have done them. Another missionary of still earlier time identifies Iouskeha with the supreme deity Atahocan : ' Iouskeha,' he says, ' is good and gives growth and fair weather ; his grandmother Eatahentsic is wicked and spoils.'[1] Thus in early Iroquois legend, the Sun and Moon, as god and god-

[1] Brebeuf in ' Rel. des Jésuites dans la Nouvelle France,' 1635, p. 34, 1636, p. 100. Sagard, ' Histoire du Canada,' Paris, 1636, p. 490. L. H. Morgan, ' Iroquois,' p. 156. See ante, vol. i. pp. 288, 349.

dess of Day and Night, had already acquired the characters of the great friend and enemy of man, the Good and Evil Deity. And as to the related cosmic legend of Day and Night, contrasted in the persons of the two brothers, the White One and the Dark One, though this was originally pure unethic nature-myth, yet it naturally took the same direction among the half-Europeanized Indians of later times, becoming a moral myth of Good and Evil. The idea comes to full maturity in the modern shaping of Iroquois religion, where the good and great deity Häwenneyu the Ruler has opposed to him a rival deity keeping the same name as in the myth, Hänegoategeh the Evil-minded. We have thus before us the profoundly interesting fact, that the rude North American Indians have more than once begun the same mythologic transition which in ancient Asia shaped the contrast of light and darkness into the contrast of righteousness and wickedness, by following out the same thought which still in the European mind arrays in the hostile forms of Light and Darkness the contending powers of Good and Evil.

Judging by such evidence, at once of the rudimentary dualism springing up in savage animism, and of the tendency of this to amalgamate with similar thought brought in by foreign intercourse, it is possible to account for many systems of the dualistic class found in the native religions of America. While the evidence may lead us to agree with Waitz that the North American Indian dualism, the most distinct and universal feature of their religion, is not to be altogether referred to a modern Christian origin, yet care must be taken not to claim as the result of primitive religious development what shows signs of being borrowed civilized theology. The records remain of the Jesuit missionary teaching under which the Algonquins came to use their native term Manitu, that is, spirit or demon, in speaking of the Christian God and Devil as the good and the evil Manitu. Still later, the Great Spirit and the Evil Spirit, Kitchi Manitu and Matchi Manitu, gained a wider place in the beliefs of North American tribes, who combined these adopted Christian conceptions with older native beliefs in powers of light and warmth and life and protection, of darkness and cold and death and destruction. Thus the two great antagonistic Beings became chiefs of the kindly and harmful spirits pervading the world and struggling for the mastery over it. Here the nature-religion of the savage was expanded and developed rather than set on foot by the foreigner. Among other American races, such combinations of foreign and native religious ideas are easy to find, though hard to analyse. In the extreme north-west, we may doubt any native origin in the semi-Christianized Kodiak's definition of Shljem Shoá the creator of heaven and earth, to whom offerings were made before and after the hunt, as contrasted with Ijak the bad spirit dwelling in the earth. In the extreme south-east may be found more originality among the Floridan Indians two or three centuries ago, for they are said to have paid solemn worship to the Bad Spirit Toia who plagued them with visions, but to have had small regard for the Good Spirit, who troubles himself little about mankind.[1] On the southern continent, Martius makes this characteristic remark as to the rude tribes of Brazil : ' All Indians have a lively conviction of the power of an evil principle over them ; in many there dawns also a glimpse of the good ; but they revere the one less than they fear the other. It might be thought that they hold the Good Being weaker in relation to the fate of man than the evil.' This generalization is to some extent supported by statements as to particular tribes. The Macusis are said to recognize the good creator Macunaima, ' he who works by night,' and his evil adversary Epel or Horiuch : of these people is is observed that 'All the powers of nature are products of the Good Spirit, when they do

[1] Waitz, ' Anthropologie,' vol. iii. pp. 182, 330, 335, 345 ; Le Jeune in ' Rel. des Jés.' 1637, p. 49 ; La Potherie, ' Hist. de l'Amér. Septentrionale,' Paris, 1722, vol. i. p. 121 ; J. G. Müller, p. 149, &c. Schoolcraft, ' Indian Tribes,' part i. p. 35, &c., 320, 412 ; Catlin, vol. i. p. 156 ; Cranz, ' Grönland,' p. 263.

not disturb the Indian's rest and comfort, but the work of evil spirits when they do.' Uauüloa and Locozy, the good and evil deity of the Yumanas, live above the earth and toward the sun ; the Evil Deity is feared by these savages, but the Good Deity will come to eat fruit with the departed and take their souls to his dwelling, wherefore they bury the dead each doubled up in his great earthen pot, with fruit in his lap, and looking toward the sunrise. Even the rude Botocudos are thought to recognize antagonistic principles of good and evil in the persons of the Sun and Moon.[1] This idea has especial interest from its correspondence on the one hand with that of the Iroquois tribes, and on the other with that of the comparatively civilized Muyscas of Bogota, whose good deity is unequivocally a mythic Sun, thwarted in his kindly labours for man by his wicked wife Huythaca the Moon.[2] The native religion of Chili is said to have placed among the subaltern deities Meulen, the friend of man, and Huecuvu the bad spirit and author of evil. These people can hardly have learnt from Christianity to conceive their evil spirit as simply and fully the general cause of misfortune : if the earth quakes, Huecuvu has given it a shock ; if a horse tires, Huecuvu has ridden him ; if a man falls sick, Huecuvu has sent the disease into his body, and no man dies but that Huecuvu suffocates him.[3]

In Africa, again, allowing for Moslem influence, dualism is not ill represented in native religion. An old account from Loango describes the natives as theoretically recognizing Zambi the supreme deity, creator of good and lover of justice, and over against him Zambi-anbi the destroyer, the counsellor of crime, the author of loss and accident, of disease and death. But when it comes to actual worship, as

---

[1] Martius, ' Ethnog. Amer.' vol. i. pp. 327, 485, 583, 645, see 247, 393, 427, 696. See also J. G. Müller, ' Amer. Urrelig.' pp. 259, &c., 403, 423 ; D'Orbigny, ' L'Homme Américain,' vol. i. p. 405, vol. ii. p. 257 ; Falkner, ' Patagonia,' p. 114 ; Musters, ' Patagonians,' p. 179 ; Fitzroy, ' Voy. of Adventure and Beagle,' vol. i. pp. 180, 190.

[2] Piedrahita, ' Hist. de Neuv. Granada,' part i. book i. ch. 3.

[3] Molina, ' Hist. of Chili,' vol. ii. p. 84 ; Febres, ' Diccionario Chileño,' s.v.

the good god will always be favourable, it is the god of evil
who must be appeased, and it is for his satisfaction that men
abstain some from one kind of food and some from another.[1]
Among accounts of the two rival deities in West Africa, one
describes the Guinea negroes as recognizing below the Supreme Deity two spirits (or classes of spirits), Ombwiri and
Onyambe, the one kind and gentle, doing good to men and
rescuing them from harm, the other hateful and wicked,
whose seldom mentioned name is heard with uneasiness and
displeasure.[2] It would be scarcely profitable, in an enquiry
where accurate knowledge of the doctrine of any insignificant tribe is more to the purpose than vague speculation on
the theology of the mightiest nation, to dwell on the enigmatic traces of ancient Egyptian dualism. Suffice it to say
that the two brother-deities Osiris and Seti, Osiris the beneficent solar divinity whose nature the blessed dead took on
them, Seti perhaps a rival national god degraded to a Typhon,
seem to have become the representative figures of a contrasted scheme of light and darkness, good and evil; the sculp-
tured granite still commemorates the contests of their long-
departed sects, where the hieroglyphic square-eared beast of
Seti has been defaced to substitute for it the figure of Osiris.[3]

The conception of the light-god as the good deity in contrast to a rival god of evil, is one plainly suggested by
nature, and naturally recurring in the religions of the world.
The Khonds of Orissa may be counted its most perfect
modern exponents in barbaric culture. To their supreme
creative deity, Būra Pennu or Bella Pennu, Light-god or
Sun-god, there stands opposed his evil consort Tari Pennu
the Earth-goddess, and the history of good and evil in the
world is the history of his work and her counterwork. He
created a world paradisaic, happy, harmless ; she rebelled
against him, and to blast the lot of his new creature, man,

[1] Proyart, 'Loango,' in Pinkerton, vol. xvi. p. 504. Bastian, 'Mensch,'
vol. ii. p. 109. See Kolbe, ' Kaap de Goede Hoop,' part i. xxix. : Waitz,
vol. ii. p. 342 (Hottentots).
[2] J. L. Wilson, ' W. Afr.' pp. 217, 387. Waitz, vol. ii. p. 173.
[3] Birch, in Bunsen, vol. v. p. 136. Wilkinson, ' Ancient Eg.' &c.

she brought in disease, and poison, and all disorder, ' sowing the seeds of sin in mankind as in a ploughed field.' Death became the divine punishment of wickedness, the spontaneously fertile earth went to jungle and rock and mud, plants and animals grew poisonous and fierce, throughout nature good and evil were commingled, and still the fight goes on between the two great powers. So far all Khonds agree, and it is on the practical relation of good and evil that they split into their two hostile sects of Būra and Tari. Būra's sect hold that he triumphed over Tari, in sign of her discomfiture imposed the cares of childbirth on her sex, and makes her still his subject instrument wherewith to punish ; Tari's sect hold that she still maintains the struggle, and even practically disposes of the happiness of man, doing evil or good on her own account, and allowing or not allowing the Creator's blessings to reach mankind.[1]

Now that the sacred books of the Zend-Avesta are open to us, it is possible to compare the doctrines of savage tribes with those of the great faith through which of all others Dualism seems to have impressed itself on the higher nations. The religion of Zarathustra was a schism from that ancient Aryan nature-worship which is represented in a pure and early form in the Veda, and in depravity and decay in modern Hinduism. The leading thought of the Zarathustrian faith was the contest of Good and Evil in the world, a contrast typified and involved in that of Day and Night, Light and Darkness, and brought to personal shape in the warfare of Ahura-Mazda and Anra-Mainyu, the Good and Evil Deity, Ormuzd and Ahriman. The prophet Zarathustra said : ' In the beginning there was a pair of twins, two spirits, each of a peculiar activity. These are the good and the base in thought, word, and deed. Choose one of these two spirits. Be good, not base ! ' The sacred Vendidad begins with the record of the primæval contest of the two principles. Ahura-Mazda created the best of regions

[1] Macpherson, ' India,' p. 84.

and lands, the Aryan home, Sogdia, Bactria, and the rest ;
Anra-Mainyu against his work created snow and pestilence,
buzzing insects and poisonous plants, poverty and sickness,
sin and unbelief. The modern Parsi, in passages of his
formularies of confession, still keeps alive the old antagonism.
I repent, he says, of all kind of sins which the evil Ahriman
produced amongst the creatures of Ormazd in opposition.
' That which was the wish of Ormazd the Creator, and I
ought to have thought and have not thought, what I ought
to have spoken and have not spoken, what I ought to have
done and have not done ; of these sins repent I with
thoughts, words, and works, corporeal as well as spiritual,
earthly as well as heavenly, with the three words : Pardon,
O Lord, I repent of sin. That which was the wish of
Ahriman, and I ought not to have thought and yet have
thought, what I ought not to have spoken and yet have
spoken, what I ought not to have done and yet have done ;
of these sins repent I with thoughts, words, and works,
corporeal as well as spiritual, earthly as well as heavenly,
with the three words : Pardon, O Lord, I repent of sin.'
. . . ' May Ahriman be broken, may Ormazd increase.'[1]
The Izedis or Yezidis, the so-called Devil-worshippers, still
remain a numerous though oppressed people in Mesopotamia
and adjacent countries. Their adoration of the sun and
horror of defiling fire accord with the idea of a Persian
origin of their religion (Persian ized = god), an origin underlying more superficial admixture of Christian and Moslem
elements. This remarkable sect is distinguished by a
special form of dualism. While recognizing the existence
of a Supreme Being, their peculiar reverence is given to
Satan, chief of the angelic host, who now has the means of
doing evil to mankind, and in his restoration will have the
power of rewarding them. ' Will not Satan then reward
the poor Izedis, who alone have never spoken ill of him, and
have suffered so much for him ? ' Martyrdom for the rights

[1] Avesta, tr. by Spiegel. Vendidad, i. ; ' Khorda-Avesta.' xlv. xlvi,
Max Müller, ' Lectures,' 1st Ser. p. 208.

of Satan ! exclaims the German traveller to whom an old
white-bearded devil-worshipper thus set forth the hopes of
his religion.[1]

Direct worship of the Evil Principle, familiar as it is to
low barbaric races, is scarcely to be found among people
higher in civilization than these persecuted and stubborn
sectaries of Western Asia. So far as such ideas extend in
the development of religion, they seem fair evidence how
far worship among low tribes turns rather on fear than love.
That the adoration of a Good Deity should have more and
more superseded the propitiation of an Evil Deity, is the
sign of one of the great movements in the education of
mankind, a result of happier experience of life, and of
larger and more gladsome views of the system of the
universe. It is not, however, through the inactive systems
of modern Parsism and Izedism that the mighty Zoroastrian
dualism has exerted its main influence on mankind. We
must look back to long-past ages for traces of its contact
with Judaism and Christianity. It is often and reasonably
thought that intercourse between Jews and ancient Persians
was an effective agent in producing that theologic change
which differences the later Jew of the Rabbinical books from
the earlier Jew of the Pentateuch, a change in which one important part is the greater prominence of the dualistic scheme.
So in later times (about the fourth century), the contact of
Zoroastrism and Christianity appears to have been influential
in producing Manichæism. Manichæism is known mostly on
the testimony of its adversaries, but thus much seems clear,
that it is based on the very doctrine of the two antagonistic
principles of good and evil, of spirit and matter. It sets on
the one hand God, original good and source of good alone,
primal light and lord of the kingdom of light, and on the
other hand the Prince of Darkness, with his kingdom of
darkness, of matter, of confusion, and destruction. The
theory of ceaseless conflict between these contending

[1] Layard, ' Nineveh,' vol. i. p. 297 ; Ainsworth, ' Izedis,' in ' Tr. Eth. Soc.'
vol. i. p. 11.

powers becomes a key to the physical and moral nature and course of the universe.[1] Among Christian or semi-Christian sects, the Manichæans stand as representatives of dualism pushed to its utmost development. It need scarcely be said, however, that Christian dualism is not bounded by the limits of this or that special sect. In so far as the Evil Being, with his subordinate powers of darkness, is held to exist and act in any degree in independence of the Supreme Deity and his ministering spirits of light, so far theological schools admit, though in widely different grades of importance, a philosophy of nature and of life which has its basis rather in dualism than in monotheism.

We now turn to the last objects of our present survey, those theological beliefs of the lower tribes of mankind which point more or less distinctly toward a doctrine of Monotheism. Here it is by no means proposed to examine savage ideas from the point of view of doctrinal theology, an undertaking which would demand arguments quite beyond the present range. Their treatment is limited to classifying the actual beliefs of the lower races, with some ethnographic considerations as to their origin and their relation to higher religions. For this purpose it is desirable to distinguish the prevalent doctrines of the uncultured world from absolute monotheism. At the outset, care is needed to exclude an ambiguity of which the importance often goes unnoticed. How are the mighty but subordinate divinities, recognized in different religions, to be classed ? Beings who in Christian or Moslem theology would be called angels, saints, demons, would under the same definitions be called deities in polytheistic systems. This is obvious, but we may realize it more distinctly from its actually having happened. The Chuwashes, a race of Tatar affinity, are stated to reverence a god of Death, who takes to himself the souls of the departed, and whom they call Esrel ; it is curious that Castrén, in mentioning

[1] Beausobre, 'Hist. de Manichée,' &c. Neander, 'Hist. of Christian Religion,' vol. ii. p. 157, &c.

this, should fail to point out that this deity is no other than Azrael the angel of death, adopted under Moslem influence.[1] Again, in the mixed Pagan and Christian religion of the Circassians, which at least in its recently prevalent form would be reckoned polytheistic, there stand beneath the Supreme Being a number of mighty subordinate deities, of whom the principal are Iele the Thunder-god, Tleps the Fire-god, Seoseres the god of Wind and Water, Misitcha the Forest-god, and Mariam the Virgin Mary.[2] If the monotheistic criterion be simply made to consist in the Supreme Deity being held as creator of the universe and chief of the spiritual hierarchy, then its application to savage and barbaric theology will lead to perplexing consequences. Races of North and South America, of Africa, of Polynesia, recognizing a number of great deities, are usually and reasonably considered polytheists, yet under this definition their acknowledgment of a Supreme Creator, of which various cases will here be shown, would entitle them at the same time to the name of monotheists. To mark off the doctrines of monotheism, closer definition is required, assigning the distinctive attributes of deity to none save the Almighty Creator. It may be declared that, in this strict sense, no savage tribe of monotheists has been ever known. Nor are any fair representatives of the lower culture in a strict sense pantheists. The doctrine which they do widely hold, and which opens to them a course tending in one or other of these directions, is polytheism culminating in the rule of one supreme divinity. High above the doctrine of souls, of divine manes, of local nature-spirits, of the great deities of class and element, there are to be discerned in barbaric theology shadowings, quaint or majestic, of the conception of a Supreme Deity, henceforth to be traced onward in expanding power and brightening glory along the history of religion. It is no unimportant task, partial as it is, to select and group the typical data

---

[1] Castrén, ' Finn. Myth.' p. 155.
[2] Klemm, ' Cultur-Gesch.' vol. vi. p. 85.

which show the nature and position of the doctrine of supremacy, as it comes into view within the lower culture.

On the threshold of the investigation, there meets us the same critical difficulty which obstructs the study of primitive dualism. Among low tribes who have been in contact with Christianity or Mohammedanism, how are we to tell to what extent, under this foreign influence, dim, uncouth ideas of divine supremacy may have been developed into more cultured forms, or wholly foreign ideas implanted ? We know how the Jesuit missionaries led the native Canadians to the conception of the Great Manitu ; how they took up the native Brazilian name of the divine Thunder, Tupan, and adapted its meaning to convey in Christian teaching the idea of God. Thus, again, we find most distinctly-marked African ideas of a Supreme Deity in the West, where intercourse with Moslems has actually Islamized or semi-Islamized whole negro nations, and the name of Allah is in all men's mouths. The ethnographer must be ever on the look-out for traces of such foreign influence in the definition of the Supreme Deity acknowledged by any uncultured race, a divinity whose nature and even whose name may betray his adoption from abroad. Thus the supreme Iroquois deity, Neo or Hawaneu, the pre-existent creator, has been triumphantly adduced to show the monotheism underlying the native creeds of America. But it seems that this divinity was introduced by the French Catholic missionaries, and that Niio is an altered form of Dieu.[1] Among the list of supreme deities of the lower races who are also held to be first ancestors of man, we hear of Louquo, the uncreate first Carib, who descended from the eternal heaven, made the flat earth, and produced man from his own body. He lived long on earth among men, died and came to life again after three days, and returned to heaven.[2] It would be hardly reasonable

[1] ' Études Philologiques sur quelques Langues Sauvages de l'Amérique,' par N. O. (J. A. Cuoq.) Montreal, 1866, p. 14. Brinton, 'Myths of New World,' p. 53. Schoolcraft, 'Iroquois,' p. 33.

[2] De la Borde, 'Caraibes,' p. 524. J. G. Müller, 'Amer. Urrel.' p. 228.

to enumerate, among genuine deities of native West Indian
religion, a being with characteristics thus on the face of
them adopted from the religion of the white men. Yet
even in such extreme cases, it does not necessarily follow
that the definitions of these deities, vitiated as they are for
ethnographical use by foreign influence, have not to some extent a native substratum. In criticising details, moreover, it
must not be forgotten how largely the similarities in the religions of different races may be of independent origin, and
how closely allied are many ideas in the rude native theologies of savages to ideas holding an immemorial place in the
religions of their civilized invaders. For the present purpose, however, it is well to dwell especially on such evidence
as by characteristic traits or early date is farthest removed
from suspicion of being borrowed from a foreign source.

In surveying the peoples of the world, the ethnographer
finds many who are not shown to have any definite conception of a supreme deity ; and even where such a conception
is placed on record, it is sometimes so vaguely asserted, or
on such questionable authority, that he can but take note
of it and pass on. In numerous cases, however, illustrated
by the following collection from different regions, certain
leading ideas, singly or blended, may be traced. There
are many savage and barbaric religions which solve their
highest problem by the simple process of raising to divine
primacy one of the gods of polytheism itself. Even the
system of the manes-worshipper has been stretched to reach
the limit of supreme deity, in the person of the primæval
ancestor. More frequently, it is the nature-worshipper's
principle which has prevailed, giving to one of the great
nature-deities the precedence of the rest. Here, by no recondite speculation, but by the plain teaching of nature,
the choice has for the most part lain between two mighty
visible divinities, the all-animating Sun and the all-encompassing Heaven. In the study of such schemes, we are on
intellectual terra firma. There is among the religions of
the lower races another notable group of systems, seemingly

in close connexion with the first. These display to us a heavenly pantheon arranged on the model of an earthly political constitution, where the commonalty are crowds of human souls and other tribes of world-pervading spirits, the aristocracy are great polytheistic gods, and the King is the supreme Deity. To this comparatively intelligible side of the subject, a more perplexed and obscure side stands contrasted. Among thoughtful men whose theory of the soul animating the body has already led them to suppose a divine spirit animating the huge mass of earth or sky, this idea needs but a last expansion to become a doctrine of the universe as animated by one greatest, all-pervading divinity, the World-Spirit. Moreover, where speculative philosophy grapples with the vast fundamental world-problem, the solution is attained by ascending from the Many to the One, by striving to discern through and beyond the Universe a First Cause. Let the basis of such reasoning be laid in theological ground, then the First Cause is realized as the Supreme Deity. In such ways, the result of carrying to their utmost limits the animistic conceptions which among low races and high pervade the philosophy of religion, is to reach an idea of as it were a soul of the world, a shaper, animator, ruler of the universe. Entering these regions of transcendental theology, we are not to wonder that the comparative distinctness belonging to conceptions of lower spiritual beings here fades away. Human souls, subordinate nature-spirits, and huge polytheistic nature-gods, carry with the defined special functions they perform some defined character and figure, but beyond such limits form and function blend into the infinite and universal in the thought of supreme divinity. To realize this widest idea, two especial ways are open. The first way is to fuse the attributes of the great polytheistic powers into more or less of common personality, thus conceiving that, after all, it is the same Highest Being who holds up the heavens, shines in the sun, smites his foes in the thunder, stands first in the human pedigree as the divine ancestor. The second way is to remove the limit of theologic speculation into the region of the indefinite and the inane. An unshaped divine entity looming vast, shadowy, and calm beyond and over the material world, too benevolent or too exalted to need human worship, too huge, too remote, too indifferent, too supine, too merely existent, to concern himself with the petty race of men,—this is a mystic form of formlessness in which religion has not seldom pictured the Supreme.

Thus, then, it appears that the theology of the lower races already reaches its climax in conceptions of a highest of the gods, and that these conceptions in the savage and barbaric world are no copies stamped from one common type, but outlines widely varying among mankind. The degeneration-theory, in some instances no doubt with justice, may claim such beliefs as mutilated and perverted remnants of higher religions. Yet for the most part, the development-theory is competent to account for them without seeking their origin in grades of culture higher than those in which they are found existing. Looked upon as products of natural religion, such doctrines of divine supremacy seem in no way to transcend the powers of the low-cultured mind to reason out, nor of the low-cultured imagination to deck with mythic fancy. There have existed in times past, and do still exist, savage or barbaric peoples who hold such views of a highest god as they may have attained to of themselves, without the aid of more cultured nations. Among these races, Animism has its distinct and consistent outcome, and Polytheism its distinct and consistent completion, in the doctrine of a Supreme Deity.

The native religions of South America and the West Indies display a well-marked series of types. The primacy of the Sun was long ago well stated by the Moluches when a Jesuit missionary preached to them, and they replied, ' Till this hour, we never knew nor acknowledged anything greater or better than the Sun.'[1] So when a later mis-

[1] Dobrizhoffer, ' Abipones,' vol. ii. p. 89.

sionary argued with the chief of the Tobas, ' My god is good and punishes wicked people,' the chief replied, ' My God (the Sun) is good likewise ; but he punishes nobody, satisfied to do good to all.'[1] In various manifestations, moreover, there reigns among barbarians a supreme being whose characteristics are those of the Heaven-god. It is thus with the Tamoi of the Guaranis, ' that beneficent deity worshipped in his blended character of ancestor of mankind and ancient of heaven, lord of the celestial paradise.'[2] It is so with the highest deity of the Arauca-nians, Pillan the Thunder or the Thunderer, called also Huenu-Pillan or Heaven-Thunder, and Vuta-gen or Great Being. ' The universal government of Pillan,' says Molina, ' is a prototype of the Araucanian polity. He is the great Toqui (Governor) of the invisible world, and as such has his Apo-Ulmenes, and his Ulmenes, to whom he entrusts the administration of affairs of less importance. These ideas are certainly very rude, but it must be acknow-ledged that the Araucanians are not the only people who have regulated the things of heaven by those of the earth.'[3] A different but not less characteristic type of the Supreme Deity is placed on record among the Caribs, a beneficent power dwelling in the skies, reposing in his own happi-ness, careless of mankind, and by them not honoured nor adored.[4]

The theological history of Peru, in ages before the Spanish conquest, has lately had new light thrown on it by the researches of Mr. Markham. Here the student comes into view of a rivalry full of interest in the history of barbaric religion, the rivalry between the Creator and the divine Sun. In the religion of the Incas, precedence was given to Uiracocha, called Pachacamac, ' Creator of the World.' The Sun (with whom was coupled his sister-

[1] Hutchinson, ' Chaco Ind.' in ' Tr. Eth. Soc.' vol. iii. p. 327.

[2] D'Orbigny, ' L'Homme Américain,' vol. ii. p. 319.

[3] Molina, ' Hist. of Chili,' vol. ii. p. 84, &c. Compare Febres, ' Diccionario Chileño.'

[4] Rochefort, ' Iles Antilles,' p. 415. Musters, ' Patagonians,' p. 179.

wife the Moon) was the divine ancestor, the dawn or origin, the totem or lar, of the Inca family. The three great deities were the Creator, Sun, and Thunder ; their images were brought out together at great festivals into the square of Cuzco, llamas were sacrificed to all three, and they could be addressed in prayer together, ' O Creator, and Sun, and Thunder, be for ever young, multiply the people, and let them always be at peace.' Yet the Thunder and Lightning was held to come by the command of the Creator, and the following prayer shows clearly that even ' our father the Sun ' was but his creature :—

'Uiracocha ! Thou who gavest being to the Sun, and afterwards said let there be day and night. Raise it and cause it to shine, and preserve that which thou hast created, that it may give light to men. Grant this, Uiracocha !
' Sun ! Thou who art in peace and safety, shine upon us, keep us from sickness, and keep us in health and safety.'

Among the transitions of religion, however, it is not strange that a subordinate God, by virtue of his nearer intercourse and power, should usurp the place of the supreme deity. Among the various traces of this taking place under the Incas, are traditions of the great temple at Cuzco called ' The Golden Place,' where Manco Ccapac originally set up a flat oval golden plate to signify the Creator; Mayta Ccapac, it is said, renewed the Creator's symbol, but Huascar Inca took it down, and set up in its stead in the place of honour a round golden plate like the sun with rays. The famous temple itself, Ccuricancha the ' Golden Place,' was known to the Spaniards as the Temple of the Sun ; no wonder that the idea has come to be so generally accepted, that the Sun was the chief god of Peru. There is even on record a memorable protest made by one Inca, who dared to deny that the Sun could be the maker of all things, comparing him to a tethered beast that must make ever the same daily round, and to an arrow that must go whither it is sent, not whither it will. But what availed philosophic protest, even from the head of church and state himself, against a state church of which the world has seldom seen the equal for stiff and solid organization ? The Sun reigned in Peru till Pizarro overthrew him, and his splendid golden likeness came down from the temple wall to be the booty of a Castilian soldier, who lost it in one night at play.[1]

Among rude tribes of the North American continent, evidence of the primacy of the divine Sun is not unknown. Father Hennepin's account of the Sioux worshipping the Sun as the Creator is explicit enough, and agrees with the argument of the modern Shawnees, that the Sun animates everything, and therefore must be the Master of Life or Great Spirit.[2] It is the widespread belief in this Great Spirit which has long and deservedly drawn the attention of European thinkers to the native religions of the North American tribes. The name of the Great Spirit originates with the equivalent term Kitchi Manitu in the language of the Algonquin Indians. Before the European intercourse in the 17th century, these tribes had indeed no deity so called, but as has been already pointed out, the term came first into use by the application of the native word manitu, meaning demon or deity, to the Christian God. During the following centuries, the name of the Great Spirit, with the ideas belonging to the name, travelled far and wide over the continent. It became the ordinary expression of Europeans in their descriptions of Indian religion, and in discourse carried on in English words between Europeans and Indians, and was more or less naturalized among the Indians themselves. On their religions it had on the one

---

[1] 'Narratives of the Rites and Laws of the Yncas,' trans. from the original Spanish MSS., and ed. by C. R. Markham, Hakluyt Soc. 1873, p. ix. 5, 16, 30, 76, 84, 154, &c. The above remarks are based on the early evidence here printed for the first time, and on private suggestions for which I am also indebted to Mr. Markham. The title Pachacamac has been also considered to mean Animator or Soul of the World, camani = I create, camac = creator, cama = soul (note to 2nd ed.). Garcilaso de la Vega, lib. i., ii. c. 2, iii. c. 20 ; Herrera, dec. v. 4 ; Brinton, 'Myths of New World,' p. 177, see 142 ; Rivero and Tschudi, 'Peruvian Antiquities,' ch. vii. ; Waitz, vol. iv. p. 447 ; J. G. Müller, p. 317, &c.

[2] Sagard, 'Hist. du Canada,' p. 490. Hennepin, 'Voy. dans l'Amérique,' p. 302. Gregg, 'Commerce of Prairies,' vol. ii. p. 237.

hand a transforming influence, while on the other hand, as is usual in the combination of religions, the new divinity incorporated into himself the characteristics of native divinities, so that native ideas remained in part represented in him. A divine being whose characteristics are often so unlike what European intercourse would have suggested, could be hardly altogether of foreign origin.[1] Again, among the Greenlanders, Torngarsuk or Great Spirit (his name is an augmentative of 'torngak'—'demon') was known to the early Danish missionary Egede as the oracular deity of the angekoks, to whose under-world souls hope to descend at death. He so far held the place of supreme deity in the native mind, that, as Cranz the missionary relates somewhat afterwards, many Greenlanders hearing of God and his almighty power were apt to fall on the idea that it was their Torngarsuk who was meant ; but he was eventually identified with the Devil.[2] In like manner, Algonquin Indians, early in the 17th century, hearing of the white man's Deity, identified him with one known to their own native belief, Atahocan the Creator. When Le Jeune the missionary talked to them of an almighty creator of heaven and earth, they began to say to one another, ' Atahocan, Atahocan, it is Atahocan ! ' The traditional idea of such a being seems indeed to have lain in utter mythic vagueness in their thoughts, for they had made his name into a verb, ' Nitatahocan,' meaning, ' I tell a fable, an old fanciful story.'[3]

In late times, Schoolcraft represents the Great Spirit as a Soul of the Universe, inhabiting and animating all things, recognized in rocks and trees, in cataracts and clouds, in thunder and lightning, in tempest and zephyr, becoming incarnate in birds and beasts as titular deities, existing in the world under every possible form, animate and inani-

---

[1] Le Jeune, ' Rel. des Jés.' 1637, p. 49 ; Brinton, p. 52 ; Lafitau, ' Mœurs des Sauvages Amériquains,' vol. i. pp. 126, 145 (note to 3rd ed.).

[2] Egede, ' Descr. of Greenland,' ch. xviii. ; Cranz, ' Grönland,' p. 263 ; Rink, ' Eskimoiske Eventyr,' &c., p. 28.

[3] Le Jeune, 1633, p. 16 ; 1634, p. 13.

mate.[1] Whether the Red Indian mind even in modern times really entertained this extreme pantheistic scheme, we may well doubt. In early times of American discovery, the records show a quite different and more usual conception of a supreme deity. Among the more noteworthy of these older documents are the following. Jacques Cartier, in his second Canadian voyage (1535), speaks of the people having no valid belief in God, for they believe in one whom they call Cudouagni, and say that he often speaks with them, and tells them what the weather will be ; they say that when he is angry with them he casts earth in their eyes. Thevet's statement somewhat later is as follows : ' As to their religion, they have no worship or prayer to God, except that they contemplate the new moon, called in their language Osannaha, saying that Andouagni calls it thus, sending it little by little to advance or retard the waters. For the rest, they fully believe that there is a Creator, greater than the Sun, the Moon, and the Stars, and who holds all in his power. He it is whom they call Andouagni, without however having any form or method of prayer to him.[2] In Virginia about 1586, we learn from Heriot that the natives believed in many gods, which they call ' mantoac,' but of different sorts and degrees, also that there is one chief god who first made other principal gods, and afterwards the sun, moon, and stars as petty gods. In New England, in 1622, Winslow says that they believe, as do the Virginians, in many divine powers, yet of one above all the rest ; the Massachusetts call their great god Kiehtan, who made all the other gods ; he dwells far westerly above the heavens, whither all good men go when they die ; ' They never saw *Kiehtan*, but they hold it a great charge and dutie, that one age teach another ; and to him they make feasts, and cry and sing for plentie and victorie, or anything is good.' Another famous native

---

[1] Schoolcraft, ' Indian Tribes,' part i. p. 15.

[2] Cartier, ' Relation ; ' Hakluyt, vol. iii. p. 212 ; Lescarbot, ' Nouvelle France,' p. 613. Thevet, 'Singularitez de la France Antarctique,' Paris, 1558, ch. 77. See also J. G. Müller, p. 102. Andouagni is perhaps a miscopied form of Cudouagni. Other forms, Cudruagni, &c., occur.

American name for the supreme deity is Oki. Captain John Smith, the hero of the colonization of Virginia in 1607, he who was befriended by Pocahontas, ' La Belle Sauvage,' thus describes the religion of the country, and especially of her tribe, the Powhatans : ' There is yet in Virginia no place discovered to be so Savage in which they haue not a Religion, Deer, and Bow and Arrowes. All things that are able to doe them hurt beyond their prevention, they adore with their kinde of divine worship ; as the fire, water, lightning, thunder, our Ordnance peeces, horses, &c. But their chiefe god they worship is the Devill. Him they call *Okee*, and serue him more of feare than loue. They say they haue conference with him, and fashion themselves as neare to his shape as they can imagine. In their Temples they haue his image evill favouredly carved, and then painted and adorned with chaines of copper, and beads, and covered with a skin in such manner as the deformities may well suit with such a God.'[1] This quaint account deserves to be quoted at length as an example of the judgment which a half-educated and whole-prejudiced European is apt to pass on savage deities, which from his point of view seem of simply diabolic nature. It is known from other sources that Oki, a word belonging not to the Powhatan but to the Huron language, was in fact a general name for spirit or deity. We may judge the real belief of these Indians better from Father Brebeuf's description of the Heaven God, cited here in a former chapter : they imagine in the heavens an Oki, that is, a Demon or power ruling the seasons of the year, and controlling the winds and waves, a being whose anger they fear, and whom they call on in making solemn treaties.[2]

[1] Smith, ' Hist. of Virginia,' London, 1632, in Pinkerton, ' Voyages,' vol. xiii. pp. 13, 18, 244 (New Eng.) ; see Arber's edition. Priority has been claimed for E. Strachey (see Lang, ' Making of Religion,' p. 254), but this copyist seems only to have copied Capt. Smith's ' Map of Virginia ' (1608). Brinton, p. 58 ; Waitz, vol. iii. p. 177, &c. J. G. Müller, pp. 99, &c. ; Loskiel, part i. pp. 33, 43.

[2] Brebeuf in ' Rel. des Jés.' 1636, p. 107 ; see above, p. 255. Sagard, p. 494 ; Cuoq, p. 176 ; J. G. Müller, p. 103. For other mention of a Supreme Deity among North American tribes see Joutel, ' Journal du Voyage,' &c., aris, 1713, p. 224 (Louisiana) ; Sproat in ' Tr. Eth. Soc.' vol. v. p. 253 (Vancouver's I.).

About a century later, Father Lafitau wrote passages which illustrate well the transformation of native animistic conceptions under missionary influence into analogues of Christian theology. Such general terms for spiritual beings as 'oki' or 'manitu' had become to him individual names of one supreme being. ' This great Spirit, known among the Caribs under the name of *Chemiin*, under that of *Manitou* among the Algonquin nations, and under that of *Okki* among those who speak the Huron tongue . . .' &c. All American tribes, he says, use expressions which can only denote God : they call him the great Spirit, sometimes the Master and Author of Life . . .' &c.[1] The longer rude tribes of America have been in contact with European belief, the less confidently can we ascribe to purely native sources the theologic scheme their religions have settled into. Yet the Greeks towards the end of the 18th century preserved some elements of native faith. They believed in the Great Spirit, the Master of Breath (a being whom Bartram represents as a soul and governor of the universe) : to him they would address their frequent prayers and ejaculations, at the same time paying a kind of homage to the sun, moon, and stars, as the mediators or ministers of the Great Spirit, in dispensing his attributes for their comfort and well-being in this life.[2] In our own day, among the wild Comanches of the prairies, the Great Spirit, their creator and supreme deity, is above Sun and Moon and Earth ; towards him is sent the first puff of tobacco-smoke before the Sun receives the second, and to him is offered the first morsel of the feast.[3]

Turning from the simple faiths of savage tribes of North America to the complex religion of the half-civilized Mexican nation, we find what we might naturally except, a cumbrous polytheism complicated by mixture of several national pantheons, and beside and beyond this, certain

[1] Lafitau, ' Mœurs des Sauvages Amériquains,' 1724, vol. i. pp. 124-6.
[2] Bartram in ' Tr. Amer. Eth. Soc.' vol. iii. pp. 20, 26.
[3] Schoolcraft, ' Ind. Tribes,' part ii. p. 127.

appearances of a doctrine of divine supremacy.   But these doctrines seem to have been spoken of more definitely than the evidence warrants.   A remarkable native development of Mexican theism must be admitted, in so far as we may receive the native historian Ixtlilxochitl's account of the worship paid by Nezahualcoyotl, the poet king of Tezcuco, to the invisible supreme Tloque Nahuaque, he who has all in him, the cause of causes, in whose star-roofed pyramid stood no idol, and who there received no bloody sacrifice, but only flowers and incense.   Yet it would have been more satisfactory were the stories told by this Aztec panegyrist of his royal ancestor confirmed by other records.   Traces of divine supremacy in Mexican religion are especially associated with Tezcatlipoca, ' Shining Mirror,' a deity who seems in his original nature the Sun-God, and thence by expansion to have become the soul of the world, creator of heaven and earth, lord of all things, Supreme Deity.   Such conceptions may in more or less measure have arisen in native thought, but it should be pointed out that the remarkable Aztec religious formulas collected by Sahagun, in which the deity Tezcatlipoca is so prominent a figure, show traces of Christian admixture in their material, as well as of Christian influence in their style.   For instance, all students of Mexican antiquities know the belief in Mictlan, the Hades of the dead.   But when one of these Aztec prayer-formulas (concerning auricular confession, the washing away of sins, and a new birth) makes mention of sinners being plunged into a lake of intolerable misery and torment, the introduction of an idea so obviously European condemns the composition as not purely native. The question of the actual developments of ideas verging on pantheism or theism, among the priests and philosophers of native Mexico, is one to be left for further criticism.[1]

In the islands of the Pacific, the idea of Supreme Deity

[1] Prescott, ' Mexico,' book i. ch. vi.   Sahagun, ' Hist. de Nueva España,' lib. vi. in Kingsborough, vol. v. ;   Torquemada, ' Monarq. Ind.' lib. x. c. 14. Waitz, vol. iv. p. 136 ;   J. G. Müller, p. 621, &c.

is especially manifested in that great mythologic divinity of
the Polynesian race, whom the New Zealanders call Tangaroa, the Hawaiians Kanaroa, the Tongans and Samoans
Tangaloa, the Georgian and Society islanders Taaroa.
Students of the science of religion who hold polytheism to
be but the mis-development of a primal idea of divine
unity, which in spite of corruption continues to pervade it,
might well choose this South Sea Island divinity as their
aptest illustration from the savage world. Taaroa, says
Moerenhout, is their supreme or rather only god ; for all
the others, as in other known polytheisms, seem scarcely
more than sensible figures and images of the infinite attributes united in his divine person. The following is given
as a native poetic definition of the Creator. ' He was ;
Taaroa was his name ; he abode in the void. No earth, no
sky, no men. Taaroa calls, but nought answers ; and alone
existing, he became the universe. The props are Taaroa ;
the rocks are Taaroa ; the sands are Taaroa ; it is thus he
himself is named.' According to Ellis, Taaroa is described
in the Leeward Islands as the eternal parentless uncreate
Creator, dwelling alone in the highest heaven, whose bodily
form mortals cannot see, who after intervals of innumerable
seasons casts off his body or shell and becomes renewed.
It was he who created Hina his daughter, and with her aid
formed the sky and earth and sea. He founded the world
on a solid rock, which with all the creation he sustains by
his invisible power. Then he created the ranks of lesser
deities such as reign over sea and land and air, and govern
peace and war, and preside over physic and husbandry, and
canoe-building, and roofing, and theft. The version from
the Windward Islands is that Taaroa's wife was the rock,
the foundation of all things, and she gave birth to earth and
sea. Now, fortunately for our understanding of this myth,
the name of Taaroa's wife, with whom he begat the lesser
deities, was taken down in Tahiti in Captain Cook's time.
She was a rock called Papa, and her name plainly suggests
her identity with Papa the Earth, the wife of Rangi the

Heaven in the New Zealand myth of Heaven and Earth, the great first parents. If this inference be just, then it seems that Taaroa the Creator is no personification of a primæval theistic idea, but simply the divine personal Heaven transformed under European influence into the supreme Heaven-god. Thus, when Turner gives the Samoan myths of Tangaloa in heaven presiding over the production of the earth from beneath the waters, or throwing down from the sky rocks which are now islands, the classic name by which he calls him is that which rightly describes his nature and mythic origin—Tangaloa, the Polynesian Jupiter. Yet in island district after district, we find the name of the mighty heavenly creator given to other and lesser mythic beings. In Tahiti, the manes-worshipper's idea is applied not only to lesser deities, but to Taaroa the Creator himself, whom some maintained to be but a man deified after death. In the New Zealand mythology, Tangaroa figures on the one hand as Sea-god and father of fish and reptiles, on the other as the mischievous eaves-dropping god who reveals secrets. In Tonga, Tangaloa was god of artificers and arts, and his priests were carpenters ; it was he who went forth to fish, and dragged up the Tonga islands from the bottom of the sea. Here, then, he corresponds with Maui, and indeed Tangaroa and Maui are found blending in Polynesia even to full identification. It is neither easy nor safe to fix to definite origin the Protean shapes of South Sea mythology, but on the whole the native myths are apt to embody cosmic ideas, and as the idea of the Sun preponderates in Maui, so the idea of the Heaven in Taaroa.[1] In the Fiji Islands, whose native mythology is on the whole distinct from that of Polynesia proper, a strange weird figure takes the supreme place among the gods. His name is Ndengei,

[1] Moerenhout, ' Voy. aux Iles du Grand Océan,' vol. i. pp. 419, 437. Ellis, ' Polyn. Res.' vol. i. p. 321, &c. J. R. Forster, ' Voyage round the World,' pp. 540, 567. Grey, ' Polyn. Myth.' p. 6. Taylor, ' New Zealand,' p. 118 ; see above, vol. i. p. 322. Turner, ' Polynesia,' p. 244. Mariner, ' Tonga Is.' vol. ii. pp. 116, 121. Schirren, ' Wandersagen der Neuseeländer,' pp. 68, 89.

the serpent is his shrine, some traditions represent him with
a serpent's head and body and the rest of him stone. He
passes a monotonous existence in his gloomy cavern, feeling
no emotion nor sensation, nor any appetite but hunger ; he
takes no interest in any one but Uto, his attendant, and
gives no sign of life beyond eating, answering his priest,
and changing his position from one side to the other. No
wonder Ndengei is less worshipped than most of the inferior
gods. The natives have even made a comic song about
him, where he talks with his attendant, Uto, who has been
to attend the feast at Rakiraki, where Ndengei has especially his temple and worship.

Ndengei. ' Have you been to the sharing of food to-day ? '
Uto.   ' Yes : and turtles formed a part ; but only the under-shell
            was shared to us two.'
Ndengei. ' Indeed, Uto ! This is very bad. How is it ? We made them
            men, placed them on the earth, gave them food, and yet
            they share to us only the under-shell. Uto, how is
            this ? ' [1]

The native religion of Africa, a land pervaded by the doctrines of divine hierarchy and divine supremacy, affords apt
evidence for the problem before us. The capacity of the
manes-worshipper's scheme to extend in this direction may
be judged from the religious speculations of the Zulus,
where may be traced the merging of the First Man, the
Old-Old-One, Unkulunkulu, into the ideal of the Creator,
Thunderer, and Heaven-god.[2] If we examine a collection
of documents illustrating the doctrines of the West African
races lying between the Hottentots on the south and the
Berbers on the north, we may fairly judge their conceptions, evidently influenced as these have been by Christian intercourse, to be nevertheless based on native ideas
of the personal Heaven.[3] Whether they think of their

[1] Williams, ' Fiji,' vol. i. p. 217.
[2] Callaway, ' Religion of Amazulu,' part i. See ante, pp. 116, 313.
[3] See especially Waitz, vol. ii. p. 167, &c. ; J. L. Wilson, ' W. Afr.'
pp. 209, 387 ; Bosman, Mungo Park, &c. Comp. Ellis, ' Madagascar,'
vol. i. p. 390.

supreme deity as actively pervading and governing his universe, or as acting through his divine subordinates, or as retiring from his creation and leaving the lesser spirits to work their will, he is always to their minds the celestial ruler, the Heaven-god. Examples may be cited, each in its way full of instruction. In the mind of the Gold-coast negro, tendencies towards theistic religion seem to have been mainly developed through the idea of Nyongmo, the personal Heaven, or its animating personal deity. Heaven, wide-arching, rain-giving, light-giving, who has been and is and shall be, is to him the Supreme Deity. The sky is Ny-ongmo's creature, the clouds are his veil, the stars his face-ornaments. Creator of all things, and of their animating powers whose chief and elder he is, he sits in majestic rest surrounded by his children, the wongs, the spirits of the air who serve him and represent him on earth. Though men's worship is for the most part paid to these, reverence is also given to Nyongmo, the Eldest, the Highest. Every day, said a fetish-man, we see how the grass and corn and trees spring forth by the rain and sunshine that Nyongmo sends, how should he not be the Creator? Again, the mighty Heaven-god, far removed from man and seldom roused to interfere in earthly interests, is the type on which the Guinea negroes may have modelled their thoughts of a Highest Deity who has abandoned the control of his world to lesser and evil spirits.[1] The religion of another district seems to show clearly the train of thought by which such ideas may be worked out. Among the Kimbunda race of Congo, Suku-Vakange is the highest being. He takes little interest in mankind, leaving the real government of the world to the good and evil kilulu or spirits, into whose ranks the souls of men pass at death. Now in that there are more bad spirits who torment, than good who favour living men, human misery would be unbearable, were it not that from

---

[1] Steinhauser, 'Religion des Negers,' in 'Mag. der Miss.' Basel, 1856. No. 2, p. 128. J. L. Wilson, 'W. Afr. 'pp. 92, 209; Römer, 'Guinea,' p. 42. See also Waitz, vol. ii. pp. 171, 419.

time to time Suku-Vakange, enraged at the wickedness of
the evil spirits, terrifies them with thunder, and punishes
the more obstinate with his thunderbolts. Then he returns
to rest, and lets the kilulu rule again.[1] Who, we may ask,
is this divinity, calm and indifferent save when his wrath
bursts forth in storm, but the Heaven himself ? The relation of the Supreme Deity to the lesser gods of polytheism is
graphically put in the following passage, where an American
missionary among the Yorubas describes the relation of
Olorung, the Lord of Heaven, to his lesser deities (orisa),
among whom the chief are the androgynous Obatala, representing the reproductive power of nature, and Shango the
Thunder-god. 'The doctrine of idolatry prevalent in
Yoruba appears to be derived by analogy from the form and
customs of the civil government. There is but one king in
the nation, and one God over the universe. Petitioners to
the king approach him through the intervention of his
servants, courtiers, and nobles : and the petitioner con-
ciliates the courtier whom he employs by good words and
presents. In like manner no man can directly approach
God ; but the Almighty himself, they say, has appointed
various kinds of orisas, who are mediators and intercessors
between himself and mankind. No sacrifices are made to
God, because he needs nothing ; but the orisas, being much
like men, are pleased with offerings of sheep, pigeons, and
other things. They conciliate the orisa or mediator that he
may bless them, not in his own power, but in the power
of God.'[2]

Rooted as they are in the depths of nature-worship, the
doctrines of the supreme Sun and Heaven both come to the
surface again in the native religions of Asia. The divine
Sun holds his primacy distinctly enough among the rude
indigenous tribes of India. Although one sect of the
Khonds of Orissa especially direct their worship to Tari

[1] Magyar, ' Reisen in Süd-Afrika,' pp. 125, 335.
[2] Bowen, ' Gr. and Dic. of Yoruba,' p. xvi. in ' Smithsonian Contr.'
vol. i.

Pennu the Earth-goddess, yet even they agree theoretically with the sect who worship Bura Pennu or Bella Pennu, Light-god or Sun-god, in giving to him supremacy above the manes-gods and nature-gods, and all spiritual powers.[1] Among the Kol tribes of Bengal, the acknowledged primate of all classes of divinities is the beneficient supreme deity, Sing-bonga, Sun-god. Among some Munda tribes his authority is so real that they will appeal to him for help where recourse to minor deities has failed ; while among the Santals his cultus has so dwindled away that he receives less practical worship than his malevolent inferiors, and is scarce honoured with more than nominal dignity and an occasional feast.[2] These are rude tribes who, so far as we know, have never been other than rude tribes. The Japanese are a comparatively civilized nation, one of those so instructive to the student of culture from the stubborn conservatism with which they have consecrated by traditional reverence, and kept up by state authority, the religion of their former barbarism. This is the Kami-religion, Spirit-religion, the ancient but mixed faith of divine spirits of ancestors, nature-spirits, and polytheistic gods, which still holds official place by the side of the imported Buddhism and Confucianism. The Sun-goddess, Amaterasu, ' Heaven-shiner,' though but sprung from the left eye of the parent Izanagi, came to be honoured above all lesser kamis or gods, while by a fiction of ancestor-worship the solar race, as in Peru, became the royal family, her spirit descending to animate the Mikado. Kaempfer, in his ' History of Japan,' written early in the 18th century, showed how absolutely the divine Tensio Dai Sin, represented below on the imperial throne, was looked upon as ruler of the minor powers; he mentions the Japanese tenth month, called the ' godless month,' because then the lesser gods are considered to be away from their temples, gone to pay their annual homage to the Dairi. He describes, as it

[1] Macpherson, ' India,' p. 84, &c.
[2] Dalton, ' Kols,' in ' Tr. Eth. Soc.' vol. vi. p. 32. Hunter, ' Rural Bengal,' p. 184.

was in his time, the great Japanese place of pilgrimage, Yse. There was to be seen the small cavern in a hill near the sea, where the divine Sun once hid herself, depriving the world of light, and thus showing herself to be supreme above all gods. Within the small ancient temple hard by, of which an account and a picture are given from a Japanese book, there were to be seen round the walls the usual pieces of cut white paper, and in the midst nothing but a polished metal mirror.[1]

Over the vast range of the Tatar races, it is the type of the supreme Heaven that comes prominently into view. Nature-worshippers in the extreme sense, these rude tribes conceived their ghosts and elves and demons and great powers of the earth and air to be, like men themselves, within the domain of the divine Heaven, almighty and all-encompassing. To trace the Samoyed's thought of Num the personal Sky passing into vague conceptions of pervading deity ; to see with the Tunguz how Boa the Heaven-god, unseen but all-knowing, kindly but indifferent, has divided the business of his world among such lesser powers as sun and moon, earth and fire ; to discern the meaning of the Mongrel Tengri, shading from Heaven into Heaven-god, and thence into god or spirit in general ; to follow the records of Heaven-worship among the ancient Turks and Hiong-nu ; to compare the supremacy among the Lapps of Tiermes, the Thunderer, with the supremacy among the Finns of Jumala and Ukko, the Heaven-god and heavenly Grandfather—such evidence seems good ground for Castrén's argument, that the doctrine of the divine Sky underlay the first Turanian conceptions, not merely of a Heaven-god, but of a highest deity who in after ages of Christian conversion blended into the Christian God.[2] Here, again, we may have

---

[1] Siebold, ' Nippon.' Kaempfer, ' Hist. of Japan,' 1727, book I. ch. I, IV. For accurate modern information, see papers of Chamberlain and Satow in ' Tr. As. Soc. Japan,' and Murray's Handbook (note to 3rd ed.).

[2] Castrén, ' Finn. Myth.' p. 1, &c. Klemm, ' Cultur-Gesch.' vol. iii. p. 101. ' Samoiedia,' in Pinkerton, vol. i. p. 531. ' Georgi, Reise im Russ. Reich.' vol. i. p. 275.

the advantage of studying among a cultured race the survival of religion from ruder ancient times, kept up by official ordinance. The state religion of China is in its dominant doctrine the worship of Tien, Heaven, identified with Shang-ti, the Emperor-above, next to whom stands Tu, Earth ; while below them are worshipped great nature-spirits and ancestors. It is possible that this faith, as Professor Max Müller argues, may be ethnologically and even linguistically part and parcel of the general Heaven-worship of the Turanian tribes of Siberia. At any rate, it is identical with it in its primary idea, the adoration of the supreme Heaven. Dr. Legge charges Confucius with an inclination to substitute in his religious teaching the name of Tien, Heaven, for that known to more ancient religion and used in more ancient books, Shang-ti, the personal ruling Deity. But it seems rather that the sage was in fact upholding the traditions of the ancient faith, thus acting according to the character on which he prided himself, that of a transmitter and not a maker, a preserver of old knowledge, not a new revealer. It is in accordance with the usual course of theologic development, for the divine Heaven to reign in rude mythologic religion over the lesser spirits of the world before the childlike poetic thought passes into the statesman's conception of a Celestial Emperor. As Plath well remarks, ' It belongs to the Chinese system that all nature is animated by spirits, and that all these follow one order. As the Chinese cannot think of a Chinese Empire with an Emperor only, and without the host of vassal-princes and officials, so he cannot think of the Upper Emperor without the host of spirits.' Developed in a different line, the idea of a supreme Heaven comes to pervade Chinese philosophy and ethics as a general expression of fate, ordinance, duty. ' Heaven's order is nature '—' The wise man readily awaits Heaven's command '—' Man must first do his own part ; when he has done all, then he can wait for Heaven to complete it '—' All state officers are Heaven's workmen, and represent him '— 'How does Heaven speak ? The four seasons have their course, the hundred things arise, what speaks he?'—'No, Heaven speaks not; by the course of events he makes himself understood, no more.'[1]

These stray scraps from old Chinese literature are intelligible to European ears, for our Aryan race has indeed worked out religious ideas from the like source and almost in the like directions. The Samoyed or Tunguz Heaven-god had his analogue in Dyu, Heaven, of the Vedic hymns. Once meaning the sky, and the sky personified, this Zeus came to mean far more than mere heaven in the minds of Greek poets and philosophers, when it rose toward 'that conception which in sublimity, brightness, and infinity transcended all others as much as the bright blue sky transcended all other things visible upon earth.' At the lower level of mythic religion, the ideal process of shaping the divine world into a monarchic constitution was worked out by the ancient Greeks, on the same simple plan as among such barbarians as the Kols of Chota-Nagpur or the Gallas of Abyssinia ; Zeus is King over Olympian gods, and below these again are marshalled the crowded ranks of demigods, heroes, demons, nymphs, ghosts. At the higher level of theologic speculation, exalted thoughts of universal cause and being, of physical and moral law, took personality under the name of Zeus. It is in direct derivation along this historic line, that the classical heaven-cultus still asserts itself in song and pageant among us, in that quaintest of quaint survivals, the factitious religion of the Italian Opera, where such worship as artistic ends require is still addressed to the divine Cielo. Even in our daily talk, colloquial expressions call up before the mind of the ethnographer outlines of remotest religious history. Heaven grants, forbids, blesses still in phrase, as heretofore in fact.

Vast and difficult as is the research into the full scope and history of the doctrine of supremacy among the higher

[1] Plath, ' Rel. der Alten Chinesen,' part i. p. 18, &c. See Max Müller, ' Lectures on Science of Religion,' No. III. in ' Fraser's Mag.' 1870. Legge, ' Confucius,' p. 100.

nations, it may be at least seen that helpful clues exist to lead the explorer. The doctrine of mighty nature-spirits, inhabiting and controlling sky and earth and sea, seems to expand in Asia into such ideas as that of Mahâtman the Great Spirit, Paramâtman the Highest Spirit, taking personality as Brahma the all-pervading universal soul[1]—in Europe into philosophic conceptions of which a grand type stands out in Kepler's words, that the universe is a harmonious whole, whose soul is God. There is a saying of Comte's that throws strong light upon this track of speculative theology : he declares that the conception among the ancients of the Soul of the Universe, the notion that the earth is a vast living animal, and in our own time, the obscure pantheism which is so rife among German metaphysicians, are only fetishism generalized and made systematic.[2] Polytheism, in its inextricable confusion of the persons and functions of the great divinities, and in its assignment of the sovereignty of the world to a supreme being who combines in himself the attributes of several such minor deities, tends toward the doctrine of fundamental unity. Max Müller, in a lecture on the Veda, has given the name of kathenotheism to the doctrine of divine unity in diversity which comes into view in these instructive lines :—

> ' Indram Mitram Varunam Agnim âhur atho
> divyah sa suparno Garutmân :
> Ekam sad viprâ bahudha vadanti Agnim
> Yamam Mâtariçvânam âhuh.'

'They call him Indra, Mitra, Varuna, Agni; then he is the beautiful-winged heavenly Garutmat : That which is One the wise call it in divers manners ; they call it Agni, Yama, Mâtariçvan.'[3]

[1] See Colebrooke, ' Essays,' vol. ii. Wuttke, ' Heidenthum,' part i. p. 254. Ward, ' Hindoos,' vol. i. p. xxi. vol. ii. p. 1.

[2] Comte, ' Philosophie Positive.' Cf. Bp. Berkeley's ' Siris ' ; and for a modern dissertation on the universal æther as the divine soul of the world, see Phil. Spiller, ' Gott im Lichte der Naturwissenschaften,' Berlin, 1873 (note to 2nd ed.).

[3] ' Rig-Veda,' i. 164, 46. Max Müller, ' Chips,' vol. i. pp. 27, 241.

The figure of the supreme deity, be he Heaven-god, Sun-god, Great Spirit, beginning already in uncultured thought to take the form and function of a divine ruler of the world, represents a conception which it becomes the age-long work of systematic theology to develop and to define. Thus in Greece arises Zeus the highest, greatest, best, ' who was and is and shall be,' ' beginning and chief of all things,' ' who rules over all mortals and immortals,' ' Zeus the god of gods.'[1] Such is Ahura Mazda in the Persian faith, among whose seventy-two names of might are these : Creator, Protector, Nourisher, Holiest Heavenly One, Healing Priest, Most Pure, Most Majestic, Most Knowing, Most Ruling at Will.[2] There may be truth in the assertion that the esoteric religion of ancient Egypt centred in a doctrine of divine unity, manifested through the heterogeneous crowd of popular deities.[3] It may be a hopeless task to disentangle the confused personalities of Baal, Bel, and Moloch, and no antiquary may ever fully solve the enigma how far the divine name of El carried in its wide range among the Jewish and other Semitic nations a doctrine of divine supremacy.[4] The great Syro-Phœnician kingdoms and religions have long since passed away into darkness, leaving but antiquarian relics to vouch for their former might. Far other has been the history of their Jewish kindred, still standing fast to their ancient nationality, still upholding to this day their patriarchal religion, in the midst of nations who inherit from the faith of Israel the belief in one God, highest, almighty, who in the beginning made the heavens and the earth, whose throne is established of old, who is from everlasting to everlasting.

Before now bringing these researches to a close, it will be well to state compactly the reasons for treating the animism of the modern savage world as more or less representing the

[1] See Welcker, ' Griech. Götterlehre,' pp. 143, 175.
[2] Avesta ; trans. by Spiegel, ' Ormazd-Yasht.' 12.
[3] Wilkinson, ' Ancient Eg.' vol. iv. ch. xii. ; Bunsen, ' Egypt,' vol. iv. p. 325.
[4] Movers, ' Phönizier,' vol. i. p. 169, &c.

animism of remotely ancient races of mankind. Savage animism, founded on a doctrine of souls carried to an extent far beyond its limits in the cultivated world, and thence expanding to a yet wider doctrine of spiritual beings animating and controlling the universe in all its parts, becomes a theory of personal causes developed into a general philosophy of man and nature. As such, it may be reasonably accounted for as the direct product of natural religion, using this term according to the sense of its definition by Bishop Wilkins : ' I call that Natural Religion, which men might know, and should be obliged unto, by the meer principles of Reason, improved by Consideration and Experience, without the help of Revelation.'[1] It will scarcely be argued by theologians familiar with the religions of savage tribes, that they are direct or nearly direct products of revelation, for the theology of our time would abolish or modify their details till scarce one was left intact. The main issue of the problem is this, whether savage animism is a primary formation belonging to the lower culture, or whether it consists, mostly or entirely, of beliefs originating in some higher culture, and conveyed by adoption or degradation into the lower. The evidence for the first alternative, though not amounting to complete demonstration, seems reasonably strong, and not met by contrary evidence approaching it in force. The animism of the lower tribes, self-contained and self-supporting, maintained in close contact with that direct evidence of the senses on which it appears to be originally based, is a system which might quite reasonably exist among mankind, had they never any-

[1] ' Of the Principles and Duties of Natural Religion,' London, 1678, book i. ch. vi. Johnson's Dictionary, s.v. The term ' natural religion ' is used in various and even incompatible senses. Thus Butler in his ' Analogy of Religion, Natural and Revealed, to the Constitution and Course of Nature,' signifies by ' natural religion ' a primæval system which he expressly argues to have been not reasoned out, but taught first by revelation. This system, of which the main tenets are the belief in one God, the Creator and Moral Governor of the World, and in a future state of moral retribution, differs in the extreme from the actual religions of the lower races.

where risen above the savage condition. Now it does not seem that the animism of the higher nations stands in a connexion so direct and complete with their mental state. It is by no means so closely limited to doctrines evidenced by simple contemplation of nature. The doctrines of the lower animism appear in the higher often more and more modified, to bring them into accordance with an advancing intellectual condition, to adapt them at once to the limits of stricter science and the needs of higher faith ; and in the higher animism these doctrines are retained side by side with other and special beliefs, of which the religions of the lower world show scarce a germ. In tracing the course of animistic thought from stage to stage of history, instruction is to be gained alike from the immensity of change and from the intensity of permanence. Savage animism, both by what it has and by what it wants, seems to represent the earlier system in which began the age-long course of the education of the world. Especially is it to be noticed that various beliefs and practices, which in the lower animism stand firm upon their grounds as if they grew there, in the higher animism belong rather to peasants than philosophers, exist rather as ancestral relics than as products belonging to their age, are falling from full life into survival. Thus it is that savage religion can frequently explain doctrines and rites of civilized religion. The converse is far less often the case. Now this is a state of things which appears to carry a historical as well as a practical meaning. The degradation-theory would expect savages to hold beliefs and customs intelligible as broken-down relics of former higher civilization. The development-theory would expect civilized men to keep up beliefs and customs which have their reasonable meaning in less cultured states of society. So far as the study of survival enables us to judge between the two theories, it is seen that what is intelligible religion in the lower culture is often meaningless superstition in the higher, and thus the development-theory has the upper hand. Moreover, this evidence fits with the teaching of prehistoric archæology. Savage life, carrying on into our own day the life of the Stone Age, may be legitimately claimed as representing remotely ancient conditions of mankind, intellectual and moral as well as material. If so, a low but progressive state of animistic religion occupies a like ground in savage and in primitive culture.

Lastly, a few words of explanation may be offered as to the topics which this survey has included and excluded. To those who have been accustomed to find theological subjects dealt with on a dogmatic, emotional, and ethical, rather than an ethnographic scheme, the present investigation may seem misleading, because one-sided. This one-sided treatment, however, has been adopted with full consideration. Thus, though the doctrines here examined bear not only on the development but the actual truth of religious systems, I have felt neither able nor willing to enter into this great argument fully and satisfactorily, while experience has shown that to dispose of such questions by an occasional dictatorial phrase is one of the most serious of errors. The scientific value of descriptions of savage and barbarous religions, drawn up by travellers and especially by missionaries, is often lowered by their controversial tone, and by the affectation of infallibility with which their relation to the absolutely true is settled. There is something pathetic in the simplicity with which a narrow student will judge the doctrines of a foreign religion by their antagonism or conformity to his own orthodoxy, on points where utter difference of opinion exists among the most learned and enlightened scholars. The systematization of the lower religions, the reduction of their multifarious details to the few and simple ideas of primitive philosophy which form the common groundwork of them all, appeared to me an urgently needed contribution to the science of religion. This work I have carried out to the utmost of my power, and I can now only leave the result in the hands of other students, whose province it is to deal with such evidence in wider schemes of argument. Again, the intellectual rather than the emotional side of religion has here been kept in view. Even in the life of the rudest savage, religious belief is associated with intense emotion, with awful reverence, with agonizing terror, with rapt ecstasy when sense and thought utterly transcend the common level of daily life. How much the more in faiths where not only does the believer experience such enthusiasm, but where his utmost feelings of love and hope, of justice and mercy, of fortitude and tenderness and self-sacrificing devotion, of unutterable misery and dazzling happiness, twine and clasp round the fabric of religion. Language, dropping at times from such words as soul and spirit their mere philosophic meaning, can use them in full conformity with this tendency of the religious mind, as phrases to convey a mystic sense of transcendent emotion. Yet of all this religion, the religion of vision and of passion, little indeed has been said in these pages, and even that little rather in incidental touches than with purpose. Those to whom religion means above all things religious feeling, may say of my argument that I have written soullessly of the soul, and unspiritually of spiritual things. Be it so : I accept the phrase not as needing an apology, but as expressing a plan. Scientific progress is at times most furthered by working along a distinct intellectual line, without being tempted to diverge from the main object to what lies beyond, in however intimate connexion. The anatomist does well to discuss bodily structure independently of the world of happiness and misery which depends upon it. It would be thought a mere impertinence for a strategist to preface a dissertation on the science of war, by an enquiry how far it is lawful for a Christian man to bear weapons and serve in the wars. My task has been here not to discuss Religion in all its bearings, but to portray in outline the great doctrine of Animism, as found in what I conceive to be its earliest stages among the lower races of mankind, and to show its transmission along the lines of religious thought.

The almost entire exclusion of ethical questions from

this investigation has more than a mere reason of arrange-
ment. It is due to the very nature of the subject. To
some the statement may seem startling, yet the evidence
seems to justify it, that the relation of morality to religion
is one that only belongs in its rudiments, or not at all, to
rudimentary civilization. The comparison of savage and
civilized religions bring into view, by the side of a deep-
lying resemblance in their philosophy, a deep-lying contrast
in their practical action on human life. So far as savage
religion can stand as representing natural religion, the
popular idea that the moral government of the universe is
an essential tenet of natural religion simply falls to the
ground. Savage animism is almost devoid of that ethical
element which to the educated modern mind is the very
mainspring of practical religion. Not, as I have said, that
morality is absent from the life of the lower races. Without
a code of morals, the very existence of the rudest tribe
would be impossible ; and indeed the moral standards of
even savage races are to no small extent well-defined and
praiseworthy. But these ethical laws stand on their own
ground of tradition and public opinion, comparatively independent of the animistic belief and rites which exist
beside them. The lower animism is not immoral, it is
unmoral. For this plain reason, it has seemed desirable to
keep the discussion of animism, as far as might be, separate
from that of ethics. The general problem of the relation of
morality to religion is difficult, intricate, and requiring immense array of evidence, and may be perhaps more profit-
ably discussed in connexion with the ethnography of morals.
To justify their present separation, it will be enough to
refer in general terms to the accounts of savage tribes
whose ideas have been little affected by civilized intercourse ; proper caution being used not to trust vague statements about good and evil, but to ascertain whether these
are what philosophic moralists would call virtue and vice,
righteousness and wickedness, or whether they are mere
personal advantage and disadvantage. The essential con-

nexion of theology and morality is a fixed idea in many minds. But it is one of the lessons of history that subjects may maintain themselves independently for ages, till the event of coalescence takes place. In the course of history, religion has in various ways attached to itself matters small and great outside its central scheme, such as prohibition of special meats, observance of special days, regulation of marriage as to kinship, division of society into castes, ordinance of social law and civil government. Looking at religion from a political point of view, as a practical influence on human society, it is clear that among its greatest powers have been its divine sanction of ethical laws, its theological enforcement of morality, its teaching of moral government of the universe, its supplanting the 'continuance-doctrine' of a future life by the 'retribution-doctrine' supplying moral motive in the present. But such alliance belongs almost or wholly to religions above the savage level, not to the earlier and lower creeds. It will aid us to see how much more the fruit of religion belongs to ethical influence than to philosophical dogma, if we consider how the introduction of the moral element separates the religions of the world, united as they are throughout by one animistic principle, into two great classes, those lower systems whose best result is to supply a crude childlike natural philosophy, and those higher faiths which implant on this the law of righteousness and of holiness, the inspiration of duty and of love.

CHAPTER XVIII

RITES AND CEREMONIES

RELIGIOUS rites fall theoretically into two divisions, though these blend in practice. In part, they are expressive and symbolic performances, the dramatic utterance of religious thought, the gesture-language of theology. In part, they are means of intercourse with and influence on spiritual beings, and as such, their intention is as directly practical as any chemical or mechanical process, for doctrine and worship correlate as theory and practice. In the science of religion, the study of ceremony has its strong and weak sides. On the one hand, it is generally easier to obtain accurate accounts of ceremonies by eye-witnesses, than anything like trustworthy and intelligible statements of doctrine ; so that very much of our know-ledge of religion in the savage and barbaric world consists in acquaintance with its ceremonies. It is also true that some religious ceremonies are marvels of permanence, holding substantially the same form and meaning through age after age, and far beyond the range of historic record. On the other hand, the signification of ceremonies is not to be rashly decided on by mere inspection. In the long and varied course in which religion has adapted itself to new intellectual and moral conditions, one of the most marked processes has affected time-honoured religious customs, whose form has been faithfully and even servilely kept up, while their nature has often undergone transformation. In the religions of the great nations, the natural difficulty of following these changes has been added to by the sacer-dotal tendency to ignore and obliterate traces of the in-evitable change of religion from age to age, and to convert into mysteries ancient rites whose real barbaric meaning is too far out of harmony with the spirit of a later time. The embarrassments, however, which beset the enquirer into the ceremonies of a single religion, diminish in a larger com-parative study. The ethnographer who brings together examples of a ceremony from different stages of culture can often give a more rational account of it, than the priest, to whom a special signification, sometimes very unlike the original one, has become matter of orthodoxy. As a contribution to the theory of religion, with especial view to its lower phases as explanatory of the higher, I have here selected for ethnographic discussion a group of sacred rites, each in its way full of instruction, different as these ways are. All have early place and rudimentary meaning in savage culture, all belong to barbaric ages, all have their representatives within the limits of modern Christendom. They are the rites of Prayer, Sacrifice,

Fasting and other methods of Artificial Ecstasy, Orientation, Lustration.

Prayer, ' the soul's sincere desire, uttered or unexpressed,' is the address of personal spirit to personal spirit. So far as it is actually addressed to disembodied or deified human souls, it is simply an extension of the daily intercourse between man and man ; while the worshipper who looks up to other divine beings, spiritual after the nature of his own spirit, though of place and power in the universe far beyond his own, still has his mind in a state where prayer is a reasonable and practical act. So simple and familiar indeed is the nature of prayer, that its study does not demand that detail of fact and argument which must be given to rites in comparison practically insignificant. It has not indeed been placed everywhere on record as the necessary outcome of animistic belief, for especially at low levels of civilization there are many races who distinctly admit the existence of spirits, but are not positively known to pray to them. Beyond this lower level, however, animism and ceremonial prayer become nearly conterminous ; and a view of their relation in their earlier stages may be best gained from a selection of actual prayers taken down word for word, within the limits of savage and barbaric life. These agree with an opinion that prayer appeared in the religion of the lower culture, but that in this its earlier stage it was unethical. The accomplishment of desire is asked for, but desire is as yet limited to personal advantage. It is at later and higher moral levels, that the worshipper begins to add to his entreaty for prosperity the claim for help toward virtue and against vice, and prayer becomes an instrument of morality.

In the Papuan Island of Tanna, where the gods are the spirits of departed ancestors, and preside over the growth of fruits, a prayer after the offering of first-fruits is spoken aloud by the chief who acts as high priest to the silent assembly : ' Compassionate father ! Here is some food for you ; eat it ; be kind to us on account of it ! ' Then all shout together.[1] In the Samoan Islands, when the libation of ava was poured out at the evening meal, the head of the family prayed thus :—

'Here is ava for you, O gods! Look kindly towards this family : let it prosper and increase; and let us all be kept in health. Let our plantations be productive; let food grow; and may there be abundance of food for us, your creatures. Here is ava for you, our war gods! Let there be a strong and numerous people for you in this land.

'Here is ava for you, O sailing gods (gods who come in Tongan canoes and foreign vessels). Do not come on shore at this place; but be pleased to depart along the ocean to some other land.'[2]

Among the Indians of North America, more or less under European influence, the Sioux will say, ' Spirits of the dead, have mercy on me ! ' then they will add what they want, if good weather they say so, if good luck in hunting, they say so.[3] Among the Osages, prayers used not long since to be offered at daybreak to Wohkonda, the Master of Life. The devotee retired a little from the camp or company, and with affected or real weeping, in loud uncouth voice of plaintive piteous tone, howled such prayers as these :— ' Wohkonda, pity me, I am very poor ; give me what I need ; give me success against mine enemies, that I may avenge the death of my friends. May I be able to take scalps, to take horses ! &c.' Such prayers might or might not have allusion to some deceased relative or friend.[4] How an Algonquin Indian undertakes a dangerous voyage, we may judge from John Tanner's account of a fleet of frail Indian bark canoes setting out at dawn one calm morning on Lake Superior. We had proceeded, he writes, about two hundred yards into the lake, when the canoes all stopped together, and the chief, in a very loud voice, addressed a prayer to the Great Spirit, entreating him to

[1] Turner, ' Polynesia,' p. 88 ; see p. 427.
[2] Ibid. p. 200; see p. 174. See also Ellis, ' Polyn. Res.' vol. i. p. 343. Mariner, ' Tonga Is.' vol. ii. p. 235.
[3] Schoolcraft, ' Ind. Tribes,' part iii. p. 237.
[4] M'Coy, ' Baptist Indian Missions,' p. 359.

give us a good look to cross the lake. ' You,' said he, ' have made this lake, and you have made us, your children ; you can now cause that the water shall remain smooth while we pass over in safety.' In this manner he continued praying for five or ten minutes ; he then threw into the lake a small quantity of tobacco, in which each of the canoes followed his example.[1] A Nootka Indian, preparing for war, prayed thus : ' Great Quahootze, let me live, not be sick, find the enemy, not fear him, find him asleep, and kill a great many of him.'[2] There is more pathos in these lines from the war-song of a Delaware :—

> ' O Great Spirit there above
> Have pity on my children
> And my wife !
> Prevent that they shall mourn for me !
> Let me succeed in this undertaking,
> That I may slay my enemy
> And bring home the tokens of victory
> To my dear family and my friends
> That we may rejoice together . . .
> Have pity on me and protect my life,
> And I will bring thee an offering.'[3]

The following two prayers are among those recorded by Molina, from the memory of aged men who described to him the religion of Peru under the Incas, in whose rites they had themselves borne part. The first is addressed to the Sun, the second to the World-creator :—

' O Sun ! Thou who hast said, let there be Cuzcos and Tampus, grant that these thy children may conquer all other people. We beseech thee that thy children the Yncas may be the conquerors always, for this hast thou created them.'

' O conquering Uiracocha ! Ever present Uiracocha ! Thou who art in the ends of the earth without equal ! Thou who gavest life and valour to men, saying " Let this be a man ! " and to women, saying, " Let this be a woman ! " Thou who madest them and gavest them being ! Watch over them that they may live in health and peace. Thou who art in the

---

[1] Tanner, ' Narrative,' p. 46.
[2] Brinton, ' Myths of New World,' p. 297.
[3] Heckewelder, ' Ind. Völkerschaften,' p. 354.

high heavens, and among the clouds of the tempest, grant this with long
life, and accept this sacrifice, O Uiracocha ! ' [1]

In Africa, the Zulus, addressing the spirits of their ancestors, think it even enough to call upon them without saying
what they want, taking it for granted that the spirits know,
so that the mere utterance ' People of our house ! ' is a
prayer. When a Zulu sneezes, and is thus for the moment
in close relation to the divine spirits, it is enough for him
to mention what he wants (' to wish a wish,' as our own
folklore has it), and thus the words 'A cow!' 'Children!'
are prayers. Fuller forms are such as these : ' People of
our house ! Cattle ! '—' People of our house ! Good luck
and health ! '—' People of our house ! Children ! ' On
occasions of ancestral cattle-sacrifice the prayers extend to
actual harangues, as when, after the feast is over, the headman speaks thus amid dead silence : ' Yes, yes, our people,
who did such and such noble acts, I pray to you—I pray
for prosperity after having sacrificed this bullock of yours.
I say, I cannot refuse to give you food, for these cattle
which are here you gave me. And if you ask food of me
which you have given me, is it not proper that I should
give it to you ? I pray for cattle, that they may fill this
pen. I pray for corn, that many people may come to this
village of yours, and make a noise, and glorify you. I ask
also for children, that this village may have a large population, and that your name may never come to an end.' So
he finishes.[2] From among the negro races near the equator,
the following prayers may be cited, addressed to that Supreme Deity whose nature is, as we have seen, more or less
that of the Heaven-god. The Gold Coast negro would
raise his eyes to Heaven and thus address him : ' God,
give me to-day rice and yams, gold and agries, give me

---

[1] ' Narratives of Rites and Laws of Yncas,' tr. and ed. by C. R. Markham,
pp. 31, 33. See also Brinton, p. 298.

[2] Callaway, ' Religion of Amazulu,' pp. 141, 174, 182. ' Remarks on
Zulu Lang.' Pietermaritzburg, 1870, p. 22.

slaves, riches, and health, and that I may be brisk and swift ! ' the fetish-man will often in the morning take water in his mouth and say, ' Heaven ! grant that I may have something to eat to-day ; ' and when giving medicine shown him by the fetish, he will hold it up to heaven first, and say, ' Ata Nyongmo ! (Father Heaven !) bless this medicine that I now give.' The Yebu would say, ' God in heaven, protect me from sickness and death. God give me happiness and wisdom ! '[1] When the Manganja of Lake Nyassa were offering to the Supreme Deity a basketful of meal and a pot of native beer, that he might give them rain, the priestess dropped the meal handful by handful on the ground, each time calling, in a high-pitched voice, ' Hear thou, O God, and send rain ! ' and the assembled people responded, clapping their hands softly and intoning (they always intone their prayers) ' Hear thou, O God ! '[2]

Typical forms of prayer may be selected in Asia near the junction-line of savage and barbaric culture. Among the Karens of Burma, the Harvest-goddess has offerings made to her in a little house in the paddy-field, in which two strings are put for her to bind the spirits of any persons who may enter her field. Then they entreat her on this wise : ' Grandmother, thou guardest my field, thou watchest over my plantation. Look out for men entering ; look sharp for people coming in. If they come, bind them with this string, tie them with this rope, do not let them go ! ' And at the threshing of the rice they say : ' Shake thyself, Grandmother, shake thyself ! Let the paddy ascend till it equals a hill, equals a mountain. Shake thyself, Grandmother, shake thyself ! '[3] The following are extracts from the long-drawn prayers of the Khonds of Orissa : ' O Boora Pennu ! and O Tari Pennu, and all other gods ! (naming them). You, O Boora Pennu ! created us, giving us the attribute of hunger ; thence corn food was necessary to us,

---

[1] Waitz, vol. ii. p. 169. Steinhauser, l.c. p. 129.
[2] Rowley, ' Universities' Mission to Central Africa,' p. 226.
[3] Mason, ' Karens,' l.c. p. 215.

and thence were necessary producing fields. You gave us every seed, and ordered us to use bullocks, and to make ploughs, and to plough. Had we not received this art, we might still indeed have existed upon the natural fruits of the jungle and the plain, but, in our destitution, we could not have performed your worship. Do you, remembering this—the connexion betwixt our wealth and your honour— grant the prayers which we now offer. In the morning, we rise before the light to our labour, carrying the seed. Save us from the tiger, and the snake, and from stumblingblocks. Let the seed appear earth to the eating birds, and stones to the eating animals of the earth. Let the grain spring up suddenly like a dry stream that is swelled in a night. Let the earth yield to our ploughshares as wax melts before hot iron. Let the baked clods melt like hailstones. Let our ploughs spring through the furrows with a force like the recoil of a bent tree. Let there be such a return from our seed, that so much shall fall and be neglected in the fields, and so much on the roads in carrying it home, that, when we shall go out next year to sow, the paths and the fields shall look like a young corn-field. From the first times we have lived by your favour. Let us continue to receive it. Remember that the increase of our produce is the increase of your worship, and that its diminution must be the diminution of your rites.' The following is the conclusion of a prayer to the Earth-goddess : ' Let our herds be so numerous that they cannot be housed ; let children so abound that the care of them shall overcome their parents—as shall be seen by their burned hands ; let our heads ever strike against brass pots innumerable hanging from our roofs ; let the rats form their nests of shreds of scarlet cloth and silk ; let all the kites in the country be seen in the trees of our village, from beasts being killed there every day. We are ignorant of what it is good to ask for. You know what is good for us. Give it to us ! '[1]

[1] Macpherson, ' India,' pp. 110, 128. See also Hunter, ' Rural Bengal,' p. 182 (Santals).

Such are types of prayer in the lower levels of culture, and in no small degree they remain characteristic of the higher nations. If, in long-past ages, the Chinese raised themselves from the condition of rude Siberian tribes to their peculiar culture, at any rate their consecutive religion has scarce changed the matter-of-fact prayers for rain and good harvest, wealth and long life, addressed to manes and nature-spirits and merciful Heaven.[1] In other great national religions of the world, not the whole of prayer, but a smaller or larger part of it, holds closely to the savage definition. This is a Vedic prayer : ' What, Indra, has not yet been given me by thee, Lightning-hurler, all good things bring us hither with both hands . . . with mighty riches fill me, with wealth of cattle, for thou art great ! '[2] This is Moslem : ' O Allah ! unloose the captivity of the captives, and annul the debts of the debtors : and make this town to be safe and secure, and blessed with wealth and plenty, and all the towns of the Moslems, O Lord of all creatures ! and decree safety and health to us and to all travellers, and pilgrims, and warriors, and wanderers, upon thy earth, and upon thy sea, such as are Moslems, O Lord of all creatures ! '[3] Thus also, throughout the rituals of Christendom, stand an endless array of supplications unaltered in principle from savage times—that the weather may be adjusted to our local needs, that we may have the victory over all our enemies, that life and health and wealth and happiness may be ours.

So far, then, is permanence in culture : but now let us glance at the not less marked lines of modification and new formation. The vast political effect of a common faith in developing the idea of exclusive nationality, a process scarcely expanding beyond the germ among savage tribes, but reaching its full growth in the barbaric world, is apt to have its outward manifestation in hostility to those of another

---

[1] Plath, ' Religion der Chinesen,' part ii. p. 2 ; Doolittle, vol. ii. p. 116.

[2] ' Sama-Veda,' i. 4, 2. Wuttke, ' Gesch. des Heidenthums,' part ii. p. 342.

[3] Lane, ' Modern Egyptians,' vol. i. p. 128.

creed, a sentiment which finds vent in characteristic prayers. Such are these from the Rig-Veda : ' Take away our calamities. By sacred verses may we overcome those who employ no holy hymns ! Distinguish between the Aryas and those who are Dasyus : chastising those who observe no sacred rites, subject them to the sacrificer . . . Indra subjects the impious to the pious, and destroys the irreligious by the religious.'[1] The following is from the closing prayer which the boys in many schools in Cairo used to repeat some years ago, and very likely do still : ' I seek refuge with Allah from Satan the accursed. In the name of Allah, the Compassionate, the Merciful . . . O Lord of all creatures ! O Allah ! destroy the infidels and polytheists, thine enemies, the enemies of the religion ! O Allah ! make their children orphans, and defile their abodes, and cause their feet to slip, and give them and their families and their households and their women and their children and their relations by marriage and their brothers and their friends and their possessions and their race and their wealth and their lands as booty to the Moslems ! O Lord of all creatures ! '[2] Another powerful tendency of civilization, that of regulating human affairs by fixed ordinance, has since early ages been at work to arrange worship into mechanical routine. Here, so to speak, religion deposits itself in sharply defined shape from a supersaturated solution, and crystallizes into formalism. Thus prayers, from being at first utterances as free and flexible as requests to a living patriarch or chief, stiffened into traditional formulas, whose repetition required verbal accuracy, and whose nature practically assimilated more or less to that of charms. Liturgies, especially in those three quarters of the world where the ancient liturgical language has become at once unintelligible and sacred, are crowded with examples of this historical process. Its extremest development in Europe is connected with the use of the rosary. This devotional

---

[1] ' Rig-Veda,' i. 51, 8, x. 105, 8. Muir, ' Sanskrit Texts,' part ii. ch. iii.
[2] Lane, ' Modern Egyptians,' vol. ii. p. 383.

calculating-machine is of Asiatic invention ; it had if not its origin at least its special development among the ancient Buddhists, and its 108 balls still slide through the modern Buddhist's hands as of old, measuring out the sacred formulas whose reiteration occupies so large a fraction of a pious life. It was not till toward the middle ages that the rosary passed into Mohammedan and Christian lands, and finding there conceptions of prayer which it was suited to accompany, has flourished ever since. How far the Buddhist devotional formulas themselves partake of the nature of prayer, is a question opening into instructive considerations, which need only be suggested here. By its derivation from Brahmanism and its fusion with the beliefs of rude spirit-worshipping populations, Buddhism practically retains in no small measure a prayerful temper and even practice. Yet, according to strict and special Buddhist philosophy, where personal divinity has faded into metaphysical idea, even devotional utterances of desire are not prayers ; as Köppen says, there is no ' Thou ! ' in them. It must be only with reservation that we class the rosary in Buddhist hands as an instrument of actual prayer. The same is true of the still more extreme development of mechanical religion, the prayer-mill of the Tibetan Buddhists. This was perhaps originally a symbolic ' chakra ' or wheel of the law, but has become a cylinder mounted on an axis, which by each rotation is considered to repeat the sentences written on the papers it is filled with, usually the ' Om mani padme hûm! ' Prayer-mills vary in size, from the little wooden toys held in the hand, to the great drums turned by wind or water-power, which repeat their sentences by the million.[1] The Buddhist idea, that ' merit ' is produced by the recitation of these sentences, may perhaps lead us to form an opinion of large application in the study of religion and superstition, namely, that the theory of prayers may explain the origin of charms. Charm-formulas are in very many cases actual

[1] See Köppen, ' Religion des Buddha,' vol. i. pp. 345, 556 ; vol. ii. pp. 303, 319. Compare Fergusson, ' Tree and Serpent Worship, ' pl. xlii.

prayers, and as such are intelligible. Where they are mere verbal forms, producing their effect on nature and man by some unexplained process, may not they or the types they were modelled on have been originally prayers, since dwindled into mystic sentences?

The worshipper cannot always ask wisely what is for his good, therefore it may be well for him to pray that the greater power of the deity may be guided by his greater wisdom—this is a thought which expands and strengthens in the theology of the higher nations. The simple prayer of Sokrates, that the gods would give such things as are good, for they know best what are good,[1] raises a strain of supplication which has echoed through Christendom from its earliest ages. Greatest of all changes which difference the prayers of lower from those of higher nations, is the working out of the general principle that the ethical element, so scanty and rudimentary in the lower forms of religion, becomes in the higher its most vital point; while it scarcely appears as though any savage prayer, authentically native in its origin, were ever directed to obtain moral goodness or to ask pardon for moral sin. Among the semi-civilized Aztecs, in the elaborate ritual which from its early record and its original characteristics may be thought to have a partial authenticity, we mark the appearance of ethical prayer. Such is the supplication concerning the newly-elect ruler: 'Make him, Lord, as your true image, and permit him not to be proud and haughty in your throne and court; but vouchsafe, Lord, that he may calmly and carefully rule and govern them whom he has in charge, the people, and permit not, Lord, that he may injure or vex his subjects, nor without reason and justice cause loss to any; and permit not, Lord, that he may spot or soil your throne or court with any injustice or wrong, &c.'[2] Moral prayer, sometimes appearing in rudiment, sometimes shrunk into

---

[1] Xenoph. Memorabilia Socrat. i. 3, 2.
[2] Sahagun, 'Retorica, &c., de la Gente Mexicana,' lib. vi. c. 4, in Kingsborough, 'Antiquities of Mexico,' vol. v.

insignificance, sometimes overlaid by formalism, sometimes maintained firm and vigorous in the inmost life, has its place without as well as within the Jewish-Christian scheme. The ancient Aryan prayed : ' Through want of strength, thou strong and bright god, have I gone wrong ; have mercy, almighty, have mercy ! . . . . Whenever we men, O Varuna, commit an offence before the heavenly host, whenever we break the law through thoughtlessness, have mercy, almighty, have mercy!'[1] The modern Parsi prays: 'Of my sins which I have committed against the ruler Ormazd, against men, and the different kinds of men. . . . . Deceit, contempt, idol-worship, lies, I repent of. . . . . All and every kind of sin which men have committed because of me, or which I have committed because of men ; pardon, I repent with confession!'[2] As a general rule it would be misleading to judge utterances of this kind in the religions of classic Greece and Rome as betokening the intense habitual prayerfulness which pervades the records of Judaism, Mohammedanism, Christianity. Moralists admit that prayer can be made an instrument of evil, that it may give comfort and hope to the superstitious robber, that it may strengthen the heart of the soldier to slay his foes in an unrighteous war, that it may uphold the tyrant and the bigot in their persecution of freedom in life and thought. Philosophers dwell on the subjective operation of prayer, as acting not directly on outward events, but on the mind and will of the worshipper himself, which it influences and confirms. The one argument tends to guide prayer, the other to suppress it. Looking on prayer in its effect on man himself through the course of history, both must recognize it as even in savage religion a means of strengthening emotion, of sustaining courage and exciting hope, while in higher faiths it becomes a great motive power of the ethical system, controlling and enforcing, under an ever-present sense of supernatural intercourse and aid, the emotions and energies of moral life.

[1] ' Rig-Veda,' vii. 89, 3. Max Müller, ' Chips,' vol. i. p. 39.
[2] ' Avesta,' tr. by Spiegel ; ' Khorda-Avesta,' Patet Qod.

Sacrifice has its apparent origin in the same early period of culture and its place in the same animistic scheme as prayer, with which through so long a range of history it has been carried on in the closest connexion. As prayer is a request made to a deity as if he were a man, so sacrifice is a gift made to a deity as if he were a man. The human types of both may be studied unchanged in social life to this day. The suppliant who bows before his chief, laying a gift at his feet and making his humble petition, displays the anthropomorphic model and origin at once of sacrifice and prayer. But sacrifice, though in its early stages as intelligible as prayer is in early and late stages alike, has passed in the course of religious history into transformed conditions, not only of the rite itself but of the intention with which the worshipper performs it. And theologians, having particularly turned their attention to sacrifice as it appears in the higher religions, have been apt to gloss over with mysticism ceremonies which, when traced ethnographically up from their savage forms, seem open to simply rational interpretation. Many details of offerings have already been given incidentally here, as a means of elucidating the nature of the deities they are offered to. Moreover, a main part of the doctrine of sacrifice has been anticipated in examining the offerings to spirits of the dead, and indeed the ideal distinction between soul and deity breaks down among the lower races, when it appears how often the deities receiving sacrifice are themselves divine human souls. In now attempting to classify sacrifice in its course through the religions of the world, it seems a satisfactory plan to group the evidence as far as may be according to the manner in which the offering is given by the worshipper, and received by the deity. At the same time, the examples may be so arranged as to bring into view the principal lines along which the rite has undergone alteration. The ruder conception that the deity takes and values the offering for itself, gives place on the one hand to the idea of mere homage expressed by a gift, and on the other to the negative view that the virtue lies in the worshipper depriving himself of something prized. These ideas may be broadly distinguished as the gift-theory, the homage-theory, and the abnegation-theory. Along all three the usual ritualistic change may be traced, from practical reality to formal ceremony. The originally valuable offering is compromised for a smaller tribute or a cheaper substitute, dwindling at last to a mere trifling token or symbol.

The gift-theory, as standing on its own independent basis, properly takes the first place. That most childlike kind of offering, the giving of a gift with as yet no definite thought how the receiver can take and use it, may be the most primitive as it is the most rudimentary sacrifice. Moreover, in tracing the history of the ceremony from level to level of culture, the same simple unshaped intention may still largely prevail, and much of the reason why it is often found difficult to ascertain what savages and barbarians suppose to become of the food and valuables they offer to the gods, may be simply due to ancient sacrificers knowing as little about it as modern ethnologists do, and caring less. Yet rude races begin and civilized races continue to furnish with the details of their sacrificial ceremonies the key also to their meaning, the explanation of the manner in which the offering is supposed to pass into the possession of the deity.

Beginning with cases in which this transmission is performed bodily, it appears that when the deity is the personal Water, Earth, Fire, Air, or a fetish-spirit animating or inhabiting such element, he can receive and sometimes actually consume the offerings given over to this material medium. How such notions may take shape is not ill shown in the quaintly rational thought noticed in old Peru, that the Sun drinks the libations poured out before him ; and in modern Madagascar, that the Angatra drinks the arrack left for him in the leaf-cup. Do not they see the liquids diminish from day to day ?[1] The sacrifice to Water

[1] Garcilaso de la Vega, 'Commentarios Reales,' v. 19. Ellis, 'Madagascar,' vol. i. p. 421.

is exemplified by Indians caught in a storm on the North American lakes, who would appease the angry tempest-raising deity by tying the feet of a dog and throwing it overboard.[1] The following case from Guinea well shows the principle of such offerings. Once in 1693, the sea being unusually rough, the headmen complained to the king, who desired them to be easy, and he would make the sea quiet next day. Accordingly he sent his fetishman with a jar of palm oil, a bag of rice and corn, a jar of pitto, a bottle of brandy, a piece of painted calico, and several other things to present to the sea. Being come to the sea-side, he made a speech to it, assuring it that his king was its friend, and loved the white men ; that they were honest fellows and came to trade with him for what he wanted ; and that he requested the sea not to be angry, nor hinder them to land their goods ; he told it, that if it wanted palm oil, his king had sent it some ; and so threw the jar with the oil into the sea, as he did, with the same compliment, the rice, corn, pitto, brandy, calico, &c.[2] Among the North American Indians the Earth also receives offerings buried in it. The distinctness of idea with which such objects may be given is well shown in a Sioux legend. The Spirit of the earth, it seems, requires an offering from those who perform extraordinary achievements, and accordingly the prairie gapes open with an earthquake before the victorious hero of the tale ; he casts a partridge into the crevice, and springs over.[3] One of the most explicit recorded instances of the offering to the Earth is the hideous sacrifice to the Earth-goddess among the Khonds of Orissa, the tearing of the flesh of the human victim from the bones, the priest burying half of it in a hole in the earth behind his back without

[1] Charlevoix, ' Nouv. Fr.' vol. i. p. 394. See also Smith, ' Virginia,' in ' Pinkerton,' vol. xiii. p. 41.
[2] Phillips in Astley's ' Voyages,' vol. ii. p. 411 ; Lubbock, ' Origin of Civilization,' p. 216. Bosman, ' Guinea,' in Pinkerton, vol. xvi. p. 500. Bastian in ' Ztschr. für Ethnologie,' 1869, p. 315.
[3] Schoolcraft, ' Algic Res.' vol. ii. p. 75. See also Tanner, ' Narr.' p. 193, and above, p. 270.

looking round, and each householder carrying off a particle to bury in like manner in his favourite field.[1] For offerings to the Fire, we may take for an example the Yakuts, who not only give him the first spoonful of food, but instead of washing their earthen pots allow him to clean out the remains.[2] Here is a New Zealand charm called Wangaihau, i.e., feeding the Wind :—

> ' Lift up his offering,
> To Uenga a te Rangi his offering,
> Eat, O invisible one, listen to me,
> Let that food bring you down from the sky.'[3]

Beside this may be set the quaint description of the Fanti negroes assisting at the sacrifice of men and cattle to the local fetish ; the victims were considered to be carried up in a whirlwind out of the midst of the small inner ring of priests and priestesses ; this whirlwind was, however, not perceptible to the senses of the surrounding worshippers.[4] These series of details collected from the lower civilization throw light on curious problems as to sacrificial ideas in the religions of the classic world ; such questions as what Xerxes meant when he threw the golden goblet and the sword into the Hellespont, which he had before chained and scourged ; why Hannibal cast animals into the sea as victims to Poseidon ; what religious significance underlay the patriotic Roman legend of the leap of Marcus Curtius.[5]

Sacred animals, in their various characters of divine beings, incarnations, representatives, agents, symbols, naturally receive meat and drink offerings, and sometimes other gifts. For examples, may be mentioned the sun-birds (tonatzuli), for which the Apalaches of Florida set out

---

[1] Macpherson, ' India,' p. 129.

[2] Billings, ' Exp. to Northern Russia,' p. 125. Chinese sacrifices buried for earth spirits, see ante, vol. i. p. 107 ; Plath, part ii. p. 50.

[3] Taylor, ' New Zealand,' p. 182.

[4] Römer, ' Guinea,' p. 67.

[5] Herod. vii. 35, 54. Liv. vii. 6. Grote, ' Hist. of Greece,' vol. x. p. 589, see p. 715.

crushed maize and seed;[1] the Polynesian deities coming
incarnate in the bodies of birds to feed on the meat-offerings
and carcases of human victims set out upon the altar-
scaffolds;[2] the well-fed sacred snakes of West Africa, and
local fetish animals like the alligator at Dix Cove which
will come up at a whistle, and follow a man half a mile if he
carries a white fowl in his hands, or the shark at Bonny
that comes to the river bank every day to see if a human
victim has been provided for his repast;[3] in modern India
the cows reverently fed with fresh grass, Durga's meat-
offerings laid out on stones for the jackals, the famous
alligators in their temple-tanks.[4] The definition of sacred
animal from this point of view distinctly includes man.
Such in Mexico was the captive youth adored as living representative of Tezcatlipoca, and to whom banquets were
made during the luxurious twelvemonth which preceded his
sacrifice at the festival of the deity whom he personated :
such still more definitely was Cortes himself, when Monte-
zuma supposed him to be the incarnate Quetzalcoatl come
back into the land, and sent human victims accordingly to
be slaughtered before him, should he seem to lust for blood.[5]
Such in modern India is the woman who as representative
of Radha eats and drinks the offerings at the shameless
orgies of the Saktas.[6] More usually it is the priest who as
minister of the deities has the lion's share of the offerings
or the sole privilege of consuming them, from the Fijian
priest who watches for the turtle and puddings apportioned
to his god,[7] and the West African priest who carries the
allowances of food sent to the local spirits of mountain, or
river, or grove, which food he eats himself as the spirit's

[1] Rochefort, ' Iles Antilles,' p. 367.
[2] Ellis, ' Polyn. Res.' vol. i. pp. 336, 358. Williams, ' Fiji,' vol. i. p. 220.
[3] Bosman, ' Guinea,' in Pinkerton, vol. xvi. p. 494 ; J. L. Wilson, ' W.
Afr.' p. 218 ; Burton, ' W. & W. fr. W. Afr.' p. 331.
[4] Ward, ' Hindoos,' vol. ii. p. 195, &c.
[5] Clavigero, ' Messico,' vol. ii. p. 69. J. G. Müller, p. 631.
[6] Ward, vol. ii. p. 194 ; ' Mem. Anthrop. Soc.' vol. i. p. 332.
[7] Williams, ' Fiji,' vol. i. p. 226.

proxy,[1] to the Brahmans who receive for the divine ancestors the oblation of a worshipper who has no sacred fire to consume it, 'for there is no difference between the Fire and a Brahman, such is the judgment declared by them who know the Veda.'[2] It is needless to collect details of a practice so usual in the great systematic religions of the world, where priests have become professional ministers and agents of deity, as for them to partake of the sacrificial meats. It by no means follows from this usage that the priest is necessarily supposed to consume the food as representative of his divinity ; in the absence of express statement to such effect, the matter can only be treated as one of ceremonial ordinance. Indeed, the case shows the caution needed in interpreting religious rites, which in particular districts may have meanings attached to them quite foreign to their general intent.

The feeding of an idol, as when Ostyaks would pour daily broth into the dish at the image's mouth,[3] or when the Aztecs would pour the blood and put the heart of the slaughtered human victim into the monstrous idol's mouth,[4] seems ceremonial make-believe, but shows that in each case the deity was somehow considered to devour the meal. The conception among the lower races of deity, as in disembodied spiritual form, is even less compatible with the notion that such a being should consume solid matter. It is true that the notion does occur. In old times it appears in the legend of Bel and the Dragon, where the footprints in the strewn ashes betray the knavish priests who come by secret doors to eat up the banquet set before Bel's image.[5] In modern centuries, it may be exemplified by the negroes of Labode, who could hear the noise of their god Jimawong emptying one after another the bottles of brandy handed in

---

[1] J. L. Wilson, ' W. Afr.' p. 218.
[2] Manu, iii. 212. See also ' Avesta,' tr. by Spiegel, vol. ii. p. lxxvii. (sacrificial cakes eaten by priest).
[3] Ysbrants Ides, ' Reize naar China,' p. 38. Meiners, vol. i. p. 162.
[4] Clavigero, vol. ii. p. 46. J. G. Müller, p. 631.
[5] Bel and the Dragon.

at the door of his straw-roofed temple;[1] or among the Ostyaks, who, as Pallas relates, used to leave a horn of snuff for their god, with a shaving of willow bark to stop his nostrils with after the country fashion ; the traveller describes their astonishment when sometimes an unbelieving Russian has emptied it in the night, leaving the simple folk to conclude that the deity must have gone out hunting to have snuffed so much.[2] But these cases turn on fraud, whereas absurdities in which low races largely agree are apt to have their origin rather in genuine error. Indeed, their dominant theories of the manner in which deities receive sacrifice are in accordance not with fraud but with facts, and must be treated as strictly rational and honest developments of the lower animism. The clearest and most general of these theories are as follows.

When the deity is considered to take actual possession of the food or other objects offered, this may be conceived to happen by abstraction of their life, savour, essence, quality, and in yet more definite conception their spirit or soul. The solid part may die, decay, be taken away or consumed or destroyed, or may simply remain untouched. Among this group of conceptions, the most materialized is that which carries out the obvious primitive world-wide doctrine that the life is the blood. Accordingly, the blood is offered to the deity, and even disembodied spirits are thought capable of consuming it, like the ghosts for whom Odysseus entering Hades poured into the trench the blood of the sacrificed ram and black ewe, and the pale shades drank and spoke;[3] or the evil spirits which the Mintira of the Malay Peninsula keep away from the wife in childbirth by placing her near the fire, for the demons are believed to drink human blood when they can find it.[4] Thus in Virginia the Indians (in pretence or reality) sacrificed children, whose blood the oki or spirit was said

[1] Römer, ' Guinea,' p. 47.
[2] Bastian, ' Mensch,' part ii. p. 210.
[3] Homer, Odyss. xi. xii.
[4] ' Journ. Ind. Archip.' vol. i. p. 270.

to suck from their left breast.[1] The Kayans of Borneo used to offer human sacrifice when a great chief took possession of a newly built house ; in one late case, about 1847, a Malay slave girl was bought for the purpose and bled to death, the blood, which alone is efficacious, being sprinkled on the pillars and under the house, and the body being thrown into the river.[2] The same ideas appear among the indigenes of India, alike in North Bengal and in the Deccan, where the blood alone of the sacrificed animal is for the deities, and the votary retains the meat.[3] Thus, in West Africa, the negroes of Benin are described as offering a cock to the idol, but it receives only the blood, for they like the flesh very well themselves;[4] while in the Yoruba country, when a beast is sacrificed for a sick man, the blood is sprinkled on the wall and smeared on the patient's forehead, with the idea, it is said, of thus transferring to him the victim's life.[5] The Jewish law of sacrifice marks clearly the distinction between shedding the blood as life, and offering it as food. As the Israelites themselves might not eat with the flesh the blood which is the life, but must pour it on the earth as water, so the rule applies to sacrifice. The blood must be sprinkled before the sanctuary, put upon the horns of the altar, and there sprinkled or poured out, but not presented as a drink offering—' their drink-offerings of blood will I not offer.'[6]

Spirit being considered in the lower animism as somewhat of the ethereal nature of smoke or mist, there is an

---

[1] Smith, ' Virginia,' in Pinkerton, vol. xiii. p. 41 ; see J. G. Müller, p. 143 ; Waitz, vol. iii. p. 207. Comp. Meiners, vol. ii. p. 89. See also Bollaert in ' Mem. Anthrop. Soc.' vol. ii. p. 96.

[2] ' Journ. Ind. Archip.' vol. iii. p. 145. See also St. John, ' Far East,' vol. i. p. 160.

[3] Hodgson, ' Abor. of India,' p. 147 ; Hunter, ' Rural Bengal,' p. 181 ; Forbes Leslie, ' Early Races of Scotland,' vol. ii. p. 458.

[4] Bosman, ' Guinea,' letter xxi. in Pinkerton, vol. xvi. p. 531. See also Waitz, vol. ii. p. 192.

[5] Bastian, ' Psychologie,' p. 96.

[6] Levit. i. &c. ; Deuteron. xii. 23 ; Psalm xvi. 4.

obvious reasonableness in the idea that offerings reduced to this condition are fit to be consumed by, or transmitted to, spiritual beings towards whom the vapour rises in the air. This idea is well shown in the case of incense, and especially a peculiar kind of incense offered among the native tribes of America. The habit of smoking tobacco is not suggestive of religious rites among ourselves, but in its native country, where it is so widely diffused as to be perhaps the best point assignable in favour of a connexion in the culture of the northern and southern continent, its place in worship is very important. The Osages would begin an undertaking by smoking a pipe, with such a prayer as this : ' Great Spirit, come down to smoke with me as a friend ! Fire and Earth, smoke with me and help me to overthrow my foes ! ' The Sioux in Hennepin's time would look toward the Sun when they smoked, and when the calumet was lighted, they presented it to him, saying : ' Smoke, Sun ! ' The Natchez chief at sunrise smoked first to the east and then to the other quarters ; and so on. It is not merely, however, that puffs from the tobacco-pipe are thus offered to deities as drops of drink or morsels of food might be. The calumet is a special gift of the Sun or the Great Spirit, tobacco is a sacred herb, and smoking is an agreeable sacrifice ascending into the air to the abode of gods and spirits.[1] Among the Caribs, the native sorcerer evoking a demon would puff tobacco-smoke into the air as an agreeable perfume to attract the spirit ; while among Brazilian tribes the sorcerers smoked round upon the bystanders and on the patient to be cured.[2] How thoroughly incense and burnt-offering are of the same nature, the Zulus well show, burning incense together with the fat of the caul of the slaughtered beast, to give the spirits of the people a sweet

---

[1] Waitz, vol. iii. p. 181. Hennepin, ' Voyage,' p. 302. Charlevoix, ' Nouvelle France,' vol. v. p. 311, vi. p. 178. Schoolcraft, ' Ind. Tribes,' part i. p. 49, part ii. p. 127. Catlin, vol. i. pp. 181, 229. Morgan, ' Iroquois,' p. 164. J. G. Müller, p. 58.

[2] Rochefort, ' Iles Antilles,' pp. 418, 507. Lery, ' Voy. en Brésil,' p. 268. See also Musters in ' Journ. Anthrop. Inst.' vol. i. p. 202 (Patagonians).

savour.[1] As to incense more precisely of the sort we are familiar with, it was in daily use in the temples of Mexico, where among the commonest antiquarian relics are the earthen incense-pots in which ' copalli ' (whence our word copal) and bitumen were burnt.[2] Though incense was hardly usual in the ancient religion of China, yet in modern Chinese houses and temples the ' joss-stick ' and censer do honour to all divine beings, from the ancestral manes to the great gods and Heaven and Earth.[3] The history of incense in the religion of Greece and Rome points the contrast between old thrift and new extravagance, where the early fumigations with herbs and chips of fragrant wood are contrasted with the later oriental perfumes, myrrh and cassia and frankincense.[4] In the temples of ancient Egypt, numberless representations of sacrificial ceremony show the burning of the incense-pellets in censers before the images of the gods; and Plutarch speaks of the incense burnt thrice daily to the Sun, resin at his rising, myrrh at his meridian, kuphi at his setting.[5] The ordinance held as prominent a place among the Semitic nations. At the yearly festival of Bel in Babylon, the Chaldæans are declared by Herodotus to have burned a thousand talents of incense on the large altar in the temple where sat his golden image.[6] In the records of ancient Israel, there has come down to us the very recipe for compounding incense after the art of the apothecary. The priests carried every man his censer, and on the altar of incense, overlaid with gold, standing before the vail in the tabernacle, sweet spices

[1] Callaway, ' Religion of Amazulu,' pp. 11, 141, 177. See also Casalis, ' Basutos,' p. 258.

[2] Clavigero, ' Messico,' vol. ii. p. 39. See also Piedrahita, part i. lib. i. c. 3 (Muyscas).

[3] Plath, ' Religion der alten Chinesen,' part ii. p. 31. Doolittle, ' Chinese.'

[4] Porphyr. de Abstinentia, ii. 5. Arnob. contra Gentes. vii. 26. Meiners, vol. ii. p. 14.

[5] Wilkinson, ' Ancient Egyptians,' vol. v. pp. 315, 338. Plutarch. de Is. et Osir.

[6] Herodot. i. 183.

were burned morn and even, a perpetual incense before
the Lord.[1]

The sacrifice by fire is familiar to the religion of North
American tribes. Thus the Algonquins knew the practice
of casting into the fire the first morsel of the feast; and
throwing fat into the flames for the spirits, they would pray
to them ' make us find food.' Catlin has described and
sketched the Mandans dancing round the fire where the first
kettleful of the green-corn is being burned, an offering to
the Great Spirit before the feast begins.[2] The Peruvians
burnt llamas as offerings to the Creator, Sun, Moon, and
Thunder, and other lesser deities. As to the operation of
sacrifice, an idea of theirs comes well into view in the
legend of Manco Ccapac ordering the sacrifice of the most
beautiful of his sons, ' cutting off his head, and sprinkling
the blood over the fire, that the smoke might reach the
Maker of heaven and earth.'[3] In Siberia the sacrifices of
the Tunguz and Buraets, in the course of which bits of
meat and liver and fat are cast into the fire, carry on the
same idea.[4] Chinese sacrifices to sun and moon, stars and
constellations, show their purpose in most definite fashion;
beasts and even silks and precious stones are burned, that
their vapour may ascend to these heavenly spirits.[5] No less
significant, though in a different sense, is the Siamese offering to the household deity, incense and arrack and rice
steaming hot; he does not eat it all, not always any part of
it, it is the fragrant steam which he loves to inhale.[6] Looking now to the records of Aryan sacrifice, views similar to
these are not obscurely expressed. When the Brahman
burns the offerings on the altar-fire, they are received by

---

[1] Exod. xxx., xxxvii. Lev. x. 1, xvi. 12, &c.
[2] Smith, ' Virginia,' in Pinkerton, vol. xiii. p. 41. Le Jeune in ' Rel.
des Jés.' 1634, p. 16. Catlin, ' N. A. Ind.' vol. i. p. 189.
[3] ' Rites and Laws of Incas,' p. 16, &c., 79; see ' Ollanta, an ancient Ynca
Drama,' tr. by C. R. Markham, p. 81. Garcilaso de la Vega, lib. i. ii. vi.
[4] Klemm, ' Cultur-Gesch.' vol. iii. pp. 106, 114.
[5] Plath, part ii. p. 65.
[6] Latham, ' Descr. Eth.' vol. i. p. 191.

Agni the divine Fire, mouth of the gods, messenger of the All-knowing, to whom is chanted the Vedic strophe, 'Agni ! the sacrifice which thou encompassest whole, it goes unto the gods!'[1] The Homeric poems show the plain meaning of the hecatombs of old barbaric Greece, where the savour of the burnt offering went up in wreathing smoke to heaven, 'Κνίσση δ' οὐρανὸν ἷκεν ἑλισσομένη περὶ καπνῷ.'[2] Passed into a far other stage of history, men's minds had not lost sight of the archaic thought even in Porphyry's time, for he knows how the demons who desire to be gods rejoice in the libations and fumes of sacrifice, whereby their spiritual and bodily substance fattens, for this lives on the steam and vapours and is strengthened by the fumes of the blood and flesh.[3]

The view of commentators that sacrifice, as a religious act of remote antiquity and world-wide prevalence, was adopted, regulated, and sanctioned in the Jewish law, is in agreement with the general ethnography of the subject. Here sacrifice appears not with the lower conception of a gift acceptable and even beneficial to deity, but with the higher significance of devout homage or expiation for sin. As is so usual in the history of religion, the offering consisted in general of food, and the consummation of the sacrifice was by fire. To the ceremonial details of the sacrificial rites of Israel, whether prescribing the burning of the carcases of oxen and sheep or of the bloodless gifts of flour mingled with oil, there is appended again and again the explanation of the intent of the rite ; it is 'an offering made by fire, of a sweet savour unto the Lord.' The copious records of sacrifice in the Old Testament enable us to follow its expansion from the simple patriarchal forms of a pastoral tribe, to the huge and complex system organized to carry on the ancient service in a now populous and settled kingdom. Among writers on the Jewish religion, Dean Stanley has vividly por-

[1] 'Rig-Veda,' i. 1, 4.   [2] Homer, Il. i. 317.
[3] Porphyr. De Abstinentia, ii. 42 ; see 58.

trayed the aspect of the Temple, with the flocks of sheep and droves of cattle crowding its courts, the vast apparatus of slaughter, the great altar of burnt-offering towering above the people, where the carcases were laid, the drain beneath to carry off the streams of blood. To this historian, in sympathy rather with the spirit of the prophet than the ceremony of the priest, it is a congenial task to dwell upon the great movement in later Judaism to maintain the place of ethical above ceremonial religion.[1] In those times of Hebrew history, the prophets turned with stern rebuke on those who ranked ceremonial ordinance above weightier matters of the law. ' I desired mercy and not sacrifice, and the knowledge of God more than burnt offerings.' ' I delight not in the blood of bullocks, or of lambs, or of he goats . . . Wash you, make you clean ; put away the evil of your doings from before mine eyes. Cease to do evil, learn to do well.'

Continuing the enquiry into the physical operation ascribed to sacrifice, we turn to a different conception. It is an idea well vouched for in the lower culture, that the deity, while leaving apparently untouched the offering set out before him, may nevertheless partake of or abstract what in a loose way may be described as its essence. The Zulus leave the flesh of the sacrificed bullock all night, and the divine ancestral spirits come and eat, yet next morning everything remains just as it was. Describing this practice, a native Zulu thus naïvely comments on it : ' But when we ask, " What do the Amadhlozi eat ? for in the morning we still see all the meat," the old men say, " The Amatongo lick it." And we are unable to contradict them, but are silent, for they are older than we, and tell us all things and we listen ; for we are told all things, and assent without seeing clearly whether they are true or not.'[2] Such imagination

---

[1] Stanley, ' Jewish Church,' 2d Ser. pp. 410, 424. See Kalisch on Leviticus ; Barry in Smith's ' Dictionary of the Bible,' art. ' sacrifice.'

[2] Callaway, ' Religion of Amazulu,' p. 11 (amadhlozi or amatongo = ancestral spirits).

was familiar to the native religion of the West Indian islands. In Columbus' time, and with particular reference to Hispaniola, Roman Pane describes the native mode of sacrifice. Upon any solemn day, when they provide much to eat, whether fish, flesh, or any other thing, they put it all into the house of the cemis, that the idol may feed on it. The next day they carry all home, after the cemi has eaten. And God so help them (says the friar), as the cemi eats of that or anything else, they being inanimate stocks or stones. A century and a half later, a similar notion still prevailed in these islands. Nothing could show it more neatly than the fancy of the Caribs that they could hear the spirits in the night moving the vessels and champing the food set out for them, yet next morning there was nothing touched ; it was held that the viands thus partaken of by the spirits had become holy, so that only the old men and considerable people might taste them, and even these required a certain bodily purity.[1] Islanders of Pulo Aur, though admitting that their banished disease-spirits did not actually consume the grains of rice set out for them, nevertheless believed them to appropriate its essence.[2] In India, among the indigenes of the Garo hills, we hear of the head and blood of the sacrificed animal being placed with some rice under a bamboo arch covered with a white cloth ; the god comes and takes what he wants, and after a time this special offering is dressed for the company with the rest of the animal.[3] The Khond deities live on the flavours and essences drawn from the offerings of their votaries, or from animals or grain which they cause to die or disappear.[4] When the Buraets of Siberia have sacrificed a sheep and boiled the mutton, they set it up on a scaffold for the gods while the shaman is

---

[1] Roman Pane, ch. xvi. in ' Life of Colon,' in Pinkerton, vol. xii. p. 86. Rochefort, ' Iles Antilles,' p. 418 ; see Meiners, vol. ii., p. 516 ; J. G. Müller, p. 212.

[2] ' Journ. Ind. Archip.' vol. iv. p. 194.

[3] Eliot in ' As. Res.' vol. iii. p. 30.

[4] Macpherson, ' India,' pp. 88, 100.

chanting his song, and then themselves fall to.[1]   And thus,
in the folklore of mediæval Europe, Domina Abundia would
come with her dames into the houses at night, and eat and
drink from the vessels left uncovered for their increase-
giving visit, yet nothing was consumed.[2]

The extreme animistic view of sacrifice is that the soul
of the offered animal or thing is abstracted by or transmitted to the deity.   This notion of spirits taking souls is
in a somewhat different way exemplified among the Binua
of Johore, who hold that the evil River-spirits inflict
diseases on man by feeding on the ' semangat,' or unsubstantial body (in ordinary parlance the spirit) in which his
life resides,[3] while the Karen demon devours not the body
but the ' la,' spirit or vital principle ; thus when it eats a
man's eyes, their material part remains, but they are blind.[4]
Now an idea similar to this furnished the Polynesians with
a theory of sacrifice.   The priest might send commissions
by the sacrificed human victim; spirits of the dead are
eaten by the gods or demons ; the spiritual part of the
sacrifices is eaten by the spirit of the idol (i.e. the deity
dwelling or embodied in the idol) before whom it is presented.[5]   Of the Fijians it is observed that of the great
offerings of food native belief apportions merely the soul to
the gods, who are described as being enormous eaters ; the
substance is consumed by the worshippers.   As in various
other districts of the world, human sacrifice is here in fact
a meat-offering ; cannibalism is a part of the Fijian religion,
and the gods are described as delighting in human flesh.[6]
Such ideas are explicit among Indian tribes of the American
lakes, who consider that offerings, whether abandoned or
consumed by the worshippers, go in a spiritual form to the

1 Klemm, ' Cultur-Gesch.' vol. iii. p. 114.
2 Grimm, ' Deutsche Myth.' p. 264.
3 ' Journ. Ind. Archip.' vol. i. p. 27.
4 Mason, ' Karens,' l.c. p. 208.
5 Bastian, ' Mensch,' vol. ii. p. 407.   Ellis, ' Polyn. Res.' vol. i. p. 358.
Taylor, ' New Zealand,' pp. 104, 220.
6 Williams, ' Fiji,' vol. i. p. 231.

spirit they are devoted to. Native legends afford the clearest illustrations. The following is a passage from an Ottawa tale which recounts the adventures of Wassamo, he who was conveyed by the spirit-maiden to the lodge of her father, the Spirit of the Sand Downs, down below the waters of Lake Superior. ' Son-in-law,' said the Old Spirit, ' I am in want of tobacco. You shall return to visit your parents, and can make known my wishes. For it is very seldom that those few who pass these Sand Hills, offer a piece of tobacco. When they do it, it immediately comes to me. Just so,' he added, putting his hand out of the side of the lodge, and drawing in several pieces of tobacco, which some one at that moment happened to offer to the Spirit, for a smooth lake and prosperous voyage. ' You see,' he said, ' every thing offered me on earth, comes immediately to the side of my lodge.' Wassamo saw the women also putting their hands to the side of the lodge, and then handing round something, of which all partook. This he found to be offerings of food made by mortals on earth. The distinctly spiritual nature of this transmission is shown immediately after, for Wassamo cannot eat such mere spirit-food, wherefore his spirit-wife puts out her hand from the lodge and takes in a material fish out of the lake to cook for him.[1] Another Ottawa legend, the already cited nature-myth of the Sun and Moon, is of much interest not only for its display of this special thought, but as showing clearly the motives with which savage animists offer sacrifices to their deities, and consider these deities to accept them. Onowuttokwutto, the Ojibwa youth who has followed the Moon up to the lovely heaven-prairies to be her husband, is taken one day by her brother the Sun to see how he gets his dinner. The two look down together through the hole in the sky upon the earth below, the Sun points out a group of children playing beside a lodge, at the same time throwing a tiny stone to hit a beautiful boy. The child falls, they see him carried into the lodge, they

[1] Schoolcraft, ' Algic Researches,' vol. ii. p. 140 ; see p. 190.

hear the sound of the sheesheegwun (the rattle), and the song and prayer of the medicine-man that the child's life may be spared. To this entreaty of the medicine-man, the Sun makes answer, ' Send me up the white dog.' Then the two spectators above could distinguish on the earth the hurry and bustle of preparation for a feast, a white dog killed and singed, and the people who were called assembling at the lodge. While these things were passing, the Sun addressed himself to Onowuttokwutto, saying,' There are among you in the lower world some whom you call great medicine-men ; but it is because their ears are open, and they hear my voice, when I have struck any one, that they are able to give relief to the sick. They direct the people to send me whatever I call for and when they have sent it, I remove my hand from those I had made sick.' When he had said this, the white dog was parcelled out in dishes for those that were at the feast ; then the medicine-man when they were about to begin to eat, said, ' We send thee this, Great Manito.' Immediately the Sun and his Ojibwa companion saw the dog, cooked and ready to be eaten, rising to them through the air—and then and there they dined upon it.[1] How such ideas bear on the meaning of human sacrifice, we may perhaps judge from this prayer of the Iroquois, offering a human victim to the War-god : 'To thee, O Spirit Arieskoi, we slay this sacrifice, that thou mayst feed upon the flesh, and be moved to give us henceforth luck and victory over our enemies ! '[2] So among the Aztec prayers, there occurs this one addressed to Tezcatlipoca-Yautl in time of war: 'Lord of battles ; it is a very certain and sure thing, that a great war is beginning to make, ordain, form, and concert itself ; the War-god opens his mouth, hungry to swallow the blood of many who shall die in this war ; it seems that the Sun and the Earth-God Tlatecutli desire to rejoice ; they desire to give meat and drink to the gods of Heaven and Hades, making them a

---

[1] Tanner's ' Narrative,' pp. 286, 318. See also Waitz, vol. iii. p. 207.
[2] J. G. Müller, p. 142 ; see p. 282.

banquet of the flesh and blood of the men who are to die in this war,' &c.[1] There is remarkable definiteness in the Peruvian idea that the souls of human victims are transmitted to another life in divine as in funeral sacrifice ; at one great ceremony, where children of each tribe were sacrificed to propitiate the gods, ' they strangled the children, first giving them to eat and drink, that they might not enter the presence of the Creator discontented and hungry.'[2] Similar ideas of spiritual sacrifice appear in other regions of the world. Thus in West Africa we read of the tree-fetish enjoying the spirit of the food-offering, but leaving its substance, and an account of the religion of the Gold Coast mentions how each great wong or deity has his house, and his priest and priestess to clean the room and give him daily bread kneaded with palm-oil, ' of which, as of all gifts of this kind, the wong eats the invisible soul.'[3] So, in India, the Limbus of Darjeeling make small offerings of grain, vegetables, and sugar-cane, and sacrifice cows, pigs, fowls, &c., on the declared principle ' the life breath to the gods, the flesh to ourselves.'[4] It seems likely that such meaning may largely explain the sacrificial practices of other religions. In conjunction with these accounts, the unequivocal meaning of funeral sacrifices, whereby offerings are conveyed spiritually into the possession of spirits of the dead, may perhaps justify us in inferring that similar ideas of spiritual transmission prevail extensively among the many nations whose sacrificial rites we know in fact, but cannot trace with certainty to their original significance.

Having thus examined the manner in which the operation of sacrifice is considered to take physical effect, whether indefinitely or definitely, and having distinguished its actual transmission as either substantial, essential, or spiritual,

[1] Sahagun, lib. vi. in Kingsborough, vol. v.

[2] ' Rites and Laws of Yncas,' tr. and ed. by C. R. Markham, pp. 55, 58, 166. See ante, p. 385 (possible connexion of smoke with soul).

[3] Waitz, vol. ii. pp. 188, 196. Steinhauser, l.c. p. 136. See also Schlegel, ' Ewe-Sprache,' p. xv. ; Magyar, ' Süd-Afrika,' p. 273.

[4] A. Campbell in ' Tr. Eth. Soc.' vol. vii. p. 153.

let us now follow the question of the sacrificer's motive in presenting the sacrifice. Important and complex as this problem is, its key is so obvious that it may be almost throughout treated by mere statement of general principle. If the main proposition of animistic natural religion be granted, that the idea of the human soul is the model of the idea of deity, then the analogy of man's dealings with man ought, *inter alia*, to explain his motives in sacrifice. It does so, and very fully. The proposition may be maintained in wide generality, that the common man's present to the great man, to gain good or avert evil, to ask aid or to condone offence, needs only substitution of deity for chief, and proper adaptation of the means of conveying the gift to him, to produce a logical doctrine of sacrificial rites, in great measure explaining their purpose directly as they stand, and elsewhere suggesting what was the original meaning which has passed into changed shape in the course of ages. Instead of offering a special collection of evidence here on this proposition, it may be enough to ask attentive reference to any extensive general collection of accounts of sacrifice, such for instance as those cited for various purposes in these volumes. It will be noticed that offerings to divinities may be classed in the same way as earthly gifts. The occasional gift made to meet some present emergency, the periodical tribute brought by subject to lord, the royalty paid to secure possession or protection of acquired wealth, all these have their evident and well-marked analogues in the sacrificial systems of the world. It may impress some minds with a stronger sense of the sufficiency of this theory of sacrifice, to consider how the transition is made in the same imperceptible way from the idea of substantial value received, to that of ceremonial homage rendered, whether the recipient be man or god. We do not find it easy to analyse the impression which a gift makes on our own feelings, and to separate the actual value of the object from the sense of gratification in the giver's good-will or respect, and thus we may well scruple to define closely how

uncultured men work out this very same distinction in their
dealings with their deities. In a general way it may be
held that the idea of practical acceptableness of the food or
valuables presented to the deity, begins early to shade into
the sentiment of divine gratification or propitiation by a
reverent offering, though in itself of not much account to
so mighty a divine personage. These two stages of the
sacrificial idea may be fairly contrasted, the one among the
Karens who offer to a demon arrack or grain or a portion
of the game they kill, considering invocation of no avail
without a gift,[1] the other among the negroes of Sierra
Leone, who sacrifice an ox ' to make Gòd glad very much,
and do Kroomen good.'[2]

Hopeless as it may be in hundreds of accounts of sacrifice
to guess whether the worshipper means to benefit or merely
to gratify the deity, there are also numbers of cases in which
the thought in the sacrificer's mind can scarcely be more
than an idea of ceremonial homage. One of the best-
marked sacrificial rites of the world is that of offering by
fire or otherwise morsels or libations at meals. This ranges
from the religion of the North American Indian to that of
the classic Greek and the ancient Chinese, and still holds
its place in peasant custom in Europe.[3] Other groups of
cases pass into yet more absolute formality of reverence.
See the Guinea negro passing in silence by the sacred tree
or cavern, and dropping a leaf or a sea-shell as an offering
to the local spirit;[4] the Talein of Burma holding up the
dish at his meal to offer it to the nat, before the company
fall to;[5] the Hindu holding up a little of his rice in his
fingers to the height of his forehead, and offering it in

[1] O'Riley, in ' Journ. Ind. Archip.' vol. iv. p. 592. Bastian, ' Oestl. Asien,'
vol. ii. p. 12.

[2] R. Clarke, ' Sierra Leone,' p. 43.

[3] Smith, ' Virginia,' in Pinkerton, vol. xiii. p. 41. Welcker, ' Griech.
Götterlehre,' vol. ii. p. 693. Legge, ' Confucius,' p. 179. Grohmann,
' Aberglauben aus Böhmen,' p. 41, &c.

[4] J. L. Wilson, ' W. Afr.' p. 218 ; Bosman, ' Guinea,' in Pinkerton, vol.
xvi. p. 400.

[5] Bastian, ' Oestl. Asien,' vol. ii. p. 387.

thought to Siva or Vishnu before he eats it.[1] The same
argument applies to the cases ranging far and wide through
religion, where, whatever may have been the original intent
of the sacrifice, it has practically passed into a feast. A
banquet where the deity has but the pretence and the worshippers the reality, may seem to us a mere mockery of
sacrifice. Yet how sincerely men regard it as a religious
ceremony, the following anecdote of a North American
Indian tribe will show. A travelling party of Potawatomis,
for three days finding no game, were in great distress for
want of food. On the third night, a chief, named Saugana,
had a dream, wherein a person appearing to him showed
him that they were suffering because they had set out without a sacrificial feast. He had started, on this important
journey, the dreamer said, ' as a white man would,' without
making any religious preparation. Therefore the Great
Spirit had punished them with scarcity. Now, however,
twelve men were to go and kill four deer before the sun was
thus high (about nine o'clock). The chief in his dream had
seen these four deer lying dead, the hunters duly killed
them, and the sacrificial feast was held.[2] Further illustrative examples of such sacred banquets may be chosen
through the long range of culture. The Zulus propitiate
the Heaven-god above with a sacrifice of black cattle,
that they may have rain ; the village chiefs select the
oxen, one is killed, the rest are merely mentioned ; the
flesh of the slaughtered ox is eaten in the house in perfect
silence, a token of humble submission ; the bones are burnt
outside the village ; and after the feast they chant in
musical sounds, a song without words.[3] The Serwatty
Islanders sacrifice buffaloes, pigs, goats, and fowls to the
idols when an individual or the community undertakes an
affair or expedition of importance, and as the carcases are
devoured by the devotees, this ensures a respectable

[1] Roberts, ' Oriental Illustrations,' p. 545.
[2] M'Coy, ' Baptist Indian Missions,' p. 305.
[3] Callaway, ' Religion of Amazulu,' p. 59. See Casalis, p. 252.

attendance when the offerings are numerous.[1] Thus among rude tribes of Northern India, sacrifices of beasts are accompanied by libations of fermented liquor, and in fact sacrifice and feast are convertible words.[2] Among the Aztecs, prisoners of war furnished first an acceptable sacrifice to the deity, and then the staple of a feast for the captors and their friends;[3] while in ancient Peru whole flocks of sacrificed llamas were eaten by the people.[4] The history of Greek religion plainly records the transition from the early holocausts devoted by fire to the gods, to the great festivals where the sacrifices provided meat for the public banquets held to honour them in ceremonial homage.[5]

Beside this development from gift to homage, there arises also a doctrine that the gist of sacrifice is rather in the worshipper giving something precious to himself, than in the deity receiving benefit. This may be called the abnegation-theory, and its origin may be fairly explained by considering it as derived from the original gift-theory. Taking our own feelings again for a guide, we know how it satisfies us to have done our part in giving, even if the gift be ineffectual, and how we scruple to take it back if not received, but rather get rid of it in some other way—it is corban. Thus we may enter into the feelings of the Assinaboin Indians, who considered that the blankets and pieces of cloth and brass kettles and such valuables abandoned in the woods as a medicine-sacrifice, might be carried off by any friendly party who chanced to discover them;[6] or of the Ava Buddhists bringing to the temples offerings of boiled rice and sweetmeats and coco-nut fried

[1] Earl in ' Journ. Ind. Archip.' vol. iv. p. 174

[2] Hodgson, ' Abor. of India,' p. 170, see p. 146 ; Hooker, ' Himalayan Journals,' vol. ii. p. 276.

[3] Prescott, ' Mexico,' book i. ch. iii.

[4] ' Rites and Laws of Yncas,' p. 33, &c.

[5] Welcker, ' Griech. Götterlehre,' vol. ii. p. 50 ; Pauly, ' Real-Encyclopedie,' s.v. ' Sacrificia.'

[6] Tanner's ' Nar.' p.154 ; see also Waitz. vol. iii. p. 167.

in oil, and never attempting to disturb the crows and wild dogs who devoured it before their eyes;[1] of the modern Moslems sacrificing sheep, oxen, and camels in the valley of Muna on their return from Mekka, it being a meritorious act to give away a victim without eating any of it, while parties of Takruri watch around like vultures, ready to pounce upon the carcases.[2] If the offering to the deity be continued in ceremonial survival, in spite of a growing conviction that after all the deity does not need and cannot profit by it, sacrifice will be thus kept up in spite of having become practically unreasonable, and the worshipper may still continue to measure its efficacy by what it costs him. But to take this abnegation theory as representing the primitive intention of sacrifice would be, I think, to turn history upside down. The mere fact of sacrifices to deities, from the lowest to the highest levels of culture, consisting to the extent of nine-tenths or more of gifts of food and sacred banquets, tells forcibly against the originality of the abnegation-theory. If the primary motive had been to give up valuable property, we should find the sacrifice of weapons, garments, ornaments, as prevalent in the lower culture as in fact it is unusual. Looking at the subject in a general view, to suppose men to have started by devoting to their deities what they considered practically useless to them, in order that they themselves might suffer a loss which none is to gain, is to undervalue the practical sense of savages, who are indeed apt to keep up old rites after their meaning has fallen away, but seldom introduce new ones without a rational motive. In studying the religion of the lower races, men are found dealing with their gods in as practical and straightforward a way as with their neighbours, and where plain original purpose is found, it may well be accepted as sufficient explanation. Of the way in which gift can pass into abnegation, an instructive example is forth-

---

[1] Symes, ' Ava,' in Pinkerton, vol. ix. p. 440 ; Caron, ' Japan,' ib. vol. vii. p. 629.

[2] Burton, ' Medinah,' &c., vol. iii. p. 302 ; Lane, ' Mod. Eg.' vol. i. p.132.

coming in Buddhism. It is held that sinful men are liable to be re-born in course of transmigration as wandering, burning, miserable demons (preta). Now these demons may receive offerings of food and drink from their relatives, who can further benefit them by acts of merit done in their name, as giving food to priests, unless the wretched spirits be so low in merit that this cannot profit them. Yet even in this case it is held that though the act does not benefit the spirit whom it is directed to, it does benefit the person who performs it.[1] Unequivocal examples of abnegation in sacrifice may be best found among those offerings of which the value to the offerer utterly exceeds the value they can be supposed to have to the deity. The most striking of these found among nations somewhat advanced in general culture, appear in the history of human sacrifice among Semitic nations. The king of Moab, when the battle was too sore for him, offered up his eldest son for a burnt-offering on the wall. The Phœnicians sacrificed the dearest children to propitiate the angry gods, they enhanced their value by choosing them of noble families, and there was not wanting among them even the utmost proof that the efficacy of the sacrifice lay in the sacrificer's grievous loss, for they must have for yearly sacrifice only-begotten sons of their parents (Κρόνῳ γὰρ Φοίνικες καθ' ἕκαστον ἔτος ἔθυον τὰ ἀγαπητὰ καὶ μονογενῆ τῶν τέκνων). Heliogabalus brought the hideous Oriental rite into Italy, choosing for victims to his solar divinity high-born lads throughout the land. Of all such cases, the breaking of the sacred law of hospitality by sacrificing the guest to Jupiter hospitalis, Ζεὺς ξένιος, shows in the strongest light in Semitic regions how the value to the offerer might become the measure of acceptableness to the god.[2] In such ways, slightly within the range of the lower culture, but strongly in the religion of the higher

---

[1] Hardy, 'Manual of Budhism,' p. 59.

[2] 2 Kings iii. 27. Euseb. Præp. Evang. i. 10, iv. 156; Laud. Constant. xiii. Porphyr. De Abstin. ii. 56, &c. Lamprid. Heliogabal. vii. Movers, 'Phönizier,' vol. i. p. 300, &c.

nations, the transition from the gift-theory to the abnegation theory seems to have come about. Our language displays it in a word, if we do but compare the sense of presentation and acceptance which 'sacrificium' had in a Roman temple, with the sense of mere giving up and loss which 'sacrifice' conveys in an English market.

Through the history of sacrifice, it has occurred to many nations that cost may be economized without impairing efficiency. The result is seen in ingenious devices to lighten the burden on the worshipper by substituting something less valuable than what he ought to offer, or pretends to. Even in such a matter as this, the innate correspondence in the minds of men is enough to produce in distant and independent races so much uniformity of development, that three or four headings will serve to class the chief divisions of sacrificial substitution among mankind.

To give part for the whole is a proceeding so closely conformed to ordinary tribute by subject to lord, that in great measure it comes directly under the gift-theory, and as such has already had its examples here. It is only when the part given to the gods is of contemptible value in proportion to the whole, that full sacrifice passes gradually into substitution. This is the case when in Madagascar the head of the sacrificed beast is set up on a pole, and the blood and fat are rubbed on the stones of the altar, but the sacrificers and their friends and the officiating priest devour the whole carcase ; [1] when rich Guinea negroes sacrifice a sheep or goat to the fetish, and feast on it with their friends, only leaving for the deity himself part of the entrails; [2] when Tunguz, sacrificing cattle, would give a bit of liver and fat and perhaps hang up the hide in the woods as the god's share, or Mongols would set the heart of the beast before the idol till next day. [3] Thus the most ancient whole

---

[1] Ellis, ' Madagascar,' vol. i. p. 419.

[2] Römer, ' Guinea,' p. 59. Bosman in Pinkerton, vol. xvi. p. 399.

[3] Klemm, ' Cultur-Gesch.' vol. iii. p. 106 ; Castrén, ' Finn. Myth.' p. 232.

burnt-offering of the Greeks dwindled to burning for the gods only the bones and fat of the slaughtered ox, while the worshippers feasted themselves on the meat, an economic rite which takes mythic shape in the legend of the sly Prometheus giving Zeus the choice of the two parts of the sacrificed ox he had divided for gods and mortals, on the one side bones covered seemly with white fat, on the other the joints hidden under repulsive hide and entrails.[1] With a different motive, not that of parsimony, but of keeping up in survival an ancient custom, the Zarathustrian religion performed by substitution the old Aryan sacrifice by fire. The Vedic sacrifice Agnishtoma required that animals should be slain, and their flesh partly committed to the gods by fire, partly eaten by sacrificers and priests. The Parsi ceremony Izeshne, formal successor of this bloody rite, requires no animal to be killed, but it suffices to place the hair of an ox in a vessel, and show it to the fire.[2]

The offering of a part of the worshipper's own body is a most usual act, whether its intention is simply that of gift or tribute, or whether it is considered as a *pars pro toto* representing the whole man, either in danger and requiring to be ransomed, or destined to actual sacrifice for another and requiring to be redeemed. How a finger-joint may thus represent a whole body, is perfectly shown in the funeral sacrifices of the Nicobar islanders ; they bury the dead man's property with him, and his wife has a finger-joint cut off (obviously a substitute for herself), and if she refuses even this, a deep notch is cut in a pillar of the house.[3] We are now concerned, however, with the finger-offering, not as a sacrifice to the dead, but as addressed to other deities. This idea is apparently worked out in the Tongan custom of tutu-nima, the chopping off a portion of the little finger with a hatchet or sharp stone as a sacrifice to the gods, for the recovery of a sick relation of higher rank ; Mariner saw

[1] Hesiod. Theog. 537. Welcker, vol. i. p. 764 ; vol. ii p. 51.
[2] Haug, ' Parsis,' Bombay, 1862, p. 238.
[3] Hamilton in ' As. Res.' vol. ii. p. 342.

children of five years old quarrelling for the honour of having it done to them.[1] In the Mandan ceremonies of initiation into manhood, when the youth at last hung sense-less and (as they called it) lifeless by the cords made fast to splints through his flesh, he was let down, and coming to himself crawled on hands and feet round the medicine-lodge to where an old Indian sat with hatchet in his hand and a buffalo skull before him ; then the youth, holding up the little finger of his left hand to the Great Spirit, offered it as a sacrifice, and it was chopped off, and sometimes the fore-finger afterwards, upon the skull.[2] In India, probably as a Dravidian rather than Aryan rite, the practice with full meaning comes into view ; as Siva cut off his finger to appease the wrath of Kali, so in the southern provinces mothers will cut off their own fingers as sacrifices lest they lose their children, and one hears of a golden finger being allowed instead, the substitute of a substitute.[3] The New Zealanders hang locks of hair on branches of trees in the burying-ground, a recognised place for offerings.[4] That hair may be a substitute for its owner is well shown in Malabar, where we read of the demon being expelled from the possessed patient and flogged by the exorcist to a tree ; there the sick man's hair is nailed fast, cut away, and left for a propitiation to the demon.[5] Thus there is some ground for interpreting the consecration of the boy's cut hair in Europe as a representative sacrifice.[6] As for the formal shedding of blood, it may represent fatal bloodshed, as when

---

[1] Mariner's ' Tonga Is.' vol. i. p. 454 ; vol. ii. p. 222. Cook's ' 3rd Voy.' vol. i. p. 403. Details from S. Africa in Bastian, ' Mensch,' vol. iii. pp. 4, 24 ; Scherzer, ' Voy. of Novara,' vol. i. p. 212.

[2] Catlin, ' N. A. Ind.' vol. i. p. 172; Klemm, 'Cultur-Gesch.' vol. ii. p. 170. See also Venegas, ' Noticia de la California,' vol. i. p. 117 ; Garcilaso de la Vega, lib. ii. c. 8 (Peru).

[3] Buchanan, ' Mysore,' &c., in Pinkerton, vol. viii. p. 661 ; Meiners, vol. ii. p. 472 ; Bastian, l.c. See also Dubois, ' India,' vol. i. p. 5.

[4] Polack, ' New Zealand,' vol. i. p. 264.

[5] Bastian, ' Psychologie,' p. 184.

[6] Theodoret. in Levit. xix. ; Hanusch, ' Slaw. Myth.' Details in Bastian, ' Mensch,' vol. ii. p. 229, &c.

the Jagas or priests in Quilombo only marked with spears the children brought in, instead of running them through;[1] or when in Greece a few drops of human blood had come to stand instead of the earlier and more barbaric human sacrifice ;[2] or when in our own time and under our own rule a Vishnuite who has inadvertently killed a monkey, a garuda, or a cobra, may expiate his offence by a mock sacrifice, in which a human victim is wounded in the thigh, pretends to die, and goes through the farce of resuscitation, his drawn blood serving as substitute for his life.[3] One of the most noteworthy cases of the survival of such formal bloodshed within modern memory in Europe must be classed as not Aryan but Turanian, belonging as it does to the folklore of Esthonia. The sacrificer had to draw drops of blood from his forefinger, and therewith to pray this prayer, which was taken down verbatim from one who remembered it :—' I name thee with my blood and betroth thee with my blood, and point thee out my buildings to be blessed, stables and cattle-pens and hen-roosts ; let them be blessed through my blood and thy might ! ' ' Be my joy, thou Almighty, upholder of my forefathers, my protector and guardian of my life ! I beseech thee by strength of flesh and blood ; receive the food that I bring thee to thy sustenance and the joy of my body ; keep me as thy good child, and I will thank and praise thee. By the help of the Almighty, my own God, hearken to me ! What through negligence I have done imperfectly toward thee, do thou forget! But keep it truly in remembrance, that I have honestly paid my gifts to my parents' honour and joy and requital. Moreover falling down I thrice kiss the earth. Be with me quick in doing, and peace be with thee hitherto!'[4] These various rites of finger-cutting, hair-cutting, and blood-letting, have required mention here from the special point of view of their

---

[1] Bastian, ' Mensch,' vol. iii. p. 113 (see other details).
[2] Pausan. viii. 23 ; ix. 8.
[3] ' Encyc. Brit.' art. ' Brahma.' See ' Asiat. Res.' vol. ix. p. 387.
[4] Boecler, ' Ehsten Aberglaübische Gebraüche,' &c., p. 4.

connexion with sacrifice. They belong to an extensive
series of practices, due to various and often obscure motives,
which come under the general heading of ceremonial muti-
lations.

When a life is given for a life, it is still possible to offer a
life less valued than the life in danger. When in Peru the
Inca or some great lord fell sick, he would offer to the deity
one of his sons, imploring him to take this victim in his
stead.[1] The Greeks found it sufficient to offer to the gods
criminals or captives;[2] and the like was the practice of the
heathen tribes of northern Europe, to whom indeed Christian
dealers were accused of selling slaves for sacrificial purposes.[3]
Among such accounts, the typical story belongs to Punic
history. The Carthaginians, overcome and hard pressed
in the war with Agathokles, set down the defeat to divine
wrath. Now Kronos had in former times received his
sacrifice of the chosen of their sons, but of late they had
put him off with children bought and nourished for the
purpose. In fact they had obeyed the sacrificer's natural
tendency to substitution, but now in time of misfortune
the reaction set in. To balance the account and condone
the parsimonious fraud, a monstrous sacrifice was celebrated.
Two hundred children, of the noblest of the land, were
brought to the idol. ' For there was among them a brazen
statue of Kronos, holding out his hands sloping downward,
so that the child placed on them rolled off and fell into
a certain chasm full of fire.'[4] The Phœnician god here
called Kronos is commonly though not certainly identified
with Moloch. Next, it will help us to realize how the
sacrifice of an animal may atone for a human life, if we
notice in South Africa how a Zulu will redeem a lost child
from the finder by a bullock, or a Kimbunda will expiate
the blood of a slave by the offering of an ox, whose blood

---

[1] Rivero and Tschudi, p. 196. See ' Rites of Yncas,' p. 79.
[2] Bastian, p. 112, &c.; Smith's 'Dic. of Gr. and Rom. Ant.' art. 'Sacrificium.'
[3] Grimm, ' Deutsche Myth.' p. 40.
[4] Diodor. Sic. xx. 14.

will wash away the other.[1]   For instances of the animal substituted for man in sacrifice the following may serve. Among the Khonds of Orissa, when Colonel Macpherson was engaged in putting down the sacrifice of human victims by the sect of the Earth-goddess, they at once began to discuss the plan of sacrificing cattle by way of substitutes. Now there is some reason to think that this same course of ceremonial change may account for the following sacrificial practice in the other Khond sect.   It appears that those who worship the Light-god hold a festival in his honour, when they slaughter a buffalo in commemoration of the time when, as they say, the Earth-goddess was prevailing on men to offer human sacrifices to her, but the Light-god sent a tribe-deity who crushed the bloody-minded Earth-goddess under a mountain, and dragged a buffalo out of the jungle, saying, ' Liberate the man, and sacrifice the buffalo!'[2]   This legend, divested of its mythic garb, may really record a historical substitution of animal for human sacrifice.   In Ceylon, the exorcist will demand the name of the demon possessing a demoniac, and the patient in frenzy answers, giving the demon's name, ' I am So-and-so, I demand a human sacrifice and will not go out without ! '   The victim is promised, the patient comes to from the fit, and a few weeks later the sacrifice is made, but instead of a man they offer a fowl.[3]   Classic examples of substitution of this sort may be found in the sacrifice of a doe for a virgin to Artemis in Laodicæa, a goat for a boy to Dionysos at Potniæ.   There appears to be Semitic connexion here, as there clearly is in the story of the Æolians of Tenedos sacrificing to Melikertes (Melkarth) instead of a new-born child a new-born calf, shoeing it with buskins and tending the mother-cow as if a human mother.[4]

One step more in the course of substitution leads the

[1] Callaway, ' Zulu Tales,' vol. i. p. 88 ; Magyar, ' Süd-Afrika,' p. 256.
[2] Macpherson, ' India,' pp. 108, 187.
[3] De Silva in Bastian, ' Psychologie,' p. 181.
[4] Details in Pauly, ' Real-Encyclop.' s.v. ' Sacrificia'; Bastian, ' Mensch,' vol. iii. p. 114 ; Movers, ' Phönizier,' vol. i. p. 300.

worshipper to make his sacrifice by effigy. An instructive example of the way in which this kind of substitution arises may be found in the rites of ancient Mexico. At the yearly festival of the water-gods and mountain-gods, certain actual sacrifices of human victims took place in the temples. At the same time, in the houses of the people, there was celebrated an unequivocal but harmless imitation of this bloody rite. They made paste images, adored them, and in due pretence of sacrifice cut them open at the breast, took out their hearts, cut off their heads, divided and devoured their limbs.[1] In the classic religions of Greece and Rome, the desire to keep up the consecrated rites of ages more barbaric, more bloodthirsty, or more profuse, worked itself out in many a compromise of this class, such as the brazen statues offered for human victims, the cakes of dough or wax in the figure of the beasts for which they were presented as symbolic substitutes.[2] Not for economy, but to avoid taking life, Brahmanic sacrifice has been known to be brought down to offering models of the victim-animals in meal and butter.[3] The modern Chinese, whose satisfaction in this kind of make-believe is so well shown by their despatching paper figures to serve as attendants for the dead, work out in the same fanciful way the idea of the sacrificial effigy, in propitiating the presiding deity of the year for the cure of a sick man. The rude figure of a man is drawn on or cut out of a piece of paper, pasted on a slip of bamboo, and stuck upright in a packet of mock-money. With proper exorcism, this representative is carried out into the street with the disease, the priest squirts water from his mouth over patient, image, and mock-money, the two latter are burnt, and the company eat up the little feast

[1] Clavigero, 'Messico,' vol. ii. p. 82 ; Torquemada, 'Monarquia Indiana,' x. c. 29; J. G. Müller, pp. 502, 640. See also ibid. p. 379 (Peru); 'Rites and Laws of Yncas,' pp. 46, 54.

[2] Grote, vol. v. p. 366. Schmidt in Smith's ' Dic. of Gr. and Rom. Ant.' art. ' Sacrificium.' Bastian, l.c.

[3] Bastian, ' Oestl. Asien,' vol. iii. p. 501.

laid out for the year-deity.[1] There is curious historical significance in the custom at the inundation of the Nile at Cairo, of setting up a conical pillar of earth which the flood washes away as it rises. This is called the arûseh or bride, and appears to be a substitute introduced under humaner Moslem influence, for the young virgin in gay apparel who in older time was thrown into the river, a sacrifice to obtain a plentiful inundation.[2] Again, the patient's offering the model of his diseased limb is distinctly of the nature of a sacrifice, whether it be propitiatory offering before cure, or thank-offering after. On the one hand, the ex-voto models of arms and ears dedicated in ancient Egyptian temples are thought to be grateful memorials,[3] as seems to have been the case with metal models of faces, breasts, hands, &c., in Bœotian temples.[4] On the other hand, there are cases where the model and, as it were, substitute of the diseased part is given to obtain a cure; thus in early Christian times in Germany protest was made against the heathen custom of hanging up carved wooden limbs to a helpful idol for relief,[5] and in modern India the pilgrim coming for cure will deposit in the temple the image of his diseased limb, in gold or silver or copper according to his means.[6]

If now we look for the sacrificial idea within the range of modern Christendom, we shall find it in two ways not obscurely manifest. It survives in traditional folklore, and it holds a place in established religion. One of its most remarkable survivals may be seen in Bulgaria, where sacrifice of live victims is to this day one of the accepted rites of the land. They sacrifice a lamb on St. George's day, telling to account for the custom a legend which combines the episodes of the offering of Isaac and the miracle of the Three Children.

---

[1] Doolittle, ' Chinese,' vol. i. p. 152.
[2] Lane, ' Modern Eg.' vol. ii. p. 262. Meiners, vol. ii. p. 85.
[3] Wilkinson, ' Ancient Eg.' vol. iii. p. 395 ; and in Rawlinson's Herodotus, vol. ii. p. 137. See 1 Sam. vi. 4.
[4] Grimm, ' Deutsche Myth.' p. 1131.
[5] Ibid.
[6] Bastian, vol. iii. p. 116.

On the feast of the Panagia (Virgin Mary) sacrifices of lambs, kids, honey, wine, &c., are offered in order that the children of the house may enjoy good health throughout the year. A little child divines by touching one of three saints' candles to which the offering is to be dedicated ; when the choice is thus made, the bystanders each drink a cup of wine, saying ' Saint So-and-So, to thee is the offering.' Then they cut the throat of the lamb, or smother the bees, and in the evening the whole village assembles to eat the various sacrifices, and the men end the ceremony with the usual drunken bout.[1] Within the borders of Russia, many and various sacrifices are still offered ; such is the horse with head smeared with honey and mane decked with ribbons, cast into the river with two millstones to its neck to appease the water-spirit, the Vodyany, at his spiteful flood-time in early spring ; and such is the portion of supper left out for the house-demon, the domovoy, who if not thus fed is apt to turn spirit-rapper, and knock the tables and benches about at night.[2] In many another district of Europe, the tenacious memory of the tiller of the soil has kept up in wondrous perfection heirlooms from præ-Christian faiths. In Franconia, people will pour on the ground a libation before drinking ; entering a forest they will put offerings of bread and fruit on a stone, to avert the attacks of the demon of the woods, the ' bilberry-man ; ' the bakers will throw white rolls into the oven flue for luck, and say, ' Here, devil, they are thine ! ' The Carinthian peasant will fodder the wind by setting up a dish of food in a tree before his house, and the fire by casting in lard and dripping, in order that gale and conflagration may not hurt him. At least up to the end of the 18th century this most direct elemental sacrifice might be seen in Germany at the midsummer festival in the most perfect form ; some of the porridge

[1] St. Clair and Brophy, ' Bulgaria,' p. 43. Compare modern Circassian sacrifice of animal before cross, as substitute for child, in Bell, ' Circassia,' vol. ii.

[2] Ralston, ' Songs of Russian People,' pp. 123, 153, &c.

from the table was thrown into the fire, and some into running water, some was buried in the earth, and some smeared on leaves and put on the chimney-top for the winds.[1] Relics of such ancient sacrifice may be found in Scandinavia to this day ; to give but one example, the old country altars, rough earth-fast stones with cup-like hollows, are still visited by mothers whose children have been smitten with sickness by the trolls, and who smear lard into the hollows and leave rag-dolls as offerings.[2] France may be represented by the country-women's custom of beginning a meal by throwing down a spoonful of milk or bouillon ; and by the record of the custom of Andrieux in Dauphiny, where at the solstice the villagers went out upon the bridge when the sun rose, and offered him an omelet.[3] The custom of burning alive the finest calf, to save a murrain-struck herd, had its last examples in Cornwall in the 19th century ; the records of bealtuinn sacrifices in Scotland continue in the Highlands within a century ago ; and Scotchmen still living remember the corner of a field being left untilled for the Goodman's Croft (i.e., the Devil's), but the principle of ' cheating the devil ' was already in vogue, and the piece of land allotted was but a worthless scrap.[4] It is a remnant of old sacrificial rite, when the Swedes still bake at yule-tide a cake in the shape of a boar, representing the boar sacrificed of old to Freyr, and Oxford to this day commemorates the same ancestral ceremony, when the boar's head is carried in to the Christmas feast at Queen's College, with its appointed carol, ' Caput apri defero, Reddens laudes Domino.'[5] With a lingering recollection of the old

[1] Wuttke, 'Deutsche Volksaberglaube,' p. 86. See also Grimm, 'Deutsche Myth.' pp. 417, 602.

[2] Hyltén-Cavallius, ' Wärend och Wirdarne,' part i. pp. 131, 146, 157, &c.

[3] Monnier, ' Traditions Populaires,' pp. 187, 666.

[4] R. Hunt, ' Pop. Rom. of W. of England,' 1st Ser. p. 237. Pennant, ' Tour in Scotland,' in Pinkerton, vol. iii. p. 49. J. Y. Simpson, Address to Soc. Antiq. Scotland, 1861, p. 33 ; Brand, ' Pop. Ant.' vol. iii. pp. 74, 317.

[5] Brand, vol. i. p. 484. Grimm, ' D. M.' pp. 45, 194, 1188, see p. 250 ; ' Deutsche Rechtsalterthümer,' p. 900 ; Hyltén-Cavallius, part i. p. 175.

libations, the German toper's saying still runs that heeltaps are a devil's offering.[1]

As for sacrificial rites most fully and officially existing in modern Christendom, the presentation of ex-votos is one. The ecclesiastical opposition to the continuance of these classic thank-offerings was but temporary and partial. In the 5th century it seems to have been usual to offer silver and gold eyes, feet, &c., to saints in acknowledgment of cures they had effected. At the beginning of the 16th century, Polydore Vergil, describing the classic custom, goes on to say : ' In the same manner do we now offer up in our churches sigillaria, that is, little images of wax, and oscilla. As oft as any part of the body is hurt, as the hand, foot, breast, we presently make a vow to God, and his saints, to whom upon our recovery we make an offering of that hand or foot or breast shaped in wax, which custom has so far obtained that this kind of images have passed to the other animals. Wherefore so for an ox, so for a horse, so for a sheep, we place puppets in the temples. In which thing any modestly scrupulous person may perhaps say he knows not whether we are rivalling the religion or the superstition of the ancients.'[2] In modern Europe the custom prevails largely, but has perhaps somewhat subsided into low levels of society, to judge by the general use of mock silver and such-like worthless materials for the dedicated effigies. In Christian as in præ-Christian temples, clouds of incense rise as of old. Above all, though the ceremony of sacrifice did not form an original part of Christian worship, its prominent place in the ritual was obtained in early centuries. In that Christianity was recruited among nations to whom the conception of sacrifice was among the deepest of religious ideas, and the ceremony of sacrifice among the sincerest efforts of worship, there arose an observance suited to supply the vacant place.

[1] Grimm, ' D. M.' p. 962.
[2] Beausobre, vol. ii. p. 667. Polydorus Vergilius, De Inventoribus Rerum (Basel, 1521), lib. v. 1.

This result was obtained not by new introduction, but by transmutation. The solemn eucharistic meal of the primitive Christians in time assumed the name of the sacrifice of the mass, and was adapted to a ceremonial in which an offering of food and drink is set out by a priest on an altar in a temple, and consumed by priest and worshippers. The natural conclusion of an ethnographic survey of sacrifice, is to point to the controversy between Protestants and Catholics, for centuries past one of the keenest which have divided the Christian world, on this express question whether sacrifice is or is not a Christian rite.

The next group of rites to be considered comprises Fasting and certain other means of producing ecstasy and other morbid exaltation for religious ends. In the foregoing researches on animism, it is frequently observed or implied that the religious beliefs of the lower races are in no small measure based on the evidence of visions and dreams, regarded as actual intercourse with spiritual beings. From the earliest phases of culture upward, we find religion in close alliance with ecstatic physical conditions. These are brought on by various means of interference with the healthy action of body and mind, and it is scarcely needful to remind the reader that, according to philosophic theories antecedent to those of modern medicine, such morbid disturbances are explained as symptoms of divine visitation, or at least of superhuman spirituality. Among the strongest means of disturbing the functions of the mind so as to produce ecstatic vision, is fasting, accompanied as it so usually is with other privations, and with prolonged solitary contemplation in the desert or the forest. Among the ordinary vicissitudes of savage life, the wild hunter has many a time to try involuntarily the effects of such a life for days and weeks together, and under these circumstances he soon comes to see and talk with phantoms which are to him visible personal spirits. The secret of spiritual intercourse thus learnt, he has thenceforth but to reproduce the cause in order to renew the effects.

The rite of fasting, and the utter objective reality ascribed to what we call its morbid symptoms, are shown in striking details among the savage tribes of North America. Among the Indians (the accounts mostly refer to the Algonquin tribes), long and rigorous fasting is enjoined among boys and girls from a very early age ; to be able to fast long is an enviable distinction, and they will abstain from food three to seven days, or even more, taking only a little water. During these fasts, especial attention is paid to dreams. Thus Tanner tells the story of a certain Net-no-kwa, who at twelve years old fasted ten successive days, till in a dream a man came and stood before her, and after speaking of many things gave her two sticks, saying, ' I give you these to walk upon, and your hair I give it to be like snow ; ' this assurance of extreme old age was through life a support to her in times of danger and distress. At manhood the Indian lad, retiring to a solitary place to fast and meditate and pray, receives visionary impressions which stamp his character for life, and especially he waits till there appears to him in a dream some animal or thing which will be henceforth his ' medicine,' the fetish-representative of his manitu or protecting genius. For instance, an aged warrior who had thus in his youth dreamed of a bat coming to him, wore the skin of a bat on the crown of his head henceforth, and was all his life invulnerable to his enemies as a bat on the wing. In after life, an Indian who wants anything will fast till he has a dream that his manitu will grant it him. While the men are away hunting, the children are sometimes made to fast, that in their dreams they may obtain omens of the chase. Hunters fasting before an expedition are informed in dreams of the haunts of the game, and the means of appeasing the wrath of the bad spirits ; if the dreamer fancies he sees an Indian who has been long dead, and hears him say, ' If thou wilt sacrifice to me thou shalt shoot deer at pleasure,' he will prepare a sacrifice, and burn the whole or part of a deer, in honour of the apparition. Especially the ' medī ' or 'medicine-man' receives in fasts much of his qualification for his sacred office. The Ojibwa prophetess, known in after life as Catherine Wabose, in telling the story of her early years, relates how at the age of womanhood she fasted in her secluded lodge till she went up into the heavens and saw the spirit at the entrance, the Bright Blue Sky ; this was the first supernatural communication of her prophetic career. The account given to Schoolcraft by Chingwauk, an Algonquin chief deeply versed in the mystic lore and picture-writing of his people, is as follows : 'Chingwauk began by saying that the ancient Indians made a great merit of fasting. They fasted sometimes six or seven days, till both their bodies and minds became free and light, which prepared them to dream. The object of the ancient seers was to dream of the sun, as it was believed that such a dream would enable them to see everything on the earth. And by fasting long and thinking much on the subject, they generally succeeded. Fasts and dreams were at first attempted at an early age. What a young man sees and experiences during these dreams and fasts, is adopted by him as truth, and it becomes a principle to regulate his future life. He relies for success on these revelations. If he has been much favoured in his fasts, and the people believe that he has the art of looking into futurity, the path is open to the highest honours. The prophet, he continued, begins to try his power in secret, with only one assistant, whose testimony is necessary should he succeed. As he goes on, he puts down the figures of his dreams and revelations, by symbols, on bark or other material, till a whole winter is sometimes passed in pursuing the subject, and he thus has a record of his principal revelations. If what he predicts is verified, the assistant mentions it, and the record is then appealed to as proof of his prophetic power and skill. Time increases his fame. His *kee-keé-wins*, or records, are finally shown to the old people, who meet together and consult upon them, for the whole nation believe in these revelations. They in the end give their approval, and declare that he is gifted as a prophet—is inspired with wisdom, and is fit to lead the opinions of the nation. Such, he concluded, was the ancient custom, and the celebrated old war-captains rose to their power in this manner.' It remains to say that among these American tribes, the ' jossakeed ' or soothsayer prepares himself by fasting and the use of the sweating-bath for the state of convulsive ecstasy in which he utters the dictates of his familiar spirits.[1]

The practice of fasting is described in other districts of the uncultured world as carried on to produce similar ecstasy and supernatural converse. The account by Roman Pane in the Life of Colon describes the practice in Hayti of fasting to obtain knowledge of future events from the spirits (cemi) ; and a century or two later, rigorous fasting formed part of the apprentice's preparation for the craft of ' boyé ' or sorcerer, evoker, consulter, propitiator, and exorciser of spirits.[2] The ' keebèt ' or conjurers of the Abipones were believed by the natives to be able to inflict disease and death, cure all disorders, make known distant and future events, cause rain, hail, and tempests, call up the shades of the dead, put on the form of tigers, handle serpents unharmed, &c. These powers were imparted by diabolical assistance, and Father Dobrizh offer thus describes the manner of obtaining them :—' Those who aspire to the office of juggler are said to sit upon an aged willow, over-hanging some lake, and to abstain from food for several days, till they begin to see into futurity. It always appeared probable to me that these rogues, from long fasting, contract a weakness of brain, a giddiness, and kind

---

[1] Tanner's ' Narrative,' p. 288. Loskiel, ' N. A. Ind.' part i. p. 76, School-craft, ' Ind. Tribes,' part i. pp. 34, 113, 360, 391 ; part iii. p. 227. Catlin, ' N. A. Ind.' vol. i. p. 36. Charlevoix, ' Nouv. Fr.' vol. ii. p. 170 ; vol. vi. p. 67. Klemm, ' Cultur-Gesch.' vol. ii. p. 170. Waitz, ' Anthropologie,' vol. iii. pp. 206, 217.

[2] Colombo, ' Vita,' ch. xxv. Rochefort, ' Iles Antilles,' p. 501. See also Meiners, vol. ii. p. 143 (Guyana).

of delirium, which makes them imagine that they are gifted
with superior wisdom, and give themselves out for magicians. They impose upon themselves first, and afterwards
upon others.'[1] The Malay, to make himself invulnerable,
retires for three days to solitude and scanty food in the
jungle, and if on the third day he dreams of a beautiful
spirit descending to speak to him, the charm is worked.[2]
The Zulu doctor qualifies himself for intercourse with the
' amadhlozi,' or ghosts, from whom he is to obtain direction in his craft, by spare abstemious diet, want, suffering,
castigation, and solitary wandering, till fainting fits or coma
bring him into direct intercourse with the spirits. These
native diviners fast often, and are worn out by fastings,
sometimes of several days' duration, when they become
partially or wholly ecstatic, and see visions. So thoroughly
is the connexion between fasting and spiritual intercourse
acknowledged by the Zulus, that it has become a saying
among them, ' The continually stuffed body cannot see
secret things.' They have no faith in a fat prophet.[3]

The effects thus looked for and attained by fasting among
uncultured tribes continue into the midst of advanced civilization. No wonder that, in the Hindu tale, king Vasava-
datta and his queen after a solemn penance and a three
days' fast should see Siva in a dream and receive his gra-
cious tidings ; no wonder that, in the actual experience of
to-day, the Hindu yogi should bring on by fasting a state
in which he can with bodily eyes behold the gods.[4] The
Greek oracle-priests recognized fasting as a means of bringing on prophetic dreams and visions ; the Pythia of Delphi
herself fasted for inspiration ; Galen remarks that fasting
dreams are the clearer.[5] Through after ages, both cause

---

[1] Dobrizhoffer, ' Abipones,' vol. ii. p. 68.
[2] St. John, ' Far East,' vol. i. p. 144.
[3] Döhne, ' Zulu Dic.' s.v. ' nyanga ; ' Grout, ' Zulu-land,' p. 158 ; Callaway, ' Religion of Amazulu,' p. 387.
[4] Somadeva Bhatta, tr. Brockhaus, vol. ii. p. 81. Meiners, vol. ii. p. 147.
[5] Maury, ' Magie,' &c., p. 237 ; Pausan. i. 34 ; Philostrat. Apollon. Tyan.
i. ; Galen. Comment. in Hippocrat. i.

and consequence have held their places in Christendom.
Thus Michael the Archangel, with sword in right hand
and scales in left, appears to a certain priest of Siponte,
who during a twelvemonth's course of prayer and fasting
had been asking if he would have a temple built in his
honour:—

'precibus jejunia longis
Addiderat, totoque orans se afflixerat anno.'[1]

Reading the narratives of the wondrous sights seen by
St. Theresa and her companions, how the saint went in
spirit into hell and saw the darkness and fire and unutterable despair, how she had often by her side her good patrons
Peter and Paul, how when she was raised in rapture above
the grate at the nunnery where she was to take the sacrament, Sister Mary Baptist and others being present, they
saw an angel by her with a golden fiery dart at the end
whereof was a little fire, and he thrust it through her heart
and bowels and pulled them out with it, leaving her wholly
inflamed with a great love of God—the modern reader
naturally looks for details of physical condition and habit
of life among the sisterhood, and as naturally finds that
St. Theresa was of morbid constitution and subject to
trances from her childhood, in after life subduing her flesh
by long watchings and religious discipline, and keeping
severe fast during eight months of the year.[2] It is needless
to multiply such mediæval records of fasts which have produced their natural effects in beatific vision—are they not
written page after page in the huge folios of the Bollandists?
So long as fasting is continued as a religious rite, so long
its consequences in morbid mental exaltation will continue
the old and savage doctrine that morbid phantasy is supernatural experience. Bread and meat would have robbed
the ascetic of many an angel's visit; the opening of the
refectory door must many a time have closed the gates of
heaven to his gaze.

[1] Baptist. Mantuan. Fast. ix. 350.
[2] 'Acta Sanctorum Bolland.' S. Theresa.

It is indeed not the complete theory of fasting as a religious rite, but only an important and perhaps original part of it, that here comes into view. Abstinence from food has a principal place among acts of self-mortification or penance, a province of religious ordinance into which the present argument scarcely enters. Looking at the practice of fasting here from an animistic point of view, as a process of bringing on dreams and visions, it will be well to mention with it certain other means by which ecstatic phenomena are habitually induced.

One of these means is the use of drugs. In the West India Islands at the time of the discovery, Columbus describes the religious ceremony of placing a platter containing 'cohoba' powder on the head of the idol, the worshippers then snuffing up this powder through a cane with two branches put to the nose. Pane further describes how the native priest, when brought to a sick man, would put himself in communication with the spirits by thus snuffing cohoba, ' which makes him drunk, that he knows not what he does, and so says many extraordinary things, wherein they affirm that they are talking with the cemis, and that from them it is told them that the infirmity came.' On the Amazons, the Omaguas have continued to modern times the use of narcotic plants, producing an intoxication lasting twenty-four hours, during which they are subject to extraordinary visions ; from one of these plants they obtain the ' curupa ' powder which they snuff into their nostrils with a Y-shaped reed.[1] Here the similar names and uses of the drug plainly show historical connexion between the Omaguas and the Antilles islanders. The Californian Indians would give children narcotic potions, in order to gain from the ensuing visions information about their enemies ; and thus the Mundrucus

---

[1] Colombo, ' Vita,' ch. lxii. ; Roman Pane, ibid. ch. xv. ; and in Pinkerton, vol. xii. Condamine, ' Travels,' in Pinkerton, vol. xiv. p. 226 ; Martius, ' Ethnog. Amer.' vol. i. pp. 441, 631 (details of snuff-powders among Omaguas, Otomacs, &c. ; native names curupá, paricá, niopo, nupa ; made from seeds of Mimosa acacioides, Acacia niopo).

of North Brazil, desiring to discover murderers, would administer such drinks to seers, in whose dreams the criminals appeared.[1] The Darien Indians used the seeds of the Datura sanguinea to bring on in children prophetic delirium, in which they revealed hidden treasure. In Peru the priests who talked with the ' huaca ' or fetishes used to throw themselves into an ecstatic condition by a narcotic drink called ' tonca,' made from the same plant, whence its name of ' huacacacha ' or fetish-herb.[2] The Mexican priests also appear to have used an ointment or drink made with seeds of ' ololiuhqui,' which produced delirium and visions.[3] In both Americas tobacco served for such purposes. It must be noticed that smoking is more or less practised among native races to produce full intoxication, the smoke being swallowed for the purpose. By smoking tobacco, the sorcerers of Brazilian tribes raised themselves to ecstasy in their convulsive orgies, and saw spirits ; no wonder tobacco came to be called the ' holy herb.'[4] So North American Indians held intoxication by tobacco to be supernatural ecstasy, and the dreams of men in this state to be inspired.[5] This idea may explain a remarkable proceeding of the Delaware Indians. At their festival in honour of the Fire-god with his twelve attendant manitus, inside the house of sacrifice a small oven-hut was set up, consisting of twelve poles tied together at the top and covered with blankets, high enough for a man to stand nearly upright within it. After the feast this oven was heated with twelve red-hot stones, and twelve men crept inside. An old man threw twelve pipefulls of tobacco on these stones, and when the patients had borne to the utmost

[1] Maury, ' Magie,' &c., p. 425.
[2] Seemann, ' Voy. of Herald,' vol. i. p. 256. Rivero and Tschudi, ' Peruvian Antiquities,' p. 184. J. G. Müller, p. 397.
[3] Brasseur, ' Mexique,' vol. iii. p. 558 ; Clavigero, vol. ii. p. 40 ; J. G. Müller, p. 656.
[4] J. G. Müller, ' Amer. Urrelig.' p. 277 ; Hernandez, ' Historia Mexicana,' lib. v. c. 51 ; Purchas, vol. iv. p. 1292.
[5] D. Wilson, ' Prehistoric Man,' vol. i. p. 487.

the heat and suffocating smoke, they were taken out, generally falling in a swoon.[1] This practice, which was carried
on in the last century, is remarkable for its coincidence
with the Scythian mode of purification after a funeral, as
described by Herodotus. He relates that they make their
hut with three stakes sloping together at the top and
covered in with wooden felts ; then they cast red-hot stones
into a trough placed within and throw hemp-seed on them,
which sends forth fumes such as no Greek vapour-bath
could exceed, and the Scyths in their sweating-hut roar
with delight.[2]

Not to dwell on the ancient Aryan deification of an
intoxicating drink, the original of the divine Soma of the
Hindus and the divine Haoma of the Parsis, nor on the
drunken orgies of the worship of Dionysos in ancient
Greece, we find more exact Old World analogues of the
ecstatic medicaments used in the lower culture. Such are
the decoctions of thalassægle which Pliny speaks of as
drunk to produce delirium and visions ; the drugs mentioned by Hesychius, whereby Hekate was evoked ; the
mediæval witch-ointments which brought visionary beings
into the presence of the patient, transported him to the
witches' sabbath, enabled him to turn into a beast.[3] The
survival of such practices is most thorough among the
Persian dervishes of our own day. These mystics are not
only opium-eaters, like so large a proportion of their
countrymen ; they are hashish-smokers, and the effect of
this drug is to bring them into a state of exaltation passing
into utter hallucination. To a patient in this condition,
says Dr. Polak, a little stone in the road will seem a great
block that he must stride over ; a gutter becomes a wide
stream to his eyes, and he calls for a boat to ferry him

---

[1] Loskiel, ' Ind. of N. A.' part i. p. 42.
[2] Herodot. iv. 73-5.
[3] Maury, ' Magie,' &c., l.c. ; Plin. xxiv. 102 ; Hesych. s.v. 'ὠπήτειρα.'
See also Bastian, ' Mensch,' vol. ii. p. 152, &c. ; Baring-Gould, ' Werewolves,' p. 149.

across ; men's voices sound like thunder in his ears ; he fancies he has wings and can rise from the ground. These ecstatic effects, in which miracle is matter of hourly experience, are considered in Persia as high religious developments ; the visionaries and their rites are looked on as holy, and they make converts.[1]

Many details of the production of ecstasy and swoon by bodily exercises, chanting and screaming, &c., have been incidentally given in describing the doctrine of demoniacal possession. I will only further cite a few typical cases to show that the practice of bringing on swoons or fits by religious exercises, in reality or pretence, is one belonging originally to savagery, whence it has been continued into higher grades of civilization. We may judge of the mental and bodily condition of the priest or sorcerer in Guyana, by his preparation for his sacred office. This consisted in the first place in fasting and flagellation of extreme severity ; at the end of his fast he had to dance till he fell senseless, and was revived by a potion of tobacco-juice causing violent nausea and vomiting of blood ; day after day this treatment was continued till the candidate, brought into or confirmed in the condition of a ' convulsionary,' was ready to pass from patient into doctor.[2] Again, at the Winnebago medicine-feast, members of the fraternity assemble in a long arched booth, and with them the candidates for initiation, whose preparation is a three days' fast, with severe sweating and steaming with herbs, under the direction of the old medicine-men. The initiation is performed in the assembly by a number of medicine-men. These advance in line, as many abreast as there are candidates ; holding their medicine-bags before them with both hands, they dance forward slowly at first, uttering low guttural sounds as they approach the candidates, their step and voice increasing in energy, until with a violent ' Ough ! ' they thrust their medicine-

[1] Polak, ' Persien,' vol. ii. p. 245 ; Vambéry in ' Mem. Anthrop. Soc.' vol. ii. p. 20 ; Meiners, vol. ii. p. 216.

[2] Meiners, vol. ii. p. 162.

bags at their breasts. Instantly, as if struck with an electric shock, the candidates fall prostrate on their faces, their limbs extended, their muscles rigid and quivering. Blankets are now thrown over them, and they are suffered to lie thus a few moments ; as soon as they show signs of recovering from the shock, they are assisted to their feet and led forward. Medicine-bags are then put in their hands, and medicine-stones in their mouths ; they are now medicine men or women, as the case may be, in full communion and fellow-ship ; and they now go round the bower in company with the old members, knocking others down promiscuously by thrusting their medicine-bags at them. A feast and dance to the music of drum and rattle carry on the festival.[1] Another instance may be taken from among the Alfurus of Celebes, inviting Empong Lembej to descend into their midst. The priests chant, the chief priest with twitching and trembling limbs turns his eyes towards heaven; Lembej descends into him, and with horrible gestures he springs upon a board, beats about with a bundle of leaves, leaps and dances, chanting legends of an ancient deity. After some hours another priest relieves him, and sings of another deity. So it goes on day and night till the fifth day, and then the chief priest's tongue is cut, he falls into a swoon like death, and they cover him up. They fumigate with benzoin the piece taken from his tongue, and swing a censer over his body, calling back his soul ; he revives and dances about, lively but speechless, till they give him back the rest of his tongue, and with it his power of speech.[2] Thus, in the religion of uncultured races, the phenomenon of being ' struck ' holds so recognised a position that impostors will even counterfeit it. In its morbid nature, its genuine cases at least plainly correspond with the fits which history records among the convulsionnaires of St. Medard and the enthusiasts of the Cevennes. Nor need we go even a gene-

---

[1] Schoolcraft, ' Indian Tribes,' part iii. p. 286.
[2] Bastian, ' Mensch,' vol. ii. p. 145. Compare ' Oestl. Asien,' vol. ii. p. 247 (Aracan).

ration back to see symptoms of the same type accepted as signs of grace among ourselves. Medical descriptions of the scenes brought on by fanatical preachers at ' revivals ' in England, Ireland, and America, are full of interest to students of the history of religious rites. I will but quote a single case. ' A young woman is described as lying extended at full length ; her eyes closed, her hands clasped and elevated, and her body curved in a spasm so violent that it appeared to rest arch-like upon her heels and the back portion of her head. In that position she lay without speech or motion for several minutes. Suddenly she uttered a terrific scream, and tore handfuls of hair from her uncovered head. Extending her open hands in a repelling attitude of the most appalling terror, she exclaimed, " Oh, that fearful pit ! " During this paroxysm three strong men were hardly able to restrain her. She extended her arms on either side, clutching spasmodically at the grass, shuddering with terror, and shrinking from some fearful inward vision ; but she ultimately fell back exhausted, nerveless, and apparently insensible.'[1] Such descriptions carry us far back in the history of the human mind, showing modern men still in ignorant sincerity producing the very fits and swoons to which for untold ages savage tribes have given religious import. These manifestations in modern Europe indeed form part of a revival of religion, the religion of mental disease.

From this series of rites, practical with often harmful practicality, we turn to a group of ceremonies whose characteristic is picturesque symbolism. In discussing sun-myth and sun-worship, it has come into view how deeply the association in men's mind of the east with light and warmth, life and happiness and glory, of the west with darkness and chill, death and decay, has from remote ages rooted itself in religious belief. It will illustrate and confirm this view to observe how the same symbolism of east and west has taken shape in actual ceremony, giving rise to a series of practices

[1] D. H. Tuke in ' Journal of Mental Science,' Oct. 1870, p. 368.

concerning the posture of the dead in their graves and the living in their temples, practices which may be classed under the general heading of Orientation.

While the setting sun has shown to men, from savage ages onward, the western region of death, the rising sun has displayed a scene more hopeful, an eastern home of deity. It seems to be the working out of the solar analogy, on the one hand in death as sunset, on the other in new life as sunrise, that has produced two contrasted rules of burial, which agree in placing the dead in the sun's path, the line of east and west. Thus the natives of Australia have in some districts well-marked thoughts of the western land of the dead, yet the custom of burying the dead sitting with face to the east is also known among them.[1] The Samoans and Fijians, agreeing that the land of the departed lies in the far west, bury the corpse lying with head east and feet west;[2] the body would but have to rise and walk straight onward to follow its soul home. This idea is stated explicitly among the Winnebagos of North America; they will sometimes bury a dead man sitting up to the breast in a hole in the ground, looking westward; or graves are dug east and west, and the bodies laid in them with the head eastward, with the motive ' that they may look towards the happy land in the west.'[3] With these customs may be compared those of certain South American tribes. The Yumanas bury their dead bent double with faces looking toward the heavenly region of the sunrise, the home of their great good deity, who they trust will take their souls with him to his dwelling;[4] the Guarayos bury the corpses with heads turned to the east, for it is in the eastern sky that their god Tamoi, the Ancient of Heaven, has his happy hunting-grounds where the dead will meet again.[5]

[1] Grey, ' Australia,' vol. ii. p. 327.
[2] Turner, ' Polynesia,' p. 230. Seemann, ' Viti,' p. 151.
[3] Schoolcraft, ' Indian Tribes,' part iv. p. 54.
[4] Martius, ' Ethnog. Amer.' vol. i. p. 485.
[5] D'Orbigny, ' L'Homme Américain,' vol. ii. pp. 319, 330.

On the other hand the Peruvian custom was to place the dead huddled up in a sitting posture and with faces turned to the west.[1] Barbaric Asia may be represented by the modern Ainos of Yesso, burying the dead lying robed in white with the head to the east, ' because that is where the sun rises ; ' or by the Tunguz who bury with the head to the west ; or by the mediæval Tatars, raising a great mound over the dead, and setting up thereon a statue with face turned toward the east, holding a drinking-cup in his hand before his navel ; or by the modern Siamese, who do not sleep with their heads to the west, because it is in this significant position that the dead are burned.[2] The burial of the dead among the ancient Greeks in the line of east and west, whether according to Athenian custom of the head toward the sunset, or the converse, is another link in the chain of custom.[3] Thus it is not to late and isolated fancy, but to the carrying on of ancient and widespread solar ideas, that we trace the well-known legend that the body of Christ was laid with the head toward the west, thus looking eastward, and the Christian usage of digging graves east and west, which prevailed through mediæval times and is not yet forgotten. The rule of laying the head to the west, and its meaning that the dead shall rise looking toward the east, are perfectly stated in the following passage from an ecclesiastical treatise of the 16th century : ' Debet autem quis sic sepeliri, ut capite ad occidentem posito, pedes dirigat ad orientem, in quo quasi ipsa positione orat : et innuit quod promptus est, ut de occasu festinet ad ortum : de mundo ad seculum.'[4]

---

[1] Rivero and Tschudi, ' Peruvian Antiquities,' p. 202. See also Arbousset and Daumas, ' Voyage,' p. 277 (Kafirs).

[2] Bickmore, in ' Tr. Eth. Soc.' vol. vii. p. 20. Georgi, ' Reise,' vol. i. p. 266. Gul. de Rubruquis in Hakluyt vol. i. p. 78. Bastian, ' Oestl. Asien,' vol. iii. p. 228.

[3] Ælian. Var. Hist. v. 14, vii. 19 ; Plutarch. Solon, x. ; Diog. Laert. Solon ; Welcker, vol. i. p. 404.

[4] Beda in Die S. Paschæ. Durand, Rationale Divinorum Officiorum, lib. vii. c. 35-9. Brand, ' Popular Antiquities,' vol. ii. pp. 295, 318.

Where among the lower races sun-worship begins to con-
solidate itself in systematic ritual, the orientation of the
worshipper and the temple becomes usual and distinct.
The sun-worshipping Comanches, preparing for the war-
path, will place their weapons betimes on the east side of
the lodge to receive the sun's first rays ; it is a remnant of
old solar rite, that the Christianized Pueblo Indians of New
Mexico turn to the sun at his rising.[1]   It has been already
noticed how in old times each morning at sunrise the Sun-
chief of the Natchez of Louisiana stood facing the east at
the door of his house, and smoked toward the sun first,
before he turned to the other three quarters of the world.[2]
The cave-temple of the sun-worshipping Apalaches of
Florida had its opening looking east, and within stood the
priests on festival days at dawn, waiting till the first rays
entered to begin the appointed rites of chant and incense
and offering.[3]   In old Mexico, where sun-worship was the
central doctrine of the complex religion, men knelt in prayer
towards the east, and the doors of the sanctuaries looked
mostly westward.[4]   It was characteristic of the solar worship
of Peru that even the villages were habitually built on slopes
toward the east, that the people might see and greet the
national deity at his rising.   In the temple of the sun at
Cuzco, his splendid golden disc on the western wall looked
out through the eastern door, so that as he rose his first
beams fell upon it, reflected thence to light up the sanctuary.[5]

In Asia, the ancient Aryan religion of the sun manifests
itself not less plainly in rites of orientation.   They have
their place in the weary ceremonial routine which the Brah-

[1] Gregg, ' Commerce of Prairies,' vol. i. pp. 270, 273 ; vol. ii. p. 318.
[2] Charlevoix, ' Nouvelle France,' vol. vi. p. 178.
[3] Rochefort, ' Iles Antilles,' p. 365.
[4] Clavigero, ' Messico,' vol. ii. p. 24 ; J. G. Müller, p. 641. See Oviedo,
Nicaragua,' p. 29.
[5] J. G. Müller, p. 363 ; Prescott, ' Peru,' book i. ch. 3.   Garcilaso de la
Vega, ' Commentarios Reales,' lib. iii. c. 20, says it was at the east end ; cf.
lib. vi. c. 21 (llama sacrificed with head to east).

man must daily accomplish.   When he has performed the dawn ablution, and meditated on the effulgent sun-light which is Brahma, the supreme soul, he proceeds to worship the sun, standing on one foot and resting the other against his ankle or heel, looking toward the east, and holding his hands open before him in a hollow form.   At noon, when he has again adored the sun, it is sitting with his face to the east that he must read his daily portion of the Veda ; it is looking toward the east that his offering of barley and water must be first presented to the gods, before he turns to north and south ; it is with first and principal direction to the east that the consecration of the fire and the sacrificial implements, a ceremony which is the groundwork of all his religious acts, has to be performed.[1]   The significance of such reverence paid by adorers of the sun to the glorious eastern region of his rising, may be heightened to us by setting beside it a ceremony of a darker faith, displaying the awe-struck horror of the western home of death.   The antithesis to the eastward consecration by the orthodox Brahmans is the westward consecration by the Thugs, worshippers of Kali the death-goddess.   In honour of Kali their victims were murdered, and to her the sacred pickaxe was consecrated, wherewith the graves of the slain were dug. At the time of the suppression of Thuggee, Englishmen had the consecration of the pickaxe performed in make-believe in their presence by those who well knew the dark ritual.   On the dreadful implement no shadow of any living thing must fall, its consecrator sits facing the west to perform the fourfold washing and the sevenfold passing through the fire, and then it being proved duly consecrated by the omen of the coco-nut divided at a single cut, it is placed on the ground, and the bystanders worship it, turning to the west.[2]

These two contrasted rites of east and west established

[1] Colebrooke, ' Essays,' vol. i., iv. and v.

[2] ' Illustrations of the History and Practices of the Thugs,' London, 1837, p. 46.

themselves and still remain established in modern European religion. In judging of the course of history that has brought about this state of things, it scarcely seems that Jewish influence was effective. The Jewish temple had the entrance in the east, and the sanctuary in the west. Sun-worship was an abomination to the Jews, and the orientation especially belonging to it appears as utterly opposed to Jewish usage, in Ezekiel's horror-stricken vision : ' and, behold, at the door of the temple of Jehovah, between the porch and the altar, about five-and-twenty men, with their backs toward the temple of Jehovah, and their faces toward the east, and they worshipped the sun toward the east.'[1] Nor is there reason to suppose that in later ages such orientation gained ground in Jewish ceremony. The solar rites of other nations whose ideas were prominent in the early development of Christianity, are sufficient to account for the rise of Christian orientation. On the one hand there was the Asiatic sun-worship, perhaps specially related to the veneration of the rising sun in old Persian religion, and which has left relics in the east of the Turkish empire into modern years ; Christian sects praying toward the sun, and Yezidis turning to the east as their kibleh and burying their dead looking thither.[2] On the other hand, orientation was recognized in classic Greek religion, not indeed in slavish obedience to a uniform law, but as a principle to be worked out in converse ways. Thus it was an Athenian practice for the temple to have its entrance east, looking out through which the divine image stood to behold the rising sun. This rule it is that Lucian refers to, when he talks of the delight of gazing toward the loveliest and most longed-for of the day, of welcoming the sun as he peeps forth, of taking one's fill of light through the wide-open doors, even as the

---

[1] Ezek. viii. 16 ; Mishna, ' Sukkoth,' v.   See Fergusson in Smith's ' Dictionary of the Bible,' s.v. ' Temple.'

[2] Hyde, ' Veterum Persarum Religionis Historia,' ch. iv.   Niebuhr, ' Reisebeschreibung nach Arabien,' vol. i. p. 396.   Layard, ' Nineveh,' vol. i. ch. ix.

ancients built their temples looking forth. Nor was the contrary rule as stated by Vitruvius less plain in meaning; the sacred houses of the immortal gods shall be so arranged, that if no reason prevents and choice is free, the temple and the statue erected in the cell shall look toward the west, so that they who approach the altar to sacrifice and vow and pray may look at once toward the statue and the eastern sky, the divine figures thus seeming to arise and look upon them. Altars of the gods were to stand toward the east.[1]

Unknown in primitive Christianity, the ceremony of orientation was developed within its first four centuries. It became an accepted custom to turn in prayer toward the east, the mystic region of the Light of the World, the Sun of Righteousness. Augustine says, ' When we stand at prayer, we turn to the east, where the heaven arises, not as though God were only there, and had forsaken all other parts of the world, but to admonish our mind to turn to a more excellent nature, that is, to the Lord.' No wonder that the early Christians were thought to practise in substance the rite of sun-worship which they practised in form. Thus Tertullian writes : ' Others indeed with greater truth and verisimilitude believe the sun to be our God. . . . . the suspicion arising from its being known that we pray toward the region of the east.' Though some of the most ancient and honoured churches of Christendom stand to show that orientation was no original law of ecclesiastical architecture, yet it became dominant in early centuries. That the author of the 'Apostolical Constitutions' should be able to give directions for building churches toward the east (ὁ οἶκω ἔστω ἐπιμηκής, κατ᾿ ἀνατολὰς τετραμμένος), just as Vitruvius had laid down the rule as to the temples of the gods, is only a part of that assimilation of the church to the temple which took effect so largely in the scheme of worship. Of all Christian ceremony, however, it was in the rite of baptism that orientation took its fullest and most picturesque

[1] Lucian. De Domo, vi. Vitruv. de Architectura, iv. 5. See Welcker, vol. i. p. 403.

form. The catechumen was placed with face toward the west, and then commanded to renounce Satan with gestures of abhorrence, stretching out his hands against him, or smiting them together, and blowing or spitting against him thrice. Cyril of Jerusalem, in his ' Mystagogic Catechism,' thus depicts the scene : ' Ye first came into the ante-room of the baptistery, and standing toward the west (πρὸς τὰς δυσμάς) ye were commanded to put away Satan, stretching out your hands as though he were present. . . . . And why did ye stand toward the west ? It was needful, for sunset is the type of darkness, and he is darkness and has his strength in darkness ; therefore symbolically looking toward the west ye renounce that dark and gloomy ruler.' Then turning round to the east, the catechumen took up his allegiance to his new master, Christ. The ceremony and its significance are clearly set forth by Jerome, thus: ' In the mysteries [meaning baptism] we first renounce him who is in the west, and dies to us with our sins; and so, turning to the east, we make a covenant with the Sun of righteousness, promising to be his servants.'[1] This perfect double rite of east and west, retained in the baptismal ceremony of the Greek Church, may be seen in Russia to this day. The orientation of churches and the practice of turning to the east as an act of worship, are common to both Greek and Latin ritual. In our own country they declined from the Reformation, till at the beginning of the 19th century they seemed falling out of use; since then, however, they have been restored to a certain prominence by the revived mediævalism of our own day. To the student of history, it is a striking example of the connexion of thought and ceremony through the religions of the lower and higher culture, to see surviving in our midst, with meaning dwindled into

---

[1] Augustin. de Serm. Dom. in Monte, ii. 5. Tertullian. Contra Valentin. iii. ; Apolog. xvi. Constitutiones Apostolicæ, ii. 57. Cyril. Catech. Mystag. i. 2. Hieronym. in Amos. vi. 14 ; Bingham, ' Antiquities of Chr. Church,' book viii. ch. 3, book xi. ch. 7, book xiii. ch. 8. J. M. Neale, ' Eastern Church,' part i. p. 956 ; Romanoff, ' Greco-Russian Church,' p. 67.

symbolism, this ancient solar rite. The influence of the divine Sun upon his rude and ancient worshippers still subsists before our eyes as a mechanical force, acting diamagnetically to adjust the axis of the church and turn the body of the worshipper.

The last group of rites whose course through religious history is to be outlined here, takes in the varied dramatic acts of ceremonial purification of Lustration. With all the obscurity and intricacy due to age-long modification, the primitive thought which underlies these ceremonies is still open to view. It is the transition from practical to symbolic cleansing, from removal of bodily impurity to deliverance from invisible, spiritual, and at last moral evil. Our language follows this ideal movement to its utmost stretch, where such words as cleansing and purification have passed from their first material meaning, to signify removal of ceremonial contamination, legal guilt, and moral sin. What we thus express in metaphor, the men of the lower culture began early to act in ceremony, purifying persons and objects by various prescribed rites, especially by dipping them in and sprinkling them with water, or fumigating them with and passing them through fire. It is the plainest proof of the original practicality of proceedings now passed into formalism, to point out how far the ceremonial lustrations still keep their connexion with times of life when real purification is necessary, how far they still consist in formal cleansing of the new-born child and the mother, of the man-slayer who has shed blood, or the mourner who has touched a corpse. In studying the distribution of the forms of lustration among the races of the world, while allowing for the large effect of their transmission from religion to religion, and from nation to nation, we may judge that their diversity of detail and purpose scarcely favours a theory of their being all historically derived from one or even several special religions of the ancient world. They seem more largely to exemplify independent working out, in different directions, of an idea common to mankind at large. This view may be justified by surveying lustration through a series of typical instances, which show its appearance and character in savage and barbaric culture, as being an act belonging to certain well-marked events of human life.

The purification of the new-born child appears among the lower races in various forms, but perhaps in some particular instances borrowed from the higher. It should be noticed that though the naming of the child is often associated with its ceremonial cleansing, there is no real connexion between the two rites, beyond their coming due at the same early time of life. To those who look for the matter-of-fact origin of such ceremonies, one of the most suggestive of the accounts available is a simple mention of the two necessary acts of washing and name-giving, as done together in mere practical purpose, but not as yet passed into formal ceremony—the Kichtak Islanders, it is remarked, at birth wash the child, and give it a name.[1] Among the Yumanas of Brazil, as soon as the child can sit up, it is sprinkled with a decoction of certain herbs, and receives a name which has belonged to an ancestor.[2] Among some Jakun tribes of the Malay Peninsula, as soon as the child is born it is carried to the nearest stream and washed ; it is then brought back to the house, the fire is kindled, and fragrant wood thrown on, over which it is passed several times.[3] The New Zealanders' infant baptism is no new practice, and is considered by them an old traditional rite, but nothing very similar is observed among other branches of the Polynesian race. Whether independently invented or not, it was thoroughly worked into the native religious scheme. The baptism was performed on the eighth day or earlier, at the side of a stream or elsewhere, by a native priest who sprinkled water on the child with a branch or twig ; sometimes the child was immersed. With this lustration it received its name, the priest repeating a list of

[1] Billings, ' N. Russia,' p. 175.
[2] Martius, ' Ethnog. Amer.' vol. i. p. 485.
[3] ' Journ. Ind. Archip.' vol. ii. p. 264.

ancestral names till the child chose one for itself by sneezing at it. The ceremony was of the nature of a dedication, and was accompanied by rhythmical formulas of exhortation. The future warrior was bidden to flame with anger, to leap nimbly and ward off the spears, to be angry and bold and industrious, to work before the dew is off the ground ; the future housewife was bidden to get food and go for firewood and weave garments with panting of breath. In after years, a second sacred sprinkling was performed to admit a lad into the rank of warriors. It has to be noticed with reference to the reason of this ceremonial washing, that a new-born child is in the highest degree tapu, and may only be touched by a few special persons till the restriction is removed.[1] In Madagascar, a fire is kept up in the room for several days, then the child in its best clothes is in due form carried out of the house and back to its mother, both times being carefully lifted over the fire, which is made near the door.[2] In Africa, some of the most noticeable ceremonies of the class are these. The people of Sarac wash the child three days after birth with holy water.[3] When a Mandingo child was about a week old its hair was cut, and the priest, invoking blessings, took it in his arms, whispered in its ear, spat thrice in its face, and pronounced its name aloud before the assembled company.[4] In Guinea, when a child is born, the event is publicly proclaimed, the new-born babe is brought into the streets, and the headman of the town or family sprinkles it with water from a basin, giving it a name and invoking blessings of health and wealth upon it ; other friends follow the example, till the child is thoroughly drenched.[5] In these various examples

[1] Taylor, ' New Zealand,' p. 184; Yate, p. 82; Polack, vol. i. p. 51 ; A. S. Thomson, vol. i. p. 118; Klemm, ' Cultur-Gesch.' vol. iv. p. 304. See Schirren, ' Wandersagen der Neuseeländer,' pp. 58, 183 ; Shortland, p. 145.

[2] Ellis, ' Madagascar,' vol. i. p. 152.

[3] Munzinger, ' Ost-Afrika,' p. 387.

[4] Park, ' Travels,' ch. vi.

[5] J. L. Wilson, ' Western Africa,' p. 399. See also Bastian, ' Mensch,'

of lustration of infants, the purifications by fire have especial importance ethnologically, not because this proceeding is more natural to the savage mind than that of bathing or sprinkling with water, but because this latter ceremony may sometimes have been imitated from Christian baptism. The fact of savage and barbaric lustration of infants being in several cases associated with the belief in re-birth of ancestral souls seems to mark the rite as belonging to remote pre-Christian ages.[1]

The purification of women at childbirth, &c., is ceremonially practised by the lower races under circumstances which do not suggest adoption from more civilized nations. The seclusion and lustration among North American Indian tribes have been compared with those of the Levitical law, but the resemblance is not remarkably close, and belongs rather to a stage of civilization than to the ordinance of a particular nation. It is a good case of independent development in such customs, that the rite of putting out the fires and kindling ' new fire ' on the woman's return is common to the Iroquois and Sioux in North America,[2] and the Basutos in South Africa. These latter have a well-marked rite of lustration by sprinkling, performed on girls at womanhood.[3] The Hottentots considered mother and child unclean till they had been washed and smeared after the uncleanly native fashion.[4] Lustrations with water were usual in West Africa.[5] Tatar tribes in Mongolia used bathing, while in Siberia the custom of leaping over a fire answered the purpose of purification.[6] The Mantras of the Malay Peninsula have made the bathing of the mother after

vol. ii. p. 279 (Watje); 'Anthropological Review,' Nov. 1864, p. 243 (Mpongwe); Barker-Webb and Berthelot, vol. ii. p. 163 (Tenerife).

[1] See pp. 5, 437.

[2] Schoolcraft, 'Indian Tribes,' part i. p. 261; part iii. p. 243, &c. Charlevoix, 'Nouvelle France,' vol. v. p. 425. Wilson in 'Tr. Eth. Soc.' vol. iv. p. 294.

[3] Casalis, 'Basutos,' p. 267.

[4] Kolben, vol. i. pp. 273, 283.

[5] Bosman, in Pinkerton, vol. xvi. pp. 423, 527; Meiners, vol. ii. pp. 107, 463.

[6] Pallas, 'Mongolische Völkerschaften,' vol. i. p. 166, &c.; Strahlenberg, 'Siberia,' p. 97.

childbirth into a ceremonial ordinance.[1] It is so among the indigenes of India, where both in northern and southern districts the naming of the child comes into connexion with the purification of the mother, both ceremonies being performed on the same day.[2] Without extending further this list of instances, it is sufficiently plain that we have before us the record of a practical custom becoming consecrated by traditional habit, and making its way into the range of religious ceremony.

Much the same may be said of the purification of savage and barbaric races on occasion of contamination by bloodshed or funeral. In North America, the Dacotas use the vapour-bath not only as a remedy, but also for the removal of ceremonial uncleanness, such as is caused by killing a person, or touching a dead body.[3] So among the Navajos, the man who has been deputed to carry a dead body to burial, holds himself unclean until he has thoroughly washed himself in water prepared for the purpose by certain ceremonies.[4] In Madagascar, no one who has attended a funeral may enter the palace courtyard till he has bathed, and in all cases there must be an ablution of the mourner's garments on returning from the grave.[5] Among the Basutos of South Africa, warriors returning from battle must rid themselves of the blood they have shed, or the shades of their victims would pursue them and disturb their sleep. Therefore they go in procession in full armour to the nearest stream to wash, and their weapons are washed also. It is usual in this ceremony for a sorcerer higher up the stream to put in some magical ingredient, such as he also uses in the preparation of the holy water which is sprinkled over the people with a beast's tail at the frequent public purifications. These Basutos, moreover, use fumigation with burning wood to purify growing corn, and cattle taken from the

---

[1] Bourien in 'Tr. Eth. Soc.' vol. iii. p. 81.
[2] Dalton in 'Tr. Eth. Soc.' vol. vi. p. 22 ; Shortt, ibid. vol. iii. p. 375.
[3] Schoolcraft, 'Indian Tribes,' part i. p. 255.
[4] Brinton, 'Myths of New World,' p. 127.
[5] Ellis, 'Madagascar.' vol. i. p. 241 ; see pp. 407, 419.

enemy. Fire serves for purification in cases too trifling to require sacrifice ; thus when a mother sees her child walk over a grave, she hastens to call it, makes it stand before her, and lights a small fire at its feet.[1] The Zulus, whose horror of a dead body will induce them to cast out and leave in the woods their sick people, at least strangers, purify themselves by an ablution after a funeral. It is to be noticed that these ceremonial practices have come to mean something distinct from mere cleanliness. Kaffirs who will purify themselves from ceremonial uncleanness by washing, are not in the habit of washing themselves or their vessels for ordinary purposes, and the dogs and the cockroaches divide between them the duty of cleaning out the milk-baskets.[2] Mediæval Tatar tribes, some of whom had con-scientious scruples against bathing, have found passing through fire or between two fires a sufficient purification, and the household stuff of the dead was lustrated in this latter way.[3]

In the organised nations of the semi-civilized and civi-lized world, where religion shapes itself into elaborate and systematic schemes, the practices of lustration familiar to the lower culture now become part of stringent ceremonial systems. It seems to be at this stage of their existence that they often take up in addition to their earlier cere-monial significance an ethical meaning, absent or all but absent from them at their first appearance above the reli-gious horizon. This will be made evident by glancing over the ordinances of lustration in the great national religions of history. It will be well to notice first the usages of two semi-civilized nations of America, which though they have scarcely produced practical effect on civilization at large, give valuable illustration of a transition period in culture, leaving apart the obscure question of their special civiliza-

[1] Casalis, ' Basutos,' p. 258.
[2] Grout, ' Zulu-land,' p. 147 ; Backhouse, ' Mauritius and S. Africa,' pp. 213, 225.
[3] Bastian, ' Mensch,' vol. iii. p. 75 ; Rubruquis, in Pinkerton, vol. vii. p. 82 ; Plano Carpini in Hakluyt, vol. i. p. 37.

tion having been influenced in early or late times from the Old World.

In the religion of Peru, lustration is well-marked and characteristic. On the day of birth, the water in which the child has been washed was poured into a hole in the ground, charms being repeated by a wizard or priest ; an excellent instance of the ceremonial washing away of evil influences. The naming of the child was also more or less generally accompanied with ceremonial washing, as in districts where at two years old it was weaned, baptized, had its hair ceremonially cut with a stone knife, and received its childname ; Peruvian Indians still cut off a lock of the child's hair at its baptism. Moreover, the significance of lustration as removing guilt is plainly recorded in ancient Peru ; after confession of guilt, an Inca bathed in a neighbouring river and repeated this formula, ' O thou River, receive the sins I have this day confessed unto the Sun, carry them down to the sea, and let them never more appear.'[1] In old Mexico, the first act of ceremonial lustration took place at birth. The nurse washed the infant in the name of the water-goddess, to remove the impurity of its birth, to cleanse its heart and give it a good and perfect life ; then blowing on water in her right hand she washed it again, warning it of forthcoming trials and miseries and labours, and praying the invisible Deity to descend upon the water, to cleanse the child from sin and foulness, and to deliver it from misfortune. The second act took place some four days later, unless the astrologers postponed it. At a festive gathering, amid fires kept alight from the first ceremony, the nurse undressed the child sent by the gods into this sad and doleful world, bade it receive the life-giving water, and washed it, driving out evil from each limb and offering to the deities appointed prayers for virtue and blessing. It

[1] Rivero and Tschudi, ' Peruvian Antiquities,' p. 180 ; J. G. Müller, ' Amer. Urrelig.' p. 389 ; Acosta, ' Ind. Occ.' v. c. 25 ; Brinton, p. 126. See account of the rite of driving out sicknesses and evils into the rivers, ' Rites and Laws of Incas,' tr. and ed. by C. R. Markham, p. 22.

was then that the toy instruments of war or craft or household labour were placed in the boy's or girl's hand (a custom
singularly corresponding with one usual in China), and the
other children, instructed by their parents, gave the new-
comer its child-name, here again to be replaced by another
at manhood or womanhood. There is nothing unlikely in
the statement that the child was also passed four times
through the fire, but the authority this is given on is not
sufficient. The religious character of ablution is well
shown in Mexico by its forming part of the daily service
of the priests. Aztec life ended as it had begun, with
ceremonial lustration ; it was one of the funeral ceremonies
to sprinkle the head of the corpse with the lustral water of
this life.[1]

Among the nations of East Asia, and across the more civilized Turanian districts of Central Asia, ceremonial lustration comes frequently into notice ; but it would often bring
in difficult points of ethnography to attempt a general judgment how far these may be native local rites, and how far ceremonies adopted from foreign religious systems. As examples
may be mentioned in Japan the sprinkling and naming of
the child at a month old, and other lustrations connected
with worship;[2] in China the religious ceremony at the first
washing of the three days' old infant, the lifting of the bride
over burning coals, the sprinkling of holy-water over sacrifices and rooms and on the mourners after a funeral;[3] in
Burma the purification of the mother by fire, and the annual
sprinkling-festival.[4] Within the range of Buddhism in its
Lamaist form, we find such instances as the Tibetan and

---

[1] Sahagun, 'Nueva España,' lib. vi. ; Torquemada, ' Monarquia Indiana,'
lib. xii. ; Clavigero, vol. ii. pp. 39, 86, &c. ; Humboldt, ' Vues des Cordillères,' Mendoza Cod. ; J. C. Müller, p. 652.

[2] Siebold, ' Nippon,' v. p. 22 ; Kempfer, ' Japan,' ch. xiii. in Pinkerton,
vol. vii.

[3] Doolittle, ' Chinese,' vol. i. p. 120, vol. ii. p. 273. Davis, vol. i. p.
269.

[4] Bastian, ' Oestl. Asien,' vol. ii. p. 247 ; Meiners, vol. ii. p. 106 ; Symes
in Pinkerton, vol. ix. p. 435.

Mongol lustration of the child a few days after birth, the lama blessing the water and immersing the child thrice, and giving its name; the Buraet consecration by threefold washing; the Tibetan ceremony where the mourners returning from the funeral stand before the fire, wash their hands with warm water over the hot coals, and fumigate themselves thrice with proper formulas.[1] With this infant baptism of Tibetans and Mongols may be compared the rite of their ethnological kinsfolk in Europe. The Lapps in their semi-Christianized state had a form of baptism, in which a new name, that of the deceased ancestor who would live again in the child, as the mother was spiritually informed in a dream, was given with a threefold sprinkling and washing with warm water where mystic alder-twigs were put. This ceremony, though called by the Scandinavian name of ' laugo ' or bath, was distinct from the Christian baptism to which the Lapps also conformed.[2] The natural ethnographic explanation of these two baptismal ceremonies existing together in Northern Europe, is that Christianity had brought in a new rite, without displacing a previous native one.

Other Asiatic districts show lustration in more compact and characteristic religious developments. The Brahman leads a life marked by recurring ceremonial purification, from the time when his first appearance in the world brings uncleanness on the household, requiring ablution and clean garments to remove it, and thenceforth through his years from youth to old age, where bathing is a main part of the long minute ceremonial of daily worship, and further washings and aspersions enter into more solemn religious acts, till at last the day comes when his kinsfolk, on their way home from his funeral, cleanse themselves by a final bath from their contamination by his remains. For the means

---

[1] Köppen, ' Religion des Buddha,' vol. ii. p. 320; Bastian, ' Psychologie,' pp. 151, 211; ' Mensch,' vol. ii. p. 499.

[2] Leems, ' Finnmarkens Lapper.' Copenhagen, c. xiv., xxii., and Jessen, c. xiv.; Pinkerton, vol. i. p. 483; Klemm, ' Cultur-Gesch.' vol. iii. p. 77.

of some of his multifarious lustrations the Hindu has recourse to the sacred cow, but his more frequent medium of
removing uncleanness of body and soul is water, the divine
waters to which he prays, ' Take away, O Waters, whatsoever is wicked in me, what I have done by violence or curse,
and untruth ! '[1] The Parsi religion prescribes a system of
lustrations which well shows its common origin with that
of Hinduism by its similar use of cow's urine and of water.
Bathing or sprinkling with water, or applications of 'nirang'
washed off with water, form part of the daily religious rites,
as well as of such special ceremonies as the naming of the
new-born child, the putting on of the sacred cord, the purification of the mother after childbirth, the purification of
him who has touched a corpse, when the unclean demon,
driven by sprinkling of the good water from the top of the
head and from limb to limb, comes forth at the left toe and
departs like a fly to the evil region of the north.   It is,
perhaps, the influence of this ancestral religion, even more
than the actual laws of Islam, that makes the modern
Persian so striking an example of the way in which ceremony may override reality.   It is rather in form than in
fact that his cleanliness is next to godliness.   He carries
the principle of removing legal uncleanness by ablution so
far, that a holy man will wash his eyes when they have been
polluted by the sight of an infidel.   He will carry about a
water-pot with a long spout for his ablutions, yet he depopu-
lates the land by his neglect of the simplest sanitary rules,
and he may be seen by the side of the little tank where
scores of people have been in before him, obliged to clear
with his hand a space in the foul scum on the water, before
he plunges in to obtain ceremonial purity.[2]

[1] Ward, ' Hindoos,' vol. ii. pp. 96, 246, 337 ; Colebrooke, ' Essays,'
vol. ii. Wuttke, ' Gesch. des Heidenthums,' vol. ii. p. 378. ' Rig-Veda,' i.
22, 23.
[2] Avesta, Vendidad, v.-xii. ; Lord, in Pinkerton, vol. viii. p. 570 ;
Naoroji, ' Parsee Religion ' ; Polak, ' Persien,' vol. i. p. 355, &c., vol. ii.
p. 271. Meiners, vol. ii. p. 125.

Over against the Aryan rites of lustration in the religions of Asia, may be set the well-known types in the religions of classic Europe. At the Greek amphidromia, when the child was about a week old, the women who had assisted at the birth washed their hands, and afterwards the child was carried round the fire by the nurse, and received its name ; the Roman child received its prænomen with a lustration at about the same age, and the custom is recorded of the nurse touching its lips and forehead with spittle. To wash before an act of worship was a ceremony handed down by Greek and Roman ritual through the classic ages : καθαραῖς δὲ δρόσοις, ἀφυδρανάμενοι στχείετε ναούς—eo lavatum, ut sacrificem. The holy-water mingled with salt, the holy-water vessel at the temple entrance, the brush to sprinkle the worshippers, all belong to classic antiquity. Romans, their flocks and herds and their fields, were purified from disease and other ill by lustrations which show perfectly the equivalent nature of water and fire as means of purification ; the passing of flocks and shepherds through fires, the sprinkling water with laurel branches, the fumigating with fragrant boughs and herbs and sulphur, formed part of the rustic rites of the Palilia. Bloodshed demanded the lustral ceremony. Hektor fears to pour with unwashen hands the libation of dark wine, nor may he pray bespattered with gore to cloud-wrapped Zeus ; Æneas may not touch the household gods till cleansed from slaughter by the living stream. It was with far changed thought that Ovid wrote his famous reproof of his too-easy countrymen, who fancied that water could indeed wash off the crime of blood :—

> ' Ah nimium faciles, qui tristia crimina cædis
> Fluminea tolli posse putetis aqua.'

Thus, too, the mourner must be cleansed by lustration from the contaminating presence of death. At the door of the Greek house of mourning was set the water-vessel, that those who had been within might sprinkle themselves and be clean ; while the mourners returning from a Roman funeral, aspersed with water and stepping over fire, were by this double process made pure.[1]

The ordinances of purification in the Levitical law relate especially to the removal of legal uncleanness connected with childbirth, death, and other pollutions. Washing was prescribed for such purposes, and also sprinkling with water of separation, water mingled with the ashes of the red heifer. Ablution formed part of the consecration of priests, and without it they might not serve at the altar nor enter the tabernacle. In the later times of Jewish national history, perhaps through intercourse with nations whose lustrations entered more into the daily routine of life, ceremonial washings were multiplied. It seems also that in this period must be dated the ceremony which in after ages has held so great a place in the religion of the world, their rite of baptism of proselytes.[2] The Moslem lustrations are ablutions with water, or in default with dust or sand, performed partially before prayer, and totally on special days or to remove special uncleanness. They are strictly religious acts, belonging in principle to prevalent usage of Oriental religion ; and their details, whether invented or adopted as they stand in Islam, are not carried down from Judaism or Christianity.[3] The rites of lustration which have held and hold their places within the pale of Christianity are in well-marked historical connexion with Jewish and Gentile ritual. Purification by fire has only appeared as an actual ceremony

---

[1] Details in Smith's ' Dic. of Gr. and Rom. Ant.' and Pauly, ' Real-Encyclopedie,' s.v. ' amphidromia,' ' lustratio,' ' sacrificium,' ' funus ' ; Meiners, ' Gesch. der Religionen,' book vii. ; Lomeyer, ' De Veterum Gentilium Lustrationibus ' ; Montfaucon, ' L'Antiquité Expliquée,' &c. Special passages ; Homer, Il. vi. 266 ; Eurip. Ion. 96 ; Theocrit. xxiv. 95 ; Virg. Æn. ii. 719 ; Plaut. Aulular. iii. 6 ; Pers. Sat. ii. 31 ; Ovid. Fast. i. 669, ii. 45, iv. 727 ; Festus, s.v. ' aqua et ignis,' &c. The obscure subject of lustration in the mysteries is here left untouched.

[2] Ex. xxix. 4, xxx. 18, xl. 12 ; Lev. viii. 6, xiv. 8, xv. 5, xxii. 6 ; Numb. xix. &c. ; Lightfoot in ' Works,' vol. xi. ; Browne in Smith's ' Dic. of the Bible,' s.v. ' baptism ; ' Calmet, ' Dic.' &c.

[3] Reland, ' De Religione Mohammedanica ; ' Lane, ' Modern Eg.' vol. i. p. 98, &c.

among some little-known Christian sects, and in the European folklore custom of passing children through or over fire, if indeed we can be sure that this rite is lustral and not sacrificial.[1] The usual medium of purification is water. Holy-water is in full use through the Greek and Roman churches. It blesses the worshipper as he enters the temple, it cures disease, it averts sorcery from man and beast, it drives demons from the possessed, it stops the spirit-writer's pen, it drives the spirit-moved table it is sprinkled upon to dash itself frantically against the wall ; at least these are among the powers attributed to it, and some of the most striking of them have been lately vouched for by papal sanction. This lustration with holy-water so exactly continues the ancient classic rite, that its apologists are apt to explain the correspondence by arguing that Satan stole it for his own wicked ends.[2] Catholic ritual follows ancient sacrificial usage in the priest's ceremonial washing of hands before mass. The priest's touching with his spittle the ears and nostrils of the infant or catechumen, saying, ' Ephphatha,' is obviously connected with passages in the Gospels ; its adoption as a baptismal ceremony has been compared, perhaps justly, with the classical lustration by spittle.[3] Finally, it has but to be said that ceremonial purification as a Christian act centres in baptism by water, that symbol of initiation of the convert which history traces from the Jewish rite to that of John the Baptist, and thence to the Christian ordinance. Through later ages adult baptism carries on the Jewish ceremony of the admission of the proselyte, while infant baptism combines this with the lustration of the new-born infant. Passing through a range of meaning such as separates the sacrament of the Roman

---

[1] Bingham, ' Antiquities of Christian Church,' book xi. ch. 2. Grimm, ' Deutsche Mythologie,' p. 592 ; Leslie, ' Early Races of Scotland,' vol. i. p. 113 ; Pennant, in Pinkerton, vol. iii. p. 383.

[2] Rituale Romanum ; Gaume, ' L'Eau Bénite ; ' Middleton, ' Letter from Rome,' &c.

[3] Rituale Romanum. Bingham, book x. ch. 2, book xv. ch. 3. See Mark vii. 34, viii. 23 ; John ix. 6.

centurion from the sacrament of the Roman cardinal, becoming to some a solemn symbol of new life and faith, to some an act in itself of supernatural efficacy, the rite of baptism has remained almost throughout the Christian world the outward sign of the Christian profession.

In considering the present group of religious ceremonies, their manifestations in the religions of the higher nations have been but scantily outlined in comparison with their rudimentary forms in the lower culture. Yet this reversal of the proportions due to practical importance in no way invalidates, but rather aids, the ethnographic lessons to be drawn by tracing their course in history. Through their varied phases of survival, modification, and succession, they have each in its own way brought to view the threads of continuity which connect the faiths of the lower with the faiths of the higher world ; they have shown how hardly the civilized man can understand the religious rites even of his own land without knowledge of the meaning, often the widely unlike meaning, which they bore to men of distant ages and countries, representatives of grades of culture far different from his.

CHAPTER XIX

CONCLUSION

Practical results of the study of Primitive Culture—Its bearing least upon Positive Science, greatest upon Intellectual, Moral, Social, and Political Philosophy—Language—Mythology—Ethics and Law—Religion—Action of the Science of Culture, as a means of furthering progress and removing hindrance, effective in the course of Civilization.

It now remains, in bringing to a close these investigations on the relation of primitive to modern civilization, to urge the practical import of the considerations raised in their course. Granted that archæology, leading the student's mind back to remotest known conditions of human life, shows such life to have been of unequivocally savage type ; granted that the rough-hewn flint hatchet, dug out from amidst the bones of mammoths in a drift gravel-bed to lie on an ethnologist's writing-table, is to him a very type of primitive culture, simple yet crafty, clumsy yet purposeful, low in artistic level yet fairly started on the ascent toward highest development—what then? Of course the history and præ-history of man take their proper places in the general scheme of knowledge. Of course the doctrine of the world-long evolution of civilization is one which philosophic minds will take up with eager interest, as a theme of abstract science. But beyond this, such research has its practical side, as a source of power destined to influence the course of modern ideas and actions. To establish a connexion between what uncultured ancient men thought and did, and what cultured modern men think and do, is not a matter of inapplicable theoretic knowledge, for it raises the issue, how far are modern opinion and conduct based on the strong ground of soundest modern knowledge, or how far only on such knowledge as was available in the earlier and ruder stages of culture where their types were shaped. It has to be maintained that the early history of man has its bearing, almost ignored as that bearing has been by those whom it ought most stringently to affect, on some of the deepest and most vital points of our intellectual, industrial, and social state.

Even in advanced sciences, such as relate to measure and force and structure in the inorganic and organic world, it is at once a common and a serious error to adopt the principle of letting bygones be bygones. Were scientific systems the oracular revelations they sometimes all but pretend to be, it might be justifiable to take no note of the condition of mere opinion or fancy that preceded them. But the investigator who turns from his modern text-books to the antiquated dissertations of the great thinkers of the past, gains from the history of his own craft a truer view of the relation of theory to fact, learns from the course of growth in each current hypothesis to appreciate its raison d'être and full significance, and even finds that a return to older starting-points may enable him to find new paths, where the modern track seems stopped by impassable barriers. It is true that rudimentary conditions of arts and sciences are often rather curious than practically instructive, especially because the modern practitioner has kept up, as mere elementary processes, the results of the ancient or savage man's most strenuous efforts. Perhaps our tool-makers may not gain more than a few suggestive hints from a museum of savage implements, our physicians may only be interested in savage recipes so far as they involve the use of local drugs, our mathematicians may leave to the infant-school the highest flights of savage arithmetic, our astronomers may only find in the star-craft of the lower races an uninstructive combination of myth and common-place. But there are departments of knowledge, of not less consequence than mechanics and medicine, arithmetic and astronomy, in which the study of the lowest stages, as influencing the practical acceptance of the higher, cannot be thus carelessly set aside.

If we survey the state of educated opinion, not within the limits of some special school, but in the civilized world at large, on such subjects especially as relate to Man, his intellectual and moral nature, his place and function among his fellow-men and in the universe at large, we see existing side by side, as if of equal right, opinions most diverse in real authority. Some, vouched for by direct and positive evidence, hold their ground as solid truths. Others, though founded on crudest theories of the lower culture, have been so modified under the influence of advancing knowledge, as to afford a satisfactory framework for recognized facts; and positive science, mindful of the origin of its own philosophic schemes, must admit the validity of such a title. Others, lastly, are opinions belonging properly to lower intellectual levels, which have held their place into the higher by mere force of ancestral tradition; these are survivals. Now it is the practical office of ethnography to make known to all whom it may concern the tenure of opinions in the public mind, to show what is received on its own direct evidence, what is ruder ancient doctrine reshaped to answer modern ends, and what is but timehonoured superstition in the garb of modern knowledge.

Topic after topic shows at a glimpse the way in which ethnography bears on modern intellectual conditions. Language, appearing as an art in full vigour among rude tribes, already displays the adaptation of childlike devices in self-expressive sound and pictorial metaphor, to utter thoughts as complex and abstruse as savage minds demand speech for. When it is considered how far the development of knowledge depends on full and exact means of expressing thought, is it not a pregnant consideration that the language of civilized men is but the language of savages, more or less improved in structure, a good deal extended in vocabulary, made more precise in the dictionary definition of words?

The development of language between its savage and cultured stages has been made in its details, scarcely in its principle. It is not too much to say that half the vast defect of language as a method of utterance, and half the vast defect of thought as determined by the influence of language, are due to the fact that speech is a scheme worked out by the rough and ready application of material metaphor and imperfect analogy, in ways fitting rather the barbaric education of those who formed it, than our own. Language is one of those intellectual departments in which we have gone too little beyond the savage stage, but are still as it were hacking with stone celts and twirling laborious friction-fire. Metaphysical speculation, again, has been one of the potent influences on human conduct, and although its rise, and one may almost say also its decline and fall, belong to comparatively civilized ages, yet its connexion with lower stages of intellectual history may to some extent be discerned. For example, attention may be recalled to a special point brought forward in this work, that one of the greatest metaphysical doctrines is a transfer to the field of philosophy from the field of religion, made when philosophers familiar with the conception of object-phantoms used this to provide a doctrine of thought, thus giving rise to the theory of ideas. Far more fully and distinctly, the study of the savage and barbaric intellect opens to us the study of Mythology. The evidence here brought together as to the relation of the savage to the cultured mind in the matter of mythology has, I think, at any rate justified this claim. With a consistency of action so general as to amount to mental law, it is proved that among the lower races all over the world the operation of outward events on the inward mind leads not only to statement of fact, but to formation of myth. It gives no unimportant clues to the student of mental history, to see by what regular processes myths are generated, and how, growing by wear and increasing in value at secondhand, they pass into pseudo-historic legend. Poetry is full of myth, and he who will understand it analytically will do well to study it ethnographically. In so far as myth, seriously or sportively meant, is the subject of poetry, and in so far as it is couched in language whose characteristic is that wild and rambling metaphor which represents the habitual expression of savage thought, the mental condition of the lower races is the key to poetry—nor is it a small portion of the poetic realm which these definitions cover. History, again, is an agent powerful, and becoming more powerful, in shaping men's minds, and through their minds their actions in the world ; now one of the most prominent faults of historians is that, through want of familiarity with the principles of myth-development, they cannot apply systematically to ancient legend the appropriate test for separating chronicle from myth, but with few exceptions are apt to treat the mingled mass of tradition partly with undiscriminating credulity and partly with undiscriminating scepticism. Even more injurious is the effect of such want of testing on that part of traditional or documentary record which, among any section of mankind, stands as sacred history. It is not merely that in turning to the index of some book on savage tribes, one comes on such a suggestive heading as this, 'Religion—*see* Mythology.' It is that within the upper half of the scale of civilization, among the great historic religions of the world, we all know that between religion and religion, and even to no small extent between sect and sect, the narratives which to one side are sacred history, may seem to the other mythic legend. Among the reasons which retard the progress of religious history in the modern world, one of the most conspicuous is this, that so many of its approved historians demand from the study of mythology always weapons to destroy their adversaries' structures, but never tools to clear and trim their own. It is an indispensable qualification of the true historian that he shall be able to look dispassionately on myth as a natural and regular product of the human mind, acting on appropriate facts in a manner suited to the intellectual state of the people producing it, and that he shall treat it as an accretion to be deducted from professed history, whenever it is recognized by the tests of being decidedly against evidence as fact, and at the same time clearly explicable as myth. It is from the ethnographic study of savage and barbaric races that the knowledge of the general laws of myth-development, required for the carrying out of this critical process, may be best or must necessarily be gained.

The two vast united provinces of Morals and Law have been as yet too imperfectly treated on a general ethnographic scheme, to warrant distinct statement of results. Yet thus much may be confidently said, that where the ground has been even superficially explored, every glimpse reveals treasures of knowledge. It is already evident that enquirers who systematically trace each department of moral and legal institutions from the savage through the barbaric and into the civilized condition of mankind, thereby introduce into the scientific investigations of these subjects an indispensable element which merely theoretical writers are apt unscrupulously to dispense with. The law or maxim which a people at some particular stage of its history might have made fresh, according to the information and circumstances of the period, is one thing. The law or maxim which did in fact become current among them by inheritance from an earlier stage, only more or less modified to make it compatible with the new conditions, is another and far different thing. Ethnography is required to bridge over the gap between the two, a very chasm where the arguments of moralists and legists are continually falling in, to crawl out maimed and helpless. Within modern grades of civilization this historical method is now becoming more and more accepted. It will not be denied that English law has acquired, by modified inheritance from past ages, a theory of primogeniture and a theory of real estate which are so far from being products of our own times that we must go back to the middle ages for anything like a satisfactory explanation of them ; and as for more absolute

survival, did not Jewish disabilities stand practically, and
the wager of battle nominally, in our law of not many
years back ? But the point to be pressed here is, that the
development and survival of law are processes that did not
first come into action within the range of written codes of
comparatively cultured nations. Admitted that civilized
law requires its key from barbaric law ; it must be borne
in mind that the barbarian lawgiver too was guided in
judgment not so much by first principles, as by a reverent
and often stupidly reverent adherence to the tradition of
earlier and yet ruder ages.

Nor can these principles be set aside in the scientific
study of moral sentiment and usage. When the ethical
systems of mankind, from the lowest savagery upward, have
been analyzed and arranged in their stages of evolution,
then ethical science, no longer vitiated by too exclusive
application to particular phases of morality taken unreasonably as representing morality in general, will put its
methods to fair trial on the long and intricate world-history
of right and wrong.

In concluding a work of which full half is occupied by
evidence bearing on the philosophy of religion, it may well
be asked, how does all this array of facts stand toward the
theologian's special province ? That the world sorely needs
new evidence and method in theology, the state of religion
in our own land bears witness. Take English Protestantism
as a central district of opinion, draw an ideal line through
its centre, and English thought is seen to be divided as by
a polarizing force extending to the utmost limits of repul-
sion. On one side of the dividing line stand such as keep
firm hold on the results of the 16th century reformation, or
seek yet more original canons from the first Christian ages ;
on the other side stand those who, refusing to be bound by
the doctrinal judgments of past centuries, but introducing
modern science and modern criticism as new factors in
theological opinion, are eagerly pressing toward a new
reformation. Outside these narrower limits, extremer

partizans occupy more distant ground on either side. On the one hand the Anglican blends gradually into the Roman scheme, a system so interesting to the ethnologist for its maintenance of rites more naturally belonging to barbaric culture ; a system so hateful to the man of science for its suppression of knowledge, and for that usurpation of intellectual authority by a sacerdotal caste which has at last reached its climax, now that an aged bishop can judge, by infallible inspiration, the results of researches whose evidence and methods are alike beyond his knowledge and his mental grasp. On the other hand, intellect, here trampled under foot of dogma, takes full revenge elsewhere, even within the domain of religion, in those theological districts where reason takes more and more the command over hereditary belief, like a mayor of the palace supersed- ing a nominal king. In yet farther ranges of opinion, religious authority is simply deposed and banished, and the throne of absolute reason is set up without a rival even in name ; in secularism the feeling and imagination which in the religious world are bound to theological belief, have to attach themselves to a positive natural philosophy, and to a positive morality which shall of its own force control the acts of men. Such, then, is the boundless divergence of opinion among educated citizens of an enlightened country, in an age scarcely approached by any former age in the possession of actual knowledge and the strenuous pursuit of truth as the guiding principle of life. Of the causes which have brought to pass so perplexed a condition of public thought, in so momentous a matter as theology, there is one, and that a weighty one, which demands mention here. It is the partial and one-sided application of the historical method of enquiry into theological doctrines, and the utter neglect of the ethnographical method which carries back the historical into remoter and more primitive regions of thought. Look- ing at each doctrine by itself and for itself, as in the abstract true or untrue, theologians close their eyes to the instances which history is ever holding up before them, that one phase of a religious belief is the outcome of another, that in all times religion has included within its limits a system of philosophy, expressing its more or less transcendental conceptions in doctrines which form in any age their fittest representatives, but which doctrines are liable to modification in the general course of intellectual change, whether the ancient formulas still hold their authority with altered meaning, or are themselves reformed or replaced. Christendom furnishes evidence to establish this principle, if for example we will but candidly compare the educated opinion of Rome in the 5th with that of London in the 19th century, on such subjects as the nature and functions of soul, spirit, deity, and judge by the comparison in what important respects the philosophy of religion has come to differ even among men who represent in different ages the same great principles of faith. The general study of the ethnography of religion, through all its immensity of range, seems to countenance the theory of evolution in its highest and widest sense. In the treatment of some of its topics here, I have propounded special hypotheses as to the order in which various stages of doctrine and rite have succeeded one another in the history of religion. Yet how far these particular theories may hold good, seems even to myself a minor matter. The essential part of the ethnographic method in theology lies in admitting as relevant the compared evidence of religion in all stages of culture. The action of such evidence on theology proper is in this wise, that a vast proportion of doctrines and rites known among mankind are not to be judged as direct products of the particular religious systems which give them sanction, for they are in fact more or less modified results adopted from previous systems. The theologian, as he comes to deal with each element of belief and worship, ought to ascertain its place in the general scheme of religion. Should the doctrine or rite in question appear to have been transmitted from an earlier to a later stage of religious thought, then it should be tested, like any other point of culture, as to its place in development.

The question has to be raised, to which of these three categories it belongs :—is it a product of the earlier theology, yet sound enough to maintain a rightful place in the later?—is it derived from a cruder original, yet so modified as to become a proper representative of more advanced views ?—is it a survival from a lower stage of thought, imposing on the credit of the higher by virtue not of inherent truth but of ancestral belief ? These are queries the very asking of which starts trains of thought which candid minds should be encouraged to pursue, leading as they do toward the attainment of such measure of truth as the intellectual condition of our age fits us to assimilate. In the scientific study of religion, which now shows signs of becoming for many a year an engrossing subject of the world's thought, the decision must not rest with a council in which the theologian, the metaphysician, the biologist, the physicist, exclusively take part. The historian and the ethnographer must be called upon to show the hereditary standing of each opinion and practice, and their enquiry must go back as far as antiquity or savagery can show a vestige, for there seems no human thought so primitive as to have lost its bearing on our own thought, nor so ancient as to have broken its connection with our own life.

It is our happiness to live in one of those eventful periods of intellectual and moral history, when the oft-closed gates of discovery and reform stand open at their widest. How long these good days may last, we cannot tell. It may be that the increasing power and range of the scientific method, with its stringency of argument and constant check of fact, may start the world on a more steady and continuous course of progress than it has moved on heretofore. But if history is to repeat itself according to precedent, we must look forward to stiffer duller ages of traditionalists and commentators, when the great thinkers of our time will be appealed to as authorities by men who slavishly accept their tenets, yet cannot or dare not follow their methods through better evidence to higher ends. In either case, it is for those among us whose minds are set on the advancement of civilization, to make the most of present opportunities, that even when in future years progress is arrested, it may be arrested at the higher level. To the promoters of what is sound and reformers of what is faulty in modern culture, ethnography has double help to give. To impress men's minds with a doctrine of development, will lead them in all honour to their ancestors to continue the progressive work of past ages, to continue it the more vigorously because light has increased in the world, and where barbaric hordes groped blindly, cultured men can often move onward with clear view. It is a harsher, and at times even painful, office of ethnography to expose the remains of crude old culture which have passed into harmful superstition, and to mark these out for destruction. Yet this work, if less genial, is not less urgently needful for the good of mankind. Thus, active at once in aiding progress and in removing hindrance, the science of culture is essentially a reformer's science.

INDEX TO VOLUMES I AND II